Achieving Federated and Self-Manageable Cloud Infrastructures:

Theory and Practice

Massimo Villari
Università Degli Studi di Messina, Italy

Ivona Brandic
Vienna University of Technology, Austria

Francesco Tusa
Università Degli Studi di Messina, Italy

T0350104

Managing Director:	Lindsay Johnston
Senior Editorial Director:	Heather A. Probst
Book Production Manager:	Sean Woznicki
Development Manager:	Joel Gamon
Development Editor:	Hannah Abelbeck
Acquisitions Editor:	Erika Gallagher
Typesetter:	Adrienne Freeland
Cover Design:	Nick Newcomer, Lisandro Gonzalez

Published in the United States of America by
Business Science Reference (an imprint of IGI Global)
701 E. Chocolate Avenue
Hershey PA 17033
Tel: 717-533-8845
Fax: 717-533-8661
E-mail: cust@igi-global.com
Web site: http://www.igi-global.com

Copyright © 2012 by IGI Global. All rights reserved. No part of this publication may be reproduced, stored or distributed in any form or by any means, electronic or mechanical, including photocopying, without written permission from the publisher. Product or company names used in this set are for identification purposes only. Inclusion of the names of the products or companies does not indicate a claim of ownership by IGI Global of the trademark or registered trademark.

Library of Congress Cataloging-in-Publication Data

Achieving federated and self-manageable cloud infrastructures: theory and practice / Massimo Villari, Ivona Braidic, and Francesco Tusa, editors.
  p. cm.
Includes bibliographical references and index.
Summary: "This book presents an overview of current developments in cloud computing concepts, architectures, infrastructures and methods, focusing on the needs of small to medium enterprises"--Provided by publisher.
ISBN 978-1-4666-1631-8 (hardcover) -- ISBN 978-1-4666-1632-5 (ebook) -- ISBN 978-1-4666-1633-2 (print & perpetual access)
  1. Cloud computing. I. Villari, Massimo, 1972- II. Brandic, Ivona, 1977- III. Tusa, Francesco, 1983-
  QA76.585.A25 2012
  004.6782--dc23
            2012003502

British Cataloguing in Publication Data
A Cataloguing in Publication record for this book is available from the British Library.

All work contributed to this book is new, previously-unpublished material. The views expressed in this book are those of the authors, but not necessarily of the publisher.

Editorial Advisory Board

Nik Bessis, *University of Derby, UK*
Alex Galis, *University College London, UK*
Ignacio M. Llorente, *Universidad Complutense de Madrid, Spain*
Philippe Massonet, *Cetic: Centre d'Excellence en Technologies de l'Information et de la Communication, Belgium*
Gabriel Mateescu, *Ecole Polytechnique Fédérale de Lausanne, Switzerland*
Benny Rochwerger, *IBM Haifa Research Lab, Israel*

Table of Contents

Foreword..xvii

Preface..xix

Acknowledgment... xxv

Section 1
Theory

Chapter 1
Toward Cloud Federation: Concepts and Challenges.. 1
> Antonio Celesti, Università Degli Studi di Messina, Italy
> Francesco Tusa, Università Degli Studi di Messina, Italy
> Massimo Villari, Università Degli Studi di Messina, Italy

Chapter 2
Interoperable Resource Management for Establishing Federated Clouds............................ 18
> Gabor Kecskemeti, Laboratory of Parallel and Distributed Systems of the MTA-SZTAKI, Hungary
> Attila Kertesz, Laboratory of Parallel and Distributed Systems of the MTA-SZTAKI, Hungary
> Attila Marosi, Laboratory of Parallel and Distributed Systems of the MTA-SZTAKI, Hungary
> Peter Kacsuk, Laboratory of Parallel and Distributed Systems of the MTA-SZTAKI, Hungary

Chapter 3
Understanding Decentralized and Dynamic Brokerage in Federated Cloud Environments................. 36
> Nicolò Maria Calcavecchia, Politecnico di Milano, Italy
> Antonio Celesti, Universit Degli Studi di Messina, Italy
> Elisabetta Di Nitto, Politecnico di Milano, Italy

Chapter 4
Implementing Distributed, Self-Managing Computing Services Infrastructure using a Scalable,
Parallel and Network-Centric Computing Model 57
> Rao Mikkilineni, Kawa Objects Inc., USA
> Giovanni Morana, DIEEI, University of Catania, Italy
> Ian Seyler, Return Infinity Inc., Canada

Chapter 5

The Cloud@Home Volunteer and Interoperable Cloud through the Future Internet............................ 79

    Salvatore Distefano, Politecnico di Milano, Italy

    Antonio Puliafito, Università degli Studi di Messina, Italy

Chapter 6

Cloud Monitoring... 97

    Peer Hasselmeyer, NEC Laboratories Europe, Germany

    Gregory Katsaros, National Technical University of Athens, Greece

    Bastian Koller, High Performance Computing Centre Stuttgart, Germany

    Philipp Wieder, Gesellschaft fuer wissenschaftliche Datenverarbeitung mbH Goettingen, Germany

Chapter 7

Monitoring in Federated and Self-Manageable Clouds 117

    Stefanos Koutsoutos, National Technical University of Athens, Greece

    Spyridon V. Gogouvitis, National Technical University of Athens, Greece

    Dimosthenis Kyriazis, National Technical University of Athens, Greece

    Theodora Varvarigou, National Technical University of Athens, Greece

Chapter 8

Availability Analysis of IaaS Cloud Using Analytic Models... 134

    Francesco Longo, Università degli Studi di Messina, Italia

    Rahul Ghosh, Duke University, USA

    Vijay K. Naik, IBM T. J. Watson Research Center, USA

    Kishor S. Trivedi, Duke University, USA

Chapter 9

The Security of Cloud Infrastructure 158

    Massimo Civilini, Cisco Systems® Inc., USA

Chapter 10

Security Issues in Cloud Federations... 176

    Massimiliano Rak, Second University of Naples, Italy

    Massimo Ficco, Second University of Naples, Italy

    Jesus Luna, TU Darmstadt, Germany

    Hamza Ghani, TU Darmstadt, Germany

    Neeraj Suri, TU Darmstadt, Germany

    Silviu Panica, Institute e-Austria Timisoara, Romania

    Dana Petcu, Institute e-Austria Timisoara, Romania

Section 2
Practice

Chapter 11
On the use of the Hybrid Cloud Computing Paradigm 196
    Carlos Martín Sánchez, Complutense University of Madrid, Spain
    Daniel Molina, Complutense University of Madrid, Spain
    Rafael Moreno Vozmediano, Complutense University of Madrid, Spain
    Ruben S. Montero, Complutense University of Madrid, Spain
    Ignacio M. Llorente, Complutense University of Madrid, Spain

Chapter 12
CLEVER: A Cloud Middleware Beyond the Federation 219
    Francesco Tusa, Università degli Studi di Messina, Italy
    Maurizio Paone, Università degli Studi di Messina, Italy
    Massimo Villari, Università degli Studi di Messina, Italy

Chapter 13
Monitoring Services in a Federated Cloud: The RESERVOIR Experience 242
    Stuart Clayman, University College London, UK
    Giovanni Toffetti, University College London, UK
    Alex Galis, University College London, UK
    Clovis Chapman, University College London, UK

Chapter 14
Achieving Flexible SLA and Resource Management in Clouds 266
    Vincent C. Emeakaroha, Vienna University of Technology, Austria
    Marco A. S. Netto, IBM Research, Brazil
    Rodrigo N. Calheiros, The University of Melbourne, Australia
    César A. F. De Rose, PUCRS, Brazil

Chapter 15
Resource Management Mechanisms to Support SLAs in IaaS Clouds 288
    David Breitgand, IBM Haifa Research Lab, Israel
    Amir Epstein, IBM Haifa Research Lab, Israel
    Benny Rochwerger, IBM Haifa Research Lab, Israel

Chapter 16
Economic Analysis of the SLA Mapping Approach for Cloud Computing Goods 308
    Michael Maurer, Vienna University of Technology, Austria
    Vincent C. Emeakaroha, Vienna University of Technology, Austria
    Ivona Brandic, Vienna University of Technology, Austria

Chapter 17
Deploying and Running Enterprise Grade Applications in Federated Cloud 328
    Benoit Hudzia, SAP, UK
    Jonathan Sinclair, SAP, UK
    Maik Lindner, SAP, UK

Chapter 18
Towards Energy-Efficient, Scalable, and Resilient IaaS Clouds 350
    Eugen Feller, INRIA Centre Rennes - Bretagne Atlantique, France
    Louis Rilling, Kerlabs, France
    Christine Morin, INRIA Centre Rennes - Bretagne Atlantique, France

Chapter 19
Self-Management of Applications and Systems to Optimize Energy in Data Centers 372
    Frederico Alvares de Oliveira Jr., ASCOLA Research Team (INRIA-Mines Nantes, LINA), France
    Adrien Lèbre, ASCOLA Research Team (INRIA-Mines Nantes, LINA), France
    Thomas Ledoux, ASCOLA Research Team (INRIA-Mines Nantes, LINA), France
    Jean-Marc Menaud, ASCOLA Research Team (INRIA-Mines Nantes, LINA), France

Chapter 20
Access Control in Federated Clouds: The Cloudgrid Case Study 395
    Valentina Casola, University of Naples "Federico II", Italy
    Antonio Cuomo, University of Sannio, Italy
    Umberto Villano, University of Sannio, Italy
    Massimiliano Rak, Second University of Naples, Italy

Compilation of References 418

About the Contributors 445

Index 460

Detailed Table of Contents

Foreword..xvii

Preface..xix

Acknowledgment..xxv

Section 1
Theory

Chapter 1

Toward Cloud Federation: Concepts and Challenges.. 1
Antonio Celesti, Università Degli Studi di Messina, Italy
Francesco Tusa, Università Degli Studi di Messina, Italy
Massimo Villari, Università Degli Studi di Messina, Italy

Federation in cloud computing is an emerging topic. Currently, all over the world in both academia and industry contexts many operators are picking up the advantages of cloud computing and federation in planning the Internet of the future. Nevertheless, cloud federation is at the early stage, and the scientific community is not fully aware how the federation will impact the cloud computing scenario. In this chapter, the authors try to clarify the ideas and discuss the main future challenges regarding cloud federation.

Chapter 2

Interoperable Resource Management for Establishing Federated Clouds.. 18
Gabor Kecskemeti, Laboratory of Parallel and Distributed Systems of the MTA-SZTAKI, Hungary
Attila Kertesz, Laboratory of Parallel and Distributed Systems of the MTA-SZTAKI, Hungary
Attila Marosi, Laboratory of Parallel and Distributed Systems of the MTA-SZTAKI, Hungary
Peter Kacsuk, Laboratory of Parallel and Distributed Systems of the MTA-SZTAKI, Hungary

Cloud Computing builds on the latest achievements of diverse research areas, such as Grid Computing, Service-oriented computing, business process modeling and virtualization. As this new computing paradigm was mostly lead by companies, several proprietary systems arose. Recently, alongside these commercial systems, several smaller-scale privately owned systems are maintained and developed. This chapter focuses on issues faced by users with interests in Multi-Cloud use and by Cloud providers with highly dynamic workloads. The authors propose a Federated Cloud Management architecture that provides unified access to a federated Cloud that aggregates multiple heterogeneous IaaS Cloud providers in a transparent manner. The architecture incorporates the concepts of meta-brokering, Cloud brokering, and on-demand service deployment. The meta-brokering component provides transparent service execution for the users by allowing the interconnection of various Cloud brokering solutions. Cloud-Brokers manage the number and the location of the Virtual Machines performing the user requests. In order to decrease Virtual Machine instantiation time and increase dynamism in the system, the service deployment component optimizes service delivery by encapsulating services as virtual appliances allowing their decomposition and replication among IaaS Cloud infrastructures. The architecture achieves service provider level transparency through automatic virtual appliance replication and Virtual Machine management of Cloud-Brokers.

Chapter 3

Understanding Decentralized and Dynamic Brokerage in Federated Cloud Environments................. 36

Nicolò Maria Calcavecchia, Politecnico di Milano, Italy

Antonio Celesti, Universit Degli Studi di Messina, Italy

Elisabetta Di Nitto, Politecnico di Milano, Italy

The advent of the cloud computing paradigm offers different ways both to sell services and to exploit external computational resources according to a pay-per-use economic model. Nowadays, cloud computing clients can buy various form of IaaS, PaaS, and SaaS from cloud providers. Besides this form of pay-per-use, the perspective of cloud federation offers further business opportunities for small/medium providers which hold physical datacenters. Considering the cloud computing ecosystem, besides large cloud providers, smaller ones are also becoming popular even though their own virtualization infrastructures (i.e., deployed in their datacenters) cannot directly compete with the bigger market leaders. The result is that often small/medium clouds have to exploit the services of mega-providers in order to develop their business logic and their cloud-based services. To this regard, a possible future alternative scenario is represented by the promotion of cooperation among small/medium cloud providers, thus enabling the sharing of computational and storage resources. However, in order to achieve such an environment, several issues have to be addressed. One of these challenges is how to plan brokerage strategies allowing cloud providers to discover other providers for partnership establishment. This chapter focuses on different possible centralized and decentralized approaches in designing a brokerage strategy for cloud federation, analyzing their features, advantages and disadvantages.

Chapter 4

Implementing Distributed, Self-Managing Computing Services Infrastructure using a Scalable, Parallel and Network-Centric Computing Model 57

Rao Mikkilineni, Kawa Objects Inc., USA

Giovanni Morana, DIEEI, University of Catania, Italy

Ian Seyler, Return Infinity Inc., Canada

This chapter introduces a new network-centric computing model using Distributed Intelligent Managed Element (DIME) network architecture (DNA). A parallel signaling network overlay over a network of self-managed von Neumann computing nodes is utilized to implement dynamic fault, configuration, accounting, performance, and security management of both the nodes and the network based on business priorities, workload variations and latency constraints. Two implementations of the new computing model are described which demonstrate the feasibility of the new computing model. One implementation provides service virtualization at the Linux process level and another provides virtualization of a core in a many-core processor. Both point to an alternative way to assure end-to-end transaction reliability, availability, performance, and security in distributed Cloud computing, reducing current complexity in configuring and managing virtual machines and making the implementation of Federation of Clouds simpler.

Chapter 5

The Cloud@Home Volunteer and Interoperable Cloud through the Future Internet.......................... 79

    Salvatore Distefano, Politecnico di Milano, Italy

    Antonio Puliafito, Università degli Studi di Messina, Italy

Cloud computing is the new consolidated trend in ICT, often considered as the panacea to all the problems of existing large-scale distributed paradigms such as Grid and hierarchical clustering. The Cloud breakthrough is the service oriented perspective of providing everything "as a service". Different from the others large-scale distributed paradigms, it was born from commercial contexts, with the aim of selling the temporarily unexploited computing resources of huge datacenters in order to reduce the costs. Since this business model is really attractive and convenient for both providers and consumers, the Cloud paradigm is quickly growing and widely spreading, even in non commercial context. In fact, several activities on the Cloud, such as Nimbus, Eucalyptus, OpenNEbula, and Reservoir, etc., have been undertaken, aiming at specifying open Cloud infrastructure middleware.

Chapter 6

Cloud Monitoring... 97

    Peer Hasselmeyer, NEC Laboratories Europe, Germany

    Gregory Katsaros, National Technical University of Athens, Greece

    Bastian Koller, High Performance Computing Centre Stuttgart, Germany

    Philipp Wieder, Gesellschaft fuer wissenschaftliche Datenverarbeitung mbH Goettingen, Germany

The management of the entire service landscape comprising a Cloud environment is a complex and challenging venture. There, one task of utmost importance, is the generation and processing of information about the state, health, and performance of the various services and IT components, something which is generally referred to as monitoring. Such information is the foundation for proper assessment and management of the whole Cloud. This chapter pursues two objectives: first, to provide an overview of monitoring in Cloud environments and, second, to propose a solution for interoperable and vendor-independent Cloud monitoring. Along the way, the authors motivate the necessity of monitoring at the different levels of Cloud infrastructures, introduce selected state-of-the-art, and extract requirements for Cloud monitoring. Based on these requirements, the following sections depict a Cloud monitoring solution and describe current developments towards interoperable, open, and extensible Cloud monitoring frameworks.

Chapter 7

Monitoring in Federated and Self-Manageable Clouds 117

    Stefanos Koutsoutos, National Technical University of Athens, Greece

    Spyridon V. Gogouvitis, National Technical University of Athens, Greece

    Dimosthenis Kyriazis, National Technical University of Athens, Greece

    Theodora Varvarigou, National Technical University of Athens, Greece

The emergence of Service Clouds and the Future Internet has lead to a lot of research taking place in the area of Cloud frameworks and solutions. The complexity of these systems has proven to be a challenge for the design of a successful platform that will be capable of meeting all possible needs and require the minimum time and effort put to its management. Current trends in the field move away from models of human managed networks and towards the self-manageable, cooperating Clouds. This goal is synonymous to building software that is able to make decisions required to reconfigure itself in a way that it resists failures and, at the same time, makes optimal use of the resources available to it. The heart of each decision making mechanism is always the data that is fed to it, which assigns a very central role to Monitoring mechanisms in federated and self-manageable Clouds.

Chapter 8

Availability Analysis of IaaS Cloud Using Analytic Models... 134

Francesco Longo, Università degli Studi di Messina, Italia

Rahul Ghosh, Duke University, USA

Vijay K. Naik, IBM T. J. Watson Research Center, USA

Kishor S. Trivedi, Duke University, USA

Cloud based systems are inherently large scale. Failures in such a large distributed environment are quite common phenomena. To reduce the overall Cloud downtime and to provide a seamless service, providers need to assess the availability characteristics of their data centers. Such assessments can be done through controlled experimentations, large scale simulations and via analytic models. In the scale of Cloud, conducting repetitive experimentations or simulations might be costly and time consuming. Analytic models, on the other hand, can be used as a complement to small scale measurements and simulations since the analytic results can be obtained quickly. However, accurate analytic modeling requires dealing with large number of system states, leading to state-space explosion problem. To reduce the complexity of analysis, novel analytic methods are required. This chapter introduces the reader to a novel approach using interacting analytic sub-models and shows how such approach can deal with large scale Cloud availability analysis. The chapter puts the work in perspective of other existing and ongoing research in this area, describe how such approach can be useful to Cloud providers, especially in the case of federated scenarios, and summarize the open research questions that are yet to be solved.

Chapter 9

The Security of Cloud Infrastructure 158

Massimo Civilini, Cisco Systems® Inc., USA

The development of commercial Cloud environments has been fueled by the introduction of new technologies which have changed the interactions between the base components of a legacy IT infrastructure: computing, networking, and storage. In particular, the security of data and operations has been impacted by these changes, making the legacy security infrastructure no longer adequate to support new scenarios. This chapter illustrates how base infrastructure operations like software provisioning and resource virtualization are critical from a security viewpoint. It will also discuss the mitigation solutions available in guaranteeing an adequate level of security in the Cloud.

Chapter 10

Security Issues in Cloud Federations 176

Massimiliano Rak, Second University of Naples, Italy

Massimo Ficco, Second University of Naples, Italy

Jesus Luna, TU Darmstadt, Germany

Hamza Ghani, TU Darmstadt, Germany

Neeraj Suri, TU Darmstadt, Germany

Silviu Panica, Institute e-Austria Timisoara, Romania

Dana Petcu, Institute e-Austria Timisoara, Romania

The cloud paradigm, based on the idea of delegating to the network any kind of computational resources, is showing a considerable success. The estimated trend is that the number of different cloud-based solutions, approaches, and service providers (CSP) will continue growing. Despite the big number of different cloud solutions that currently exist, most of them are "walled gardens" unable to interoperate. On the other side, a large effort is taking place in the cloud community to develop and identify open solutions and standards. In such a context the concept of cloud federation, an architecture that combines the functionalities of different CSP, is a hot topic. This chapter presents an overview of the cloud federation topic, with special focus on its most important security challenges. Furthermore, it proposes a taxonomy of possible approaches to federation. Then it proposes a comparison of security problems in cloud and grid environment, and a detailed analysis of two relevant security problems, identity management and Cyber Attacks analysis, trying to outline how they can be applied in a federated context.

Section 2
Practice

Chapter 11
On the use of the Hybrid Cloud Computing Paradigm 196

Carlos Martín Sánchez, Complutense University of Madrid, Spain

Daniel Molina, Complutense University of Madrid, Spain

Rafael Moreno Vozmediano, Complutense University of Madrid, Spain

Ruben S. Montero, Complutense University of Madrid, Spain

Ignacio M. Llorente, Complutense University of Madrid, Spain

This chapter analyzes the Hybrid Cloud computing model, a paradigm that combines on-premise Private Clouds with the resources of Public Clouds. This new model is not yet fully developed, and there is still a lot of work to be done before true multi-Cloud installations become mature enough to be used in production environments. A review of some of its limitations and the challenges that have to be faced is done in this chapter, and some common techniques to address the challenges studied are also included. It also presents a Hybrid Cloud architecture based on the OpenNebula Cloud toolkit, trying to overcome some of the challenges, and present some real-life experiences with this proposed architecture and Amazon EC2.

Chapter 12
CLEVER: A Cloud Middleware Beyond the Federation 219

Francesco Tusa, Università degli Studi di Messina, Italy

Maurizio Paone, Università degli Studi di Messina, Italy

Massimo Villari, Università degli Studi di Messina, Italy

This chapter describes both the design and architecture of the CLEVER cloud middleware ,pointing out the possibilities it offers towards enlarging the concept of federation in more directions. CLEVER is able to accomplish such an enlargement enabling the interaction among whatever type of electronic device connected to Internet, thus offering the opportunity of implementing the Internet of Things. Together with this type of perspective, CLEVER aims to "aggregate" heterogeneous computing infrastructure by putting together Cloud and Grid as an example. The chapter starts with a description of the cloud projects related to CLEVER, followed by a discussion on the middleware components that mainly focuses on the innovative features they have, in particular the communication mechanisms adopted. The second part of the chapter presents a real use case that exploits the CLEVER features that allow easy creation of federated clouds' infrastructures that can be also based on integration with existing Grids; it is demonstrated thanks to the "oneshot" CLEVER deploying mechanism. It is possible to scale dynamically the cloud resources by taking advantage of the existing Grid infrastructures, and minimizing the changes needed at the involved management middleware.

Chapter 13

Monitoring Services in a Federated Cloud: The RESERVOIR Experience 242

    Stuart Clayman, University College London, UK

    Giovanni Toffetti, University College London, UK

    Alex Galis, University College London, UK

    Clovis Chapman, University College London, UK

This chapter presents the need, the requirements, and the design for a monitoring system that is suitable for supporting the operations and management of a Federated Cloud environment. The chapter discusses these issues within the context of the RESERVOIR Service Cloud computing project. It first presents the RESERVOIR architecture itself, then introduces the issues of service monitoring in a federated environment, together with the specific solutions that have been devised for RESERVOIR. It ends with a review of the authors' experience in this area by showing a use-case application executing on RESERVOIR, which is responsible for the computational prediction of organic crystal structures.

Chapter 14

Achieving Flexible SLA and Resource Management in Clouds 266

    Vincent C. Emeakaroha, Vienna University of Technology, Austria

    Marco A. S. Netto, IBM Research, Brazil

    Rodrigo N. Calheiros, The University of Melbourne, Australia

    César A. F. De Rose, PUCRS, Brazil

One of the key factors driving Cloud computing is flexible and on-demand resource provisioning in a pay-as-you-go manner. This resource provisioning is based on Service Level Agreements (SLAs) negotiated and signed between customers and providers. Efficient management of SLAs and Cloud resources to reduce cost, achieve high utilization, and generate profit is challenging due to the large-scale nature of Cloud environments and complex resource provisioning processes. In order to advance the adoption of this technology, it is necessary to identify and address the issues preventing proper resource and SLA management. The authors purport that monitoring is the first step towards successful management strategies. Thus, this chapter identifies the SLA management and monitoring challenges in Clouds and federated Cloud environments, and proposes a novel resource monitoring architecture as a basis for resource management in Clouds. It presents the design and implementation of this architecture and presents the evaluation of the architecture using heterogeneous application workloads.

Chapter 15

Resource Management Mechanisms to Support SLAs in IaaS Clouds 288

    David Breitgand, IBM Haifa Research Lab, Israel

    Amir Epstein, IBM Haifa Research Lab, Israel

    Benny Rochwerger, IBM Haifa Research Lab, Israel

The chapter discusses horizontal elasticity support in IaaS, its relationship to SLA protection, VM placement optimization, and efficient capacity management to improve cost-efficiency of cloud providers. Elastic services comprise multiple virtualized resources that can be added and deleted on demand to match variability in the workload. A Service owner profiles the service to determine its most appropriate sizing under different workload conditions. This variable sizing is formalized through a service level agreement (SLA) between the service owner and the cloud provider. The Cloud provider obtains maximum benefit when it succeeds to fully allocate the resource set demanded by the elastic service subject to its SLA. Failure to do so may result in SLA breach and financial losses to the provider. The chapter defines a novel combinatorial optimization problem called elastic services placement problem to maximize the provider's benefit from SLA compliant placement. It demonstrates the feasibility of our approach through a simulation study, showing that we are capable of consistently obtaining good solutions in a time efficient manner. In addition, we discuss how resource utilization level can be improved through an advanced capacity management leveraging elastic workload resource consumption variability.

Chapter 16

Economic Analysis of the SLA Mapping Approach for Cloud Computing Goods 308
Michael Maurer, Vienna University of Technology, Austria
Vincent C. Emeakaroha, Vienna University of Technology, Austria
Ivona Brandic, Vienna University of Technology, Austria

Because of the large number of different types of service level agreements (SLAs), computing resource markets face the challenge of low market liquidity. The authors therefore suggest restricting the number of different resource types to a small set of standardized computing resources to counteract this problem. Standardized computing resources are defined through SLA templates. SLA templates specify the structure of an SLA, the service attributes, the names of the service attributes, and the service attribute values. However, since existing approaches working with SLA templates are static so far, these approaches cannot reflect changes in user needs. To address this shortcoming, the chapter presents a novel approach to adaptive SLA matching. This approach adapts SLA templates based on SLA mappings of users. It allows Cloud users to define mappings between a public SLA template, which is available in the Cloud market, and their private SLA templates, which are used for various in-house business processes. Besides showing how public SLA templates are adapted to the demand of Cloud users, the chapter also analyzes the costs and benefits of this approach. Costs are incurred every time a user has to define a new SLA mapping to a public SLA template that has been adapted. In particular, it investigates how the costs differ with respect to the public SLA template adaptation method. The simulation results show that the use of heuristics for adaptation methods allows balancing the costs and benefits of the SLA mapping approach.

Chapter 17

Deploying and Running Enterprise Grade Applications in Federated Cloud 328
Benoit Hudzia, SAP, UK
Jonathan Sinclair, SAP, UK
Maik Lindner, SAP, UK

The notion of cloud computing is a paradigm shift from local machines and networks to virtualization technologies with services as a technical and business concept. This shift introduces major challenges when using cloud for deploying and running enterprise applications in the current Enterprise ecosystems. For companies, picking and choosing the right cloud to meet requirements is hard, and no solution is likely to provide the end-to-end specific IT services delivery and an end-to-end IT solution. Conversely cloud federation assists in providing flexibility to the customer and enables them to lower their TCO by shifting from one cloud to another while mitigating risks associated with a single cloud approach.In order to create competitive differentiation, small businesses require multiple software systems to both meet minimal data management and creative expectations. At the other end of the enterprise ecosystem spectrum, large companies rely on thousands of services in order to meet the needs of everything from simple departmental database applications to core Enterprise Resource planning and Customer Relationship Management systems on which the enterprise itself is managed. As an optimal adoption decision cannot be established for all individual cases, the authors propose to analyze three different use cases for deployment of enterprise applications such as SAP, on the cloud in order to provide some valuable pointers to navigate the emerging cloud ecosystem: rapid provisioning, elasticity and live migration of enterprise applications.

Chapter 18

Towards Energy-Efficient, Scalable, and Resilient IaaS Clouds 350

    Eugen Feller, INRIA Centre Rennes - Bretagne Atlantique, France

    Louis Rilling, Kerlabs, France

    Christine Morin, INRIA Centre Rennes - Bretagne Atlantique, France

With increasing numbers of energy hungry data centers, energy conservation has now become a major design constraint for current and future Infrastructure-as-a-Service (IaaS) cloud providers. In order to efficiently manage such large-scale environments, three important properties have to be fulfilled by the management frameworks: (1) scalability, (2) fault-tolerance, and (3) energy-awareness. However, the scalability and fault tolerance capabilities of existing open-source IaaS cloud management frameworks are limited. Moreover, they are far from being energy-aware. This chapter first surveys existing efforts on building IaaS platforms. This includes both, system architectures and energy-aware virtual machine (VM) placement algorithms. Afterwards, it describes the architecture and implementation of a novel scalable, fault-tolerant, and energy-aware VM manager called Snooze. Finally, a nature-inspired energy-aware VM placement approach based on the Ant Colony Optimization is introduced.

Chapter 19

Self-Management of Applications and Systems to Optimize Energy in Data Centers 372

    Frederico Alvares de Oliveira Jr., ASCOLA Research Team (INRIA-Mines Nantes, LINA), France

    Adrien Lèbre, ASCOLA Research Team (INRIA-Mines Nantes, LINA), France

    Thomas Ledoux, ASCOLA Research Team (INRIA-Mines Nantes, LINA), France

    Jean-Marc Menaud, ASCOLA Research Team (INRIA-Mines Nantes, LINA), France

As a direct consequence of the increasing popularity of cloud computing solutions, data centers are growing amazingly and hence have to urgently face with the energy consumption issue. Available solutions are focused basically on the system layer, by leveraging virtualization technologies to improve energy efficiency. Another body of works relies on cloud computing models and virtualization techniques to scale up/down applications based on their performance metrics. Although those proposals can reduce the energy footprint of applications and by transitivity of cloud infrastructures, they do not consider the internal characteristics of applications to finely define a trade-off between applications Quality of Service and energy footprint. In this paper, the authors propose a self-adaptation approach that considers both application internals and system to reduce the energy footprint in cloud infrastructure. Each application and the infrastructure are equipped with control loops, which allow them to autonomously optimize their executions. The authors implemented the control loops and simulated them in order to show their feasibility. In addition, the chapter shows how the solution fits in federated clouds through a motivating scenario. Finally, it provides some discussion about open issues on models and implementation of the proposal.

Chapter 20

Access Control in Federated Clouds: The Cloudgrid Case Study 395

    Valentina Casola, University of Naples "Federico II", Italy

    Antonio Cuomo, University of Sannio, Italy

    Umberto Villano, University of Sannio, Italy

    Massimiliano Rak, Second University of Naples, Italy

Resource sharing problem is one of the most important aspects of Cloud architectures whose primary goal is to fully enable the concept of accessing computing resources on-demand. Access control and resource federation are hot research topics and a lot of open issues should be addressed on functionalities, technological interoperability, quality of services, and security of the federated infrastructures. This chapter aims at offering a view on the problems of access control on federated Clouds; since they strongly depend on chosen architectures and platforms, the chapter will discuss some solutions applied on a real case study: the PerfCloud framework, which is based on the integration of Grid and Cloud platforms. The proposed architecture is based on the adoption of an interoperability system to cope with identity federation and access control, it is strictly related to the adopted framework nevertheless it helps the reader to have an idea of the involved open issues and available solutions in commercial or experimental clouds.

Compilation of References 418

About the Contributors 445

Index 460

Foreword

Starting with the good news: We are currently looking at five years of successful implementation and deployment of cloud computing, 5 YEARS. Although there seems to be a lot of hype in this young and widely immature field of cloud computing, this hype is mostly seen in the press and in laymen's view. In contrast, science, engineering, and business communities are moving forward into clouds, *in big steps,* driven by the many benefits and factors like virtualization and easy access, and accelerated by an ever increasing number of cloud use cases, success stories, growing number of cloud start-ups, and established IT firms offering standard cloud services. And many cloud service users are often not aware that the services they use today are sitting right in the cloud. They enjoy cloud benefits, like business flexibility, scalability of IT, reduced capex, and resource availability on demand and pay per use, at their finger tip. *So far so good!*

Looking closer into the current cloud offerings and the uses of clouds in research and industry, however, we anticipate a whole set of problems or *barriers to cloud adoption.* To name a few, major ones: lack of trust, which is caused mainly by security concerns; the attitude of "never changing a running system"; painful legal regulations when crossing political boundaries; stiff software licensing models and cost; and securing intellectual property and other corporate assets.

And, *another cloud challenge* arises at the horizon, far beyond the current state of the mega-providers' monolithic clouds: with more and more cloud service providers, with richer and deeper cloud services crowding the cloud market, in the near future, how do I get my data out of one cloud to continue processing it in another cloud? Or, how does an independent service provider (or cloud broker) interconnect different services from different cloud providers most efficiently? Such scenarios happen, for example, with *federated (web) services,* which consist of different service components sitting in different clouds. How do I manage this cloud workflow? How do I monitor, control, and manage the underlying cloud infrastructure and the complex applications running there? How far can I get with least manual intervention, plus taking into account user requirements and service level agreements?

And that's what this book is all about: Achieving federated and self-manageable cloud infrastructures, in theory and practice. In 20 chapters, written exclusively by renowned experts in their field, the book thoroughly discusses the concepts of federation in clouds, resource management and brokerage, new cloud middleware, monitoring in clouds, and security concepts. The book presents practical implementations, studies, and solutions such as cloud middleware implementations and use, monitoring in clouds from a practical point of view, enterprise experience in cloud, energy constrains, and applicable solution for securing clouds.

That's what makes this book so important, for the *researcher*, but also for the *practitioner* to develop and operate these cloud infrastructures, and for the *user* of these clouds: For the researcher it contributes to the most important actual and open research areas in federated clouds as mentioned above. For the practitioner and user it provides real use cases demonstrating how to build, operate and use federated clouds, which are based on real experience of the authors themselves, practical insight and guidance, lessons learned, and valuable recommendations.

Wolfgang Gentzsch
DEISA (Distributed European Initiative for Supercomputing Applications), Germany

Wolfgang Gentzsch *is a Consultant for HPC, Grid and Cloud and the Chairman of the ISC Cloud Conferences. He was Advisor to EU project DEISA, directed the German D-Grid Initiative, was a member of the Board of Directors of the OGF Open Grid Forum, and a member of the US President's Council of Advisors for Science and Technology, PCAST. He founded the e-School Project aiming at developing an interactive Web 2.0 simulation laboratory for K-20 science and engineering education. Before, Wolfgang was a professor of computer science and mathematics at several universities in the US and Germany, and held leading positions at the North Carolina Grid and Data Center, Sun Microsystems in California, Gridware, Genias, the DLR German Aerospace Center, and MPI for Plasmaphysics. Wolfgang studied Mathematics and Physics at the Technical Universities in Aachen and Darmstadt, and got his PhD in numerical methods for partial differential equations.*

Preface

Cloud Computing represents a novel and promising approach for implementing scalable ICT systems for individual-, communities- and business-use. Resources are pooled and offered on-demand with ubiquitous network access to rapidly configurable and elastic IT capabilities. Resources are provided following three basic delivery models: access to applications (SaaS), provision of platforms to create applications (PaaS), and provision of infrastructures for data processing, storing, and communication (IaaS).

Software as a Service (SaaS), also known as Application as a Service (AaaS), is the model in which an application is hosted as a service and customers access it using Internet protocols. It is the opposite of the Software as a Product model, currently used worldwide. Already, classical examples of SaaSs have emerged, including office automation applications, accounting systems, online video conferencing, web analytics or web content management tools.

Platform as a Service (PaaS), also known as Cloudware, offers the resources required to build new applications and services, without locally installing software. The current offer includes services for application design, development, testing, deployment, hosting for team collaboration, services for database integration, scalability, and versioning for state management.

(IaaS), also known as Hardware as a Service (HaaS), allows the renting of CPU cycles, server space, network equipment, memory and storage space. The major benefit is the fact that the infrastructure can be dynamically scaled up and down depending on the users' needs.

Looking at the three different service delivery models that have been described, the Cloud Computing paradigm shakes up the market of IT services by its pay-per-use concept for the leased resources and its promise to cut operational and capital costs. The resources, either infrastructure, platforms or software, are available over the network and their providers use a multi-tenant model and virtualization techniques.

In 2010, Gartner, Inc. has identified Cloud Computing as the most important strategic technology. The key benefits of providing *aaS using Clouds are in fact mainly related to: the avoidance of expensive computer systems configured to cope with peak performance; pay-as-you-go solutions for computing cycles requested on-demand; and avoidance of idle computing resources, resulting in novel business models.

Another type of classification can be made in the Cloud scenario, considering the deployment model. *Private Clouds* are enterprise owned or leased, *Public Clouds*, are sold to the public, including multi-tenant arbitrary-scale infrastructure, and *Hybrid Clouds*, result from the combined usage of multiple Cloud types.

In the Cloud scenario, stakeholders include among others: Cloud providers, Cloud resellers, and Cloud users, which might be *private users,* e.g., using Clouds to store private pictures, *community users,* e.g., using Clouds to deploy and provide communication portals as in case of academic portals, and *business users,* e.g., using Clouds to store business data or to host complex enterprise systems.

People might wonder why Cloud Computing is gaining a lot interest in the last couple of years. The answer to this question can be found in the opportunity it offers for creating new business for universities, organizations, governments and ICT societies: sharing part of the resources between cloud providers using the *aaS model represents a new way for providers to make money; the possibility to rely on a self-management system contribute to push down costs and at the same time to increase the revenues.

In such a context, the maximum profits may be reached looking at the perspective of the cloud federation where small/medium cloud providers may acquire resources on demand to deal with users peak requests to overcome their limited amount of physical resources.

This trend has also been stated in Gartner Blog Network (T. Bittman) where has been hypothesized the cloud computing evolution in three subsequent stages:

- **Stage 1:** "Monolithic" (now), where cloud services are based on independent proprietary architectures - islands of Cloud services delivered by mega-providers (this is what Amazon, Google, Salesforce, Rackspace and Microsoft look like today);
- **Stage 2:** "Vertical Supply Chain", where Cloud providers will leverage Cloud services from other providers - the Clouds will be proprietary infrastructure yet, but the ecosystem building is starting slowly;
- **Stage 3:** "Horizontal Federation", smaller, medium, and large cloud providers will federate themselves to gain economies of scale and an enlargement of their capabilities in order to build up services.

Thus, the current development of the Cloud computing markets results in the gap between the mega-providers like Amazon, Google etc. which have monolithic infrastructures provided to the public use and SMEs Cloud providers which have to federate, in- or outsource their infrastructures, maybe combine on demand offers of different mega-providers and act as Cloud resellers providing guarantees not only on functional but also non functional properties of their services.

This book addresses the new challenges existing in the future alternative scenario based on the concept of cooperating clouds constituting the federation. Federation has always had both political and historical implications: the term refers, in fact, to a type of system characterized by an aggregation of partially "self-governing" entities with "central government". In a federation, each self-governing status of the component entities is typically independent and may not be altered by a unilateral decision of the "central government". Federation is also a concept, which is adopted in many information systems. Considering small/medium independent self-governing cloud providers, federation means a cooperation enabling the sharing of part of their computational and storage resources with the purpose to provide new business opportunity.

This book is mainly addressed to two different categories of audience: business manager and research or academic people. To the first category belongs the Enterprise Business Manager who, reading the book will gain knowledge about the basic concepts on Cloud Computing and the Cloud federations issues, mainly focusing on the alternative solution of using distributed federated Clouds instead of relying on monolithic mega-providers. The same category might also include IT Enterprise Business Manager who can understand how it might be possible to migrate their own services on Cloud platforms in order to better optimize costs and resources usage. They might also look towards the new models of distributed federated Clouds instead of the monolithic one and understand how to earn profit from a set of unused hardware resources building a federated Cloud.

Research and Academic readers may have a good starting point to understand which issues the Cloud computing involves and the main research topics related to Cloud federation. Once the main issues regarding Cloud federation have been understood, these readers could propose his own solution for solving them.

The book is composed of two main parts: Theory and Practice.

The Theory part highlights federation concepts in cloud, analyzing them from a theoretical point of view and considering what nowadays is crucial in cloud computing scenarios. Several chapters present theoretic studies and possible new frameworks falling into cooperating clouds. In particular, this part contains ten chapters dealing with the following topics:

- Concepts of Federation in Clouds,
- Resource Management and Brokerage,
- New cloud Middleware,
- Monitoring in Clouds: its importance and operation.
- Theoretical Security Concepts.

In the Practical part, starting from the concepts of the Theoretical one, the attention is focused on practical implementations along with practical studies dealing with the possible solutions challenging cloud contexts. In particular this part contains ten chapters covering the following topics:

- Cloud Middleware implementations and use.
- Monitoring in Clouds from a practical point of view,
- Enterprise experience in Cloud,
- How to face Energy Constrains in Cloud,
- Applicable solution for Securing Clouds.

Regarding the first theoretical part, the authors in Chapter 1 "Toward Cloud Federation: Concepts and Challenges" introduce the main concept regarding the cloud federation and tries to clarify the ideas discussing its future challenges.

The authors in Chapter 2 "Interoperable Resource Management for establishing Federated Clouds" focus on issues faced by users with interests on Multi-Cloud use and by Cloud providers with highly dynamic workloads. The chapter proposes a Federated Cloud Management architecture that provides unified access to a federated Cloud that aggregates multiple heterogeneous IaaS Cloud providers in a transparent manner.

The authors in Chapter 3 "Understanding Decentralized and Dynamic Brokerage in Federated Cloud Environments" analyze a scenario represented by the promotion of cooperations among small/medium cloud providers, for enabling the sharing of computational and storage resources. In this scenario, the chapter focuses on different possible centralized and decentralized approaches in designing a brokerage strategy for cloud federation, analyzing their features, advantages and disadvantages.

The authors in Chapter 4 "Implementing Distributed, Self-Managing Computing Services Infrastructure using a Scalable, Parallel and Network-Centric Computing Model" introduce a new network-centric computing model using Distributed Intelligent Managed Element (DIME) network architecture (DNA).

The Chapter proposes two alternative implementations to assure end-to-end transaction reliability, availability, performance and security in distributed Cloud computing, reducing current complexity in configuring and managing virtual machines and making the Cloud Federation implementation simpler.

The authors in Chapter 5 "The Cloud@Home Volunteer and Interoperable Cloud through the Future Internet" propose the idea to implement a volunteer-Cloud, in which the infrastructure is obtained by merging heterogeneous resources that could be provided by different domains and/or providers such as other Clouds, Grid farms, clusters, datacenters, ..., till single desktops. The chapter presents the Cloud@ Home paradigm, providing a general overview and identifying all its aims and goals.

The authors in Chapter 6 "Cloud Monitoring" pursue two objectives: first, to provide an overview of monitoring in Cloud environments and, second, to propose a solution for interoperable and vendor-independent Cloud monitoring. The Chapter also motivates the necessity of monitoring at the different levels of Cloud infrastructures, introduces selected state-of-the-art, and extracts requirements for Cloud monitoring.

The authors in Chapter 7 "Monitoring in Federated and Self-Manageable Clouds" investigate the goal of building software that is able to make decisions required to reconfigure itself in a way that it resists failures and, at the same time, makes optimal use of the resources available to it. The authors identify the heart of each decision making mechanism as the data that are fed to it, which assigns to Monitoring mechanisms in federated and self-manageable Clouds a very central role.

The authors in Chapter 8 "Availability Analysis of IaaS Cloud Using Analytic Models" introduce the reader with a novel approach using interacting analytic sub-models and show how such approach can deal with large scale Cloud availability analysis. The authors put their work in perspective of other existing and ongoing research in this area, describe how such approach can be useful to Cloud providers, especially in the case of federated scenarios, and summarize the open research questions that are yet to be solved.

The author in Chapter 9 "The Security of Cloud Infrastructure" illustrates how base infrastructure operations like software provisioning and resource virtualization are critical from a security viewpoint. He also discusses the mitigation solutions available in guaranteeing an adequate level of security in the Cloud.

The authors in Chapter 10 "Security Issues in Cloud Federations" present an overview of the cloud federation topic, with special focus on its most important security challenges. Furthermore, they propose a taxonomy of possible approaches to federation and a comparison of security problems in cloud and grid environment. A detailed analysis of two relevant security problems, identity management and Cyber Attacks analysis is provided, trying to outline how they can be applied in a federated context.

The practical part starts with Chapter 11, "On the use of the Hybrid Cloud Computing Paradigm ", where the analysis of the Hybrid Cloud computing model is addressed. It combines on-premise Private Clouds with the resources of Public Clouds. The authors remark this new model is not yet fully developed and there is still a lot of work to be done before true multi-Cloud installation. As they stated, the federation of clouds needs to be mature enough to be used in production environments. For such a motivation they present a real Hybrid Cloud architecture based on the OpenNebula Cloud toolkit that tries to fill this gap. Furthermore they provide the description of some real-life experiences with the proposed architecture and Amazon EC2.

The Chapter 12 is in-line with the topic of the previous chapter. It presents the design of a cloud architecture operating at IaaS level and called CLEVER. As the authors claimed this cloud middleware was conceived for accomplishing federation mechanism at basis. The authors are using this framework also for satisfying more needs not only simply related to Cloud. The Chapter "CLEVER: A Cloud Middleware Beyond the Federation" pointing out the possibilities to enlarge the concept of federation in more directions. The chapter shows how CLEVER is able to "aggregate" heterogeneous computing infrastructure unifying together the computation resources of Cloud and Grid in a dynamic way.

A concrete experience is described in the Chapter 13, where the authors, involved in the European Project RESERVOIR on Service Cloud computing, were in charge for setup an efficient monitoring system. Moreover, they have faced the design of a monitoring system that is suitable for supporting the operations and management of a Federated Cloud environment. They first present the RESERVOIR architecture itself, then introduce the issues of service monitoring in a federated environment, together with the specific solutions that have been devised for RESERVOIR. The authors remark that reviewing their experience in this area it is possible to notice that further work is still needed.

Having good cloud middleware and efficient systems of monitoring it is possible to opportunely manage physical resources in clouds and meet the cloud customers' requirements. This is the main aim of the Chapter 14, "Achieving Flexible SLA and Resource Management in Clouds".

The authors try to accomplish a flexible Cloud computing where the resource provisioning is considered on-demand following the pay-as-you-go philosophy. Furthermore, their resource provisioning is based on Service Level Agreements (SLAs) negotiated and signed between customers and providers. Efficient management of SLAs and Cloud are aimed to cost reduction and high resource utilization. In order to advance the adoption of this technology, it is necessary to identify and address the issues preventing proper resource and SLA management. In the chapter the authors identify the SLA management and monitoring challenges in Clouds related to federated environments and propose a novel resource monitoring architecture as a basis for a new type of resource management.

Another concrete experience addressed during the EU funded project RESERVOIR is described in Chapter 15, which is the "Resource Management Mechanisms to Support SLAs in IaaS Clouds". The chapter focuses on the Infrastructure as a Service (IaaS) model that epitomizes many of the generic resource management problems arising in cloud computing.

The authors face the issue related to the elastic multi-VM workloads corresponding to multi-tier application. They study the fundamental problems of VM placement optimization, subject to policy constraints, elasticity requirements, and performance SLAs. They report a combinatorial optimization problem called elastic services placement problem to maximize the provider's benefit from SLA compliant placement.

Satisfy the even more complex SLAs in Clouds is not easy at all. The Chapter 16, "Economic Analysis of the SLA Mapping Approach for Cloud Computing Goods" tries to give an answer on such a problem reducing the SLA complexity. The authors propose a restriction of the number of different resource types to a small set of standardized computing resources. As they stated this approach appears to be the appropriate solution to counteract this problem. The SLA template defines the structure of an SLA, the service attributes, the names of the service attributes, and the service attribute values. The existing research results have only introduced static SLA templates but it cannot reflect changes in user needs and market structures. To address this shortcoming, they present an approach of adaptive SLA matching. Indeed their approach should adapt SLA templates based on SLA mappings of users, allowing Cloud users to define mappings between public SLA templates. In the chapter they investigate how the costs differ with respect to the public SLA template adaptation method.

An industrial experience on how to shift Enterprises' applications on clouds is reported in Chapter 17, "Deploying and running Enterprise Grade Applications in Federated Cloud".

The chapter describes what are the major challenges when it is necessary to use cloud for deploying and running enterprise applications. They highlight that for companies, picking and choosing the right cloud to meet requirements is hard, and no solution is likely to provide the end-to-end specific IT services deliver and end-to-end IT solution. Cloud federation assists in providing flexibility to the customer and enables them to lower their Total Cost of Ownership by shifting from one cloud to another while mitigating risks associated with a single cloud approach. The work focuses on three different use cases for the deployment of enterprise applications such as *SAP Enterprise*, on the cloud in order to provide some valuable pointers to navigate the emerging cloud ecosystem: rapid provisioning, elasticity and live migration of enterprise applications.

One of the *long-standing* issue on cloud is represented from the reduction of CO_2 footprint. The energy consumption in clouds heavily affects this negative outcome. The next two chapters address this grave problem and provide possible solutions for reducing the impact on the Environment in using clouds. The chapter 18 surveys existing efforts on building IaaS platforms, but evaluating such systems from the energy consumption point of view, assessing energy-aware virtual machine placement algorithms. The authors in "Towards Energy-Efficient, Scalable, and Resilient IaaS Clouds", describe the architecture and implementation of a scalable, fault-tolerant and energy-aware VM manager called *Snooze*. It follows the approach of the nature-inspired energy-aware VM placement mechanism based on the Ant Colony Optimization.

Chapter 19 treats the "Self-Management of Applications and Systems to Optimize Energy in Data Centers", where a self-adaptation approach is used that considers both users' applications and the computation system to reduce the energy footprint in cloud infrastructures. The authors consider each application and the infrastructure as one system with control closed-loop, which allows them to autonomously optimize their executions. They implemented the control loops and simulated them in order to show their feasibility. In addition, they show how the provided solution fits in federated clouds through a motivating scenario.

The last Chapter, 20, illustrates a practical way for securing clouds. It deals with the "Access Control in Federated Clouds: The Cloudgrid Case Study". The chapter offers a view on the problems of access control on federated Clouds. The PerfCloud framework is presented which is based on the integration of Grid and Cloud platforms. The authors proposed an architecture able to make up an interoperable system coping with identity federation and access control. The dissertation should help the reader to have an idea on what are the security open issues and available solutions in commercial or experimental clouds.

This book will provide an overview about the current cloud technologies that can be applied by the industry as well as academia. On one hand, decision makers from the industry will get an overview about trends and challenges for investment and utilization of Cloud technologies in their companies. On the other hand, academia will get an overview about recent developments in and challenging research fields in Cloud computing. The chapters present as follows mainly threat the Federation challenges at IaaS level.

Massimo Villari
Università Degli Studi di Messina, Italy

Ivona Brandic
Vienna University of Technology, Austria

Francesco Tusa
Università Degli Studi di Messina, Italy

Acknowledgment

First of all and foremost we say thank you very much to all contributors that allowed us to concretize this book. We are grateful with them for the time, efforts, abnegation, and patience they've shown during the phases of selection, revisions, and finalization of their chapters.

We would like to say thank you also to the members of the book Editorial Advisory Board for their assistance in making a good result. In particular, to Dr. Walfang Gaentz for his illuminating foreword conceived for this book.

The chapters included in this book have been reviewed in double-blind process, with three reviewers for each chapter. We remark the authors have addressed point by point the detailed and valuable comments of the reviewers involved in the evaluation phase. We also say thank you to members of the MDSLAB Messina, Università degli Studi di Messina, who helped us on chapters' reviews and book organization.

Massimo would like to thank Carmen, his wife, who bears and supports him during his very stressing commitments, and to his sweet daughter, Gaia, who gives him beautiful smiles and carefree moments. A particular thank you is also due to Villari and Nazzari families; Massimo's relatives who always sustain him.

Francesco would like to say thanks both to his kind partner in love, Miriam, and his relatives, for their patience and support provided while the book has been written.

Ivona would like to thank Manda, Ivo, Igor, and Harald for their invaluable support and love.

Massimo Villari
Università Degli Studi di Messina, Italy

Ivona Brandic
Vienna University of Technology, Austria

Francesco Tusa
Università Degli Studi di Messina, Italy

Section 1
Theory

Chapter 1
Toward Cloud Federation:
Concepts and Challenges

Antonio Celesti
Università Degli Studi di Messina, Italy

Francesco Tusa
Università Degli Studi di Messina, Italy

Massimo Villari
Università Degli Studi di Messina, Italy

ABSTRACT

Federation in cloud computing is an emerging topic. Currently, all over the world in both academia and industry contexts many operators are picking up the advantages of cloud computing and federation in planning the Internet of the future. Nevertheless, cloud federation is at the early stage, and the scientific community is not fully aware how the federation will impact the cloud computing scenario. In this chapter, the authors try to clarify the ideas and discuss the main future challenges regarding cloud federation.

INTRODUCTION

The success of cloud computing is due to the fact that it leverages new business opportunities for ICT societies, governments, organizations, and universities. Nowadays, more and more capital investments have been done in both academia and industry areas, and at the same time more and more research works and commercial applications are rising on the market.

In such a context, perspectives of cloud federation and self-management are again destined

to change the Future Internet scenario, bringing new business opportunities. On one hand the possibility to share part of resources between cloud providers, considering computational and storage capabilities according to a utility-as-a-service model, brings new ways for providers to make money. On the other hand the possibility to rely on a self-management system contributes to push down costs and at the same time to increase the revenues. For example, if a cloud provider has run out its storage and computing capabilities it can ask for resources to other clouds establishing a partnership with them according to business agreements.

DOI: 10.4018/978-1-4666-1631-8.ch001

Copyright © 2012, IGI Global. Copying or distributing in print or electronic forms without written permission of IGI Global is prohibited.

Hence, the advantage of transforming a physical datacenter in a cloud virtualization infrastructure in the perspective of cloud federation is relevant indeed. Small/medium cloud providers, often characterized by a limited amount of physical resources, may rent resources from other providers optimizing the use of their infrastructure. Even more, external small/medium cloud providers can elastically scale up/down their logical virtualization infrastructure borrowing capabilities and paying them to other providers only when they need.

Commonly the sentence "Time is money" is widely referred to the notion that time is valuable, especially in business area, and it remains valid for cloud computing markets. For this reason a reactive cloud infrastructure able to optimize itself according to changes of the surrounding environment, on one hand enables providers to save money, for example migrating services from a server to another into another clouds in order to turn off physical appliances, whereas on the other hand a more reactive provider can improve its revenues answering to a federation request faster than other providers. For example, for Quality of Service (QoS) constraints a cloud provider, which needs external capabilities, might very likely choose the cloud provider which first response to the partnership establishment request.

Cloud computing is a rapidly and continuously evolving paradigm, which embrace different research fields. Typical research topics are QoS, security, trusted computing, policy management, self-management, monitoring, service brokerage, service composition, service negotiation, service migration, networking, data export control, green computing, naming and information retrieval, standard compliance, and many others. Many researchers and ICT business operators believe that the next step in the evolution of cloud computing is represented by federation, but currently it is not clear which will be the impact of the federation on the traditional cloud computing paradigm,

including a "sea of thousand of independent cloud islands".

In this chapter, the authors try to identify which the main research topics in cloud computing are analyzing available solutions in the traditional scenario including single independent cloud providers. After that, the chapter analyzes how the perspective of cloud federation impacts each of these research topics, highlighting new opportunities and challenges in those areas. The rest of the chapter is organized as follows. Firstly, it discusses the new business opportunities and new cloud federation scenarios. After that, it presents the main phases for performing the federation establishment process. Then, the chapter analyzes the main research topics in cloud computing especially considering federation, highlighting both new challenges in the perspective of cloud federation. After a discussion of the current standards, the chapter ends with conclusions.

BACKGROUND

Cloud federation does not always have the same meaning. This section provides the base information for classifying a cloud federation, according to an agreed service level and related to the partnership establishment.

Why Federation in Cloud Computing?

The concept of federation has always had both political and historical implications. The term refers, in fact, to a type of system organization characterized by a joining of partially "self-governing" entities united by a "central government". In a federation, each self-governing status of the component entities is typically independent and may not be altered by a unilateral decision of the "central government".

The components of a federation are in some sense "sovereign" with a certain degree of autonomy from the "central government": this is why a federation can be intended as more than a mere loose alliance of independent entities.

Until now, the cloud ecosystem has been characterized by the steady rising of hundreds of independent and heterogeneous cloud providers, managed by private subjects which yield various services to their clients. Using this computing infrastructure it is possible to pursue new levels of efficiency in delivering services (SaaS, PaaS, and IaaS) to clients such as IT companies, organizations, universities, generic single end-user which can range from desktop to mobile users, and so on. For shortness, in the rest of the chapter, we will also refer to these services with the term *aaS.

Despite that such an ecosystem includes hundreds of independent, heterogeneous clouds, many business operators have predicted that the process toward interoperable federated cloud scenarios will begin in the near future. Imagine a scenario where different clouds, belonging to different administrative domains, could interact each other becoming themselves both "users" and "resource providers" at the same time. Obviously the interaction and cooperation among the entities of this scenario might be complex and needs to be deeply investigated: this is why the term "federation" is also in the IT world and cloud computing.

The current gap between the current scenario including thousands of independent cloud providers and the futuristic scenario of federated clouds, is reflected by the cloud infrastructure developments in US and Europe. While US cloud landscape is dominated by the "mega- providers" like Amazon, Azure and Google, in Europe the cloud providers are generally Telcos developing their private clouds and Enterprises which offer their infrastructures to specific groups of users with specific needs.

Economic Aspects: The Rising of a New Market

Even though the idea of creating federated infrastructures seems to be very profitable, bridging such gap could not be straightforward: on one hand, in fact, highly scalable infrastructures are required to comply with the varying load, software, and hardware failures using Cloud federation scenarios. On the other hand, autonomic managed infrastructures are required to adapt, manage, and utilize cloud ecosystems in an efficient way.

Considering the cloud computing ecosystem, besides large cloud providers, also smaller/medium providers are becoming popular even though the virtualization infrastructures they have deployed in their datacenters cannot directly compete with the bigger counterparts including mega-providers. A way to overcome these resource limitations is represented by the promotion of federation and cooperation mechanisms among small/medium cloud providers, thus enabling the sharing of computational and storage resources. This allows another form of pay-per-use economic model for ICT societies, universities, research centers and organizations that commonly do not fully exploit the resources of their own physical infrastructure.

Federation brings new business opportunities for clouds. Besides the traditional market where cloud providers offer cloud-based services to their clients, federation triggers a new market where cloud providers can buy and/or sell computing/storage capabilities and services to other clouds. This means that groups of federated small/medium size cloud providers could become as competitive as mega-providers and overcome the current gap.

The new business opportunities of cloud federation may promote the rising of a new form of web companies providing service to cloud federation providers. An example is represented by "resource capability brokers" acting as mediator between cloud providers. These brokers would interact both with providers offering capabilities and providers requiring capabilities. In a world-wide cloud federation scenario, the presence of different heterogeneous cloud providers is very likely. These brokers would provide discovery and mediation services, since they would be always up-to-date about the market of cloud capabilities.

Use Cases Overview

Cloud federation may be applied to different business scenarios. Here, an overview of possible use cases which can leverage the advantages of cloud federation is provided. Such use cases are: "running out of capabilities", "service composition", and "service migration".

- **Running out of Capabilities:** Typically, datacenters are under-utilized during the night and over-utilized during the morning. Therefore, as in many cases, the datacenter cannot be turned off, and the cloud provider may decide to turn the problem into a business opportunity. This case may be applied to many different organizations, such as, universities, governments and ICT companies. Hence, the advantage of transforming a physical datacenter in a cloud virtualization infrastructure in the perspective of cloud federation is twofold. On the one hand, small/medium cloud providers that rent resources to other providers can optimize the use of their infrastructure, which are often underutilized. On the other hand, external small/medium cloud providers can elastically scale up/down their logical virtualization infrastructure by borrowing resources and paying them to other providers. This situation is motivated by the fact that clouds do not have infinite resources. There are three main situations which can take place when a cloud temporarily runs out of its own storage and computing capabilities:

  ◦ The cloud is not able to satisfy any further *aaS instantiation requests.
  ◦ The cloud is not able to satisfy the Service Level Agreements (SLA) a prior established with the client concerning the utilization terms of the *aaS.
  ◦ The cloud is not able to satisfy a SLA modification request sent by its client who needs to increase the capabilities and features of its *aaS.

  The three situations imply that, for a period of time, the cloud is not able to satisfy the requests of its clients as long as some of its resources are not released. This can have a serious negative economic impact especially for small and medium clouds. Such a problem can be solved recurring to partnership establishment, as each cloud provider is able to transparently enlarge and optimize its own resource capabilities, increasing the number of instantiable virtual environments, also balancing the workload so that clouds can never deny services to their clients.

- **Distributed Service Composition:** According to the size of a virtualization infrastructure we can distinguish among small, medium, and large clouds. Small and medium clouds are held by small and medium size companies, while large clouds are held by large size companies (e.g., Amazon Europe or Rackspace). The latter are able to provide distributed large-scale IaaS, PaaS, and SaaS. (generalizing ``D*aaS"). A distributed cloud service is an instance composed of a set of VMs spread over a wide geographical area, orchestrated in order to achieve a target purpose, and which is provided on-demand to a cloud client to meet his business needs. In this perspective federation can also give to both small and medium clouds the opportunity to offer distributed services to their clients. By means of federation, small and medium cloud providers can enlarge their virtualization capabilities using the virtualization infrastructures of other ones for a given business purpose, becoming as competitive as large clouds. In this scenario the reason driving clouds to establish partnerships is that they need to have several resources placed in given geographical locations. In order to arrange and provide distributed cloud service composed of several VMs, they need to be hosted in different clouds placed in target geographical areas. An example of distributed cloud-based service can be a Content Delivery Network (CDN) including mirrors of a main web server in different cities.

- **Service Migration:** Even though cloud computing has been thought only for the optimization of the resources in data centers, considering the benefits of the independent cloud, there could be situations where federation along with resource migration can increase the business profits of providers. Resource migration implies the movement of VMs from a cloud provider to another one. In such situations it is important for cloud providers to rely on trust partners to migrate their services. This scenario can be very useful in different situations including power saving, fault tolerance, security, and backup.

Power saving can be done according to green computing strategies.

Service migration can reduce the energy consumptions of datacenter. For example, if a provider has only a VM running in a physical server, it will save money migrating the VM into another cloud if the money needed to maintain the active server is more than the money needed for the external hosting. Thanks to the migration in federated environments, cloud providers can rely on powerful trusted backup services in order to react to failures and cyber attacks. To this regard, if a cloud provider is attacked and it realizes that the security of its infrastructure is violated, it can decide either to migrate its services in real time to other federated cloud providers or switch to the backup of its system hosted in other federated providers.

FEDERATION ESTABLISHMENT PROCESS

The previous sections introduced the concept of cloud federation. The following will try to understand which requirements should be satisfied for allowing the establishment of cooperation among clouds.

A cloud federation is an interconnection among homogeneous and heterogeneous clouds, each laying out its own set of resources, managed using a specific middleware and probably accessible through different security mechanisms. Due to the high dynamism that could characterize this type of federation, several different platforms and technologies should coexist and be able to address all such issues that might consist in the employment of middleware: the ability to grant interoperability, automatism, and scalability features.

In a typical federation scenario, it could be possible that new clouds, offering available resources could appear, while others could disappear. Taking into account such a dynamism, when a given cloud needs to "lease" external resources from another one, the first phase it will perform refers to the *discovery* of the cloud which properly *matches* (phase 2) its requirements (both in terms of available resources, technologies, policies, and supported authentication mechanisms, etc). Once these two phases have been performed, and the best exploitable clouds have been found, in order to establish a secure interaction between the involved entities, an authentication process (phase 3) will begin.

The accomplishment of the authentication process leads to the establishment of a secure and direct connection between the cloud that is requesting more resources and the cloud selected for satisfying this resource provisioning. As consequence, the first cloud will be able to instantiate (or migrate) VMs on the second one in a secure environment.

Thus the federation process can be summarized as the accomplishment of a sequence of three different phases: discovery, match-making and authentication.

Discovery

The goal of this first phase consists of exploring the dynamic environment in order to discover all the clouds that are available for taking part into the federation.

This environment can not be known *a priori*, but it is pretty flexible and dynamic. The most convenient way to accomplish the discovery process should be based on the employment of a distributed approach: the middlewares of all the clouds which aim to attend the federation should communicate by exploiting a peer-to-peer (p2p) mechanism, based conveniently on the presence concept.

The latter is indeed an enabling technology for p2p interactions, whose implementation follows the software design pattern known as publish-and-subscribe (pub-sub): an application publishes its own set of information to a centralized location (even though such a location is logically centralized, it is implemented in a distributed fashion, also granting fault-tolerance mechanisms), from which only a set of authorized (subscribed) entities are able to retrieve it.

The employment of these mechanisms might represent a valid starting point to address the cloud discovery problem in a federation scenario: each cloud middleware broadcasts on-demand information about its supported features and states

its resources to other peers aiming to attend the federated environment.

When a given cloud needs to know the other clouds available to start the federation in a certain moment, along with the related capabilities, its management middleware will merely check the shared area on which this information is stored. To accomplish this mechanism, the cloud middleware should be required to integrate a specific component acting as presence daemon. It may exploit one or more presence protocols, in order to distribute information about its features, state, and availability as widely as possible.

Match-Making

Once the discovery phase is done, the more convenient cloud(s) wherewith to establish a high cooperation federation has to be chosen. In order to accomplish this task, another specific component of the cloud middleware should be responsible of managing and enforcing the policies defined by the clouds.

In fact, both the cloud that requests the resources and the other available (discovered) clouds may be associated with a set of data containing a several policies, each composed of a set of rules respectively describing which resources are required and which ones are offered according to some conditions.

For example a cloud could require a certain amount of CPU and storage, with a certain QoS, supporting some security policies, from 0.00 am to 8.00 am. At the same time, a cloud could offer resources with a certain QoS, with a target security policy, at any time, denying the requests sent by certain clouds.

In order to enable the middleware to evaluate which of the available (discovered) clouds are the ones that best "fit" the requested requirements, policy matching should be performed.

To accomplish the policy matching mechanism, each cloud middleware should evaluate the applicable policies by returning authorization decisions and performing an access control by enforcing the stated authorization decisions.

For instance, the cloud policies might be expressed by means of an extensible policy language able to integrate different policy formats using transformation algorithms.

Authentication

During the last phase, once the cloud with which to establish the federation has been selected, a mechanism for creating a security context between the cloud that requested new resources and the one chosen for satisfying that request should be accomplished. When the authentication phase begins, the component responsible of the authentication on the requesting cloud will contact its "peer" on the "destination" cloud: the authentication process will be lead exchanging authentication information in form of meta-data, involving trusted third parties in the process. In a distributed scenario composed of hundreds of clouds, the credential managements could be very hard: each cloud should manage hundreds of credentials which can change over the time, each needed for the authentication with the other federation members.

In order to accomplish these mechanisms, the cloud middlewares could use the Identity Provider/ Service Provider (IdP/SP) model. Such a model defines the exchange of authentication assertions between security domains, more specifically, between an IdP or asserting party (a producer of assertions) and a SP or relying party (a consumer of assertions). The model assumes that a subject, a person, or a software/hardware entity (i.e., in our case the cloud requering federation) holds at least one digital identity on an IdP which supplies SSO authentication services. SSO is the property by means of an entity and is able to perform the authentication once accessing to the resources of different SPs (i.e., in our case the clouds offering resources). As the SPs are trusted with the IdP, the subject is able to perform the log-in once gaining the access to all the required resources (hosted inside the SPs).

CHALLENGES: ISSUES, CONTROVERSIES, PROBLEMS?

The following section aims to provide an overview about a set of issues that are deeply involved in the cloud computing scenario. More specifically, the section introduces and analyzes the monitoring of the resources, the Service Level Agreement management, the autonomous systems applicability and the involved networking issues. Finally the section highlights security and standards.

Monitoring and History

Considering the set of services constituting a cloud, it appears straightforward that one of the most important tasks to be accomplished for assuring its management consists of the generation and processing of information about the state, health, and performance of its various involved services and IT components. Such information is the foundation for proper assessment and management of distributed computing systems and is generally known as *monitoring*. More specifically, the term monitoring refers to the process of collecting measures of different parameters of the infrastructures that are then forwarded to the control process of the management for adjusting the infrastructure configuration. Since the monitoring provides information needed to perform appropriate control decisions, it can be considered a fundamental process for achieving control of the whole distributed infrastructure.

Proper management should be based on the measurement coming from the set of components involved in the service delivery, i.e. hardware, storage, and software modules. More specifically, these measurements include metrics related to CPU utilization, memory and bandwidth consumptions. The collected information allows to evaluate the current state of the infrastructure and to predict also its future behavior in terms of requirements and utilization.

As already stated in the previous sections, the cloud service landscape is separated into IaaS, PaaS, and SaaS. This brief dissertation mainly deals with IaaS although some considerations might be also assumed with PaaS and SaaS.

In a typical IaaS scenario, an IaaS provider has a contract with a service provider which, in turn, has a contract with an end-user. The services of the service provider are supported by the infrastructure made available from the IaaS provider. Since the quality of service offered by the service provider depends on the quality of service supported by the IaaS provider, both parties need adequate monitoring to ensure the required service levels.

In particular, the focus of IaaS providers is to keep their system running at an operating point that allows profit maximization. Therefore they need to retrieve information about the health of their physical infrastructure and about the resource usage of customers' virtual resources.

IaaS customers, on the other hand, need low-level information about their virtual infrastructure as well as all the software that is running on top of it. Unfortunately, even though a little overlap exists between the two sets of information needed by providers and customers, only some measurement are shared. In order to build a complete overview of the state of the applications and services deployed in the cloud, any additional information the customers may need must be retrieved by the customers themselves.

A solution to the above problem is the installation of monitoring and management software on the virtual machine images. Although this solution appears to be the easiest, it does not exploit the benefits of the cloud paradigm. In this environment, monitoring would be externally supplied by the provider or an external third-party in order to exempt the customers from the annoying task of deploying and maintaining their own monitoring solution.

Orthogonal to the requirement of additional monitoring capabilities for the customers, is the rising need for monitoring solutions to able to retrieve information from multiple cloud slices spanning multiple independent cloud providers. As cloud providers offer different features, different quality-of-service levels, and different pricing strategies, customers want to mix and match those parts of the various clouds for achieving the best satisfaction of their requirements. At present, federated cloud monitoring still lies far in the future. The major obstacle to achieve this is the lack of interoperability. All cloud providers support their own proprietary monitoring systems only.

Service Level Agreements

A service-level agreement (SLA) is a part of a service contract in which is formally defined the delivery time and performance of a service. It is thus an agreement stipulated between two parties: a customer and a service provider. The SLA records a common understanding about services, priorities, responsibilities, guarantees, and warranties. Each area of service scope should have the "level of service" defined. The SLA may specify the levels of availability, serviceability, performance, operation, or other attributes of the service, such as billing. The "level of service" can also be specified as "target" and "minimum," which allows customers to be informed of what to expect (the minimum), while providing a measurable (average) target value that shows the level of organization performance. In some contracts, penalties may be agreed upon in the case of non-compliance with the SLA. It is important to note that the "agreement" relates to the services the customer receives, and not how the service provider delivers that service.

In the cloud computing scenario, dynamically scalable computing infrastructures are provided to the customers exploiting the concept of virtualization. Cloud resources and services are provisioned based on SLAs, which are contracts specified and signed between cloud providers and their customers detailing the terms of the agreement including non-functional requirements, such as Quality of Service (QoS) and penalties in case of violations. Since the service provisioning within a cloud can be realized at different levels (Iaas, PaaS and SaaS), a flexible and reliable management of both the resource provisioning and SLA agreements has to be employed in a transverse way, regardless of the level the services are provided to, in order to help providers avoid SLA penalties due to contract violations. The SLAs of customer applications are guaranteed by providers using complex and sophisticated resource monitoring strategies that are also able to provide information about the current SLA, by consequently adjusting the management process.

An IaaS cloud scenario allows a cloud provider to host end-user applications in a cost-efficient way thanks to resource pooling. This mechanism is based on the idea that, since different user workloads do not peak all at the same time, the available resources can be allocated to them, used and then returned to the pool. Obviously, this paradigm can be implemented using a real-time monitoring of resource availability, utilization and user workloads quality of service. All this information has to be retrieved by means of a monitoring system and then has to be analyzed by a resource management engine that will consequently take resources allocation decisions. One of the risks coming from this paradigm is the possibility of temporarily assigning a lot of resources to the customer workload that is requesting them, and decreasing the quality of service and breaking SLA compliance with the other customers.

The current SLA solutions employed by all the main IaaS vendors offer the so called up-time SLAs to their customers. SLAs for VMs stipulate a specific percentile of billing period when a VM started by a user is supposed to be up and running (also known as up-time SLAs); the customer himself is responsible for detecting and reporting a problem with the SLA. A close look at the current cloud SLA practices reveals that these SLAs are difficult for the customer to understand and evaluate due to obfuscation of vendor's commitments. Usual tricks include annualizing service unavailability periods, vaguely defining outages, obscuring maintenance periods and having non-transparent refund policies.

The SLAs management will grow in complexity if we consider cloud environments including dozens of independent, heterogeneous data centers cooperating together toward an interoperable federated Cloud.

This is expected as a result of inefficiencies in the independent Cloud environments and the drive to exploit the full potentials of Cloud computing. For instance, if a provider does not have enough local resources to fulfill its customers' requirements, the provider will start denying the acceptance of new customers or cancelling some low-priority applications in order to guarantee the SLA of the high priority ones. This eventually leads to low profit for the provider and dissatisfaction for the customers.

Brokerage

Before the provisioning of a cloud-based service between the cloud provider and its client, a preliminary phase of negotiation, in which agreements and constrains are established between them, is required. This negotiation phase can take place between the provider and the client itself, or through a third party broker. SLAs may regard functional and non-functional requirements that the cloud-based service has to guarantee. For example, a client, represented by an ICT society can require an IaaS including, for example, four Linux-based VMs, each one with CPU 2,6 GHz, RAM 4GB, with KVM virtualization technology, connected by means of a virtual network, from 8:00 a.m. to 22:00 p.m.

In the phase of negotiation the client has to consider the costs for supplying the IaaS, the guaranteed QoS, and the security. All these required factors have to match the offer of the cloud provider. Often the client has to find the right compromise between its demand and the offers of different cloud providers. For example, sometimes the client is willing to pay more in order to have a better QoS, and in other cases the client is willing to have a worse QoS in order to save money.

Currently, cloud computing is still evolving so that new specific negotiation mechanisms among service providers are needed for enabling effective collaboration, allowing the process of serving consumers to be more efficient. Alhamad, M. & Dillon, T. & Chang, E. (2010) investigate the negotiation strategies between cloud providers and cloud consumers and propose a method to maintain the trust and reliability between each of the parties involved in the negotiation process. Brandic, I. (2009) proposed an architecture for the implementation of self-manageable cloud services, focusing on service mediation by means of a matching between the meta negotiation document of a service consumer and the one of service provider. Paletta, M.& Herrero, P. (2009) present a negotiation mechanism that allows a cloud to achieve an effective collaboration among its internal services by means of a multi-agent architecture.

Cloud federation raises several new challenges in service brokerage. Apart from the typical service negotiation which happens between a cloud provider and its clients, the federated scenario also requires a negotiation between different cloud providers for the establishment of partnerships. If for example a cloud run out of its resources or simply needs external resources for other business reasons, the cloud provider requiring the federation need to choose the provider that better satisfy its requirements in term of SLAs.

Considering a worldwide federation cloud scenario, besides the issues already picked up regarding service negotiation, the brokerage between different cloud providers raises issue due to technology compliance. Considering heterogeneous providers from the technological point of view, mediation mechanisms are required. A possible solution is including such mechanisms in the cloud providers themselves. In this case each provider has to manage the discovery, mediation, and negotiation by itself. Another possible approach is to delegate such functionalities to third party federation brokers acting as mediator between different heterogeneous clouds. In this case, if a cloud wants to look for another cloud for federation, it has only to contact the federation broker specifying its required SLAs.

A hybrid scenario combining the two aforementioned approaches is also possible.

Self-CHOP

Evolved cloud providers have to manage complex and unpredictable situations. Clouds should be able to react to peaks of requests, failures, internal policy and SLA violation. A peak of requests can happen when suddenly the provider receives more requests than usual. Failures can regard both the hardware and software cloud infrastructure. Cloud providers should be able to recover disasters either in a proactive or reactive way. Internal policy violation can regard load balancing, infrastructure management, or power saving strategies in force on the cloud provider. SLA violation can happen when an agreement established between a cloud provider and its users is broken. Solutions addressing all these situations can come from the autonomic computing system theory. Autonomic Computing Systems are systems which are capable of adapting themselves to changes in their working environment in order to maintain required service level agreements, protect the execution of the system from external attacks, or prevent and recover failures.

As a typical autonomic system, a cloud provider should be able to leverage the advantages of self-management performing, self-provisioning, self-healing, self-protection, and self-optimization strategies (all together known as self-CHOP). Autonomic systems are developed as control loops which monitor and analyze the execution of the whole system and then plan and execute changes if needed in order to adapt the system to its dynamic environment. Typically control loops are implemented as MAPE (monitoring, analysis, planning, and execution) functions. The monitor collects state information and prepares it for the analysis. If deviations to the desired state are discovered during the analysis, the planner elaborates change plans, which are passed to the executor which executes the required operation.

In an autonomic system two important elements for the self-management are sensors and actuators. Sensors collect data monitoring the cloud infrastructure and services; instead actuators execute the instructions given by the executor according to target policy rearranging the cloud infrastructure and cloud-based services when required. Cloud providers can take advantage of the autonomic system in order to self-optimize both their infrastructures and their cloud-based services. A cloud provider should be capable of controlling the life-cycle of its systems and instantiated service.

More specifically, considering cloud-based services built on top of one or more virtualized environments, a cloud provider should be able to guarantee target SLAs established with the user according to target functional and non-functional requirements. In order to achieve such a goal, the provider should be characterized by self-provisioning and self-optimization features. When the cloud provider receives a service allocation coming from its user, it has to self-provision the service, composing it by aggregating several components that can be hosted in one or more virtual environments. In order to minimize the waste of resources and make the service efficient, the provider has to self-optimize the service also considering its resource consumption rate. On the contrary, when a cloud service is overloaded due to a peak in utilization, the provider has to enhance the performance of the service, for example elastically creating service replications allocating additional instances in other virtual environments in order to achieve load balancing. Moreover, when the cloud-based service is not needed anymore, the provider has to deallocate the instance, releasing the resources. Nevertheless, the autonomic management of cloud infrastructures and services is not simple depending on the specific problems that the autonomic management attempts to solve.

Recently a few works have been made regarding the application of the autonomic system concepts in cloud computing environments. Solomon, B. & Ionescu, D. & Litoiu, M. & Iszlai, G. (2010) propose an approach for the designing of autonomic management systems for cloud computing. Using a compassable strategy, the authors discuss how their development approach can be easily reconfigured in order to achieve self-management for Web Services and self-optimization for server virtualization. Paton, N. & De Aragão, M. & Lee, K. & Fern, A. & Sakellariou, R. (2009) describe how utility functions can be used to make explicit the desirability of different workload evaluation strategies, and how optimization can be used to select between such alternatives.

Self-management implies new challenges considering cloud federation. Different from the traditional case including a single cloud provider, in a cloud federation, services can be spread over different providers.

In this perspective the autonomic management of services cannot be easy, because coordination and technology compliance between different cloud infrastructures are required. From the point of view of partnerships between different clouds, providers have to face relationship establishment, management, and breaking. In order to establish a partnership, it needs to automatically discover other clouds and select the ones matching target requirements and SLAs. Once the partnership is established, it needs to check that it satisfies such SLAs, and in case of violation, break the relationship. In the end, when a partnership is broken it is needed to free the used resources.

Security: The Overlapping of Definitions among Initiatives in Cloud and Security

Security management in the IT world represents one of the main challenges in distributed systems, in particular for Cloud Computing environments. This emerging digital globalization has not only raised the legal stakes and ownership concerns, but also heralded the need of developing new security models to assure resilience, security, and privacy of data in the peculiar characteristics of Cloud computing such as multi-tenancy, federation, and workload mobility, and so on. Resilience is the ability of a system (network, service, infrastructure, etc) to provide and maintain an acceptable level of service in the face of various faults and challenges to normal operation. Security is the ability to protect user data and information systems from unauthorized access, use, disclosure, and disruption, modification or destruction, and to respond and recover in case of an incident or fault. Data security and service resilience are considered when defining the acceptable level of service for each organization. A service can be considered end-to-end secure and resilient when it performs as described in the service level specification (SLS).

Currently many initiatives are taking place for addressing issues related to cloud computing and security. It is possible to notice an overlapping among initiatives that are attempting to clarify what security means in Cloud Computing paradigm. The information below briefly highlights such an overlap, describing that often IT argumentations are generally hard to treat with respect to cloud issues and concerns. Four initiatives for pointing out these concepts were selected. A survey was conducted by GARTNER along with the view point of: CSA, NIST, and ENISA.

The GARNTER was the early company highlighting problems that customers identified adopting cloud technology. They are listed as follows:

Privileged user access is where mostly IT administrators have greater access rights compared to the other system users. Cloud managers have to properly address this issue. *Regulatory compliance* is a very significant issue that requires careful consideration of the legislation that governs the handling of data and information in secure and ethical ways. *Data location*, the knowledge of the physical location of data, is important in various perspectives. It is necessary to know where particular data is stored to assure data export control for sensitive data. Moreover it is necessary to assure the privacy of business data especially in the case of outsourcing back-office operations. *Data segregation* is equivalent to the partition of a given dataset into a number of subsets and enables the application of the principle of least privilege. Given the hosting nature of cloud computing providers, consumers need mechanisms and warranties so that their applications are isolated from others that are being hosted in the same infrastructure. *Recovery* is linked to system resilience. This is an important virtue of massive and autonomic systems where human-interventions are kept at the minimum level so as to achieve significant performance. Cloud deployments require that the normal state has to be restored after a failure. In *Investigative support* the security requirements are generally seen as preventive measures that are meant to contrast any security breach. Failure of security services is reasonably possible in real life situations but a post-accident scenario should be conceived and necessary investigative support should be provided. *Long-term viability* is important to define the protection cycle of the data stored over the clouds especially in the context of digital curation. The security and confidentiality of the data should be assured throughout their lifecycle.

The Cloud Security Alliance (CSA,2009) is a non-profit organization formed to promote and provide education on the uses of Cloud Computing to help secure all other forms of computing. The Cloud Security Alliance is comprised of many subject matter experts from a wide variety disciplines, united in four objectives: a) promote a common level of understanding between the consumers and providers of cloud computing regarding the necessary security requirements and attestation of assurance; b) promote independent research into best practices for cloud computing security; c) launch awareness campaigns and educational programs on the appropriate uses of cloud computing and cloud security solutions; d) create consensus lists of issues and provide guidance for cloud security assurance. CSA has defined 13 different domains dealing with clouds. Some of them are aimed at the description of clouds, while others fall into security constrains. The complete list is as follows:

1. Cloud Computing Architectural Framework
2. Governance and Enterprise Risk Management
3. Legal and Electronic Discovery
4. Compliance and Audit
5. Information Lifecycle Management
6. Portability and Interoperability
7. Traditional Security, Business Continuity, and Disaster Recovery
8. Data Center Operations
9. Incident Response, Notification, and Remediation
10. Application Security
11. Encryption and Key Management
12. Identity and Access Management
13. Virtualization

The National Institute of Standards & Technology form US (NIST, 2011) is really active in Cloud context formalization: IaaS, PaaS and SaaS are their definition. The NIST has recently produced its *"Guidelines on Security and Privacy in Public Cloud Computing"*. The authors reported a list of issues needing to be addressed in Cloud Computing context, that is: *Compliance, Trust, Identity* and *Access Management, Software Isolation, Data Protection, Availability*, and *Incident Response*.

In January 2011, the European Network and Information Security Agency (ENISA, 2001)

members has provided some highlights on such areas along with the report Security & Resilience in Governmental Clouds. The report identifies a decision-making model that can be used by senior management to determine how information security requirements and legal aspects may allow the identification of the architectural solution that suits the needs of their organization. The report objectives are:

1. Highlighting the pros and cons, with regard to information security and resilience, of community, private and public cloud computing delivery models;
2. Guiding public governments in the definition of their requirements for information security and resilience when evaluating cloud computing. In the context of this study that means that a service should provide: a level of *data confidentiality*, *integrity*, and availability according to specified requirements; a level of service *availability* and *reliability* according to specified requirements; *compliance* with the applicable law.

An overlap of definitions may be noticed, along with concerns and issues described in the world wide initiatives dealing with clouds and security.

The overlapping of security concerns may encourage standardization works, help cloud companies to meet as much as possible the cloud customers' requirements, and open new clear businesses where new enterprises may fill the existing gaps present in securing clouds. The situation becomes much more complex if federated scenarios in which different administration domains that need to interact with each other are considered. Issues as Data Export Control, Regulatory Compliance, Data Protection, and so far are situations where seamless resources aggregation is aspired but satisfying the customer security requirements is a must. However, in such context a cloud federation can be seen as an accelerator of new solutions in this area IT companies have to use same standards in order to accomplish collaborations, guarantee similar security level, and provide partners with all the information on how their systems are working, by reaching a good level of introspection. These accomplishments are not ideals because as mentioned just above, at this stage the boundaries are well defined, that is the cloud world is less complex indeed, with respect to how it appears. In the end, no any guidelines and/or security solutions can represent the panacea of the overall ills, each use-case deployed on cloud has to be investigated separately, keeping in mind that the Internet has given an early effect of worldwide involvement of citizens and governments, clouds may exacerbate such an effect.

A Brief Survey on Standards

Cloud Computing is finding a wide consensus among IT operators, because behind its computation model it is possible to advise a real business model. One of the main reasons for the Grid Computing failure, seen under the economic perspectives, was the inapplicability of any business model within it. Currently in the IT world we are assisting to a progressive mixing of meaningful efforts among operators, scientific communities and organizations for standards (as well: DMTF, IEEE, IETF, ITU, etc.) to enforce this new distributed computation infrastructure.

The standardization of the rate of proposals is also showing a huge interest of IT stockholders. The concept of interoperability needs to be enforced at any level of the Cloud Stackthat should provide Application Program Interfaces (APIs) which enable the full control and monitoring of cross-cloud virtual resources. In this scenario the federation has to be considered as a new opportunity for increasing and optimizing physical resources, although the federation among Clouds makes sense if each Cloud Operator can dynamically join the federation. Since the federation

can exist if there is a high level infrastructure that allows this aggregation. Giving a look at the classical cloud stack representation (IaaS, PaaS, SaaS), currently the main efforts for standardization processes are aimed to define new protocols at IaaS level. It is possible to consider it as the base level for clouds. Giving a look at Figure 1 we can see how complex is this part of the *cloud world.*

OVF

The working group in DMTF Standards is defining the Cloud Incubator Initiative for Cloud Management Standards. It was formed to address management interoperability for Cloud Systems. The DMTF organization has began the initiatives in Virtualization environments with Open Virtual Format. The format (OVF, 2011) represents an early descriptor able to define the customer requirements, in terms of number of VMs to instantiate; memory, CPUs, storage and etcetera to allocate and so far. This format permits the interaction from IaaSs and their customers. Inside DMTF board many IT companies are also trying to add standards in the cloud particularly useful for their businesses. For instance VMware has introduced the VCloud API, while Telefonica their TCloud API and other cloud operators (as Amazon, Rackspace, Google, Oracle, Citrix and Microsoft) embraced OVF as well. Such proposals should guarantee a set of new parameters useful for cross interaction. Moreover in this way, many more functionalities should be addressed, such as: load balancing, fault tolerance (VMs replication), network configuration, firewalling policies, etc. The main feature of such standards is the adoption of OVF as the base, to meet customers' requirements and constrains, without the heavy translation among different descriptor files. It supports the full range of virtual hard disk formats used for VMs today, and is extensible to deal with future formats.

Figure 1. Cloud: World Wide Standardization Boards

CIMI

In DMTF another initiative is taking place for explicit formalized cloud API for creating and managing VMs.

The initiative is identified under the name of Cloud Infrastructure Management Interface (CIMI). This interface is based on a RESTful model over HTTP. Some typical operations that are possible to perform through CIMI are: Create a New Machine, Retrieve the list of Machine Images, Query new Machine, Start and Stop a Machine. This working progress standard has a privileged position because a lot of experience came from the early formalization of the OVF standard; hence CIMI is the natural evolution.

OCCI

Another example of API standardization process is the Open Cloud Computing Interface (OCCI,

2011) standard. The OCCI standard is proposed inside the Open Grid Forum (OGF), and it should guarantee an exposition of virtual infrastructure manager capabilities. OCCI should guarantee *Interoperability*, allowing different Cloud providers to work together without data schema or format translation between APIs and understanding the dependency on multiple APIs. OCCI should allow *Portability* where there is not any vendor lock-in. Enabling services to move between providers allows clients to easily switch between providers based on business objectives (e.g., cost) with minimal technical costs, thus enabling and fostering competition and *Integration* where the specification can be implemented with both the latest infrastructures or legacy ones. However OCCI does appear to be neither particularly flexible nor fully oriented to cloud customers' requirements. In the same cases it needs a translation from OVF.

CDMI

SNIA is a world-wide Storage Networking Industry Association, and it is defining the Cloud Data Management Interface (CDMI, 2011) for enforcing the adoption of a common API aimed at data storage for clouds. Furthermore it defines the functional interface that applications will use to create, retrieve, update, and delete data elements from the Cloud. As part of this interface the client will be able to discover the capabilities of the cloud storage offering and use this interface to manage containers and the data that is placed in them. In addition, metadata can be set on containers and their contained data elements through this interface. This interface is also used by administrative and management applications to manage containers, accounts, security access, and monitoring/billing information, even for storage that is accessible by other protocols. The capabilities of the underlying storage and data services are exposed so that clients can understand the offering.

All the standards presented above are based on XML in order to guarantee the portability and interoperability in heterogeneous systems.

Standards de Facto

Due to the lack of standards in the cloud main big operators, as Amazon, Rackspace, Google, Microsoft are moving really forward for providing cloud services using their implementations. In the history all the times that companies offer solutions on IT markets. Anticipating the work of standardization boards, such solutions become standards the facto filling existing gaps. Although standards de facto might be not represent the best technical solution but, often they are widely used, since their market penetration determines their success. Some example include the videotape format war in the late 1980 years, VHS against V2000 and Betamax both having lost that competition.

In the cloud arena Amazon may be highlighted for proposing a way for VMs management (EC2),

whereas the S3 web-interface for data storage API is on the cloud (Amazon uses REST and SOAP APIs). Rackspace has its APIs REST based, while Amazon S3 is storage for the Internet. It is designed to make web-scale computing easier for developers. Amazon S3 provides a simple web services interface that can be used to store and retrieve any amount of data, at any time, from anywhere on the web. It gives any developer access to the same highly scalable, reliable, secure, fast, and inexpensive infrastructure that Amazon uses to run its own global network of web sites. The service aims to maximize benefits of scale and to pass those benefits on to developers.

CONCLUSION

In this chapter, an overview to cloud federation was provided. Firstly, the possible business scenarios taking advantages of the partnership establishment between cloud providers was discussed. After that, a discussion regarding the main research challenges was proposed. More specifically, topics such as QoS, security, brokerage, and autonomic computing were discussed, highlighting the emerging concerns considering federation. In the end, a discussion of the main current standards was provided. Nevertheless, there is still a long way to go toward the adoption of this new paradigm in the industry field.

The authors hope to succeed in stimulating the interest of both the scientific and industrial communities regarding cloud federation.

REFERENCES

Achemlal, M., Gharout S., & Gaber, C. (2011). Trusted platform module as an enabler for security in cloud computing. *Network and Information Systems Security Conference*, 1-6.

Alhamad, M., Dillon, T., & Chang, E. (2010). Conceptual SLA framework for cloud computing. *4th IEEE International Conference on Digital Ecosystems and Technologies (DEST)*, 606-610, doi:10.1109/DEST.2010.5610586

Berger, S., Caceres, R., Goldman, K., Perez, R., Sailer, R., & Van Doorn, L. (2006). vTPM: Virtualizing the Trusted PlatformModule. *Proceedings of the 15th conference on USENIX Security Symposium*, 1 –6.

Brandic, I. (2009). Towards Self-Manageable Cloud Services. *33rd Annual IEEE International Computer Software and Applications Conference*, 128-133.

Cloud Data Management Interface. (CDMI, 2011) Specification Version 1.0.1. Retrieved September 15, 2011, from: http://cdmi.sniacloud.com/

Cloud Security Alliance, C. S. A. (2009) Security Guidance for Critical Areas of Focus in Cloud Computing V2.1 Retrieved November 30, 2011, from https://cloudsecurityalliance.org/csaguide.pdf

Computing (CLOUD), vol., no., pp.123-130, 5-10 July 2010.

DMTF's Open Virtualization Format. (OVF, 2011), Retrieved November 30, 2011 from: http://www.dmtf.org/standards/ovf

European Network and Information Security Agency. ENISA (2011). Security & Resilience in Governmental Clouds. Making an informed decision. Annex III Reservoir Architecture Description. Retrieved May 15, 2011, from http://www.reservoir-fp7.eu/uploads/Documents/Security%20%20Resilience%20in%20Governmental%20Clouds_ENISA.pdf

GATNER. (2008), Seven cloud-computing security risks. Retrieved November 30, 2011, from: http://www.gartner.com/

Goiri, I.; Guitart, J.; Torres, J.; (2010). Characterizing Cloud Federation for Enhancing Providers' Profit, In Proceedings of the 2010 IEEE 3rd International Conference on Cloud

National Institute of Standards and Technology (NIST), Guidelines on Security and Privacy in Public Cloud Computing. Retrieved September 15, 2011, from http://csrc.nist.gov/publications/drafts/800-144/Draft-SP-800-144_cloud-computing.pdf

Open Cloud Computing Interface. (OCCI, 2011) An open community-lead specifications delivered through the Open Grid Forum (OGF). Retrieved November 30, 2011, from: http://occi-wg.org/

Paletta, M., & Herrero, P. (2009). A MAS-Based Negotiation Mechanism to Deal with Service Collaboration in Cloud Computing. *International Conference on Intelligent Networking and Collaborative Systems*,147-153, doi: 10.1109/INCOS.2009.21.

Paton, N., De Aragão, M., Lee, K., Fern, A., & Sakellariou, R. (2009). Optimizing utility in cloud computing through autonomic workload execution. *IEEE Data Eng. Bull.*

Shen, Z., Li, L., Yan, F., & Wu, X. (2010). Cloud computing system based on trusted computing platform. *International Conference on Intelligent Computation Technology and Automation (ICICTA)*, 942 –945.

Solomon, B., Ionescu, D., Litoiu, M., & Iszlai, G. (2010). Designing autonomic management systems for cloud computing. *International Conference on Computational Cybernetics and Technical Informatics*, 631-636, doi: 10.1109/ICCCYB.2010.5491335

Chapter 2
Interoperable Resource Management for Establishing Federated Clouds

Gabor Kecskemeti
Laboratory of Parallel and Distributed Systems of the MTA-SZTAKI, Hungary

Attila Kertesz
Laboratory of Parallel and Distributed Systems of the MTA-SZTAKI, Hungary

Attila Marosi
Laboratory of Parallel and Distributed Systems of the MTA-SZTAKI, Hungary

Peter Kacsuk
Laboratory of Parallel and Distributed Systems of the MTA-SZTAKI, Hungary

ABSTRACT

Cloud Computing builds on the latest achievements of diverse research areas, such as Grid Computing, Service-oriented computing, business process modeling and virtualization. As this new computing paradigm was mostly lead by companies, several proprietary systems arose. Recently, alongside these commercial systems, several smaller-scale privately owned systems are maintained and developed. This chapter focuses on issues faced by users with interests in Multi-Cloud use and by Cloud providers with highly dynamic workloads. The authors propose a Federated Cloud Management architecture that provides unified access to a federated Cloud that aggregates multiple heterogeneous IaaS Cloud providers in a transparent manner. The architecture incorporates the concepts of meta-brokering, Cloud brokering, and on-demand service deployment. The meta-brokering component provides transparent service execution for the users by allowing the interconnection of various Cloud brokering solutions. Cloud-Brokers manage the number and the location of the Virtual Machines performing the user requests. In order to decrease Virtual Machine instantiation time and increase dynamism in the system, the service deployment component optimizes service delivery by encapsulating services as virtual appliances allowing their decomposition and replication among IaaS Cloud infrastructures. The architecture achieves service provider level transparency through automatic virtual appliance replication and Virtual Machine management of Cloud-Brokers.

DOI: 10.4018/978-1-4666-1631-8.ch002

Copyright © 2012, IGI Global. Copying or distributing in print or electronic forms without written permission of IGI Global is prohibited.

1. INTRODUCTION

Highly dynamic service environments (Di Nitto, 2008) require a novel infrastructure that can handle the on demand deployment and decommission of service instances. Cloud Computing (Buyya, 2009) offers simple and cost effective outsourcing in dynamic service environments and allows the construction of service-based applications extensible with the latest achievements in diverse research areas, such as Grid Computing, Service-oriented computing, and business processes and virtualization. Virtual appliances (VA) encapsulate metadata (e.g., network requirements) with a complete software system (e.g., operating system, software libraries and applications or services) prepared for execution in Virtual Machines (VM). IaaS Cloud systems provide access to remote computing infrastructures by allowing their users to instantiate virtual appliances (as a result, deploy service instances) on their virtualized resources as Virtual Machines.

Nowadays, several public and private IaaS systems co-exist and to realize dynamic service environments, users frequently envisage a federated Cloud that aggregates capabilities of various IaaS Cloud providers. These IaaS systems are offered either by public service providers – e.g. (Amazon EC2, 2011) or (Rackspace, 2011) – or by private entities (e.g. universities or startup companies who typically offer smaller scale infrastructures). There are several scenarios to accomplish Cloud federations – e.g., Hybrid-, Community- or Multi-Clouds (A. J. Ferrer et. al., 2012). This chapter, focuses only on the Multi-Cloud federation scenario where the Cloud user plays a central role, because the different infrastructure providers are used separately.

This chapter identifies two major scenarios when users switch IaaS systems: dissatisfaction end extension. When the users get dissatisfied with their currently used provider, they inevitably face the issue of provider lock in – all its applications

and data are stored at the specific provider. This chapter is focused on compute intensive applications only; therefore, data lock in is not discussed. However, there is a need for an efficient way to transform applications for new providers. As Cloud adoption becomes more widespread, more and more users start using privately constructed proprietary IaaS systems. Nevertheless, users with strong workloads face the limitation of these providers. In mission critical situations or high demand periods, these users are willing to outsource a small percentage of their workloads to third party providers. This chapter identifies the following challenges for federated Cloud usage: *(i)* single IaaS entry point, *(ii)* Cloud selection, *(iii)* Virtual Machine management (termination, reuse or repurposing policies and IaaS specific VM operations), *(iv)* demand based virtual appliance distribution, *(v)* coping with software and hardware failures and varying load of user requests, *(vi)* establishing interoperability and *(vii)* minimizing Cloud usage costs. The way these challenges are addressed is detailed in the next paragraphs.

This chapter proposes and conceptually discusses an autonomic resource management solution that serves as an entry point to Cloud federations by providing transparent service execution for users. This solution incorporates and builds on top of the already proven concepts of meta-brokering (Kertesz, 2010), Cloud brokering (Marosi, 2011) and automated on-demand service deployment (Kecskemeti, 2011). Thus this chapter concentrates on the techniques that led these concepts towards the formation of Cloud federations. The meta-brokering component directly interacts with the user and acts as the *single entry point* to the system (the challenge *(i)*). Its interface offers *Cloud selection* facilities (the challenge *(ii)*) to identify the suitable IaaS providers for user requests. Cloud-Brokers are responsible for *managing* (challenge *(iii)*) and *optimizing* the usage costs (challenge *(vii)*) of the

Virtual Machine instances of the particular virtual appliances hosted on a specific IaaS system. Last, virtual appliance *distribution* is organized by the automatic service deployment component of the architecture. This component decomposes appliances and then replicates them to the repositories of the IaaS systems based on the current *demand* for the specific services in the system (the challenge *(iv)*).

The architecture presented in this chapter aims at the remaining two challenges by multiple components. *Software and hardware level faults and varying workloads* (the challenge *(v)*) are handled by the meta-broker with directing requests to less problematic IaaS systems. On the level of Cloud-Brokers, the system handles faults and workloads by intelligent VM queue management (e.g. extra load is handled by deciding on creating new VMs according to the cost restrictions of the system). The architecture also supports *interoperability* (challenge *(vi)*) by its three components. First, it translates user requests (expressed in the language of the meta-broker) to the proprietary APIs of the selected IaaS system. Next, it offers multiple Cloud-Brokers each aimed for a specific IaaS provider. Finally, it uses the on-demand deployment solution to transform the code of the requested services into formats understood by IaaS providers. These last two challenges also follow future research directions, (e.g., interoperability of VM migration solutions) to be revealed in the conclusions section.

This chapter is organized as follows: first, it introduces the related research results in Section 2. Then, in section 3.1 it details the issues and manual usage problems of Multi-Cloud systems. Next, it focuses on an advanced use case in Section 3.2 that involves the proposed architecture and discusses its advantages in comparison to previous research results. Next, it details the operational roles of the brokering components in our architecture in Section 3.3 and Section 3.4. Afterwards, in Section 3.5, it discusses virtual appliance delivery scenarios supported by the system and an approach to rebuild virtual appliances within the Virtual Machine that is used to execute them. Finally, we the research is concluded in Section 4.

2. BACKGROUND

2.1. Cloud Federations

Bernstein et al. (2009) define two use case scenarios that exemplify the problems faced by users of Multi-Cloud systems. First, they define the case of VM Mobility where they identify the networking, the specific Cloud VM management interfaces and the lack of mobility interfaces as the three major obstacles. Next, they discuss the storage interoperability and federation scenario in which storage provider replication policies are subject to change when a Cloud provider initiates subcontracting. Through these use case scenarios they recognize obstacles in the fields of addressing, naming, identity management, and reliable messaging, and Virtual Machine formats and time synchronization. However, they offer interoperability solutions only for low-level functionality of the Clouds that are not focused on recent user demands but on solutions for IaaS system operators.

Buyya et al. (2010) suggest a Cloud federation oriented, just in time, opportunistic, and scalable application services provisioning environment called InterCloud. They envision utility oriented federated IaaS systems that are able to predict application service behavior for intelligent down and up-scaling infrastructures. Then, they list the research issues of flexible service to resource mapping, user and resource centric QoS optimization, integration with in-house systems of enterprises, and scalable monitoring of system components. Later, their paper presents a market-oriented approach to offer InterClouds including Cloud exchanges and brokers that bring together producers and consumers. Producers are offering domain specific enterprise Clouds that are connected and managed within the federation with their Cloud Coordinator component. Finally, they have implemented a CloudSim based simulation that evaluates the performance of the federations created using InterCloud technologies. The InterCloud architecture focuses on meeting providers and users demands during service execution. However, users already face several federation related issues (e.g. VM reuse strategies, appliance propagation to new Cloud systems – see Section 3.1 for details) before execution, therefore, the concept of InterClouds cannot be applied for the user scenarios this chapter is targeting. In an earlier work (Ranjan, 2009), they discuss scalability issues and decentralized operation of Cloud federations in an approach called Aneka-Federation. They show that this decentralized solution can enhance scalability and fault-tolerance. The authors believe that such peer-to-peer techniques are not necessary for the proposed solutions, and introducing them can raise additional security and management problems. In addition the approach is not fully centralized: the authors propose a multi-layer brokering approach, in which different Cloud brokers are responsible for managing various IaaS systems, and a top-layer meta-broker mediates among them. It is not likely that the number of managed Cloud brokers will go beyond thousands-scale.

Rochwerger et al. (2009) introduce the reader to the internal operation of the RESERVOIR project and its federated Infrastructure as a Service Cloud management model. They introduce the federated Cloud model from the perspective of shared Grid resources and propose that commercial Cloud providers could also temporarily lease excess capacities during high-demand periods. From the customer point of view, they present the security problems as the biggest issue in federated Clouds and offer isolation on several hardware layers: Virtual Machines, virtual networks and virtual storage. Next, they investigate the problems faced by federated Cloud management solutions: *(i)* dynamic service elasticity - scaling up/down service instances, *(ii)* admission control - reducing the probability of resource congestion, *(iii)* policy-driven placement optimization - revenue maximization and service level agreement violation penalties, *(iv)* Cross-Cloud virtual networks - virtual application networks and VLAN, *(v)* Cross-Cloud monitoring, and *(vi)* Cross-Cloud live migration. Finally, they present the case study of on-demand enterprise systems (constructing a SAP system in the Cloud). Nevertheless, in contrast to our contributions, the paper mostly discusses issues and solutions targeted towards infrastructure providers and the users are rarely considered.

Simarro et al. (2011) investigate the optimization of Virtual Machine deployment in a multi-Cloud scenario to reduce total cost. They use Amazon EC2 spot instances for evaluation of their future price prediction that relies on historical values. Their approach is trend-following, where they define the current trend based on the previous three price data. Their predicted price is the average price multiplied by a constant based on the current trend. They also address performance degradation of Virtual Machines by introducing two restrictions: a distance and a load balancing constraint. The distance constraint limits the number of Virtual Machines to relocate to a defined percentage. It ensures that a certain number of resources will be running regardless of migrations due to price fluctuations in different Cloud fabrics. The load balancing constraint guarantees that a certain percentage of the total resource count will be allocated to and stay in every utilized Cloud system. Their evaluation shows that their scheduler can save up to 5% of the total cost per day compared to manual placement of instances, but they do not consider the deployment cost of instances and the overhead for the VA's caused by the migration.

2.2. Cloud Brokering and VM Management Strategies

Matthias Schmidt et al. (2010) investigate different strategies for distributing Virtual Machine images within a data center: unicast, multicast, binary tree distribution, and peer-to-peer distribution based on BitTorrent. They found the multicast method the most efficient, but in order to be able to distribute images over network boundaries ("Cross-Cloud") they choose BitTorrent. They also propose to use layered Virtual Machine images for virtual appliances consisting of three layers: user, vendor, and base. By using the layers and a copy-on-write method, they were able to avoid the retransmission of images already present at the destination and thus decrease instantiation time and network utilization. The authors investigated distribution methods only within the boundaries of a single data center, going beyond that remained future work.

There are several related works focusing on providing dynamic pool of resources. Paul Marshall et al. (2010) describe an approach for developing an "elastic site" model where batch schedulers, storage and web services can utilize such resources. They introduce different basic policies for allocating resources, that can be "on-demand" meaning resources are allocated when a service call or task arrives, "steady stream" assumes steady utilization, thus leaves some elastic resources continuously running, regardless of the (temporary) shortage of tasks, or "bursts" for fluctuating load. They concentrate on dynamically increasing and decreasing the number of resources, but rely on third party logic for balancing the load among the allocated resources. Vazquez et al. (2011) are building complex Grid infrastructures on top of IaaS Cloud systems that allow them to adjust the number of Grid resources dynamically. They focus on the capability of using resources from different Cloud providers and on the capability of providing resources for different Grid middleware, but Meta scheduling between the utilized infrastructures and developing a model

that considers the different Cloud provider characteristics is not addressed.

Bellur et al. (2010) present two algorithms for Virtual Machine placement in data centers. They treat the placement as a multi-dimensional vector bin-packaging problem. They represent physical machines by d-dimensional vectors with the magnitude of one along each dimension (bins) where each dimension represents a resource class (e.g., CPU, memory). D-dimensional vectors also represent Virtual Machine instantiation requests. The goal is to minimize the number of bins in such way that the sum of vectors (coordinate-wise) for each bin is less or equal to the vector of the bin. Their evaluation shows that their algorithms always yield the optimal solution and that they are an improvement over the existing approaches.

In 2009, Amazon Web Services launched Amazon CloudWatch (2011) that is a supplementary service for Amazon EC2 instances that provides monitoring services for running Virtual Machine instances. It allows gathering information about the different characteristics (traffic shape, load, disk utilization, etc.) of resources. Users and services can dynamically start or release instances based on the collected information to match demand as utilization goes over or below predefined thresholds. The main shortcoming of this solution is that it is tied to a specific IaaS Cloud system and introduces a monetary overhead, since the service charges a fixed hourly rate for each monitored instance.

Salehi, Buyya (2010) focus on the so called marketing-oriented scheduling policies that can provision extra resources when the local cluster resources are not sufficient to meet the user requirements. Former scheduling policies used in Grids are not working effectively in Cloud environments, mainly because Infrastructure-as-a-Service providers are charging users in a pay-as-you-go manner in an hourly basis for computational resources. To find the trade-off between buying acquired additional resources from IaaS and reusing existing local infrastructure resources, they propose two scheduling policies (cost and time optimization scheduling policies) for mixed (commercial and non-commercial) resource environments. Two different approaches were identified on provisioning commercial resources. The first approach is offered by the IaaS providers at resource provisioning level (user/application constraints are neglected: deadline, budget, etc.), the other approach deploys resources focusing at user level (time and/or cost minimization, estimating the workload in advance, etc.).

RightScale (2010) offers a Multi-Cloud management platform that enables users to exploit the unique capabilities of different Clouds, which has a similar goal to this chapter's approach. It is able to manage complete deployments of multiple servers across more Clouds, using an automation engine that adapts resource allocation as required by system demand or system failures. They provide server templates to automatically install software on other supported Cloud infrastructures. They also advertise disaster recovery plans, low-latency access to data, and support for security and SLA requirements. RightScale users can select, migrate and monitor their chosen Clouds from a single management environment. They support Amazon Web Services, Eucalyptus Systems, Flexiscale, GoGrid, and VMware. The direct access to IaaS systems is performed by the so-called Multi-Cloud Engine, which is supposed to perform brokering capabilities related to VM placement. Unfortunately, we are not aware of any publications that detail the brokering operations of these components; therefore, we cannot provide any deeper comparisons to our approach.

EnStratus (2011) offers a similar platform as RightScale, but supports provisioning, management and monitoring of applications on multiple Clouds on a SaaS level. EnStratus supports multiple Clouds like Amazon EC2, CloudSigma, GoGrid, OpenStack, etc. The platform consists of three main components, first the web based Console is used for reporting, automation and management. It allows specifying configuration, application architecture and objectives like uptime

and deploying applications in different Clouds. The Provisioning System enacts on behalf of the user: executes requests from the Console, scales up and down based on supplied criteria, and it is advertised to support disaster recovery and Cross-Cloud backup as well. Finally, the Credential System stores all authentication data and encryption credentials and it is advertised as a component that is isolated ("not routable from the Internet") and stores all data encrypted using customer-specific keys. Unfortunately, similarly to RightScale, no publications with specific details were available and thus any deeper comparisons cannot be provided.

3. ESTABLISHING CLOUD FEDERATIONS

3.1 Manually Executed User Scenario

This chapter is aimed at solving user problems that occur in several scenarios while users execute compute intensive tasks in IaaS Cloud systems. It only focuses on compute intensive tasks because currently available commercial and academic IaaS systems are mostly targeted at them. The following two subsections identify common user related issues that the architecture proposed in this chapter is aimed at.

3.1.1. Manual Usage Problems in Distinct Cloud Systems

Even in the simplest use cases users need to select the IaaS provider that meets their application's requirements. From the user point of view, IaaS providers can be differentiated on pricing, on supported Virtual Machine monitors (Xen, VMWare, etc.), on offered service level (e.g. availability, compensation in case of service failures), on the VM types (possible resource configurations for a requested VM). Inexperienced users already face the problem of prioritizing between their requirements and the IaaS offerings and prices.

After IaaS selection, users face the problem of porting their applications to the selected Cloud. This operation requires users to identify the planned usage frequency of their applications. If applications are planned for single use then users could start a third party appliance and extend it with the application. As a result, applications are going to be available in the Cloud until their Virtual Machines are running. Appliance extension expects users to investigate the available third party appliances and pick one that is extensible and will be able to support their application. A more permanent and reusable solution, that supports more frequent usage, requires users to create a new virtual appliance encapsulating the application. To create the virtual appliance users have to be aware of the virtual appliance creation tools and techniques in the selected IaaS system. For both the appliance extension and creation cases users have to know the IaaS system's virtual appliance instantiation methods (VM creation).

Based on the pricing model of the selected IaaS system, users must decide when to destroy their running VMs. We identified three strategies applied by users for VM destruction: *(i)* destruct after use, *(ii)* allow frequent reuse and *(iii)* allow repurposing. In the first case, users create Virtual Machines for every single task and after task termination they destruct the VM. Next, if users realize a single application will receive multiple tasks sequentially, then they only destruct the Virtual Machine after the last task of the application arrives. Finally, if users find several low demand applications with distinct uses (the applications receive tasks that never overlap), then they can repurpose the VM created for the application with the first task. After repurposing the VM will offer a different application that serves the following tasks. As these strategies are all assuming frequent use of the requested applications, their manual handing reduces the overall performance of the system.

3.1.2. Issues with Manual Multi-Cloud Usage

Nowadays, IaaS Cloud offerings start to raise further issues for advanced users: *(i)* application migration between Clouds, and *(ii)* Multi-Cloud use. First, users face *application migration* issues when they become dissatisfied with the pricing, the performance, or the actual service level of a particular IaaS system, therefore they decide on switching Cloud providers. As the different Cloud providers do not provide live migration capabilities, users first have to transfer all their appliances and data files stored in the original Cloud system to the new Cloud provider. Consequently, they not only need to calculate the future operation costs and gains but they also need to evaluate the costs of appliance and data transfer. In case of appliances, the IaaS providers frequently use proprietary appliance formats, so users first need to transform their appliances between the old and the new format. If the old appliance was tightly integrated with the original IaaS system (e.g. proprietary APIs were used), then users either have to re-implement the tight integration for the newly selected IaaS system, or they have to choose an IaaS system that also offers the same type of integration options as the original did.

Second, applications with dynamic workloads are often good candidates for *Multi-Cloud* systems. Users frequently host their applications on their small-scaled Private Cloud that is extended with commercial Cloud offerings during high demand periods. In such cases user applications have to be prepared to scale to multiple Virtual Machines. Also, users have to select commercial Clouds resembling their Private Clouds the most.

3.2. Federated Cloud Management Architecture

Figure 1 shows the Federated Cloud Management (FCM) architecture and its connections to the corresponding components that together repre-

Figure 1. The Federated Cloud Management architecture

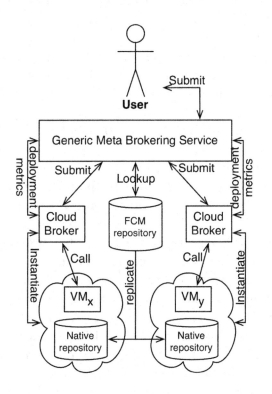

operation and the input parameters to exploit the advanced selection capabilities of the system. Then the GMBS checks, if a virtual appliance, corresponding to the user specified service interface, has been uploaded to *"FCM Repository"*. The repository stores virtual appliances alongside with metadata that enables the GMBS service to determine the list of IaaS systems that already host the appliance. From this list, the GMBS initiates a matchmaking procedure that considers the past performance, pricing and reliability of the suitable Cloud systems. Consequently, GMBS automatically handles *Multi-Cloud usage* for its users (e.g. it handles the switch between Private and Public Cloud infrastructures according to predefined policies). After the most suitable IaaS system is selected, the GMBS passes the user request to the Cloud-Broker component of the architecture.

The main goal of the *"Cloud-Broker"* is to manage the Virtual Machines according to their respective service demand (thus accomplishing our challenge *(iii)* identified in Section 1). Cloud-Brokers are associated with specific IaaS systems and are responsible offering various Virtual Machine *termination, reuse, and repurposing* strategies within their Cloud. To allow Virtual Machine reuse, this chapter assumes that virtual appliances only offer standard stateless web services. Cloud-Brokers manage user requests (incoming service calls) separately from Virtual Machines, therefore when a new request arrives they are responsible to associate and dispatch the call with a currently unoccupied Virtual Machine. The system dynamically creates and destructs Virtual Machines with the Virtual Machine Handler component that translates and forwards Virtual Machine related requests to the corresponding IaaS system. This component is a Cloud infrastructure-specific one that uses the public interface of the IaaS system to deploy or decommission virtual appliances stored in the *native repository* of the specific Cloud.

First, virtual appliances are stored in the generic repository called FCM Repository. This repository

sent an interoperable solution for establishing a federated Cloud environment. The FCM targets the problem area outlined in the Introduction, and provides solutions for the listed open issues. With FCM, users are able to execute services deployed on Cloud infrastructures transparently, in an automated way.

The architecture provides a *single entry point* (the challenge *(i)* from Section 1) to Cloud federations through the *"Generic Meta Brokering Service"* (GMBS). The role of GMBS is to manage autonomously the interconnected Cloud infrastructures with the help of the Cloud-Brokers by forming a federation. This service is responsible of *Cloud selection* (the challenge *(ii)* from Section 1), load balancing under *varying workloads* (the challenge *(v)* from Section 1) and submission using a well-defined interface. To reduce the pressure on users, the GMBS requires users to specify only the service interface, the is capable of *minimizing the virtual appliance storage costs* (see challenge *(vii)* listed in Section 1) by decomposing the appliances and only storing their unique parts in the system. Then, based on the deployment and decommission requests of the Cloud-Brokers in the system, the FCM Repository optimizes service deployments in highly dynamic service environments by automatically replicating the necessary appliance parts to the native repositories (thus addresses the *demand based appliance distribution* challenge identified in Section 1). Before the replication can be started, the FCM Repository automatically checks and *transforms* (Kecskemeti, 2011) the appliance to the format (e.g. OVF, AMI) required by the IaaS provider. With the help of the minimal manageable virtual appliances (MMVA – further discussed in Section 3.5) the Virtual Machine Handler is able to rebuild these decomposed parts in the IaaS system on demand. This results in faster VA deployment and in a reduced storage requirement in the native repositories. Storage costs are further reduced during replication because the repository only replicates the complete VA to a native repository if it is frequently requested by the Cloud-Broker.

The following, subsections detail how resource management is carried out in this architecture. At the top-level, a meta-broker is used to select from the available Cloud providers based on performance metrics, while at the bottom-level, IaaS-specific Cloud-Brokers are used to schedule VA instantiation and deliver the service calls to the Clouds.

3.2.1. Meta-Brokering in FCM

As already mentioned in the scenario discussed in the previous section, brokering takes place at two levels in the FCM architecture. First, service calls are submitted to the Generic Meta-Brokering Service (GMBS – that is a revised and extended version of the work described in Kertesz (2010)), where a meta-level decision is made to which Cloud infrastructure calls should be forwarded.

Then the service call is placed in the queue of the selected Cloud-Broker, where the low-level brokering is carried out to select the VM that performs the actual service execution. This low-level brokering and the detailed introduction of the architecture of the Cloud-Broker are discussed later in Section 3.4.

3.2.2. The Architecture of GMBS

Now, the chapter turns its attention to the role of GMBS. An overview of its architecture is shown in Figure 2. This meta-brokering service has five major components. The *Meta-Broker Core* is responsible for managing the interaction with the other components and handling user interactions (by providing the *single point of entry* – see the challenge *(i)* in Section 1 - to multiple federated IaaS systems). Users should name the service they would like to invoke, which has to match the WSDL (2011) description of a user's VA stored in the repository. The GMBS is implemented as a web-service that is independent from middleware-specific components, and it uses standards for information gathering, management and user interaction.

Figure 2. The architecture of the Generic Meta-Brokering Service

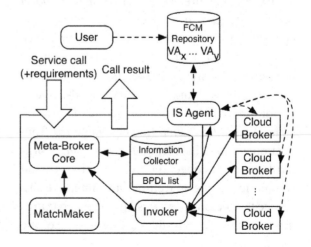

The *MatchMaker* component performs the scheduling of the calls by selecting a suitable Cloud managed by a broker. This decision-making is based on aggregated static and dynamic data stored by the *Information Collector* (IC) component in a local database. The Information System (*IS*) *Agent* is implemented as a listener service of GMBS. It is responsible for regularly updating static information from the FCM Repository on service availability, and aggregated dynamic information collected from the Cloud-Brokers based on various metrics, including average VA deployment and service execution times. The *Invoker* component forwards the service call to the selected Cloud-Broker and receives the service response from it. According to the success or failure of the actual response, it updates the historical performance value of the appropriate broker in the local database.

3.2.3. The Matchmaking Process of GMBS

Each Cloud-Broker is described by an XML-based Broker Property Description Language (BPDL) document containing basic broker properties (e.g., name, managed IaaS Cloud), and the gathered aggregated dynamic properties. More information on this document format can be read in Kertesz (2010). The scheduling-related attributes are typically stored in the *PerformanceMetrics* field of BPDL. Namely, the following metrics are stored in this field for each Cloud-Broker:

Estimated availability time: This metric is represented by a numeric value calculated for a specific virtual appliance retrieved from the FCM Repository and to be placed in a native repository. The following values may be given:

- **-1:** if the native repository of the IaaS Cloud does not support the VA, therefore it cannot be transferred there.
- **0:** if the VA is already transferred to the native repository, thus available right away.

- **A positive integer:** representing the estimated transfer time between the FCM repository and a native one assuming there is no burden for the transfer.

Average deployment and execution time: Average times are stored for each VA regarding the deployment from the native repository to a VM of the appropriate Cloud system, and the execution of the service in a running VA. These values are provided by the Cloud-Brokers.

Historical performance value: This value denotes the success rate of previous service executions in a VA, which is regularly updated by the IS Agent based on the responses of the Cloud-Brokers.

The scheduling process is performed by the *MatchMaker* component of GMBS. The metrics described above is used for calculating a rank for each broker, and then the Cloud-Broker with the highest rank is selected for forwarding the service request.

3.3. Improvements on Cloud Selection

As we have seen from this description, the role of GMBS is to select a suitable IaaS Cloud environment (the challenge *(ii)* from Section 1), and adapt the selection process to performance fluctuations propagated from lower levels through pre-defined metrics. These metrics are extensible as the architecture becomes more widely adopted and more and more Clouds will be supported. For example, if IaaS systems provide an estimate on the rest of the available VM slots in a Cloud, then the GMBS considers them during matchmaking in order to better distribute load among different Clouds.

User requirements for certain IaaS Cloud functionalities (e.g. live Virtual Machine migration or resource allocation change) are supported though a special scheduling related description language called MBSDL (more information can be found in Kertesz (2010)) that can express such require-

Figure 3. Internal behavior of a Cloud-Broker

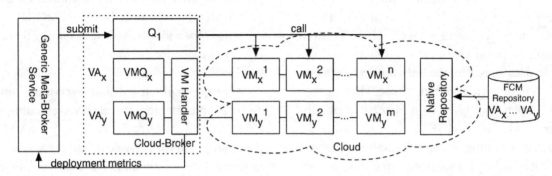

ments of the service call. Using this information and the user specified requirements, the GMBS performs a pre-filtering process, and withholds the unsuitable Cloud systems from participating in the matchmaking process.

As mentioned in Section 2.1, it is not expected to experience scalability problems in the hierarchically centralized architecture. Nevertheless, the applicability of peer-to-peer technologies to our meta-brokering approach has been investigated in Kertesz (2008), which may be further developed and implemented in the future. This solution will be able to avoid possible future bottlenecks and will be capable of serving thousands of users accessing a single GMBS instance.

Regarding performance issues some preliminary evaluations for federated management of different distributed systems (including Clouds) have already been conducted, and it was experienced that the approach provides additional performance gains (Kertesz, 2011).

3.4. Cloud-Broker

The Cloud-Broker handles and dispatches service calls to resources and performs resource management within a single IaaS system, it is an extended version of the system described in Marosi (2011).

The architecture of the Cloud-Broker is shown in Figure 3. Its first task is to dynamically create or destroy Virtual Machines (VM_x^i) and VM queues (VMQ_x) for the different used virtual appliances

(consequently it solves our challenge *(iii)* from Section 1). To do that, first, the VA has to be replicated to the native repository of the IaaS system from the FCM Repository (an alternative method is discussed in Section 3.5).

Alongside the appliance, the FCM Repository also stores additional static requirements about its future instances, like its minimum resource demands (e.g., architecture, operating system, disk, CPU and memory), that are needed by the Cloud-Broker. This data is not replicated to the native repository, rather the FCM Repository is queried.

A VM queue stores references to either requests for resources or resources capable of handling a specific service call, thus instances of a specific VA ($VA_x \rightarrow VMQ_x$). Status of a VM i in VM queue j ($S_{i,j}$) is as follows. New resource requests are new entries inserted into the queue of the appropriate VM ($S_{i,j} \leftarrow WAITING$), and an instance will be started when there are enough resources available ($S_{i,j} \leftarrow INIT$). Once the instance is successfully started ($S_{i,j} \leftarrow RUNNING$) it will accept service requests, if the instance cannot start it will wait ($S_{i,j} \leftarrow WAITING$) and later restarted. Resource destruction requests are modification of entries representing an already running resource ($S_{i,j} \leftarrow CANCEL$). On permanent error the VM's status is set accordingly ($S_{i,j} \leftarrow ERROR$), and it will be restarted or on permanent failure removed from the queue similar to decommissioned instances ($S_{i,j} \leftarrow TERMINATED$). Since the FCM repository contains validated and working VA's the users ideally will never meet the permanent error status ($S_{i,j} \leftarrow ERROR$), but developers might get it during VA development and testing. The VM Queue entries are managed by the Virtual Machine Handler ("*VM Handler*") that is a Cloud fabric specific component designed to interact with the public interface of a single IaaS system. Each VA contains a monitoring component that allows the Cloud-Broker to gather basic monitoring information (e.g., CPU, disk and memory usage) about the running Virtual Machines along with the average deployment time for each VA and average service execution times. This data can be queried by the IS Agent of the GMBS.

The service call queue (Q_l) stores incoming service requests and, for each request, a reference to a VA in the FCM Repository. There is a single service call queue in each Cloud-Broker, while there are many VM queues. Dynamic requirements for the VA may be specified with the service call:

- Additional resources (e.g., CPU, memory and disk);
- An UUID, that allows to identify service calls originating from the same entity (e.g., to identify batches of requests).

The UUID binds different service calls together, this allows meeting user demands, e.g., to enforce a total cost limit on Public Clouds, or to comply with deadlines for the service calls of a batch. If dynamic requirements are present, the Cloud-Broker treats the VA as a new VA type, thus creating a new VM queue and starts a VM. The service calls may now be dispatched to the appropriate VMs. Some IaaS systems provide the possibility to define how much of each resource type should be allocated to the VM, but most IaaS systems offer only predefined classes of resources (e.g., CPU, memory and disk capacity) not adjustable by the user. In this case, the Cloud-Broker selects the resource class that has at least the requested resources available. This may lead

to allocating excess resources in some cases (e.g., the resource class has twice the memory requested to meet the CPU capacity requirement). In all cases the Cloud-Broker selects resource classes or allocate resources, thus both dynamic and static resource requirements for the VA are satisfied.

The Cloud-Broker also performs the scheduling of service call requests to VM's and the life-cycle management of resources. The scheduling decision is based on the *(a)* monitoring information gathered from the resources; *(b)* number of requests waiting in the queue and *(c)* resource demands. If the service request cannot be scheduled to any resource within a threshold, then the Cloud-Broker may decide to start a new VM capable of serving the request. The decision is based on the following:

- The number of running VM's available to handle the service call (referred as *n,m* on Figure 3);
- The number of waiting calls for a specific service in the call queue;
- Resource limits in Private Clouds for deploying new VA's;
- The average execution time of service calls;
- The average deployment time of VA's;
- And additional constraints (e.g., total budget, deadline).

For VM decommission, the Cloud-Broker also takes into account the billing period of the IaaS system. Shutdown is performed shortly before the end of this period considering the average decommission time for the system. We define T_x as the end of the *x*-th billing period of the IaaS system for the instance, T_u as the uptime, T_D as the decommission time and T_w as the time wasted by an early shutdown. Instances are shutdown only in proximity of T_x-T_D to keep T_w minimal: [T_x-T_D-T_g, T_x-T_D*(1+ε)], where $0 < \varepsilon \ll 1$ defines the precision and $T_g > \varepsilon * T_D$ is a configurable time period. This defines the time window when an instance can be decommissioned so that minimum part of the billing period is wasted (T_w is minimal). The decommission decision in not made based solely on this, rather this only gives one constraint, defines a possible time window to perform it. Other constraints are defined by:

- The number of waiting service calls in the queue for the a specific service;
- Number of running VM's in the VM queue of the a specific service;
- Idle time elapsed since the last service call on the instance;
- And the average service call execution time.

The current implementation of the Cloud-Broker supports the de facto standard Amazon EC2 interface (both the REST and SOAP API's) and it is tested and supports Amazon EC2, Eucalyptus, OpenNebula and OpenStack. It is open source and available for download packaged with the EDGeS 3G Bridge (2011).

3.5. Virtual Appliance Delivery Optimization

Our architecture builds on the Automated Virtual appliance creation Service (or AVS – Kecskemeti, 2011) of the ASD subsystem. This service offers three major functionalities: *(i)* initial virtual appliance creation and upload, *(ii)* an appliance size optimization facility and finally, *(iii)* an active repository. The AVS supports the appliance developers in creating a virtual appliance that conforms to the publication requirements of the FCM repository. However, before publishing the appliance this chapter assumes that appliances are optimized with the size optimization facility. As a result, the FCM repository only stores virtual appliances that are built up from a Just enough Operating System – JeOS (Geer, 2009) – and from the Service's code that the appliance represents. The FCM repository behaves as an active

repository in the system and it is capable of *(a)* decomposing virtual appliances to smaller parts, *(b)* merging appliance parts, *(c)* destroying unnecessarily decomposed parts and *(d)* replicating parts to repositories that could better serve them.

IaaS systems instantiate Virtual Machines based on appliances stored in their native repositories only. Therefore, the architecture offers two distinct methods for delivering appliances to native repositories. First, it discusses techniques that replicate parts or the entire appliance to the native repositories. Second, it discusses how the system avoids the need for replication by utilizing extensible virtual appliances and two-phased instantiation.

3.5.1. Appliance Replication

First, the architecture allows users to upload their virtual appliances to the FCM Repository that organizes the contents of the native repositories with its replication functionality. This functionality distributes appliances by balancing between reduced appliance storage costs in the native repositories and reduced virtual machine instantiation time. For reduced storage, the FCM repository aims at minimizing the unnecessary replication to native repositories. For reduced VM instantiation time, the repository ensures the availability of the required appliances in a repository closest to the IaaS system. As a result, the repository currently offers the support for four VA replication strategies: *(i)* background replication, *(ii)* Cloud-Broker initiated replication, *(iii)* extensible virtual appliance use and *(iv)* combined replication.

If the repository uses the *background replication* strategy, then it organizes the replication of entire virtual appliances to the native repositories according to the current service demand. The FCM repository replicates those services that are frequently called. In contrast, when the demand for a service decreases the FCM repository erases appliances from native repositories that are bound to IaaS systems without a running service instance.

As a result, the GMBS always queries the FCM repository to identify those native repositories that already store the appliance of the requested service. Then, the GMBS restricts its brokering decision to the Cloud-Brokers responsible for the IaaS systems with the identified repositories.

In case of *Cloud-Broker initiated* replication, the Meta-broker component does not consider the service availability in the various native repositories and the FCM repository does not initiate replication autonomously. Therefore, it is the task of the Cloud-Brokers to initiate the replication of the appliance with the requested service. If the Cloud-Broker receives a request to a service without an appliance in the native repository, then it requests the FCM repository to replicate the requested service to the native repository. After the FCM repository confirms the completion of the replication the Cloud-Broker can proceed with the Virtual Machine creation for the requested service.

Next, if the *extensible virtual appliance use* based strategy is applied, then the system uses a two-phased appliance instantiation technique. First, the FCM repository ensures the availability of necessary extensible virtual appliances in all native repositories. The FCM repository also decomposes the appliances offering the requested service into at least two parts: the extensible virtual appliance as the *base* and the offered service with its dependencies as an *extension*. This decomposition allows the Cloud-Broker to avoid the replication of the entire appliance. Instead, it instantiates the extensible appliance in a Virtual Machine first, matching the requirements of the requested service. Then, the Cloud-Broker applies the *extension* on the newly created Virtual Machine (this technique is further discussed in the following sub-section). Finally, if the extension is frequently queried from a specific IaaS system then the FCM repository replicates the appliance of the requested service to the native repository automatically.

Finally, with *combined replication*, the Cloud-Broker either initiates the replication of the appli-

ances or uses extensible virtual appliances. The Cloud-Broker automatically decides between the two options by analyzing the current contents of the service request queue. If multiple queries exist to the service then it considers replication, otherwise it chooses to use an extensible VA.

3.5.2. Two-Phased Appliance Instantiation

Centralized virtual appliance storage would require the VM Handler to first download the entire appliance to a native repository, then instantiate the appliance with the IaaS system. To avoid the first transfer, but keep the convenience of a single repository for our users, options to rebuild virtual appliances (VA_r) in already running Virtual Machines have been investigated. Two distinct approaches for rebuilding have been identified: *(i)* native appliance reuse and *(ii)* minimal manageable virtual appliances. Both approaches follow a *two-phased appliance instantiation* procedure: in the *first phase* they require the VM Handler to instantiate an appliance (VA_b) that shares common roots with VA_r, next, in the *second phase*, they extend the newly instantiated Virtual Machines (VM_b) with the differences of VA_b and VA_r. The only difference between these approaches is the used VA_b appliance. The first approach utilizes already available virtual appliances in the native repositories. In contrast, the second approach introduces a brand new appliance that is tailored to offer maximal extensibility and minimal impact on the delivery of VA_r.

The first approach requires the FCM repository (R_f) to analyze the publicly available virtual appliances ($VA_p \in R_n$) of each native repository (R_n). Then find the appliances (VA_e) that are extensible while running. *Extensible virtual appliances* is defined by the abilities of *(i)* adding new content – e.g. files or software packages –, *(ii)* configuring the newly added content and *(iii)* removing unnecessary content – and allows VMs to be repurposed and avoids the expensive

VM destruction and instantiation procedures (see challenge *(iii)* from Section 1). Before appliance rebuilding, as one of its background processes, the FCM repository automatically calculates all file hashes of these extensible appliances. To maintain hash correctness, this approach requires the FCM repository to continuously monitor if there were changes in the available extensible appliances in all native repositories.

The second approach proposes the minimal manageable virtual appliance (MMVA – VA_m) that is defined as extensible virtual appliance with the following two extra properties:

- Offers monitoring capabilities allowing VMs based on this appliance to analyze their current state and provide access to their CPU load, free disk space, network usage and other properties. This feature is utilized during high level decision making in the Cloud-Broker and GMBS components of the architecture.
- Optimally sized: only those files present in the appliance that are required to offer the management and monitoring capabilities and allows its extensibility by appliance developers.

MMVAs are created in two ways: either by *constructing* them as new appliances or by *intersecting* extensible appliances (VA_e). Constructing MMVAs is a simple appliance development task and it is not discussed in this chapter in detail. Appliance intersection assumes that available native repositories contain more than one extensible appliance and they all offer at least basic monitoring capabilities. In such cases, our architecture proposes MMVAs as the intersection between any pair of the already extensible appliances in the system: $VA'_m = VA_{e1} \cap VA_{e2}$. If the proposed VA'_m still remains extensible then the FCM repository automatically registers it. Therefore, the proposed appliance becomes available for future intersections. The FCM architecture recommends new

appliances to be developed by using an MMVA as their *base*, because they enable the advanced features of the higher-level FCM components.

To further support the *two-phased appliance instantiation*, the architecture avoids the transfer of extensible virtual appliances during the first phase of instantiation. For each appliance offering a service requested in a specific IaaS system, the FCM repository checks if the native repository of the IaaS system offers an extensible appliance that could host the requested service. If the native repository does not offer the necessary extensible appliances then the FCM repository replicates them. The continuous scanning and replication processes of the FCM repository are executed independently from the current appliance instantiation procedures. The replicated appliances are utilized during the first phase of the appliance instantiation by delivering the *base* part of the decomposed service appliance.

Native repositories might hold multiple extensible appliances as possible candidates to form the basis for the requested service's appliance. If the VM Handler identifies such case, then it looks for the *ideal extensible virtual appliance* by filtering the available extensible appliances. The ideal extensible virtual appliance must be selected for every service appliance in every native repository. We define the ideal extensible VA as an appliance that shares the most common files with the appliance under instantiation (VA_r). To find the common files the AVS stores all file hashes of VA_r in the FCM repository, and during the registration of the extensible appliances, the repository also calculates the hashes for their contents. Therefore, in practice, the system identifies the ideal extensible appliance by selecting the extensible appliance that offers the largest sized intersection between the hash sets of the VA_r and VA_e. Consequently, when the ideal extensible appliance is used in the first phase of the instantiation of the VA_r, then the second phase of the instantiation requires the smallest extension on the VM created in the first phase.

4. FUTURE RESEARCH DIRECTIONS

Regarding future works, the authors plan to investigate various scenarios that arise during handling federated Cloud infrastructures using the FCM architecture (e.g., the interactions and interoperation of public and private IaaS systems). It is also planned to increase the autonomous behavior of the various layers in the system allowing federations to be more flexible, to better cope with unexpected situations (e.g. failures and irregular demands – see the challenge *(v)* in Section 1) and to be more user friendly. Next, issues of providing feedback mechanisms from the deployed services are investigated (monitoring their Cloud and Virtual Machine type specific performance) and the received feedback incorporated into the matchmaking and VM queuing mechanisms of the architecture. Even though the chapter has already addressed several issues of interoperability (like different IaaS system interfaces or virtual appliance formats), it plans to deeper investigate further interoperability issues (e.g., support for Cross Cloud VPNs, Inter Cloud VM migration or federation aware service level agreement management). Finally, it also aims to extend the architecture towards future IaaS capabilities such as VM migration and resizing.

5. CONCLUSION

This chapter proposed a Federated Cloud Management solution that acts as an entry point to Cloud federations. It started by identifying the seven main issues of Cloud federations in current systems: single entry point, Cloud selection, Virtual Machine management, virtual appliance distribution, handling failures, and varying loads on multiple levels, interoperability, and cost optimization. Then, it revealed the current struggles users regularly meet when using multiple Cloud providers (e.g. when to terminate Virtual Machines,

how to migrate virtual appliances). Afterwards, it presented the federated Cloud management architecture that offers a solution for these issues by incorporating the concepts of meta-brokering, Cloud brokering and on-demand service deployment. The meta-brokering component provides transparent service execution for the users by allowing the system to interconnect the various Cloud broker solutions managed by aggregating capabilities of these IaaS Cloud providers. The chapter has shown how Cloud-Brokers manage the number and the location of the utilized Virtual Machines for the various service requests they receive. In order to accelerate Virtual Machine instantiation, the architecture uses the automatic service deployment component that is capable of optimizing its delivery by decomposing and replicating it among the various IaaS Cloud infrastructures.

REFERENCES

Amazon CloudWatch. (2011). Website, retrieved July 20, 2011 from http://aws.amazon.com/cloudwatch/

Amazon Web Services LLC. (2011). Amazon elastic compute cloud. Website, retrieved July 20, 2011 from http://aws.amazon.com/ec2/

Bellur, U., Rao C. S. & S.D, M. K. (2010). Optimal Placement Algorithms for Virtual Machines. *Arxiv preprint arXiv 1011 5064, (Vm)*, pp 1-16. Retrieved from http://arxiv.org/abs/1011.5064

Bernstein, D., Ludvigson, E., Sankar, K., Diamond, S., & Morrow, M. (2009). Blueprint for the Intercloud – Protocols and Formats for Cloud Computing Interoperability. In *Proceedings of The Fourth International Conference on Internet and Web Applications and Services*. 328-336.

Buyya, R., Ranjan, R., & Calheiros, R. N. (2010). Lecture Notes in Computer Science: *Vol. 6081. InterCloud: Utility-Oriented Federation of Cloud Computing Environments for Scaling of Application Services*. Algorithms and Architectures for Parallel Processing.

Buyya, R., Yeo, C. S., Venugopal, S., Broberg, J., & Brandic, I. (2009). Cloud computing and emerging it platforms: Vision, hype, and reality for delivering computing as the 5th utility. *Future Generation Computer Systems*, 25(6), 599–616. doi:10.1016/j.future.2008.12.001

Di Nitto, E., Ghezzi, C., Metzger, A., Papazoglou, M., & Pohl, K. (2008). A journey to highly dynamic, self-adaptive service-based applications. *Automated Software Engineering*, 25, 313–341. doi:10.1007/s10515-008-0032-x

EDGeS 3G Bridge (2011). Website: http://source-forge.net/projects/edges-3g-bridge/

EnStratus. (2011). Website, retrieved July 20, 2011 from http://www.enstratus.com/

Ferrer, A. J. (2012). OPTIMIS: a Holistic Approach to Cloud Service Provisioning. *Future Generation Computer Systems*, 28(1), 66–77. doi:10.1016/j.future.2011.05.022

Geer, D. (2009). The OS faces a brave new world. *Computer*, 42(10), 15–17. doi:10.1109/MC.2009.333

Kecskemeti, G., Terstyanszky, G., Kacsuk, P., & Nemeth, Zs. (2011). An approach for virtual appliance distribution for service deployment. *Future Generation Computer Systems*, 27(3), 280–289. doi:10.1016/j.future.2010.09.009

Kertesz, A., & Kacsuk, P. (2010). GMBS: A new middleware service for making grids interoperable. *Future Generation Computer Systems*, 26(4), 542–553. doi:10.1016/j.future.2009.10.007

Kertesz, A., Kacsuk, P., Iosup, A. & Epema, D. H. J. (2008). Investigating peer-to-peer meta-brokering in Grids, *Technical report*, TR-0170, Institute on Resource Management and Scheduling, *Core-GRID* – Network of Excellence.

Kertesz, A., Kecskemeti, G., & Brandic, I. (2011). Autonomic SLA-aware Service Virtualization for Distributed Systems, In proceedings of the 19th Euromicro International Conference on Parallel, Distributed and Network-Based Computing, *IEEE Computer Society*, 503-510.

Lucas-Simarro, J. L., Moreno-Vozmediano, R., Montero, R. S., & Llorente, I. M. (2011). Dynamic Placement of Virtual Machines for Cost Optimization in Multi-Cloud Environments. *In Proceedings of the 2011 International Conference on High Performance Computing & Simulation (HPCS 2011)*. 1-7.

Marosi, A. Cs. & Kacsuk, P. (2011). Workers in the clouds. In *Proceedings of the 2011 19th Euromicro Conference on Parallel, Distributed and Network-based Processing*, 519–526.

Marshall, P., Keahey, K., & Freeman, T. (2010). Elastic site: Using clouds to elastically extend site resources. In *Proceedings of the 2010 10th IEEE/ACM International Conference on Cluster, Cloud and Grid Computing*. 43–52.

Rackspace Cloud. (2011). Website, retrieved July 20, 2011 from http://www.rackspace.com/cloud/

Ranjan, R., & Buyya, R. (2009). *Decentralized Overlay for Federation of Enterprise Clouds. Handbook of Research on Scalable Computing Technologies* (Li, K., Eds.). USA: IGI Global.

RightScale. (2011). Website, retrieved July 20, 2011 from http://www.rightscale.com/

Rochwerger, B., Berltgand, D., Epstein, A., Hadas, D., Loy, I., & Nagin, K. (2011). Reservoir – When One Cloud is not enough. *Computer*, 44(3), 44–51. doi:10.1109/MC.2011.64

Salehi, M. A., & Buyya, R. (2010). Lecture Notes in Computer Science: *Vol. 6081. Adapting market-oriented scheduling policies for cloud computing* (pp. 351–362). Algorithms and Architectures for Parallel Processing.

Schmidt, M., Fallenbeck, N., Smith, M., & Freisleben, B. (2010). Efficient distribution of Virtual Machines for cloud computing. In *Proceedings of the 2010 18th Euromicro Conference on Parallel, Distributed and Network-based Processing.* 564-574.

Vázquez, C., Huedo, E., Montero, R. S., & Llorente, I. M. (2011). On the use of clouds for grid resource provisioning. *Future Generation Computer Systems, 27*(5), 600–605. doi:10.1016/j.future.2010.10.003

Web Service Description Language – WSDL. (2011), Website, retrieved July 20, 2011 from http://www.w3.org/TR/wsdl

ADDITIONAL READING

Armbrust, M., Fox, A., Griffith, R., Joseph, A. D., Katz, R. H., Konwinski, A., Lee, G., Patterson, D. A., Rabkin, A., Stoica, I. & Zaharia, M. (2009). Above the Clouds: A Berkeley View of Cloud Computing. UCB/EECS-2009-28.

Elmroth, E., Marquez, F. G., Henriksson, D., & Ferrera, D. P. (2009). Accounting and Billing for Federated Cloud Infrastructures. *In Proceedings of the Eight International Conference on Grid and Cooperative Computing*, 268-275

Foster, I., Zhao, Y., Raicu, I., & Lu, S. (2008). Cloud computing and grid computing 360-degree compared. *In proceedings of the Grid Computing Environments Workshop (GCE08).*

Keahey, K., Tsugawa, M., Matsunaga, A., & Fortes, J. (2009). Sky computing. *IEEE Internet Computing, 13*(5), 43–51. doi:10.1109/MIC.2009.94

Leavitt, N. (2009). Is Cloud Computing Really Ready for Prime Time? *Computer, 42*(1), 15–20. doi:10.1109/MC.2009.20

Moreno-Vozmediano, R., Montero, R. S., & Llorente, I. M. (2011). Multi-Cloud Deployment of Computing Clusters for Loosely-Coupled MTC Applications. *IEEE Transactions on Parallel and Distributed Systems, 22*(6), 924–930. doi:10.1109/TPDS.2010.186

Vaquero, L. M., Rodero-Merino, L., Caceres, J., & Lindner, M. (2008). A break in the clouds: towards a cloud definition. *SIGCOMM Computer Communication Review, 39*, 50–55. doi:10.1145/1496091.1496100

KEY TERMS AND DEFINITIONS

Appliance Instantiation: The means of creating and starting a virtual machine that utilizes and executes a specific virtual appliance.

Cloud-Brokering: This task involves the dynamic creation and destruction of virtual machine according to their respective service demand.

Combined Replication: The strategy that ensures the availability of particular virtual appliances on the target cloud infrastructures either using extensible virtual appliances or the intelligence in cloud-brokers.

Matchmaking: This is a process of mapping service calls to provisioned services of virtual appliances.

Meta-Brokering: This method means a high-level, autonomous management of interconnected infrastructures with the help of brokers by forming a federation. Its tasks include automatic infrastructure selection, load balancing under varying workloads and service call submission using a well-defined interface.

Repository: A storage entity that keeps and offers virtual appliances for its users.

Virtual Appliance: Stored form of a virtual machine state that encapsulates services with their support environment.

Chapter 3
Understanding Decentralized and Dynamic Brokerage in Federated Cloud Environments

Nicolò Maria Calcavecchia
Politecnico di Milano, Italy

Antonio Celesti
Universit Degli Studi di Messina, Italy

Elisabetta Di Nitto
Politecnico di Milano, Italy

ABSTRACT

The advent of the cloud computing paradigm offers different ways both to sell services and to exploit external computational resources according to a pay-per-use economic model. Nowadays, cloud computing clients can buy various form of IaaS, PaaS, and SaaS from cloud providers. Besides this form of pay-per-use, the perspective of cloud federation offers further business opportunities for small/medium providers which hold physical datacenters. Considering the cloud computing ecosystem, besides large cloud providers, smaller ones are also becoming popular even though their own virtualization infrastructures (i.e., deployed in their datacenters) cannot directly compete with the bigger market leaders. The result is that often small/medium clouds have to exploit the services of mega-providers in order to develop their business logic and their cloud-based services. To this regard, a possible future alternative scenario is represented by the promotion of cooperation among small/medium cloud providers, thus enabling the sharing of computational and storage resources. However, in order to achieve such an environment, several issues have to be addressed. One of these challenges is how to plan brokerage strategies allowing cloud providers to discover other providers for partnership establishment. This chapter focuses on different possible centralized and decentralized approaches in designing a brokerage strategy for cloud federation, analyzing their features, advantages and disadvantages.

DOI: 10.4018/978-1-4666-1631-8.ch003

Copyright © 2012, IGI Global. Copying or distributing in print or electronic forms without written permission of IGI Global is prohibited.

INTRODUCTION

The advent of the cloud computing paradigm offers different ways for buying/selling services by exploiting computational resources offered by third parties according to a pay-per-use economic model. Nowadays, cloud computing clients can buy services at various levels of abstraction from cloud providers. Examples include: IaaS, that is, VMs and storage, PaaS that is, the possibility of deploying applications fulfilling specific architectural and programming models, and SaaS, that is, pure application services.

Considering the cloud computing ecosystem, besides large cloud providers, smaller/medium providers are also becoming popular even though the virtualization infrastructures they have deployed in their datacenters cannot directly compete with the bigger counterparts including mega-providers such as: Amazon, Rackspace, Google, and Salesforce. A way to overcome these resource limitations is represented by the promotion of federation and cooperation mechanisms among small/medium cloud providers, thus enabling the sharing of computational and storage resources. This allows another form of pay-per-use economic model for ICT societies, universities, research centers, and organizations that commonly do not fully exploit the resources of their own physical infrastructure.

Federation brings new business opportunities for clouds. In fact besides, the traditional market where cloud providers offer cloud-based services to their clients, federation triggers a new market where cloud providers can buy and/or sell computing/storage capabilities and services to other clouds. For example, a cloud might need to buy resources from other clouds for the following reasons:

- The cloud runs out of its storage/computing resources. In order to continue providing cloud-based service to its clients, it decides to buy resources from other clouds.

- The cloud needs to deploy a distributed cloud-based service in different geographical locations; hence, it acquires resources placed in those target locations.
- The cloud needs to migrate cloud-based service instances in other clouds in order to accomplish service relocation, power saving, backup, etc.

At the same time, a cloud can decide to provide resources to other clouds when it realizes that its datacenter is under-utilized at given times. Typically, datacenters are under-utilized during the night and over-utilized during the morning. Therefore, as the datacenter cannot be turned off, the cloud provider may decide to turn the problem into a business opportunity. This case may be applied to many different organizations, such as, universities, public administrations, and enterprises.

Hence, the advantage of transforming a physical datacenter in a cloud virtualization infrastructure, in the perspective of cloud federation, is twofold. On the one hand, small/medium cloud providers that rent resources to other providers can optimize the use of their infrastructure, which are often underutilized. On the other hand, external small/medium cloud providers can elastically scale up/down their logical virtualization infrastructure borrowing resources and paying them to other providers.

The federation partnership establishment process can be schematized according to the following three main phases: (i) discovery, the cloud looks for other available clouds for federation; (ii) match-making, the cloud selects between the discovered clouds the ones that fit as much as possible its requirements; (iii) authentication, the cloud establishes a trust context with the selected clouds.

When the federation is established, a new phase becomes very relevant, that is, the "management" of the federated resources. All above phases can be executed in various ways and are complicated by the fact that the involved cloud platforms can be heterogeneous in the technology they use and in the level of abstraction (IaaS, PaaS, SaaS) at which they offer their services.

Currently, cloud federation is at the early stage. All over the word, at the time of writing of this chapter, some research initiatives are focusing on different specific aspects of cloud federation including architectures, security, QoS, volunteer computing, and business profits, etc. This chapter, tries to identify the main issues concerning the establishment of a federation in a decentralized and dynamic way focusing on the way in which the brokerage takes place between cloud providers for the establishment of federation. More specifically, it presents centralized and decentralized brokerage approaches including cloud providers and brokers, also arguing how cloud providers might find out partners for federation in a dynamic fashion.

The chapter is organized as follows. Firstly, it discusses about four orthogonal factors that characterize the federation of cloud environments. After that, it analyzes the state to the orthogonal factors.

Then, it focuses on the decentralized and dynamic brokerage discussing advantages and disadvantages. In order to better understand the dynamic decentralized brokerage between cloud providers, it analyzes different possible strategies and the main involved factors. Future research challenges and conclusion end the Chapter.

DIMENSIONS FOR THE ESTABLISHMENT OF A CLOUD FEDERATION

Considering cloud computing, federation is a wide problem which has different facets. In order to better understand the cloud federation from an architectural point of view, and understand what research works, and industry initiatives conceived for federation and how they accomplish it, this section defines four dimensions characterizing the cloud federation: Service Level, Technology, Brokerage Strategy, and Scope.

Service Level

Federation of clouds can happen at the three typical levels of abstraction IaaS, PaaS, and SaaS.

IaaS Federation is a partnership between clouds for the borrowing/lending of virtual infrastructures, e.g., physical virtualization appliances (i.e., servers, storages, networks, etc), VMs, virtual clusters, and virtual networks, etc. From the technological point of view, such a federation requires the definition of an abstraction layer that enables the access and the management of the external clouds resources in a seamless way, across different operating systems and virtualization mechanisms.

PaaS Federation refers to a partnership where clouds borrow/rent PaaS from/to other clouds. This case is more complex than the previous one as the current PaaS middleware supports quite different programming abstractions. If they are not carefully solved, these differences in the programming abstractions impact the way the applications deployed in the federated environment should be built. So, at the current stage, only federations between PaaS supporting the same programming abstractions seem to be feasible, but an effort to uniform the various programming abstractions would be more than welcomed.

Finally, SaaS federation corresponds to what in the SOA domain is called a *service composition* (Di Nitto et al, 2008) and is regulated by the standards defined for service interaction.

Technology

An important element affecting the design of the mechanisms for establishing and managing a federation depends on the type of architecture, middleware and technologies used by the involved cloud providers. Clearly, the more the architectural and technological choices of cloud providers are similar, the more the establishment and the management of the federation are simplified.

As cloud providers can be heterogeneous, technology compliance is a sensitive topic. In fact, it involves the communication interfaces between clouds, the protocols used in cloud-based services, virtualization technologies (e.g., KVM, Xen, VmWare, Virtual Box, Virtul PC, etc), adopted security models and technologies (e.g., Username/Password, Digital Certificate, PKI schemes, SAML, OpenID, Shibboleth, etc), and so on.

Brokerage Strategy

Brokerage is defined as the discovery and match-making phase needed for the creation of a federation of clouds. The authors envisage four possible federation schemas in which this brokerage may take place: *centralized*, that is, a single broker common to all clouds is in charge of establishing the federation, *hierarchical*, that is, a number of brokers interact among each other to establish the federation, *decentralized*, that is, the brokerage function is embedded within all clouds that do not need any third party to perform it, and *mixed*, that is, a combination of hierarchical and decentralized.

In the centralized scheme the broker is a third-party entity allowing a cloud to look for other clouds for federation according to its requirements. It has interfaces toward several different heterogeneous clouds and its main task is to perform a matching between a cloud requiring federation and clouds offering federation. Figure 1 depicts an example where cloud 1, 2, and N establish a partnership by means of a broker. Hence, using the capabilities and services made available by partners, each cloud provides IaaS, PaaS, or SaaS to their own clients.

The hierarchical scheme, depicted in Figure 2, is an extension of the previous one: clouds are connected to a broker, and, at the same time, each broker can also interact with other brokers in order to look for clouds whose requirements match the requirements of clouds requesting partnerships.

In the decentralized scheme clouds negotiate the partnership by themselves. They manage discovery, communication, negotiation of agree-

Figure 1. Centralized federation scheme using a broker

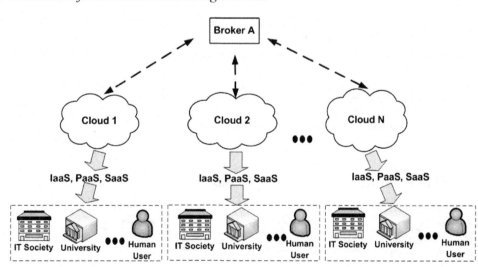

ments, and matching and selection of the best partners for federation according to their requirements by themselves. This scheme appears to be the most flexible one, but it is also hard to achieve as it has the biggest impact on cloud providers middleware. Figure 3 depicts an example where cloud 1, 2, and 3 establish partnerships by themselves.

Of course, mixed situations where some clouds rely on some broker and others manage the fed-

eration by themselves are also possible. In Figure 4, clouds 1, 2, 3 exploit a decentralized brokerage scheme. The same applies to clouds 4, 5 and 6 and to clouds 7, 8 and 9. At the same time clouds 2, 4, and 7 rely also on some brokers that allow them to participate in other federations. If a federation between cloud 4 and 7 is established, then a centralized brokerage approach is exploited. If the federation also involves cloud 2, then a hierarchical brokerage mechanism can be exploited.

Figure 2. Hierarchical federation scheme

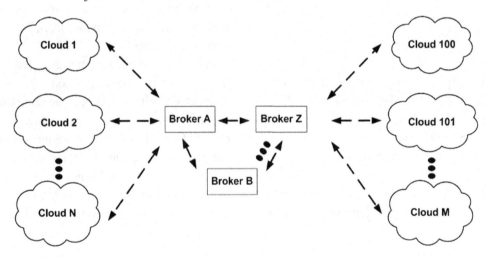

Figure 3. Decentralized federation scheme

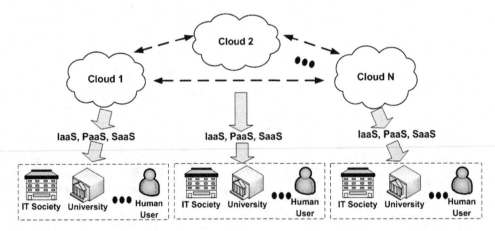

Figure 4. Combination of the centralized and decentralized brokerage schemes

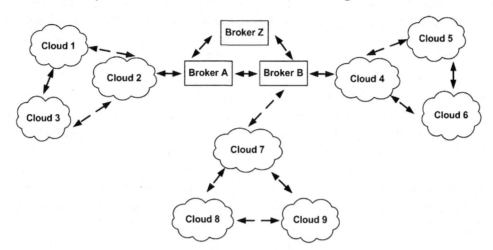

Scope

An important element of a federation is the definition of the policy to grant access to new partners. Access can be limited to a set of predefined partners (this case is called *closed*) or it can be *open* to every provider able to fulfill the required SLA.

In the closed case, cloud providers establish a priori agreements with other clouds forecasting possible peak of workload due to particular events in the target period of time. The involved operators configure the partnership manually. The selection of partners can either be performed autonomously or by exploiting the services of one or more federation brokers. This preconfigured federation is accomplished by selecting clouds according to constraints regarding the type of required capabilities/service, technology compliance, security, QoS, etc. Another aspect regards the level of trustiness of cloud providers. In fact, operators choose their partners according to reputation and history.

After the establishment of a closed federation, the runtime management costs are relatively low as the SLAs are established and maintained off-line.

In the open case, a new stakeholder can enter in a federation if it is able to fulfill the required constraints and to offer the required services. These requirements should be publicly available to give to any cloud provider the possibility of entering into the cloud, and they should be described in a widely understood language. Of course, some automatic access control mechanisms would be very important in this case. They should be able to process the federation requirements description and to check the fulfillment of these requirements by the newcomers. This check can be performed in various ways. It can be limited to verifying that what the new cloud provider declares is compliant with the requirements or it may involve more complex runtime checks including monitoring of the cloud provider activity and verification of its trustworthiness.

APPLYING DIMENSIONS TO CLASSIFY EXISTING APPROACHES

Technological solutions for cloud computing infrastructures are increasing day by day, and the vision where companies use computational facilities according to a pay-per-use model, similar to other utilities like electricity, gas, and water, is becoming true.

However, the concept of cloud federation is quite recent. Cloud federation refers to mesh of clouds that are interconnected based on open standards to provide a universal decentralized computing environment where everything is driven by constraints and agreements in a ubiquitous, multi-provider infrastructure.

This section provides an overview of currently existing solutions in the field, taking into account initiatives born in academia, industry and major research projects. Most of the work in the field concerns the study of architectural models able to efficiently support the collaboration between different cloud providers focusing on various aspects of the federation.

In Ranjan and Buyya (2009), the authors propose a decentralized technique using a structured peer-to-peer network supporting discovery, deployment and output data collection of a (PaaS) middleware (Aneka). The system is structured as a set of Aneka coordinator peers deployed in each cloud (or in the extreme case on each node of the cloud) offering discovery and coordination mechanisms useful for federation. A central point is represented by the Distributed Hash Table (DHT) overlay which is adapted in order to take into account multi-dimensional queries (e.g., "find all nodes with Linux operating system, two cores with 2.0 GHz and 2GB or RAM"). However, it is not clear how this approach deals with dynamism as discovery and matchmaking are carried out by a third party node (imposed by the DHT), which can be subject to failures.

Celesti, Tusa, Villari and Puliafito (2010) propose an architectural solution for federation by means of a Cross-Cloud Federation Manager (CCFM), a software component in charge of executing the three main functionalities required for a federation. In particular, the component explicitly manages: i) the discovery phase in which information about other clouds are received and sent, ii) the match-making phase performing the best choice of the provider according to some utility measure and iii) the authentication phase creating a secure channel between the federated clouds.

In Buyya, Ranjan and Calheiros (2010), the authors propose a more articulated model for federation composed of three main components. A Cloud Coordinator manages a specific cloud and acts as interface for the external clouds by exposing well-defined cloud operations. The Cloud Exchange component implements the functionality of a registry by storing all necessary information characterizing cloud providers together with demands and offers for computational resources. Lastly, the Cloud Broker represents the touch point for users to enact the federation process; it interacts with the Cloud Exchange to find appropriate cloud providers and with the Cloud Coordinator to define the resource allocation satisfying the needed QoS.

A FP7 European Project focusing on cloud federation is RESERVOIR. In Rochwerger et al (2009), the authors define a RESERVOIR cloud as decentralized federation of collaborating sites. RESERVOIR introduces an abstraction layer that allows developing a set of high level management components that are not tied to any specific environment. In RESERVOIR, several sites can share physical infrastructure resources on which service applications can be executed. Each site is partitioned by a virtualization layer into virtual execution environments (VEEs). These environments are fully isolated runtime modules that abstract away the physical characteristics of the resource and enable sharing. The virtualized computational resources, alongside with the virtualization layer and all the management enablement components, are referred to as the VEE Host. In RESERVOIR a service application is a set of software components which work to achieve a common goal in which each one can be deployed in the same or in different sites. A RESERVOIR cloud federation is homogeneous (i.e., each site has to run the same middleware) and decentralized. It occurs at the IaaS level and needs a static a-priori configuration in each site.

Goiri, Guitart, and Torres (2010) focus on the problem of deciding if to select the local resources or the resources offered by the federation and if to make the local resources available for external usage. In particular, the authors' approach is based on a global scheduler deployed on each cloud. The scheduler continuously analyzes the status of the system, taking into account the incoming workload, and identifies the most appropriate action to be taken, among deploying the service in the local cloud, outsourcing the service or offering unused resources to other providers.

The problem of cloud federation includes also several semantic issues due to the diversity of existent cloud infrastructures. Thus, a common ontology unifying cloud concepts belonging to different clouds could be beneficial. Loutas, Peristeras, Bouras, Kamateri, Zeginis and Tarabanis (2010) focus on this challenge and propose a reference semantic-aware architecture for cloud interoperability. Their solution relies on semantic annotations (implemented with standardized languages such as OWL or RDF) for cloud deployed services and cloud resources (e.g. components, data, interfaces, etc.); annotations are then interpreted by a semantic interoperability engine capable of solving mismatches and incompatibilities among clouds. Starting from the analysis of literature the authors also propose a set common APIs which captures the majority of functionalities found in available technological solutions.

An even more decentralized vision is offered by Cloud@Home (Distefano, Cunsolo, Puliafito, Scarpa (2010)). This is a PRIN Project founded by the Italian Ministry of Education facing the cloud federation problem from the point of view of the volunteer computing paradigm. Here, along with cloud providers and datacenter owners (i.e., enterprises, organizations, universities, governments, etc) also single desktop/mobile volunteer entities can join the Cloud&Home federation. The scenario includes several coexisting and interoperable open, commercial and hybrid Clouds. Open Clouds identify groups of shared resources and services operating for free Volunteer computing; commercial Clouds characterize entities or companies selling their computing resources for business; hybrid Clouds can both sell or give for free their services. Both open and hybrid Clouds can interoperate with any other Cloud, also commercial ones, creating federations of Clouds. The federation takes place at IaaS level and is coordinated by a centralized entity including service management and SLA modules. The Cloud&Home federation is self-managed, and does not require a priori configuration in each volunteer entity.

The problem of reliable and scalable cloud storage is studied in Bermbach, Klems, Tai, Menzel (2011), where federation is reducing the vendor lock-in problem. In particular, the proposed solution, called MetaStorage, is able to provide storage operations (e.g., GET, PUT, DELETE and LISTFILES) according to an eventually consistent scheme, spreading multiple copies of data over different cloud providers. The system is composed of two kinds of nodes: i) Coordinator/Distributor nodes (organized in a decentralized fashion) representing the interface to the operations of data replication and retrieval and ii) MetaStorage nodes wrapping available storage services (e.g., Amazon S3) with a common interface.

A similar problem is addressed by a recent FP7 European Project, VISION Cloud, which aims to introduce a powerful ICT infrastructure for reliable and effective delivery of PaaS and SaaS data-intensive storage services. This infrastructure supports the setup and deployment of data and storage services on demand, at competitive costs, across disparate administrative domains, while providing QoS and security guarantees. The VISION architecture includes two layers: access interface layer and operating layer. Federation should take place in the last one, but at the moment of writing of this chapter, there are no further details on the system architecture.

Comparison Table

As previously discussed, a decentralized brokerage strategy for federated cloud environments is strongly needed. However, the topic is not deeply addressed in the literature. Table 1 depicts an analysis of the main research and industry projects initiatives facing the problem of cloud federation. The analysis considers three of the four dimensions identified in the third section of this chapter, that is, "Service Level", "Brokerage Strategy", and "Technology". The fourth dimension, i.e., "Scope", is left undefined for all approaches as all of them are orthogonal to it and each of them can be used to develop both open and closed federations; however, no approach explicitly deals with this aspect. The Table is not completely filled in, because it has not been possible to classify all works according to all dimensions due to the lack of specific information.

Table 1 shows how each approach focuses on one or more particular service levels. Nevertheless, in Buyya, Ranjan, Calheiros (2010) and Loutas et al (2009) it is not clear how the federation impacts on IaaS, PaaS, SaaS. Instead, other works, such as Rochwerger et al (2009) and Bermbach, Klems, Tai, Menzel (2011), focus on a particular service level in a detailed way. Regarding technology, almost all related works face the federation adopting homogeneous protocols and software solutions. The only exception is represented by Loutas et al (2010), where the authors assume the federation as an environment of heterogeneous cloud providers.

The adopted brokerage strategy deserves a specific discussion. From the analysis of related work it is evident that not all the approaches consider a decentralized brokerage strategy. In Buyya, Ranjan, Calheiros (2010), Distefano, Cunsolo, Puliafito, Scarpa (2010), and Bermbach, Klems, Tai, Menzel (2011) a centralized scheme for federation brokerage is considered. The other approaches we have analyzed, apart from Vision-Cloud whose strategy has not clarified yet, adopt a decentralized Cloud2Cloud scheme for brokerage, but they do not provide detailed information about how the decentralized brokerage take place.

Another important aspect concerns the dynamicity of decentralized brokerage. Apart from Rochwerger et al (2009), where the brokerage between RESERVOIR-based sites has to be established by administrators, the other approaches assume the presence of a dynamic brokerage, though, without providing detailed information. Furthermore, Hierarchical and Mixed Brokerage schemes have not been adopted in cloud federation yet. For these reasons, the authors think it is worthwhile to better investigate the different strategies of decentralized dynamic brokerage,

Table 1. Classification of the current research works and industry initiatives

	Service Level	Technology	Brokerage Strategy	Scope
Celesti, Tusa, VIllari, Puliafito (2010)	IaaS	-	Decentralized C2C scheme	-
Buyya, Ranjan, Calheiros (2010)	IaaS, PaaS, SaaS	-	Centralized scheme	-
Ranjan, Buyya (2009)	PaaS	Homogeneous	Decentralized C2C scheme	-
Rochwerger et al (2009)	IaaS	Homogeneous	Decentralized C2C scheme	-
Loutas et al (2010)	IaaS, PaaS, SaaS	Heterogeneous	Decentralized C2C scheme	-
Distefano, Cunsolo, Puliafito, Scarpa (2010)	IaaS	Homogeneous	Centralized scheme	-
Goiri, Guitart, Torres (2010)	-	-	Decentralized C2C scheme	-
Bermbach, Klems, Tai, Menzel (2011)	PaaS	Homogeneous	Centralized Scheme	-
VisionCloud (2011)	PaaS, SaaS	Homogeneous	-	

considering their impact on a cloud federation. The reminder of this chapter will focus on this topic.

TOWARD DECENTRALIZED AND DYNAMIC BROKERAGE

As discussed in the previous sections, the establishment of a cloud federation implies that a number of cloud providers encounter themselves through the accomplishment of some discovery and matchmaking activities. As highlighted in Table 1, a common factor of the aforementioned cloud federation initiatives is the need for decentralized brokerage strategies. Clearly, on one hand, decentralized brokerage strategies require more intelligence than centralized ones, but allow a Cloud provider to leverage new business opportunities. As a drawback, decentralized brokerage strategies require a greater degree of complexity than centralized strategies. However, the current literature lacks exhaustive works regarding the issues facing the decentralized brokerage in federated cloud environments. The rest of this chapter will try to clear up this aspect, providing an overview of the possible decentralized brokerage scheme which could be adopted in planning out a federated cloud environment.

Advantages of the Dynamic Decentralized Brokerage

The following section provides a few possible advantages deriving from the possible adoption of a dynamic decentralized brokerage.

- **Reaction to Partnership Breaking:** In cloud federations, changes in partnerships can frequently occur for many reasons. The joining and leaving of cloud providers to/from the federation relationships can happen due to faults, Service Level Agreement (SLA) violation, and reconfiguration, security, etc. These latter are only a few of the possible situations which can trigger the need to re-arrange particular federation relationships between cloud providers. Hence an up-to-date decentralized dynamic brokerage can be useful to address such situations.

- **Federation Management:** After a federation has been established, it has to be managed in the proper way. In particular, the usage of the federated resources has to be controlled and auto-scaling techniques similar to those used within a single cloud have to be put in place. The ability of the federated cloud environment to perform self-management is of utmost importance. In fact, the management of complex federated environments is quite difficult for humans. Instead, with a decentralized dynamic brokerage strategy, cloud providers should be capable of self-management performing self-provisioning, self-healing, self-protection, and self-optimization strategies (all together there are known as self-CHOP), automatically exploiting or releasing the resources of the federation as needed. We can envisage such a management thanks to a distributed C2C brokerage strategy where each cloud provider manages directly the usage of the federated resources, continuously making decisions about the opportunity of using its own resources or those of the federation it belongs to. Also, if a cloud is active in more than one federation, the selection of the federation to exploit could vary from time to time, depending on the requirements of a certain application and on the SLAs associated to each federation. Similarly to the distributed C2C brokerage case, we can also envisage decentralized hierarchical and mixed schemes where some third party brokers build a proper abstraction layer managing the federation on behalf of cloud providers.

- **Response Time:** Basically, federation relationships can be established either a priori, reserving resources, or service according to probabilistic forecasts, or in real-time. In the first case the reserved resources can be used or not, instead in the second case the resource are requested on-demand when needed. When a cloud provider needs to establish in real time a partnership with other providers, the response time of the providers available for federation can determine the choice of the cloud requesting the partnership. Hence, federation-available providers can lose money if they do not respond promptly to a request. For these reasons a decentralized dynamic brokerage is strongly required.
- **Enhanced Market Competitiveness:** A decentralized and dynamic brokerage can promote a new form of competitiveness between cloud providers. This could be possible by means of the rising of a market for cloud resources, where small and medium size clouds could offer their storage and computing capabilities dynamically joining and leaving federation partnerships. In this way, they could automatically loan/borrow resources to/from other providers promoting their business without barriers all over the world.

Disadvantages of the Dynamic Decentralized Brokerage

Regardless the obvious advantages of a dynamic decentralized brokerage, there are several issues that need to be addressed. First of all, we need to tackle the complexity in design and the management of the federation process. The cloud computing scenario is complicated by the introduction of new subject, federation brokers and, at the same time, cloud architectures have to be enhanced by means of new features in order to support different brokerage scenarios. In this way, providers

should be able to find out partners by themselves or by means of third party brokers. To this regard discovery algorithms are strongly required. To complicate the scenario, the discovery process could take place applying search filters according to the cloud requirements, either in a reactive or passive way.

In the first case, cloud providers perform a real-time discovery applying research criteria options only when they realize to need external resources. Instead in the second one, providers perform a continuous passive discovery, hence performing a sort of monitoring of the federation environment, that way, when they realize to need external resources, they can carry out a search on the data already picked up applying the required search criteria options.

At the moment of writing this book, as well as for other challenges in decentralized federation, the lack of standards is another important issue for decentralized brokerage strategies in a heterogeneous federated cloud environment. These standards should offer linguistic tools for the definition of the general conditions for the federation, including the constraints regulating the access to the federation (e.g., the required virtualization technologies, QoS, security, etc), the conditions under which the resources and the services of the federation can be exploited, and the billing policy to be applied (i.e., flat contracts, pay-per-use, etc).

PLANNING DECENTRALIZED DYNAMIC BROKERAGE STRATEGIES

This section studies how the issue of cloud federation brokerage can be solved using a decentralized, dynamic, and autonomic approach by identifying major characteristics of the problem and efficiently applying existing techniques to this scenario. As described in Section 3, by decentralized brokerage the authors intend each federation process in which some or all of the interactions between participants (i.e., cloud providers or brokers) take place without a central coordinating entity.

This chapter envisions that an efficient technique to face the problem of cloud federation brokerage should satisfy the following properties:

- **Decentralization:** Cloud federation happens when two or more cloud providers decide to share their computational resources, thus producing some gain from this collaboration. However, the general scenario happening in cloud federation can involve hundreds of cloud providers, each one working independently of the others, which are potentially competitors. For this reason relying on a single central entity, trusted by all clouds, could not be realistic as it imposes a strong dependency on the central component. Conversely a decentralized technique leaves the maximum freedom among cloud providers, which can decide with whom to cooperate, thus ensuring independency from third party entities.

- **Dynamic:** The context of federation is intrinsically dynamic as it involves dynamic systems. In particular, cloud providers can suffer of outages and may not be available for some time; and as a consequence the federation with some providers could not be possible. Moreover, resources and conditions offered by the cloud itself vary with time (e.g. prices, SLAs, computational power, security, etc.) and should be timely reported to other clouds wishing to engage a federation process.

- **Autonomic:** A set of properties that a cloud federation technique should support is the one envisioned by the autonomic computing research field (i.e. self-* properties). For example the federation should be self-configuring in the sense that no manual intervention by the administrators should be required whenever new clouds join and leave the system; the federation should be self-protecting in order to avoid that other clouds voluntarily or through malicious behaviors can negatively influence the process of federation. Self-healing is also important as crashes or network partitioning in cloud providers may happen and the task of cloud federation is expected to take the appropriate actions in order to fix possible problems. Finally, self-optimization is also desirable, as the federation process should improve with time, for example, by observing past interactions with other clouds and learning which ones best fit for next federations.

The required property of decentralization, however, imposes new challenges that must be taken into account while designing the federation technique. As a consequence the designer of a federation procedure should pay attention to these aspects. Here we present a list of the major ones:

- **Lack of global knowledge:** One possible problem deriving by the use of decentralized techniques is represented by the potential lack of a global knowledge at various nodes involved in the federation. In particular, it may happen that some of the nodes involved in the federation do not have a complete view of the system state (e.g. existing clouds, resources offered, etc.); those nodes incur the risk of taking suboptimal choices during the matchmaking phase because of their limited knowledge about other clouds.

- **Data dynamicity:** As previously mentioned, data representing the system state continuously changes with time. Differently from a centralized approach, where the state is typically stored and updated in the central entity, in a decentralized one the global state is spread all over the system nodes. A major challenge is thus the timely propagation of the partial state representing a given provider.

- **Discovery:** The decentralization imposes that each cloud provider must take into account the federation functionalities that in a centralized approach are delegated to a central entity. In a decentralized approach providers are connected among them forming an emergent topology where each node is a cloud provider (or broker in the case of more complex schemas); the discovery of providers together with their current resource offering is not trivial as queries (or updates) about cloud state should be carefully forwarded over the network topology.

Strategies for Decentralized Dynamic Brokerage

This section analyzes the major design decisions that must be taken in the design process for a decentralized federation scheme. It mainly focuses on the discovery phase, as it is the one that mainly impacts the federation in a decentralized structure. These design decisions can be used as guidelines for future designers of decentralized federation schemes.

Below is a list describing what problems they address and the related advantages and disadvantages to each choice.

Structured vs. Unstructured Networks

One of the first choices to perform while considering decentralized federation techniques involves the topology interconnecting clouds and brokers. This aspect affects the way peers participating in the federation are interconnected each other (e.g. circular, mesh-like, toroid-like, random, scale-

free, etc.) and the rules regulating search queries in those networks.

In particular there are two main categories of networks: *structured networks* and *unstructured networks*. Structured networks (also known as Distributed Hash Tables, DHTs) impose a rigid structure on the topology interconnecting node as well as the data that each node contains. Queries among nodes typically have a deterministic execution time and scale well; however, as outlined also in Ranjan and Buyya (2009), they do not specifically handle range queries (i.e. queries involving a set of results satisfying a given property) which are important in a cloud context (a range query could be for example "find all providers offering computing power greater than a certain threshold with price below a given value"). Moreover very dynamic environments (i.e. nodes joining and leaving the network) can highly impact performances and quality of queries of these systems. In the case of unstructured networks, nodes have less restrictive rules regulating interconnections and data locations. Searches are performed by forwarding queries to neighbors, which, in turn, apply the same policy; range queries are typically supported by unstructured networks and are typically resistant to high level of peer dynamism.

Discovery Mode

The objective of the discovery phase is to obtain a list of all the available cloud providers with their resource availability and characteristics (e.g. price, location, SLA, trustiness, etc.). Specifically, whenever a cloud provider wants to start a federation (e.g. need more resources) it needs to compare its requested resources and conditions with other providers.

By discovery mode we refer to the rules regulating the interactions between clouds requesting resources and clouds offering them; this aspect is orthogonal from the topology adopted as it can be applied to both structured and unstructured networks.

Figure 5. Sequence of interactions in a active discovery process involving three clouds

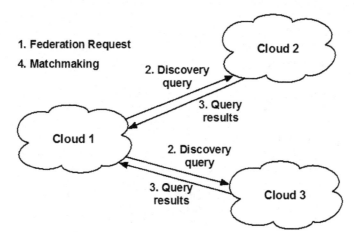

We envision three ways to carry out the discovery in a decentralized federation scheme:

1. *"active"* in which each provider proactively begins a discovery process due to an internal federation need; the provider directly queries other known providers asking their current state. The matchmaking phase is then performed on the set of retrieved results. The advantage of an active search is represented by the quality of results; in fact, since the request is performed on demand the retrieved results are very likely to be up to date. On the other hand the discovery process can take some time in order to be completed thus delaying the federation process. Figure 5 depicts the Sequence of interactions in an active discovery process involving three clouds.

2. *"passive"* in this case the provider desiring to enact a federation process is updated about the state of other clouds passively; information are periodically forwarded by clouds offering resources. In this case the matchmaking can be directly performed on the locally available information, which are stored on each cloud provider or broker. This aspect represents the main advantage of this discovery mode as the matchmaking can be immediately computed; however, local information may be outdated leading to suboptimal or denied federation requests. Figure 6 depicts the sequence of interactions in a passive discovery process involving three clouds.

3. *"hybrid"* is a combination of the previously described strategies; in this case both previously described approaches are used. Depending on the specific implementation chosen it is possible to achieve a good tradeoff between the advantages and disadvantages of both active and passive techniques.

Figure 7 depicts the sequence of interactions in a hybrid discovery process involving three clouds.

Discovery with Filtering

Discovery can be enhanced with filtering techniques. In this case the cloud provider looking for cloud resources describes the resources it is interested in through a common language. This description is later used during the search in order to improve the process and immediately filter out cloud resource offers that are not of interest for the requestor cloud. Filtering can improve the

Figure 6. Sequence of interactions in a passive discovery process involving three clouds

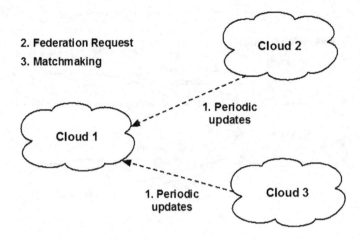

Figure 7. Sequence of interactions in a hybrid discovery process involving three clouds

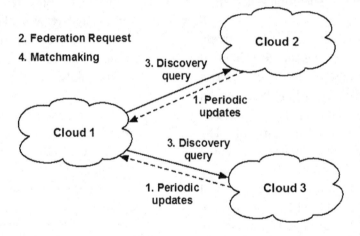

discovery process by accelerating the federation process and saving network messages. It is an independent aspect from the previous ones as it can be applied to both active (i.e. the description of requested resource is included in the search message), passive discovery mode (i.e. the cloud declares the resources in which it is interested in) and network structure.

Broker vs. Cloud Match-Making

The role of the broker can be in general interpreted as the entity acting as a representative for a cloud performing discovery, matchmaking and possibly a translation among different standards. However some of these features can be extracted from the broker such as the matchmaking phase; in particular the location of the actual matchmaking can be varied. There are two possible choices in this case: broker matchmaking or cloud matchmaking. In the first case the broker fully implements the federation intermediation resulting into the choice of a single cloud provider. In this case the provider requesting the federation completely delegates the matchmaking phase and trusts the results returned by the broker. Conversely in the cloud matchmaking each cloud provider performs a local choice on the results of the discovery phase. In this way, cloud providers have the advantage to customize the matchmaking policies and have full control on all cloud offers.

Resource Description Languages

An important aspect in cloud federation is represented by the language adopted by clouds and brokers to communicate each other about computational resources and their characteristic (e.g. price, availability, region, SLA, and trustiness, etc.). This language can be mainly used to accomplish two tasks: describing resources that a cloud provider is offering and describing resources that are needed by a provider to start the federation. The language adopted for the second task could also include an expressive query language to better define the requested resources. Moreover, depending on the federation brokerage adopted the federation technique may support different languages. For example, in the case of decentralized through brokerage and fully decentralized federations, we may think that clouds connected to a broker adopt the same language which can be different from language adopted by another set of clouds connected to different broker. In this case brokers need to implement a translation service among languages; the advantage is represented by the fact that clouds do not need to change the way resources are described without compromising federation compatibilities. Figure 8 depicts an example with three brokers implementing a translation service for three different resource description languages.

The remaining part of this section highlights existing technologies and approaches that fit some of the design choices outlined before. It supports the idea that most of these techniques can be easily adapted to the context of cloud federation and represent a solid base in order to offer efficient and robust solutions for future implementations and research activities in this field.

Considering the aspect of the network topology many works exist in literature facing the problem of searching in both structured and unstructured networks. In particular in Sahin, Gupta, Agrawal, Abbadi (2004), Bharambe, Agrawal, and Seshan (2004) and Andrzejak, Xu (2002) range queries are applied to structured networks while in Lv, Cao, Cohen, Li (2002), and Shenker and Gkantsidis and Mihail (2005) focus is given to search in unstructured networks. Most of these works also take into account both the network overlay managements, thus ensuring a network with some robustness properties.

Filtering can also be achieved by considering classic publish/subscribe techniques. In this kind of systems nodes sending (or receiving) messages do not specify the receiver (or sender) of the message but only the class of messages they are sending (receiving). In a cloud federation environment this loose coupling is of great help: for example, a cloud offering resources can publish messages containing the resource description they want to offer, while a cloud requesting resources can define a filter over messages thus accepting only messages matching the needed resources (content-based publish/subscribe). The literature offers many solutions developed for the publish/subscribe problem, an overview can be found in Baldoni, Querzoni and Virgillito (2005).

A relevant contribution that can be exploited in order to define decentralized federation techniques comes from the field of web service discovery; indeed, similar problems have been studied in this area where the main objective was to find a web service satisfying a given description or property. Some of the available works focus on the definition of techniques able to find similar services with respect to some similarity-criteria based on interface, structure, behavior, etc. Nonetheless, other techniques face the search and coordination problems.

For example in Baresi, Miraz, and Plebani (2008) an infrastructure allowing the cooperation of decentralized web service registries is presented.

Figure 8. An example with three brokers implementing a translation service for three different resource description languages

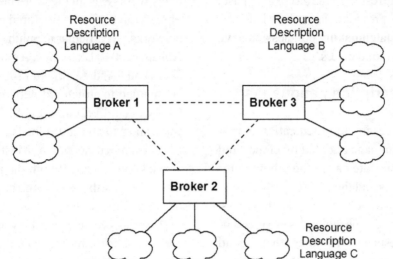

The approach proposes the use of a publish/subscribe cooperation bus in order to carry out the communication tasks. Registries have the ability to federate among them in order to create a share context for the participants in the federations.

Other similar aspects related to the web service discovery can be found in Zisman, Spanoudakis, and Dooley (2008) where a framework supporting the dynamic web service discovery is proposed. Finally, the QoS aware architecture for peer-to-peer service discovery presented in Di Stefano, Morana, and Zito (2009) can be easily adopted in the context of cloud federation to achieve the discovery phase and the SLA management task.

OTHER CHALLENGES ON DECENTRALIZED FEDERATION

Apart from decentralized brokerage, in the cloud federation panorama, several issues need to be addressed. In the following we provide an overview of the major challenges on a decentralized federation:

- **Interoperability:** In a heterogeneous cloud federation scenario, interoperability is a key concept. The current Cloud Computing solutions have not been built with interoperability as a primary concern, A. Sheth et al (2010). Current Cloud computing offerings usually "lock" customers into a single Cloud infrastructure, platform, or application, preventing the portability of data or software created by them. The increasing competition between the leading vendors in the Cloud market, such as Amazon, Microsoft, Google, and SalesForce, each of which promotes its own, incompatible Cloud standards and formats, prevents them from agreeing on a widely accepted, standardized way to input/output Cloud details and specifications, G. Sperb et al (2009). For the same reason small and medium enterprises are reluctant to enter the Cloud market. An interoperable Cloud environment would benefit providers, as they could migrate their VMs, data, and applications between other Cloud providers without setting data at risk. Moreover, they would be able to compare

Cloud offerings with different characteristics, such as resource, pricing, or Quality of Server (QoS) model, and to choose the most cost-effective offering. Besides creating a competitive market for Cloud customers, interoperability could also attract more SMEs to the Cloud market and a new business federation models among Cloud providers could emerge according to demand. At the moment of writing this book, the standardization bodies are working to create standard interfaces that will enable interaction between distributed sites, allowing the federation of infrastructures. In April 2011, IEEE announced the raising of two working groups (i.e., P2301, P2302) aiming to define portability and cooperation mechanisms among different clouds. Other initiatives for enhancing the cooperation between Europe and USA in defining cloud standards were promoted in September 2011 by the EC and ETSI in partnership with NIST, EuroCIO and Eurocloud.

- **Auto-Scaling:** With the advent of the cloud computing, providers are not bound to physical assets anymore, but can enlarge their computing and storage capabilities by acquiring external virtualized resources as VMs and services from other providers.. In fact, Cloud Computing, thanks to the concepts of virtualization and elasticity, allows ICT companies to automatically enlarge their capabilities by automatically scaling up/down their infrastructure when required according to their instantaneous workload. However, federation can potentially involve thousands of cloud providers with each one offering data centers of considerable dimensions. In such a scenario scalability raises several challenges. If on one hand centralized brokerage strategies can introduce bottlenecks, but on the other

hand decentralized strategies can complicate the management of the whole system. In addition, cloud providers may join and leave federation environments in an unpredictable way due to several reasons (i.e., faults, resource unavailability, network partitions, etc.). Hence, the process of "joining" and "leaving" federation partnerships should be accomplished in an automatic fashion without the need of a central brokerage or static configurations.

- **Monitoring and Billing:** In federated cloud environments, cloud-based service instances can be spread over different cloud providers. In such a context, when a cloud borrows computing and storage resources from other providers, it should be able to monitor the leased resources. In this way, cloud providers should be able to monitor application instance running in VMs which can also be hosted in other providers. The ability to monitor internal and external resources determines the expertise for a Cloud provider to enforce and guarantee SLAs both with other federated clouds and with end-users. This practice is not so trivial at all, because cloud providers are reluctant to provide access to their physical assets to other providers, and new strategies have to be planned.

- **Security:** The European Network and Information Security Agency (ENISA) has recognized the lock-in problem of commercial providers as a high risk that Cloud infrastructures inherit from the existing systems, D. Catteddu et al (2009). Decentralized federation raises several concerns related to Authentication and Identity Management (IdM). IdM represents the first issue to be overcome, in order to perform authentication among heterogeneous clouds establishing a partnership. Such a task is not trivial, because a high level of interoperability is required between different security technologies. In fact, each cloud could use different IdM mechanisms separate from each other. Moreover, in order to accomplish IdM in cloud computing, an indispensable requirement is to set up a trusted third party responsible both for storing the access credentials and securing them, H. Takabi et al (2010). To this regard several works are leveraging the Identity Provider/Service Provider (IdP/SP) model to cloud environments, adopting technologies such as WS-Security, SAML, Shibboleth, and OpenID. Another interesting challenge regards how to manage the propagation of trustiness among federated clouds. As in a federated environment, resources can be spread across different providers and both physical and virtual assets have to be secured. To this regard, traditional authentication systems will not be sufficient. In order to address such challenges, several initiatives are recently trying to apply the emerging concept of Trusted Computing to Clouds, W. Han-zhang (2010). This is possible by integrating Trusted Computing Modules (TPMs), i.e., physical CHIPs integrated in the motherboard of servers whose trustiness is guaranteed by third-party certification authorities. Trusted computing, thanks to TPMs allowed to develop a software layer, is able to guarantee security in both software and hardware.

CONCLUSION

This chapter analyzed the problem of cloud federation focusing, in particular, on the federation establishment issue. A federation can be established either manually or automatically, either statically or dynamically. Moreover, the mechanisms needed for managing the identification and matchmaking of counterparts can be more or less centralized. As highlighted in the chapter, decentralized techniques for discovery and matchmaking provide advantages in specific situations where many small cloud providers get together to address specific and transitory issues.

However the problem of cloud federation is a complex one due to the heterogeneity of considered actors and technologies. For example, the research community still has not examined problems of security and authentication between different clouds; this is, however, a key point in the actuation of federation concepts in real scenarios. Furthermore, cloud paradigm also brings to attention economic aspects; indeed, providers can have many differences such as: costs, pay models, and APIs, etc. A fundamental aspect here is the definition of a common ground on which various federation techniques can refer to.

ACKNOWLEDGMENT

This research has been partially funded by the following projects funded by the European Commission: Project 227077-SMScom, Programme IDEAS-ERC (http://www.erc-smscom.org), the FP7 Integrated Project 216556-SLA@SOI (http://sla-at-soi.eu/).

REFERENCES

Andrzejak, A., & Xu, Z. (2002). Scalable, Efficient Range Queries for Grid Information Services. In *Second IEEE International Conference on Peer-to-Peer Computing*. Washington, DC: IEEE Press.

Baldoni, R., Querzoni, L., & Virgillito, A. (2005). *Distributed Event Routing in Publish/Subscribe Communication Systems: a Survey. Technical Report TR-1/06*. Rome, Italy: Universita di Roma

Baresi, L., Miraz, M., & Plebani, P. (2008). A Flexible and Semantic-Aware Publication Infrastructure for Web Services. In *Proceedings of the 20th international conference on Advanced Information Systems Engineering* (CAiSE '08). New York, NY: Springer

Bermbach, D., Klems, M., Tai, S., & Menzel, M. (2011). MetaStorage: A Federated Cloud Storage System to Manage Consistency-Latency Tradeoffs. In *IEEE 4th Conference on Cloud Computing (CLOUD). 2011.* Washington, DC: IEEE Press.

Bharambe, A. R., Agrawal, M., & Seshan, S. (2004). Mercury: Supporting scalable multi-attribute range queries. In *Proceedings of the ACM SIGCOMM*, New York, NY: ACM Press.

Buyya, R., Ranjan, R., & Calheiros, R. N. (2010). InterCloud: Utility-Oriented Federation of Cloud Computing Environments for Scaling of Application Services. In *Proceedings of the 10th International Conference on Algorithms and Architectures for Parallel Processing (ICA3PP 2010),* New York, NY: Springer.

Catteddu, D., & Hogben, G. (2009). Cloud Computing-Benefits, risks and recommendations for information security. In *ENISA*. Heraklion, Greece: ENISA. doi:10.1007/978-3-642-16120-9_9

Celesti, A., Tusa, F., Villari, M., & Puliafito, A. (2010). How to Enhance Cloud Architectures to Enable Cross-Federation. In *IEEE 3rd Conference on Cloud Computing (CLOUD). 2010.* Washington, DC: IEEE Press.

Di Nitto, E., Ghezzi, C., Metzger, A., Papazoglou, M., & Pohl, K. (2008). A journey to highly dynamic, self-adaptive service-based applications. Automated Software Engineering Journal, 2008.

Di Stefano, A., Morana, G., & Zito, D. (2009). A P2P strategy for QoS discovery and SLA negotiation in Grid environment. In *Future Generation Computer Systems Journal 25*, (8)862-875

Distefano, S., Cunsolo, V., Puliafito, A., & Scarpa, M. (2010). Cloud@Home: A New Enhanced Computing Paradigm. In Furht, B., & Escalante, A. (Eds.), *Handbook of Cloud Computing*, (pp. 575–594). New York, NY: Springer. doi:10.1007/978-1-4419-6524-0_25

Gkantsidis, C., & Mihail, M. (2005). Hybrid search schemes for unstructured peer-to-peer networks. In *INFOCOM 2005, 24th Annual Joint Conference of the IEEE Computer and Communications Societies.* Washington, DC: IEEE Press

Goiri, Í., Guitart, J., & Torres, J. (2010). Characterizing cloud federation for Enhancing Providers' Profit. Paper presented at IEEE 3rd International Conference on Cloud Computing, Miami, Florida, USA.

Han-Zhang, W., & Liu-Sheng, H. (2010). An improved trusted cloud computing platform model based on daa and privacy ca scheme. In International Conference on Computer Application and System Modeling (ICCASM), pp. V13–33 – V13–39, 2010.

Loutas, N., Peristeras, V., Bouras, T., Kamateri, E., Zeginis, D., & Tarabanis, K. (2010). Towards a Reference Architecture for Semantically Interoperable Clouds. In Cloud Computing Technology and Science (CloudCom), 2010 IEEE Second International Conference on.

Lv, Q., Cao, P., Cohen, E., Li, K., & Shenker, S. (2002). Search and replication in unstructured peer-to-peer networks. In Proceedings of the 16th international conference on Supercomputing (ICS '02).

Ranjan, R., & Buyya, R. (2009). Decentralized Overlay for Federation of Enterprise Clouds. In Li, K. (Eds.), *Handbook of Research on Scalable Computing Technologies*. Hershey, PA: IGI Global. doi:10.4018/978-1-60566-661-7.ch009

Rochwerger, B., Breitgand, D., Levy, E., Galis, A., Nagin, K., Llorente, I. M., et al. Càceres, J., Ben-Yehuda, M., Emmerich, W., & Galàn, F. (2009). The reservoir model and architecture for open federated cloud computing. In *IBM Journal of Research and Development. 53* (4)

Sahin, O. D., Gupta, A., Agrawal, D., & El Abbadi, A. (2004). A Peer-to-peer Framework for Caching Range Queries. In *20th International Conference on Data Engineering (ICDE'04)*, Washington, DC: IEEE Press.

Sheth, A., & Ranabahu, A. (2010). Semantic Modeling for Cloud Computing, Part I & II. In *IEEE Internet Computing Magazine, 14*, 81-83.

Sperb Machado, G., Hausheer, D., & Stiller, B. (2009). *Considerations on the Interoperability of and between Cloud Computing Standards. In 27th Open Grid Forum (OGF27), G2CNet Workshop: From Grid to Cloud Networks*. New York, NY: Springer.

Takabi, H., Joshi, J. B., & Ahn, G. J. (2010). In Security and privacy challenges in cloud computing environments, *IEEE Security and Privacy*, 824–31.

Zisman, A., Spanoudakis, G., & Dooley, J. (2008). A Framework for Dynamic Service Discovery. In *Proceedings of the 2008 23rd IEEE/ACM International Conference on Automated Software Engineering (ASE '08)* Washington, DC: IEEE Press.

Chapter 4
Implementing Distributed, Self-Managing Computing Services Infrastructure using a Scalable, Parallel and Network-Centric Computing Model

Rao Mikkilineni
Kawa Objects Inc., USA

Giovanni Morana
DIEEI, University of Catania, Italy

Ian Seyler
Return Infinity Inc., Canada

ABSTRACT

This chapter introduces a new network-centric computing model using Distributed Intelligent Managed Element (DIME) network architecture (DNA). A parallel signaling network overlay over a network of self-managed von Neumann computing nodes is utilized to implement dynamic fault, configuration, accounting, performance, and security management of both the nodes and the network based on business priorities, workload variations and latency constraints. Two implementations of the new computing model are described which demonstrate the feasibility of the new computing model. One implementation provides service virtualization at the Linux process level and another provides virtualization of a core in a many-core processor. Both point to an alternative way to assure end-to-end transaction reliability, availability, performance, and security in distributed Cloud computing, reducing current complexity in configuring and managing virtual machines and making the implementation of Federation of Clouds simpler.

DOI: 10.4018/978-1-4666-1631-8.ch004

Copyright © 2012, IGI Global. Copying or distributing in print or electronic forms without written permission of IGI Global is prohibited.

INTRODUCTION

A federation is a group of parties that collaborate to achieve a common goal. Enterprises use federated systems to collaborate and execute common business processes spanning across distributed resources belonging to different owners. A federated business model mandates a foundation of trust among the participants. Trust in terms of service collaboration mandated by the business process is often negotiated in terms of service level agreements with specific requirements of service availability, performance, security, and cost. Federated systems, in essence, are distributed computing networks of stored program control (SPC) computing elements whose resources are shared to execute business processes to accomplish a common goal. Sharing of resources and collaboration, while they provide leverage and synergy, also pose problems such as contention for same resources, issues of trust, and management of the impact of latency in communication among the participants. These problems are well articulated in literature and the discipline of distributed computing (Tanenbaum and van Steen, 2002) is devoted to addressing them. There are four major problems often cited as key issues in designing distributed systems:

1. **Connection Management:** Collaboration with distributed shared resources can only be possible with a controlled way to assure connection during the period of collaboration. In addition, the reliability, availability, utilization accounting, performance, and security of the resources have to be assured so that the users can depend on the service levels. This is known as FCAPS (Fault, Configuration, Accounting, Performance and Security) management. Connection management allows proper allocation of resources to appropriate users consistent with business priorities, workload requirements, and latency constraints. It also assures that the connection maintains the service levels that are negotiated between the consumers and the suppliers of the resources.

2. **Transparency:** The shared resources in a distributed system may be physically deployed in different containers and the components may be geographically separated. Any distributed systems design must provide the users and resources, access-, location- and physical container-transparency. The users must be able to specify service levels in terms of agreed upon parameters such as business priorities, workload requirements and latency constraints.

3. **Openness:** In an ideal environment, resources are offered as services and users who consume services will be able to choose the right services that meet their requirements, or the consumers will specify their requirements and the service providers can tailor the services that meet consumer's requirements. The specification and execution of services must support an open process where service can be discovered and service levels are matched to consumer requirements without depending on underlying mechanisms in which services are implemented. In addition, service composition mechanisms must be available to dynamically create new value added services by the consumers.

4. **Scalability:** As the requirements in the form of business priorities, workload variations, or latency constraints change, the distributed system must be designed to scale accordingly. The scaling may involve the dialing-up or dialing-down of resources, geographically migrating them and administratively extending the reach based on policies that support centralized or locally autonomous or a hybrid management with coordinated orchestration.

Current generation server, networking, and storage equipment and their management systems have evolved from server-centric and bandwidth limited network architectures to today's Cloud computing architecture with virtual servers and broadband networks. During last six decades, many layers of computing abstractions have been introduced to map the execution of complex computational workflows to a sequence of 1s and 0s that eventually get stored in the memory and operated upon by the CPU to achieve the desired result. These include process definition languages, programming languages, file systems, and databases, operating systems etc.

While this has helped in automating many business processes, the exponential growth in services in the consumer market also has introduced severe strains on current IT infrastructures. This chapter argues that the lack of "telecom grade trust" in current distributed systems design is a more fundamental architecture issue related to the lack of resiliency than being just an operational failure. Telecommunication services provide a benchmark of trust which assures managed resources on-demand with high availability, performance and security. Today, as soon as the user goes on hook, the telecommunication network recognizes the profile based on the dialing telephone number. As soon as the dialed party number is dialed, the network recognizes the destination profile and provisions all the network resources required to make the desired connection, to commence billing, to monitor, and to assure the connection availability, performance and security till one of the parties initiates a disconnect. The continuous visibility and control of the connection allows service assurance even in critical situations. Call waiting, call forwarding, 800 service call model, and multiparty conferencing—all these features contribute to the telecom-grade trust that the telecommunication network has come to symbolize. The same cannot be said about the current IT infrastructure and its management. The vulnerability of current Internet and Cloud-based computing infrastructure is known (Morris, 2011; Thibodeau and Vijayan, 2011). In addition, up to

70% to 80% of current IT budget is devoted to IT operation & management.

The limitations of the SPC computing architecture were clearly on his mind when von Neumann gave his lecture at the Hixon symposium in 1948 in Pasadena, California. "The basic principle of dealing with malfunctions in nature is to make their effect as unimportant as possible and to apply correctives, if they are necessary at all, at leisure. In our dealings with artificial automata, on the other hand, we require an immediate diagnosis. Therefore, we are trying to arrange the automata in such a manner that errors will become as conspicuous as possible, and intervention and correction follow immediately." (von Neumann, 1987, p. 408)

Comparing the computing machines and living organisms, he points out that the computing machines are not as fault tolerant as the living organisms. He goes on to say "It's very likely that on the basis of philosophy that every error has to be caught, explained, and corrected, a system of the complexity of the living organism would not run for a millisecond" (von Neumann, 1987, p. 408).

This chapter will revisit the design of distributed systems with a new computing model (called Distributed Intelligent Managed Element (DIME) Network computing model) that integrates computational workflows with a parallel implementation of management workflows and provide dynamic real-time control of connecting consumers and distributed resources. This model also provides a service composition scheme that allows designing agile, scalable, open and transparent distributed systems with high reliability, availability, performance and security.

The authors believe that the manageability of DIMEs can be exploited for designing a new generation of cloud environments. In particular, as explained in the following sections, the ability of DIME network in composing and aggregating, in an easy way, multiple local and global management policies makes the DIME-based approach suitable for implementing and managing Federation of Clouds.

The chapter compares this network-centric computing model with current state-of-the-art and science of distributed systems design today that evolved from server-centric computational models, operating systems, (OSs) and frameworks. The final section presents new ways to leverage the DIME network-centric computing model to design self-configuring, self-monitoring, self-healing, self-protecting, and self-optimizing distributed systems with seamlessly integrated execution of computational and management workflows.

BACKGROUND

It is clear that von Neumann recognized a problem in the way computing systems are designed.

"Normally, a literary description of what an automaton is supposed to do is simpler than the complete diagram of the automaton. It is not true a priori that this always will be so. There is a good deal in formal logic which indicates that when an automaton is not very complicated the description of the function of the automaton is simpler than the description of the automaton itself, as long as the automaton is not very complicated, but when you get to high complications, the actual object is much simpler than the literary description." (von Neumann, 1987, pp. 454-457).

He remarked, "It is a theorem of Gödel that the description of an object is one class type higher than the object and is therefore asymptotically infinitely longer to describe." (von Neumann, 1987, pp. 454-457).

The conjecture of von Neumann leads to the fact that "one cannot construct an automaton which will predict the behavior of any arbitrary automaton" (von Neumann, 1987, p. 456).

This is so with the Turing machine implemented by the SPC model.

Current generation distributed systems are implemented using a network of Turing machines in which the service and its management are intermixed as shown in Figure 1. The resources utilized by the nodes in a network are often controlled by a plethora of management systems which are outside the purview of the service workflow that is utilizing the resources. Thus the end to end service transaction response is controlled by these management systems which introduce a layer of complexity in coordination and contention resolution, making the service much simpler than its management.

It turns out that the description and the execution of the described function play a crucial role in cellular organisms, giving them the capability to replicate, repair, recombine, and reconfigure themselves.

As Waldrop explains in his book on Complexity:

"The DNA residing in a cell's nucleus was not just a blue-print for the cell – a catalog of how to make this protein or that protein. DNA was actually the foreman in charge of construction. In effect, was a kind of molecular-scale computer that directed how the cell was to build itself and repair itself and interact with the outside world." (Waldrop, 1992, p. 218)

The conjecture of von Neumann leads to the fact that the SPC computing model alone is not adequate for self-replication and self-repair. Organisms somehow have managed to precisely encapsulate the descriptions of building and running a complex system such as a human being in a simpler vehicle such as a set of genes. They have also managed to invent mechanisms for replication, repair, recombination, and rearrangement to execute the descriptions precisely.

As Dyson (1997) observes "The analog of software in the living world is not a self-reproducing organism, but a self-replicating molecule of DNA (p. 123).

Figure 1. The service and its management using a Turing Machine network

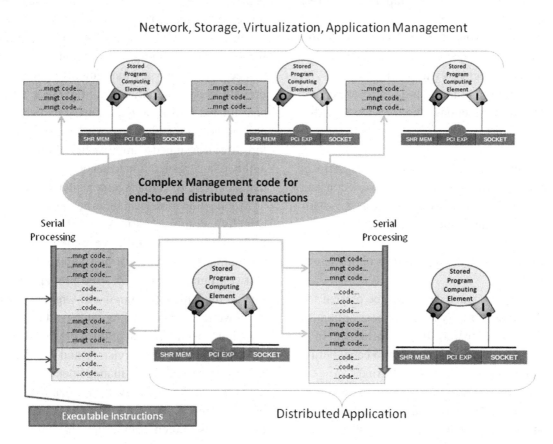

Biological organisms, even single-celled organisms, do not replicate themselves; they host the replication of genetic sequences that assist in reproducing an approximate likeness of themselves.

According to Dawkins:

DNA molecules do two important things. Firstly, they replicate, that is to say they make copies of themselves [...] This brings me to the second important thing DNA does. It indirectly supervises the manufacture of a different kind of molecule – protein. (Dawkins, 1989, p. 23)

The indirect supervision task mentioned by Dawkins is underlined also by Carroll.

This DNA determines when, where, and how much of a gene's product is made. (Carroll, 2005, p. 12)

The orchestration is accomplished by "parallel and sequential actions of tool kit genes--dozens of genes acting at the same time and same place, many more genes acting in different places at the same time, and hundreds of toolkit genes acting in sequence." (Carroll, 2005, p. 106).

Therefore, a new generation of distributed systems should learn from the nature and take into account the key abstractions of cellular architecture:

1.   The spelling out of computational workflow components as a stable sequence of patterns that accomplishes a specific purpose,

2.   A parallel management workflow specification with another sequence of patterns that assures the successful execution of the

system's purpose (the computing network) and

3. A signaling mechanism that controls the execution of the workflow for gene expression (the regulatory network)

4. Real-time monitoring and control to execute genetic transactions which provide the self-* properties

Another example of a distributed system is the human network. The human network consists of a group of individuals operating as a system (PegasusCommunications, 2010)

1. Every system has a purpose within a larger system

2. All of a system's parts must be present for the system to carry out its purpose optimally

3. A system's parts must be arranged in a specific way for the system to carry out its purpose (separation of concerns)

4. Systems change in response to feedback (collect information, analyze information and control environment using specialized resources)

5. Systems maintain their stability (in accomplishing their purpose) by making adjustments based on feedback

Humans have created organizational frameworks through evolution. An organization (Malone, 1990) establishes goals, segments the goals into separate activities to be performed by different agents, and connects different agents and activities to accomplish the overall goals. Scalability is accomplished through hierarchical segmentation of activities and specialization. Efficiency of the organization is achieved through specialization and segmentation. Dynamic reconfiguration is accomplished using signaling abstractions such as addressing, alerting, supervision, and mediation. Both efficiency and agility are achieved through a management framework that addresses Fault, Configuration, Accounting (utilization), Perfor-

mance, and Security of all network elements (in this case the agents).

Project management is a specific example where Fault, configuration, accounting, performance, and security are individually managed to provide an optimal network configuration with a coordinated workflow. Functional organizations, and hierarchical and matrix organizational structures are all designed to improve the efficiency and agility of an organization to accomplish the goals using both FCAPS management and signaling.

Connection management is achieved through effective communications framework. Over time, human networks have evolved various communications schemes and signaling forms that configure, reconfigure, and provide agility for the fundamental framework. Organizational frameworks are designed to implement the same signaling abstractions mentioned previously (addressing, alerting, supervision, and mediation) using distributed object management in human networks. Signaling allows prioritization of the network objectives and allocates resources in the form of distributed computing elements to accomplish the objectives and provides management control to mitigate risk. Elaborate workflows are implemented using the signaling mechanism to specialize and distribute tasks to various elements. The elements are used to collect information, analyze it, and control themselves as a group to accomplish the required goals.

Thus organizational hierarchies, project management, and process implementation through workflows are all accomplished through the network object model with FCAPS abstractions and signaling. Signaling allows prioritization of resources and contention resolution using a parallel communication and control channel as in traffic management and train track-control examples. Signaling and FCAPS management also play a very central role in telecommunication network management.

The next section defines a new computing model that implements a parallel signaling network overlay over a network of von Neumann computing nodes which allows programming dynamic fault, configuration, accounting, performance, and security management of both the nodes (consisting of an SPC element) and a network of such nodes based on business priorities, workload variations and latency constraints.

A New Computing Model for Distributed Systems Design – The DIME Network Architecture (DNA)

The *raison d'etre* for the DIME (Distributed Intelligent Managed Element) computing model is to fully exploit the parallelism, distribution, and massive scaling possible with multicore processor based devices supporting hardware-assisted virtualization, and create a computing architecture in which the services and their management are decoupled from the hardware infrastructure and its management in real-time. Derived from the observations on gene replication and human network organization, the DIME computing model makes possible the creation of a next generation services creation, delivery and assurance with massive scaling, distribution, and parallelism using the new multi-core architectures and OSs.

There are three reasons why there is a new search for a different operating system or computing strategy for many-core servers:

1. Application response time, unlike in a single-CPU server (or a few CPUs the OS can see), is no longer a function of application software and the operating system that provides the computing, network, and storage resources. It depends on run-time workload fluctuations and latency constraints in a shared infrastructure. The wild fluctuations caused by massive consumer demand on web-based services place a heavy burden on the management of shared infrastructure. Conventional server-centric operating systems that have evolved from their single-core origins are no longer

the primary drivers of resource administration to influence the response time. The myriad intervening layered management systems have usurped their role.

2. The marriage of server-centric OS security, which is mainly focused on isolating the shared resources allocated to different applications, with network-centric security which is, focused on isolating access to multiple servers, network devices, and storage devices providing the required application resources, has resulted in a web of security management systems that require shared run-time resources along with applications. This has resulted in ad-hoc implementation of parallel application execution and application management workflows.

3. The evolution of single-thread operating system data structures to support multi-threaded operating system data structures has resulted, over time, in a large and complex code-base dealing with choosing correct lock granularity for performance, reasoning about correctness, and deadlock prevention. Resulting difficulties in extending the large-scale lock-based OS code for multi-core systems is well documented (Wentzlaff and Agarwal, 2009).

The proposed model lends itself to be implemented i) from scratch to exploit the many core servers and ii) in current generation servers exploiting features available in current operating systems. This section, describes the DIME network architecture and both proof-of-concept implementations to demonstrate its feasibility.

The DIME Computing Model

A DIME is a managed Turing machine enabled with signaling abstractions. Each DIME is an autonomous computing entity endowed with self FCAPS management capabilities along with computing capabilities. It communicates with other DIMEs via two parallel channels:

1. One for signaling each other to implement DIME network management which configures, secures, monitors, repairs, and optimizes the workflow based on workload characteristics, latency constraints, and business priorities specified as service management profiles (we call this profile the Service Regulator SR) and

2. Another for communicating with each other to implement a distributed business workflow as a directed acyclic graph, DAG, (in the von Neumann SPC Computing model). The tasks implemented by the DIME node are specified as a DAG (called the Service Package SP).

Signaling, used to monitor and control the business workflow implementation using the parallelism, provides a powerful approach in extending the current Service Oriented Archi-tectures (SOA). By integrating computation and its management at the computing element level, and at the network level, this model exploits distributed resources, parallelism, and networking to provide real-time telecom grade availability, reliability, performance, and security management of distributed workflow services execution. Each DIME is implemented as group of multi-process, multi-thread components, as shown in Figure 2.

The DIME network architecture consists of four components:

1. A DIME node which encapsulates the von Neumann computing element with self-management of fault, configuration, accounting, performance and security shown in Figure 3

2. Signaling capability that allows intra-DIME and Inter-DIME communication,

3. An infrastructure that allows implementing distributed service workflows as a set of tasks, arranged or organized in a DAG and

Figure 2. The anatomy of a DIME

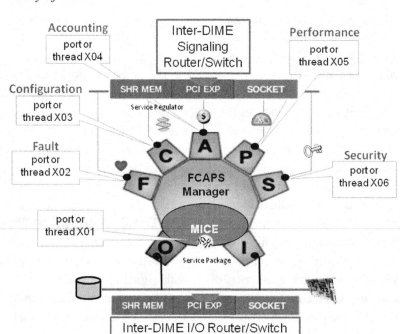

executed by a managed network of DIMEs and

4. An infrastructure that assures DIME network management using the signaling network overlay over the computing workflow

5. The self-management and task execution (using MICE, the Managed Intelligent Computing Element) are performed in parallel using the SPC computing devices.

The DIME orchestration template provides the description for instantiating the DIME using an SPC computing device with appropriate resources required (CPU, memory, network bandwidth, storage capacity, throughput and IOPs). The description contains the resources required, the constraints and the addresses of executable modules for various components and various run time commands the DIME obeys.

The service regulator provides the description for instantiating the DIME services with appropriate resources required. The description contains the resources required, the constraints and the addresses of executable modules for various components and various run time commands the service obeys. The configuration commands provide the ability for the MICE to be set up with appropriate resources and I/O communication

network to be set up to communicate with other DIME components to become a node in a service delivery network implementing a workflow. Figure 4 shows the service implementation.

Signaling allows groups of DIMEs to collaborate with each other and implement global policies. The signaling abstractions are:

1. **Addressing:** each FCAPS aware DIME has a globally unique address and any services platform using DIMEs must provide name service management.

2. **Alerting:** each DIME provides a published alerting interface that describes various alerting attributes.

3. **Supervision:** each DIME is a member of a network with a purpose and role. Supervision allows contention resolution based on roles and purpose. It also allows policy monitoring and control.

4. **Mediation:** when the DIMEs are contending for resources, the supervision hierarchy is assisted with mediation object network that provides global policy enforcement.

The DIME network architecture supports the genetic transactions of replication, repair, recombination and rearrangement. A single node of a

Figure 3. Distributed Intelligent Managed Element Network with parallel implementation of service and its management

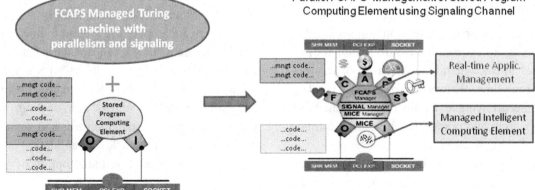

Figure 4. Service regulator and service package execution by a DIME

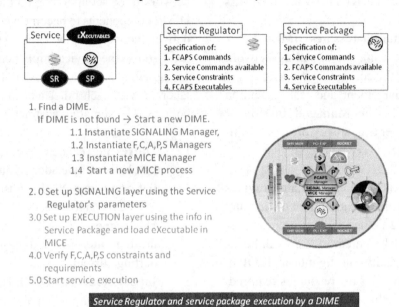

Service Regulator and service package execution by a DIME

DIME can execute a workflow by itself or by instantiating a sub-network and provides a way to implement a managed DAG executing a workflow. Replication is implemented by executing the same service as shown in Figure 5 (steps 1 and 2). Any DIME can be controlled by the FCAPS threads at runtime which allows reconfiguration by stopping the service and loading and executing a new service.

By defining service S1 to execute itself, S1 is replicated in DIME 2. In addition, dynamic FCAPS (parallel service monitoring and control) management allows changing the behavior of any instance from outside (using the signaling infrastructure) to alter the service that is executed. Figure 5 shows dynamic service reconfiguration in steps 3 and 4. The ability to execute the control commands in parallel allows dynamic replacement of services during run time. We can also redirect I/O during run time allowing dynamic reconfiguration of worker input and output thus providing computational network control.

The dynamic configuration at DIME node level and the ability to implement at each node,

a managed directed acyclic graph using a DIME sub-network provides a powerful paradigm for designing and deploying managed services. The next two sections describe two implementations of DNA.

Service Virtualization Using DIME Network Architecture (DNA) Using Linux Operating System

The DIME computing model offers a simple way to implement service virtualization independent of current generation virtualization technologies. One implementation (Morana and Mikkilineni, 2011) uses the multi-process, multi-thread support in the Linux operating system to implement the DIME network. By encapsulating a Linux based processes with parallel FCAPS management and providing a parallel signaling channel, this implementation allows auto-scaling, self-repair, performance management, and dynamic reconfiguration of workflows, replicating all the functionalities offered by the adoption of VMs

Figure 5. DIME replication and reconfiguration

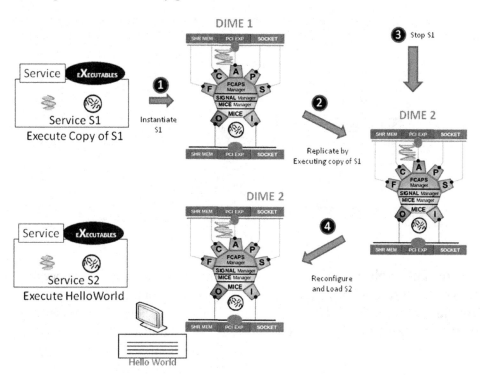

without the need for a Hypervisor-based server virtualization.

Two points are worth noting about this implementation:

1. The workflow assigned to a DIME network consists of a set of tasks arranged in a DAG. Each node of this DAG contains both the task executables and the profile DAG as a tuple < task (SP), profile (SR)>, i.e. the blueprint for both management and execution levels. This makes it easy to design self-configuring, self-monitoring, self-protecting, self-healing, and self-optimizing distributed service networks.
2. An ad hoc DIME network with parallel signaling and computing workflows is implemented using two classes of DIMEs. Signaling DIMEs responsible for the management layer at the network level are of the type Supervisor and the Mediator. The Supervisor sets up and controls the function-

ing of the sub network of DIMEs where the workflow is executed. It coordinates and orchestrates the DIMEs through the use of the Mediators. A Mediator is a specialized DIME for providing predefined roles such as fault or configuration or accounting or performance or security management. Worker DIMEs constituting the highly configurable "execution" layer of the network perform domain specific tasks that are assigned to them.

The deployment of DIMEs in the network, the number of signaling DIMEs involved in the management level, the number of available worker DIMEs and the division of the roles are established on the basis of the number and the type of tasks constituting the workflow and, overall, on the basis of the management profiles related to each task. Figure 6 shows a DIME encapsulation of Linux processes.

Figure 6. Encapsulating a Linux Process in a DIME

 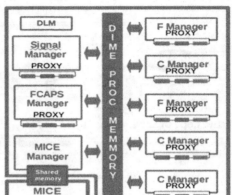

Implementing DIME Network Architecture in a Many-Core Server Using Parallax, a New Scalable, Distributed and Parallel Operating System

To address the many issues with current operating systems (Baumann et al., 2009), the Parallax operating system (Mikkilineni and Seyler, 2011) takes a different approach, by exploiting the parallelism and performance of the many-core processors. The new operating system implements the DIME network computing model directly at the core using the assembler language for effectively exploiting the hardware and C/C++ programming interfaces for high-level programming. By converting each core into a DIME with self-management and signaling abilities, the operating system is designed to address scaling, resource monitoring, dynamic configuration, and self-repair of many-core chip based servers to support distributed computational tasks. This approach is different from many of the current efforts in designing a new OS for many-core servers such as Tessellation (Colmenares at Al., 2010), Barrellfish (Baumann et al., 2009), Factored Operating System (FOS) (Wentzlaff and Agarwal, 2009), Corey (Mao et al., 2008) and many others in that the signaling and FCAPS management of DIME network exploits the parallelism offered by the many-core processors to provide dynamic reconfiguration at run-time.

Figure 7 shows the Parallax implementation of the DNA in a multi-core server.

The proof-of-concept prototype system consists of three components:

1. A service component development program that takes assembler or C/C++ programs and compiles them to be executed on an Intel Xeon multi-core Servers
2. Parallax Operating System that is used to boot the servers with Intel Xeon cores and create the DIME Network with each core acting as a DIME. The DIME allows dynamic provisioning of memory for each DIME. It supports executing multiple threads concurrently to provide DIME FCAPS management over a signaling channel. It enables fault management by broadcasting a heartbeat over the signaling network. It allows loading, executing, and stopping an executable on demand. It supports DIME discovery through signaling channel.
3. A run-time service external service orchestrator implemented under Linux which allows the DIME network management across multiple many-core servers.

Figure 7. Parallax implementation in a multi-core server

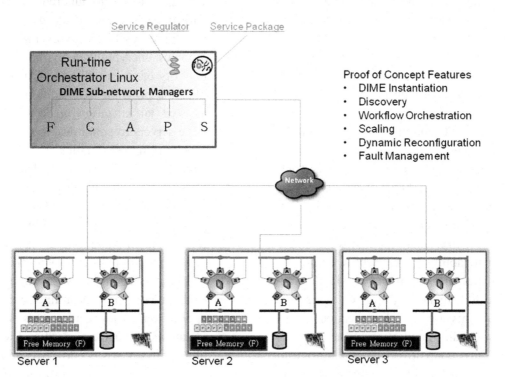

The Parallax approach provides four differentiators from other OS efforts:

1. The operating system encapsulates each core in a multi-core or many-core server with FCAPS management providing finer granularity for multi-tenancy down to a single core.

2. The operating system by providing a network management paradigm inside the server with many cores acting as nodes in a network enables visibility and control across all resources with uniformity. The same network management capability provides uniformity across servers and across geographical locations.

3. The signaling overlay and parallel implementation of service control based on service description at run-time provides the dynamism using the genetic transactions of replication, repair, recombination and reconfiguration.

4. The inclusion of service description, service regulation and service execution modules in the run-time service package provides the ability to implement global and local policies in the service workflow using network management.

EVOLUTION OF FEDERATED SYSTEMS AND THE DNA FOR NEXT GENERATION FEDERATED SERVICES VIRTUALIZATION

Business Drivers

There are two major business drivers that are forcing new approaches to meet the global demand to deliver distributed services:

1. The consumer appetite for new generation of Internet hosted applications such as Twitter,

Facebook, YouTube, and Animoto are driving the need for service providers to address the need to support massive scalability and wild fluctuations in demand. Service providers are looking to support massive scaling on a global scale with a very high degree of agility.

2. Success of Cloud based business applications such as SalesForce.com is forcing companies such as SAP and other CRM vendors to re-architect their applications and become Cloud based. The ease and flexibility of on-demand service like SalesForce.com however cannot match the richness, customizability, visibility of real-time performance and control of availability and privacy demanded by large enterprises for certain mission critical applications. In addition, trading applications which thrive on real-time competitive differentiation are not going to put their future in the hands of Public Cloud providers unless they are assured of real-time visibility and control of availability, reliability, performance, and security of the computing, network, storage, and application resources. Therefore, enterprises are starting to deploy their own Private Clouds and in some cases use Hybrid Clouds that combine both Private and Public Clouds. The massive scalability and the economics of multi-tenancy through increased shared resource utilization are forcing enterprises to re-architect their data centers to leverage globally distributed resources.

Technical Drivers

There are three key technology trends that are also contributing to the re-engineering of current services development, delivery and assurance infrastructure:

1. **Multicore Technology:** According to Intel, in 2015, a typical processor chip will likely consist of dozens to hundreds of cores and parts of each core will be dedicated to specific purposes like network management, graphics, encryption, decryption etc. and a majority of cores will be available for application programs. In addition, hardware assisted virtualization made available in large servers to small desktop, laptop and mobile computing platforms makes it possible to deploy software independent of physical infrastructure with features such as "live migration". These hardware advances provide a unique opportunity for a new class of distributed systems that can leverage distributed computing, network and storage Clouds transcending physical and geographical boundaries and constrained only by the application latency requirements, workload variations and business priorities. The decoupling of business workflow execution from the underlying hardware infrastructure also demands the decoupling of infrastructure management from the workflow management itself and offers an opportunity for a new generation of distributed systems design that exploits parallelism, distribution and scaling of resource utilization.

2. **High performance servers:** With hundreds of multicore processors coupled with high bandwidth networks, the high performance servers alter the current data center landscape by providing consolidation of unparalleled proportion. A large server containing hundreds of multicores with a DS3 pipe can eliminate a host of current generation networking equipment and the associated complexity if the processes inside the server can scale and exploit the parallelism. In addition, high bandwidth access to mini-Clouds aggregating virtualized desktops, laptops and mobile devices offers seamless connectivity and interoperability thus enabling a new class of distributed systems that span across multiple Clouds.

3. **Current generation of software development environments:** Both on web based delivery platforms and mobile broadband delivery platforms, the software development environments have radically transformed the way business and consumer applications are developed and delivered. They have unleashed a new generation of service developers outside the conventional business application domains. Web based or mobile platform based applications can be developed with such ease that we have a proliferation of social networks, games, and educational services made available on a massive scale to consumer market. This has created a need for new application architectures to meet the massive scaling and low cost constraints dictated by the consumer market. In the past, services development was in the purview of specialized programmers and IT development organizations. The service developers can now focus on their domain and not on programming detail. The domain workflows can be translated to executing services and deployed on web services platforms today much faster than application development in IT organizations that used to consume months and years in the past. The massive scale of services development and deployment also has necessitated the need for services management to meet the mass scale usage, workload fluctuations, latency constraints imposed by the speed of light in delivering services across the globe and the business priorities.

Service Creation, Delivery and Assurance Using DNA

In summary, the dynamic configuration at DIME node level and the ability to implement at each node, a managed DAG using a DIME sub-network provides a powerful paradigm for designing and deploying distributed managed services transcend-

ing physical, geographical and corporate boundaries with telecom grade trust. The DIME network computing model just generalizes the SPC model to construct a managed Turing machine network (borrowing heavily from the computing models deployed by the biological DNA and the Genes) that can be programmed to self-configure, self-secure self-monitor, self-heal, and self-optimize based on business priorities, workload variations and latency constraints implemented as local and global policies. The infrastructure can be implemented using any of the standard Operating Systems that are available today or with a new operating system that exploits the many-core chips. The key abstractions that are leveraged in this model are:

1. Parallel implementation of self-management and computing element at the (DIME) node level and
2. Parallel implementation of signaling based DIME network management and workflow implementation as a managed DAG

The parallelism and signaling allow the dynamism required to implement the genetic transactions which provide the self-* features that are the distinguishing characteristics of living organisms:

1. **Specialization:** each computing entity is specialized to perform specific tasks. The intelligence is embedded locally that can be utilized to perform collection, computing and control functions with an analog interface to the real world.
2. **Separation of concerns:** groups of computing entities combine their specializations through mediation to create value added services
3. **Priority based mediation:** the mediation is supervised to resolve contention for resources based on overall group objectives to optimize resource utilization

4. **Fault tolerance, security and reliability:** using alerting, supervision, and mediation, a high degree of resiliency to the workflow is added.

The DIME computing model does not replace any of the computing workflows that are implemented using the SPC computing model today. It provides a self-* infrastructure to implement them with the dynamism of living organisms. The DIME computing model focuses only on the reliable execution of stable patterns that are described as managed DAGs. It does not address how to discover more stable patterns from existing workflows (with lower entropy).

The objective of operating systems and programming languages is to reduce the semantic gap between business workflow definitions and their executions in a von Neumann computing device. As mentioned earlier, the important consequences of current upheaval in hardware with multi-core and many-core architectures on a monolithic OS that shares data structures across cores are well articulated by (Baumann et al, 2010). They also introduce the need for making the OS structure, hardware-neutral. "The irony is that hardware is now changing faster than software, and the effort required to evolve such operating systems to perform well on new hardware is becoming prohibitive." They argue that single computers increasingly resemble networked systems, and should be programmed as such.

As the number of cores increase to hundreds and thousands in the next decade, current generation operating systems cease to scale and full-scale networking architecture has to be brought inside the server. The DIMEs enable the execution of distributed and managed workflows within a server or across multiple servers with its unifying network computing model. Exploiting this, the Parallax operating system leverages chip-level hardware assistance provided to virtualize, manage, secure, and optimize computing at the core. While this work is in its infancy, the new OS also seems to exploit fully the parallelism and multithread execution capabilities offered in these computing elements to implement the managed DAGs with parallel signaling control network. Figure 8 shows a service infrastructure using DIME network architecture. The service workflow (S1) which monitors the temperature gauge and controls the fan is managed by the management workflows (W1, W2, W3 and W4) which monitor and control the service workflow parameters. In parallel, The DIME FCAPS managers assure the DIME infrastructure which is facilitating the service and management workflows to provide DIME FCAPS management.

Application of DIME Network Architecture to Cloud Computing

The DNA implements a managed Turing machine to exploit the parallelism and high bandwidth available in the many-core chips. The DNA approach potentially offers many new directions of research to provide next level of scaling in operating systems, telecom grade trust through end-to-end service FCAPS optimization and reduced complexity in developing, deploying and managing distributed federated software systems executing business workflows. The prototypes discussed in this chapter demonstrate the use of signaling in enabling the architectural resiliency of cellular organisms with fewer layers of management systems and decoupling of services management from the underlying hardware infrastructure management.

While the DIME network architecture is designed to improve the resiliency, efficiency and scaling of many-core server based services infrastructure, it also is applicable to both conventional physical server based computing network and to a virtual server based Cloud computing network. In the case of conventional data center without virtualization infrastructure, the DIME network architecture provides auto-scaling, self-repair, live-migration and end to end transaction integrity using either DIMEs on Linux or Parallax native

Figure 8. A service creation, delivery and assurance infrastructure using DIME Network Architecture

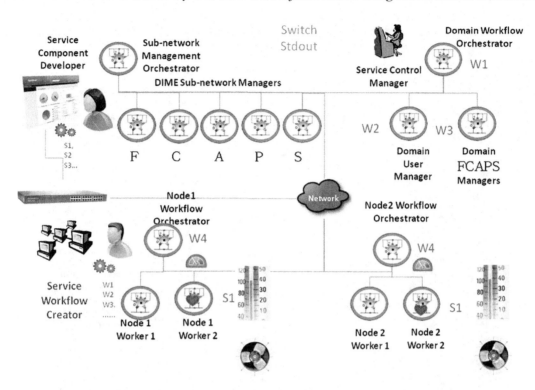

OS without the need for Hypervisors, virtual machines, and layers of virtual server management. In the case of exhisting Cloud computing, the DIME network architecture still can be used to provide same benefits at the process level by encapsulating it with FCAPS management and enabling signaling based policy management. The DIME network architecture in a virtual server still eliminates the need for virtual machine movement by replacing it with DIME movement which does not include the OS image. In addition the multi-tenancy granularity with FCAPS management is at the DIME level and is independent of the virtual server and associated operating system.

Table 1 shows a comparison between the three approaches:

Figure 9 shows the results obtained using LAMP (Linux-Apache-MySQL-PHP) architecture implemented using a DIME Network. The Apache webserver is encapsulated in a DIME as are the DNS server and the MySQL database. A

configuration manager DIME implements the self-repair, auto-scaling and live migration policies. When the average response time grows decisively with an increasing workload, and exceeds a given threshold, the DIME containing the Apache server asks DNA Supervisor for a replica. When a new DIME with the replica of Apache is started and the DNS server updated, the response time decreases.

When the response time increases again with further increase in workloads, the system instantiates new replicas of Apache and maintains the response time within the given threshold. Self-repair is implemented by watching the heartbeats of all DIMEs by the FCAPS manager.

This implementation demonstrates not only the scalability of the DIME-based solution but also its ability to reconfigure itself at run-time (e.g. by changing the content of DNS config file).

The DIME network management offers better optimization of resources when the latency of

Table 1. Comparison between conventional computing, cloud computing and DIME network architecture

	Conventional Computing	Cloud Computing	DIME Computing	
			Linux	Parallax
Managed Computing Entity	Physical Server	Virtual Server	A Process	A Core
Computing Network	IP/Shared Memory/PCI Express	IP/Shared Memory/PCI Express	IP/Shared Memory/PCI Express	IP/Shared Memory/PCI Express
Management Network	Uses Same Computing Network	Uses Same Computing Network	Parallel Signaling Network Overlay	Parallel Signaling Network Overlay
Computing Model	von Neumann Turing Machine	von Neumann Turing Machine	Managed Turing Machine	Managed Turing Machine
Server Hardware Management (FCAPS)	Labor Intensive	Automated	Service Management Decoupled from Server Management	Service Management Decoupled from Server Management
Network Hardware Management (FCAPS)	Labor Intensive	Automated	Service Management Decoupled from Network Management	Service Management Decoupled from Network Management
Storage Hardware Management (FCAPS)	Labor Intensive	Automated	Service Management Decoupled from Storage Management	Service Management Decoupled from Storage Management
Operating System	Server-centric	Virtual Server-centric	Network-centric Process management in node-centric Linux OS	Network-centric Core management transcending physical server boundaries
Service Management (FCAPS)	Labor Intensive	Automated workflows	Autonomic Policy Based Transaction FCAPS Management	Autonomic Policy Based Transaction FCAPS Management
Management Latency	T(Management) >> T(Service Transaction)	T(Management) > T(Service Transaction)	T(Management) = T(Service Transaction)	T(Management) = T(Service Transaction)

Figure 9. Response time vs. number of requests in a DIME-based LAMP

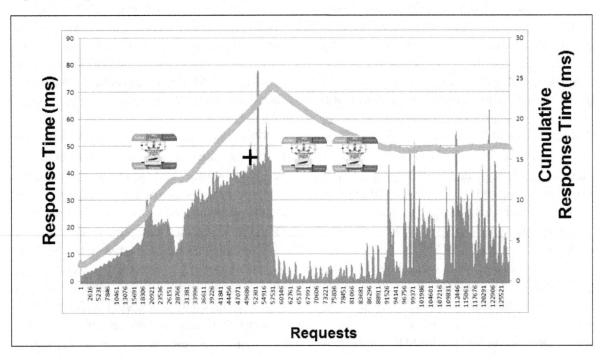

management transactions and the latency of service transactions are close together. Interestingly enough, the DNA is operating system agnostic and can be implemented even in the Cloud as it exists and we suggest here some ideas for future research:

1. First, implementing DIMEs in Linux in a virtual server in the current Cloud infrastructure provides an alternative to current layers of management systems providing virtual machine FCAPS management. The DIMEs provide FCAPS managed multi-tenancy at the process level with a finer granularity than the virtual machines (VMs). The DIME network management provides FCAPS management at the end-to-end transaction level. The services management in the DNA will decoupled from the virtual machine management.

2. Second, as Tusa et al (2011) pointed out, the signaling channel, FCAPS, and the self management features of the DNA for achieving the single sign-on (SSO) authentication across multiple administrative domains.

3. Third, the service management decoupling from underlying infrastructure management provides a vehicle to implement inter-Cloud and intra-Cloud service FCAPS monitoring and control independent of hardware or virtual machine infrastructure FCAPS monitoring and control. This could provide a vehicle to implement reliable services even on not so reliable commodity hardware infrastructure and obviate the need for high reliability special purpose hardware and clustered hardware configurations.

CONCLUSION

As is clear from the discussions presented in this chapter, conventional computing uses a physical server or a computing device with an administrative paradigm that is suited for human administration albeit with some automation. It worked well when the management transaction times are very much larger than the computation transaction times. Applications running on these devices cannot dynamically manage resources without administrative assistance to meet changing workloads, business priorities or latency constraints. Current Cloud computing is an improvement over conventional computing in improving the management of computing resources by automating manual processes. However, it increases complexity through layers of management systems necessitating orchestrator of orchestrators. It requires Hypervisors and the Virtual Machine management. As mentioned earlier, still 70% to 80% of total operational budget in the data centers is spent on operation management tasks. While the virtual server provides improvement of multi-tenancy by increasing the number of virtual servers in a physical server and provides auto-scaling, live-migration etc., the Cloud is still lacking in telecom grade trust because, it has the same isolate, diagnose, and fix philosophy as conventional computing. It is not well suited to leverage many-core servers where hundreds of cores are in the same processor and tens of processes in the same server. The computing networks inside the enclosure then are at a high bandwidth and support parallelism. The Cloud management with its origin from server-centric and bandwidth limited origins is not ideal for deploying it inside the many-core server. When the whole Cloud migrates to being inside a server in many-core servers, it is hard to believe that one would want to replicate the complex Cloud management infrastructure inside the server. This requires a reexamination of the fundamental distributed computing architecture. The authors look to biology where autonomic computing is a rule than an exception.

Evolution of living organisms teaches that the difference between survival and extinction is the information processing ability of the organism to:

1. Discover and encapsulate the sequences of stable patterns that have lower entropy, which allow harmony with the environment providing the necessary resources for its survival,
2. Replicate the sequences so that the information (in the form of best practices) can propagate from the survived to the successor,
3. Execute with precision the sequences to reproduce itself,
4. Monitor itself and its surroundings in real-time, and
5. Utilize the genetic transactions of repair, recombination and rearrangement to sustain existing patterns that are useful.

That the computing models of living organisms utilize sophisticated methods of information processing, was recognized by von Neumann who proposed the stored program control computing model and the self-replicating cellular automata. Later Chris Langton (1989) created computer programs that demonstrated self-organization and discovery of patterns using evolutionary rules which led to the field of artificial life and theories of complexity.

This paper, focused on another aspect learned from the genes in living organisms that deals with precise replication and execution of encapsulated DNA sequences. This approach allows utilizing a parallel distributed computing model to implement service virtualization and workflow execution practiced in current business process implementation in IT where a workflow is implemented as a set of tasks, arranged or organized in a DAG. The DIME approach is new with proof of concept prototypes demonstrating its feasibility. Further research, analysis, and validation are required to prove its applicability in mission critical environments. An investigation into managed Turing machine networks and von Neumann's comments regarding Gödel's theorem alluded to earlier may also throw some theoretical light on the validity and applicability of the DIME computing model in distributed computing spanning across many-core servers. Perhaps it is also worthwhile to investigate its relationship to the new models of computation (Wegner and Eberbach, 2004) proposed to provide higher expressiveness than Turing machines to model interactive, dynamic systems.

REFERENCES

Baumann, A., Barham, P., Dagand, P., Harris, T., Isaacs, R., Peter, S., et al. (2010) *The Multikernel: A new OS architecture for scalable multicore systems, In the 22nd ACM Symposium on OS Principles*, Big Sky, MT, USA, October.

Baumann, A., & Peter, S. Schüpbach, A., Singhania, A., Roscoe, T., Barham, P., and Isaacs. R., (2009). Your computer is already a distributed system. Why isn't your OS? *In 12th Workshop on Hot Topics in Operating Systems*, May.

Carroll, S. B. (2005). *The New Science of Evo Devo - Endless Forms Most Beautiful.* New York: W. W. Norton & Co.

Colmenares, J. A., Bird, S., Cook, H., Pearce, P., Zhu, D., Shalf, J., et al. (2010). Tesselation: Space-Time Partitioning in a Manycore Client OS *In 2nd USENIX Workshop on Hot Topics in Parallelism (HotPar'10).* Berkeley, CA, USA. June.

Dawkins, R. (1989). *The Selfish Gene.* New York: Oxford University Press.

Dyson, G. B. (1997). *Darwin among the Machines, the evolution of global intelligence*, Reading, MA, Helix Books, Addition Wesley Publishing Company

Langton, C. G. (1989). Artificial Life. In *Santa Fe Institute Studies in the Sciences of Complexity* (*Vol. 6*). Addison Wesley.

Malone, T. W. (1990). Organizing information systems: Parallels between human organizations and computer systems. Scott P. Robertson (Ed.), *Cognition, Computing and Cooperation*. Greenwood Publishing Company.

Mao, O., Kaashoek, F., Morris, R., Pesterev, A., Stein, L., Wu, M., et al. (2008) Corey: an operating system for many cores, *In the 8th USENIX Symposium on Operating Systems Design and Implementation* OSDI '08, San Diego, California, December.

Mikkilineni, R., Seyler, I., (2011), "*Parallax - A New Operating System Prototype Demonstrating Service Scaling and Service Self-Repair in Multicore Servers,*" Enabling Technologies: Infrastructure for Collaborative Enterprises (WETICE), 2011 20th IEEE International Workshops on, vol., no., pp.104-109, 27-29.

Mitchell, W. M. (1992). *Complexity: The Emerging Science at the Edge of Order and Chaos* (p. 218). London: Penguin Books.

Morana, G., Mikkilineni, R., (2011), "*Scaling and Self-repair of Linux Based Services Using a Novel Distributed Computing Model Exploiting Parallelism,*" Enabling Technologies: Infrastructure for Collaborative Enterprises (WETICE), 2011 20th IEEE International Workshops on, vol., no., pp.98-103, 27-29

Morris, C. (2011). *Sony PlayStation Facing Yet Another Security Breach*, New York, from http://www.cnbc.com/id/43079509

Pegasus Communications. (2010). The *Systems Thinker*, from www.thesystemsthinker.com

Tanenbaum, A. S., & van Steen, M. (2002). *Distributed Systems Principles and Paradigms*. Saddle River, New Jersey: Prentice Hall.

Thibodeau, P., & Vijayan, J. (2011). Amazon EC2 service outage reinforces Cloud doubts. *Computerworld* from http://www.computerworld.com/s/article/356212/

Tusa, F., Celesti, A., & Mikkilineni, R. (2011), "*AAA in a Cloud-Based Virtual DIME Network Architecture (DNA),*" Enabling Technologies: Infrastructure for Collaborative Enterprises (WETICE), 20th IEEE International Workshops on, vol., no., pp.110-115, 27-29 June 2011

von Neumann, J. (1966). *Theory of Self-Reproducing Automata* (Burke, A. W., Ed.). Chicago, Illinois: University of Illinois Press.

von Neumann, J. (1987). *General and Logical Theory of Automata*. William Aspray and Arthur Burks (Ed.), MIT Press

von Neumann, J. (1987). *Papers of John von Neumann on Computing and Computing Theory, Hixon Symposium*, September 20, 1948, Pasadena, CA, The MIT Press, p454, p457

Wegner, P., & Eberbach, E. (2004). New Models of Computation. *The Computer Journal*, *47*(1). doi:10.1093/comjnl/47.1.4

Wentzlaff, D., & Agarwal, A. 2009). Factored operating systems (fos): the case for a scalable operating system for multicores. *In SIGOPS Operating System Review*, vol 43(2):pp. 76–85.

ADDITIONAL READING

Distributed Systems:

Chow, R., & Johnson, T. (1997). *Distributed Operating Systems and Algorithms*. Reading, MA: Addison Wesley.

Geihs, K. (2001). Middleware Challenges Ahead. *IEEE Computer*, *34*(6), 24–31. doi:10.1109/2.928618

Federated Systems:

Beasley, M., Cameron, J., Girling, G., Hoffner, Y., van der Linden, R., & Thomas, G. (1994) Establishing Co-operation in Federated Systems. *ICL Technical Journal*, from www.ansa.co.uk

Buyya, R., & Ranjan, R. (2010). Special section: Federated resource management in Grid and Cloud computing systems. *Future Generation Computer Systems, 26,* 1189–1191. doi:10.1016/j. future.2010.06.003

Meinecke, J., Gaedke, M., & Majer, F. Brändle, A., (2006) Capturing the Essentials of Federated Systems. *In WWW Conference,* May 23–26, 2006, Edinburgh, Scotland

Many-core Chips:

Hsu, C.-H., & Malyshkin, V. (Eds.). (2010) Methods and Tools of Parallel Programming Multicomputers, *In Second Russia-Taiwan Symposium,* Berlin, Springer-Verlag

Computing Models & OS Design:

Edmund, B. Nightingale, Orion Hodson, Ross McIlroy, Chris Hawblitzel, and Galen Hunt, "Helios: Heterogeneous Multiprocessing with Satellite Kernels", ACM, SOSP'09, October 11–14, 2009, Big Sky, Montana, USA

Goldstine, H. H., & von Neumann, J. (1983) "On the principles of large scale computing machines," Taub, A. H., (Ed.) *John von Neumann Collected Works*, the Macmillan Co., New York, 1963, Volume V.

Genes:

Jacob, F., & Monod, J. (1961). Genetic regulatory mechanisms in the synthesis of proteins. *Journal of Molecular Biology, 3,* 318–356. doi:10.1016/S0022-2836(61)80072-7

Singer, M., & Berg, P. (1991). *Genes & genomes: a changing perspective*. Mill Valley, CA: University Science Books.

KEY TERMS AND DEFINITIONS

DIME: Distributed Intelligent Managed Element is a computing unit that represents a managed Turing Machine with self-management of fault configuration, accounting, performance and security of the von Neumann stored program computing node and signaling capability to collaborate with other DIMEs.

Directed Acyclic Graph: A directed acyclic graph (commonly abbreviated to DAG), is a directed graph with no directed cycles. That is, it is formed by a collection of vertices and directed edges, each edge connecting one vertex to another, such that there is no way to start at some vertex v and follow a sequence of edges that eventually loops back to v again DAGs may be used to model several different kinds of structure in mathematics and computer science. DAGs may be used to model processes in which information flows in a consistent direction through a network of processors.

DNA: DIME Network Architecture that allows programming a set of DIMEs to implement a collaborative fault, configuration, accounting, performance and security of a distributed transaction.

FCAPS: Fault, configuration, accounting, performance and security of networked elements. The term is derived from telecommunications network implementation of distributed voice service.

Signaling: A communication scheme used by distributed systems to implement system-wide policies. The basic abstractions of addressing, alerting, mediation and supervision are used by both cellular organisms and human organizations.

Telecom Grade Trust: Telecommunication services provide a benchmark of trust which assures managed resources on-demand with high availability, performance and security.

Turing Machine: A theoretical device that manipulates symbols on a strip of tape according to a table of rules. Despite its simplicity, a Turing machine can be adapted to simulate the logic of any computer algorithm, and is particularly useful in explaining the functions of a CPU inside a computer.

Chapter 5
The Cloud@Home Volunteer and Interoperable Cloud through the Future Internet

Salvatore Distefano
Politecnico di Milano, Italy

Antonio Puliafito
Università degli Studi di Messina, Italy

ABSTRACT

Cloud computing is the new consolidated trend in ICT, often considered as the panacea to all the problems of existing large-scale distributed paradigms such as Grid and hierarchical clustering. The Cloud breakthrough is the service oriented perspective of providing everything "as a service". Different from the others large-scale distributed paradigms, it was born from commercial contexts, with the aim of selling the temporarily unexploited computing resources of huge datacenters in order to reduce the costs. Since this business model is really attractive and convenient for both providers and consumers, the Cloud paradigm is quickly growing and widely spreading, even in non commercial context. In fact, several activities on the Cloud, such as Nimbus, Eucalyptus, OpenNEbula, and Reservoir, etc., have been undertaken, aiming at specifying open Cloud infrastructure middleware.

INTRODUCTION

In this context, the idea is to implement a volunteer-Cloud, in which the infrastructure is obtained by merging heterogeneous resources that could be provided by different domains and/or providers such as other Clouds, Grid farms, clusters, and datacenters, etc, till single desktops. Such a new paradigm has to implement the characteristics of the Cloud paradigm (service oriented interface, dynamic service provisioning, and QoS guaranteed offer, etc.) as well as all the mechanisms for aggregating, enrolling, and managing the resources also considering SLA and QoS requirements.

DOI: 10.4018/978-1-4666-1631-8.ch005

Copyright © 2012, IGI Global. Copying or distributing in print or electronic forms without written permission of IGI Global is prohibited.

It can be considered a mix between Cloud and volunteer computing, thus it is named Cloud@ Home. In order to accomplish its mission, Cloud@ Home has to be supported by adequate technology, especially for concerns regarding the Internet and the directions identified by the Future Internet.

This chapter presents the Cloud@Home paradigm, providing a general overview and identifying all its aims and goals. Thus, the chapter tries to address the main issues and challenges of Cloud@ Home into a specific middleware architecture composed of several modules. It therefore discusses some possible implications of Cloud@Home in the Future Internet, some possible application scenarios and finally it provides a critical overview of the paradigm against existing Cloud solutions.

Cloud Computing is emerging as a promising paradigm capable of providing a flexible, dynamic, resilient and cost effective infrastructure for both academic and business environments. It aims at raising the level of abstraction of physical resources toward a "user-centric" perspective, focused on the concept of service as the elementary unit for building any application. All the Cloud's resources, both physical/hardware and logical/ abstract (software, data, etc) are therefore considered "as a service" and so all Cloud's design and implementation choices follow a "service oriented" philosophy.

Cloud is actually a real, operating, and effective solution in commercial and business context, offering computing resources and services for rent, accessed through the Web according to a client-server paradigm regulated by specific SLA. In fact, several commercial solutions and infrastructure providers make business on the Cloud, such as Amazon EC2 and S3, Microsoft Azure, Rackspace, and so on. Recently Cloud computing is quickly and widely spreading also in open contexts such as scientific, academic, and social communities, due to the increasing demand of computing resources required by their users. As an example, there are several research activities and projects on Cloud, such as RESERVOIR (The

RESERVOIR Consortium, 2011), OpenNEbula (Universidad Complutense de Madrid, 2011), Eucalyptus (Nurmi et al., 2008), Nimrod/G (MeSsAGE Lab-Monash eScience and Grid Engineering Laboratory, 2011), OpenQRM (openQRM Developer Community, 2011), Hadoop (Apache Software Foundation, 2011), CLEVER (Tusa, Paone, Villari, & Puliafito, 2010), OpenCyrrus (HP, Intel, Yahoo!, 2011) and OpenStack (The Openstack Community, 2011), OCCI (OCCI Work Group, 2011), etc., aiming at implementing their open infrastructure providing specific middleware.

Among the reasons behind the success of Cloud, excepting the low costs, there are: the user-centric interface that acts as a unique, user friendly, point of access for users' needs and requirements; on-demand service provision; the QoS guaranteed offer, and the autonomous system for managing hardware, software and data transparently to users (Wang et al., 2008).

On the other hand, there are different open problems in Cloud infrastructures that inhibit their use, mainly concerning information security (confidentiality and integrity), trustiness, interoperability, and reliability, availability, and other quality of service (QoS) requirements specified in the service level agreement (SLA), etc., only partially addressed or sometimes still uncovered. To further complete the scenario, consider that, in the last few years, several organizations made important investments in Grid and similar distributed infrastructures: what should be done with these? Discard or reuse? How can they be reused?

Moreover, the rise of the "techno-utility complex" and the corresponding increase in demand for computing resources, in some cases growing dramatically faster than Moore's Law, as predicted by the Sun CTO Greg Papadopoulos in the red shift theory for IT (Martin, 2007), could lead to, in the near future, an oligarchy, a lobby, or a trust of a few big companies controlling the whole computing resources market.

To avoid such a pessimistic but likely scenario, the authors suggest addressing the problem in a different way: instead of building costly private data centers, such as those that the Google CEO, Eric Schmidt, likes to compare to the prohibitively expensive cyclotrons (Baker, 2008), the authors propose a more "democratic" form of Cloud computing, in which the computing resources of a single user, company, and/or community accessing the Cloud can be shared with the others, in order to contribute to the elaboration of complex problems.

In order to implement such an idea, a possible source of inspiration could be the Volunteer computing paradigm. Volunteer computing (also called Peer-to-Peer computing, Global computing, or Public computing) uses computers volunteered by their owners, as a source of computing power and storage to provide distributed scientific computing (Anderson & Fedak, 2006).

Thus, the core idea of such project is to implement a volunteer Cloud, an infrastructure built on resources voluntarily shared (for free or by charge) by their owners or administrators, following a volunteer computing approach, and provided to users through a Cloud interface, i.e. QoS guaranteed-on demand services. Since this new paradigm merges Volunteer and Cloud computing goals, it has been named Cloud@Home. It can be considered a generalization and a maturation of the @home philosophy, knocking down the (hardware and software) barriers of Volunteer computing, and also allowing the sharing more general services. In this new paradigm, the user resources/data center are not only passive interface to Cloud services, but they can interact (for free or by charge) with one or more Clouds, and therefore must be able to interoperate.

The Cloud@Home paradigm could also be applied to commercial Clouds, establishing an open computing-utility market where users can both buy and sell their services. Since the computing power can be described by a "long-tailed" distribution, in which a high-amplitude population (Cloud providers and commercial data centers) is followed by a low-amplitude population (small data centers and private users) which gradually "tails off" asymptotically, Cloud@Home can catch the Long Tail effect (Anderson, 2004), providing similar or higher computing capabilities than commercial providers' data centers, by grouping small computing resources from many single contributors.

Therefore it is believed that the Cloud@Home paradigm is applicable also at lower scales, from the single contributing user, that shares his/her desktop, to research groups, public administrations, social communities, and small and medium enterprises, which make available their distributed computing resources to the Cloud.

Both free sharing and pay-per-use models can be adopted in such scenarios. In order to open the computing market to single users resources/desktops adequate Internet access technology is required. This is the main challenge facing the Cloud@Home project and the Future Internet community.

BACKGROUND

The core idea of Cloud@Home is to implement a volunteer-Cloud, mixing aspects of both Volunteer and Cloud computing.

Great interest in Cloud computing has been manifested from both academic and private research centers, and numerous projects from the industry and academia have been proposed. The fact that the biggest ICT companies make investments in the Cloud is symptomatic of the impact and the strategic interest this new paradigm has attracted. Examples are: Amazon (Amazon Web Services-AWS (Amazon Web Services, 2011): Elastic Compute Cloud-EC2, Secure storage System-S3), IBM (IBM Cloud (IBM, 2011)), VMWARE (vCloud (VMWare, 2011)), Oracle/Sun (Oracle Cloud Computing (Oracle 2011)), Microsoft (Azure (Mircrosoft, 2011)), Google (PAAS Google App Engine (Google, 2011)), Dell (Cloud computing solutions (Dell 2011)), and Cisco (Cisco, 2011). There are also several open scientific activities and projects such as: Nimbus-Stratus-Wispy-Kupa (University Masaryk of Chicago, University of Florida, & Purdue University, 2011), RESERVOIR (The RESERVOIR Consortium, 2011), OpenNEbula (Universidad Complutense de Madrid, 2011), Eucalyptus (Nurmi et al., 2008), Nimrod/G (MeSsAGE Lab-Monash eScience and Grid Engineering Laboratory, 2011), OpenQRM (openQRM Developer Community, 2011), Hadoop (Apache Software Foundation, 2011), CLEVER (Tusa, Paone, Villari, & Puliafito, 2010), OpenCyrrus (HP, Intel, Yahoo!, 2011), and OpenStack (The Openstack Community, 2011).

The University of Chicago's Globus Nimbus (University Masaryk of Chicago et al., 2011), is widely recognized as having pioneered the field. This, like the Nimrod/G project (MeSsAGE Lab-Monash eScience and Grid Engineering Laboratory, 2011) and satellite projects, starts from a strong background in Grid, that extends with the concept of virtual workspace. Eucalyptus (Nurmi et al., 2008) is an open-source software-infrastructure project that imitates the experience of using EC2 but lets users run programs on their own resources and provides a detailed view of what would otherwise be the black box of cloud-computing services. RESERVOIR (The RESERVOIR Consortium, 2011) is an European Cloud-computing initiative for developing an open interoperable Cloud computing middleware starting from open-source components, such as OpenNebula (Universidad Complutense de Madrid, 2011), a tool for managing the virtual machines within a Cloud. OpenQRM (openQRM Developer Community, 2011) is an open-source data-center management platform offering a pluggable architecture focused on automatic, rapid- and appliance-based deployment, monitoring, and high-availability, Cloud computing, and especially on supporting and conforming multiple virtualization technologies. CLEVER (Tusa, Paone, Villari,

& Puliafito, 2010) is another attempt to develop a Cloud middleware with intrinsic new features for Cloud federation and QoS management. An interesting alternative is Hadoop, (Apache Software Foundation, 2011) an open-source software for reliable, scalable, and distributed computing, mainly oriented for clusters or datacenters and with several developments and customizations for specific application templates such as MapReduce. OpenStack is a software for provisioning and managing large-scale deployments of compute and storage instances. It is written in Python, us-ing the Tornado and Twisted frameworks, and relies on the standard AMQP messaging protocol as well as the Redis distributed key-value store. The code base for OpenStack is evolving at a very rapid pace. The current OpenStack release, known as Diablo, is functionally complete for infrastructure as a service (Nova) and object storage services (Swift).

Also some companies, such as Enomaly (Enomaly, 2011), Google (Google, 2011) and 10gen (10gen, 2011), develop open-source Cloud-computing IAAS/PAAS middlewares, or support research activities such as Open Cirrus, (HP, Intel, Yahoo!, 2011) an open cloud-computing research testbed designed to support research into the design, provisioning, and management of services at a global, multi-datacenter scale.

All of them provide and implement an on-demand computing paradigm, in the sense that a user submits his/her requests to the Cloud that remotely, in a distributed fashion, processes them and gives back the results. These tools could let companies build and customize their own private Clouds to work alongside more powerful commercial solutions.

On the other hand, the other element of the Cloud@Home recipe is Volunteer computing. The key idea of Volunteer computing is to harvest the idle time of Internet connected computers, which may be widely distributed across the world, to run a very large and distributed application (Fedak,

Germain, Neri, & Cappello, 2001). It is behind the "@home" philosophy of sharing/donating network connected resources for supporting distributed scientific computing.

Aims and Goals

The Cloud@Home paradigm is inspired to the Volunteer computing one. The latter is born for supporting the philosophy of open public computing, implementing an open distributed environment in which resources (not services as in the Cloud) can be shared. Volunteer computing is behind the "@ home" philosophy of sharing/donating network connected resources for supporting distributed scientific computing. On the other hand, Cloud@ Home can be considered as the enhancement of the grid-utility vision of Cloud computing. In this new paradigm, user's hosts are not passive interface to Cloud services anymore, but they can interact (for free or by charge) with other Clouds. The scenario we prefigure is composed of several coexisting and interoperable Clouds. Open Clouds identify groups of shared resources and services operating for free Volunteer computing; commercial Clouds characterize entities or companies selling their computing resources for business; hybrid Clouds can both sell or give for free their services. Both open and hybrid Clouds can interoperate with any other Cloud, also commercial ones, constituting Clouds' federations. In this way an open market of computing resources could be established: a private Cloud, which may require computing resources, can buy these from third parties; otherwise, it can sell or freely give its resources to the others.

Figure 1 depicts the Cloud@Home reference scenario, identifying different stakeholder characterized by their role: consuming and/or contributing. Arrows outgoing from the Cloud represent consuming resources, from which a Cloud@Home client submits its requests; otherwise, arrows incoming to the Cloud represent contributing resources providing their services to Cloud@Home clients. Therefore, infrastructure providers, datacenters, Grids, clusters, servers, till desktops and mobile devices can both contribute and consume. In fact, it is believed that the Cloud@ Home paradigm is widely applicable, from research groups, public administrations, social communities, SMEs, which make available their distributed computing resources to the Cloud, till, and potentially, the single contributing user, that autonomously decide to share his/her resources.

The widest Cloud@Home scenario, involving single contributing user, could be achievable if supported by an adequate development of the Internet. The volunteer nature of Cloud@Home implies that the underlying infrastructure is highly dynamic, due to unexpected and unpredictable join and leave of contributing users. In order to deal with this problem, adequate redundancy and replication techniques have to be used. It is therefore necessary to duplicate and migrate virtual machines, and so to transfer a huge amount of data in short time. This is a challenge for the Future Internet.

Therefore, the Cloud@Home software system has to provide readily available functionalities in the areas of directory/information services, security and management of resources. In order to implement such a form of computing the following issues should be taken into consideration:

- Resources management;
- User interface;
- Security, accounting, identity management;
- Virtualization;
- Network configuration;
- Interoperability among heterogeneous Clouds;
- Business models, billing, QoS and SLA management.

A possible rationalization of the tasks and the functionalities the Cloud@Home middleware has to implement can be performed by considering the layered view shown in Figure 2. Three

Figure 1. Cloud@Home Reference Scenario

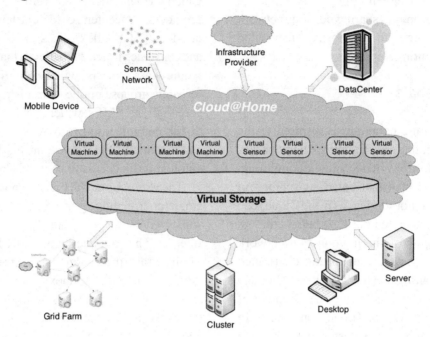

separated layers are identified in order to apply a separation of concerns and therefore to improve the middleware development process. These are:

- The Frontend Layer that globally manages resources and services (coordination, discovery, enrollment), implements the user interface for accessing the Cloud (ensuring security reliability and interoperability), and provides QoS and business models and policies management facilities.

- The Virtual Layer that implements a homogeneous view of the distributed Cloud system offered to the higher frontend layer (and therefore to users) in form of two main basic services: the execution service that allows to set up a virtual machine, and the storage service that implements a distribut-

Figure 2. Cloud@home Logic View

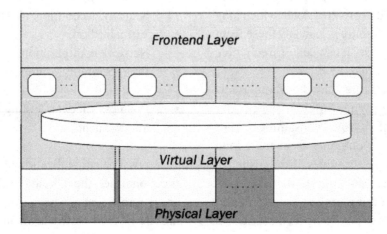

ed storage Cloud to store data and files as a remote disk, locally mounted, or accessed via Web. Virtual Sensors provide the access points to the sensing infrastructure. The access is characterized by abstraction and independence from the actual sensing process and equipment. From the network point of view it is necessary to reach all the virtualized resources by the Internet. A possible solution could be to implement a specific C@H overlay network such as a VPN.

- The bottom Physical Layer that provides both the physical resources for elaborating the requests and the software for locally managing such resources. It is composed of a "cloud" of generic nodes and/or devices geographically distributed across the Internet.

The CloudHome Middleware Architecture

The Cloud@Home logic view of Figure 2 describes a high level functional architecture organization. The modules implementing such functional architecture are depicted in the layered

model of Figure 3, that implements the separation of concerns among the modules; the modules in a layer can communicate and cooperate each other, moreover, they provide services to the modules in the layer above, and invoke services of modules in the layer below.

From the implementation perspective, a different decomposition has been applied to such a model, identifying two subsystems:

- Management subsystem is the backbone of the overall system management and coordination.
- Resource subsystem provides primitives for locally managing the resources (distributed operations), offering different services over the same resources: the execution Cloud and the storage Cloud.

The two subsystems are strictly interconnected: the management subsystem implements the upper layer of the functional architecture, while the resource subsystem implements the lower level functionalities.

Figure 3. Core Structure of a Cloud@Home Server

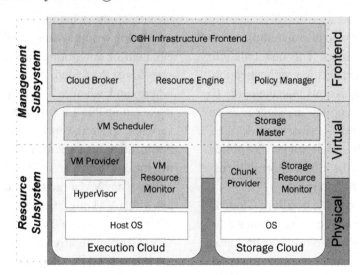

Management Subsystem

In order to enroll and manage the distributed resources and services of a Cloud, and provide a unique point of access for them, it is necessary to adopt a centralized approach that is implemented by the management subsystem. It is composed of four parts: the user frontend (UF), the Cloud broker, the resource engine, and the policy manager.

The user frontend provides tools for Cloud@ Home-user interactions. It collects and manages the users' requests issued by the Cloud@Home clients. All such requests are transferred to the blocks composing the underlying layer (resource engine, Cloud broker, and policy manager) for processing.

An important task carried out by the user frontend is the Clouds interoperability, implemented by point-to-point connecting the interface of the Clouds wishing to interoperate. In case one of the Clouds does not have the Cloud@Home core structure of Figure 3, it is necessary to translate the requests between Cloud@Home and foreign Clouds formats, a task delegated by the user frontend to the Cloud broker. The Cloud broker collects and manages information about the available Clouds and the services they provide (both functional and non-functional parameters, such as QoS, costs, and reliability,and request formats' specifications for Cloud@Home-foreign Clouds translations, etc.).

The policy manager provides and implements the Cloud's access facilities. This task falls into the security scope of identification, authentication, authorization, and permissions management. To achieve this target, the policy manager uses an infrastructure based on PKI, smartcard devices, Certification Authority, and SSO. The policy manager also manages the information about users' QoS policies and requirements.

The resource engine is the hearth of Cloud@ Home. It is responsible for the resources' management, the equivalent of a Grid resource broker in a broader Cloud environment. To meet this goal,

the resource engine applies a hierarchical policy. It operates at higher level, in a centralized way, indexing all the resources of the Cloud. Incoming requests are delegated to VM schedulers or storage masters that, in a distributed fashion, manage the computing or storage resources, respectively, coordinated by the resource engine.

In order to manage QoS policies and to perform the resources discovery, the resource engine collaborates with both Cloud broker and policy manager.

Resource Subsystem

The resource subsystem contains all the blocks implementing the local and distributed management functionalities of Cloud@Home. This subsystem can be logically split into two parts offering different software infrastructure services: the execution Cloud and the storage Cloud. The management subsystem is also able to merge them providing a unique Cloud that can offer both execution and/or storage services.

The execution Cloud provides tools for managing virtual machines according to users' requests and requirements coming from the management subsystem. It is composed of four blocks: VM scheduler, VM provider, VM resource monitor, and hypervisor.

The VM Scheduler is a peripheral resource broker of the Cloud@Home infrastructure, to which the resource engine delegates the management of computing/execution resources and services of the Cloud. It establishes which, what, where, and when a VM is allocated, moreover it is responsible for moving and managing VM services. From the end user point of view, a VM is allocated somewhere on the Cloud, therefore its migration is transparent for the end user that is not aware of any VM migration mechanism. Problems can affect VM migrations into the Cloud@Home environment. Since the nodes implementing the Cloud are, generally, widely distributed across the Internet, while migrating a VM with its entire context from a node to another (remote) node, great transfer delays are introduced. In a highly dynamic environment where VM migrations could be highly frequent, this could become a serious problem. A possible solution for facing such a problem is the introduction of technique-based difference algorithms, similar to the one implemented into the union file system (UnionFS) (Zadok, Iyer, Joukov, Sivathanu, & Wright, 2011). In the Cloud@Home infrastructure, redundant basic VM images must be available (if it is possible) in each node contributing to the execution Cloud. Thus, in case of migration based on the selected data/files comparison algorithm (diff), instead of transferring the whole VM with its context, a lighter (diff) file only containing the differences between a new VM and the one to migrate is sent to the destination host, which recomposes the original VM starting from a new VM instance and runs it. This technique can considerably reduce the amount of data to transfer and, consequently, the corresponding transfer times.

The association between resources and scheduler is made locally. Since a scheduler can become a bottleneck if the system grows, distributed scheduling algorithms can be implemented to avoid the congestion from becoming further decentralized. Possible strategies and tricks for facing the problem are:

- Implementing a hierarchy of schedulers with geographic characterization: local, zone (as termed by Amazon), meta-zones (Eucalyptus), area, and region, etc.;
- Replicating schedulers, which can communicate each other for synchronization;
- Autonomic scheduling.

The VM provider, the VM resource monitor, and the hypervisor are responsible for managing a VM locally to a physical resource. A VM provider exports functions for allocating, managing, migrating, and destroying a virtual machine on the corresponding host. The VM resource moni-

tor allows it to take control of the local computing resources, according to requirements and constraints negotiated in the setup phase with the contributing user. If during a virtual machine execution the local resources crash or become insufficient to keep the virtual machine running, the VM resource monitor asks the scheduler to migrate the VM elsewhere.

In order to implement the storage Cloud, the authors specify the Cloud@Home file system (FS), adopting an approach similar to the Google FS (Ghemawat, S., Gobioff, H., & Leung, 2011). The Cloud@Home FS splits data and files into chunks of fixed or variable size, depending on the storage resources available. The architecture of the storage file system is hierarchical: data chunks are physically stored on chunk providers and corresponding storage masters index the chunks through specific file indexes (FI). The storage master is the directory server, indexing the data stored in the associated chunk providers. It directly interfaces with the resource engine to discover the resources storing data. In this context the resource engine can be considered, in its turn, as the directory server indexing all the storage masters. To improve the storage Cloud reliability, storage masters must be replicated. Moreover, a chunk provider can be associated with more than one storage master.

In order to avoid a storage master becoming a bottleneck, once the chunk providers have been located, data transfers are implemented by directly connecting end users and chunk providers. Similar techniques to the ones discussed about VM schedulers can be applied to storage masters for improving performance and reliability of the storage Clouds.

Chunk providers physically store the data that, as introduced above, are encrypted in order to achieve the confidentiality goal. Data reliability can be improved by replicating data chunks and chunk providers, consequently updating the corresponding storage masters. In this way, a corrupted data chunk can be automatically recovered and restored through the storage masters, without involving the end user.

In order to achieve QoS/SLA requirements in a storage Cloud, it is necessary to periodically monitor its storage resources, as done in the execution Cloud for VM. For this reason, in the Cloud@Home core structure of Figure 3, we introduce a specific storage resource monitor block. Since it monitors the state of a chunk provider, it is physically located and deployed and into each chunk provider composing the storage Cloud. The choice of replicating the resource monitor in both execution and storage Clouds is motivated by the fact that we want to implement two different, separated and independent services.

Cloud@Home, Interoperability, InterCloud, Brokering and Federation

Even if Cloud computing is still an emerging field, the need for moving out from the limitations of provisioning from a single provider is gaining growing interest both in academic and commercial research.

In Kirby, Dearle, Macdonald, & Fernandes,(2010), the authors move from a data center model (in which clusters of machines are dedicated to running Cloud infrastructure software) to an ad-hoc model for building Clouds. The proposed architecture aims at providing management components to harvest resources from nondedicated machines already in existence within an enterprise.

The need for intermediary components (Cloud coordinators, brokers, and exchange) is explained in R. Buyya, R. Ranjan, R. Calheiros, (2010) where the authors outline an architecture for a federated network of Clouds (the InterCloud). The evaluation is conducted on a simulated environment modeled through the CloudSim framework, showing significant improvements in average turnaround time and makespan in some test scenarios.

Another approach is to specify a unique, standard interface for Cloud interoperability.

The Open Cloud Computing Interface (OCCI) (OCCI Work Group, 2011) is the most authoritative and important attempt in such direction. OCCI is a family of specifications and standards for Cloud interfaces, geared towards interoperability and extensibility, by means of a definition of a *Core* model, and a suite of already developed documents, falling under two categories: *Renderings* and *Extensions*, the former aimed at definition and description of interaction methods and APIs (RESTful Rendering is done), the latter for extending the model with new resource types, attributes, and available actions (there's already an IaaS Extension). Extensibility, and especially dynamic behaviour, through reconfiguration and addition of new capabilities to instances at runtime, is enabled through use of OO mixins, following the rules laid out in the Core model. Semantic renderings (i.e. JSON, RDF/RDFa, etc..), Monitoring, Billing, advanced Reservation, and Negotiation/Agreement features are already in the works. Among other advantages, there are already tools for testing of compliant implementations, and solutions for easing development, like readymade ANTLR grammar definitions.

As discussed above, Cloud@Home addresses the Cloud interoperability issue by mainly defining a specific component in its infrastructure: the Cloud broker. The approach thus followed is through an intermediary, a broker, interposed among the Clouds to be federated. In the specific literature some authors used the term "brokering" to identify such approach. Altough such definition does not properly fit with the broker tasks, it is an acceptable way to identify the technique. Indeed, it can be considered as a particular interpretation of such term, which aims at redefining the meaning associated to the resource broker in distributed computing i.e., an entity that acts as an agent of resources. The resource broker would negotiate the resources need for an organization or project, ensuring that the necessary resources were available at the right time to complete the objectives. An example is the Grid resource broker, gathering

Grid resources for satisfying incoming requests of a specific Virtual Organization.

In Cloud@Home the Cloud broker mainly implements an interface to different Cloud provider infrastructures. A Cloud infrastructure that wants to interoperate with another infrastructure can use the service provided by Cloud@Home. In other words, a Cloud can reach all the Clouds supported by Cloud@Home by just interfacing to the latter. On the other side, when a new Cloud provider requests to interface to Cloud@Home a specific plug-in has to be developed in Cloud@Home in order to translate the source Cloud format into the destination Cloud format. In this case it can be based on an intermediate model (OCCI) which translates the input format, therefore translating the intermediate model into the target model.

This is a well known benefit of intermediate model: by decoupling the input and output formats to translate by an intermediate model with *i* inputs and *o* outputs, by translating a new *i+1* input format into the intermediate model format we automatically obtain the translataion of the *i+1*-th format into the *o* output formats. This contrasts to the *all-to-all* (*-*) approach of defining a specific interface for each Cloud that has to be federated. According to such perspective, our approach can be instead considered a *one-to-all* (1-*) technique.

However, the interface-interoperability is just an aspect of the problem, the first to be addressed but not the only one. Several other issues have to be considered such as: identity management, accounting, security, privacy, trustiness, SLA management, QoS, and billing, etc. Most of them are strictly related and partially overlapped. The best approach for solving such problems is to recur to a distributed solution coordinate by Cloud@Home. More specifically, this means that Cloud@Home has to implement a service for splitting incoming requests, according to their requirements, into *n* underlying Cloud requests that will be directly managed by the corresponding providers. This is an allocation problem aiming at optimally satis-fying the user requirements. Such task is instead assigned to the resource engine that queries the Cloud providers about resources and policies.

Cloud@Home, Internet and Future Internet

The fact that Internet is strategic on the success of Cloud is widely accepted, as well as the fact that further developments are required in order Cloud can continue its rise to the success. Several issues and challenges are requested by the Cloud community to the Future Internet, most of them, more or less, also by Cloud@Home.

The Cloud requirements and needs to Future Internet concern both lower and higher layers of the current Internet stack:

- At physical layer, adequate solutions are required for dealing with the increasing traffic generated by apps, services, and social networks, etc. mainly hosted in Cloud infrastructures, as also remarked in (Jacobson et al., 2009) by in depth analyses. Moreover, since Clouds are geographically distributed infrastructures and therefore Internet connected, the issue of migrating virtual machines or generic contexts can dramatically worsen the problem. This problem is particularly felt in Cloud@Home due to the contributing resources dynamics, characterized by frequent join-and-leave having a considerable impact on the migrations traffic.
- At network and transport layers, since the QoS is a topical Cloud concept, adequate techniques at network and transport layers (routing algorithms, data redundancy, replica management, and retransmission protocols, etc.) have to be implemented. Other aspects to take into account could be the ones related to green computing such as energy-efficient cloud networking and

low energy routing. The Cloud@home dynamic SLA and QoS management requires that such algorithms should also be dynamic, allowing adaptive changes to the required parameters in order to meet users' requirements

- At application layer,the focus is to provide facilities for supporting the service oriented computing paradigm. Some refer to the specific topic as Internet of Services, i.e. a multitude of connected IT services, which are offered, bought, and sold, used, repurposed, and composed by a worldwide network of service providers, consumers, aggregators, and brokers, resulting in a new way of offering, using, and organizing IT supported functionalities. The Web 2.0 (O'Reilly, 2005) is the Web characterization of the Internet of Service philosophy, aggregating simple Web services into more complex, composed Web services.

In the specifics of Cloud@Home, particular (virtual networking) mechanisms are required for aggregating and connecting the (virtual) resources. This aspect probably has to be faced at the application layer, by implementing overlay networks that have to ensure the connectivity among all the resources, also considering the dynamics of a physical node. Moreover, adequate virtualized network resource management mechanisms and tools have to be provided. This means that, if a node leaves the CloudHome infrastructure, all the resources hosted by the node have to be restarted or a replica has to be retrieved, and the corresponding endpoint references have to be assigned to the new resources, transparently, to the final user. The virtual cloud storage aspect also has to be taken into account in Cloud@Home.

Problems of identity management, trustiness and security among different domains are required in Cloud@Home, obviously with several implications in Internet-networking, especially at network, transport, and application layers (secure routing, threats and countermeasures, virtual network security, inter-Clouds, and Cloud computing support for mobile users), as also recognized in Villari, Latanicki, Massonet, Naqvi & Rochwerger(2010). Other cross layer aspects to develop are related to measurement-based network management such as traffic engineering, network anomaly detection and usage-based pricing.

Another Future Internet goal shared with Cloud@Home is the Internet of things. The idea of aggregating mobile devices and sensors in Cloud@Home could be a way for achieving such an interesting target, considered by the perspective of separating the infrastructure, composed of voluntarily contributing devices, by the service provisioning, in order to implement on-demand, context-aware computing, with possible application in ubiquitous and pervasive computing (smart cities, smart living, smart energy, smart health, and smart enterprises, smart transportation, smart manufacturing, etc.).

Application Scenarios

Several possible application scenarios can be imagined for Cloud@Home:

- **Research centers, public administrations, and communities:** the Volunteer computing inspiration of Cloud@Home provides means for the creation of open, interoperable Clouds for supporting scientific purposes, overcoming the portability and compatibility problems highlighted by the @home projects. Similar benefits could be experienced in public administrations and open communities (social network, peer-to-peer, and gaming, etc). Through Cloud@Home it could be possible to implement resources and services management policies with QoS requirements (characterizing the scientific project importance) and specifications (QoS classification of resources and services available).

A new deal for Volunteer computing, since this latter does not take into consideration QoS, following a best effort approach.

- **Enterprises:** planting a Cloud@Home computing infrastructure in business-commercial environments can bring considerable benefits, especially in small and medium but also in big enterprises. It could be possible to implement its own data center with local, existing, and off the shelf resources: usually in every enterprise there exists a capital of stand-alone computing resources dedicated to a specific task (office automation, monitoring, designing. and so on). Since such resources are only (partially) used in office hours, with the Internet connecting them it becomes altogether possible to build up a Cloud@Home data center, in which allocate shared services (web server, file server, archive, and database, etc) without any compatibility constraints or problems. The interoperability among Clouds allows computing resources to be purchased from commercial Cloud providers if needed or, otherwise, to sell the local Cloud computing resources to the same or different providers. This allows to reduce and optimize business costs according to QoS/SLA policies, improving performances and reliability. For example, this paradigm allows to deal with peaks or burst of workload: data centers could be sized for managing the medium case and worst cases (peaks) could be managed by buying computing resources from Cloud providers. Moreover, Cloud@Home drives towards a resources rationalization: all the business processes can be securely managed by web, allocating resources and services where needed. In particular this fact can improve marketing and trading (E-commerce) by making a lot of customizable services available to sellers and customers. The interoperability could also

point out another scenario, in which private companies buy computing resources in order to resell them (subcontractors).

- **Ad-hoc networks, wireless sensor networks, home automation:** the Cloud computing approach, in which both software and computing resources are owned and managed by service providers, eases the programmers' efforts in facing the device heterogeneity problems. Mobile application designers should start to consider that their applications, besides to be usable on a small device, will need to interact with the Cloud. Service discovery, brokering, and reliability are important issues, and services are usually designed to interoperate (The Programmable Web, 2011). In order to consider the arising consequences related to the access of mobile users to service-oriented grid architecture, researchers have proposed new concepts such as a mobile dynamic virtual organization (Waldburger & Stiller, 2006). New distributed infrastructures have been designed to facilitate the extension of Clouds to the wireless edge of the Internet. Among them, the Mobile Service Clouds enable dynamic instantiation, composition, configuration, and reconfiguration of services in an overlay network to support mobile computing (Samimi, McKinley, & Sadjadi, 2006). A still open research issue is whether or not a mobile device should be considered a service provider of the Cloud itself. The use of modern mobile terminals such as smartphones not just as Web service requesters, but also as mobile hosts that can themselves offer services in a true mobile peer-to-peer setting is also discussed in Srirama, Jarke, & Prinz (2006). Context aware operations involving control and monitoring, data sharing, synchronization, etc, could be implemented and exposed as Cloud@Home Web services involving wireless and

Bluetooth devices, laptop, Ipod, cellphone, household appliances, and so on. Cloud@ Home could be a way for implementing Ubiquitous and Pervasive computing: many computational devices and systems can be engaged simultaneously for performing ordinary activities, and may not necessarily be aware that they are doing so.

DISCUSSION AND CONCLUSION

The main innovations of Cloud@Home with regard to the existing Cloud paradigm are the volunteer computing contribution and interoperability. Most of Cloud middleware introduced above, both commercial and open source, mainly implement infrastructure providers, but none of them introduce volunteer contribution aspects, and only some of them (i.e. RESERVOIR) partially face the issue of interoperability, particularly felt in Cloud@Home.

Thus, Cloud@Home is the first attempt in merging Volunteer and Cloud computing paradigms. The benefits of such a mix result in both commercial and non-commercial environments: in commercial context a new, open computing utility market can be established, in which both single users and data-centers or infrastructure providers can sell or buy their resources; in non-commercial context, anyone can provide its resources and services for supporting a specific project, joining the community, the university, the organization, and the public administration, etc., promoting the project.

With regards to the industrial/commercial environment, one of the main source of costs and complexity for companies is related to expanding, tuning, and optimizing the hardware resources in order to effectively satisfy high demand, domain-specific technical software and ensure adequate productivity levels.

The Cloud@Home technology will enable companies to adequately organize their comput-

ing resources, which are sometimes distributed over several sites, to meet the demands of the mentioned software.

Through its volunteer approach, Cloud@ Home allows a company to aggregate their sites into a federation, to which each individual site can voluntarily contribute with its available and unused hardware resources.

In open contexts a possible scenario that magnifies the Cloud@Home features and its volunteer philosophy can be specified in academic applications.

Suppose that several universities or, in general, research institutions worldwide need to collaborate on a scientific project, for which a huge amount of hardware resources is required.

Suppose also that each institution owns a datacenter, made up of heterogeneous computing resources, each having a different level of utilization (depending on their geographic coordinates, during a given hour of the day some datacenters may be underexploited in comparison to others).

Cloud@Home will provide the institutions with tools to build up a federation of datacenters acting as a Cloud broker, where each partner can voluntarily contribute to the project with its own available (i.e., not utilized) computing resources.

Pushing the volunteer approach to its limits, one can also imagine letting private users's computing resources (mainly desktop computers) to be federated and, then, shared for each other's needs; Cloud@Home is not intend to address this last scenario.

Independently of the scenario, the basic infrastructure (volunteer resources) is made up of intermittently-available and volatile computing resources over fairly unstable networks, and so the implementation of a federation is a particularly challenging problem.

In the discussed scenarios, the rationale behind the build up of a federation is that such a solution will be efficient from a cost perspective (when needed, resources can be "borrowed" from the federation, thus avoiding the need to purchase them from outside) and sufficiently reliable, as mechanisms for guaranteeing the QoS will also be implemented.

Interoperability issues are strictly connected to the idea of volunteer Cloud, since as many Clouds can exist as the necessity of allowing such Clouds to interoperate grows. By Cloud@Home, each (commercial or non-commercial) organization that builds its own Cloud can easily add new resources, that can be provided by the other organizations for free or by charge. With regard to interoperability, a significant problem in the Cloud context is standardization. In Cloud@Home we try to provide a solution to this problem by specifying a Cloud broker, that will implement complex tasks such as request format translation and Cloud discovery, mainly following a totally distributed approach.

From a technical point of view, the Cloud@Home paradigm can also be considered as an extension of Volunteer Desktop Grids in which the light weight Desktop Grid Clients are replaced with still light weight Cloud computing clients that provide Virtual Machine functionality. This process is favoured by the growth of the desktop computers systems at home and in small companies. The processing capacity is growing, today mainly by adding cores, the memory is growing, already several Gbytes per computer, and not far from having Tbyte hard disks in regular use. In addition, the networking capacity is growing, with a move to broadband and cable, and fiber-to-the-home steadily growing. The larger systems allow for larger, more complex Desktop Clients. Instead of small computational sand boxes, VMs could now be used. Cloud@Home will lead this development.

Another important and innovative aspect of Cloud@Home with regard to Volunteer computing is the introduction of the concept of QoS in systems that traditionally are best effort. This aspect concerns the more general topic of QoS/SLA, business models and credit systems.

The feasibility of the Cloud@Home is strongly related to the progress of the Internet. In order to face the problem of transferring great amount of data, referring to virtual machine or generic context migrations, adequate bandwidth is required. The network management is another challenge of Cloud@Home for Future Internet. It is necessary to ensure the reachability of the resources in virtual contexts, managing problems of data security and reliability, and also taking into account that a contributing resource can join and leave asynchronously, as required by its owners, and/or that its context can migrate transparently to the final Cloud user that has to be always able to interact with this.

FUTURE RESEARCH DIRECTIONS

Cloud@Home is the first step toward a new computing paradigm that can actively involve

- Any *resource type* (including desktops, laptops, farms, clusters, and data centers, network-attached storage, storage or system area networks, and sensor networks, mobile devices, or the Internet of Things);
- All known and emerging *distributed paradigms* (including Cloud, grid, peer-to-peer, or volunteer computing); and
- *Stakeholders* of any kind (business, academic, community, or public).

This requires further efforts, such as a synergy between projects aimed at implementing open communication infrastructures as for example Commotion (https://tech.chambana.net/projects/commotion) and Netsukuku (http://netsukuku.freaknet.org).

The authors are currently working on the design and development of a framework for achieving the Cloud@Home goals, adopting an aspect-oriented approach and following an agile software development process. They hope to define a specific Cloud software development process.

ADDITIONAL READING

Other interesting references mainly related to volunteer Clouds at large are suggested in the following.

In (Chandra & Weissman, 2009) the authors present the idea of leveraging volunteer resources to build a form of dispersed Clouds, or "nebulas", as they call them. Those nebulas are not intended to be general purpose, but to complement the offering of traditional homogeneous Clouds in some areas where a more flexible, less guaranteed approach can be beneficial, like in testing environments or in application where data are intrinsically dispersed and centralizing them would be costly. Some requirements and possible solutions are presented. BoincVM (Segal et al., 2009), is an integrated Cloud computing platform that can be used to harness volunteer computing resources such as laptops, desk- tops and server farms, for computing CPU intensive scientific applications. It leverages on existing technologies i.e., the BOINC platform and VirtualBox along with some projects currently under development: VMWrapper, VM-Controller and CernVM. Thus, it is a kind of volunteer-on-Cloud approach, whereas C@H can be classified as a Cloud-on-volunteer model.

In (Andrzejak, Kondo, & Anderson, 2010) the authors investigate how a mixture of dedicated (and so highly available) hosts and non-dedicated (and so highly volatile) hosts can be used to provision a processing tier of a large-scale Web service. They propose an operational model that guarantees long-term availability despite of host churn, by ranking non-dedicated hosts according to their availability behavior. They also study the tradeoff between a larger share of dedicated hosts vs. higher migration rate in terms of costs and SLA objectives. Through experimental simulation results they demonstrate that the technique is effective in finding a suitable balance between costs and service quality.

An approach that can be categorized as volunteer Cloud is P2P Cloud. It has been proposed in several papers as the ones cited above, and particularly in storage Cloud contexts. An interesting implementation of such idea is proposed in (Graffi et al., 2010). In particular, this work specifically focuses on the peer reliability, proposing a distributed mechanism in order to en- able churn resistant reliable services that allows to reserve, to monitor and to use resources provided by the unreliable P2P system and maintains long- term resource reservations through controlled redundant resource provision. The evaluation results obtained through simulation show that using KAD measurements on the prediction of the lifetime of peers allows for 100% successful reservations under churn with very low traffic overhead.

REFERENCES

Amazon Inc. (2011), *Amazon Web Services, Amazon Corporation Inc*, Retrieved from: http://aws.amazon.com

Anderson, C. (2011). *The Long Tail: How Endless Choice Is Creating Unlimited Demand*. New York, NY: Random House Business Books.

Anderson, D. P., & Fedak, G. (2006). The computational and storage potential of volunteer computing. In *CCGRID '06* (pp. 73–80). Washington, DC: IEEE Computer Society.

Andrzejak, A., Kondo, D., & Anderson, D. (2010), Exploiting non-dedicated resources for cloud computing, in: *Network Operations and Management Symposium (NOMS* (pp. 341–348). doi:10.1109/NOMS.2010.5488488.

Apache Software Foundation. (2011). *The Apache Hadoop Project* Retrieved from: http://www.hadoop.apache.org

Baker, S. (2008), Google and the Wisdom of Clouds. *BusinessWeek* Retrieved from: http://www.businessweek.com/magazine/content/07 52/b4064048925836.htm

Buyya, R., Ranjan, R., & Calheiros, R. (2010). Intercloud: Utility-oriented federa- tion of cloud computing environments for scaling of application services. In *Algorithms and Architectures for Parallel Processing* (pp. 13–31). New York, NY: Springer. doi:10.1007/978-3-642-13119-6_2

Chandra, A., & Weissman, J. (2009), Nebulas: using distributed voluntary resources to build Clouds, in: *Proceedings of the 2009 conference on Hot topics in cloud computing*, (p 2) Berkley, CA: USENIX Association

Cisco Inc. (2011). *Cisco Cloud Computing* Retrieved from: http://www.cisco.com/en/US/netsol/ns976/index.html

Dell Inc. (2011), *Dell cloud computing solutions* http://www.dell.com/cloudcomputing

Enomaly Inc. (2011), *Enomaly Elastic Computing Platform (ECP)* Retrieved from: http://www.enomaly.com/

Fedak, G., Germain, C., Neri, V., & Cappello, F. (2001): Xtremweb: a generic global computing system. Cluster Computing and the Grid, 2001. In *Proceedings. First IEEE/ACM International Symposium* (pp. 582–587) Washington, DC: IEEE Press

10gen (2011) *10gen PAAS* Retrieved from: www.10gen.com

Ghemawat, S., Gobioff, H., Leung, S.T. The Google File System. *SIGOPS Oper. Syst. Rev. 37*(5) 29–43

Google Inc. (2011), *Google app engine* Retrieved from: http://code.google.com/appengine/

Graffi, K., Stingl, D., Gross, C., Nguyen, H., & Kovacevic, A. Steinmetz, R. (2010), Towards a p2p cloud: Reliable resource reservations in un- reliable p2p systems, In: *Parallel and Distributed Systems (ICPADS), IEEE 16th International Conference* (pp. 27–34)doi:10.1109/ICPADS.2010.34.

HP. Intel, Yahoo! (2011), *Open Cirrus Open Cloud Computing Research Testbed* Retrieved from: https://opencirrus.org/

Inc, I. B. M. (2011), *IBM Cloud* Retrieved from: http://www.ibm.com/ibm/cloud/

Jacobson, V., Smetters, D. K., Thornton, J. D., Plass, M. F., Briggs, N. H., & Braynard, R. L. (2009), Networking named content. In: *Proceedings of the 5th international conference on Emerging networking experiments and technologies.* (pp. 1–12)., New York, NY: ACM, http://doi.acm.org/10.1145/1658939.1658941

Kirby, G., Dearle, A., Macdonald, A., & Fernandes, A. (2010). *An Approach to Ad hoc Cloud Computing.* St. Andrews, Scotland: University of St Andrews.

Martin, R. (2007), The Red Shift Theory. *InformationWeek* Retrieved from: http://www.informationweek.com/news/hardware/showArticle.jhtml?articleID=201800873

MeSsAGE Lab-Monash eScience and Grid Engineering Laboratory (2011), *Nimrod/G* Retrieved from: http://www.messagelab.monash.edu.au/NimrodG

Microsoft Inc. (2011), *Azure services platform* Retrieved from: http://www.microsoft.com/cloud/

Nurmi, D., Wolski, R., Grzegorczyk, C., Obertelli, G., Soman, S., Youseff, L., & Zagorodnov, D. (2008), The eucalyptus open-source cloud-computing system. In: *Proceedings of Cloud Computing and Its Applications (October 2008)*, Retrieved from: http://eucalyptus.cs.ucsb.edu/wiki/Presentations

OCCI Work Group. (2011), *The Open Cloud Computing Interface* Retrieved from: http://occi-wg.org/

OpenQRM Developer Community. (2011), *openQRM open-source Data-center management platform* Retrieved from: http://www.openQRM.com

ORACLE Inc. (2011), *ORACLE Cloud Computing* Retrieved from: http://www.oracle.com/us/technologies/cloud/index.htm

Samimi, F. A., McKinley, P. K., & Sadjadi, S. M. (2006). Mobile service clouds: A self-managing infrastructure for autonomic mobile computing services. In *LCNS 3996* (pp. 130–141). Berlin, Germany: Springer-Verlang.

Segal, B., Buncic, P., Quintas, D., Gonzalez, D., Harutyunyan, A., Rantala, J., & Weir, D. (2009). Building a volunteer Cloud. In *Conferencia Latinoamericana de Computacion de Alto Rendimiento*. CLCAR.

Srirama, S. N., Jarke, M., & Prinz, W. (2006), Mobile web service provisioning. In: *AICT-ICIW '06: Proceedings of the Advanced Int'l Conference on Telecommunications and Int'l Conference on Internet and Web Applications and Services*. (p. 120) Washington, DC: IEEE Computer Society

The Openstack Community. (2011), *OpenStack Cloud Software: open source software for building private and public clouds*. Retrieved from: http://www.openstack.org/

The Programmable Web. (2011) Retrieved from: http://www.programmableweb.com

The RESERVOIR Consortium. (2011), *RESERVOIR Project* Retrieved from: www.reservoir-fp7.eu/

Tim O'Reilly. (2006), *What is WEB 2.0* Retrieved from: http://www.oreillynet.com/pub/a/oreilly/tim/news/2005/09/30/what-is-web-20.html

Tusa, F., Paone, M., Villari, M., & Puliafito, A. (2010), Clever: A cloud-enabled virtual environment. In: Computers and Communications (ISCC), 2010 IEEE Symposium on. pp. 477–482

Universidad Complutense de Madrid. (2011), *Distributed Systems Architecture Research Group: OpenNEbula Project* Retrieved from: http://www.opennebula.org/

University Masaryk of Chicago - University of Florida - Purdue University. (2011), *Nimbus – Stratus – Wispy - Kupa Projects* Retreived from: http://workspace.globus.org/clouds/nimbus.html/, http://www.rcac.purdue.edu/teragrid/resources/#wispy, http://www.acis.ufl.edu/vws/, http://meta.cesnet.cz/cms/opencms/en/docs/clouds

Villari, M., Latanicki, J., Massonet, P., & Naqvi, S. Rochwerger, B. (2010), Scalable Cloud Defenses For Detection, Analysis and Mitigation Of DDOS Attacks, chap. 13, pp. 127–137. FIA book, IOS Press, towards the future internet - emerging trends from european research 2010 edn.

VMWare Inc. (2011), *Vmware vcloud* Retrieved from: http://www.vmware.com/products/vcloud/

Waldburger, M., & Stiller, B. (2006) Toward the mobile grid: service provisioning in a mobile dynamic virtual organization. In: *IEEE International Conference on Computer Systems and Applications*. (pp. 579–583) Washington, DC: IEEE Press

Wang, L., Tao, J., Kunze, M., Castellanos, A. C., Kramer, D., & Karl, W. (2008). Scientific Cloud Computing: Early Definition and Experience. In *HPCC '08* (pp. 825–830). Washington, DC: IEEE Computer Society. doi:10.1109/HPCC.2008.38

Zadok, E., Iyer, R., Joukov, N., Sivathanu, G., & Wright, C. P. (2006). On incremental file system development. *ACM Transactions on Storage, 2*(2), 161–196. doi:10.1145/1149976.1149979

Chapter 6
Cloud Monitoring

Peer Hasselmeyer
NEC Laboratories Europe, Germany

Gregory Katsaros
National Technical University of Athens, Greece

Bastian Koller
High Performance Computing Centre Stuttgart, Germany

Philipp Wieder
Gesellschaft fuer wissenschaftliche Datenverarbeitung mbH Goettingen, Germany

ABSTRACT

The management of the entire service landscape comprising a Cloud environment is a complex and challenging venture. There, one task of utmost importance, is the generation and processing of information about the state, health, and performance of the various services and IT components, something which is generally referred to as monitoring. Such information is the foundation for proper assessment and management of the whole Cloud. This chapter pursues two objectives: first, to provide an overview of monitoring in Cloud environments and, second, to propose a solution for interoperable and vendor-independent Cloud monitoring. Along the way, the authors motivate the necessity of monitoring at the different levels of Cloud infrastructures, introduce selected state-of-the-art, and extract requirements for Cloud monitoring. Based on these requirements, the following sections depict a Cloud monitoring solution and describe current developments towards interoperable, open, and extensible Cloud monitoring frameworks.

INTRODUCTION

Network and systems management has been an important topic for data center and communication service providers for decades. Appropriate management does not only ensure continued service availability and superior quality levels; it can also be a competitive advantage ensuring a quick response to customer requests and reduced costs for operations.

Management is typically separated into the two functional areas of monitoring and control. Monitoring is concerned with taking measurements of various parameters of the infrastructure,

DOI: 10.4018/978-1-4666-1631-8.ch006

Copyright © 2012, IGI Global. Copying or distributing in print or electronic forms without written permission of IGI Global is prohibited.

Figure 1. A typical service provisioning value chain

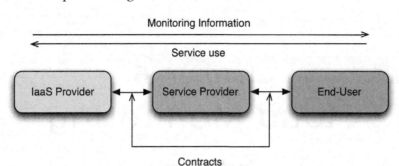

while control is about adjusting the infrastructure's configuration. Monitoring provides the information needed to reach appropriate control decisions. Monitoring is therefore essential to properly control the infrastructure.

Monitoring is typically done by adding instrumentation to the hardware and software infrastructure. The instrumentation provides measurements that relate to key performance indicators (KPIs) of the operator's systems. Proper management requires information from the complete set of components involved in service delivery, usually including hardware such as servers, network, and storage, and software such as operating system, middleware, and applications. Measurements include diverse metrics such as CPU utilization, network bandwidth consumption, transaction throughput, and the number of active users. From the collected information, the current state of the infrastructure can be assessed and, ideally, future requirements and utilization can be predicted in order to proactively adjust the available resources and their configurations to meet future demand.

Cloud computing has recently received a lot of attention as a new paradigm for the use of computational power, electronic services, and storage resources. In such scenarios, an IaaS provider has a contract with a service provider while the service provider in turn has a contract with an end-user, who can be private or an enterprise (Figure 1). The services of the service provider are supported by the infrastructure from the IaaS provider. The

quality of service offered by the service provider depends on the quality of service that the IaaS provider supports. The service provider therefore relies on the infrastructure provider, and both parties need adequate monitoring to ensure the required service levels.

As initially stated, monitoring is the basis for resource control which in turn is required to ensure proper operation of the infrastructure in order to ensure adequate service provisioning. The need for monitoring is not shrinking in the Cloud. In fact, it becomes even more important as performance parameters become less predictable with the use of shared, virtualized resources. Ideally, the Cloud infrastructure provides the same information as local installations do, combined with the ease of use of Clouds.

Although the acquisition, use, and decommission of virtual machines are well addressed by commercial providers and open-source software packages, monitoring of the rented Cloud infrastructure is not as advanced as their deployment. Some basic capabilities are offered, but they are usually much more limited than what is commonly available on locally operated hardware. In particular, the capabilities are mainly geared towards the need of the Cloud operator, not the Cloud users.

The focus of IaaS providers is on keeping their systems running at an operating point that maximizes their profits. They are therefore only interested in low-level information about the health of their physical infrastructure. In addition, they need information about the resource usage of customers' virtual resources, mainly for billing purposes but also to see how the Virtual Machines behave, and to evaluate their performance and quality on their system. IaaS customers, on the other hand, need low-level information about their virtual infrastructure as well as all the software that is running on top of it. It is obvious that in most cases there is little overlap of the sets of information needed by providers and customers. Only some low-level measurements of virtual infrastructure parameters are shared. Only these parts are made available by Cloud providers to their customers. This is clearly not enough to get a complete overview of the state of applications and services deployed in the Cloud. Any additional information needed by customers must be dealt with by customers themselves.

A partial solution to the problem is to install traditional monitoring and management software onto virtual machine images. Although this is a viable option and has the advantage of being able to reuse existing management software, this solution is very conservative and does not exploit the benefits of the Cloud paradigm. In a Cloud-inspired system, monitoring would be outsourced to the provider or another specialized third party in order to relieve the customer from the burden of deploying and maintaining their own monitoring solution. After all, getting rid of configuration burdens was one of the reasons to use the Cloud in the first place. Currently, every customer has to design, test, install, and maintain his own solution. In an ideal Cloud system, an optimized solution would be deployed and configured only once to be then used by all customers.

Orthogonal to the desire of improved monitoring capabilities is the rising need of monitoring solutions that cover Cloud slices spanning multiple independent Cloud providers. As Cloud providers offer different features, different quality-of-service levels, and different pricing strategies, customers want to mix and match those parts of the various Cloud offerings that fulfill their requirements best. Holistic monitoring spanning all pieces of the Cloud federation is then becoming a must.

At present, federated Cloud monitoring still lies far in the future. The major obstacle to achieving this is the lack of interoperability. All Cloud providers only support their own proprietary monitoring systems. Exchanging monitoring information is therefore tedious if not economically impossible. While deployment functions are quickly converging towards de jure or de facto standards, there is no such movement in sight in the monitoring domain.

Still, federated monitoring is not a new field. There has been substantial work on this topic in the Grid community. As the Grid is a federated system, by design requiring information from all participating sites, federated monitoring is a necessity in such systems. The Cloud community can therefore learn from the experiences in the Grid domain. Nevertheless, transfer of solutions has to be well thought through as most Grid solutions assume far-reaching access to information of remote sites. Such access is reasonable for academic institutions but not feasible in commercial deployments as certain information, e.g. on resource utilization, is deemed a trade secret (Hasselmeyer, 2007).

This book chapter presents an overview of the current state of Cloud monitoring solutions. It points out areas of improvement which would bring Cloud monitoring to the same level of sophistication that the Cloud workload management technologies have already reached. Last but not least, potential solutions are introduced and their merits are discussed.

BACKGROUND

This section provides an overview of the available monitoring functions for Cloud infrastructures. It is non-comprehensive, but it provides selected background information for different kinds of monitoring solutions that are applicable for Clouds. This chapter differentiates between three different categories: (i) monitoring solutions tailored for Clouds, (ii) monitoring solutions incorporated into hypervisor management software, and (iii) Grid monitoring solutions potentially applicable to Clouds. This section is considered to be representative of the current state of the art in the Cloud monitoring landscape.

A fourth category would include general monitoring frameworks that are used for hardware-level, OS-level, or service-level monitoring. Well-known representatives are, for example, Ganglia (http://ganglia.sourceforge.net/), Nagios (http://www.nagios.org/), Zabbix (http://www.zabbix.com/), or Zenoss (http://community.zenoss.org/index.jspa). Such frameworks often serve as 'sensors' providing unfiltered and un-aggregated data about services and infrastructure. As they do not directly deliver Cloud-related monitoring the generic monitoring solutions are not covered here, even though Cloud coverage is increasing through extensions and commercial offers built upon these frameworks, such as Zenoss Service Dynamics (http://www.zenoss.com/).

Cloud Monitoring

Amazon Web Services (AWS; http://aws.amazon.com/) are probably the most popular set of Cloud services. AWS allow customers to acquire compute and storage resources following the pay-as-you-go usage model. Some of the services, including computation, Elastic Compute Cloud (EC2; http://aws.amazon.com/ec2), and block storage, Elastic Block Storage (EBS; http://aws.amazon.com/ebs/), can be monitored using the CloudWatch service (http://aws.amazon.com/cloudwatch/). It can be used through its web interface or programmatically via an API.

The monitored services send various metrics to CloudWatch. Monitoring data provided by the storage system EBS consists of the number of bytes read/written, the number of read/write requests, the aggregated time needed to execute all read/write requests, the idle time of the storage, and the number of pending requests. All metrics are supplied every five minutes.

The monitoring data provided by EC2 consists of the CPU utilization, the number of bytes read from/written to disk, the number of disk read/write operations, and the number of bytes received from/sent to the network. Data can be provided in five-minute as well as in one-minute intervals, with the more detailed monitoring generating additional costs.

Some of the other services that Amazon is offering provide their own, specific metrics. These services include the Relational Database Service (RDS), the Auto Scaling service, and the Elastic Load Balancing service. Furthermore, Amazon has recently introduced an API that allows user-supplied applications to send arbitrary kinds of measurements to CloudWatch. This application-specific information is processed just like other CloudWatch monitoring information and can therefore be accessed via the aforementioned interfaces either programmatically or via the web interface.

With the growing commercial success of Cloud offerings, the number of monitoring solutions also increases. Looking at one major competitor of AWS, Windows Azure (http://www.microsoft.com/windowsazure/), a variety of monitoring solutions can be seen. This includes the Azure Diagnostics Manager (http://www.cerebrata.com/Products/AzureDiagnosticsManager/Default.aspx), which provides a management console for Azure-based infrastructures and applications and which targets administrators and application developers. Another example is the Subscription Manager for Azure (http://communities.quest.com/docs/DOC-9911) that allows users and Cloud administrators to assess the utilization of their Azure resources. Similar monitoring tools exist for other Cloud providers.

CloudStatus (http://www.hyperic.com/products/cloud-status-monitoring), though, pursues a different approach. Based on Hyperic HQ, a monitoring and management tool for web-based infrastructures, CloudStatus provides a means to monitor the performance and health of a variety of Cloud services, including AWS and Google App Engine services. At the time of writing (end-2011), only a limited selection of services is supported, but others are likely to be included in the future. CloudStatus offers a vendor-independent solution and represents a generic approach towards monitoring of Clouds with a coarse granularity.

Hypervisor Management

Virtualization solutions are the foundation of all IaaS offerings. Data centers adopting virtualization need proper management for both the physical and the virtual domains. All virtualization platforms are therefore complemented by appropriate management systems. For example, VMware offers vCenter (Soundararaja & Govil, 2010), Citrix offers XenCenter (http://community.citrix.com/xencenter), and Xen-enabled servers can be managed using one of many solutions, including Xen Admin (http://xen-admin.de/) and Ganeti (http://code.google.com/p/ganeti/).

All these systems primarily focus on the management of the lifecycle of virtual machines (VMs). They contain functions for creating, starting, stopping, migrating, cloning, and deleting VMs. Assignment of VMs to physical resources, including VM migration and high availability, is also supported. To ensure proper VM management, knowledge of the underlying physical resources is needed. VM management systems therefore include components for monitoring physical resources, including CPU, memory, and storage.

The management tools are aimed primarily at data center operators. Although they support managing the virtual machines of multiple users, only few support management by multiple administrators. VMware's vCenter is an exception as it supports multiple users and fine-grained access control. It allows assigning management privileges

to users, and restricting access to certain VMs and certain functions. This multi-tenant function in conjunction with the possibility to cluster multiple installations allows the use of vCenter in Cloud environments. Citrix is working on similar functions with its Self-Service Manager.

The monitoring features of all the mentioned tools are restricted to physical and virtual machine parameters. They include mainly CPU utilization, memory utilization, disk utilization, and network utilization. Application-specific monitoring parameters or user-defined metrics are not supported.

Grid Monitoring

Although there are many differences, Grid computing pursues a similar target as Cloud computing: the provisioning of resources on demand. Monitoring has been an active area of research in the Grid community for quite some time as this forms the basis of workload management. It is therefore instructive to look at the solutions developed by that community.

A large number of different monitoring solutions have been developed (Zanikolas, & Sakellariou, 2005). They offer different capabilities and features, sometimes overlapping, sometimes complementary. Being solutions for Grids, they are able to integrate monitoring information originating from multiple sites into a single view. Many solutions can work with arbitrary data spanning compute resources, the network, applications, and others. For completeness, two important examples are briefly introduced.

First, the Globus Monitoring and Discovery Service (Globus MDS) (Schopf et al., 2006) can be used with arbitrary information supplied by arbitrary sources formatted according to the XML. Arbitrary structures of information providers and aggregators can be set up to fulfill the needs of different user communities. Access to monitoring information is provided directly at the information provider as well as in cached and aggregated form at index services.

Another important example is the Grid Monitoring Architecture (GMA) as defined by the Open Grid Forum (OGF) (Tierney et al., 2002). The document describes an architectural blueprint which can be realized with different technologies and setups. The architecture contains a directory service which allows producers and consumers of monitoring information to find each other. The actual monitoring information is then exchanged directly between the two entities. Intermediaries that aggregate information are possible.

While the topic of monitoring in Grids is fairly old and there are numerous scientific publications dealing with this field, to the section lists a select few that were considered interesting. In (Andreozzi et al., 2003) GridICE is introduced as a centralized system that periodically queries Grid nodes for extracting information. For real-time job execution monitoring, a very interesting monitoring system is presented in (Colling et al., 2010) which has a stable performance even with a large number of requests.

The main problem of transferring Grid monitoring solutions to the Cloud space is that Grid monitoring systems were designed with assumptions different from those of Clouds. A main tenet of Grids is the collaboration between different provider and user sites. As such, the monitoring systems' main focus is on integrating monitoring information from multiple sites into a single monitoring system. For individual Clouds, this functionality is not needed. For federated Clouds, this functionality is required and the concepts and architectures developed by the Grid community, e.g. the Grid Monitoring Architecture, can be transferred to the federated Cloud domain.

A major obstacle to using Grid monitoring systems in Cloud environments is that sharing of information in Grids is mainly a given and not seen as a security breach as it would be in Cloud environments. Access rights to monitoring information in Grids do only sometimes exist; and if they exist, they usually have coarse granularity (e.g., clusters) and are mainly separated by virtual organizations, not by individuals. In particular, information about the status of the resources operated by a Grid provider is routinely handed out to users of the Grid. Cloud providers treat such information as corporate secrets and reluctant to provide this information to customers (Hasselmeyer, 2007).

Another difference between Grids and Clouds is the common assumption in Grids that compute resources are handed out in a non-virtualized way. Associated with that approach is that monitoring information is related to physical hosts and comes with the granularity of physical machines, not virtual machines. In Clouds, monitoring information on physical hosts is only interesting to resource providers, not to customers.

Furthermore, a main purpose of many Grid monitoring systems is to enhance decisions on job scheduling. The Grid scheduler tries to send jobs to a Grid site that it considers optimal with respect to some criteria, including available hardware resources and installed software. The decision on where to place a particular VM inside a single Cloud is always the decision of the particular Cloud provider. The user's decision on which Cloud to use depends on the criteria the individual user is selecting, usually including performance, price and reputation. Availability of resources is always assumed and is therefore not an issue.

RELATED SCIENTIFIC CONTRIBUTIONS

Besides the APIs, systems and services presented here for Cloud, Hypervisor, and Grid monitoring, there are several research efforts which are worth mentioning. Lindner et al. (2010) present a complete Cloud-enabled framework that incorporates information management, monitoring, accounting and billing. While the authors provide a good analysis of the requirements for monitoring in Cloud environments, the paper lacks in implementation details and performance measurements.

Katsaros, Kübert, and Gallizo (2011) introduce an IaaS monitoring mechanism that is based on available systems like Nagios and libvirt. They also highlight the need for high level information management in Clouds and the definition of a common data model. The architecture of the monitoring solution designed and implemented in the RESERVOIR project is presented in Clayman, et al. (2010). The proposed framework (called "Lattice") offers libraries and tools through which one could build its own monitoring system. It is also stated that the solution could serve monitoring of federated service Clouds.

A Summary of Current Cloud Monitoring Solutions

In general, existing monitoring solutions for Clouds feature particular vendors, particular services, or particular roles. What is missing is a vendor-independent solution that allows interoperation between different Cloud infrastructures and eases the migration of applications and services. The section that follows investigates and analyzes the requirements for such a monitoring solution and sketches a framework that fulfills these requirements and provides an interoperable monitoring for Cloud infrastructures. In addition, it will present how those requirements are being addressed by the current research initiatives that are active in Europe and finally discuss the future steps towards the realization of our proposal.

A PROPOSAL FOR MONITORING OF CLOUD INFRASTRUCTURES

Monitoring systems have been in operation for decades. It is therefore not directly obvious, why Cloud computing warrants a fresh look at monitoring. Examining the main differences between Cloud computing and preceding computing paradigms reveals a number of areas that have so far not been prime objectives for develop-

ing monitoring systems. This chapter highlights the main differences of Cloud computing when compared to previous computing paradigms and shows their impact on monitoring systems. Appropriate requirements on monitoring systems are then derived.

Even though a variety of Cloud monitoring offerings already exists (see also the related section on Cloud Monitoring in the Background subchapter), they often provide only very limited capabilities in terms of monitored parameters. In particular, parameters are often restricted to particular levels of the XaaS family. Depending on which level is chosen, monitoring data may be on a more or less abstract level. The selection of the abstraction level may or may not fit the purposes of the Cloud customer.

With the advent of Cloud computing, the evolution from single Cloud offerings to federated Clouds has progressed but requires enhanced mechanisms in the management of Cloud services, including a proper monitoring adapted to the needs of end users.

Among the main concerns of Cloud customers is the danger of vendor lock-in. Currently, there are no generally accepted standards for accessing Cloud resources, although Amazon's EC2 interface is used by other Cloud software as well and the Open Cloud Computing Interface (OCCI) (Nyren, Edmonds, Papaspyrou, & Metsch, 2011) is implemented in a number of software products. When it comes to monitoring, a standard way to interact with the monitoring system is similarly desired. The state of standardization of monitoring systems is even less mature than the compute, storage, and networking interfaces. The danger of vendor-lock-in is therefore even more pronounced for monitoring systems than it is for VM management systems.

Aggregated monitoring is a topic of high priority as current developments are putting a focus on federated Clouds, but also on a hybrid use of grids/HPC and Clouds (so-called HPC Clouds). With this, the assumption of having either a single monitoring data source or at least all monitoring data provided in the same format is no more valid.

Current activities such as the BonFIRE and the OPTIMIS projects are dealing with some of the mentioned issues. Within BonFIRE, five different sites from all over Europe operated by Hewlett Packard, the University of Edinburgh, the University of Stuttgart, IBBT and INRIA are combined to provide a European Cloud test-bed for Cloud experiments. The main challenge is to bring (at least) five heterogeneous resource/Cloud types together and to bundle them in a way that hides the heterogeneity, making the data provided to end users homogeneous. Further complexity is introduced by the requirement to not only include computing resources in the monitoring, but the network as well.

The OPTIMIS (Optimized Services Infrastructure Services) project is developing concepts and tools for managing Hybrid Clouds (Private and Public) in an optimal way. The complete lifecycle of services and their interactions are addressed and enhanced by value added services including trust management and energy efficiency optimization. These services require particular monitoring information that is not commonly conveyed, such as energy consumption. The project therefore has the requirements that the monitoring system needs to support such new parameters in addition to more traditional parameters such as CPU utilization which are obviously still needed. As the integration of Public and Private Clouds is a particular instance of the Cloud federation space, the ideas and solutions generated by the OPTIMIS project are applicable to the general Cloud federation problem.

Requirements for Cloud Monitoring

Before potential solutions for monitoring Cloud infrastructures are presented, one needs to understand the requirements such a solution has to fulfill. The chapter therefore reflects on the needs of the various stakeholders in Cloud systems and

their roles in systems monitoring. Complementary to that it discusses properties particular to Cloud systems and how those map to requirements on Cloud monitoring systems.

Roles in Monitoring Systems

The role model provided here is aligned with the one provided by Schubert et al. in the report "Future of Cloud Computing" (Schubert, et al., 2010). As mentioned above, the best way to understand the requirements ton Cloud monitoring and by that the functionalities that need to be provided is to look at the different roles within the Cloud universe and their respective desires.

Role A: Infrastructure Provider: Infrastructure Providers offer physical resources either directly as a service (IaaS) or indirectly for Application/Service Providers to base their respective offerings on.

Requirements of the Infrastructure Provider

The Infrastructure Provider should have full flexibility on configuring monitoring components. This can cover the use of provisioned monitoring components by a Cloud monitoring offering, but also the integration of his own monitoring tools. In terms of parameters, plain infrastructure parameters such as CPU usage should be provided by the monitoring system as well as higher level, VM-related data.

Role B: Application/Service Provider: Application or Service Providers use Cloud infrastructures to provide their own applications or services which are then sold to End Users/Customers.

Requirements of the Application/ Service Provider

The Application or Service Provider needs a monitoring interface which provides the necessary monitoring data related to the application/service provided to the End User/Customer. This typically includes information about the performance of the (virtual) machine the application/service is running on as well as service-specific data.

Role C: End User/Customer: The End User/Customer is the direct user of the Cloud offerings. This role is not at all involved in any service provisioning; it is just consuming services.

Requirements of the End User/Customer

The End User/Customer either has no access to monitoring data at all or, in case it is agreed within a contractual relationship, has access to a tailored subset of the monitoring information pertaining to its slice of service during the time of service use.

Cloud-Specific Requirements

Cloud systems have specific capabilities and requirements and cater for particular requirements. The monitoring system must offer features matching these requirements and capabilities. An investigation of the differences between regular monitoring systems and Cloud monitoring systems (Hasselmeyer & d'Heureuse, 2010) revealed the following requirements that go beyond the requirements and capabilities of regular monitoring solutions.

Multi-Tenancy

As Clouds are inherently designed to be used by multiple users, monitoring systems for Clouds must equally support multiple tenants. Having large numbers of independent consumers of monitoring information is perhaps the biggest difference of Cloud monitoring systems when compared to previous systems. Monitoring systems must ensure that monitoring information from particular tenants cannot be accessed by other tenants. Every tenant must have the illusion that he is the exclusive user of the monitoring system, while, in reality, he might share it with thousands of others. Traditional monitoring systems were not designed with multi-tenancy in mind. Some do offer different levels of privileges, but they were introduced for a different aim: they were designed to support a small number of administrators from the same company. The proliferation of administrators with distinct access rights is not well supported with such a scheme. Besides support for the sheer number of administrators, Cloud monitoring systems must allow automated management of users and access rights.

The provider of IaaS infrastructure is special as he is the only participant in the system who can access monitoring information related to the physical state of the infrastructure. All other tenants only get information about the state of their part of the virtual infrastructure hosted on the physical systems. With that special role, providers might utilize a monitoring system that is separate (and potentially different) from the system all the tenants are using. A consequence of this approach is that at least two monitoring systems would need to be installed and maintained. Another solution would be the use of the same monitoring system as everybody else in the system, albeit with elevated access rights.

Dynamism

A major consequence of multi-tenancy is the dynamism in the set of users and resources as well as their assignment. Users in Cloud environments can be added and removed at any time. As the number of users is large, so is the number of changes in the set of users. The monitoring system must be able to adapt to a changing set of users. Such adaptation must happen automatically in order to ensure timeliness as well as cost efficiency.

In addition to user dynamism, the set of resources is constantly changing as virtual machines are created and removed. Although the assignment of VMs to users is static, the assignment of slices of physical resources changes as VMs are started, stopped, and migrated.

With the variety of resources in the Cloud, the types of monitoring information are dynamically changing as well. As every resource potentially provides different types of monitoring information, the monitoring system must be able to deal with this variety and ideally process any kind of monitoring information.

Scalability

Clouds are based on economies of scale. Lessons learnt within activities such as the BonFIRE project (setting up a European Cloud Testbed) have shown that there is a demand for a variety of different VM images sizes coming from Cloud customers. With only a small installation the provided services are likely to become niche services which tend to be of a higher price to allow for profits.

To ensure proper monitoring, the monitoring system must be at least as scalable as the Cloud infrastructure. Scalability here relates to a number of domains, specifically the number of physical resources, the number of virtual resources, and the number of tenants.

Comprehensiveness

The monitoring system should cover information from the complete stack of monitored objects, including the physical infrastructure, the virtual objects, and the applications. Comprehensiveness does also apply to the set of users of the monitoring system. As monitoring information is needed by Cloud operators as well as Cloud customers, the monitoring system should ideally cover all the stakeholders in need of monitoring information.

Comprehensiveness can be achieved by either having one system covering everything or multiple systems covering particular aspects. It seems preferable to have just a single system as its use and maintenance are expected to be easier than dealing with multiple systems each having their own interface and peculiarities.

Simplicity

Arguably, one of the main reasons of Cloud adoption is its simplicity of use. A Cloud monitoring system should follow the idea of simplicity. It should be easy to set up, to retrieve information from it, and to feed information into it. Looking from the operator perspective, it is desirable to have a monitoring system that is easy to install, to maintain, and to provide to customers.

Summary of the Requirements

As a summary of the abovementioned requirements five main requirements which need to be fulfilled by a Cloud Monitoring System can be defined.

R1: Comprehensive Monitoring: The monitoring system must be able to deal with data originating from different levels and parts of the infrastructure – from the plain physical infrastructure level to Virtual Machine related data up to the service/application level.

R2: Scalability: A main tenet of the Cloud is dynamic scalability. The monitoring system must be able to keep up with the scalability of the underlying resource assignments.

R3: Extensibility and adaptability of the monitoring solution: Independent of the already installed data sources (e.g. Nagios or Ganglia), the monitoring system must allow for use of adapters to integrate these sources into the monitoring system. This avoids the replacement of already existing components within a domain. Furthermore, the set of adapters needs to be dynamically extensible in order to cater for the inclusion of future monitoring probes.

R4: Authorization of data access: As the support of several different stakeholders acting in various roles is faced, it is mandatory to ensure that only authorized access to data sets is possible. This might be enforced by components outside the monitoring sub system but interfaces for their integration must be available.

R5: Customizable Interfaces: Depending on the role, interactive and programmatic interfaces need to be provided which provide access to the monitoring data. The interfaces need to be tailored to the respective users and their roles. The interfaces need to be easy to use yet powerful to provide maximum productivity to consumers of monitoring information.

Solutions and Recommendations

The solution presented in this section addresses the abovementioned requirements. Due to the nature of the problem space, the solution will be split in two subparts, namely the Cloud Monitoring Architecture and the Cloud Monitoring Schema as shown in Figure 2.

The following presents a high level monitoring architecture which has been realized by a concrete implementation. A data schema allowing the transfer of arbitrary monitoring data is introduced.

The Cloud Monitoring Architecture proposed by the authors contains components for collecting and processing the monitored parameters from a variety of data sources. Figure 3 depicts a rough sketch of the architecture.

The architecture covers all the mentioned requirements with dedicated conceptual components. On the lowest level we distinguish two types of nodes – virtual and physical hosts, both providing monitoring data through components labeled monitoring tools. These can be realized by general monitoring software such as Nagios,

Figure 2. The components of the Cloud monitoring framework

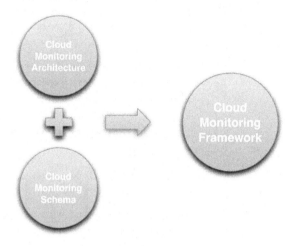

Ganglia or Zabbix, by monitoring tools already in operation within the infrastructure of a provider, or by newly developed probes. Generally it is not foreseen that Cloud monitoring solutions will provide such tools. Rather, it is expected that existing tools will be integrated into the monitoring framework.

No matter where monitoring information originates from, it is propagated to a high level monitoring tool which acts as the single source of monitoring information for connected components making use of monitoring data, such as applications, services and graphical user interfaces.

What will be provided on the lower level within this architecture is the possibility to store the monitored data into a database. This is mandatory for later evaluation including accounting and billing, auditing, contract violation discovery, and service assessment.

A direct transfer of the low level monitored data to a higher level monitoring component is not possible, as the data formats provided by the different tools are diverse and the technical means to transfer data are different. To tackle the heterogeneity a layer in between is introduced – the data aggregation layer. It takes the plain data as provided by the tools and converts it into a com-

Figure 3. Conceptual architecture of Cloud monitoring

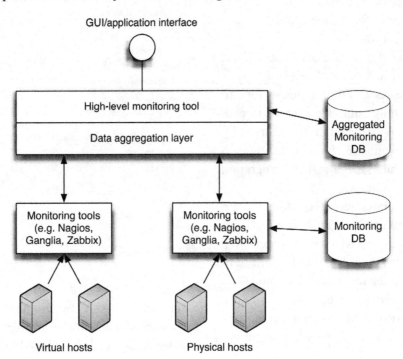

mon format, which can be processed by the high level monitoring tool.

Even though there needs to be a common format, the Cloud monitoring systems must be usable with a diverse range of data sources. The full range of data types cannot be anticipated at the time of implementation or deployment of the monitoring system. The monitoring system should therefore ideally support arbitrary types of data. An analysis of monitoring systems and data revealed that there are some parameters that are common to all monitoring information while others are specific to the various probes and events. The data structure used for holding monitoring information was therefore split into two sections, one part carrying the common information and one carrying arbitrary, event-specific data.

The common information consists of an identifier of the information source, a time stamp, a data type identifier, and a tenant identifier. The source identifier allows monitoring applications to know which part of the system a particular monitoring

message pertains to, e.g. which physical host it relates to. Queries are usually scoped by this parameter to include, for example, physical hosts or email applications only.

The time stamp is used to serialize event notifications. As the authors do not assume strictly synchronized clocks, time stamps are only relevant when issued by the same information source. The data type identifier uniquely specifies what kind of data is transferred inside an event notification, e.g., the temperature in degrees centigrade or the number of shopping transactions per second. The tenant identifier is needed to separate information of different tenants and to ensure that monitoring information can only be seen by authorized parties.

The specific part of event notifications can be realized with various data encoding mechanisms and schemata. Possible technologies for encoding are XML (extensible markup language) and JSON (JavaScript object notation). Various schemata exist, but they are commonly restricted to particular domains. An example of a schema covering high-

Figure 4. Monitoring system components

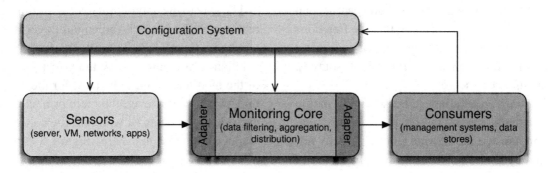

performance computing job requirements is the GLUE specification (Andreozzi, 2009). To cover a wide variety of monitoring domains, the parallel use of multiple schemata is warranted.

In terms of communication, the architecture does not prescribe a particular exchange pattern between the monitoring tools and the data aggregation layer, but it is assumed that the support of both pull and push communication depends on the capabilities of the lower layer monitoring tools. Once aggregated, the data can be handed over to the high level monitoring tool for further processing. Similar to the low level monitoring data storage, the authors also foresee an aggregated monitoring database on this level to store and retrieve the data for later retrieval and analysis.

The aggregated and normalized monitoring information needs to be provided by the monitoring system to monitoring data consumers. Our architecture allows this through a dedicated interface to the high level monitoring tool component. Communication at this interface can again happen in push and pull fashion, depending on the requirements of the monitoring applications.

Monitoring System Implementation

The monitoring architecture has been prototypically implemented by one of the authors to show its viability (Hasselmeyer, & d'Heureuse, 2010). The components involved are shown in Figure 4. The monitoring core has been realized on top of a data stream management system (Hyde, 2010) to cater for high throughput data processing, selection, and aggregation. The system has been integrated with a number of monitoring sensors covering measurements from servers, the network, and applications. Visualization of monitoring has been done via Web-based user interfaces which were tailored to specific stakeholders of the system.

The monitoring system and its components are subject to configuration. A configuration system is taking care of appropriately setting notification frequency, access control, and aggregation optimization. The configuration system takes into consideration policies set by the monitoring system provider (usually the Cloud operator) and the consumers of monitoring information who request information with certain fidelity. As the configuration system has complete overview of the monitoring system configuration, it can control and optimize information flow inside the system. It is therefore an important component for security and performance of the system.

The actual monitoring data is expressed in XML. XML offers the desired flexibility in information structure and content described earlier. The monitoring system is mainly forwarding the arbitrary data. In addition, the monitoring system is able to aggregate monitoring events carrying simple data types (i.e. integer and floating point numbers). Different functions are available for aggregation, including the maximum, the minimum, and the average. Aggregation can happen over time and space, meaning that the functions are applied to a series of data originating over a period of time or from a set of related data sources, e.g. a number of servers.

The implementation addresses most of the requirements stated in the previous section. Comprehensive monitoring (R1) is directly addressed by the use of XML and the inclusion of arbitrarily structured data in monitoring event notifications. Extensibility (R3) is ensured by a loosely-coupled infrastructure which allows the dynamic introduction of new sensors via adaptors. Authorization (R4) is handled by the explicit use of tenant identifiers and the strict enforcement of access control at the egress points of the monitoring system.

Customized interfaces (R5) is only partially addressed. There currently exists only a simple programming interface to extract monitoring information and to register for event notifications. Other interfaces need to be built on top of the given ones. Scalability (R2) is realized only partially. The system scales arbitrarily in the number of providers and consumers of monitoring information, but the number of processed events is restricted by the capabilities of the data stream management system (DSMS). A solution to this restriction is the use of multiple DSMS instances and the assignment of various producers and consumers to them.

Progressing the Presented Work

Several other research activities are currently working on the realization of Cloud Monitoring, some aligned to the presented high-level architecture. Examples are the German SLA4D-Grid or the European OPTIMIS project. SLA4D-Grid is, though being completely Grid-related, working on a solution which takes into account the requirements of Cloud environments and can be used to handle the monitoring of pure Grid, pure Cloud

or Hybrid (Grid and Cloud) systems (Tenschert, 2011). Due to the nature of the project (aiming to realize a Service Level Agreement Layer for the German national Grid – D-Grid), their monitoring solution is targeting mainly the post-processing of the monitored data to be used for the evaluation of SLAs. However, the main principles and derived components fit well into the conceptual architecture presented here. Figure 5 shows a high-level overview of the architecture.

Within the project, results from the D-Mon project (http://www.d-grid-gmbh.de/index.php?id=52&L=1) are re-used as lower level monitoring tools. The monitored data is then processed and delivered in a format which can be processed by an SLA monitoring implementation based on WSAG4J (https://packcs-e0.scai.fraunhofer.de/wsag4j/index.html), an implementation of the WS-Agreement specification (Andrieux, 2011).

The OPTIMIS project is – in contrast to SLA4D-Grid – focused on the optimization of Cloud environments, including optimal monitoring of different levels such as the application/service level, the virtual environment level and last but not least the physical IT infrastructure. The conceptual design of the OPTIMIS monitoring approach is presented in Figure 6. The first prototype of this system has been already delivered, implemented mainly as a set of RESTful Java Web Services.

The OPTIMIS design explicitly includes energy efficiency information in its architectural design. According to requirement R3 (extensibility), such information must be supported by a Cloud monitoring system. The implementation described above will be able to handle such information without needing to upgrade the monitoring system itself. Obviously, appropriate adaptors are needed to feed such information into the monitoring system.

What is quite obvious in the OPTIMIS design is the fact that monitored data can be processed in several ways to give feedback on diverse proper-

Figure 5. The SLA4D-Grid high-level monitoring architecture

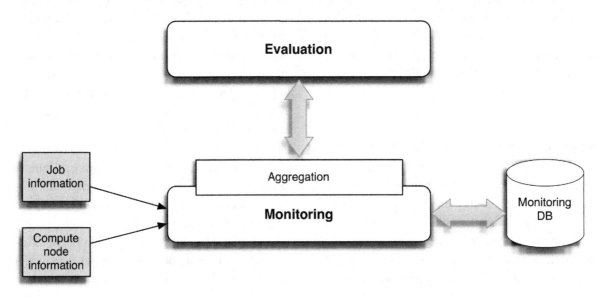

Figure 6. The OPTIMIS high-level monitoring architecture

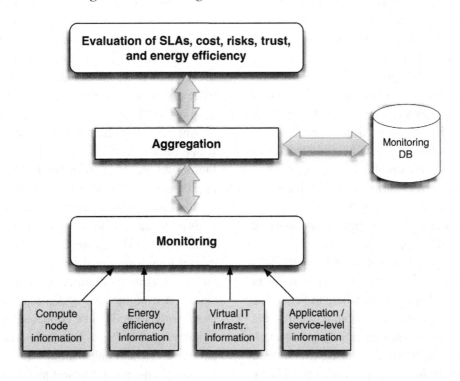

ties of a system and the provided services. Some examples are given in Figure 6, such as the risk assessment which aims to provide estimation of risks of services not running as planned based on monitoring data. Another example is cost estimation based on the performance and current use of the system.

Support of Federated Clouds

Cloud customers that are using multiple Cloud infrastructures for hosting their applications require a monitoring system that spans all the infrastructures involved and that can deal with monitoring information from those infrastructures. For most users, it is desirable to have aggregated information that covers the complete set of Clouds used. Such aggregation can happen in various ways. All such aggregation methods have to address two areas of potential heterogeneity.

The first problem of integration is the heterogeneity of communication protocols. In order to exchange monitoring information with a Cloud, the protocol spoken by that Cloud needs to be used. But as each Cloud could have its own protocol, some form of integration must happen. The other integration problem stems from the heterogeneity of monitoring information. As mentioned before, monitoring information can be encoded using various methods and can therefore vary between Clouds. In order to be able to use monitoring information from different sources, the data needs to be transformed into a common language understood by the consumer of the information.

Integrating monitoring information and bridging the gaps between different protocols and data encodings must happen somewhere in Federated Clouds. At the extremes, this can happen at the client side or at the monitoring infrastructure level. Various solutions in between those extremes can be developed, including, in particular, third party monitoring information brokers/integrators.

Aggregating monitoring information at the client side means that the monitoring systems at different Clouds are completely separated and an integration of the monitoring information only happens outside the Clouds at the client. Such a model can be realized directly and does not need any changes on the Cloud monitoring infrastructure side. Only the client needs to be able to perform proper data acquisition and to understand the monitoring data.

Aggregating monitoring information at the infrastructure level means that monitoring systems at different Clouds cooperate and exchange monitoring information that pertains to the infrastructure belonging to a particular client.

No matter where the integration of monitoring information happens, standardized protocols and data models can help in this work. Standard protocols remove the need to implement multiple protocols to talk to different Clouds. Similarly, the use of standard data models and encodings obviates the need for translating between them.

The architecture as shown in Figure 3 can also be applied to the monitoring of Federated Clouds. In such an environment, the monitoring tools are spread across the Clouds involved in the federation. The data aggregation layer needs to be able to deal with the various data formats used in the Clouds.

Implementing the architecture in a Federated Cloud setting requires more effort. In particular, the monitoring information needs to be distributed to all the Cloud monitoring systems involved in a federation, which then make the data available to its consumers. The so-far isolated monitoring systems need to be enhanced by components that extract monitoring information from one Cloud and inject it into the monitoring system of another Cloud. As monitoring systems allow arbitrary monitoring sources to be connected to it, such a monitoring "pipe" can be easily created as just another source and sink of monitoring information.

Besides the technical problems, policy issues can exist which restrict the free flow of monitoring information. Some Cloud provider might be reluctant to hand out monitoring information to a competitor. Some data might not be allowed to flow to a different jurisdiction. A possible solution is to anonymize such data or pass it on in aggregated format only. Such changes to the data further complicate the process of integrating data and need to be observed by application that are using the monitoring data.

FUTURE RESEARCH DIRECTIONS

The solution proposed in this chapter describes a Cloud monitoring architecture that enables the development of interoperable and vendor-independent monitoring frameworks. Interoperability, though, is not only reached by design, but other aspects have to be considered, too. With user-friendly and open solutions in mind, the authors think that standards are the right way to tackle this problem and to channel research into consistent solutions. With respect to monitoring, valuable candidates for standardization are the monitoring data format and the interfaces between (i) the sensors and the monitoring service and (ii) the monitoring service and the consumer.

Although there is no standard for a Cloud monitoring data format, a number of standards exist that are used to describe the capabilities of IT infrastructures and services. Two examples are the Common Information Model (DMTF, 2003) and the aforementioned GLUE specification (Andreozzi, 2009). Both are used to describe services and resources, advertise them through registries, and match them with consumer requests. Whether these two (or other) standards fulfill the requirements specific to Cloud monitoring, whether they could be extended, or whether some new standard would be the appropriate solution is still subject of future research.

Speaking of Cloud monitoring data formats, most likely more than one will co-exist. On the hand, general monitoring frameworks like Ganglia or Nagios and other sensors that produce monitoring data without using a common standard (and without one being developed as of today)exist. On the other hand, there are also Cloud monitoring services normalizing, aggregating and filtering monitoring data. These services, also, use vendor-specific data formats and no standardization activity is underway. As the latter is the information that is exchanged between Cloud providers and Cloud users, the latter is seen as more important for interoperable consumer-oriented solutions and would direct future research towards a standardized data format covering this level.

Looking at standardized interfaces, we think that targeting the consumer-oriented level is valuable for future research. End-user applications and value-added services have to operate independent of the underlying Cloud environment and Cloud management framework. One solution is the use of standardized interfaces (ideally delivering data formatted according to a standardized data format) like, for example, the Open Cloud Computing Interface (OCCI; http://occi-wg.org/). Although it is currently primarily used to interact with IaaS and is integrated into IaaS management tools like OpenNebula (Milojicic, 2011), OCCI has been designed to also operate on PaaS and SaaS level. It is therefore a suitable solution to integrate monitoring into the Cloud service stack and to offer a standardized interface to Cloud users.

CONCLUSION

Monitoring is an important aspect of systems management in any kind of IT system. Clouds are no exception and Cloud monitoring adds a few of its own twists to the topic. In particular, multi-tenancy, dynamism, and scalability are at the heart of Cloud computing and need to be supported by the monitoring system. This chapter described these properties and their influence on monitoring systems. Five major requirements were derived which taken together establish boundaries for monitoring systems adequate for Cloud use.

A high-level architecture is introduced which caters for all the mentioned requirements. An exemplary implementation of the architecture shows the viability of the architecture and proves that the requirements can be fulfilled. Some other implementation efforts following a similar architecture are introduced and compared.

The recent progress in Cloud monitoring systems has shown that there is an increasing need for appropriately monitoring Cloud installations, both by providers and by consumers. The current research is centered around finding appropriate architectures for Cloud monitoring. What will be needed in the future for the broad adoption of Cloud monitoring is interoperability between monitoring systems, Cloud providers, and management applications. Standardization of Cloud monitoring has just begun, but should enable such interoperability.

REFERENCES

Andreozzi, S., De Bortoli, N., Fantinel, S., Ghiselli, A., Tortone, G., & Vistoli, C. (2003). GridICE: A Monitoring Service for the Grid. In *Third Cracow Grid Workshop* (pp. 220–226).

Andrieux, A., Czajkowski, K., Dan, A., Keahey, K., Ludwig, H., Nakata, T., et al. (2011). GFD-R.192: Web Services Agreement Specification (WS-Agreement). *The Open Grid Forum Full Recommendation*. Retrieved November 15, 2011, from http://www.ogf.org/documents/GFD.192.pdf.

Armbrust, M., Fox, A., Griffith, R., Joseph, A. D., Katz, R., Konwinski, A., et al. (2009). Above the Clouds: A Berkeley view of Cloud Computing. *Technical Report EECS-2009-28, EECS Department*, Berkley, CA: University of California

Clayman, S., Galis, A., Chapman, C., Toffetti, G., Rodero-Merino, L., & Vaquero, L. M. (2010). Monitoring Service Clouds in the Future Internet. In Tselentis, G., Galis, A., Gavras, A., Krco, S., Lotz, V., & Simperl, E. (Eds.), *Towards the Future Internet - Emerging Trends from European Research* (pp. 115–126). Amsterdam, The Netherlands: IOS Press.

Colling, D. J., Martyniak, J., McGough, A. S., Krenek, A., Sitera, J., & Mulac, M., & Dvorák, F. (2010). Real time monitor of grid job executions. *Journal of Physics: Conference Series, 219*(6). doi:10.1088/1742-6596/219/6/062020

DMTF. (2003). CIM Concepts White Paper CIM Versions 2.4+. *Technical Report DSP0110*, Distributed Management Task Force

Hasselmeyer, P. (2007). Removing the Need for State Dissemination in Grid Resource Brokering. In *5th International Workshop on Middleware for Grid Computing (MGC 2007)*. New York, NY ACM Press.

Hasselmeyer, P., & d'Heureuse, N. (2010). Towards Holistic Multi-Tenant Monitoring for Virtual Data Centers. In *2010 IEEE/IFIP Network Operations and Management Symposium Workshops* (pp. 350-356). Piscataway, NJ: IEEE.

Katsaros, G., & Gallizo, G. Kübert, R., Wang, T., Fitó, J.O., & Henriksson, D. (2011). A Multi-level Architecture for Collecting and Managing Monitoring Information in Cloud Environments. In *1st International Conference on Cloud Computing and Services Science (CLOSER 2011)*.

Katsaros, G., Kübert, R., & Gallizo, G. (2010). Building a Service-Oriented Monitoring Framework with REST and Nagios. In *IEEE International Conference on Services Computing (SCC)* Washington, DC: IEEE Press.

Lindner, M., Marquez, F. G., Chapman, C., Clayman, S., Henriksson, D., & Elmroth, E. (2010). The Cloud Supply Chain: A Framework for Information, Monitoring, Accounting and Billing. In *2nd International ICST Conference on Cloud Computing (CloudComp 2010)*.

Mell, P., & Grance, T. (2011). *The NIST Definition of Cloud Computing (Draft)* (NIST Special Publication 800-145 (Draft)). Retrieved July 13, 2011, from http://csrc.nist.gov/publications/drafts/800-145/Draft-SP-800-145_cloud-definition.pdf.

Milojicic, D., Lorente, I. M., & Montero, R. S. (2011). OpenNebula: A Cloud Management Tool. *IEEE Internet Computing*, *15*(2), 11–14. doi:10.1109/MIC.2011.44

Nyren, A., Edmonds, A., Papaspyrou, A., & Metsch, T. (2011). GFD-P-R.183: Open Cloud Computing Interface - Core. *The Open Grid Forum Proposed Recommendation*. Retrieved August 8, 2011, from http://www.ogf.org/documents/GFD.183.pdf.

Schopf, J. M., Raicu, I., Pearlman, L., Miller, N., Kesselman, C., Foster, I., & D'Arcy, M. (2006). *Monitoring and Discovery in a Web Services Framework: Functionality and Performance of Globus Toolkit MDS4*. MCS Preprint #ANL/MCS-P1315-0106. Retrieved August 8, 2011, from http://www.mcs.anl.gov/uploads/cels/papers/P1315.pdf.

Schubert, L., Jeffery, K., & Neidecker-Lutz, B. (2010). *The Future of Cloud Computing*. Brussels, BE: European Commission.

Soundararajan, V., & Govil, K. (2010). Challenges in Building Scalable Virtualized Datacenter Management. *ACM SIGOPS Operating Systems Review*, *44*(4), 95–102. doi:10.1145/1899928.1899941

Tenschert, A., et al. (2011). *VERSION II der Architektur der SLA-Schicht; Official Report from the SLA4D-Grid project*. Retrieved August 8, 2011, from http://www.sla4d-grid.de/sites/default/files/SLA4D-Grid_Version-II_Architektur.pdf.

Tierney, B., Aydt, R., Gunter, D., Smith, W., Swany, M., Taylor, V., & Wolski, R. (2002). *GFD-I.7: A Grid Monitoring Architecture*. The Open Grid Forum Informational Document. Retrieved August 8, 2011, from http://www.ogf.org/documents/GFD.7.pdf.

Zanikolas, S., & Sakellariou, R. (2005). A Taxonomy of Grid Monitoring Systems. *Future Generation Computer Systems*, *21*, 163–188. doi:10.1016/j.future.2004.07.002

ADDITIONAL READING

Clayman, S., Galis, A., Chapman, C., Toffetti, G., Rodero-Merino, L., & Vaquero, L. M. (2010). Monitoring Service Clouds in the Future Internet. In Tselentis, G., Galis, A., Gavras, A., Krco, S., Lotz, V., & Simperl, E. (Eds.), *Towards the Future Internet - Emerging Trends from European Research* (pp. 115–126). IOS Press.

Comuzzi, M., Kotsokalis, C., Spanoudakis, G., & Yahyapour, R. (2009). Establishing and Monitoring SLAs in Complex Service Based Systems. In *IEEE International Conference on Web Services, 2009 (ICWS 2009)* (pp. 783 -790).

De Chaves, S. A., Uriarte, R. B., & Westphall, C. B. (2011). Toward an architecture for monitoring private clouds. *IEEE Communications Magazine*, *49*(12), 130–137. doi:10.1109/MCOM.2011.6094017

Emeakaroha, V. C., Brandic, I., Maurer, M., & Dustdar, S. (2010). Low level Metrics to High level SLAs - LoM2HiS framework: Bridging the gap between monitored metrics and SLA parameters in cloud environments. In *2010 International Conference on High Performance Computing and Simulation (HPCS)* (pp. 48-54).

Foster, H., & Spanoudakis, G. (2011). Dynamic Creation of Monitoring Infrastructures. In Wieder, P., Butler, J., Teilmann, W., & Yahyapour, R. (Eds.), *Service Level Agreements for Cloud Computing* (pp. 123–138). New York, NY, US: Springer New York. doi:10.1007/978-1-4614-1614-2_8

Kennedy, J., Edmonds, A., Bayon, V., Cheevers, P., Lu, K., Stopar, M., & Murn, D. (2011). SLA-Enabled Infrastructure Management. In Wieder, P., Butler, J., Teilmann, W., & Yahyapour, R. (Eds.), *Service Level Agreements for Cloud Computing* (pp. 271–287). New York, NY, US: Springer New York. doi:10.1007/978-1-4614-1614-2_16

Larsson, L., Henriksson, D., & Elmroth, E. (2011). Scheduling and monitoring of internally structured services in Cloud federations. In *IEEE Symposium on Computers and Communications (ISCC)* (pp. 173-178).

Mahbub, K., Spanoudakis, G., & Tsigkritis, T. (2011). Translation of SLAs into Monitoring Specifications. In Wieder, P., Butler, J., Teilmann, W., & Yahyapour, R. (Eds.), *Service Level Agreements for Cloud Computing* (pp. 79–101). New York, NY, US: Springer New York. doi:10.1007/978-1-4614-1614-2_6

Massie, M. L., Chun, B. N., & Culler, D. E. (2003). The Ganglia Distributed Monitoring System: Design, Implementation And Experience. *Parallel Computing*, *30*(7), 817–840. doi:10.1016/j.parco.2004.04.001

Massonet, P., Naqvi, S., Ponsard, C., Latanicki, J., Rochwerger, B., & Villari, M. (2011). A Monitoring and Audit Logging Architecture for Data Location Compliance in Federated Cloud Infrastructures. In *IEEE International Symposium on Parallel and Distributed Processing Workshops and Phd Forum (IPDPSW)* (pp. 1510-1517).

Moses, J., Iyer, R., Illikkal, R., Srinivasan, S., & Aisopos, K. (2011). Shared Resource Monitoring and Throughput Optimization in Cloud-Computing Datacenters. In *IEEE International Parallel & Distributed Processing Symposium (IPDPS)* (pp. 1024–1033).

Reese, G. (2009). *Cloud application architectures*. O'Reilly Media, Inc.

Shao, J., Wei, H., Wang, Q., & Mei, M. (2010). A Runtime Model Based Monitoring Approach for Cloud, In *3rd International Conference on Cloud Computing (CLOUD)* (pp. 313-320).

Spring, J. (2011). Monitoring Cloud Computing by Layer, Part 1. *IEEE Security & Privacy*, *9*(2), 66–68. doi:10.1109/MSP.2011.33

Spring, J. (2011). Monitoring Cloud Computing by Layer, Part 2. *IEEE Security & Privacy*, *9*(3), 52–55. doi:10.1109/MSP.2011.57

Wang, L., Ranjan, R., Chen, J., & Benatallah, B. (Eds.). (2011). *Cloud Computing. Methodology, Systems, and Applications*. CRC Press.

Chapter 7
Monitoring in Federated and Self-Manageable Clouds

Stefanos Koutsoutos
National Technical University of Athens, Greece

Spyridon V. Gogouvitis
National Technical University of Athens, Greece

Dimosthenis Kyriazis
National Technical University of Athens, Greece

Theodora Varvarigou
National Technical University of Athens, Greece

ABSTRACT

The emergence of Service Clouds and the Future Internet has lead to a lot of research taking place in the area of Cloud frameworks and solutions. The complexity of these systems has proven to be a challenge for the design of a successful platform that will be capable of meeting all possible needs and require the minimum time and effort put to its management. Current trends in the field move away from models of human managed networks and towards the self-manageable, cooperating Clouds. This goal is synonymous to building software that is able to make decisions required to reconfigure itself in a way that it resists failures and, at the same time, makes optimal use of the resources available to it. The heart of each decision making mechanism is always the data that is fed to it, which assigns a very central role to Monitoring mechanisms in federated and self-manageable Clouds.

INTRODUCTION

Research in the fields of Grid Computing, Service Oriented Architectures (SOA) as well as Virtualization technologies has driven the emergence of Cloud (Mell & Grance, 2009) service models such as Infrastructure-as-a-Service (IaaS), Platform-as-a-Service (PaaS) and Software-as-a-Service (SaaS). This classification of services provision has in turn led to the emergence of new business roles, potentially with differing interests. The efficient service provisioning through Clouds

DOI: 10.4018/978-1-4666-1631-8.ch007

Copyright © 2012, IGI Global. Copying or distributing in print or electronic forms without written permission of IGI Global is prohibited.

adhering to these models, while maintaining the constraints set by each such business, has driven the development of novel architectures for tools which are capable of addressing the challenges set forth. To briefly explain these three service models, as seen from the point of view of the service provider, SaaS offers an application as a service over a Cloud environment to the end users. PaaS offers a service platform supporting storage and giving access onto various Cloud infrastructures, without the need to buy and manage the underlying hardware and software. IaaS offers resources on demand, including storage, hardware, servers and networking components, depending on each deployed instance. In all cases any applications that are able to run on these systems must be adapted to them. This is achieved by describing their characteristics and requirements in a machine-understandable way. Therefore the service provider can enable them to be executed in virtualized environments. It is common ground that all these services are provided with specific, predefined, Quality of Service (QoS). In all cases a Service Level Agreement (SLA) (Skene, Lamanna, & Emmerich, 2004) is signed prior to the service provision initiation for each individual client.

The goal of achieving self-manageability in Clouds requires several features to be present. Self-manageability means adaptation to new situations as they arise, so as to ensure the Cloud's service characteristics, i.e. the continuation of the service at the required quality level. In order to perform this task a Cloud must react intelligently to events that occur at runtime, without any human intervention. Proper decision making mechanisms are employed which ensure such features. These mechanisms vary in their responsibilities depending on the aspect of the Cloud that they manage. However, they all have one thing in common, as they need to have an up-to-date view of the Cloud resources, maybe at different granularities. Thus, Monitoring mechanisms, able to collect and

propagate information and events, are an integral part of Cloud solutions.

The following section will analyze in detail the Cloud monitoring environment and its purpose. Then, the requirements posed by the required features and sub-systems of the Cloud will be discussed. The next section discusses available techniques and technologies in the area of monitoring for distributed systems. A detailed view of the monitoring solutions developed within the context of two EU projects follows, while a proposal for a new monitoring system is presented in next section. Lastly, future research directions are presented and conclusions drawn.

BACKGROUND

Regardless of the service model of any given Cloud, let it be IaaS, PaaS or SaaS, some common architectural components are shared in all. All Clouds can be seen as pools of resources, which serve requests for allocating those to their clients and making sure they receive a minimum Quality of Service. To realize that, each Cloud must have components dedicated to allocation and relocation of resources so as to meet the needs of their clients and ensure their smooth operation. Such components are decision making mechanisms which solve optimization problems over the set of available and required resources, costs and time requirements for placement and relocation. In addition to these, all Clouds contain components which are responsible for accounting the actions of their clients and billing them. Of course, depending on each individual Cloud's feature list others may or may not be present. The Monitoring mechanism is required to exist in all Cloud platforms, since it offers a very basic functionality that is crucial for the Cloud operation.

The Monitoring mechanism's exact responsibilities vary in different Cloud platforms, but there is a common set of services provided. It's this module which monitors physical & virtual resources and produces events, aggregates those events, and notifies any other modules interested in them. It is very common to have the corresponding monitoring system perform additional tasks, like logging the events or extracting other, more high level events from the ones received, using some kind of intelligent mechanism.

The diversity of Cloud environments, as well as the variety of consumers of the monitored events, usually results in a hard set of requirements for a monitoring module. Depending on the platform, a number of probes exist per physical host and per virtual resource. Virtual resources range from services which are parts of the Cloud framework and virtual machines or similar resources, to the applications which run over each specific Cloud instance. The number of these probes is analogous to the Cloud's size and their location depends on both its physical and virtual layout. They can be all gathered in a single cluster of physical hosts, or span networks and geographies.

Similarly the consumers of events pose their own requirements on Monitoring, since each one is interested in a different set of events and they need them at different granularities in terms of time or aggregation resolution. For example, SLA violation detection mechanism requires events at a greater frequency than that of accounting and billing. In addition, billing a customer is usually concerned with aggregated events at the Cloud level, while the resource placement decision making module would normally require events at the per physical host level.

The following sections will analyze the possible set of requirements posed by a Cloud environment to their respective Monitoring mechanism. This analysis will go beyond self-manageability and federation in Clouds, highlighting requirements important in any end product or framework.

REQUIREMENTS

Distributed Systems

Various readily available monitoring systems, such as Nagios (Nagios, n.d.), Hyperic (SpringSource Hyperic, n.d.), Ganglia (Massie, Chun, & Culler, 2004), OpenNMS (About OpenNMS, n.d.), Globus Toolkit (Foster, 2005) and GridICE (Andreozzi et al., 2005) offer a sufficient set of capabilities when it comes to monitor a Grid, or large cluster. Such systems cover a range of requirements, which, depending on each implementation, usually include:

- **Scalability:** The monitoring mechanism should be able to cope with both a large number of nodes and a large number of probes hosted in them.
- **Robustness:** The monitoring mechanism should be able to overcome node and network failures, with proper failover mechanisms.
- **Manageability:** The monitoring mechanism should be able to be managed by the human operators easily and especially the time and effort required for this management should not be analogous to the size of the monitored system.
- **Portability:** The monitoring mechanism should support different operating systems and underlying hardware platforms.
- **Overhead:** The monitoring mechanism should incur low overhead on the nodes it operates upon and also should require low bandwidth to transmit the information gathered.
- **Extensibility:** The monitoring mechanism should be able to be extended by adding new probes to read from.

Cloud Systems

The aforementioned requirements are all present in a Cloud environment too. However, Cloud platforms also put their own constraints on top of these, or make some constraints even harder than they usually are in a distributed system. In a usual Cloud platform the monitoring mechanism should be able to drive other components, crucial to the overall operation. The whole system is constantly changing with services migrating from one host to another. Each single service may be the result of cooperating components whose instances lie in different clusters, networks or geographies. The rate of changes in a Cloud is a lot higher than that of a distributed system. In addition, when federation comes into the foreground, services to be monitored may even be hosted by different Cloud providers.

The most important factor that comes into consideration in Cloud monitoring is the tight integration of itself as a component with the rest of the modules comprising the platform. The Monitoring mechanism feeds with data those components responsible for decision making and service management. The latter are those responsible for various important tasks, often associated with real-time constraints, such as SLA, QoS, placement and service provision. Therefore the role of the Monitoring mechanism in a Cloud platform is more crucial, compared to a distributed system.

The requirements which follow the aforementioned constraints are harder than the ones referred in the list provided above. The following list provides a few more requirements, as well as some adjusted definitions for points already present.

- **Elasticity:** The monitoring mechanism should be able to correctly monitor the Cloud resources created and destroyed when expanding the Cloud or joining it with others.

- **Migration:** The monitoring mechanism should be able to track the Cloud resources which move from one physical or virtual host to another.
- **Adaptability:** The monitoring mechanism should be able to adapt itself to the load of the hosts and networks it operators upon so as not to be invasive.
- **Manageability/Autonomous Monitoring:** The monitoring mechanism should be able to keep running without intervention and reconfiguration.
- **Federation:** The monitoring mechanism should be able to correctly monitor any Cloud resource which resides on another Cloud, joined with the initial one.

One aspect of monitoring, often neglected in related analysis, is security. Cloud monitoring and security are bound in two ways. The first one the requirement that monitored information should be made available only to those physical or virtual entities which are authorized to access it. The other one is the ability to monitor changes in security policies made in the Cloud, since the later may be information which affects the operation of other Cloud components implementing decision making mechanisms.

The requirements regarding the kinds of data monitored may differ cross different Cloud platforms. The most simplistic assumption is that the data fetched from the low level probes are transmitted as-is to the client modules of monitoring. Such a solution may not scale well in large Clouds, especially when the data need to travel across different network to reach their consumer. Instead, a Monitoring mechanism may employ data aggregation techniques, or even filter data. In addition, there have been proposed mechanisms that achieve the monitoring of functions of data, like Sharfman, Schuster and Keren (2007) and Keren, Sharfman and Livne (2011).

Finally, some requirements result from the kind of monitored information consumers. There are three kinds of consumers, other Cloud components, the Cloud administrator and the Cloud clients (both human and their software, if any). Depending on the nature of the consumer, there are differences in the format that the monitored data are communicated to their target (like UIs & friendly alerts, as opposed to a REST API), as well as the amount of historical information that has to be kept by the monitoring mechanism (real time feeds, as opposed to batch analysis). In addition, providing monitoring information to the Cloud platform's clients set another set of requirements, mostly regarding security, since the Monitoring mechanism is publicly visible, but also they may have to do with SLA.

The aforementioned list of requirements should make it obvious that the realization of a Monitoring mechanism which covers all of them requires a very delegate design of its architecture. There is no solution, to the best of our knowledge, which addresses all of the above, without making compromises at some point.

EXISTING MONITORING FRAMEWORKS

Overview

A presentation of the mostly used and well known existing frameworks for monitoring distributed systems follows. Some of them have successfully been employed in Cloud monitoring, while others are specifically designed for them. In the following discussion the tools are presented from the less suitable for Cloud monitoring to the most promising solutions.

The most simplistic approach to Cloud monitoring is of course to ignore any Cloud specific requirements and treat it as a large distributed system. This approach can work for specific kinds of Clouds, depending on the provided services. Such systems would have a very narrow set of requirements for their monitoring mechanism,

which would primarily serve as a system monitor rather than an integrated system component. This task can be undertaken by tools like Collectd (Collectd - The system statistics collection daemon, n.d.) and Ntop (What is ntop, n.d.), the later only monitoring network resources. These tools would need a great deal of time and effort put to managing them, since they offer no support for several features, notably failover, interoperability with other instances of themselves, no notion of elasticity or resource migration, and they are not autonomous. However, it should be noted that these solutions are among the ones which have the less overhead on the monitored host or network.

One step further lie tools which have been designed for monitoring large clusters of nodes. Such systems are Nagios and Ganglia, both open source solutions. They are all modular solutions to allow for custom and extensible list of probes. They also excel in scalability, able to manage thousands of nodes. As such, they are easier to manage at the cluster level. They lack all Cloud specific features like resource elasticity and migration, adaptability and autonomous monitoring. Also, no interoperability with multiple instances of themselves is supported. On the other hand, all of them provide a very comprehensive way to present the collected data to a human operator, making the managing of the system tractable. According to their makers they are used to generate alerts and in general help the system administrator easily and timely identify possible issues and problems in the infrastructure they manage. Nevertheless, a considerable amount of effort is required for the Cloud administrator when making use of these tools. If used as-is, the Cloud administrator will have to track as many instances of the tools as there are running in the Cloud. It should be noted that they are quite extensive in the way they provide the information gathered, so another software layer can be built on top of them to provide for aggregation.

Two tools which address the issue of manageability in very large systems are OpenNMS and

Hyperic. Both of these tools add to the feature list of the ones mentioned above the automatic discovery of resources. OpenNMS targets network resources monitoring only, which makes it an incomplete solution for a service Cloud. However, it is able to cooperate with Hyperic. The later provides several features that are required by a Cloud monitoring mechanism. Specifically it supports high availability mode (failover), deployment automation, including the ability to copy and reuse monitoring configurations and global alert templates, to bring resources under management in a short time. Among all tools discussed so far, Hyperic is the only one that claims it is designed for being deployed in a Cloud. In addition it puts a considerable focus on the security aspect of monitoring, as well as monitoring the security aspects of the Cloud.

Two systems which specifically target Cloud monitoring are Gomez (The Gomez Platform, n.d.) and LogicMonitor (Automated Monitoring, n.d.). They are both designed to be very easy to administer both at deploy time and at runtime. However, they target the Cloud administrator mostly and are not designed to be an integrated component of the Cloud.

Of course, all tools, which cover the requirements of Grid monitoring, do provide resource discovery and failover mechanisms and are designed for easily managing very large networks of nodes. Two notable software solutions are GridICE and and the monitoring facilities of Globus Toolkit. GridICE is a pure grid monitoring framework, which means that the whole Cloud should be designed to operate with a Grid's standards. Therefore, its use would pose a set of architecture constraints in the Cloud that would use it. In a similar fashion, the Globus Toolkit is a Grid solution framework which includes, but is not restricted to, a Grid monitoring mechanism. Employing any of these two solutions in a Cloud platform is therefore restrictive for the Cloud architecture.

On the other hand, MonALISA (Legrand et al., 2009; Newman, Legrand, Galvez, Voicu, & Cirstoiu, 2003; Newman, Legrand, & Bunn, 2001) is designed for distributed systems, but covers a wide range of requirements mentioned in the previous section. Specifically, its multi-agent design poses virtually no constraints in the architecture of the Cloud, while allowing for scalability, manageability, and autonomous monitoring, robustness, failover, extensibility, and adaptability. It is however notable that MonALISA can interact with any other services and Cloud components to provide information custom formatted based on the information gathered, all in near real-time. It is also very flexible regarding the type of collected information, since its Agent system can be used to develop higher level decision services, implemented as a distributed network of communicating agents, to perform global optimization tasks. Thus, MonALISA can be used as a framework to implement various others components, or their integral parts, with high degree of efficiency.

Finally, a notable Cloud Monitoring mechanism is Amazon CloudWatch (Amazon CloudWatch, n.d.) Amazon CloudWatch is part of the Amazon Web Services (AWS) Cloud services. It supports all of the features required from a Cloud monitoring mechanism, besides that of federation. The important aspect of CloudWatch is that any customer of AWS can use it to monitor his/her own resources. The information provided can be fed into programs running onto AWS, so as to be exploited in decision making employed by the customer, therefore allowing for the maximum of integration and information exploitation of monitoring data.

A listing of the frameworks and their capabilities in terms of the requirements and features layed out in the previous section can be found in Table 1.

Table 1. Comparison of Monitoring Frameworks

	Scalability	Robustness	Manageability	Portability	Overhead	Extensibility	Elasticity	Migration	Adaptability	Autonomicity	Federation
Collectd	-	-	-	-	+	-	-	-	-	-	-
Ntop	-	-	-	-	+	-	-	-	-	-	-
Nagios	+	-	+	+	+	+	-	-	-	-	-
Ganglia	+	-	+	+	+	+	-	-	-	-	-
OpenNMS	+	-	+	+	+	+	-	-	-	-	-
Hyperic	+	+	+	+	+	+	-	-	-	-	-
Gomez	+	-	+	+	+	+	-	-	-	-	-
LogicMonitor	+	-	+	+	+	+	-	-	-	-	-
GridICE	+	+	+	+	+	+	-	-	+	+	-
Globus	+	+	+	+	+	+	-	-	+	+	-
MonALISA	+	+	+	+	+	+	+	+	+	+	+
CloudWatch	+	+	+	+	+	+	+	+	+	+	-

A Detailed View of Two Monitoring Solutions: IRMOS an RESERVOIR

The Cloud monitoring solutions presented in this section have been chosen due to the set of requirements they cover. They are the result of two successful EU funded projects, namely IRMOS (Boniface et al. 2010; Kyriazis et al., 2011) and RESERVOIR (Rochwerger et al., 2009), which have addressed the challenges in today's Cloud platform development.

IRMOS Monitoring

The IRMOS project mainly addresses real-time service provision in a Cloud infrastructure (mainly referring to multimedia and interactive applications) for all Service models, namely IaaS, PaaS and SaaS. Besides, the main project objective was to bridge the gap between the application developers and end users and the infrastructure providers. Among its other results, the project defined a service-oriented architecture consisting of a suite of tools and services that together provide a core Platform-as-a-Service (PaaS) functionality. This suite of tools provides capabilities such as resource provider discovery, advance reservation, workflow execution management, monitoring, Service Level Agreement (SLA) management, performance estimation, and application modeling among others. A view of its architecture can be seen in Figure 1.

The IRMOS Monitoring mechanism (Katsaros, 2010) is a two-layer approach which applies to Service Oriented platforms that includes a "virtualization" layer, composed of Virtual Machine Units (VMUs). The components related with an application workflow execution and the instance of the monitoring framework are deployed in these VMUs (Gogouvitis, 2012). The mechanism consists of six components:

Monitoring Framework Service (MFS): This component is part of the IRMOS platform's framework. It is used to start and stop the operation through the interfaces it exposes. In addition, it has access both to the collected data from both the infrastructure level and the application level and also the aggregated information through the

Figure 1. IRMOS Monitoring Architecture

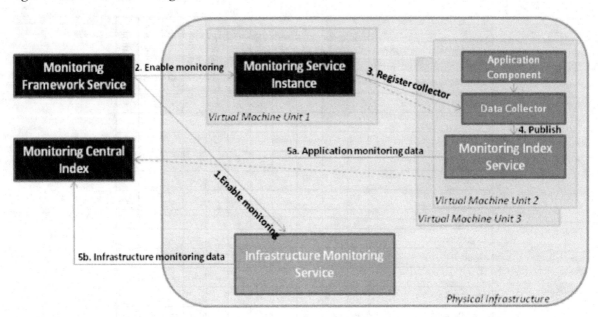

Monitoring Central Index. It serves a major role in the Cloud since it orchestrates the monitoring of all applications towards the virtual environment. It serves different and concurrent applications that are being deployed in separated virtual environments.

Monitoring Service Instance (MSI): The MSI is located within the Virtual Environment and is specific to every application workflow deployment. It is started by the MFS, which makes use of a specific interface exposed to it, so as to initiate the application monitoring. The MFS is also responsible to provide the parameters for configuring the workflow monitoring of the application. These parameters include, for example, the private IP addresses of the VMUs and the time granularity used by the Data Collector of each component.

Data Collector: The Data Collector is deployed in the same VMU with each application component in order to collect data from the application execution and publish them into the local Monitoring Index. Data Collectors are expected to be implemented by the Application developers and are not provided as part of the Cloud platform

itself. They should periodically generate an XML message which contains the parameters collected by them (names, values, measurement units, etc). The collection / generation period is set by the MFS to MSI at monitoring initiation time. The XML generated is stored in the local Monitoring Index.

Monitoring Index Service: This service is used as a local repository for the monitored parameters of each application component. Since it needs to communicate with the Data Collectors of each application, it is deployed in the same VMU as the application and the collectors, therefore allowing their direct communication and exchange of the high level information gathered. At every communication the parameter values are updated with the new ones provided by the collectors. It is the responsibility of the Monitoring Index Service to publish all application monitoring parameters to the Central Monitoring Index, at the time they are received.

Infrastructure Monitoring Service: This component collects the low level information of the VMUs execution on each physical host. The data collected are all published to the Monitoring Central Index. This is part of the IaaS provider.

Figure 2. The Lattice Monitoring Framework

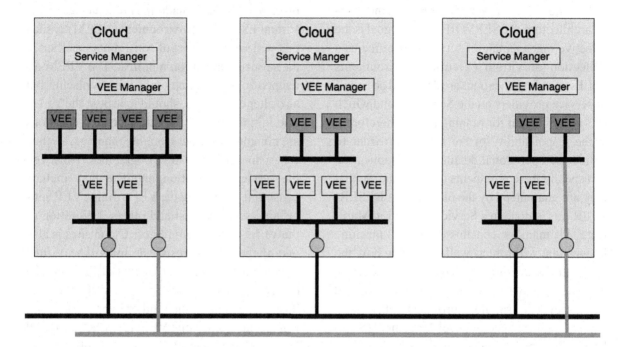

Monitoring Central Index: This serves the role of the global repository of the platform. The Monitoring Index Service and Infrastructure Monitoring Service are publishing to this index. Therefore, it is populated with both the high level monitored parameters of all application components and the low level parameters of the infrastructure. It follows from the way the application workflow monitoring starts that the refresh rate of the Central index differs per each individual application, since the MFS can set the collection time granularity differently.

The implementation of the framework presented is based on KVM (Kivity, Lublin, & Liguori, 2007) for the VMUs and the Globus Toolkit 4 (GT4) for the rest of the services. The GT4's Monitoring and Discovery Service (MDS) was employed for service discovery and the GT4 Indexing services were used for local and global monitoring indexes implementation.

The IRMOS Monitoring mechanism was tested and evaluated in several scenarios with real time requirements. Its primary evaluation had to do with a real-time distributed color correction system on live video streams. The system was shown to perform very well and timely in all of its tests, with response time in the order of milliseconds. When put under stress conditions, setting the data collection periods too low for all sub-systems involved, it still performed well, however there was a 0.5% chance to lose a report (the stress test was 30 minutes long).

RESERVOIR Monitoring

The RESERVOIR project is to enable the deployment of complex services on a Service Cloud that spans infrastructure providers and geographies, while ensuring QoS and security guarantees. That way a significant increase of the effectiveness of the compute utility is achieved. The architecture of the Lattice Monitoring Framework, upon which the RESERVOIR Monitoring has been built, is shown in Figure 2.

To analyze the monitoring system of RESERVOIR, the chapter first briefly presents the overall architecture. RESERVOIR primary goal is the effective management of services specified as a collection of virtual execution environments (VEEs). Such applications are deployed on behalf of service providers on the Service Cloud which acts as a platform for running them. Therefore it is the responsibility of the service provider to define the operational details of the application and specify its requirements to the Cloud, so that they are guaranteed by the platform. In RESERVOIR this is done in a Service Definition Manifest. This manifest contains the virtual machine images that will run, as well as specify how the application scales in the Cloud, trough the Elasticity Rules, and which are the minimum required service level that should be provided by the Cloud site, through the Service Level Agreement (SLA) Rules. The management functionality, required for both the provided services as well as for the infrastructure, is realized by a Service Manager (SM) and a VEE Manager (VEEM), both present in each Cloud site.

Service application instantiation requests originate from the Service Manager (SM). A VEE is created and configured per service component present in the manifest. The execution of the service applications is monitored in real-time. This information is exploited by the Service Manager in order to evaluate and execute the elasticity rules and ensure SLA compliance (Sahai, Graupner, Machiraju, & Van Moorsel, 2003). Elasticity of a service is managed by adjusting the application capacity. This effect is achieved by the addition or removal of service components and/or the change of the resource requirements for a particular component according to the load and measurable application behavior. The placement of VEEs into VEE hosts (VEEHs) is the responsibility of the Virtual Execution Environment Manager (VEEM). The later exposes an interface to the Service Manager, which support the creation of new VEEs and the resizing of existing ones. The placement decision made and implemented by the Virtual Execution Environment (VEEM) is such that will satisfy the set of constraints specified in the service application manifest. The VEEM attempts to optimize each site by initially placing, but also alter on moving, should it be best, the VEEs. The initial and subsequent placement decisions are not constraint but from the manifest, so they can span networks and geographies. However, the service application manifest may include constraints regarding the VEE affinity, VEE anti-affinity, security, cost and others. Federation of the VEEs to and from remote Cloud sites is also one of the VEEM responsibilities. The Virtual Execution Environment Hosts (VEEHs) can be categorized based on the type of VEEs they can host. For example, the kind of hypervisor in use is important, since one VEEH may be controlled by Xen hypervisor (Barham et al., 2003), while another is controlled by the KVM hypervisor (Kivity, Lublin, & Liguori, 2007). Moreover is is expected that in each Cloud site, several VEEHs are grouped together as a cluster.

The aforementioned components are the main ones found in the RESERVOIR architecture. In terms of interfaces the Service Manager exposes its interface (SMI) to the Service Provider. In the RESERVOIR platform, the Service Provider is the responsible entity for specifying the execution configuration and requirements for its application. It does so, by supplying the Service Definition Manifest. The Virtual Execution Environment Manager exposes its interface (VMI) to the Service Manager. In addition this interface is used for the site-to-site federation, so that the VEEMs communicate with each other. Finally the Virtual Execution Environment Hosts (VEEHs) expose their interface (VHI) to their controlling VEEM.

The Virtual Execution Environment Manager constantly attempts to optimize the resource utilization in the Cloud. This is attempted through the relocation of VEEs in a Cloud site or cross

Cloud site. Monitoring data are exploited towards the direction of meeting the application requirements specified in the manifest. The management components run its optimization processes autonomously, without any need for human intervention. To achieve this, a variety of measurement data are required to be fetched from a number of sources. The RESERVOIR Monitoring mechanism is designed to optimally monitor and provide these pieces of data to their respective consumers.

In order to cover the set of requirements from the monitoring component of the RESERVOIR architecture, the Lattice Monitoring Framework has been put in use. It is open source software. The Lattice Monitoring Framework offers a number of features, such as it is designed around producers & consumers, it separates data sources from probes and it creates a distribution network which focuses on optimal and minimal network resource utilization, as well as timely delivery of data to their destination(s).

The monitoring system used in the RESERVOIR project has been built on top of the Lattice Monitoring Framework. In order for this to happen, three kinds of probes had to be built, due to the kind of data that are required to b monitored (as explained above). These probes are designed to monitor (a) physical resources, (b) virtual resources, and (c) application specific resources. The physical resources are tracked by probes on the VEEHs which provide metrics such as CPU and memory utilization. The virtual resources are measure by probes installed in VEEs. These probes work in cooperation with the hypervisor in use. The application specific resources are embedded into the software actually running on the VEE.

Employing all these techniques the RESERVOIR Monitoring system nearly covers all of the requirements set in the previous sections. Its evaluation shows that it performs well and it proves that this performance and qualitative results are the result of its delegate architecture (Clayman et al., 2010).

A NEW PROPOSAL: THE VISION CLOUD MONITORING SOLUTION

The VISION CLOUD project (Kolodner et al., 2012) aims to support the setup and deployment of data and storage services on demand, at competitive costs, across disparate administrative domains, providing QoS and security guarantees. To analyze the monitoring system of VISION CLOUD, this section first briefly presents the overall architecture.

VISION Cloud Architecture

At the highest level, the VISION CLOUD architecture consists of one or more independent Storage Clouds, where each Cloud consists of one or more data centers, each containing physical compute and storage resources. Each Cloud defines a single administrative domain. One of the key features of this architecture, advancing over the state-of-the-art, is the capability to federate, i.e., logically connect disparate Clouds across administrative domains.

The architecture introduces two complementary services, namely the Data Service and the Management Service, which together provide the functions of VISION CLOUD as a Cloud for data-intensive services. The Data Service, including the Data Access Layer (DAL) and the Data Operating Layer (DOL), enables manipulation of data objects and their properties, computation on storage, mobility, availability, reliability and security. This service is distributed across the federated Clouds. The DAL provides unified interface to data across the Clouds, and encapsulates the DOL which realises the data service over a set of distributed heterogeneous physical resources.

The Management Service, including the Management Interface Layer (MIL) and the Management Operating Layer (MOL), enables service provisioning and monitoring, accounting and billing, security management and transformation of user-specified service level requirements

Figure 3. The VISION Monitoring Framework

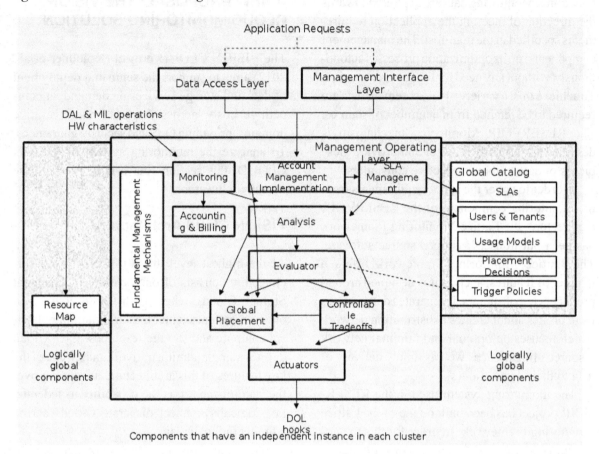

to management operations on the underlying infrastructure level. This service is also distributed across the federated Clouds. The MIL, just like the DAL, provides a unified interface to management of services across disparate federated Clouds, and encapsulates the MOL which realises the management service over a set of distributed heterogeneous physical resources. The MIL deploys management models that translate business level objectives into operating level settings and tasks.

Monitoring in VISION CLOUD

The monitoring component is responsible for the receipt and transmission of all events generated by the system to their appropriate listeners. The component itself goes beyond being a simple messaging system to aggregating, applying rules and extracting valuable information from the events received, therefore generating new events, which represent more complex states the VISION CLOUD can be at, and delivers them appropriately (see Figure 3).

The component is built around a hierarchical distributed stack of metering-dispatcher pair sub-systems responsible for the receipt of events from their sources and delivering them to their registered listeners. These sub-systems are identical, but operate in different layers of the VISION CLOUD, i.e. the cluster, the data center and the Cloud. They are configurable in that various listeners are registered with them and they specify the events that they are interested in are. These sub-systems are then capable of delivering those events to them.

In addition the monitoring component is also composed of an evaluation sub-system, which is modular. Its modules are able generate events from the ones received. Such modules include:

- **Aggregator:** This module is able to generate events which are themselves collections of a number of other events receipt over a period of time.
- **Rule System:** This is a rule application system on the events received.
- **Analysis:** This is a "clever" module which detects repeatable patterns on the receipt event sequence and is able to predict future states the VISION CLOUD will achieve (with a degree of certainty).

Furthermore, there exists a database, where certain events are stored as they are generated. Again, which events have this behavior is configurable.

The monitoring subsystem interface is split into three parts, for registration, event transmission and for configuring the evaluators.

- The Registration Interface is used for components' registration with the monitoring as listeners of a certain events' range. This interface allows a component to register either itself, or another one as listener.
- The Event Transmission Interface is used by the monitoring and its registered components to transmit events that are to be delivered to the later ones.
- This Evaluation Configuration Interface is used by external components of the monitoring, to setup any configuration parameters for the evaluator modules. Examples of such configuration include the rules used by the rule engine module, or the parameters for event aggregation (needed by the aggregation module).

The monitoring component interacts with a number of other components of the VISION CLOUD. They are mostly event consumers, although they can also act as systems which configure the monitoring. One important aspect of this binding is that the interacting components may "plug" with monitoring at the level they are running. For example the placement component will require getting events from monitoring at two levels. The data center placement will receive events which have to do with the respective data center, while the Cloud placement component will receive events which are generated at its own level.

The SLA management component is both an event consumer of monitoring and also acts as a configuration system for it. As an event consumer, it requires information on SLA status and especially the events which have to do with the violation of an SLA. As a configuration mechanism, it is the component responsible to set appropriate rules and policies to the base monitoring framework, as well as to the monitoring evaluation modules, which are in accordance to the SLAs at hand.

The accounting and billing component is an event consumer of monitoring, since it requires a view of per user actions, in order to bill the user according to their billing policy.

The decision mechanisms component is an event consumer of monitoring, since it requires a view of what's going on the system in order to reach a decision about placement & similar requests.

The storlet engine is an event consumer of monitoring in order to manage the storlets lifecycle.

The innovation of the VISION CLOUD Monitoring architecture lies in the way aggregation is achieved. The system will merge two technologies, one of the Rule Engines, making use of the RETE algorithm (Forgy, 1979) and that of geometric monitoring in Cloud environments. The RETE algorithm is an efficient pattern matching algorithm. It is based on building a network of logical filters or tuples which are subsequently used for in more filters and finally end up in evaluating certain conditions over a set of data. It is a well-known and widely used algorithm, with many variations to its original form, depending on the implementation and application domain.

The Geometric approach to monitoring offers also an efficient way to go beyond monitoring aggregated values of the raw data taken from the installed probes, like frequencies of events. The algorithm is based on applying a set of constraints locally on each of the data streams. These constraints filter out data increments which leave the monitoring result invariant, so as to save communication resources. The result of this method is the efficient monitoring of threshold functions over distributed data streams.

The VISION CLOUD Monitoring mechanism will merge these two techniques. It must be underlined that such a system is very extensive and adaptable, since all of the monitored functions / conditions can be re-configured at run-time, without affecting the performance of the system. Although making some compromises in the expressiveness of the patterns that can be matched, compared to using the original RETE algorithm (which allows for virtually any truth statement), is necessary, the outcome will be a very expressive language for specifying the conditions that should be monitored, allowing for other VISION CLOUD components to (a) offload some of their condition tracking logic for monitored data, (b) save bandwidth and storage for events, and (c) allow for a more intelligent system to be built around it, by integrating this Monitoring mechanism into the Cloud and making use of it by the decision making components.

FUTURE RESEARCH DIRECTIONS

The aforementioned solutions show that the goal of designing a Monitoring mechanism which both addresses autonomous operation and federation is not achieved yet. Research should continue in this field, addressing more than a single sub-domain. It is the view of the authors that the self-manageability is a task that will be achieved through a tighter integration of the monitoring mechanism and the decision making modules, in terms of the first allowing to the later more expressive power over what should be monitored. Decision making is as powerful as the input data it receives. Therefore, the more intelligently structured data and customized to the consuming decision making mechanisms, the more effective the decision making will be. In addition, advances in this area can lead to better behaved applications deployed on the Cloud, should the later be able to exploit the information gathered from the monitoring mechanism.

Another domain that needs to be advanced is the self-awareness of the Monitoring mechanism. Self-awareness is not limited to failover and error resistance. The system should be able to adapt to the variable loads of the Cloud, which alone puts a decision making module inside Monitoring. It is crucial to realize that the goal of such a step is to make Monitoring less invasive to the overall operation of the Cloud, but not lesser its service quality. Instead proper reconfiguration of itself should take place that will both lower the required resources and also ensure no information is lost. However, today's monitoring mechanisms lack a key piece of information required for achieving this goal, which is the knowledge of how the produced information is going to be used and what is the effect of each possible reconfiguration.

One key aspect of Cloud Monitoring which requires further research is Cloud federation. Maybe this is the most difficult task to achieve, when facing the variety and differences in the existing Cloud technologies employed today. The authors believe that some attempts to standardization of Monitoring APIs should be pursued, as has already happened in other domains of the Cloud technology (Cloud Data Management Interface (SNIA, 2009). However, the authors also believe that the full potential of monitoring solutions has not been explored yet; therefore constructing a broad enough API is quite a difficult task.

CONCLUSION

It is be made obvious from the presentation of the existing technologies, projects and frameworks that several solutions exist in most of the problems mentioned, but still there is no single recipe to achieve everything without making some compromises here and there. It is however our view that the active research on the field has led to very promising results, upon which the solutions for the Future Internet applications will be based upon. Beginning from very restrictive monitoring mechanisms tailored for the needs of an administrator of a distributed network, the advances of today's systems allow for mechanisms able to fully support and empower intelligent decision making systems, which constantly solve optimization problems to allow for the maximum use of the resources at hand. Such solutions lead the way to even more successful installations of Cloud sites and can make the a real difference in the end result, both in terms of the owner, by reducing their total cost of ownership (TCO), and to the customer, by both reducing their costs and also by being able to receive better service quality.

REFERENCES

About OpenNMS. (n.d.). Retrieved from http://www.opennms.org/about/

Amazon CloudWatch. (n.d.). Retrieved from http://aws.amazon.com/cloudwatch/

Andreozzi, S., De Bortoli, N., Fantinel, S., Ghiselli, A., Rubini, G. L., & Tortone, G. (2005). GridICE: a monitoring service for Grid systems. *Future Generation Computer Systems, 21*(4), 559–571. doi:10.1016/j.future.2004.10.005

Automated Monitoring. (n.d.). Retrieved from http://www.logicmonitor.com/features/automated-configuration/

Barham, P., Dragovic, B., Fraser, K., Hand, S., Harris, T., Ho, A., et al. (2003). Xen and the art of virtualization. M. L. Scott & L. L. Peterson, (Eds.)*Memory, 37*(5), 164-177. ACM. Berlin / Heidelberg. Retrieved from http://www.springerlink.com/index/10.1007/s11390-006-0513-y

Boniface, M., Nasser, B., Papay, J., Phillips, S. C., Servin, A., Xiaoyu, Y., et al. (2010, 9-15 May 2010). *Platform-as-a-Service Architecture for Real-Time Quality of Service Management in Clouds*. Paper presented at the Internet and Web Applications and Services (ICIW), 2010 Fifth International Conference on.

Clayman, S., Galis, A., Chapman, C., Toffetti, G., Rodero-Merino, L., & Vaquero, L. (2010). *Monitoring Service Clouds in the Future Internet. Framework* (pp. 115–126). Amsterdam, The Netherlands: IOS Press.

Collectd - The system statistics collection daemon. (n.d.). Retrieved from http://collectd.org/

Forgy, C. L. (1979). *On the efficient implementation of production systems*. Pittsburg, PA: Carnegie Mellon University.

Foster, I. (2005). Globus Toolkit Version 4: Software for Service-Oriented Systems. In Jin, H., Reed, D., & Jiang, W. (Eds.), *Journal of Computer Science and Technology* (*Vol. 3779*, pp. 2–13). New York, NY: Springer. doi:10.1007/11577188_2

Gogouvitis, S., Konstanteli, K., Waldschmidt, S., Kousiouris, G., Katsaros, G., & Menychtas, A. (2012). Workflow management for soft real-time interactive applications in virtualized environments. *Future Generation Computer Systems, 28*(1), 193–209. doi:10.1016/j.future.2011.05.017

Katsaros, G., Kousiouris, G., Gogouvitis, S., Kyriazis, D., & Varvarigou, T. (2010). *A service oriented monitoring framework for soft real-time applications*. Paper presented at the Service-Oriented Computing and Applications (SOCA), 2010 IEEE International Conference on. Washington, DC: IEEE Press

Keren, D., Sharfman, I., Schuster, A., & Livne, A. (2011). Shape Sensitive Geometric Monitoring. *Knowledge and Data Engineering, IEEE Transactions on, PP*(99), 1-1.

Kivity, A., Lublin, U., & Liguori, A. (2007). kvm: the Linux Virtual Machine Monitor. *Reading and Writing, 1*, 225–230.

Kolodner, E. K., Shulman-Peleg, A., Naor, D., Brand, P., Dao, M., & Eckert, A. (2012). Data-intensive Storage Services on Clouds: Limitations, Challenges and Enablers. In Petcu, D., & Poletti, J. V. (Eds.), *European Research Activities in Cloud Computing New Castle upon Tyne*. UK: Cambridge Scholars Publishing.

Kyriazis, D., Menychtas, A., Kousiouris, G., Oberle, K., Voith, T., & Boniface, M. (2011). *A Real-time Service Oriented Infrastructure. Control, 1(2)*. Global Science and Technology Forum.

Legrand, I. C., Newman, H. B., Voicu, R., Cirstoiu, C., Grigoras, C., Toarta, M., & Dobre, C. (2009). MonALISA: An agent based, dynamic service system to monitor, control and optimize distributed systems. *Computer Physics Communications, 180*(12), 2472–2498. doi:10.1016/j.cpc.2009.08.003

Massie, M. L., Chun, B. N., & Culler, D. E. (2004). The ganglia distributed monitoring system: design, implementation, and experience. *Parallel Computing, 30*(7), 817–840. doi:10.1016/j.parco.2004.04.001

Mell, P., & Grance, T. (2009). The NIST Definition of Cloud Computing. *National Institute of Standards and Technology, 53(6)*, 50. NIST. Retrieved from http://csrc.nist.gov/groups/SNS/cloud-computing/cloud-def-v15.doc

Nagios. (n.d.). Retrieved from http://nagios.org/about

Newman, H. B., Legrand, I. C., & Bunn, J. J. (2001). A distributed agent-based architecture for dynamic services. *CHEP2001 Beijing Sept.*

Newman, H. B., Legrand, I. C., Galvez, P., Voicu, R., & Cirstoiu, C. (2003). MonALISA: A Distributed Monitoring Service Architecture. *Arxiv preprint cs0306096*, cs.DC/0306, 8.

Rochwerger, B., Breitgand, D., Levy, E., Galis, A., Nagin, K., & Llorente, I. M. (2009). The Reservoir model and architecture for open federated cloud computing. *IBM Journal of Research and Development, 53*(4), 1–11. doi:10.1147/JRD.2009.5429058

Sahai, A., Graupner, S., Machiraju, V., & Van Moorsel, A. (2003). Specifying and monitoring guarantees in commercial grids through SLA. *CCGrid 2003 3rd IEEEACM International Symposium on Cluster Computing and the Grid 2003 Proceedings*, 292-299. Washington, DC: IEEE.

Sharfman, I., Schuster, A., & Keren, D. (2007). A geometric approach to monitoring threshold functions over distributed data streams. *ACM Transactions on Database Systems, 32*(4), 23. doi:10.1145/1292609.1292613

Skene, J., Lamanna, D., & Emmerich, W. (2004). *Precise Service Level Agreements*. In Proc. of the *26th nt. Conference on Software Engineering*, (pp. 179–188), Washington, DC: IEEE Computer Society Press.

SNIA. Cloud Storage Reference Model (2009). Retrieved from http://www.snia.org/tech_activities/publicreview/CloudStorageReferenceModelV03.pdf

SpringSource Hyperic. (n.d.). Retrieved from http://www.springsource.com/files/uploads/all/datasheets/S2_DataSheet_Hyperic_USLET_EN.pdf

The Gomez Platform: Overview. (n.d.). Retrieved from http://www.compuware.com/application-performance-management/the-gomez-platform.html

What is ntop? (n.d.). Retrieved from http://www.ntop.org/overview.html

ADDITIONAL READING

Autonomic Internet (AutoI) Project. Retrieved from http://www.ist-autoi.eu/, 2008-2010.

Cooke, A., Gray, A. J. G., Ma, L., Nutt, W., Magowan, J., Oevers, M., Taylor, P., et al. (2003). R-GMA: An Information Integration System for Grid Monitoring.

(2003). *CoopISDOAODBASE* (*Vol. 2888*, pp. 462–481). Springer.

Denazis, S., Bassi, A., Giacomin, P., Berl, A., Fischer, A., Srassner, J., et al. (2009). Management Architecture and Systems for Future Internet Networks. *Knowledge Creation Diffusion Utilization*, 112-122. IOS Press.

Design Principles, G. E. N. I. (2006)... *Computer*, *39*(9), 102–105. doi:10.1109/MC.2006.307

Foster, I., & Kesselman, C. (1997). Globus: A Metacomputing Infrastructure Toolkit. *International Journal of High Performance Computing Applications*, *11*(2), 115–128. doi:10.1177/109434209701100205

Future Internet Assembly (FIA). (n.d.) Retrieved from http://www.future-internet.eu/.

Future Internet Design (FIND) program. (n.d.) Retrieved from http://www.nets-find.net/.

Galis, A., Abramowicz, H., Brunner, M., Raz, D., & Chemouil, P. (2009). *Management and Service-aware Networking Architectures (MANA) for Future Internet - Position Paper: System Functions, Capabilities and Requirements. Group.* ChinaCom.

Kyriazis, D., Varvarigou, T., & Konstanteli, K. G. (2012). Achieving Real-Time in Distributed Computing: From Grids to Clouds (pp. 1-330).

KEY TERMS AND DEFINITIONS

Cloud: The Cloud is the provision of compute, storage, network and software Services to users in a virtualized way.

Cloud Management: The set of operations required for a Cloud infrastructure to operate.

Cloud Monitoring: Monitoring solutions applied to Cloud Infrastructure.

Distributed Computing: A system which performs operations in a distributed environment.

Federation: The ability to use more than one Cloud provider and have their services interoperate.

Rule Engine: A system which applies a set of rules on data and takes actions based on the results of these applications.

Virtualization: The creation & provision of resources which are virtual, rather than actual, enabling them to be used as a service.

Chapter 8
Availability Analysis of IaaS Cloud Using Analytic Models

Francesco Longo
Università degli Studi di Messina, Italia

Rahul Ghosh
Duke University, USA

Vijay K. Naik
IBM T. J. Watson Research Center, USA

Kishor S. Trivedi
Duke University, USA

ABSTRACT

Cloud based systems are inherently large scale. Failures in such a large distributed environment are quite common phenomena. To reduce the overall Cloud downtime and to provide a seamless service, providers need to assess the availability characteristics of their data centers. Such assessments can be done through controlled experimentations, large scale simulations and via analytic models. In the scale of Cloud, conducting repetitive experimentations or simulations might be costly and time consuming. Analytic models, on the other hand, can be used as a complement to small scale measurements and simulations since the analytic results can be obtained quickly. However, accurate analytic modeling requires dealing with large number of system states, leading to state-space explosion problem. To reduce the complexity of analysis, novel analytic methods are required. This chapter introduces the reader to a novel approach using interacting analytic sub-models and shows how such approach can deal with large scale Cloud availability analysis. The chapter puts the work in perspective of other existing and ongoing research in this area, describe how such approach can be useful to Cloud providers, especially in the case of federated scenarios, and summarize the open research questions that are yet to be solved.

DOI: 10.4018/978-1-4666-1631-8.ch008

Copyright © 2012, IGI Global. Copying or distributing in print or electronic forms without written permission of IGI Global is prohibited.

INTRODUCTION

Cloud computing is a model of Internet-based computing. An IaaS Cloud, such as Amazon EC2 and IBM SmatCloud Enterprise™ (Amazon EC2: http://aws.amazon.com/ec2, 2011; IBM SmatCloud Enterprise™: www.ibm.com/services/us/en/cloud-enterprise/, 2011) delivers, on-demand, operating system (OS) instances provisioning computational resources in the form of VMs deployed in the Cloud provider's data center. Requests submitted by the users are provisioned and served if the Cloud has enough available capacity in terms of physical machines (PMs). Large Cloud service providers such as IBM provide service level agreements (SLAs) regulating the availability of the Cloud service. Before committing an SLA to the customers of a Cloud, the service provider needs to carry out availability analysis of the infrastructure on which the Cloud service is hosted. This chapter shows how stochastic analytic models can be utilized for Cloud service availability analysis. It first provides a background on the subject describing how the problem is faced in the current literature. Then, it proposes an example of one-level monolithic model that can be used to analyze the availability of an IaaS Cloud. However, such monolithic models become intractable as the size of Cloud increases. To overcome this difficulty, the chapter illustrates the use of an interacting sub-models approach. Overall model solution is obtained by iteration over individual sub-model solutions. Comparison of the results with monolithic model shows that errors introduced by model decomposition are negligible. It also shows how closed form solutions of the sub-models can be obtained and demonstrate that the approach can scale for large size Clouds. The presence of three pools of PMs and the migration of them from one pool to another caused by failure events makes the model both novel, interesting and particularly suitable in federated environments. In order to automate the construction and solution of underlying Markov models, the authors use a variant of stochastic Petri net (SPN) called stochastic reward net (SRN). This paradigm is supported by SHARPE (Trivedi & Sahner, 2009) and Stochastic Petri Net Package (SPNP) (Hirel, Tuffin, & Trivedi, 2000) software packages.

Rest of the chapter is organized as follows. Section II gives a background on the subject illustrating the state of the art. Section III provides an introduction to the formalism that will be used in the following to model the considered scenario. Section IV describes Cloud system model, assumptions and problem formulation. Section V, presents the monolithic SRN model. Interacting SRN sub-models are described in Section VI and their closed form solutions are presented in Section VII. Fixed point iteration among the interacting sub-models and proof of existence of a solution is shown in Section VIII. Results obtained from monolithic approach and interacting sub-models approach are compared in Section IX. Sections X and XI discuss how the approach can be used by Cloud providers, point out future challenges and highlight the benefit of decomposed models in the analysis of federation scenarios. The chapter concludes in Section XII.

BACKGROUND

This section highlights key analytic approaches for system availability assessment. There are four main types of analytic modeling techniques (Nicol, Sanders, & Trivedi, 2004; Trivedi, 2001; Trivedi, Kim, Roy, & Medhi, 2009) that can be applied for availability analysis: non-state-space models, state-space space models, hierarchical, and fixed-point iterative models (Haring, Marie, Puigjaner, & Trivedi, 2001; Longo, Ghosh, Naik, & Trivedi, 2011; Mainkar & Trivedi, 1996; Tomek & Trivedi, 1991). Reliability block diagram (RBD), reliability graph (Relgraph), fault tree (FT) are examples of non-state-space models. Such models can be easily developed assuming statistical independence between system components and thus allowing a fast solution for system reliability, system MTTF and system availability. However, non-state space models cannot easily handle failure/repair dependencies (e.g., shared repair, warm/cold spares, imperfect coverage, etc.). In order to model complex interactions between system components, Markov chains or more generally state-space models can be used (Trivedi, 2001). Markov chains consist of state(s) and state transition(s). In Discrete Time Markov Chains (DTMC), all transition labels are probabilities. In Continuous Time Markov Chains (CTMC), all transition labels are rates. If the rates are time dependent then we have a non-homogeneous CTMC. If each label is a distribution function (Yin, Fricks, & Trivedi, 2002) then we have a Semi-Markov Process (SMP) or a Markov Regenerative Process (MRGP) (Kulkarni, 2010). Markovian and non-Markovian models may suffer from the state-space explosion problem (or largeness problem). SPNs (Trivedi, 2001) or SRNs can be used for easy specification and automated generation/solution of underlying Markov models to tolerate largeness. To avoid largeness problems, hierarchical models (Chen, Dharmaraja, Chen, Li, Trivedi, Some, & Nikora, 2002; Kim, Machida, & Trivedi, 2009; Smith, Trivedi, Tomek, & Ackaret, 2008; Tomek, Muppala, & Trivedi, 1993; Trivedi, Vasireddy, Trindade, Nathan, & Castro, 2006; Trivedi, Wang, Hunt, Rindos, Smith, & Vashaw, 2008) or interacting sub-models can be used. In interacting sub-models approach (Longo, Ghosh, Naik, & Trivedi, 2011), dependencies among the sub-models are usually resolved by fixed-point iterations (Haring, Marie, Puigjaner, & Trivedi, 2001; Mainkar & Trivedi, 1996; Tomek & Trivedi, 1991). Such interacting sub-models can be used for analysis of large scale Cloud infrastructure.

In (Vishwanath, & Nagappan, 2010), Vishwanath et al. investigated failure characteristics of servers in large Cloud data centers. They explored the relationship between the failure of a PM and other factors (e.g., age of the PM, number of disks on a PM etc.), tried to quantify the relationships

between successive failures on same PM by analyzing experimental data and finally empirically compute reliability. The analytic approach described in this chapter can be complementary to this work since it takes into consideration multiple classes of PMs and consider their failure and repair. In (Yang, Tan, Dai, & Guo, 2009), Yang et al. investigated the failure of workloads on Cloud service performance. They considered response time as the performance metric. Although, such joint analysis of availability and performance is important, the authors do not address the scalability issues. This chapter restricts itself only to the scalability of availability models. In (Bonvin, Papaioannou, & Aberer, 2009), Bonvin et al. designed a reliable and cost-effective storage system that maintains high availability guarantees despite failures of servers. The authors address interesting cost-optimization questions. Similar optimization problems can be formulated using the models and approach that is described in this chapter. In (Joshi, Bunker, Jahanian, Moorsel, & Weinman, 2009), Joshi et al. discussed the key challenges and opportunities in achieving high availability in large scale Cloud services. They outline different security threats, privacy issues and compliance requirements for a highly available Cloud. Although, the authors do not solve any specific problem, their work can provide interesting open research issues in this area.

There are limited research efforts which investigated availability in large scale infrastructure. In (Tan, Gu, & Wang, 2010), Tan et al. designed and implemented a prediction system to achieve robust hosting for production hosting infrastructure. Specifically, they designed a system called ALERT to predict anomalies in the system. In the context of this chapter, anomalies in failure-repair behavior can be viewed as a sub-problem as addressed by the Tan et al. Moreover, the modeling approach described here can be complementary to such experimental work. In (Javadi, Kondo, Vincent, & Anderson, 2010), Javadi et al. show how statistical models can be useful to predict availability of an Internet distributed system. Analytic models described in this chapter can perhaps be combined with the statistical models proposed by Javadi et al. In (Uemura, Dohi, & Kaio, 2009), Uemura et al. used discrete time semi-Markov process to describe the stochastic behavior of a scalable intrusion tolerant system. In contrast, for Cloud availability analysis, the chapter starts with Petri net (PN) based models, to facilitate automated generation of Markov chains and subsequently decompose the large PN model into small PNs and eventually to Markov chains. In (Chen, Zhou, & Xiong, 2010) Chen et al. used a deterministic and stochastic PN method to illustrate the performance of producer/consumer based application models in Cloud context. Unlike the approach proposed here, they focus only on performance behavior of Cloud. In the previous work (Ghosh, Longo, Naik, & Trivedi, 2010), the authors showed an SRN modeling approach for resiliency analysis of IaaS Cloud but scalability of such approach needs to be investigated. The key challenges in developing an analytic model for Cloud are: (i) developed models should be accurate by taking into account different system details, and (ii) the models should be scalable and tractable i.e., their solution times should be negligible, especially in the case of federated environments. The subsequent sections describe how such an analytic model can be developed.

STOCHASTIC PETRI NETS AND REWARD NETS

This section presents an overview of SPNs and SRNs. A PN can be formally defined as a 4-tuple: $PN = (P, T, A, M)$, where P is the finite set of places (represented by circles), T is the finite set of transitions (represented by bars), A is the set of arcs (connecting elements of P and T) and M is the set of markings each of which denotes the number of tokens in the places of the net. In SPN, exponentially distributed firing times can be associated to the net transitions so that the stochastic process underlying a SPN is a CTMC. In generalized SPNs (GSPN) (Marsan, Balbo, & Conte, 1984), transitions are allowed to be either timed (exponentially distributed firing time, drawn as rectangular boxes) or immediate (zero firing time, represented by thin black bars). Immediate transitions always have priority over timed transitions and if both timed and immediate transitions are enabled in a marking then timed transitions are treated as if they were not enabled. If several immediate transitions compete for firing, a specified probability mass function is used to break the tie. A marking of a GSPN is called vanishing if at least one immediate transition is enabled in it. A marking is called tangible otherwise. GSPN also introduces the concept of inhibitor arc (represented by a small hollow circle at the end of the arc) which connects a place to a transition. A transition with an inhibitor arc cannot fire if the input place of the inhibitor arc contains more tokens than the multiplicity of the arc.

SRNs (Ciardo, Blakemore, Chimento, Muppala, & Trivedi, 1993) are extensions of GSPNs. In SRNs, every tangible marking can be associated with a reward rate thus facilitating the computation of a variety of performance measures. Key features of SRNs are:

1. Each transition may have an enabling function (also called a guard) so that a transition is enabled only if its marking-dependent enabling function is true;
2. Marking dependent arc multiplicities are allowed;
3. Marking dependent firing rates are allowed;
4. Transitions can be assigned different priorities;
5. Besides traditional output measures obtained from a GSPN, such as throughput of a transition and mean number of tokens in a place, more complex measures can be computed by using reward functions.

PROBLEM DEFINITION

System Model and Assumptions

In IaaS Cloud, when a request is processed, a pre-built image is used to create one or more VM instances. When the VM instances are deployed, they are provisioned with request specific CPU, RAM, and disk capacity. VMs are deployed on PMs each of which may be shared by multiple VMs. To reduce overall VM provisioning delays and operational costs, it is a common practice to group the PMs into a certain number of tiered pools. Here, it is supposed that PMs are grouped into three pools; hot (running), warm (turned on, but not ready) and cold (turned off). Maintaining the PMs in three pools (in general, multiple tiered pools) helps to minimize power and cooling costs without incurring high startup delays for all VMs. A pre-instantiated VM can be readily provisioned and brought to ready state on a running PM (hot PM) with minimum provisioning delay. Instantiating a VM from an image and deploying it on a warm PM needs additional provisioning time. PMs in the cold pool are turned-off when not in use and deploying a VM on such a PM adds to the startup delays. A performability model of this system was presented in (Ghosh, Trivedi, Naik, & Kim, 2010) where it has been shown that the "bottleneck" model is the availability model. Hence, the objective of this chapter is to show a scalable availability model of Cloud service with the following assumptions:

1. Variety of failures/repairs can occur in a Cloud environment such as failure/repair of hardware, software, hypervisor, VM, OS and applications. Here, only the net effect of different failures and repairs of PMs in the hot, warm and cold pools are considered. The authors do not consider software and OS failures in a VM. Typically, these failures are handled by restarting the VM. Although the cause of a PM failure can be because of

variety of reasons, in the analysis the net combined effect on the PM failure rate is considered. However, it is possible to extend such availability model to capture detailed PM failure modes and recovery steps as in (Trivedi, 2001; Trivedi, Wang, Hunt, Rindos, Smith, & Vashaw, 2008).

2. It is assumed that all times to failure are exponentially distributed. Equivalent mean time to failure (MTTF) of each hot PM is $1/\lambda_h$ and that of each warm PM is $1/\lambda_w$. Typically $1/\lambda_w$ is higher than $1/\lambda_h$ by a factor of 2 to 4. Cold machines can fail with a very low failure rate $1/\lambda_c$ with $\lambda_h \gg \lambda_c$ and $\lambda_w \gg \lambda_c$. It is possible to remove the assumption of exponential distribution as done in (Wang, Fricks, & Trivedi, 2003).

3. All PMs in a pool are identical. Failure of a PM in one pool triggers migration of a PM (if available) from other pools to replace the failed one. When a hot PM fails, the failed PM needs to be repaired and at the same time the system tries to replace it by a warm PM, if available (i.e., in "UP" state). If no warm PM is available, replacement is attempted by migrating an available cold PM to the hot pool. When a warm PM fails, the failed PM undergoes repair and at the same time it is replaced by a PM from the cold pool (if there is at least one PM available in cold pool). It is assumed that the migration process is instantaneous.

4. Each pool has its own repair facilities. Within a pool, maximum number of PMs that can be repaired in parallel is assumed to be n_r. Value of n_r is assumed to be greater or equal to 1 but less than the maximum number of PMs in the pool. When the number of PM failures are higher than n_r, failed PMs are put in a queue for repair. Across different pools, repairs can be done in parallel. It is assumed that time to repair is exponentially distributed with mean $1/\mu$. Once a failed

PM is repaired, it is returned to the original pool where it belonged before failure. If a PM was borrowed from other pool to replace the failed PM; such borrowed PM is also returned to its original pool instantaneously.

Problem Formulation

Assume that n_h, n_w, and n_c PMs are initially available in the hot, warm, and cold pools, respectively. A possible definition of availability in such a context is that at least k PMs (with $1 \leq k \leq n_h + n_w + n_c$) should be available across all the pools combined in order for the system to be up. Under the failure, repair, and migration of the PMs across different pools, the authors show how to compute the average number of PMs in each pool at steady state and the effects of downtime on the Cloud service.

It starts by developing a monolithic model using the high level formalism of SRN for the automated generation and solution of the underlying Markov chain. The monolithic model is not scalable to the large size Clouds that are to be analyzed and that can be present in a federated environment. Hence, an interacting SRN sub-models approach that is scalable is shown. As an important side-benefit, the decomposition also enables the user to obtain closed form solutions of sub-models. Three key comparisons are made between these two approaches: (i) errors introduced by interacting sub-models, (ii) maximum number of PMs that each approach can handle and (iii) solution time required for both the approaches. Through systematic analysis, the authors show that interacting SRN sub-models approach is highly scalable compared to single monolithic modeling approach. Closed form solutions of the sub-models are especially useful in providing a highly scalable and fast method for the availability analysis of large sized IaaS Cloud.

MONOLITHIC AVAILABILITY MODEL

Monolithic SRN model for the availability analysis of IaaS Cloud is shown in Figure 1.

Input parameters of monolithic model are: (1) initial number of PMs in each pool (n_h, n_w, and n_c), (2) MTTFs of hot, warm, and cold PMs ($1 / \lambda_h$, $1 / \lambda_w$, and $1 / \lambda_h$, respectively), (3) number of repair facilities for each pool (n_r), (4) MTTR of a PM ($1 / \mu$). Among the input parameters, n_h, n_w, n_c and n_r are design parameters, MTTF and MTTR values are measured. Five guard functions are defined on the model and they are described in Table 1.

Places P_h, P_w, and P_c represent the hot, warm, and cold pool, respectively. Number of tokens in these places indicates the number of "UP" PMs in the corresponding pool. Transitions T_{bwhf}, T_{bchf}, and T_{hf} represent the failure event of a hot PM. Since migration of a PM is attempted upon failure of a hot PM, three cases are possible: (1) T_{bwhf} fires if a warm PM is available for migration to the hot pool, (2) T_{bchf} fires if the warm pool is empty but a cold PM is available to be borrowed, and (3) T_{hf} fires if both the warm and the cold pool are empty so that no PM is available to substitute the failed hot PM. The guard functions $[g_1]$ and $[g_2]$ model the three mutually exclusive cases. Moreover, rates of these transitions are considered to be dependent on the number of tokens in place P_h so that the overall hot PM failure rate is equal to $ë_h$ multiplied by the number of available hot PMs. These marking dependent firing rates are represented by the # symbol near the input arcs which connect the transitions T_{bwhf}, T_{bchf}, and T_{hf} to the place P_h.

Upon firing of transition T_{bwhf}, a token is removed from place P_w and the number of tokens in place P_h remains unchanged. At the same time, a token is deposited in place P_{bw}. This place keeps track of number of failed PMs that need to be repaired and given back to the warm pool at the

Figure 1. Monolithic SRN model for availability analysis of IaaS Cloud

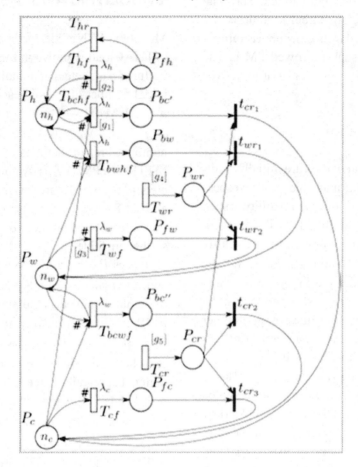

end of the repair process. Similarly, upon firing of transition T_{bchf}, a token is removed from place P_c and the number of tokens in place P_h remains unchanged. Simultaneously, a token is deposited in place $P_{bc'}$ to take into account that a PM has to be repaired and given back to the cold pool. Upon firing of transition T_{hf}, following token exchanges happen: (i) removal of a token from place P_h to model the reduction in number of available PMs in the hot pool by one and (ii) deposition of a token in place P_{fh} to model that the failed PM has to be repaired and given back to the hot pool.

Failure-repair behavior of warm pool is modeled similarly. Transitions T_{bcwf}, and T_{wf} model the failure event of a warm PM. Two cases are

possible: (1) T_{bcwf} fires if a cold PM is available for migration to warm pool, and (2) T_{wf} fires if the cold pool is empty and no PM is available to substitute the failed warm PM. The guard function $[g_3]$ models the fact that the two cases are mutually exclusive. Rates of transitions T_{bcwf} and T_{wf} are considered to be dependent on the number of tokens in place P_w so that the overall warm PM failure rate is equal to $\ddot{e}_w$ multiplied by the number of available warm PMs. Firing of T_{bcwf} removes a token from place P_c and deposits a token to place $P_{bc''}$ representing the failed PM that needs to be repaired and given back to the cold pool. Upon firing of T_{wf}, a token is removed from place P_w and a token is deposited to place P_{fw} repre-

Table 1. Guard functions defined on monolithic SRN model and interacting SRN sub-models

Guard functions	Values
g_1	1 if $\#P_w = 0$ 0 otherwise
g_2	1 if $\#P_w = 0$ and $\#P_c = 0$ 0 otherwise
g_3	1 if $\#P_c = 0$ 0 otherwise
g_4	1 if $\#P_{fw} + \#P_{bw} > 0$ 0 otherwise
g_5	1 if $\#P_{fc} + \#P_{bc'} + \#P_{bc''} > 0$ 0 otherwise

senting the failed PM that needs to be repaired and given back to the warm pool.

Transition T_{cf} fires when a cold PM fails. Rate of such transition is considered to be dependent on the number of tokens in place P_c so that the overall cold PM failure rate is equal to $\ddot{e}_c$ multiplied by the number of available cold PMs. Upon firing of T_{cf}, a token is removed from place P_c and deposited to place P_{fc}.

Transitions T_{hr}, T_{wr}, and T_{cr} model the repair of the failed PMs. Rates of these transitions are marking dependent to take into account the presence of n_r repair facilities for each pool. In particular, the rates of the above mentioned transitions are reported in Table 2. Guard functions $[g_4]$ and $[g_5]$ allow transitions T_{wr}, and T_{cr} to be enabled only when at least one PM needs to be repaired. Immediate transitions $t_{wr_1}, t_{wr_2}, t_{cr_1}, t_{cr_2}$ and t_{cr_3} model the instantaneous migrations of repaired PMs to the original pool.

Model Outputs

Outputs of the model are obtained using the Markov reward approach by assigning an appropriate reward rate to each marking of the SRN and then computing the expected reward rate both in transient and steady state as the desired measures (Trivedi, 2001). Let r_i be the reward rate assigned to marking i of the SRN in Figure 1. If $\pi_i(t)$ denotes the probability for the SRN to be in marking i at time t then the expected reward rate at time t is given by $\sum_i \pi_i(t) r_i$. The expected steady state reward rate can be computed by taking into consideration the steady state probabilities π_i of the SRN as $\sum_i \pi_i r_i$. The measures of interest are following.

1. **Mean number of PMs in each pool:** The mean number of PMs in the hot pool is given by the mean number of tokens in the corresponding place P_h ($E[P_h]$). Similarly, for the warm and the cold pool the mean number of tokens in places P_w and P_c are considered, respectively ($E[P_w]$ and $E[P_c]$). Reward assignment for this measures is shown in Table 3.

2. **Availability of Cloud service (A):** As mentioned above, the authors consider the Cloud service to be available if the total number of PMs across all hot, warm, and cold pool is greater than or equal to **k** (with

Table 2. Rates of transitions modeling the repair of failed PMs in monolithic SRN model and interacting SRN sub-models

Transitions	Rates of transitions
T_{hr}	$\#P_{fh} \cdot \mu$ if $\#P_{fh} \leq n_r$ $n_r \cdot \mu$ otherwise
T_{wr}	$(\#P_{fw} + \#P_{bw}) \cdot \mu$ if $\#P_{fw} + \#P_{bw} \leq n_r$ $n_r \cdot \mu$ otherwise
T_{cr}	$(\#P_{fc} + \#P_{bc'} + \#P_{bc''}) \cdot \mu$ if $\#P_{fc} + \#P_{bc'} + \#P_{bc''} \leq n_r$ $n_r \cdot \mu$ otherwise

$1 \leq k \leq n_h + n_w + n_c$). As a consequence, the reward assignment for this measure is the one shown in Table 3.

INTERACTING SRN SUB-MODELS

The monolithic model is decomposed into three sub-models, each of which captures the failure and repair behavior of a single pool. Here, it is described how these three sub-models interact with each other and can be used to compute the same quantities that are computed from the monolithic model. The SRN sub-models for the hot, warm and cold pool are shown in Figures 2, 3 and 4, respectively. Observe that some of the transitions of the monolithic model are present in more than one sub-model. Hence, to obtain overall model solution, sub-models exchange some of the input parameters and output measures. Guard functions $[g_1], [g_2]$ and $[g_3]$ are not present in the interacting sub-models approach while the rates of transitions T_{hr}, T_{wr}, and T_{cr} are still marking dependent according to the functions described in Table 2.

The structure of the hot pool sub-model in Figure 2 is obtained from the structure of the monolithic model by keeping the transitions that directly interact with place P_h and disregarding the others and the related places. Input parameters to this sub-model are: (i) initial number of PMs

in hot pool (n_h), (ii) hot PMs failure rate (λ_h), (iii) hot PMs repair rate (μ), (iv) number of repair facilities in the hot pool (n_r). Among these input parameters, n_h and n_r are design parameters, λ_h and μ are measured. Assume p_w and p_c are the probabilities to have at least one PM available in warm and cold pool, respectively as computed from the warm and cold pool sub-models discussed later. In the hot pool sub-model, the rate of transition T_{bwhf} is $\lambda_h p_w$. This is because, in the monolithic model, an arc is present from place P_w to such a transition. In the hot pool sub-model, place P_w is not present but still the impact of the behavior of the warm pool sub-model on the throughput of transition T_{bwhf} needs to be taken into account by scaling its rate with the quantity p_w. Similarly, the rate of transition T_{bchf} is $\lambda_h(1 - p_w)p_c$ because it is necessary to take into account the presence of the arc from place P_c (by multiplying with p_c) and the guard function $[g_1]$ (by multiplying with $1 - p_w$) as used in the monolithic model. Finally, the rate of transition T_{hf} is $\lambda_h(1 - p_w)(1 - p_c)$ because it is necessary to take into account the presence of the guard function $[g_2]$. From the hot pool sub-model the example computes $E[\#P_h]$ that represents the mean number of tokens in place P_h, i.e., mean number of available PMs in the hot pool. It will be used in the warm and cold pool

Figure 2. SRN sub-model for the availability analysis of the hot pool

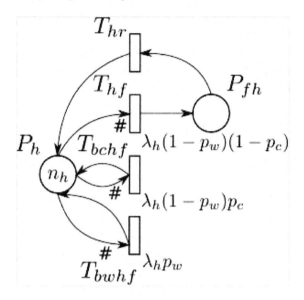

SRN sub-models to approximate the rate of transitions T_{bwhf} and T_{bchf}. Moreover, from the hot pool sub-model the example computes the probability (A_{k_h}) for the hot pool to be available, i.e., the probability for the number of tokens in place P_h to be greater or equal to k_h with $0 < k_h \leq n_h$. It will be used to compute the overall Cloud service availability from the interacting sub-models. These output measures can be computed by assigning the reward rates reported in Table 3.

Similar to the hot pool sub-model, the structure of the warm pool sub-model in Figure 3 is obtained from the structure of the monolithic model by keeping the transitions that directly interact with place P_w and disregarding the others and the related places. Input parameters to this sub-model are: (i) initial number of PMs in warm pool (n_w), (ii) warm PMs failure rate (λ_w), (iii) warm PMs repair rate (μ) and (iv) number of repair facilities for the warm pool (n_r). Among these input parameters, n_w and n_r are design parameters, λ_w and μ are measured. Computation of rate of transitions T_{bcwf} and T_{wf} is similar to the computation

of rate of transitions T_{bwhf}, T_{bchf} and T_{hf} as described for hot pool sub-model. Probability p_c is obtained from cold pool sub-model. However, the rate of transition T_{bwhf} needs to be set so that the throughput of this transition and the throughput of the transition with the same name in the hot pool sub-model are equal. In fact, the two transitions are same in the monolithic model. By equaling the throughput of such transitions, the example obtains:

$$rate_w(T_{bwhf}) = \ddot{e}_h E[\# P_h] \qquad (1)$$

where $E[\# P_h]$ is obtained from hot pool sub-model.

Outputs of warm pool sub-model are: (i) probability (p_w) to have at least one token in place P_w, i.e., at least one PM is available in the warm pool, (ii) mean number of tokens $(E[\# P_w])$ in place P_w, i.e., mean number of available PMs in the warm pool, and probability (A_{k_w}) for the number of tokens in place P_w to be greater or equal to k_w (with $0 \leq k_w \leq n_w$), i.e., availability of the warm pool. Among these output measures p_w will be used as an input parameter to the hot pool SRN sub-model to approximate the rates of transitions T_{bwhf}, T_{bchf} and T_{hf}, $E[\# P_w]$ will be used as an input parameter to the cold pool SRN sub-model to approximate the rate of transition T_{bcwf}, and A_{k_w} will be used to compute the overall Cloud service availability from the interacting sub-models. The reward rates assignment for such output measures are shown in Table 3.

Also in the case of cold pool, the structure of the sub-model in Figure 4 can be obtained from the structure of the monolithic model by keeping the transitions that directly interact with place P_c and disregarding the others and the related places. Input parameters to the cold pool sub-model are: (i) initial number of PMs in cold pool (n_c), (ii) cold PMs failure rate (λ_c), (iii) cold PMs

Figure 3. SRN sub-model for the availability analysis of the warm pool

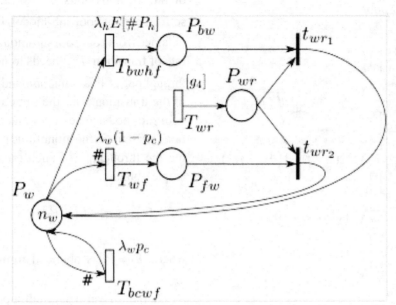

Figure 4. SRN sub-model for the availability analysis of the cold pool

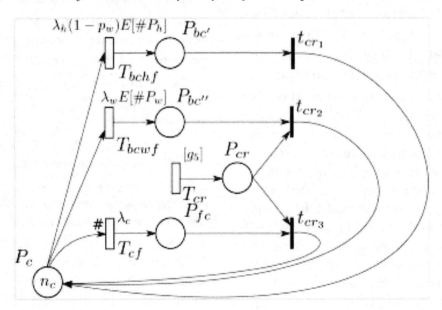

repair rate (μ) and (iv) number of repair facilities for the cold pool (n_r). Among these input parameters, n_c and n_r are design parameters, λ_c and μ are measured. Following similar arguments as in the case of warm pool, the rate of transitions T_{bchf}

and T_{bcwf} can be computed in the cold pool sub-model:

$$rate_c(T_{bchf}) = \ddot{e}_h(1 - p_w)E[\# P_h] \qquad (2)$$

Table 3. Reward rates to compute different output measures from monolithic SRN model and interacting SRN sub-models

Measures	Reward rates
Mean number of PMs in the hot pool ($E[\#P_h]$)	$\#P_h$
Mean number of PMs in the warm pool ($E[\#P_w]$)	$\#P_w$
Mean number of PMs in the cold pool ($E[\#P_c]$)	$\#P_c$
Availability of cloud service (A)	1 if $(\#P_h + \#P_w + \#P_c) \geq k$; 0 o/w
Availability of hot pool (A_{k_h})	1 if $\#P_h \geq k_h$; 0 o/w
Availability of warm pool (A_{k_w})	1 if $\#P_w \geq k_w$; 0 o/w
Availability of cold pool (A_{k_c})	1 if $\#P_c \geq k_c$; 0 o/w
Probability to have at least one PM in warm pool (p_w)	1 if $\#P_w \geq 1$; 0 o/w
Probability to have at least one PM in cold pool (p_c)	1 if $\#P_c \geq 1$; 0 o/w

and

$$rate_c(T_{bcwf}) = \ddot{e}_w E[\#P_w] \qquad (3)$$

where p_w and $E[\#P_w]$ are obtained from warm pool sub-model, and $E[\#P_h]$ is obtained from hot pool sub-model. Output measures of cold pool sub-model are: (i) probability (p_c) to have at least one token in place P_c, i.e., at least one PM is available in the cold pool, (ii) mean number of tokens $(E[\#P_c])$ in place P_c, i.e., mean number of available PMs in the cold pool, and (iii) the probability (A_{k_c}) for the number of tokens in place P_c to be greater or equal to k_c (with $0 \leq k_c \leq n_c$), i.e., the cold pool availability. p_c will be used as an input parameter to the hot and warm SRN sub-models to approximate the rate of transitions $T_{bchf}, T_{hf}, T_{bcwf}$ and T_{wf}. A_{k_c} will be used to compute the overall Cloud service availability. Reward assignments for such output measures are reported in Table 3.

All these sub-models and the interactions among them are shown as an import graph in Figure 5. The figure briefly describes the interactions among these models here. The hot pool sub-model computes the mean number of PMs in the hot pool ($E[\#P_c]$) that is needed as an input parameter to both the warm and cold pool sub-models. The warm pool sub-model compute the probability for the warm pool to have at least one available PM (p_w) and the mean number of PMs in the warm pool $(E[\#P_w])$. The former quantity is used both in the hot and cold pool sub-models while the latter is used in the cold pool sub-model. Finally, the output measure of old pool sub-model $(p_c$, i.e., the probability for the cold pool to have at least one available PM) is used both in the hot and warm pool sub-models. Observe, the import graph shows cyclic dependencies among the sub-models. Such dependencies are resolved using fixed point iteration (Mainkar & Trivedi, 1996; Tomek, & Trivedi, 1991).

Model Outputs

Once the interacting sub-models have been solved, the same output measures of interest for the availability analysis of the Cloud service that can be computed from the monolithic model can be obtained. In particular, the mean number of PMs in each pool ($E[\#P_h]$, $E[\#P_w]$, and $E[\#P_c]$) are immediately available from the hot, warm, and cold pool sub-models, respectively. The availability of Cloud service for a given k can be computed by combining the availability of hot, warm, and cold pool as computed from hot, warm,

Figure 5. Interactions among the sub-models as an import graph

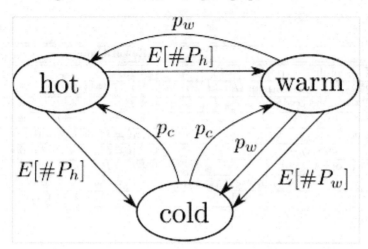

and cold pool sub-models such that $k_h + k_w + k_c \geq k$.

CLOSED FORM SOLUTION OF THE SUB-MODELS

This section shows the closed form solution for the interacting SRN sub-models approach by using equivalent Markov chain models. The Markov chains are reported in the case of $n_r{=}1$ to simplify calculations, but the closed form results can also be derived for the cases $n_r{>}1$. The SRN sub-model for the hot pool shown in Figure 2 is equivalent to the Markov chain model shown in Figure 6. In this Markov chain, state i represents the configuration of the hot pool in which i PMs are available. While solving this Markov chain for steady state probability of each state, the self-loops can be ignored (Trivedi, 2001). Hence, the Markov chain depicted in Figure 6 is a simple birth-death process where birth rate for state i is $\lambda_h (1 - p_w)(1 - p_c)i$ and death rate for all states is μ. Let

$$\lambda'_w = \lambda_h (1 - p_w)(1 - p_c) \qquad (4)$$

Let p_{h_i} be the steady state probability to be in state i for the Markov chain of Figure 6, i.e., the probability to have i PMs in the hot pool. Under such assumptions, p_{h_i} is given by:

$$p_{h_i} = \frac{\lambda'^{(n_h-i)}_h}{\mu^{(n_h-i)}} \frac{(n_h)!}{i!} p_{h_{n_h}} \text{ with } (0 \leq i \leq n_h - 1)$$

$$(5)$$

and $p_{h_{n_h}}$ is given by:

$$p_{h_{n_h}} = \frac{1}{\sum_i \lambda'^{(n_h-i)}_h \frac{(n_h)!}{\mu^{(n_h-i)} i!}} \qquad (6)$$

From the steady-state state probabilities, the mean number of PMs in the hot pool ($E[\# P_h]$) that needs to be exchanged with the other sub-models can be computed:

$$E[\# P_h] = \sum_i i p_{h_i} \qquad (7)$$

and the availability of the hot pool:

$$A_{k_h} = \sum p_{h_i} \qquad (8)$$

Figure 6. Markov chain equivalent to the hot pool SRN sub-models

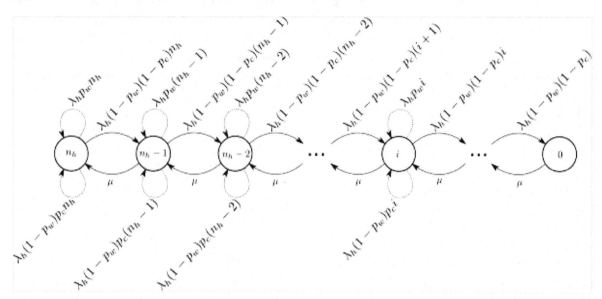

Similar solutions can be found for the warm and cold pools.

FIXED POINT ITERATION

To resolve the cyclic dependency among the interacting sub-models, one needs to use a fixed point iteration approach. Fixed point iteration variables are reported in the import graph depicted in Figure 5. The fixed point equation is given by:

$$\vec{x} = \vec{G}(\vec{x}) \tag{9}$$

where $\vec{x} = (p_w,\ p_c,\ E[\# P_h],\ E[\# P_w])$. It can be shown that all variables can be expressed as functions of p_w and p_c. Hence, the fixed point equation (9) can be rewritten as:

$$\vec{y} = \vec{F}(\vec{y}) \tag{10}$$

where $\vec{y} = (p_w, p_c)$.

Proof of existence of a solution to equation (10) implies the existence of a solution to equation (9). One uses the Brouwer's fixed point theorem (Ortega & Rheinboldt, 1970): "*Let $\vec{F} : C \subset \mathbb{R}^2 \to \mathbb{R}^2$ be continuous on the compact, convex set C, and suppose that $\vec{F}(C) \subseteq C$. Then, $\vec{F}$ has a fixed point in C.*"

In this case, given that p_w and p_c are probabilities, one can define

$$C = \{\vec{y} = (p_w, p_c) :\ p_w \in [0,1],\ p_c \in [0,1]\}.$$

By means of Heine-Borel theorem, it is straightforward to demonstrate that set C is compact and convex. Moreover, given that the component functions of $\vec{F}$ are continuous in C, then also $\vec{F}$ is continuous in C. This proves the existence of a solution for the fixed point equation $\vec{y} = \vec{F}(\vec{y})$.

NUMERICAL RESULTS

SPNP (Hirel, Tuffin, & Trivedi, 2000) can be used to solve the SRN models. Results have been obtained by solving the models for a broad range of parameter space so that they can represent large variety of Clouds. However, for space limitation, here the authors report only interesting results. Assume the MTTF of hot PMs to be in the range of 1–6 months, MTTF of warm PMs to be in the range of 3.5–12 months and MTTF of cold PMs to be in the range of 7 months - 2 years. MTTR of a PM can vary depending on type of repair process: (i) software based completely automated repair (1–30 minutes), (ii) completely manual repair (1–5 days) and (iii) combination of manual and automated repair (1–12 hours).

In Table 4, we report the state space and storage requirements for both the monolithic model and interacting sub-models. Monolithic model runs into a memory overflow problem when the number of PMs in each pool increases beyond 19. One observes that the state space size of the monolithic model increases quickly and becomes too large to construct the reachability graph even for small number of PMs. However, with interacting sub-models approach, the state space increases at a slower rate as the number of PMs in the system is increased. Table 4 also shows a comparison of non-zero entries. These entries are number of non-zero elements in the infinitesimal generator matrix of the underlying continuous time Markov chain. For the same number of PMs, number of non-zero entries in interacting sub-models is 3 − 4 orders of magnitude smaller compared to the monolithic model. Observe that, for interacting sub-models, in both cases (i.e., number of states and number of non-zero entries), this section reports only the maximum value among the three sub-models. Since three sub-models are solved separately, it is assumed that for a given execution only states and non-zero entries of only one sub-model are require to be stored in the memory. Reduction in state space and non-zero entries for interacting sub-models also leads to concomitant reduction in solution time needed. A comparison of solution times is shown in Table 5. Solution time for monolithic model increases almost exponentially with the increase in model size. Solution time for interacting sub-models remains almost constant with the increase in model size.

In Table 4, the downtime values as obtained from the monolithic model and interacting sub-models are compared. It is assumed that a Cloud is available if there are at least k "UP" PMs across all pools. For the example scenario investigated, it varies the value of k, with 10 PMs in each pool and 30 PMs in total. When k is 30, any failure of PM results in unavailability of Cloud service. For each value k, we also change the value of n_r which denotes maximum number of PMs that can be repaired in parallel. If n_r is 1, failed PMs are repaired serially, i.e., one after another. MTTFs of hot, warm and cold PMs were assumed to be 1000 hrs, 3500 hrs and 5000 hrs respectively. MTTR was assumed to be 3 hrs. Table 4 shows that results obtained from the interacting sub-models are accurate. As expected, downtime values are higher with increasing in values of k. For each k, down-

Table 4. Comparison of number of states and number of non-zero entries

#PMs in each pool in the beginning	#States in monolithic model	Maximum #states in interacting sub-models	#Non-zero entries in monolithic model	Maximum #non-zero entries in interacting sub-models
5	7056	56	44520	210
10	207636	286	1535490	1320
15	1775616	136	13948160	480
17	3508920	171	27976968	612
19	6468000	210	52189200	760
20	Memory overflow	231	Memory overflow	840
50	-	1326	-	5100
100	-	5151	-	20200
150	-	11476	-	45300
200	-	20301	-	80400

Table 5. Comparison of solution times in seconds

#PMs in each pool in the beginning	Monolithic model	Interacting sub-models
5	0.627	0.406
10	18.670	0.517
15	373.822	0.278
17	1004.494	0.279
19	2459.553	0.280
20	Memory overflow	0.281
50	-	0.296
100	-	0.377
150	-	0.564
200	-	0.948

time reduces if value of n_r is increased. This gives rise to interesting optimization problems as discussed in Section XI.

In Table 7, the mean number of PMs in each pool is shown. MTTF and MTTR values for this case were assumed to same as in the Table 6. Value of n_r was assumed to be 1 for this example

scenario. Results obtained from interacting sub-models are in good agreement with the results obtained from monolithic model. In Table 8, the effect of changing MTTF of PMs on downtime is shown. 10 PMs are assumed to be in each pool (i.e., 30 PMs in total) and maximum number of parallel repairs in each pool is 2. In this example

Table 6. Comparison of downtime values in minutes per year

Value of k	Value of n_r	Downtime (minutes per year)	
		Monolithic model	Interacting sub-models
30	1	23185.793	23178.956
	2	22904.919	22898.454
	3	22903.681	22897.219
29	1	792.475	798.651
	2	499.081	505.258
	3	497.787	503.964
28	1	24.722	25.336
	2	8.412	8.691
	3	7.118	7.396
27	1	0.740	0.778
	2	0.129	0.138
	3	0.081	0.087
26	1	0.022	0.024
	2	0.002	0.002
	3	0.0008	0.0009

Table 7. Comparison of average number of PMs in each pool

#PMs in each pool in the beginning	Avg. #PMs in pools for monolithic model			Avg. #PMs in pools for interacting sub-models		
	hot	warm	cold	hot	warm	cold
5	4.99	4.98	4.99	5.00	4.98	4.99
10	10.00	9.96	9.98	10.00	9.96	9.98
15	14.99	14.95	14.97	15.00	14.95	14.97
17	16.99	16.94	16.97	17.00	16.94	16.97
19	18.99	18.93	18.97	19.00	18.93	18.97

scenario, it further assumes that Cloud service is available when at least 28 PMs across all pools are "UP". For each value MTTF of hot PM, MTTFs of warm and cold PM were assumed to be 3.5 times and 5 times greater than that of hot PM's MTTF.

Results described so far were obtained by solving SRN models using SPNP. Next, using the closed form solutions for the interacting sub-models, one can solve large scale models (order of thousands PMs in each pool). Table 9 shows that solution time needed for solving large mod-

els increases very slowly with the model input size. Clearly, interacting sub-models approach facilitates availability analysis of large sized Clouds with a reasonably small solution time.

DECOMPOSED MODELS IN CLOUD FEDERATIONS

Cloud federations are characterized by the presence of different small and medium Private Clouds,

Table 8. Effect of varying MTTF of PMs with 10 PMs in each pool

MTTF of hot PM (hours)	Downtime (minutes per year)	
	Monolithic model	Interacting sub-models
800	16.313	16.848
1000	8.412	8.691
1200	4.892	5.055
1400	3.091	3.195
1600	2.076	2.146

Table 9. Solution time required for availability analysis of large scale Cloud using closed-form

Number of PMs in each pool	Solution time (sec)
500	0.251
1000	0.592
1500	0.911
2000	1.715
3000	2.483
4000	2.651

belonging to the same or to different organizations, that join each other to achieve a common goal, usually represented by the optimization of resources utilization. Public Clouds are usually used as backup when it is necessary to deal with load burst that cannot be managed by the Private federation. In (Bruneo, Longo, Puliafito, 2011) a methodology based on the use of SRN monolithic models to investigate the more convenient strategies to manage a federation of two or more Private or Public Clouds was shown. The final goal was to optimize energy consumption and performance in an energy-aware Green computing context. This chapter presented a monolithic SRN that can be used to model the availability of a single Cloud infrastructure composed of a certain number of pools of PMs. Both the models are characterized by scalability problems. In fact, a greater number of Cloud infrastructures and/or PMs in the scenarios that it is necessary to model corresponds to the raising of model states and to the impossibility to store and analyze the model in a common computer memory.

The solution to the state space explosion problem that was presented in the present chapter, i.e. to decompose the monolithic model in a set of interactive sub-models that can be analyzed by mean of fixed point iteration finds a perfect application in a federated environment. In fact, the presence of more than one Cloud infrastructure, each of which is characterized by two or more PM pools, would lead to an unmanageable monolithic model while is still tractable in a decomposed fashion. The advantages of the interactive sub-models approach are evident not only from an analysis point of view but also for what concerns clearness and conciseness of the representation power. In fact, while the use of SRN monolithic models to represent a Cloud federation scenario would lead to a complex and error-prone model with a huge number of places and transitions, the use of decomposed models limits the errors and the complexity of the representation. This is

even more clear if it is noted that the main functional blocks of the system to be represented (in this case a Cloud infrastructure) are usually the same among different administrative domain. For example, warm and cold pools sub-models presented in Section VI are very similar and this characteristic is still valid if one considers different Clouds. This allows the user to represent and solve a single sub-model for each of the functional block with different parameters and still be able to analyze the variety of behaviors that are present in a federated environment.

DISCUSSIONS AND FUTURE RESEARCH

The previous section compared the analytic results obtained from monolithic PN model, interacting PN sub-models and closed form solutions of Markov chains. The models developed so far can be used by Cloud service provider during design, development, testing and operational phases of IaaS Cloud. During the design and development stage, the providers can use these models to determine the pool size required to offer a specific availability SLA. During the testing and operational stages, the providers can dynamically learn, how the repair strategy should be designed (i.e., number of parallel repairs, automated vs. manual repairs etc.) to maintain the promised availability SLA.

While, this chapter outlines the existing research on Cloud availability analysis and describes a novel approach for large scale analysis, many open research questions are yet to be solved. With the fast scalable approach for modeling availability, one can extend the performability analysis described in (Ghosh, Trivedi, Naik, & Kim, 2010) to large size IaaS Clouds. Characterizing the system behavior from such a coupled pure performance and availability models with thousands of PMs taking into account workload arrival, admission control, queueing, resource provisioning decisions, VM provisioning, and run-time execution in addition to the failures is challenging. Combining the performance model with availability model, the economics of failure-repair for a given utilization rate of the PMs needs to be determined. For different utilization and failure-repair rates, there are different break-even points between loss of revenue and repair costs, which can be determined and analyzed. Optimization problems on Cloud availability can also be developed. Table 6 shows that downtime can be reduced by increasing the maximum number repairs that can be done in parallel. Since, there is a cost associated with each repair, an optimal number of repair facilities required to minimize the repair cost for acceptable value of downtime can be determined. The availability models also allow the performance of trade-off analysis of longer MTTF vs faster MTTR on system availability, the effect of having multiple concurrent repair facilities (i.e., higher labor costs) vs. higher availability but expensive components, repairing failed components vs replacing components for the a given service availability and so on. Another interesting type of analysis possible with this work is analyzing tradeoff between cost of availability SLAs vs operational costs including repair, replacement, and energy costs. These are important questions Cloud architects and designers often face. It is possible to answer these type of questions using tools based on the modeling and analysis techniques described in this chapter.

CONCLUSION

This chapter showed how analytic models can be used to analyze Cloud based systems in the context of federation. After a deep analysis of the state of the art in such field, it showed how it is possible to overcame the state space explosion problem, deriving from the largeness of scale in such scenarios, by mean of an interactive sub-models approach. The reference context is the availability analysis in the presence of multiple class of server pools. The possibility to compute closed-form solutions for the sub-models and the managing of dependencies among sub-models through the use of fixed-point iterations make the approach able to analyze IaaS Cloud systems with thousands of PMs in order of seconds. This is indeed promising in a federated environment where a great number of Clouds, each of which is composed by a certain number of pools of PMs, interact among each other in order to fulfill their business goals. After discussing the possible applications and the usefulness of the approach for Cloud providers during design, development, testing and operational phases, open research questions that are yet to be solved have been summarized and future work have been indicated.

REFERENCES

Amazon EC2. (2011). Retrieved from: http://aws.amazon.com/ec2.

Bonvin, N., Papaioannou, T. G., & Aberer, K. (2009). Dynamic cost efficient replications in data Clouds. In *1st ACM Workshop on Automated Control for Datacenters and Clouds* (ACDC) (pp. 49-56), Barcelona, Spain: ACM Press.

Bruneo, D., Longo, F., & Puliafito, A. (2011). Evaluating energy consumption in a Cloud infrastructure. In *Proceedings of the 2011 IEEE International Symposium on World of Wireless, Mobile and Multimedia Networks* (WoWMoM) (pp. 1-6), Lucca, Italy: IEEE Computer Society.

Chen, D., Dharmaraja, S., Chen, D., Li, L., Trivedi, K. S., Some, R. R., & Nikora, A. P. (2002). Reliability and availability analysis for the JPL remote exploration and experimentation system. In *Proceedings of the International Conference on Dependable Systems and Networks* (DSN) (pp. 337-342), Bethesda, MD, USA: IEEE Computer Society.

Chen, H., Zhou, C., & Xiong, N. (2010). Petri net modeling of the reconfigurable protocol stack for Cloud computing based control systems. In *Proceedings of the 1st International Conference on Cloud Computing* (CLOUDCOM) (pp. 393-400), Indianapolis, IN, USA: IEEE Computer Society.

Ciardo, G., Blakemore, A., Chimento, P. F., Muppala, J. K., & Trivedi, K. S. (1993). Automated generation and analysis of Markov reward models using stochastic reward nets. In *Linear Algebra, Markov Chains and Queuing Models* (pp. 145–191). New York, NY, USA: Springer. doi:10.1007/978-1-4613-8351-2_11

Ghosh, R., Longo, F., Naik, V. K., & Trivedi, K. S. (2010). Quantifying resiliency of IaaS Cloud. In *Proceedings of the IEEE Symposium on Reliable Distributed Systems* (SRDS) (pp. 343-347), Los Alamitos, CA, USA: IEEE Computer Society.

Ghosh, R., Trivedi, K. S., Naik, V. K., & Kim, D. S. (2010). End-to-End Performability analysis for Infrastructure-as-a-Service Cloud: An interacting stochastic models approach. In *Proceedings of the Pacific Rim International Symposium on Dependable Computing* (PRDC) (pp. 125-132), Tokyo, Japan: IEEE Computer Society.

Haring, G., Marie, R., Puigjaner, R., & Trivedi, K. S. (2001). Loss Formulae and Their Application to Optimization for Cellular Networks. In *IEEE Transaction on Vehicular Technology* (pp. 664–673). Washington, DC, USA: IEEE Computer Society.

Hirel, C., Tuffin, B., & Trivedi, K. S. (2000). SPNP: Stochastic Petri Nets. Version 6. In *Proceedings of the 11th International Conference on Technology of Object-Oriented Languages and Systems* (TOOLS) (p.354), Malaga, Spain: Springer.

IBM SmatCloud Enterprise™ (2001). Retrieved from: www.ibm.com/services/us/en/cloud-enterprise/

Javadi, B., Kondo, D., Vincent, J., & Anderson, D. (2010). Discovering statistical models of availability in large distributed systems: An empirical study of seti@home. In *IEEE Transaction on Parallel and Distributed Systems* (pp. 1896–1903). Washington, DC, USA: IEEE Computer Society. doi:10.1109/TPDS.2011.50

Joshi, K. R., Bunker, G., Jahanian, F., Moorsel, A. P. A. V., & Weinman, J. (2009). Dependability in the Cloud: Challenges and opportunities. In *Proceedings of the 39th annual IEEE/IFIP International Conference on Dependable Systems and Networks* (DSN) (pp. 103-104), Lisbon, Portugal: IEEE Computer Society.

Kim, D. S., Machida, F., & Trivedi, K. S. (2009). Availability Modeling and Analysis of a Virtualized System. In *Proceedings of the Pacific Rim International Symposium on Dependable Computing* (PRDC) (pp. 365-371), Seoul, Korea: IEEE Computer Society.

Kulkarni, V. G. (2010). *Modeling and Analysis of Stochastic Systems*. Boca Raton, FL, USA: CRC Press - Taylor & Francis Group.

Longo, F., Ghosh, R., Naik, V. K., & Trivedi, K. S. (2011). A Scalable Availability Model for Infrastructure-as-a-Service Cloud. In *Proceedings of the 41st annual IEEE/IFIP International Conference on Dependable Systems and Networks* (DSN) (pp. 335-346), Hong Kong, China: IEEE Computer Society.

Mainkar, V., & Trivedi, K. S. (1996). Sufficient conditions for existence of a fixed point in stochastic reward net-based iterative models. In *IEEE Transactions on Software Engineering* (pp. 640–653). Washington, DC, USA: IEEE Computer Society. doi:10.1109/32.541435

Marsan, M. A., Balbo, G., & Conte, G. (1984). A class of generalized stochastic petri nets for the performance evaluation of the multiprocessor systems. In *ACM Transactions on Computer Systems* (pp. 93–122). New York, NY, USA: ACM Press.

Nicol, D. M., Sanders, W. H., & Trivedi, K. S. (2004). Model-based evaluation: From dependability to security. In *IEEE Transactions on Dependable and Secure Computing* (pp. 48–65). Washington, DC, USA: IEEE Computer Society.

Ortega, J. M., & Rheinboldt, W. C. (1970). *Iterative Solution of Nonlinear Equations in Several Variables*. New York, NY, USA: Academic Press.

Smith, W. E., Trivedi, K. S., Tomek, L. A., & Ackaret, J. (2008). Availability analysis of blade server systems. In *IBM Systems Journal* (pp. 621–640). Indianapolis, IN, USA: IBM Press.

Tan, Y., Gu, X., & Wang, H. (2010). Adaptive system anomaly prediction for large-scale hosting infrastructures. In *Proceedings of the 29th ACM Symposium on Principles of distributed computing* (PODC) (pp. 173-182), Zurich, Switzerland: ACM Press.

Tomek, L., Muppala, J., & Trivedi, K. S. (1993). Modeling Correlation in Software Recovery Blocks. In *IEEE Transactions on Software Engineering* (pp. 1071–1086). Washington, DC, USA: IEEE Computer Society.

Tomek, L., & Trivedi, K. S. (1991). Fixed-Point Iteration in Availability Modeling. In *Informatik-Fachberichte* (*Vol. 283*, pp. 229–240). Berlin, Germany: Springer-Verlag.

Trivedi, K. S. (2001). *Probability and Statistics with Reliability, Queuing, and Computer Science Applications*. New York, NY, USA: John Wiley and Sons.

Trivedi, K. S., Kim, D. S., Roy, A., & Medhi, D. (2009). Dependability and security models. In *Proceedings of the 7th International Workshop on the Design of Reliable Communication Networks* (DRCN) (pp. 11-20), Washington, DC, USA: IEEE Computer Society.

Trivedi, K. S., & Sahner, R. (2009). SHARPE at the age of twenty two. In *Sigmetrics Performance Evaluation Review* (pp. 52–57). New York, NY, USA: ACM Press. doi:10.1145/1530873.1530884

Trivedi, K. S., Vasireddy, R., Trindade, D., Nathan, S., & Castro, R. (2006). Modeling High Availability Systems. In *Proceedings of the Pacific Rim International Symposium on Dependable Computing* (PRDC) (pp. 154-164), Riverside, CA, USA: IEEE Computer Society.

Trivedi, K. S., Wang, D., Hunt, D. J., Rindos, A., Smith, W. E., & Vashaw, B. (2008). Availability Modeling of SIP Protocol on IBM WebSphere. In *Proceedings of the Pacific Rim International Symposium on Dependable Computing* (PRDC) (pp. 323-330), Taipei, Taiwan: IEEE Computer Society.

Uemura, T., Dohi, T., & Kaio, N. (2009). Availability analysis of a scalable intrusion tolerant architecture with two detection modes. In *Proceedings of the 1st International Conference on Cloud Computing* (CLOUDCOM) (pp. 178-189), Beijing, China: Springer.

Vishwanath, K. V., & Nagappan, N. (2010). Characterizing Cloud computing hardware reliability. In *Proceedings of the ACM Symposium on Cloud Computing* (SOCC) (pp. 193-204), Indianapolis, IN, USA: ACM Press.

Wang, D., Fricks, R. M., & Trivedi, K. S. (2003). Dealing with non-exponential distributions in dependability models. In *Performance Evaluation - Stories and Perspectives* (pp. 273–302). Vienna, Austria: Oesterreichchische Computer Gessellschaft.

Yang, B., Tan, F., Dai, Y. S., & Guo, S. (2009). Performance evaluation of Cloud service considering fault recovery. In *Proceedings of the 1st International Conference on Cloud Computing* (CLOUDCOM) (pp. 571-576), Beijing, China: Springer.

Yin, L., Fricks, R. M., & Trivedi, K. S. (2002). Application of semi-Markov process and CTMC to evaluation of UPS system availability. In *Proceedings of the Annual Reliability and Maintainability Symposium* (pp. 584-591), Seattle, WA, USA: IEEE Computer Society.

ADDITIONAL READING

Chen, D., & Trivedi, K. S. (2001). Analysis of Periodic Preventive Maintenance with General System Failure Distribution. In Proceedings of the Pacific Rim International Symposium on Dependable Computing (PRDC) (pp. 103-107), Seoul, Korea: IEEE Computer Society.

Das, C. R., Mohapatra, P., Tien, L., & Bhuyan, L. N. (1993). An availability model for MIN-based multiprocessors. In *IEEE Transaction on Parallel and Distributed Systems* (pp. 1118–1129). Washington, DC, USA: IEEE Computer Society.

Floyd, F., & Hawkins, M. (2001). *High Availability: Design, Techniques, and Processes.* Upper Saddle River, NJ, USA: Prentice Hall.

Fricks, R., & Trivedi, K. S. (1997). Modeling Failure Dependencies in Reliability Analysis Using Stochastic Petri Nets. In Proceedings of the 11th European Simulation Multiconference (ESM), Istanbul, Turkey: ACM Press.

Goldschmidt, T., Dittrich, A., & Malek, M. (2009). Quantifying Criticality of Dependability-Related IT Organization Processes in CobiT. In Proceedings of the Pacific Rim International Symposium on Dependable Computing (PRDC) (pp. 336-341), Seoul, Korea: IEEE Computer Society.

Goseva-Popstojanov, K., & Trivedi, K. S. (2000). Stochastic Modeling Formalisms for Dependability, Performance and Performability. In *Performance Evaluation: Origins and Directions* (pp. 403–422). Berlin, Germany: Springer-Verlag. doi:10.1007/3-540-46506-5_17

Grottke, M., Nikora, A. P., & Trivedi, K. S. (2010). An Empirical Investigation of Fault Types in Space Mission System Software. In Proceedings of the International Conference on Dependable Systems and Networks (DSN) (pp. 447-456), Fairmont Chicago – Millennium Park, Chicago, IL, USA: IEEE Computer Society.

Haberkorn, M., & Trivedi, K. S. (2007). Availability Monitor for a Software Based System. In Proceedings of the 10th IEEE High Assurance Systems Engineering Symposium (HASE) (pp. 321-328), Dallas, TX, USA: IEEE Computer Society.

Kim, D. S., Machida, F., & Trivedi, K. S. (2009). Availability Modeling and Analysis of a Virtualized System. In Proceedings of the Pacific Rim International Symposium on Dependable Computing (PRDC) (pp. 365-371), Seoul, Korea: IEEE Computer Society.

Lanus, M., Yin, L., & Trivedi, K. S. (2003). Hierarchical Composition and Aggregation of State-Based Availability and Performability Models. In *IEEE Transaction on Reliability* (pp. 44–52). Washington, DC, USA: IEEE Computer Society. doi:10.1109/TR.2002.805781

Lee, F., & Marathe, M. (1999). *Beyond Redundancy: A guide to designing high-availability networks.* Indianapolis, ID, USA: Cisco Press.

Malek, M. (2008). Online Dependability Assessment through Runtime Monitoring and Prediction, Panel Contribution. In Proceedings of the 7th European Dependable Computing Conference (EDCC) (p.181), Kaunas, Lithuania: IEEE Computer Society.

Malhotra, M., & Trivedi, K. S. (1994). Power-Hierarchy of Dependability-Model Types. In *IEEE Transactions on Reliability* (pp. 493–502). Washington, DC, USA: IEEE Computer Society.

Malhotra, M., & Trivedi, K. S. (1995). Dependability Modeling Using Petri-Nets. In *IEEE Transactions on Reliability* (pp. 428–440). Washington, DC, USA: IEEE Computer Society.

Mendiratta, V. (1999). Reliability Analysis of Clustered Computing Systems. In Proceedings of the International Symposium on Software Reliability Engineering (ISSRE) (pp.268-272), Boca Reton, FL, USA: IEEE Computer Society.

Mishra, K., & Trivedi, K. S. (2006). Model Based Approach for Autonomic Availability Management. In *Service Availability* (pp. 1–16). Berlin, Germany: Springer-Verlag. doi:10.1007/11955498_1

Muppala, J., Ciardo, G., & Trivedi, K. S. (1994). Stochastic Reward Nets for Reliability Prediction. In *Reliability, Maintainability and Serviceability* (pp. 9–20). Washington, DC, USA: SAE International.

Muppala, J., Sathaye, A., Howe, R., & Trivedi, K. S. (1992). Dependability modeling of a heterogeneous VAXcluster system using stochastic reward nets. In *Hardware and Software Fault Tolerance in Parallel Computing Systems*. New York, NY, USA: Ellis Horwood.

Pecchia, A., Cotroneo, D., Kalbarczyk, Z., & Iyer, R. K. (2011). Improving Log-Based Field Failure Data Analysis of Multi-Node Computing Systems. In Proceedings of the International Conference on Dependable Systems and Networks (DSN) (pp.97-108), Hong Kong, China: IEEE Computer Society.

Sahner, R. A., Trivedi, K. S., & Puliafito, A. (1996). *Performance and Reliability Analysis of Computer Systems: An Example-Based Approach Using the SHARPE Software Package*. Norwell, MA, USA: Kluwer Academic Publishers.

Salfner, F., Lenk, M., & Malek, M. (2010). A survey of Online Failure Prediction Methods. In *ACM Computing Surveys* (pp. 1–42). New York, NY, USA: ACM Press. doi:10.1145/1670679.1670680

Smith, R. M., Trivedi, K. S., & Ramesh, A. V. (1988). Performability Analysis: Measures, an Algorithm, and a Case Study. In *IEEE Transactions on Computers* (pp. 406–417). Washington, DC, USA: IEEE Computer Society. doi:10.1109/12.2184

Stewart, W. J. (1994). *Introduction to the Numerical Solution of Markov Chains*. Princeton, NJ, USA: Princeton University Press.

Trivedi, K. S. Kim. D.S., Yin, X. (2012). Multi-State Availability Modeling in Practice. In Recent Advances in System Reliability (pp.165-180), Berlin, Germany: Springer-Verlag.

Trivedi, K. S., Kim, D. S., Roy, A., & Medhi, D. (2009). Dependability and security models. In Proceedings of the 7th International Workshop on the Design of Reliable Communication Networks (DRCN) (pp. 11-20), Washington, DC, USA: IEEE Computer Society.

KEY TERMS AND DEFINITIONS

Analytic Model: In performance and availability evaluation context, an analytic model is a mathematical tool that allows to do "what-if" analysis and predict the behavior of a real system. In contrast with simulation and measurement based approach, can provide results in smaller time.

Availability: In IaaS Cloud context, availability is the degree to which the Cloud infrastructure is able to provide VMs to clients in the face of hardware/software failures and repairs. Simply put, availability is the proportion of time the IaaS Cloud is in a functioning condition.

Fixed Point Iterations: A technique that allows to resolve cyclic dependencies among interacting sub-models to obtain model solutions without incurring significant errors. Fixed-point iterations are used to solve the equations where the unknown variables can be expressed only in implicit form. Three mathematical issues important to fixed-point iterations are: (i) existence of a solution, (ii) uniqueness of a solution and (iii) rate of convergence.

Interacting Sub-Models: A possible solution to the state-space explosion problem posed by monolithic model is to decompose the monolithic model to a set of sub-models each of which describes the behavior of one of the system components. The sub-models interact among themselves by exchanging parameters. Such interactions can be described by an import graph.

Monolithic Model: A single self-contained analytic model that allows to describe the behavior of a system and predict its performance and/or availability characteristics as a whole. In many cases, accurate analytic analysis with monolithic models usually requires dealing with large number of system states, leading to state-space explosion problem.

Petri Nets: Petri nets are high-level, graphical and mathematical formalism that allows a modeler to describe a system without explicitly enumerating its states. Compared to Markov chains and other state space formalisms, Petri nets are easy to understand for non-expert users but maintain an exact mathematical definition of their execution semantics, with a well-developed mathematical theory for process analysis. Petri-nets are used when hand-generation of Markov chain is difficult.

Stochastic Reward Nets: An extension of generalized stochastic Petri nets in which every state of the underlying Markov chain can be associated with a reward rate thus facilitating the computation of a variety of performance and availability measures.

Chapter 9
The Security of Cloud Infrastructure

Massimo Civilini
Cisco Systems® Inc., USA

ABSTRACT

The development of commercial Cloud environments has been fueled by the introduction of new technologies which have changed the interactions between the base components of a legacy IT infrastructure: computing, networking, and storage. In particular, the security of data and operations has been impacted by these changes, making the legacy security infrastructure no longer adequate to support new scenarios. This chapter illustrates how base infrastructure operations like software provisioning and resource virtualization are critical from a security viewpoint. It will also discuss the mitigation solutions available in guaranteeing an adequate level of security in the Cloud.

INTRODUCTION

The Cloud environments available today allow single home users to access extended computing and storage services as well as enterprises that outsource part of their data centers. This permits users to pay only for the resources they utilize, avoiding onerous investments in hardware, software, physical spaces, and maintenance. The Cloud concept is also appealing on a smaller scale. Because of the advantages offered by an elastic Cloud, many companies are implementing infrastructures that mimic the general Cloud concept but are personalized to their private infrastructure and needs, realizing a Cloud environment which is smaller in size, closed and private. These types of Cloud are important from a development and application viewpoint because they are extensible and allow a practical approach that is focused on customer needs, business analysis, technical solutions and marketing opportunities.

DOI: 10.4018/978-1-4666-1631-8.ch009

Copyright © 2012, IGI Global. Copying or distributing in print or electronic forms without written permission of IGI Global is prohibited.

However, these new capabilities, when connected with the Cloud concept, come at a price; the resulting environments are extremely challenging to manage from a security standpoint. The difficulty arises from the combination of the need for open network architecture and distributed resource management, thereby crossing the normal client-server security infrastructure which is at the base of everyday network security concepts.

The Cloud architecture is changing the basic interactions between the components of infrastructure and a new approach must be devised to guarantee security. Firewall, SSL and NAT are still necessary but are no longer sufficient to protect data in the Cloud. These general concerns regarding the Cloud are shared between all the different types of Cloud architectures and have an impact on the Cloud services at every level.

The Cloud infrastructure is the lowest level of deployment; Cloud services are built on top of it. A security flaw at this level has an immediate negative impact on the services. This is also the place where platforms integrate where convergence is discussed in standard committees and where commercial reasons drive the steps forward, with the result that, sometimes, the best solutions are sacrificed in favor of compatibility or revenues. These reasons explain why we still have, for example, a thirty year old BIOS infrastructure in the latest and most powerful server in the Cloud or limitations in the migration of virtual machines.

The chapter will illustrate the critical security points for a Cloud infrastructure by describing two of the main operations at infrastructure level: the provisioning of software and the virtualization of resources. These operations are at the core of the Cloud infrastructure and contain the basic problems seen on the low level side and high level side, represented by platform and applications. Provisioning deals not just with the infrastructure itself, but it regulates the possibility to offer Platform services and Software services, delivering application and VM software. In that section the problems at the base of the Cloud deployment

and security architecture are introduced: hardware identity, VM identity, virus protection, and cloud dynamics. The problems of integration among platforms and among different Cloud infrastructures are presented in the resource management section and hybrid Cloud section respectively.

BACKGROUND

The development of a fast, cost-effective network infrastructure and the availability of high performance computational and storage platforms fueled the creation of Data Centers as aggregation points for the IT infrastructure. The Cloud computing concept, favored by the heavy adoption of technologies like virtualization and self-management, has introduced the possibility of having computation and other services offered on demand. However, this transformation was not immediately apparent and the scientific community did not immediately recognize its importance, giving scarce support to the Cloud environment with analysis and proposals until recent times (Sriram & Khajeh-Hosseini, 2010). Due to this lack of support, the Cloud made its appearance only recently and was mostly driven by commercial reasons (Mohamed, 2009). The subsequent success of the idea helped create a Cloud environment which grows rapidly in term of services yet shows its limits due to the scalability of legacy infrastructures (Crump, 2010). As a result, the Cloud environment is suffering from scalability and compatibility issues connected to the difficulties of adapting legacy computing and network environments to new requirements and services.

Security in particular has been impacted heavily by the change, and the legacy methods used to ensure authentication, integrity, and privacy are no longer sufficient to cover the new functionalities and the dynamicity of the Cloud (Hu, et al., 2011). In a Cloud environment, where automation plays a primary role, concepts like hardware identity must be radically transformed and adapted to the infrastructure. Up until a few years ago, hardware identity (or any method of tracking a computing hardware), was regarded as something which threatened the privacy of the user (Markoff, 1999) (Symantec® Co., 1999). However, Cloud architecture requires a distinction between the hardware and the user of the hardware as well as the ability to authenticate an unattended computing node (Hu, et al., 2011).

This situation of inadequateness becomes even more evident in hybrid Cloud environments, where both security and network infrastructure show their limit. Solutions involving IP mobility (Silvera, Sharaby, Lorenz, & Shapira, 2009) and network Layer 2 extension (Venezia, 2010) are now under scrutiny for standardization, but the solution does not seem to be handy due to the scalability problems.

In the last few years much has been done to integrate the platforms of the Cloud infrastructure, but there are areas where this integration is still lagging, even if solutions have been defined. For example, the server's BIOS, an icon of the old computers, cannot easily be replaced because many Operating Systems in the field depend on it and are incompatible with new, Cloud-friendly products (Microsoft, 2011).

An important step ahead for a common approach to security in a Cloud environment was the creation of the Cloud Security Alliance (Messner, 2009) and the release of the guidance manual for security in the Cloud environment (Cloud Security Alliance). This is the first comprehensive document to address end-to-end security in the Cloud and is a reference for future developments (Hanna & Molina, 2010)

From a security viewpoint, the lack of synergy between platforms is well represented by the problems associated with the provisioning of software and the management of computational and storage resources that together represent the majority of the low level Cloud infrastructure operations.

THE COMPONENTS OF THE CLOUD INFRASTRUCTURE

There are three basic types of Cloud infrastructure: private, public, and hybrid. In a private Cloud, resources controlled by the infrastructure are shared among a closed set of users (or customers) usually belonging to the same organization. In this kind of Cloud, security can generally be enforced up to the user level, and operations like joining the Cloud and assigning resources are less critical. Public Cloud providers make the infrastructure available to the general public, selling services but maintaining the ownership of the infrastructure. The hybrid or federated Cloud is a combination of two or more Cloud entities which remain physically disjoined but that are able to share data and applications. One of the main reasons for creating a hybrid Cloud is to be able to extend a private Cloud to manage peaks of load without paying for costly over-dimensioned infrastructures utilized in full for short periods of time (Engates, 2009).

Although the tendency is to blend and abstract the lower levels of the architecture, a Cloud infrastructure is a combination of four basic components: a computing platform, a network infrastructure, a storage infrastructure and a management application. The resources associated with these components are distributed to groups of users (tenants) and security must be enforced to provide isolation, identity and monitoring inside and between these groups.

Computing, Network and Storage

The introduction of virtualization has radically changed the computing platform for data centers. This technology has allowed the silent partitioning of computing resources among several independent execution units, paving the road for the development of Cloud computing. Virtualization of physical resources has been realized through the virtual machine monitor (hypervisor), which sits on top of the hardware and is able to create execution environments (virtual machines, VM(s)) where the complete software stack, from applications to OS drivers, can work without any modification. The hypervisor "owns" all the hardware resources (CPU, memory, devices) and controls execution and operations. This ability to gather together in the same physical machine independent execution environments has produced the consolidation of software in VM(s), allowing savings in the number of independent hardware, their maintenance and the real estate needed to store them.

This consolidation, however, has changed the security landscape. The ability to support several VM(s) in a concurrent execution environment must be accompanied by the enforcement of their isolation. With a virtualized infrastructure, the security of the environment rests on two basic points: the safe bootstrap of the hypervisor and the ability of the hypervisor to block unauthorized accesses in run-time.

The network infrastructure is based on the OSI reference model that defines how the information moves through a network medium (Ford, Lew, Spanier, & Stevenson, 1997). The top layers deal with applications while the lower layers handle data transport. The network protocols have been defined as a set of rules and conventions and describe how endpoints exchange information. These assumptions and definitions generate a network infrastructure that is very static and the introduction of Cloud computing highlights the limits of this vision. For example, the VM migration has an impact on both session persistency and on the security of the transfer. Solutions in this particular case require a large consensus for an extension of the OSI layer 2 and the introduction of security primitives at the hypervisor level.

Storage was probably the first resource made available to generic users in the early implementation of the Cloud. The network connection between the source of the data and the Cloud is usually secured by protocols ensuring mutual authentication and privacy (Chaitanya, Butler, Sivasubramaniam,

McDaniel, & Vilayannur, 2006). Inside the Cloud, mass storage resources are usually provided by storage modules connected via network to the computing platforms and management application. The Cloud also provides some general services meant to protect data. One of the most important is data de-localization, where data is mirrored in other remote modules to ensure safe storage and provide disaster recovery.

Management Application

The integration of computing, network and storage has brought increased complexity of configuration and operations in the Cloud environment. It is not long ago that network elements were configured using command line interface (CLI(s)) or scripts allowing the administrator to specify very detailed and specific configuration solutions with server software images and storage modules statically configured. Security was insured by separating control and data planes. The integration of the environments and the possibility to request resources on demand has made that approach impractical, paving the road for a management application responsible for configuration and general operations.

The Cloud operations and configurations are now controlled by a policy-driven management application with the low-level details of the configuration hidden behind administrator-defined policies. Security is still based on the strict separation of the control and data plane, but the operations have become global, touching computing, network and storage. The administrator defines basic policies using a GUI interface and the details of the configuration remain hidden inside the application.

The autonomous management of events and procedures has greatly reduced manual intervention, making easier and faster the configuration and response to Cloud dynamics. A central point of management has also facilitated the definition of resource pools for faster response to configuration changes as well as the management of roles and privileges to increase security in the entire infrastructure. This reduction of configuration complexity spans throughout the entire Cloud structure and services. At the infrastructure level, for example, autonomous management operations take care of updating firmware versions and the boot capabilities of physical servers, and at the platform level of the virtual disk setup, it enforces roles and permissions.

This change in behavior, however, has not been (and is still not) an easy task. Administrators argue that they are losing configuration capabilities, especially on the network side, and that there is a reduced debugging capability leading to tracking problems. However, the advantages of having an automatic configuration system for such a complex environment and the need to avoid manual intervention as much as possible make the adoption of the management application a necessity.

Today, the majority of management applications offered for real deployment is designed for private Clouds and deal mostly with infrastructure management, the first step in global management. However, the trend for these applications to become distributed, multi-tenant and spanning throughout the entire Cloud structure is unavoidable.

SYSTEM BOOTSTRAP AND SOFTWARE PROVISIONING

Software provisioning is a process which involves all the platform components (computation, network and storage) and is one of the most critical from a security viewpoint. In a Cloud environment, there arc two types of software provisioning: the bare metal software provisioning that downloads the virtualization environment on the physical server and that is related to the platform services and the virtual machine software provisioning that is related to the application services. The former is most critical from a security viewpoint while

the latter can count on a security environment enforced by the synergy between the hypervisor and the management application, and is therefore less critical to the system's security.

Since the bootstrap procedure is one of the oldest BIOS procedures, it has inside all of the compatibility limitations accumulated during its thirty years of history. In its modern version, the machine can boot from local media (HDU or USB devices) or from remote media via either a fiber channel (FC) or iSCSI protocols. All of these methods aim to access a media and load in memory the master boot record (MBR) which is represented by the 512 bytes of data stored in the first sector. These bytes contain the geometry of the media and the boot loader, a small portion of code able to initiate the load of the OS in memory. Once the MBR is in memory, control is passed to the boot loader in order to begin the OS start up. After the bootstrap, the OS kernel and drivers have been loaded in memory, and they are able to interact with the portion still in the media. This portion of the OS on the media allows tracking of the state of the system so that, after a restart, the operations can be resumed from a known state. Although this is a high level description of the bootstrap procedure, it is detailed enough to be able to spot some critical points.

Master Boot Record

The goal of the bootstrap procedure, for both local and remote media disk accesses, is to load the MBR from the first sector of the device. However, there is no control over what is loaded. Even though the procedure is quite linear, it does not have anything which enables it to determine if the loaded MBR is the right one or to make assumptions about its integrity. To have a reliable mechanism to validate the MBR, it is necessary to have methods that authenticate the source and check the integrity of the data. The integrity of the code could be verified using cryptographic one-way hash functions like MD5, SHA-1 or SHA-2 (Mironov, 2005). Given an arbitrary length input document, these easy-to-calculate functions produce a compressed, easy to manipulate output of limited size (e.g., 128 bits for MD5 and 160 bits for SHA-1). These outputs also are pre-image and 2nd pre-image resistant, meaning it is computationally unfeasible to one, find any input which hashes to that output, and two, find a second image with the same output.

Although these functions can provide integrity checks for the MBR, they do not ensure source authentication: a second (malicious) entity could modify or replace the MBR and recalculate the hash function. To ensure source authentication, it is necessary to have a well defined and trusted source digitally sign the result of the hash function using cryptographic techniques. This is usually done by using a key set (public and private keys) and by encrypting the hash code using the private key and publishing the public key to a trusted and well-known certificate authority (CA).

This method can be used to calculate the hash of the document, get the public key of the source entity from the CA, decrypt the hash and verify that the two values (calculated and decrypted) are the same.

The implementation of this procedure in the boot phase of a physical machine is problematic because the BIOS environment is overloaded by compatibility constrains and it is very difficult to model since it is hardware-specific and its functionalities are limited.

BIOS modifications also require a great deal of testing to verify every possible compatibility issue as well as portability between environments. Last, but not least, there are few BIOS providers and they tend to avoid heavy customizations for a single client to maintain the full portability of the core code across different hardware and customers. Moreover, the task is difficult for the management application as well. It must take care of all the background work, from the definition of cryptographic parameters, to the signature, to public key publishing and the setup of the network. It is quite a big job if one considers that, for

security reasons, the key set should be different from machine to machine and from VM to VM.

To mitigate these problems Intel® has proposed the Trusted Execution Environment (TXT) where parts of these tasks are delegated to the hardware (Gillespie, 2009). By considering the difficulties in remotely managing a backward-compatible computing hardware, Intel has introduced Active Management Technology (AMT) which uses part of its hardware chip-set for out-of-band remote management. On top of this environment and integrated with it, Intel added a security technology to perform core encryption operations in hardware and a secure repository for cryptographic keys, delivering a complete package for the secure boot. The partnership with Citrix® for rapid access to hardware functions has opened up this technology to the Cloud. The Citrix hypervisor added automated management to a hardware-based security technology (Babcock, 2009).

In parallel with the effort of securing the actual BIOS infrastructure, Intel is proposing a new approach to the server's firmware environment with the Unified Extensible Firmware Interface (UEFI). The purpose of the UEFI is to replace the BIOS and define a common boot environment abstraction where specific images will take control of drivers and loaders (Villinger, 2011). In this environment, security is enforced by a hardware-based root of trust that allows for the screening of both the UEFI code before execution and of the code imported via network.

The UEFI environment is incompatible with the actual BIOS code, and Operating Systems must support it directly. This creates problems with the installed base in the field and although the integration of the UEFI environment started a few years ago, the compatibility problems still limit its deployment.

Hardware Identity

The same problem the booting server faces in authenticating the source of the MBR is experienced by the source to authenticate the server which allows the MBR transfer. The problem starts when the MBR is hosted in a SAN or iSCSI server and needs to be transferred via network. The authentication procedures require the booting server to have a secret that, challenged by the source, can demonstrate the authenticity of the request. Unfortunately, the booting server environment, before loading the OS, does not have anything to store a secret, either in hardware or firmware. There are unique data, but they are just obfuscated and can be easily stolen by a malicious program. Without the secret, authentication cannot take place and the server hardware cannot prove its identity.

The Intel® TXT environment has solved the problem by adding in the hardware chip-set a secure repository to store this kind of information. Its integration with the management plan allows management of both this repository and of the hardware identity. This solution works fine with a managed environment like the Cloud, but it has limitations when extended to the single home user who does not have a complete managed environment.

Intel's solution is based on the work of the Trusted Computing Group (TCG) that developed the concept of Trusted Platform Module devices (TPM) which are able to generate, store and protect cryptographic keys that in turn provide to the platform authentication and attestation capabilities.

Trusted Platform

In the previous paragraphs the concept of trusted platform has been introduced, explaining the basic limitations of servers for the base operations of bootstrap. The scope of trusted computing (Trusted Computing Group) is to create an environment where it is possible to understand the state of the system and evaluate if it is appropriate for a specific job (Grawrock, 2006). In a computing platform the trust is extended from module to module via a chain of trust, where a trusted module can measure and extend the trust to another

module. The first ring of the chain is the "root of trust" and in computing platform is represented by a protected hardware component, the trusted platform module or TPM.

TPM is a hardware device (or a portion of a device) containing internal storage memory, registers, a random number generator, a hardware-driven RSA engine and a key generator. Everything is controlled by an execution unit and microcode. The manufacturer and the platform integrator provide the keys and certificates necessary to ensure authentication and internal conformity certification. TPM can provide attestation of BIOS integrity in a pre-boot environment, enabling the execution of different portions of the code. TPM works in a chain of trust where a module is measured for integrity before its execution by the previous module. This is done by the concept of locality defined by its internal registers: each module in the BIOS writes on these registers extending their content and unlocking the key to validate the integrity of the next module. The starting point is hardware that is independent of the firmware, a characteristic which enables it to act as root of trust for the platform (Zimmer, Dasari, & Brogan, 2009).

The second component in the chain of trust is the firmware and the legacy BIOS is a weak ring (Lemos, 2006). With UEFI the monolithic and vendor-specific legacy BIOS is replaced by a code that takes care of platform initialization, diagnostic and bootstrap with drivers and module that are standard and independent and that well adapt to a propagation of the chain of trust. Other than removing the legacy BIOS limitations on the supported devices (like the network) it introduces several features that extend the capabilities of the boot operations. In terms of security the latest version of UEFI supports IPsec both for IPv4 and IPv6 protocols, the possibility to sign drivers or applications (providing policies for 3rd party image extensibility) and the user identification to facilitate platform and administrator existence (UEFI, 2011).

TPM provided trust can also extend to higher levels. In a virtual server environment the need for isolation, data security and code integrity checks suggest a need to export the TPM features to the VM level, thus enabling a virtual instance of the TPM in each VM (Berger S., Caceres, Goldman, Perez, Sailer, & Doorn, 2006). TPM virtualization is provided by a TPM driver resident in the VM (vTPM). This driver offers every function of a hardware-based TPM abstracting the hardware layer to the VM code. The vTPM drivers communicate to a vTPM manager inside the hypervisor environment that maintains instances of the drivers and provides access to the real TPM. This works well for VMs inside a physical machine but creates problems in migration, where the vTPM driver as well as all of the security context for that VM in the vTPM manager and real TPM should be migrated.

In a Cloud environment, trusted computing goes beyond TPM. It involves how it is propagated through the Cloud and how data is stored. In particular TCG has proposed an architecture to ensure endpoint integrity at the network access level (TCG, 2010), a process that has been leveraged by Cisco and Microsoft® (Bangeman, 2006). More generally, TCG, working with the guidance provided by the Cloud Security Alliance, has focused on specific areas that are key from the trusted computing viewpoint and that are critical in order to provide end-to-end security (Hanna & Molina, 2010).

Statefulness

One major security problem for all computing machines, from home desktops to laptops and servers, is the statefulness of the OS. Statefulness is the ability for the OS to keep track of operations and procedures. Although this property is very useful, it is prone to security issues and is used by viruses, worms and many malicious programs to persist through the restart operations of the computing environment.

Security software is very useful in searching for and removing these threats, but it is also limited to what it knows and on the ability of the administrator to keep it updated. This problem is highlighted in a Cloud environment, where servers are managed automatically and explicit checks are difficult. The statefulness of the environment involves not only the OS but also applications, and it cannot be avoided simply by changing configurations. Even with these structural limitations, the problem could be mitigated by using a special boot procedure and transforming the environment from stateful to stateless without modifying the OS or the applications. This does not solve the problems of having malicious programs attacking the machine, but it ensures that, after a restart, the state is clean. This is usually not acceptable for a laptop or in many offices, but it often is in a Cloud infrastructure. In the Cloud, when a machine shows signs of infection by malicious programs or simply after a certain planned time of continuous activity, it is restarted, restoring a clean state.

This ability to restart from a clean state is achieved by using special media, a Ramdisk, at bootstrap time and removing all persistent media, leaving the machine diskless. Part of the memory of the server is used to store a disk structure that is seen by the server as normal disk media. This Ramdisk has high performance and the ability to disappear through the restart of the machine, cleaning the state and requiring the bootstrap procedure to re-install everything from a fresh, safe copy.

In the computing platform, the bootstrap is controlled by BIOS, but the network is not a standard boot device and it has to rely on old compatibility methods to create the Ramdisk and download the image. The protocol used to download the disk image has been defined by Intel in the mid-1990s (pre-boot execution environment, PXE) and has remained unchanged until now. This protocol is absolutely inadequate for software provisioning in a Cloud infrastructure. Besides the problems inherent in its initial setup of the server using option ROM code, it has serious security limitations because it uses DHCP to locate the image and TFTP to download it. It also requires a special setup in the image repository storage with a server application that cannot authenticate the requestor. Solutions in today's deployments are available using a special boot loader on the computing server side (IPXE, 2010), but this is just a mitigation for a specific problem.

This situation can be changed only with a tighter integration of the platforms where each component is environment-aware and designed to be effective in a Cloud environment. To solve the specific problem of the stateless computing environment, it is necessary to have a server that is aware of the network infrastructure, a storage system open to specific operations to build bootable virtual disks and a network infrastructure able to easily create a safe transfer. At the top, everything is orchestrated by a management application that reduces the administrator manual intervention to a minimum.

Even if this could seem obvious from a high level viewpoint, it becomes very difficult to realize when one move down into the details and need to balance investments and revenues. In particular, one begins to see this transformation in the industry where Companies offering Cloud solutions are gradually extending their portfolio to products outside their classical offers. Examples include Cisco when it began to produce servers and Hewlett Packard in the acquisition of 3PAR. Unfortunately these changes take time, are pushed back by the utilization of off-shelf products, and are augmented by the need to bring know-how and the clear understanding of the details of the Cloud. Even so, the trend is well defined.

RESOURCE VIRTUALIZATION

Resource distribution in a Cloud environment is controlled by the management application through a set of policies defined by the administrator. The computing platform part of this management consists of the optimization of VM(s) activities with respect to their allocation on the physical machines. Operations like VM creation, destruction or migration require a complex interaction between different components of the environment and the policies should be complete enough to avoid ambiguities. Creating a VM, for example, does not only involve sending the right request to the hypervisor: it also requires several settings on the computing platform, the network and the storage. Beside the specific basic settings (CPU, memory, etc...), there is a need to setup the DHCP server, the internal software switch, the image to boot from and, depending on the software running, all of the security context, beginning with the firewall settings.

The VM(s) are also the minimal granularity the management application has to perform resource optimization. Based on specific policies from the administrator, the management application has the possibility to migrate the VM(s) between physical machines to optimize execution.

The Cloud infrastructure is a dynamic environment where the security is orchestrated by the management application and enforced by the different platforms and this dynamicity enhances problems connected to the integration of the platforms.

Limiting Factors for VM Migration

A virtualized server environment is created by loading a hypervisor (or virtual machine monitor) at boot time. The hypervisor takes control of the server's physical resources and shares these resources between VM(s), which are isolated software execution environments able to simulate the underlying hardware. For the OS and other applications running in the VM, this environment is indistinguishable from an old legacy desktop environment. The advantage of having a virtualized system is the reduction of physical computing hardware, while the disadvantage is the concurrent utilization of physical resources, which reduces the execution performance of the applications. The possibility of migrating (moving from a virtual environment provided by a hypervisor in a physical machine to another in a different physical machine) a VM provides a method to control consolidation.

The migration itself is performed by the hypervisor, but is started from the external environment, either by the management application or directly by the administrator using the hypervisor's console. Live migration happens if, during the migration, the applications running in the VM do not drop the network connections and there is no perceived downtime. This is distinguishable from normal migration, which stops the VM execution during migration. When the VM is created it is assigned by the hypervisor to a memory space where the software, OS and applications, are loaded. In the case of live migration, the VM continues to be active in the source machine during the migration and can take several tens of seconds: the memory pages which are not modified by the OS or application from the moment when the migration starts are moved first, leaving the few heavily modified memory pages as a last step, thus reducing the downtime to a few tenths of second.

The first limiting factor for migration is the storage associated with the VM. Local storage is usually assigned to the VM by the hypervisor, as a portion of the local disk and its contents must be migrated with the memory. This is a difficult operation because, usually, the local storage is much larger than the VM memory and the transfer time is significantly different. Also, data is exchanged between the VM and the storage during live migration and the hypervisor must track these changes carefully. For these reasons, migrating VM(s) usually do not utilize local storage but instead use disks accessed through the network. The advantage is that the content of these disks is not migrated, can be available during the migration time and there is no change in network configuration because the storage IP and MAC addresses remain the same. The real difference

between local and distributed storage is that, for local storage, security is enforced by the hypervisor while for distributed storage, it is enforced by the network. Secure protocols are available to establish a safe connection, but the management application must provide certificates management to enforce authentications for every connection. Another important limiting factor for migration is hardware compatibility between source and destination. It is important for the migrated VM to find the same hardware environment left in the source, and this means that memory, CPU and hardware devices must be the same. This check must be done by the management application which, having a list of all the hardware available, must select the appropriate destination.

However, the most important limiting factor for the Cloud is the need to migrate VM(s) inside the same network subnet so that the IP addresses associated with the VM can remain the same and active connections will not be dropped. This limitation cannot be solved at the management or administrator levels because it is due to the hierarchical IP architecture and inherited by every IP-based protocol. Solutions have been proposed to solve this problem involving existing or newly created protocols, and in general they agree to separate IP address from a second information to identify the node location. One notable example is the IEFT Mobile IP protocol (Lancki, Dixit, & Gupta, 1996) that associates to the node two IP addresses: one which is moved unchanged so that network connections are not dropped and one which is changed depending on the destination node. The same philosophy is used in the Cisco Overlay Transport Virtualization technology (OTV) (Sturdevant, 2010) where the second changing identifier is the MAC address. This method requires the extension of the Data Link layer (L2 of the OSI reference model) switching capabilities beyond the normal subnet boundary. All of these proposals are discussed at the Internet Engineering Task Force (IETF) which seeks to find a standard protocol to address this problem.

The common aim of all these methods is to leave layers 3-7 of the OSI reference model unchanged so that all of the protocols defined there and their associated security will continue to be valid.

Migration and Security

The VM is a software entity controlled by the hypervisor which ensures isolation and security. During migration, memory pages containing the VM are moved through the network as normal data. In a Cloud environment, composed of several servers and VM(s), there is a need to ensure the safe transfer of this data between hypervisors in order to avoid attacks that seek to take control of the VM via modification of data or injection of bogus VM(s). In other words, the source and destination hypervisor must provide authentication and privacy for the transfer. The migration is a hypervisor operation and security must be enforced by the hypervisors, which should form a chain of trust between themselves. For mutual authentication, the standard Public Key Infrastructure (PKI) certificates may be used. These certificates must be setup and maintained for the entire structure of hypervisors, sending or receiving VM(s); this is usually a management application task.

The process, which looks long but is straightforward, has a few complications hidden in the wrinkles of Cloud architecture. When a new physical machine is turned on, a golden copy of the hypervisor (a generic copy valid for every machine) is downloaded through the network from a repository. The use of a golden copy avoids the need to customize and store the bootstrap images for all of the machines and VMs, but the images cannot contain any data that is specific to a machine or VM, like a private key. Therefore, when the hypervisor starts up, it receives the configuration via a network channel that cannot provide authentication or privacy, leaving the hypervisor exposed to malicious attacks. The authentication cannot be provided because the hypervisor does not have a private key yet and privacy cannot be safely established because of the difficulty in a starting up machine to generate a random number for the encryption process. Mitigation of this problem can be achieved by using hardware able to store keys and making them available only on specific machine states (e.g., Trusted Platform Module hardware) or by on-fly customization of the software image during network download.

Another aspect of security connected to migration lies in the source security context of the VM. After the VM is created, the hypervisor and the management application setup the security context following policies defined by the administrator like firewall or software switch settings. If the VM is migrated to another physical server, the security context must be migrated with the VM; this must be done by a combined effort between the hypervisor and the management application.

Storage Virtualization

In a Cloud environment, remote storage capability is ensured through storage modules that are accessed by the computing platform trough the network. Although the same storage virtualization term applies both to disk resources and file resources, at the Cloud infrastructure level usually only the virtual disk resources are considered, since they are the first resource allocable to platform services. Storage local to the servers is not usually used for virtual machines in a Cloud infrastructure because of its need to move the entire storage with the VM in VM migration.

Storage modules in the Cloud infrastructure provide data storage and boot services for the computing platform via network protocols like Fiber Channel (FC) or iSCSI. The virtualization layer is provided by the management application responsible for pooling storage resources and their availability to the servers in terms of virtual disk and data services (Floyer, 2010).

The storage modules available are similar in terms of capabilities but different in term of management, thus requiring a custom approach by the management application. Usually, storage configuration is applied directly by using the GUI interface provided by the module and by manually providing the storage resources to the management application. This is, by itself, a security flaw.

Today, the security of data transport rests on the protocols used to exchange data between the server and the storage, and it relies on the capacity of the management application to safely deliver crypto parameters and setup the network (INCITS, 2006) (Winter & McDConnell). However, the autonomic management of storage virtualization does not seem to be close.

In particular there are two aspects of storage management that are still mostly manual and need a specific setup: storage data management in terms of backup and disaster recovery and the setup of bootable virtual disks. The latter one, although it is an important part of the Cloud infrastructure, is difficult to integrate because it requires boot image management, storage support to copy the image on the virtual disk and the setup to address security of the network and servers.

In the last few years, storage virtualization has progressed and we have begun to see management applications able to virtualize and manage the storage (Chan, 2011) even though the markets' great expectations have been partially missed (Rubens, 2011).

HYBRID CLOUDS

Market researches and providers' direct questions to customers indicate that security is one of the major obstacles for market penetration of the hybrid Cloud infrastructure (Parizo, 2011). Although today's technology allows an optimized utilization of the IT infrastructure, customers' diffidence, mainly due to the trust they have to give to providers of the extended Cloud, is stalling the move toward hybrid Cloud environments. The major security concerns from an enterprise viewpoint are related to how data is exchanged

between Cloud entities as well as to how this data is managed. This problem can be reduced to two separate issues: how communication is established between Cloud entities and how data is managed in the extended Cloud.

Federated Identity

The authorization for a user to access Cloud resources relies on the possibility for the provider to be able to authenticate the user and ascertain its identity. This authentication is connected to a secret used to prove identity when challenged from the resource provider and usually results in a username and password. However, the proliferation of the services offered via Internet and the consequent increases of malicious attacks on data are making the management of authentication via password unsustainable by a normal user. The best practices to mitigate security risks require users to utilize long and difficult to guess passwords, different usernames and passwords for every connection, refresh passwords often and, of course, not write any of them down. This situation resulted from the rapid evolution of Web-based technology, which was not accompanied by a similar development in terms of security. Instead, security is still anchored to firewalls and transport layer security (TLS). Ideally, a user could sign on once to enter the Internet and then have its identity safely verified for every site the user visits.

The basic idea behind the federated identity is the authentication of a user with an identity provider (IP) which will take care of every next authentication with resource providers by issuing security tokens. This is possible if the identity provider is a trusted entity and can establish a trusted relationship with the resource provider (relying party RP). In other words, federation allows identity related information to be shared between parties using a set of standards that allow for the creation and management of security tokens. Once generated, these tokens are shared between users and resource providers and are validated through a chain of trust involving the relying parties and the identity provider. This works well inside of an organization or a private Cloud, but establishing a trust relationship throughout the Internet requires a well-established background in terms of standards in order to define properties and methods. Among the few proposals in discussion for Internet-wide standardization (OpenID, 2007) (Scavo, Cantor, & Dors, 2005), the WS-Trust deserves a mention (OASIS, 2007). This is an extension of an existing standard, the Web Services Security (WSS), which utilizes instruments like Security Assertion Markup Language (SAML) to specify safe messaging between parties. The extensions provide new definitions and attributes for security tokens as well as messaging format. The major advantage of this approach which extends a private Cloud, is that the local administrator maintains complete control of the security all over the Cloud, both local and extended. Therefore, the configuration capabilities of the identity provider are extensive, and the administrator can define access and capabilities for every component of the domain.

This technology enables companies to provide custom Single Sign On feature based on a well defined architecture (Lewis & Lewis, 2009).

As an alternative to this pure-software approach, Intel recently proposed the Expressway Cloud Access 360. This method, similar in results to the federated identity, is based on the Intel TXT technology available on the Intel® hardware platforms through the Intel Identity Protection Technology. Cloud connectivity is provided through a series of standards like SAML or OAuth. The advantage of this approach is that the website or enterprise can verify the identity of the hardware in addition to the normal username and password scheme that is user and software-based.

The Customer's Perception

Hybrid Clouds are not homogeneous in terms of equipment or methodologies, creating some concerns in customers approaching external public or private Clouds to store or process sensitive data. With scalability, services and cost savings, there is the drawback that the customer cannot control the infrastructure and its ability to influence processes is limited. In a private Cloud, everything is under direct control. Moving to an external Cloud requires a certain amount of trust supported by informative knowledge from one side and transparency from the other. The situation is further complicated by the lack of any specific legislation regulating the services offered by the Cloud and everything is left to negotiations between the parties (Harris, 2011). These negotiations, in general, can have different targets, but they usually converge on a few specific and important points related to infrastructure where the customer perception of the services offered by the Provider plays a significant role.

First, data segregation is usually important. The data and processing for one customer must be separated from the data and processing of other customers. This concept, which is regulated by the management application, is the same as the VM(s) isolation in the computing area where virtual boundaries, enforced by the hypervisor, separate data and execution between VM(s). In this case, enforcement should be in the policies which regulate the allocation of resources to ensure a safe execution and storage environment, thus avoiding data leaks and poisonings.

Second, who has data access is another concern for customers moving to a hybrid Cloud. These problems involve many aspect of the Cloud, the management application, the administrator, the security implemented for roles and the authentication methodologies. The target is to restrict access to the data to a well defined group of privileged people; in the best scenario, this group would be from the customer's organization.

Lastly, end-to-end Security is an issue, as encryption and integrity are the most common concerns for data transitioning through or resting in the Cloud. Sometimes customers want complete control of the encryption process inside the entire hybrid Cloud in terms of keys, signatures and audit processes with more than one level of encryption.

Although this is an incomplete list, it gives an idea of the problems encountered in trying to outsource Cloud services. As previously said, the provider selection is difficult and mostly based on the customer's perception of the services offered by the extended network. This is a field that is beginning to gain momentum and studies are available to help customers in the selection of a provider (Pauley, 2010).

FUTURE RESEARCH DIRECTIONS

The previous paragraphs have highlighted the need for radical changes in the Cloud infrastructure to guarantee scalability, availability and security. The computing platform needs modification to remove compatibility drags, resulting in a more synergetic approach between the virtual system software and the hardware. Intel has already introduced many innovations in the servers to manage a safe hardware identity. Still, the bootstrap procedure needs better integration with remote media, software images and security. For these reasons, a few years back Intel launched the idea to replace the old BIOS with a new Unified Extensible Firmware Interface (UEFI) able to remove all compatibility issues, be fully configurable, open to every boot capability and secure (UEFI, 2011). The proposal generated many concerns because of its incompatibility with many software programs, but Intel continued to support it and software companies slowly began to release software aligned with this new firmware.

The management port and the hardware identity are also very important in a data center and generally in the Cloud, but the single user at home still faces many problems in managing security. some innovation in the hardware side on this problem is expected, even if today there is nothing in the literature. In the network platform, there are several initiatives to try to solve the scalability and security problems. There are many proposals and custom solutions (OpenFlow, 2011) (Li & Woo, 2010), but the standardization discussion is still only at the beginning. The same is happening to federated identity: there are many proposals and many custom implementations to define the trust relationship (OASIS, 2007), but the road to standardization is still long. The management application is growing with the Cloud services without a blueprint to define the basic infrastructure, making it hard to predict how it will develop, even in the near future. However, there are few things that are well-defined: it should be policy-driven and governed by a model. This is necessary in order to manage the scalability of the product and the perfect integration between all of the platforms and the administrator. Security is important for customers, with the selection of the provider often difficult, and there are already proposals on how to evaluate the security offered by a provider (Wang, Wang, Ren, & Lou, 2010). Of course this approach works if there is a standard method to apply, but the discussion has just begun and it is expected to grow in the near future.

CONCLUSION

Cloud infrastructure is moving its first steps and we are beginning to see its capabilities and its limits with actual implementation The previous paragraphs went through a general description of the components and of the limits of the infrastructure in terms of security. In particular, three cases were presented which are specific for a Cloud environment and that represent a real challenge in terms of security. Software provisioning and the federated identity have been described with the issues as well as the current proposals to mitigate the problems. It has also indicated the most important trends in research and development.

Many things remain to define, technology has to be developed, and standards still have to be accepted, but the concept of the Cloud is taking form and this process can progress to pervade all aspects of the Internet and consequently of our life.

Trademarks

Intel® is registered trademarks of Intel Corporation.

Cytrix® and Symantec® are registered trademarks of Cytrix Corporation.

Cisco® is registered trademarks of Cisco Systems, Inc.

Microsoft® is registered trademark of Microsoft Co.

Other third party trademarks referenced are the property of their respective owners

Disclaimer

The information herein is provided "as is," without any warranties or representations, express, implied or statutory, including without limitation, warranties of noninfringement, merchantability or fitness for a particular purpose.

ACKNOWLEDGMENT

I would like to thank Paul Gleichauf, Elaine Cheong and Gianluca Mardente who worked with me in the past few years and influenced me in many positive ways. Inside Cisco I would like to thank Claudio De Santi and Landon Curt Noll for reviewing the document and John McDowall for several interesting discussions. A special thank to my daughter, Maria Chiara, who helped me reviewing the document for a better wording expressions of many concepts.

REFERENCES

Babcock, C. (2009, 01 21). *Intel, Citrix To Collaborate On Virtualized Desktops*. Retrieved 04 25, 2011, from InformationWeek: http://www.informationweek.com

Bangeman, E. (2006, 09 07). *Microsoft and Cisco hook up on network security*. Retrieved 11 09, 2011, from Security: http://arstechnica.com

Berger, S., Caceres, R., Goldman, K. A., Perez, R., Sailer, R., & Doorn, L. v. (2006). vTPM: Virtualizing the Trusted Platform Module. *USENIX SS'06 - USENIX Security Symposium - Vol. 15*. Boston: Association for Computing Machinery.

Chaitanya, S., Butler, K., Sivasubramaniam, A., McDaniel, P., & Vilayannur, M. (2006). Design, implementation and evaluation of security in iSCSI-based network storage systems. *Storage Security and Survivability (StorageSS 2006)*. Alexandria, USA. doi: 10.1145/1179559.1179564

Chan, G. (2011, 11 05). *Storage Virtualization & Scale-out Technology*. Retrieved 11 08, 2011, from Enterprise Features: http://enterprisefeatures.com

Cloud Security Alliance. (2011): Retrieved 06 21, 2011 from: https://cloudsecurityalliance.org/

Crump, G. (2010, 10 21). *Articles*. Retrieved 6 14, 2011, from Storage switzerland: http://www.storage-switzerland.com

Engates, J. (2009, 07 27). *Hybrid clouds the way to go*. Retrieved 04 20, 2011, from NETWORKWORLD: http://www.networkworld.com

Floyer, D. (2010, 08 12). *Integrating Storage and Network Virtualization: A prerequisite for an effective Cloud Computing Model*. Retrieved 11 07, 2011, from Wikibon: http://wikibon.org

Ford, M., Lew, K., Spanier, S., & Stevenson, T. (1997). *Internetworking Technologies Handbook*. Indianapolis, IN: Cisco Press.

Gillespie, M. (2009, June 1). *Intel Trusted Execution Technology.* Retrieved 4 15, 2011, from Intel Software Network: http://software.intel.com

Hanna, S., & Molina, J. (2010, 03 24). *Cloud Security Questions?* Retrieved 11 07, 2011, from Cloud Computing Jornal: http://cloudcomputing. sys-con.com

Harris, D. (2011, 06 16). *Cloud legislation takes center stage on Capitol Hill.* Retrieved 06 29, 2011, from Gigaom: http://gogaom.com

Hu, F., Qiu, M., Li, J., Grant, T., Tylor, D., McCaleb, S., et al. (2011). A Review on Cloud Computing: Design Challenges in Architecture and Security. *Journal of Computing and Information Technology - CIT,* 25-55.

INCITS. (2006, 02 17). *Fiber Channel Security Protocols.* Retrieved 11 05, 2011, from T11 Project: http://www.t10.org

IPXE. (2010). *Open Source Boot Firmare.* Retrieved 11 12, 2011, from Ipxe: http://ipxe.org/

Lancki, B., Dixit, A., & Gupta, V. (1996, 08 01). *Mobile-IP: Transparent Host Migration on the Internet.* Retrieved 04 21, 2011, from LinuxJournal: http://www.linuxjournal.com

Lemos, R. (2006, 01 26). *Researchers: Rootkits headed for BIOS.* Retrieved 11 12, 2011, from Security Focus: http://www.securityfocus.com

Lewis, K. D., & Lewis, J. E. (2009). Web Single Sign-On Authentication using SAML. *Internationl Journal of Computer Science Issues, 2,* 41-48.

Li, L. E., & Woo, T. (2010). VSITE: A scalable and secure architecture for seamless L2 enterprise extension in the cloud. *Secure Network Protocols (NPSec), 5,* pp. 31-36. Kyoto. doi: 10.1109/NPSEC.2010.5634451

Markoff, J. (1999, 2 29). Intel Goes to Battle as Its Embedded Serial Number Is Unmasked. *The New York Times,* p. Retrieved from www.nyt.com on 6/7/2001.

Messner, E. (2009, 03 31). *Cloud Security Alliance Formed to Promote Best Practices.* Retrieved 06 21, 2011, from Cloud Computing: http://www. networkworld.com

Microsoft. (2011, 10 10). *Hardware.* Retrieved 11 05, 2011, from Microsoft MSDN: http://msdn.microsoft.com/en-us/windows/hardware/gg463149

Mironov, I. (2005, November). *Hash functions: Theory, attacks, and applications.* Retrieved 06 22, 2011, from Microsoft Research: http://research. microsoft.com

Mohamed, A. (2009, 06 10). *A history of cloud computing.* Retrieved 05 09, 2011, from computerweekly.com: http://www.computerweekly.com

OASIS. (2007, 03 19). *WS-Trust 1.3.* Retrieved 06 06, 2011, from OASIS: http://docs.oasis-open.org

Open, I. D. (2007, 12 05). *OpenID Authentication 2.0 - Final.* Retrieved 11 12, 2011, from Openid: http://openid.net

OpenFlow. (2011). *OpenFlow.* Retrieved 07 19, 2011, from http://www.openflow.org

Parizo, E. (2011, 06 27). *Gartner: Prepare today or face cloud computing security problems tomorrow.* Retrieved 07 02, 2011, from SearchCloudSecurity: http://searchcloudsecurity.techtarget.com

Pauley, W. A. (2010, November-December 8(6)). *Cloud Provider Transparency.* Retrieved 6 14, 2011, from Security & Privacy, IEEE: http://ieeexplore.ieee.org. doi: 10.1109/MSP.2010.140

Rubens, P. (2011, 06 16). *Does Virtualization Deliver on Its Promise?* Retrieved 11 08, 2011, from Trends: http://www.serverwatch.com

Scavo, T., Cantor, S., & Dors, N. (2005, 06 02). *Shibboleth Architecture*. Retrieved 11 08, 2011, from Internet2: http://shibboleth.internet2.edu

Silvera, E., Sharaby, G., Lorenz, D., & Shapira, I. (2009). *IP mobility to support live migration of virtual machines across subnets. SYSTOR 2009*. Haifa.

Sriram, I., & Khajeh-Hosseini, A. (2010, 01 19). *Research Agenda in Cloud Technologies*. Retrieved 05 20, 2011, from Cornell University Library: http://www.arxiv.com/abs/1001.3259

Sturdevant, C. (2010, 02 10). *Cisco OTV Extends Layer 2 Between Data Centers*. Retrieved 11 07, 2010, from Data Storage - eWeek: http://www.eweek.com

Symantec Co. (1999, 03 19). *Symantec Detects and Eliminates Recent Pentium III Serial Number Exploit*. Retrieved 06 22, 2011, from Symantec News Release: http://www.symantec.com

TCG. (2010, 09 13). *Open Standards from TNC*. Retrieved 10 21, 2011, from Trusted Computing Group: http://www.trustedcomputinggroup.org

UEFI. (2011). Retrieved 04 21, 2011, from http://www.uefi.org

Venezia, P. (2010, 02 16). *First glimpse: Cisco OTV*. Retrieved 05 20, 11, from Reuters: http://www.reuters.com

Villinger, S. (2011, 08 22). The 30-year-long Reign of BIOS is Over: Why UEFI Will Rock Your IT. *HP Feature Articles* Retrieved 11 07, 2011, from: http://h30565.www3.hp.com

Wang, C., Wang, Q., Ren, K., & Lou, W. (2010). Privacy-Preserving Public Auditing for Data Storage Security in Cloud Computing. *INFOCOM 2010. 14*, 1-9. San Diego, CA: IEEE Press. doi: 10.1109/INFCOM.2010.5462173

Winter, R., & McConnell, D. (n.d.). *Security Through Maturity: A Brief on Securing iSCSI Networks*. Retrieved 11 04, 2011, from http://www.dell.com/downloads/global/power/ps2q09-20090225-McConnell.pdf

Zimmer, V. J., Dasari, S. R., & Brogan, S. P. (2009, 09). *Trusted Platforms*. Retrieved 11 5, 2011, from EFI: http://download.intel.com/technology/efi/SF09_EFIS001_UEFI_PI_TCG_White_Paper.pdf

ADDITIONAL READING

Arregoces, M., & Portolani, M. (2004). *Data Center Fundamentals*. Indianapolis, IN: Cisco Press.

Berger, S., Caceres, R., & Goldman, K. (2006). perez, R., Sailer, R., & *vTPM: Virtualizing the Trusted Platform Module*. Yorktown Heights: IBM.

Droms, R. (1997, 03). *Dynamic Host Configuration Protocol*. (IEFT, Ed.). RFC 2131. Retrieved 07 21, 2011, from RFC-Editor: http://www.rfc-editor.org

Droms, R., & Arbaugh, W. (2001, 06). *Authentication for DHCP messages*. (IEFT, Ed.). RFC 3118. Retrieved 07 21, 2011, from RFC-Editor: http://www.rfc-editor.org

Ford, M., Lew, K., Spanier, S., & Stevenson, T. (1997). *Internetworking Technologies Handbook*. Indianapolis, IN: Cisco Press.

Grawrock, D. (2006). *The Intel Safer Computing Initiative. Hillsboro*. Intel Press.

Hammer-Lahav, E. (2010, 04). *The OAuth 1.0 Protocol*. (IEFT, Ed.). RFC 5849. Retrieved 07 21, 2011, from RFC-Editor: http://www.rfc-editor.org

Hugos, M., & Hulitzky, D. (2011). *Business in the Cloud*. Hoboken, NJ: John Wiley & Sons, Inc.

Intel Co. (1999, 09 20). *Preboot Execution Environmnet (PXE) Specification*. Retrieved 03 17, 2009, from Intel Download: http://download.intel.com

Kent, S., & Seo, K. (2005, 12). *Security Architecture for the Internet Protocol*. (IEFT, Ed.). RFC 4301. Retrieved 07 21, 2011, from RFC-Editor: http://www.rfc-editor.org

Krishnan, S. (2010). *Programming Windows Azure*. Sebastopol, CA: O'Reilly Media, Inc.

Krutz, R., & Vines, R. D. (2010). *Cloud Security*. Indianapolis, IN: Wiley Publishing, Inc.

Laet, G. D., & Schauwers, G. (2005). *Network Security Fundamentals*. Indianapolis, IN: Cisco Press.

Mather, T., Kumaraswamy, S., & Latif, S. (2009). *Cloud Security and Privacy*. Sebastopol: O'Reilly Media, Inc.

McGraw, G. (2006). *Software Security. Crawfordsville*. Addison-Wesley.

Menez, A. J., Oorschot, P. C., & Vanstone, S. A. (1997). *Handbook of Applied Cryptography*. Boca Raton, FL: CRC Press.

Murty, J. (2008). *Programming Amazon Web Services*. Sebastopol, CA: O'Reilly.

Perez, R., Doom, L. v., & Sailer, R. (2008). Virtualization and Hardware-Based Security. *Security & Privacy, IEEE, 6*(5), 24–31. doi:10.1109/MSP.2008.135

Rash, M. (2007). *Linux Firewalls*. San Francisco, CA: No Starch Press.

Rescorla, E. (2001). *SSL and TLS*. Indianapolis, IN: Addison-Wesley.

Rosenberg, J., & Mateos, A. (2011). *The Cloud at Your Service*. Greenwich, UK: Manning Publications Co.

Sollins, K. (1992, 07). *The TFTP Protocol*. (IEFT, Ed.). RFC 1350. Retrieved 07 21, 2011, from RFC-Editor: http://www.rfc-editor.org

Sportack, M. A. (2003). *IP Addressing Fundamentals*. Indianapolis, IN: Cisco Press.

Trusted Computing Group. (n.d.). *Trusted Computing*. Retrieved 07 21, 2011, from Trusted Computing Group: http://www.trustedcomputinggroup.org

Zimmer, V., Rothman, M., & Hale, R. (2006). *Beyond BIOS*. Hillsboro: Intel Press.

Chapter 10
Security Issues in Cloud Federations

Massimiliano Rak
Second University of Naples, Italy

Hamza Ghani
TU Darmstadt, Germany

Massimo Ficco
Second University of Naples, Italy

Neeraj Suri
TU Darmstadt, Germany

Jesus Luna
TU Darmstadt, Germany

Silviu Panica
Institute e-Austria Timisoara, Romania

Dana Petcu
Institute e-Austria Timisoara, Romania

ABSTRACT

The cloud paradigm, based on the idea of delegating to the network any kind of computational resources, is showing a considerable success. The estimated trend is that the number of different cloud-based solutions, approaches, and service providers (CSP) will continue growing. Despite the big number of different cloud solutions that currently exist, most of them are "walled gardens" unable to interoperate. On the other side, a large effort is taking place in the cloud community to develop and identify open solutions and standards. In such a context the concept of cloud federation, an architecture that combines the functionalities of different CSP, is a hot topic. This chapter presents an overview of the cloud federation topic, with special focus on its most important security challenges. Furthermore, it proposes a taxonomy of possible approaches to federation. Then it proposes a comparison of security problems in cloud and grid environment, and a detailed analysis of two relevant security problems, identity management and Cyber Attacks analysis, trying to outline how they can be applied in a federated context.

DOI: 10.4018/978-1-4666-1631-8.ch010

Copyright © 2012, IGI Global. Copying or distributing in print or electronic forms without written permission of IGI Global is prohibited.

INTRODUCTION

The cloud just as defined in (Mell, 2009), has increasingly become a computing/communication paradigm that seems to have the potential to change the way we consider systems and services. At the state of the art Microsoft (with Azure), Google (Google App Engine), IBM (IBM Cloud Reference Architecture), Oracle (Oracle on Demand) are just some of the "big players" offering their services for both Infrastructure as a Service (IaaS) and Platform as a Service (PaaS) solutions, which have adopted completely proprietary approaches. Because of the latter, a typical cloud user (*e.g.,* a developer) might find herself completely "locked" into a specific CSP, once she has chosen it from the available technological stack. On the other hand and in order to promote interoperability, a large effort is being spent in the cloud computing community to identify open solutions and standards through open consortiums (e.g. the Open Cloud Manifesto (OpenCloud Manifesto, 2009) and the Cloud Security Alliance (Cloud Security Alliance, 2009), open source-based solutions (*e.g.,* OpenNebula (J.Fontan, 2008)) and, standards like OCCI (Open Cloud Computing Interface (Edmonds, 2010)), and the Cloud Data Management Interface (CDMI (SNIA, 2010)).

Considerable pressure is being put by the CSP to ensure the means for using cloud services (compatible or not) from different providers. This kind of approach is desired from two different perspectives:

1. That of the application developers, who are interested to combine different cloud services from different providers or even to ensure the availability of their cloud services by replicating them to different providers;
2. That of the cloud service providers (CSP), who are interested to extend their infrastructure capabilities or to build on top of others CSP's offers.

When a cloud compliant application is distributed across two or more CSP and administrative domains simultaneously, there are two possible approaches:

*   **Federated clouds:** when the providers agree how to mutually enforce policy and governance, establishing a common trust boundary.
*   **Hybrid cloud:** when the application crosses a private-public trust boundary or spans multiple clouds (simultaneous use of multiple CSP where both, administrative domains and trust boundaries are crossed).

The main subject of this chapter is related to federation of clouds, where two use cases are already well recognized: scale-out, and mutual backup –recovery- from a disaster. In the case of scale-out scenario, if an event occurs unexpectedly or in a peak, a stable operation is possible by distributing dynamically the workloads between the resources of the local –private- cloud and the public cloud. In the case of a mutual backup and recovery from a disaster, if an event damages one provider's cloud or causes a power outage, then cloud resources in other providers are used to restore the damaged services.

A federation of clouds can be organized in different ways:

*   **Horizontal federation:** when two or more cloud providers join together to build a facility for capacity on-demand. Participants having an excess capacity share their resources (for a price agreed beforehand), with those other participants needing additional resources to deal with their workload's spikes.
*   **Intercloud:** when a federation of clouds is built with a common set of features like, e.g., addressing, naming, identity, trust, presence, messaging, multicast, time domain, and application messaging (the re-

sponsibility for communication is on the providers' side). The computing environment supports dynamic elasticity of capabilities and dynamic workload migration.

- **Cross-cloud:** when the federation is established between a cloud needing external resources and a cloud offering its resources (not necessarily agreed beforehand). This federation passes through several phases like e-discovery (looking for available clouds), matching (selecting the CSPs fitting the requirements), authentication (establishing a trust context within the selected clouds), etc..

This chapter offers an overview of the cloud federation's security issues (covering the Horizontal, Intercloud and Cross-cloud federations), with a special focus on the most important security challenges that arise when composing different cloud service providers (Cross-cloud scenario). Furthermore, it proposes a tentative problem formalization and some possible approaches, which make evident the need for layered federation solutions. As anticipated, the chapter will not enter into the detail of the (already open) technical issues related to the cloud federation approach (e.g. the need of agnostic APIs such as the one proposed in the mOSAIC project (Petcu, 2011)); by the contrary, it will rather focus on the security issues implied from the different cloud federation strategies.

The chapter starts with an identification of the main components, actors and techniques adopted in the context of cloud federations, whose will be used as a basis for offering a first survey of the security threats that this approach involves. Moreover, it offers a clear comparison between the cloud federations and the computational Grid federation approaches: in the grid community the federation problem aroused few years ago, however the different solutions and strategies developed there seem to be suitable for the cloud. Also in this chapter will be shown an analogy

between the federation of clusters (grids) and the federation of clouds (intercloud). Even at the intercloud level one will see several differences between both categories of federations, which are magnified if one takes into account the cross-clouds and the horizontal federation of clouds.

Once the security federation problem has been clearly defined and formalized, the chapter offers a vertical analysis of two of the most common security problems in such contexts: the identity and access control management (IAM), and cyber attacks.

The remainder of this chapter is structured as follows: the next section (*Background*) offers a clear taxonomy of the cloud federation problems, showing the challenges that appear when trying to federate different CSP. Afterwards, the main technical issues of this chapter are discussed in the following three sections: firstly by providing a comparison of the federation problem between cloud and grid platforms, secondly by outlining the problem of federated identity and access management and thirdly, by focusing on those cyber attacks affecting federated cloud environments. This chapter finalizes with a section summarizing the conclusions.

BACKGROUND

The "Cloud Computing Uses Cases Whitepaper" (Cloud Computing Use Case Discussion Group, 2010) proposes the following definition of cloud federation:

"Federation is the ability of multiple independent resources to act like a single resource. Cloud computing itself is a federation of resources, so the many assets, identities, configurations and other details of a cloud computing solution must be federated to make cloud computing practical."

A cloud federation is apparently a simple idea: it allows final users to access transparently a set of resources and services, distributed among several independent CSP. However, in the cloud computing context there are a lot of different interpretations for this simple idea, e.g. it is completely different if access must be given for federated resources to a final user (which implies the existence of a brokering middleware), or to a cloud application developer (which implies the adoption of agnostic APIs).

The rest of this section will propose a taxonomy for classifying the different cloud federation challenges, and also will outline the state of art related with representative cloud federation technologies. Based on the proposed taxonomy, the following sections will focus on the main security threats affecting cloud federations.

As anticipated, the first concept that it is important to define is the **Federation Visibility**, which refers to the type of actors to which the cloud federation is visible. For example, a *User Level Federation* means that final users access the cloud federation and perceive it as a single entity, while developers and other CSPs are aware of the different clouds that compose the federation. The chapter identifies the following actors according to the Federation Visibility concept:

- **Final Users:** common users which access the cloud and uses cloud services.
- **Service Providers:** acquire resources and services from the cloud in a transparent way, and offer them to Final Users.
- **Service Developers:** develop applications using the cloud's resources. Sometimes they also use services developed by other parties.
- **Cloud Service Providers:** Offer cloud resources and services.

On the opposite site to visibility is the concept of *Federation Resource*, which focuses on the type of resources being federated. For example, it is different to federate IaaS services than to federate PaaS services, even if in both cases the resulting federation has the same visibility (e.g. service developers). Under a Federation Resource it is possible to share:

- **IaaS Resources (Compute, Storage, Network):** in this case the cloud federation has the effect of delivering target resources from different CSP. This is the most widely used idea of cloud federation.
- **PaaS Resources:** the concept of federating PaaS is still in its very early days, therefore is only possible to put in evidence the following main ideas:
  - **Federation of a PaaS' API:** take for example Contrail (Jégou Y. (2011)) and Google where both offer a *mapreduce* API. A federated cloud solution enables development of applications (service developer-visibility) by using transparently both implementations. At the state of art and according to the best of our knowledge, there are not Federations of PaaS so far, however projects like mOSAIC are aiming towards creating an API to face this problem.
  - **Federation of PaaS Services:** *e.g.,* IBM, Oracle and Micrsoft offer Web-based products to deploy enterprise solutions on cloud resources. Federating them means enabling high level services to users, in order to access them independently of the "real" execution environment.

There are a lot of different ways to federate cloud solutions, however one of the main problems is still related with the kind of technologies being involved. We will call this a *Technological Federation*, which can be subdivided in:

- Federation on a fixed technology.
- Federation among different technologies.

The last, but probably the most important for this chapter, is the *Security Domains Federation* that outlines which are the relationships between the resources being federated:

- Federation between different, independent and unknown security domains.
- Federation in a set of predefined security domains.
- Federation in a single security domain.

CLOUD FEDERATION IN EUROPEAN PROJECTS

Cloud federation is a research topic of great interest in Europe, which contrary to hosting big cloud-related companies (*e.g.,* Amazon, Oracle, Google, IBM, Microsoft, RackSpace etc), usually focus on several small or medium sized CSP (Aruba, Amplidata, Cloud.bg, Cloudsigma,etc.), but an interesting list can be found in (Kiril, 2006)).

At the state of art, many EU-funded projects devoted to cloud computing face problems related with the concept of *federation*, even if they focus on proposing different approaches and terminologies to solve it. This section briefly summarizes these approaches, in particular focusing on the EU FP7 projects RESERVOIR, OPTIMIS, CONTRAIL, T-CLOUDS and mOSAIC.

In RESERVOIR project, a reference architecture was introduced in (Celesti, 2010) to address the Identity Management (IdM) problem in the Intercloud context. Moreover, another approach was proposed in (Villari, 2010) using scalability and migration of virtual machines to build scalable cloud defences against cloud DDoS attacks. These solutions have followed a deep analysis of the potential threats posed to the emerging large-scale cross border virtualization infrastructures partially presented in (Villari, 2009). The same project has presented one of the first comparisons of security issues in Grids versus Clouds in (Latanieki, 2009).

The OPTIMIS project aims at developing a framework for cloud services federation based on a deploying approach: their infrastructure is able to acquire resources from a lot of different cloud service providers, that automatically is able to deploy cloud services on them. This project aims at offering a set of tools able to manage autonomic features on the acquired federation's resources. OPTIMIS proposes the following concepts:

- **Bursted Private Cloud:** In this case a private cloud is able to acquire resources from public providers in order to face peak requests. Resources are obtained and federated from different CSP, being this solution classified as an "hybrid cloud deployment model"(according to NIST's definition (Mell, 2009)). This scenario does not extend the security domain, but only has to face the problem of Technology Federation in order to acquire resources from different cloud providers.
- **MultiCloud:** It is a broker-based solution, in which a single access point is offered to final users in order to manage the resource acquisition phase from multiple and, different clouds.
- **Federated Cloud:** In this case, resources are acquired among different cloud providers as they communicate with each other in order to synchronize themselves in a distributed manner.

The CONTRAIL project aims at building a solution dedicated to a federated cloud provider able to offer a large set of cloud services, ranging from IaaS and image management services to PaaS solutions. CONTRAIL proposes the following definition for the management of cloud federations

- **Cloud Brokering:** adoption of a broker to find the best CSP for executing an application.

- **Cloud Aggregation:** mechanism integrated on the client side, which provides the user with resources from different providers.
- **Cloud Bursting:** final users access to a single CSP, which transparently integrate resources from one or more CSP.
- **Virtual Data Center:** an organization's locally hosted data center, that has been extended to the cloud (equivalent to the hybrid solution proposed by NIST (Mell, 2009).

Note that the goal of CONTRAIL is to build up a complete cloud solution, integrating resources from existent data centers and/or external systems. They build up a single security domain using their own authentication/authorization solutions. According to the terminology proposed in this chapter, the CONTRAIL project builds up a single security domain, where the authentication credentials needed to access different CSPs (from the same security federation) are managed by the responsible of the single security domain being offered by CONTRAIL's providers to their users.

The federated cloud-of-cloud middleware of T-CLOUDS offers privacy-protection and resilience beyond any individual cloud. This expands trust from trusted (enterprise-internal) clouds to less trusted (off-shored) ones or federates a set of partially trusted providers into a trustworthy and adaptive federation. T-CLOUDS proposed in (Bugiel, 2011) an architecture and protocols that accumulate slow secure computations over time and provide the possibility to query them in parallel on demand. The user communicates with a resource-constrained Trusted Cloud (a private cloud or built from multiple secure hardware modules) which encrypts algorithms and data to be stored and later on queried in the untrusted Commodity Cloud. The Trusted Cloud performs security-critical pre-computations, while the Commodity Cloud computes the time-critical query in parallel under encryption in the query phase. T-CLOUDS' first prototype, DEPSKY (Bessani, 2011) is a system that improves the availability, integrity and confidentiality of information stored in the cloud through the encryption, encoding and replication of the data on diverse clouds that form a cloud-of-clouds.

A completely different approach is proposed in mOSAIC, which aims at developing an API to enable the development of cloud applications which are completely independent from CSP. In this case the framework is offered to cloud developers, which are in turn able to build their own federations using the computational facilities offered by the API. Security-related issues are fully delegated to mOSAIC developers.

Cloud management platforms such as that build by RightScale can provide a new dimension in the heterogeneous cloud deployments by looking forward to security issues. In this context, the simple mechanism considered in RightScale to use the security repositories from the vendors should be mentioned, but custom configurations are still needed to get the patch or workaround applied to instances.

Finally, it is also worth to mention the work performed in this area by the European Network and Information Security Agency (ENISA), in particular its report presented in January 2011 (ENISA, 2011) which highlights the pros and cons, with regards to information security and resilience of community, private and public cloud computing delivery models. This report also guides public bodies in the definition of their requirements for information security and resilience, when evaluating the different cloud computing service delivery models. ENISA has followed a previous security assessment authored also by them (ENISA, 2009), that covered the technical, policy and legal implications of security in cloud computing.

Cloud Federation in Open Source Projects

The need of free and open access to CSP is largely diffused in the open source community. In the same direction, the need of open standards for the cloud was one of the first requirements when this paradigm was born: the Open Cloud Manifesto (Open Cloud Manifesto, 2009), signed by many of the big cloud-related names, stated the need of widely adopting open and standard interfaces. Unfortunately, nowadays the Open Cloud Manifesto does not have implications in real-life and still most cloud solutions largely rely on proprietary mechanisms and de-facto standards (like the Amazon EC2 interface).

On the other hand, the open source community has replied with a large number of open frameworks which aim at offering development solutions independent from the targeted cloud provider. Jclouds (Jclouds, 2010), as an example, is a Java library which offers a single interface to many CSP in order to access their basic IaaS functionality (e.g. virtual machine management and a Blobstore interface for cloud storage). LibCloud (Paul Querna, 2010), offers similar functionalities, but using Python as the target programming language. Deltacloud offers a different approach: it provides an interface based on a Representational State Transfer (REST) architecture, that can be wrapped to many different IaaS cloud providers for virtual machine management. All the solutions surveyed in this section are essentially wrappers offering a single interface towards several CSP.

Grid Experience as Starting Point for Clouds Federation

Long disputes exist about the relationship between grids and clouds paradigms, sometimes considered as alternatives (both aims at offering a completely distributed solution for managing geographically distributed resources), sometimes like orthogonal approaches (cloud being more oriented to busi-

ness-, transaction-oriented applications, while the grid has more preference for HPC calculus and long-running applications). It is out of the scope of this chapter to add new arguments to the grid/cloud debate: from the authors' point of view both are solutions in which an incredible large amount of resources are being managed in a (semi-)automated way by several, independent administrative domains. Moreover the authors consider that grids are build as clusters of clusters based on long-running agreements to share resources in virtual organisations. A cloud is analogous to a cluster in terms of security issues from the user point of view, allowing him to build virtual clusters. The Federation of Clouds (a cluster of clouds) can follow the grid model of long-running agreements, as well a more dynamical and complex model of ad-hoc agreement (following the bursting paradigm).

The aim of this section is to try to outline how grid experiences in the field of secured grouping of disparate resources can be adapted in the cloud federation context. Following the proposed taxonomy, it will focus on two different kinds of federation problems: the Technological and Security Domain federations.

The grid solution mainly aims at solving the problem of technological federation, adopting a standard, shared interoperability solution among different Virtual Organizations. In other words, the grid mainly aims at solving the problem of technological federation using a middleware-based approach: independently from the hardware/software configuration of the HPC systems involved, they are able to cooperate and to be technologically federated using the same middleware. In order to do so, the main feature offered in such e-infrastructure is a common security layer (the most used one is GSI (Welch, 2004)) based on Public Key Infrastructures (PKIs).

The grid paradigm has widely proven its usefulness, and also has shown that interoperability between heterogeneous hardware systems is -since the end of the last century- a common solution. The grid also has proven to be not only a technology reserved for researchers and scientists, but also as one applicable to other fields like economy and eHealth.

The grid's major drawback has been the proliferation of many different middlewares (Globus, gLITE, Unicore, XtreemOS, ARC, BOINC etc), which are only partially compatible among each other. Even Globus (Foster, 2006), the first and probably most used one, has evolved in many different versions with great technological shifts (moving mainly from a non-WebService based software (up to version 2), to a WebService-based system in subsequent versions).

In cloud environments, the middleware solutions are defined as Platform as a Service (PaaS), which are being offered following the same base concepts of Service Oriented Architectures –SOA-. In these terms, grid-on-cloud solutions (like (StratusLab Consortium, 2010)) can be considered as a cloud PaaS that uses the grid as a reference platform. The "grid experience" can be considered as the key point for the problem of federation at the PaaS layer: adoption of open, shared and stable standards looks to be the only way to have full interoperability between different platforms.

Appropriateness of Grid Security Solutions for Cloud Federation

Security issues in grids and federations of clouds offer much more interesting elements for a complete comparison of both paradigms, with respect to the federation problem formalized at the beginning of this chapter. Most grid environments -at least the ones enumerated above- rely on PKI solutions with different implementations: GSI is adopted by many of the most important grid middlewares, even if exceptions exist, e.g., in XtreemOS and Unicore which adopt different security approaches (often associated to security issues related to the Proxy certificates used by GSI).

When federating different grid environments, like what is happening with the EU-EMI project (Eu-Emi Consortium, 2011) the problems to face are (i) the technological federation between the different implementations of the PKI infrastructure (as before outlined) and, (ii) the problems of trust among different security environments. The latter is strictly related to the problem of a Security domain federation, and is probably the one allowing more analogies with respect to the cloud paradigm. This problem can be formally expressed as follows: each grid's virtual organization refers to certificates issued by a given Certificate Authority (CA). The grid middleware assumes that it is possible to accept a grid host certificate generated from many different CAs, but how to select which certificates to accept or not?

In a more formal way, each CA represents a Security Domain and any user holding a certificate belonging to a given CA is consequently assigned to the correspondent Security Domain. In order to federate different grid systems, they must accept each other certificate in order to build a federated security domain.

At the state of art, identification of authorized certificates is given to each physical host in the grid by her administrator, which manually adds the public signatures of the accepted CAs in each environment. Due to the fast growing of different and independent grid systems (just think about the number of campus Grids spread around European universities belonging to EGEE (EGEE Consortium, 2004)), this solution can be hardly applied.

It is feasible to assume that the federation of security domains in grids is mainly a problem of cross-certification among different PKI, whose main limit is the need of clear, accepted quantity-based evaluation techniques for automatizing the cross-domain authentication and authorization procedures.

The grid approaches all have a common starting point: security domains are trustful because of the Policy Management Authorities (PMA), which are setting up an unified set of policies for implementing a federated security model. Groups like EUGRIDPMA (the European Grid Policy Management Authority (EUGRIDPMA, 2008)) offer a reference policy for issuing digital certificates and, validating grid PKIs which are considered secure and trusted. Few proposals exist to automate the PMA's validation procedures, like the one proposed in (Casola, 2008).

The cloud context looks more complex to be managed in these terms: first of all, there is no accepted standard (like PKI) for managing user authentication, in fact only few CSPs supports PKI-based authentication. As this chapter will later present, most CSP have adopted either open protocols (Hammer-Lahav, 2010, Ferg, 2007) or closed solutions for authentication purposes. In summary, the problem cannot be limited to cross-certification, so once more it mixes up technological and security domain federation problems. The problem of federation between public CSP can be associated to the, currently unsolved, problem of automated cross-certification in grid environments.

Different considerations can be done in the case of private clouds: this problem is similar to the problem of federation among independent grid environments (like the one faced by the EU-EMI project). In both cases physical administrators have the role of identifying the policies for administering the local resources, so federation among two different systems can be done through a cross-certification like mechanism: a common agreement among authentication and authorization mechanisms and, also another agreement related to the administrative policies for trusting each other. Experiences from the grid ecosystem in this latter case, may offer a clear know-how on both technological and administrative approaches to be taken in order to face such situations.

IDENTITY MANAGEMENT IN CLOUD FEDERATIONS

Nowadays, one of the major problems being faced by IT organizations is the management of their users' identities across the wide variety of internal systems (e.g. accounting, human resources, legacy systems, etc.). Usually this "Identity Management" (IDM) problem is tackled via centralized solutions including Single Sign-On techniques (The Open Group 2010), which typically use an identity provider (IdP) to "map" a set of identities to an unique one for accessing different service providers (SP) inside the organization.

Unfortunately, the different challenges associated with "traditional" IDMs problems are maximized when the users begin accessing cross-organizational, federated IT resources (either internal users that access external resources, or external users that access a different organization's internal resources). These new cross-organizational and cross-domain IDM issues are usually known as "Federated Identity Management" or simply FIDM, and are typically enabled via different Technological Federations (i.e. open standards and specifications) like the ones published by the Liberty Alliance (a.k.a. Kantara Initiative) (Kantara Initiative, 2009) and, the Organization for the Advancement of Structured Information Standards (OASIS, 2011).

The ultimate goal of FIDM is to enable access to Federation Resources across completely unrelated security domains (as defined by the Security Domain Federation), by sharing a limited amount of information such as security identities and policies. When it is implemented as an architectural style, FIDM is often positioned as an alternative when identity centralization is not a viable solution for involved entities (*i.e.*, Federation Visibility, according to the proposed taxonomy) (Rodriguez, 2011).

On the one hand, in federated IT environments Final Users are able to use a single set of credentials and identity information, issued under a specific single security federation, to access resources on a completely different security domain (either independent and unknown or, a predefined security domain according to the proposed taxonomy). Behind those simple principles, FIDM has been one of the most challenging aspects of IT solutions for the last few decades.

On the other hand, in a federated cloud computing environment, FIDM plays a vital role in enabling organizations to authenticate their users of cloud services using the organization's chosen identity provider (IdP). In that context, securely exchanging identity attributes between the different visible actors of the federation (*e.g.,* the service provider –SP- and the IdP) is also a requirement that rises various challenges, but also brings novel solutions to address those challenges with respect to identity lifecycle management, available authentication methods to protect confidentiality and integrity, while supporting non-repudiation and even enforcing the user's privacy rights (Kumaraswamy, 2011).

Despite the difficulty to find a common set of challenges related with cloud FIDM (in part because this topic is in its early days), the belief is that Cameron's "Laws of Identity" (Cameron, 2005) are still valid for cloud ecosystems:

1. **User Control and Consent:** Technical identity systems must only reveal information identifying a user with the user's consent.
2. **Minimal Disclosure for a Constrained Use:** The solution which discloses the least amount of identifying information and best limits its use is the most stable long term solution.
3. **Justifiable Parties:** Digital identity systems must be designed so the disclosure of identifying information is limited to parties having a necessary and justifiable place in a given identity relationship.
4. **Directed Identity:** A universal identity system must support both "omni-directional" identifiers for use by public entities and

"unidirectional" identifiers for use by private entities, thus facilitating discovery while preventing unnecessary release of correlation random identifiers.

5. **Pluralism of Operators and Technologies:** A universal identity system must channel and enable the inter-working of multiple identity technologies run by multiple identity providers.
6. **Human Integration:** The universal identity metasystem must define the human user to be a component of the distributed system integrated through unambiguous human-machine communication mechanisms offering protection against identity attacks.
7. **Consistent Experience Across Contexts:** The unifying identity metasystem must guarantee its users a simple, consistent experience while enabling separation of contexts through multiple operators and technologies.

As pointed out in (Chadwick, 2009), the former set of laws will guarantee the creation of trusted FIDM systems (either cloud-oriented or not), which will result in their general public acceptance.

It is possible to "map" Cameron's FIDM laws and, the four categories of the taxonomy proposed at the beginning of this chapter to the following challenges that are specific to cloud federations:

*   **Security:** related with the confidentiality, integrity, authentication and authorization from the Federation Visibility perspective (actors). The cloud's rapid elasticity and dynamic resource polling features (NIST, 2011), usually result in user identities moving around geographically distributed sites, most of the time with the cloud user being unaware of this. Also takes into account the trust features inherent to the Security Domains Federation and, the federated resources (Federation Resource).
*   **Privacy:** from a Federation Visibility perspective this challenge is related with the

mechanisms to protect the Final Users' PII (Personal Identifiable Information), on the different Federation Resources that possibly overlap one or more Security Federation Domains. This is also related with the cloud's geographically distributed nature, where users might need novel privacy and federation mechanisms to guarantee the privacy of their personal data.

- **Standards and Interoperability:** the technologies behind the Technological Federation category are directly mapped to this challenge.

The rest of this section explores the relevant state of the art related with the identified cloud FIDM challenges.

Security

At the state of the art, most of the security-related problems arising with cloud FIDM are related with *(i)* protocols and architectures, *(ii)* authentication and authorization mechanisms, and *(iii)* usability.

Cloud FIDM protocols and references architectures are challenging research topics nowadays, due to the cloud geographically distributed nature where the concept of "security assurance" must be provided by the CSP in order to guarantee user's trust. Apart from the protocols to be mentioned in the "Standards and Interoperability" subsection, cloud FIDM is usually related with Single Sign-On mechanisms, and in particular user-centric (from the Federation Visibility view) solutions have adopted protocols like OpenID (Ferg, 2007), OAuth (Hammer-Lahav, 2010) and Microsoft Live ID (Gopalakrishnan, 2010). According to the Security Domains Federation perspective, the enterprises have the following two federated SSO options:

- **Federated Public SSO:** Based on standards such as SAML or WS-Federation (as explained in Section "Standards and Interoperability"), enterprises can provide SSO to various cloud applications that support federation. Once again, the challenge in this area is related with the concept of "assurance", where the Identity Provider must guarantee that user identities' security levels are maintained through the federation.

- **Federated Private SSO:** Organizations using a private cloud can leverage their existing SSO architecture over a VPN tunnel or secured private connection to provide SSO to applications in the cloud.

It is also worth to mention the so-called "Interoperable IDM pattern" as described in (Gopalakrishnan, 2010), where an easy to scale identity mechanism is used, which also understands and interoperates multiple identity schemes. Architectures based on identity-brokers seem to be ideal for deploying the "Interoperable IDM pattern" (Emig 2007, Dimitrakos 2010).

On the other hand, the authentication and authorization features associated with cloud FIDM also have proved challenging in these new IT ecosystems. When organizations start to utilize Federation Resources, authenticating users (and other actors according to the Federation Visibility) in a trustworthy and manageable manner is a vital requirement. Organizations must address authentication-related challenges such as credential management, strong authentication (typically defined as multi-factor authentication), delegated authentication, and managing trust across all types of cloud resources. Based on the fact that different IdPs will authenticate users in different ways and to different strengths, some research is taking place about the use of security metrics for the cloud and, in particular with the so-called "Levels of Assurance" (Chadwick 2009, Tiffany 2009, Luna 2011), which seem an interesting mechanism to discriminate users from potential intruders in order to mitigate attacks targeting the any level of the Security Domain Federation.

The requirements for user profiles and access control policy vary depending on whether the user is acting on their own behalf (such as a consumer) or as a member of an organization (such as an employer, university, hospital, or other enterprise). The access control requirements in SPI environments include establishing trusted user profile and policy information, using it to control access within the cloud's federated resources, and doing this in an auditable way.

Finally, using the Federation Visibility terminology it has been found that cloud FIDM mechanisms are getting "closer" to the user, being designed with usability and user-centricity in order to improve their acceptance and ultimately, their trustworthiness. FIDM mechanisms like CardSpace have been designed in that way (Chappel, 2006).

Privacy

Privacy requirements varies greatly between different countries and data content, but it is always important for collaborating sites (from the same Security Domains Federation) to exchange and enforce privacy and consent directives. During cloud FIDM several privacy related issues arise, for example:

- The user identity and profile have to be transmitted to other organizations from the cloud federation.
- Multi-tenancy on the Federation Resource category becomes a privacy concern, in particular when public clouds are part of the Security Domains Federation.
- Colluding members of the cloud federation might be able to compromise a user's privacy.
- Audit logs can be exploited by potential attackers to profile a user activity, therefore violating her privacy.
- Unfortunately, some FIDM mechanisms do not follow the "minimum disclosure"

principle, by revealing more information about the user than necessary for authentication and authorization purposes.
- From a Federation Visibility perspective, despite some user-centric FIDM solutions are able to keep user attributes only in the IDP, it is true that usability has become an impediment for using them, by letting the user take privacy-related decisions without having enough information for this (*i.e.,* the informed consent principle).

In order to cope with privacy issues in cloud FIDM systems, some solutions have begun to appear. The rest of this section will survey the most representative ones.

For enterprise customers of cloud federations, the cross-enterprise Security and Privacy Authorization (XSPA) profile of XACML, currently in draft (Staggs, 2011), helps entities exchange information about privacy requirements. In this draft, privacy features for consumer users are decided and implemented locally by CSP from the federation (no matter the Security Domain Federation being taken into account).

As mentioned before, one method typically used in FIDM to provide Final User's privacy is to separate identity providers (IdPs) from service providers (SPs), and to store identity attributes with the IdPs only and not with the SPs. This approach is used both by Shibboleth (Morgan, 2004) and the Liberty Alliance protocols (Kantara Initiative, 2009). Open source cloud software like Nimbus (Nimbus, 2011) supports Shibboleth, while proposals for using Liberty's protocols in cloud federations also exist (Núñez, 2011).

As mentioned in (Takabi, 2010) it is also worth to cite promising privacy-aware FIDM approaches for the cloud, which are either mapped into the Federation Visibility category (e.g. user-centric like in (Ko, 2009)) or based on zero-knowledge proof protocols (Bertino, 2009). About the latter, it should be noted the recent advances in the so-called "Attribute Based Credentials" (Camenisch, 2006), which are also a promising approach for developing cloud FIDM that provides user-anonymity, just as shown in EU projects like ABC4Trust.

Standards and Interoperability

It is clear that a sound and comprehensive cloud FIDM solution should be interoperable, simply because of the inherent nature of cloud federations. In order to trigger interoperability it is necessary to make use of appropriate standards that can be mapped into the Technological Federation category, which guarantee that different –but compliant- technologies will be able to work together. Since the beginning of this section, it has been citing some standards that are relevant to the cloud FIDM topic, so the objective of the following paragraphs is to survey some additional standards (existing or work-in-progress) that interested readers should take into account.

On the Single Sign-On side (see Section "Security") it is important to take into account two prominent standards (i) the Security Markup and Assertion Language (SAML) (Cantor, 2005), (ii) the WS-Federation (WS-Federation, 2007) and, (iii) Liberty ID-FF (The Open Group, 2010). The latter is emerging as a widely supported federation standard and is supported by major SaaS and PaaS CSPs, however it is also common that just one version is typically supported (either SAML v1.0 or SAML v2.0). Despite it is not so as widely used as SAML, the Web Services Federation specification (WS-Federation) is another component of the Web Services Security model that defines mechanisms to allow different security realms to federate by allowing and brokering trust of identities, attributes and authentication between participating cloud services (Emig 2007, Bernstein 2010). Liberty's ID-FF standard used to represent a big hop from the initial SAML v1.0 specification (Cantor, 2005), however nowadays it is widely accepted that it is equivalent to the newer SAML v2.0 (SAMLLibertyDiffs, 2010).

Regarding to granular level authorization in the Intercloud environment, support for the eXtensible Access Control Markup Language (XACML)-compliant entitlement management is highly desirable (Bernstein, 2010). XACML (XACML, 2011) is an XML-based language for access control that has been standardized in OASIS. XACML describes both an access control policy language and a request/response language. The policy language is used to express access control policies (who can do what and when). The request/response language expresses queries about whether a particular access should be allowed (requests) and describes answers to those queries (responses). It is worth to consider that for enterprise customers of federated cloud services, the cross-enterprise Security and Privacy Authorization (XSPA) profile of XACML, helps entities exchange information about privacy requirements.

Even with an industry standard like XACML, the sender and recipient still need to agree on the names and semantics used within the requests. For example, a CSP may have a service role called "manager" or "admin" that entitles a user to specific capabilities within the service. A corporate customer may also have its own internal role of that name which is quite different. If access control policy is specified in a centralized fashion within a corporation (for the sake of visibility and manageability), a scheme will be needed to translate from corporate roles/policy to cloud federation roles/policy and to eliminate confusion caused by name conflicts. There are no standards for this task at this time, as it is highly specific to each cloud service.

CYBER-ATTACKS IN FEDERATED CLOUD

On the base of the Federation Visibility concepts presented in this chapter, a cloud computing scenario using the following classes of participants has been modelled: Final Users, Service Providers, and Cloud Service Providers. Conceptually, each participant uses/provides a specific interface of/to other participant. For instance, the Cloud Service Providers provide specific interfaces (API depending on the cloud service model, including SaaS, IaaS, and PaaS), which can be used by service instance provided by the Service Providers; a service instance provides its functionalities to a user by a dedicated interface (*e.g.,* Web Service, SSH connection). Each interface can present specific vulnerabilities that can be exploit by malicious entities (users, service instances, and cloud service providers) to perform cyber attacks (Gruschka,2010). For example:

- The interface between a service instance and an user can be considered as a client-to-server interface, that is vulnerable to all types of attacks that are possible in common client-server-architectures, including, SQL injection, buffer overflow, privilege escalation, SSL certificate spoofing, phishing attacks, and flooding attacks (Romano, 2011).

- The interface between a service instance and a Cloud Service Provider is vulnerable to all attacks that a service instance can run against its hosting cloud system, such as resource exhaustion attacks (*e.g.,* Denial-of-Service), attacks on the cloud system hypervisor (Zhou, 2010), and cloud malware injection (Jensen, 2009). In the same way, a malicious Cloud Service Provider of the Cloud Federation may perform several attacks toward service instances running on it, including availability reductions (*i.e.,* shut down service instances) and privacy related attacks, as well as provides malicious interference (*e.g.,* tampering data in process, injecting additional operations to service instance executions).

- By using its interface towards the user, a malicious Cloud Service Provider of the Cloud Federation may perform phishing-

like attempts to trigger a user into manipulating its cloud-provided services, *e.g.,* presenting the user a faked usage bill of the cloud provider.

- Finally, each Cloud Service Provider of the Cloud Federation provides interface for controlling its services. These interfaces enable Service Provider (and in general users) to add new services, delete service instances, etc. Such interface are vulnerable to attack threats similar to that one's a common cloud service has to face from a user. An example of such vulnerability was found in the control service of Amazon Elastic Cloud Computing (EC2) (Gruschka, 2009).

DENIAL OF SERVICE

Denial of Service (DoS) is a serious and growing problem for corporate and government services doing business on Internet (Ficco, 2011). Targets for DoS attacks include the computational resources, the memory buffers, the application processing logic, the communications bandwidth, and the network protocol, whereas their effects on the target system are the denial or degradation of provided services (Ficco, 2010).

In general, one of the major valuable economic benefits at the IaaS level consists in outsourcing a CSP' resources to other service providers. For example, instead of operating its own internal data centre, the paradigm of cloud computing enables companies (users) to rent computational resources on demand. Technically, this achievement can be realized by using virtual machines deployed on arbitrary data centre servers of the cloud Federation. If a company's demand for computational power rises, then it is simply fulfilled by increasing the number of virtual machines instances at the CSP.

On the other hand, from the security point of view the IaaS architecture has serious drawbacks. For example, a flooding attack, which basically consists in an attacker sending a huge amount of malicious requests to a certain service, can cause a denial of service to the federation resources (Jensen 2008, Demir 2007). When the cloud system observes the high workload on the flooded service, it is likely to start providing more computational power (*e.g.,* more virtual machines) in order to cope with it. On the other hand, to some extent, the IaaS architecture even is able to "support" an attacker by enabling him to do as much damage as possible on the cloud service's availability. Starting from a single flooding attack entry point (*i.e.,* a single cloud-based address), the attacker can perform a full loss of availability on the service, without the need to flood all the servers that provide the targeted service.

Another side effect of the flooding attacks at the IaaS level is that other services provided on the same physical servers (often known as "multi-tenancy") may suffer from the workload caused by the flooding. If the server's hardware resources are completely exhausted by processing the flooding attack requests, also other service instances on the same hardware machine could be unable to perform their tasks. Moreover, if the cloud system notices the lack of availability, it could move the affected service instances to other servers of the cloud federation. This results in additional workload for such servers, and thus the flooding attack can propagate and spread throughout the whole cloud federation.

In the worst case, an attacker could utilize cloud computing-based systems (belonging to the same or to another federation) for hosting his flooding attack application. In that case, the attack involves different cloud systems off against each other. Each cloud would provide more and more computational resources for fending and flooding respectively, until one of them reaches full loss of availability (Jensen, 2009).

However, apart from classical network layer attacks, such as TCP SYN or ICMP flooding, flooding attacks on application-layer services pose an emerging risk to cloud computing in general.

CONCLUSION

Cloud Federation is an open issue in cloud computing, which has attracted great interest both from industry and research. This chapter outlined what are the existing approaches for building trustworthy cloud federations and which are the different layers involved in each of the different solutions being proposed.

From the proposed analysis and taxonomic approach, to the authors it is clear that the state of the art does not offer an homogeneous view on the problem of technological federation, even if all the solutions have many different points in common: brokering (a single access point for final users which manage access to all the other providers) or pure federation (based on cross-certification like approaches), adoption of federation techniques mainly at the IaaS level, leaving to Platform as a Service a high degree of heterogeneity. In any case, the adopted approach is the development of a Federation framework, which offers in different ways the chance to be Cloud-provider independent (but framework-dependent).

If the technological federation is still an open problem, the security federation is a largely unexplored field. The Cloud Security Alliance Guidance (Cloud Security Alliance 2009) offers a clear identification of the cloud security domains to be explored, but few solutions are effectively available at the state of the art.

This chapter has offered a clear view of the state of art in three different contexts: the security domain federation (by comparing the grid and cloud approaches), Identity and Access Management in federation environments and an analysis of cyber attacks in federated Cloud environments. The proposed analysis is limited, as natural, nevertheless offers a clear idea of the possible research directions which are being carried on in the context of security issues in Cloud Federations.

REFERENCES

Bernstein, D., & Vij, D. (2010), Intercloud Security Considerations, In *IEEE Second International Conference on Cloud Computing Technology and Science*, (pp. 537-544).

Bertino E, Paci F, Ferrini R, and Shang N (2009), Privacy-preserving digital identity management for cloud computing, *Data Engineering 32*,(1)

Bessani, A., Correia, M., Quaresma, B., Andre, F., & Sousa, P. (2011). DEPSKY: Dependable and Secure Storage in a Cloud-of-Clouds, *Proceedings of the sixth conference on Computer systems, EuroSys'11*, (, pp. 31—46) Salzburg, Austria: ACM

Bugiel S., Nürnberger S., Sadeghi A. R., and Schneider T. (2011). TwinClouds - Secure Cloud Computing with Low Latency, In *Communications and Multimedia Security (CMS'11) conference*, LNCS.

Camenisch, J., Hohenberger, S., Kohlweiss, M., Lysyanskaya, A., & Meyerovich, M. (2006), How to win the clonewars: efficient periodic n-times anonymous authentication, in *Proceedings of the 13th ACM conference on Computer and communications security, 2006*, (pp. 201–210.) New York, NY: ACM Press

Cameron, K. (2005). *The Laws of Identity*, Retrieved July 26, 2011, from http://www.identity-blog.com/?p=352/#lawsofiden_topic3

Cantor, S., et al. (2005) Assertions and Protocols for the OASIS Security Assertion Markup Language (SAML) V2.0. *OASIS Standard*, March 2005. Document ID saml-core-2.0-os http://docs.oasis-open.org/security/saml/v2.0/saml-core-2.0-os.pdf

Casola, V., Luna, J., Manso, O., Mazzocca, N., Manel, M., & Rak, M. (2007), "Interoperable grid pkis among untrusted domains: an architectural proposal," in *Proc. of the 2nd Grid and Pervasive Conference (GPC2007)*. New York, NY: Springer

Celesti, A., Tusa, F., Villari, M., & Puliafito, A. (2010). Security And Cloud Computing: Intercloud Identity Management Infrastructure. In *Proceedings of The 19th IEEE International Workshops on Enabling Tech- nologies: Infrastructures for Collaborative Enterprises (WETICE 2010) - ETNGRID*, Washington, DC: IEEE Press

Chadwick, D. (2009). Federated identity management. *Foundations of Security Analysis and Design*, *V*, 96–120. doi:10.1007/978-3-642-03829-7_3

Chappell, D. (2006). Introducing Windows CardSpace". MSDN. April 2006. Retrieved July 26, 2011, from http://msdn.microsoft.com/en-us/library/aa480189.aspx

Cloud Computing Use Case Discussion Group. (2010). Cloud Computing Use Cases http://cloudusecases.org

Cloud Security Alliance. (2009). *Security guidance for critical areas of focus in cloud computing*. New York, NY: Springer.

Demir, O., Head, M. R., Ghose, K., & Govindaraju, M. (2007). Securing Grid Data Transfer Services with Active Network Portals. In *Proc. of the IEEE International Parallel and Distributed Processing Symposium*, (pp. 1-8.) Washington, DC: IEEE CS.

Dimitrakos, T. (2010), Common Capabilities for Service Oriented Infrastructures and Platforms: An Overview, In *Eighth IEEE European Conference on Web Services*, (pp.181-188), Washington, DC: IEEE Press.

Edmonds A., Sam Johnston, Thijs Metsch, Gary Mazzaferro (2010) Open Cloud Computing Interface - Core & Models. Retrieved from ttp://occi-wg.org/about/specification/

EGEE Consortium. (2004). *Enabling Grid for E-sciencE (EGEE) Portal*. Retreived from http://www.eu-egee.org

Emig, M., Brandt, F., Kreuzer, S., & Abeck, S. (2007). *Identity as a Service–Towards a Service-Oriented Identity Management Architecture, Dependable and Adaptable Networks and Services* (pp. 1–8). Belin, Germany: Springer.

ENISA. (2009). *Cloud Computing Risk Assessment*. ENISA.

ENISA. (2011). *Security and Resilience in Governmental Clouds. Making an informed decision.* ENISA.

Eu-Emi Consortium. (2011). *Europen Middleare Initiative (Eu-Emi) Portal*. Retreived from http://www.eu-emi.eu

EUGRIDPMA. (2008). *EU Grid PMA Charter.* Retrieved from http://www.eugridpma.org/charter

Ferg, B., & Associates. (2007). OpenID Authentication 2.0 - Final. Retrieved July 26, 2011, from http://openid.net/specs/openid-authentication-2_0.html

Ficco M. (2010). Achieving Security by Intrusion-Tolerance Based on Event Correlation, in Special Issue on Data Dissemination for Large scale Complex Critical Infrastructures, *International Journal of Network Protocols and Algorithms (NPA), 2*,(3,). 70-84.

Ficco, M., & Rak, M. (2011). Intrusion Tolerant Approach for Denial of Service Attacks to Web Services. In *Proc. of the 1st Inter. Conference on Data Compression, Communications and Processing, 2011.* Washington, DC: IEEE CS.

Fontan, J., Vazquez, T., Gonzalez, L., Montero, R., & Llorente, I. (2008). OpenNebula: The open source virtual machine manager for cluster computing. In: *Open Source Grid and Cluster Software Conference* New York, NY: Springer

Foster, I. T. (2006). Globus toolkit version 4: Software for service oriented systems. *J. Comput. Sci. Technol., 21*(4), 513–520. doi:10.1007/s11390-006-0513-y

Gopalakrishnan, A. (2009). Cloud Computing Identity Management. *SETLabs Briefings., 7,* 45–54.

Gruschka, N., & Jensen, M. (2010). Attack Surfaces: Taxonomy for Attacks on Cloud Services. In *proc. of the 3rd Int. IEEE Conf. on Cloud Computing, 2010,* (pp. 279-279). Washington, DC: IEEE CS Press.

Gruschka, N., & Lo Iacono, L. (2009). Vulnerable Cloud: SOAP Message Security Validation Revisited. In Proc. of the IEEE Int. Conf. on Web Services. Los Angeles, 2009. IEEE CS Press.

Hammer-Lahav, E. (2010). RFC 5849: The OAuth 1.0 protocol *Internet Engineering Task Force, 54*, 1–39.

Jclouds (2010). Jclouds Homepage. Retrieved from http://code.google.com/p/jclouds/

Jensen, M., & Gruschka, N. (2008). Flooding Attack Issues of Web Services and Service-Oriented Architectures. *In Proc. of the Workshop on Security for Web Services and Service-Oriented Architectures (SWSOA'08),* (pp. 117–122.)

Jensen, M., Gruschka, N., & Luttenberger, N. (2008). The Impact of Flooding Attacks on Network-based Services. In *Proceedings of the IEEE Int. Conf. on Availability, Reliability and Security (ARES), 2008.* Washington, DC: IEEE Press

Jensen, M., & Schwenk, J. (2009). The accountability problem of flooding attacks in service-oriented architectures. In Proc. of the 4th Int. Conf. on Availability, Reliability *and Security (ARES'09),* (pp. 25-32). Washington DC, USA: IEEE CS.

Jensen, M., Schwenk, J., Gruschka, N., & Lo Iacono, L. (2006). On Technical Security Issues in Cloud Computing. In *Proc. of the IEEE Inter. Conference on Cloud Computing,* (pp.109-116.) Washington, DC: IEEE CS.

Jensen, M., Schwenk, J., Gruschka, N., & Lo Iacono, L. (2009). On technical security issues in cloud computing. In *Proc. of the IEEE Int. Conf. on Cloud Computing, 2009*. Washington, DC: IEEE CS Press.

Jégou Y. (2011). Open Computing Infrastructures for Elastic Services: Contrail Approach. Invited Speak presented at the meeting 2nd Workshops on Software Services, West University of Timisoara, Timisoara, Romania

Kantara Initiative. (2009). The Kantara Initiative. Retrieved July 26, 2011, from http://kantarainitiative.org/

Kiril (2011). *Top 25 European Cloud PRoviding Rising Stars to Watch - Complete List.* Retrieved 11/08/2011 from http://www.cloudtweaks.com/2011/04/top-25-european-cloud-providing-rising-stars-to-watch-complete-list/

Ko M, and G, Shehab M. (2009) Privacy-Enhanced User-Centric Identity Management, *Proc. IEEE Int'l Conf. Communications*, (pp. 998–1002) Washington DC, USA: IEEE Press.

Kumaraswamy, S., Lakshminarayanan, S., Stein, M. R. J., & Wilson, Y. (2010), "Domain 12: Guidance for Identity & Access Management V2. 1," Retrieved July 26, 2011, from http://www.cloudsecurityalliance.org/.

Latanicki, J., & Villari, M. Massonet P., and Naqvi S. (2009). From Grids To Clouds Shift In Security Services Architecture, In *CGW '09 - Cracow Grid Workshop*, Krakow, Poland.

Luna, J., Ghani, H., Germanus, D., & Suri, N. (2011), A Security Metrics Framework for the Cloud, Proceedings of the SECRYPT 2011 Conference.

Mell, P., & Grance, T. (2009). The NIST Definition of Cloud Computing. Retrieved from http://csrc.nist.gov/groups/SNS/cloud-computing/cloud-def-v15.doc

Microsoft Corp. (2011). Windows Live ID. Retrieved July 26, 2011, from https://accountservices.passport.net/ppnetworkhome.srf?lc=1033&mkt=EN-US

Morgan, R. L., Cantor, S., Carmody, S., Hoehn, W., & Klingenstein, K. (2004). Federated Security: The Shibboleth Approach. *EDUCAUSE Quarterly, 27*(4).

Núñez D., Agudo I., Drogkaris P., and Gritzalis S. (2011), Identity Management Challenges for Intercloud Applications, in C. Lee, J.-M. Seigneur, J. J. Park, and R. R. Wagner, Eds *Secure and Trust Computing, Data Management, and Applications, vol. 187,*. (pp. 198-204.) Berlin Heidelberg, Germany: Springer,

Nimbus (2011). *The Nimbus Cloud.* Retrieved July 26, 2011, from http://www.nimbusproject.org/

NIST. (2011). *NIST Cloud Computing Standards Roadmap (NIST SP 500-291)* Retrieved 12/8/2011 from http://www.nist.gov/itl/cloud/

OASIS. (2011). *The Organization for the Advancement of Structured Information Standards.* Retrieved July 26, 2011, from http://www.oasis-open.org/

Open Cloud Manifesto. (2009). *Open Cloud Manifesto.* Retrieved from http://www.opencloudmanifesto.org

Petcu, D., Craciun, C. D., & Rak, M. (2011). TOWARDS A CROSS PLATFORM CLOUD API Components for Cloud Federation. *Paper presented at the meeting CLOSER 2011*, Noordwijkerhout, The Netherland

Querna, P. (2010). *Apache LibCloud.* Presented at the meeting Velocity Ignite 2010. Retrieved from: http://paul.querna.org/slides/libcloud-ignite.pdf

Rodriguez, J., & Klug, J. (2011). Federated Identity Patterns in a Service-Oriented world. *The Architecture Journal*. Retrieved July 26, 2011, from http://msdn.microsoft.com/en-us/library/cc836393.aspx

Romano, L., & Ficco, M. (2011). A Generic Intrusion Detection and Diagnoser System Based on Complex Event Processing. In *Proc. of the 1th International Conference on Data Compression, Communications and Processing, 2011*, (pp. 275-284.) Washington, DC:IEEE CS Press.

SAMLLibertyDiffs. (2010). *Differences Between SAML V2.0 and Liberty ID-FF 1.2*. Retrieved July 26, 2011, from https://wiki.shibboleth.net/confluence/display/SHIB/SAMLLibertyDiffs

SNIA. (2010). Cloud Data Management Interface. Retrieved from www.snia.org

Staggs, D., Saldhana, A., & DeCouteau, D. (2011). *Cross-Enterprise Security and Privacy Authorization (XSPA) TC, OASIS*. Retrieved July 26, 2011, from http://www.oasis-open.org/

Stavridou, V., Dutertre, B., Riemenschneider, R. A., & Saidi, H. (2001). Intrusion tolerant software architectures. In *Proc. of DARPA Information Survivability Conference \& Exposition II (DISCEX '01)* 2230-241.

StratusLab Consortium. (2010). StratusLab Project Homepage. Retrieved from http://stratuslab.eu/

Takabi H, Joshi J B D, and Ahn G, Security and Privacy Challenges in Cloud Computing Environments, Security & Privacy, *IEEE8*, (6) 24-31.

The Open Group. (2010). *Single Sign-On*. Retrieved July 26, 2011, from http://www.opengroup.org/security/sso/

Tiffany, E., & Madsen, P. (2009). *Level of Assurance Authentication Context Profile for SAML 2.0*. OASIS.

Tordsson, J. (2011). *OPTIMIS - towards holistic cloud*. Invited Speak presented at the meeting 2nd Workshops on Software Services, Timisoara, Romania

Villari, M., Rochwerger, B., Massonet, P., & Latanicki, J. (2010). Scalable Cloud Computing Defenses for Detection and Analysis of DDOS attacks. In Tselentis, G. (Eds.), *Towards The Future Internet* (pp. 127–137). Amsterdam, The Netherlands: IOS Press.

Villari, M., Tusa, F., Massonet, P., Naqvi, S., & Latanicki, J. (2009). Mitigating Security Threats To Large-scale Cross Border Virtualization Infrastructures, *International Conference on Cloud Computing*, 19-21 Munich, Germany

Welch, V., Foster, I., Kesselman, C., Mulmo, O., Pearlman, L., Tuecke, S., et al. (2004), X.509 proxy certificates for dynamic delegation, in *Proc. of the 3rd Annual PKI R&D Workshop*. New York, NY: Springer

WS-Federation. (2007). *Web Services Federation Language*. Retrieved July 26, 2011, from http://www.ibm.com/developerworks/library/specification/ws-fed/

XACML. (2011). eXtensible Access Control Markup Language (XACML), OASIS. Retrieved July 26, 2011, from http://www.oasis-open.org/committees/tc_home.php?wg_abbrev=xacml

Zhou, F., Goel, M., Desnoyers, P., & Sundaram, R. (2010). Scheduler Vulnerabilities and Coordinated Attacks in Cloud Computing. In *Proc. of the Int. IEEE Symposium on Network Computing and Applications*, (pp. 123-130) Washington DC, USA: IEEE CS Press

Section 2
Practice

Chapter 11
On the use of the Hybrid Cloud Computing Paradigm

Carlos Martín Sánchez
Complutense University of Madrid, Spain

Daniel Molina
Complutense University of Madrid, Spain

Rafael Moreno Vozmediano
Complutense University of Madrid, Spain

Ruben S. Montero
Complutense University of Madrid, Spain

Ignacio M. Llorente
Complutense University of Madrid, Spain

ABSTRACT

This chapter analyzes the Hybrid Cloud computing model, a paradigm that combines on-premise Private Clouds with the resources of Public Clouds. This new model is not yet fully developed, and there is still a lot of work to be done before true multi-Cloud installations become mature enough to be used in production environments. A review of some of its limitations and the challenges that have to be faced is done in this chapter, and some common techniques to address the challenges studied are also included. It also presents a Hybrid Cloud architecture based on the OpenNebula Cloud toolkit, trying to overcome some of the challenges, and present some real-life experiences with this proposed architecture and Amazon EC2.

INTRODUCTION

Nowadays, Infrastructure as a Service (IaaS) Clouds are considered a viable solution for the on-demand provisioning of computational resources. Since its popularization in 2006 by the Amazon

DOI: 10.4018/978-1-4666-1631-8.ch011

Elastic Computing Cloud (EC2), the IaaS paradigm is being adopted by many organizations not only to lease resources from a Cloud provider, but also to implement on-premise IaaS Clouds. The former, and original usage, is usually referred to as Public Clouds while the latter is commonly named Private Cloud (Sotomayor, Montero, Llorente, & Foster, 2009; Rochwerger et al., 2009).

Copyright © 2012, IGI Global. Copying or distributing in print or electronic forms without written permission of IGI Global is prohibited.

Public as well as Private Clouds have rapidly evolved since the advent of the IaaS Cloud paradigm. The public IaaS market has been enriched with multiple providers each one with different price model and offers, Cloud interfaces and APIs and even a set of disparate features. The private ecosystem is not different and multiple technologies both open-source and private can be used today to build on-premise Clouds. Again the features, characteristics and adoption levels greatly vary among these technologies (Moreno, Montero, & Llorente, 2009).

Private Clouds were designed to address specific needs that are missing in a Public Cloud, namely: (i) security, sensible data may not be stored nor processed in an external resource; (ii) legal constraints, the laws of most countries impose several limitations on the geographical location of digital data; and (iii) on-premise infrastructures, most organizations rely on their own resources to address the most important computational needs.

Although there are reasons for Private Clouds to exist, they present some of the traditional problems associated with running a data-center that Public Clouds try to mitigate, notably adjusting its dimension so the utilization is maximized while satisfying a given demand.

The solution to this problem is usually termed as Hybrid Cloud computing. A Hybrid Cloud combines an on-premise Private Cloud, to satisfy the average or sensible demands, and a Public Cloud, to outsource resources for low security or peak demands.

This chapter will analyze the Hybrid Cloud computing model, starting with its classification as a kind of Cloud Federation in the Background section. Then it will review of some of its limitations and some techniques to overcome these problems. It will also include some real-life experiences with this model using the OpenNebula Cloud toolkit and Amazon EC2. The chapter ends with a discussion on the future research directions and final conclusions.

BACKGROUND

Usually, computational resources needed by organization's services are leased in the form of Virtual Machines (VMs) from the local infrastructure. Hence, these organizations are effectively transforming their rigid infrastructure into a flexible and agile provisioning platform.

A natural step for these companies is to outsource part of the computational capacity they need from an external provider. In this way, they can face peak demands in a cost-effective manner. Also, they can better serve user requests by moving some services to an external Cloud closer to the user, or implement high availability strategies federating different Cloud infrastuctures.

The federation of Cloud infrastructures offers multiple benefits, such as the possibility of scaling-out the local data center with external resources of a remote Cloud; the possibility of aggregating resources from different Cloud infrastructures to increase the computing capacity; or the possibility of gaining access to different Cloud providers that offer different features, different types of resources, and different price schemes, allowing multi-cloud deployment of services based on cost and/or performance optimization criteria.

Although there is no general agreement on the classification of these architectures, the federation architecture models can be classified in the following four groups (Rochwerger et al., 2009):

- **Hybrid Cloud (Cloud bursting) architecture:** The Hybrid Cloud architecture, also called Cloud bursting, is a model that combines the resources of a Private Cloud with remote resources from one or more Public Clouds to provide extra capacity to satisfy peak demand periods. In this case the control over the Public Cloud resources is limited.
- **Cloud broker architecture:** This architecture is very similar to the Cloud bursting

architecture, but with no local infrastructure. The central component of this architecture is a Cloud broker that has access to several Public Cloud infrastructures. As in the previous case, the control over the resources is limited.

- **Aggregated Cloud architecture:** Cloud aggregation consists of two or more partner clouds that interoperate and aggregate their resources to provide their users with a larger virtual infrastructure. In this case the control over the remote resources depends on the terms and conditions of the contract agreed among partners.

- **Multi-tier Cloud architecture:** The multi-tier architecture consists of two or more Could sites, each one running its own infrastrucuture manager, and usually belonging to the same corporation, that are managed by a third manager following a hierarchical arrangement. The resources available in the different Cloud sites are exposed as if they were located in a single Cloud which allows advanced control over them.

The previous architectures are being explored in different research initiatives like StratusLab, BonFire, RESERVOIR (Rochwerger et al., 2009) or mOSAIC.

The following sections will analyze some of the challenges that must be faced to efficiently apply the Hybrid Cloud computing strategy to the deployment of a virtualized service.

CHALLENGES FOR HYBRID CLOUD COMPUTING

Although Hybrid Cloud computing promises the best of the Public and Private Clouds, it presents some practical difficulties that limit its application to real-life workloads, or prevent an optimal combination for a given use-case (Moreno, Montero, & Llorente, 2011). This section analyzes these challenges and reviews some common techniques to address them.

Cloud Interfaces

Cloud interoperability is probably one of the aspects that is receiving more attention by the community. The need for interoperable Clouds is two fold: first, the ability to easily move a virtualized infrastructure among different providers would prevent vendor locking; and secondly, the simultaneous use of multiple Clouds –geographically distributed– can also improve the cost-effectiveness, high availability or efficiency of the virtualized service.

The Cloud is often pictured as an infinite pool of computational resources that are always "there". But recent events like the EC2 outage of April 2011 have demonstrated that moving services to the Cloud computing paradigm is not exempt from the possibility of service downtime. This is one of the reasons why interoperability is such a big concern: to achieve replication and high availability across different Cloud providers. But the current Public Cloud ecosystem is far from being homogeneous and each provider exposes its own Cloud interface. Moreover the semantics of these interfaces are adapted to the particular services that each provider offers to its costumers. This means that apart from creating VMs, each provider has a different definition of what a storage volume is, or offers services not available in other providers, like firewall services, additional storage or specific binding to a custom IP.

Among the most known and used Cloud providers are Amazon Elastic Compute Cloud (EC2), Rackspace, and ElasticHosts. These are just three examples that offer completely different APIs, pricing models and underlying infrastructure; and of course there are many more providers to choose from like FlexiScale, Terremark, and GoGrid, etc.

These challenges have been identified by the Cloud community, see for example the "Open cloud manifesto.org", 2011, and several standardization efforts are working on different aspects of a Cloud, from formats, like the "Open virtualization format specification," 2010, (OVF) from the distributed management task force (DMTF), to Cloud interfaces, for example the "Open cloud computing interface", 2011, (OCCI) from the Open Grid Forum. In this area, there are other initiatives that try to abstract the special features of current implementations by providing a common API to interface multiple Clouds, see for example the Deltacloud project ("Deltacloud", 2011) or libcloud ("Apache libcloud python library", 2011).

A traditional technique to achieve the interoperation in this scenario, i.e. between middleware stacks with different interfaces, is the use of adapters. In this context, an adapter is a software component that allows one system to connect to and work with a given Cloud.

There are several open source and commercial virtual infrastructure managers that can manage a pool of physical resources to build an IaaS Private Cloud. Some examples are VMware vCloud Director, OpenStack or Eucalyptus.

Some of these virtual infrastructure managers can even manage both local on-premise physical resources and resources from remote Cloud providers. The remote provider could be a commercial Cloud service, such as Amazon EC2 or ElasticHosts, or a partner infrastructure running another interoperable Private IaaS Cloud. Some examples of this technology are OpenNebula or Nimbus.

The following sections will describe a Hybrid architecture based on the OpenNebula toolkit, an open-source virtual infrastructure manager that can manage remote Cloud provider resources using different pluggable drivers; presenting those remote Clouds seamlessly as if they were just another virtualization host of the local infrastructure. Users continue using the same Private and Public Cloud interfaces, so the federation is not performed at service or application level but at infrastructure level by OpenNebula; a remote Cloud provider is managed as any other OpenNebula host that may provide "infinite" capacity for the execution of VMs.

Networking

VMs running in the Private and Public Cloud are located in different networks, and may use different addressing schemes, like public addresses, or private addresses with NAT. However, the services running within those VMs usually require some of them to follow a uniform IP address scheme, e.g. to be located on the same local network. In this case it is necessary to build some kind of virtual overlay network on top of the physical network to interconnect these VMs. There is also an outstanding security concern (Pearson, 2009), since the services running on the remote Cloud provider's resources could exchange strategic business data, or sensitive customer's information.

In this context, there are some interesting research proposals like ViNe (Tsugawa, & Fortes, 2006), CLON (Matos, Sousa, Pereira, & Oliveira, 2009), etc., or some commercial tools, like VPN-Cubed ("VPN-Cubed", 2011), which provide different overlay network solutions for Grid and Cloud computing environments. This network overlay provides the VMs with the same address space by placing specialized routers in each Cloud –usually user-level virtual routers– that act as gateways for the VMs running in that Cloud. Note that these solutions do not require to modify the service VMs.

As one would expect, some Cloud providers offer extra services to protect or isolate the network connecting the customer's VMs. For instance, Amazon EC2 has a service called Amazon Virtual Private Cloud (Amazon VPC) that lets customers provision a virtual network, private and isolated from the rest of their Cloud. This service is complemented by the option to create a Hardware Virtual Private Network (VPN) connection between the on-premise infrastructure and the Virtual Private

Cloud, effectively creating the complete network scenario for hybrid deployments of services.

Again, this is a provider's specific solution, not interoperable with the similar services offered by other providers, if they are offered at all. This leaves out the possibility to deploy a service in several Public Clouds. For example, in ElasticHosts there is a private network VLANs service, but external components have to access the Cloud's virtual network through a VPN software running in the VMs.

The most flexible and provider-independent solution is to install and configure this overlay network inside the VMs, using for example OpenVPN ("OpenVPN", 2011), a cross-platform open source software. This approach requires each VM image to be configured individually.

Heterogeneous Resources

Usually each Cloud provider offers different VM instance types that differ in their processing and storing capacity. The combination of these different VMs with those obtained from the Private Cloud may lead to workload unbalance or a wrong Public-to-Private VM distribution.

Just comparing three of the main providers, EC2, ElasticHosts and Rackspace, one can see important infrastructure differences: Amazon EC2 virtualization is based on Xen, and the instances have data persistence only if they boot from an Amazon Elastic Block Storage (EBS). The VM capacity can be chosen from a list of predefined instance types with different virtual hardware configurations.

The ElasticHosts infrastructure is based on KVM, all the storage provided is persistent; and there is no notion of instance type as users can customize the hardware setup of the VMs and define arbitrary capacity for them.

Rackspace virtualization infrastructure is based on Xen and XenServer, and as with ElasticHosts the storage is persistent. There is also a list of

predefined instance type with variable amount of RAM and disk space; but unlike in EC2, there is no choice of the number of virtual processor cores.

Master Images Management

In general, a virtualized service consists in one or more components each one supported by one or more VMs. Instances of the same component are usually obtained by cloning a master image for that component, that contains a basic OS installation and the specific software required by the service.

In a Hybrid environment, the master images for the virtualized services must be available in the local infrastructure and each one of the remote Cloud providers. This presents a complex challenge, as Cloud providers use different formats and bundling methods to store these master images; and some providers allow users to upload their own image files, whereas with others only a predefined set of pristine OS installations are available as a base for customization.

There are two main strategies to prepare these images: create and customize an image manually for each one of the providers; or craft them once in the local infrastructure, and then upload the image files to each provider.

Later, the specific challenges associated with the task of converting and uploading existing image files to the Cloud providers will be reviewed; but to summarize the main complications are the lack of a common API and a common image file format. To avoid these complications, the first approach taken in the first Hybrid setup implementations (Moreno et at., 2009; Moreno et at., 2011) is to assume that suitable service component images have been previously packed and registered in each Cloud provider storage service manually. So when a VM is to be deployed in a remote Cloud the virtual infrastructure manager can skip any image conversion or transfer operation.

Note that this approach minimizes the service deployment time as no additional transfers are needed to instantiate a new service component. However there are some drawbacks associated to the storage of one master image in each Cloud provider: higher service development cycles as images have to be prepared and debug for each Cloud; higher costs as Clouds usually charge for the storage used; and higher maintenance costs as new images have to be distributed to each Cloud.

To perform this task of reproducing the same environment in the local and remote providers images, different system automation tools are available. A basic OS installation for the most common Linux distributions can be deployed in any of the existing Cloud providers, either because the provider allows users to upload any image file, or because they offer a list of images to select from. There are commercial and open-source system automation tools that use a series of scripts to install and configure a system starting from that clean OS setup; such as Puppet ("Puppet Labs", 2011), Chef ("Chef", 2011) or CFEngine ("CFEngine", 2011).

These automation tools require the remote instance to be running, and to configure the connection and credential details. Then they log into that VM to install and configure the desired software. Once the process is complete, that VM should be saved back to the provider's storage; to be instantiated as many times as needed by the local virtual infrastructure manager.

Another possibility not yet explored by any virtual infrastructure manager product would be to integrate the system automation tool into the virtual infrastructure manager. Each VM instance would start always as a base OS installation, and configured by the system automation tool right after the deployment. This approach offers some advantages and drawbacks. The clear advantage is that the administrator of the virtualized service can update the configuration scripts, and have those changes available to all the new VM instances without further effort. On the other hand, any administrator knows how to log in and manually configure a VM; and this tight coupling of the

virtual infrastructure manager and the system automation tool presents a new configuration mechanism that can be unknown and time consuming to learn. It also imposes an extra service deployment time, as each instance has to wait until the installation and configuration is complete.

The previous approach requires the user of the Hybrid Cloud architecture -that is, the administrator or developer of the service to virtualize- to be aware of the available remote providers and perform a great amount of manual configuration and testing in order to be able to take advantage of the Hybrid setup. The next step for this kind of infrastructures is to free the users of this task, and let the virtual infrastructure manager make the necessary operations to deploy a registered VM in a remote provider with the same zero configuration needed to deploy it in the local hypervisors.

This of course presents new challenges. The main obstacle is the fact that, at the time of this writing, only a few Public Cloud providers allow users to upload any generic image and instantiate VMs from it. Amazon EC2 provides a number of tools to create an Amazon Machine Image (AMI) from an existing system; once the custom AMI is created, it can be "bundled", using the EC2 API or the Web Management Console. ElasticHosts lets users upload images in raw format using their API, a ftp server, their web interface or even sending them an usb hard drive.

Each one of the above providers exposes a different API for uploading the images to their environments. Moreover, some of these providers add a custom method for bundling the images to upload them in smaller parts.

Assuming the problem of how to upload image files to different Cloud providers is solved, there is still another issue to take into consideration. The images can be uploaded to the remote infrastructures right after the user registers the new image in the local virtual infrastructure manager storage, or on-demand, only when a VM is instanced in the Cloud provider.

Uploading the images only when needed can be convenient from an economical point of view, since the providers charge for the storage services, but it can take a long time and will definitely affect the deployment time for new VMs. The other option would be to keep an updated copy of the VM image in each one of the available Cloud providers beforehand. This way the deployment times will be drastically reduced, but if the images contain non-static data then it is required to implement a mechanism to keep the remote copies updated to the latest version.

The Image files transfer can occur also in the other way, i.e. downloading existing Images from a remote Cloud provider to later deploy them in the local infrastructure. This can be interesting for organizations that already have services running in a Cloud provider, and want to migrate those instances to their Private Cloud.

This feature is meaningful by its own, even if it is implemented without the possibility to upload local images to the Cloud providers. In Amazon EC2 there is a great number of AMIs ready to use shared by the community, containing lots of different installations and configurations, so this feature would allow local infrastructure users access to a rich Image catalog.

Importing those AMIs to the local infrastructure is not an easy task. The API interoperability is again the main issue, as well as the different bundling and Image formats used by the providers. As the reader will see later, the images shared in EC2 expect the Amazon EC2 contextualization metadata server, which has to be replicated for the imported machines to work identically in the local virtualization infrastructure as in EC2.

The end of this chapter proposes a new architecture for OpenNebula that will provide this functionality using adaptors, a different set of drivers for each provider.

Virtual Image Formats

The chapter has discussed the problems associated with the existing methods to upload VM images to the Cloud providers; or download Images in a remote catalog to be registered in the local infrastructure. However, the problem is not only how to move files, but what kind of files have to be transferred. There are different kinds of image formats to represent a VM hard disk, and even depending on the hypervisor it is required to provide an image file containing a whole disk or a file for each separate partition that are mounted in separated logical volumes.

Each Cloud provider supports different formats depending on their internal architecture and the hypervisors they use. A list of the most common formats used by current hypervisors and Cloud providers has been compiled and the specification documents are listed in the References section.

RAW

A raw image file has no specific format, it only contains the raw disk data.

VMDK

The Virtual Machine Disk (VMDK) file format is a type of virtual appliance developed for VMware products.

The VMDK Image Format Specification is available to third parties, so it is natively supported by other products like QEMU, SUSE Studio and VirtualBox. Also QEMU provides the qemu-img utility to convert VMDK images to different formats.

VHD

A Virtual Hard Disk (VHD) is a virtual hard disk file format initially used only by Microsoft Virtual PC. Later Microsoft used it in Hiper-V, a hipervisor-based virtualization technology.

There are also third-party products with VHD support: VirtualBox, VMware ESX Server, WM-ware Workstation and Citrix XenServer natively support VHD format.

VDI

Virtual Desktop Image (VDI) is the name of the default storage format for VirtualBox containers. VirtualBox provides a command-line utility, VBoxManage, that transforms images from VDI to different formats, including VMDK, VHD and RAW.

QCOW

The QEMU Copy On Write (QCOW) image format is one of the disk image formats supported by the QEMU processor emulator. It is a representation of a fixed size block device in a file that delays allocation of storage until it is actually needed. The benefits that it offers in its latest version (QCOW2) over using raw dump representation include:

- Smaller file size, even on filesystems which don't support holes (i.e. sparse files)
- Copy-on-write support, where the image only represents changes made to an underlying disk image
- Snapshot support, where the image can contain multiple snapshots of the images history
- Optional zlib based compression
- Optional AES encryption

Because of the low level differences between all the above described image formats, the only solution to achieve interoperability is transform the image files for the target hypervisor or Cloud provider. There is a wide choice of applications to carry out this task, some of them reviewed in the previous list of formats. In the virtual infrastructure manager scenario, this means that before upload-ing an image to a Cloud provider, an extra step is needed to transform the image format.

There is another issue related to the way images are formatted and stored. A Linux VM requires to boot an initial ramdisk (initrd) and kernel. They can be provided as files separated from the main image or they can be included in the disk.

In a Xen environment, the VMs do not usually have bootable disks; instead, a Xen kernel stored in a different file is used to boot the VM, or DomU in Xen terminology. KVM however typically allows guest VMs to run unmodified kernels, and as a result usually are defined with disks and partitions including a boot loader such as grub installed in the master boot record (MBR).

An approach to solve this difference and be able to manage Xen images in a similar way as the KVM ones is to use a special bootloader. PyGrub enables Xen guest machines to boot from a kernel inside the image filesystem, instead of the physical host filesystem. This makes also easier to update the kernels to newer versions from the virtualized operating system.

Virtual Machine Contextualization

One of the most important features to make use of the "install-once-deploy-many" approach is the ability to pass context data to the VM at boot time. Even with a fully installed and configured VM image, it is usually necessary to perform a minimal service contextualization each time the machine is deployed.

For instance, one could register into a Hybrid setup infrastructure a VM containing a slave execution node for a Grid computing cluster, that needs to contact the head master VM at boot to register itself into the cluster. Instead of hard-coding the head node's IP, the virtual infrastructure manager can provide that IP and a small set of configuration files at boot. This allows the service users to deploy more than one Grid cluster service with only one set of registered VMs.

The instance level contextualization occurs once per VM instantiation and as such must be automated. Currently, there is no standard procedure to do this and each Cloud provider uses a different method, and even the same provider can have different methods depending on the operative system running in the VM.

Basic instance level contextualization enables access to data outside the instance. This data can be read by the VM at boot time, and used in initialization or configuration scripts to contextualize the guest operating system. Most Cloud providers use an ISO image or a Metadata Server to serve these data to the VMs.

The first option consists in mounting a CDROM device or attached disk in the VM, containing dynamically created data provided by the user. The virtualized service can then access that data using standard operating system tools. This process is managed by the infrastructure manager, and it is the one used by OpenNebula. This mechanism is compliant with the OVF standard.

The method provided by OpenNebula to give configuration parameters to a newly started VM instance is using an ISO image. This method is network agnostic so it can be used also to config-

ure network interfaces. Users can specify in the VM template the contents of the ISO file and the configuration parameters that will be written to a file for later use inside the VM instance.

In Figure 1 there is a VM with two associated disks. The Disk Image holds the filesystem where the Operating System will run from. The ISO image contains the contextualization files for that VM Instance:

- **context.sh:** file containing configuration variables, filled by OpenNebula with the parameters specified in the VM Template.
- **init.sh:** script called by the VM instance at start that will configure specific services for this instance.
- **certificates:** sample directory that contains certificates for some service.
- **service.conf:** sample file, containing service configuration.

An alternative method is to store the contextualization data in a metadata server, accessible from the VM. This is the method used by some Cloud providers such as EC2 or virtual infrastructure managers like Nimbus. The metadata server is

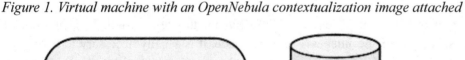

Figure 1. Virtual machine with an OpenNebula contextualization image attached

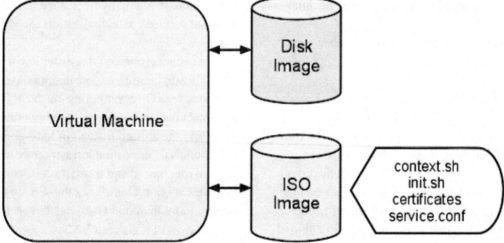

configured to allow access only from VM instance, that has to use a Query API to retrieve the data from a web server.

In a Hybrid setup, this contextualization presents a problem since the images have to prepared to use the local virtual infrastructure manger, and each one of the available Cloud providers contextualization mechanisms. The basic approach to this challenge is to have different images in the local infrastructure and remote providers, adjusted to the specific operation.

A more convenient solution is to have the virtual infrastructure manager replicate the contextualization mechanisms of the Cloud providers. The end of this chapter introduces a proposed architecture to add new functionality to Open-Nebula that will enable it to import Amazon EC2 AMIs to the local image repository, and reproduce the metadata server to properly contextualize the instances.

Non-Technical Challenges

There are several other challenges in Hybrid Cloud Computing that are not technical difficulties. The deep analysis of this kind of challenges is out of the scope of this work; but for completeness it will introduce some of them in this section.

Multiple Pricing Models

Probably the main reason to outsource peak demands to a Public Cloud is to save costs by better dimensioning the private infrastructure. However, the disparate pricing models available in the Public Cloud market make it difficult to optimize the cost scheme for the Hybrid setup, and usually requires advanced placement policies.

Not only the Cloud providers have different prices, but they also use different billing schemes. For example, Amazon EC2 offers a service called Spot Instances, in which customers bid on unused Amazon EC2 capacity and run instances for as long as their bid exceeds the current Spot Price, that changes periodically. There is no equivalent in ElasticHosts or Rackspace.

Legal Restraints

Moving the computing resources to a Hybrid Cloud setup can be a difficult task if the virtualized services manage data restrained by legal implications, such as customers private data, or company information that needs to be tightly protected.

The physical location of the data is important since different jurisdictions mean the data might be secure in one provider but may not be secure in another. What's even more, the data may be restrained by government laws that forbid it to exit the country's territory.

The virtual infrastructure manager would need to implement a strong Service Level Agreement (SLA) mechanism to cope with all the legal restraints, so the company could define that some VMs are not to leave the local infrastructure, while others could be deployed but only under certain circumstances.

PROPOSED SOLUTIONS

The Architecture of a Hybrid Cloud

This section describes a basic Hybrid Cloud setup proposal based on OpenNebula, that addresses some of the previously reviewed challenges, namely: the use of adaptors to interface multiple Cloud interfaces and the use of virtualized routers to easily interconnect private and public VMs. The following sections show two use cases where the presented architecture was implemented and it performed successfully.

The first step to achieve a Hybrid Cloud setup is to install a virtual infrastructure manager in the local infrastructure so it can be abstracted as a

IaaS Private Cloud; and then add capabilities so it can also interface with external Cloud providers.

OpenNebula is an open-source virtual infrastructure manager able to build any type of IaaS Cloud: Private, Public and Hybrid, with unique characteristics for the integration of multiple technologies. It provides the functionality needed to deploy, monitor and control VMs on a pool of distributed physical resources, usually organized in a cluster-like architecture. The OpenNebula core orchestrates three different areas to effectively control the life-cycle of a VM: virtualization, image management and networking.

OpenNebula exhibits a pluggable architecture so specific operations in each of the previous areas (e.g. shutdown a VM or clone a disk image) are performed by specialized adapters. This way, the interoperability issue is managed entirely by the drivers, so OpenNebula manages an external Public Cloud just as it was another local resource. Therefore, any virtualized service can transparently use the Public Cloud.

Local infrastructure can be supplemented with computing capacity from several external Clouds to meet service requirements, to better serve user access requests, or to implement high availability strategies. In particular the integration of a new Public Cloud requires the development of two drivers: virtualization, to interface with the Cloud provider and perform VM operations; and information, to limit the capacity that the organization wants to put in the Cloud provider.

The main components of the OpenNebula core are shown in Figure 2. The drivers are pluggable adapters, usually implemented in a scripting language. They can be listed as follows:

- Transfer Manager (TM) drivers are used to transfer, clone and remove VMs Image files. They take care of the file transfer from the OpenNebula image repository to the physical hosts. There are specific drivers for different storage configurations: shared, non-shared, lvm storage, etc.

- Virtual Machine Manager (VMM) drivers translate the high-level OpenNebula VM life-cycle management actions, like "deploy", "shutdown", etc. into specific hypervisor operations. For instance, the KVM driver will issue a "virsh create" command in the physical host. The EC2 or ElasticHosts drivers translate the actions into Amazon EC2 or ElasticHosts API calls.

- The Information Manager (IM) drivers gather information about the physical host and hypervisor status, so the OpenNebula scheduler knows the available resources and can deploy the VMs accordingly. The Amazon EC2 and ElasticHosts drivers cannot provide much details about the physical infrastructure or the available resources, since they are offered to the user as "infinite". In this case, the drivers are used to report a fixed amount of resources (CPU, free memory, etc.) to limit how many VMs are deployed in the Cloud provider. This prevents a service with a high workload to upscale without limit, which means an uncontrolled cost to the organization.

- The Image Manager (ImgM) drivers are quite similar to the Transfer Manager drivers. These drivers transfer the image files from their source location to the Image Repository when new images are registered. The Image Repository system allows OpenNebula administrators and users to set up images, which can be operative systems or data, to be used in VMs easily. These images can be used by several VMs simultaneously, and also shared with other users. This data can be then saved overwriting the original image, or as a new OpenNebula image.

Although Figure 2 shows only two different VMM and IM drivers, OpenNebula can execute any number of drivers. This allows heterogeneous

Figure 2. Internal architecture of OpenNebula. In this figure, two IM and VMM sets of drivers are represented managing local physical hosts, and a remote Cloud Provider.

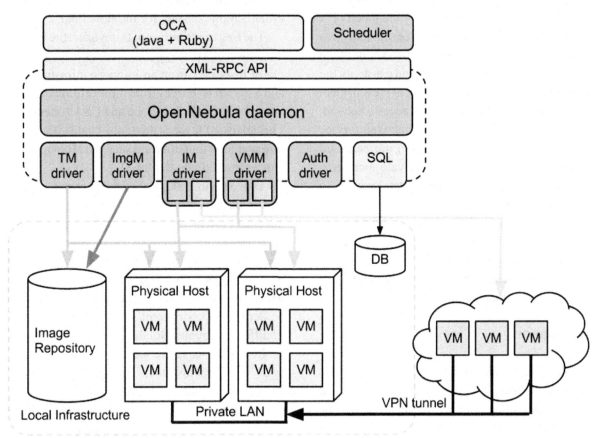

deployments to be implemented. OpenNebula can be configured to manage local hosts running different hypervisors, like KVM, Xen and VMware, and also to interact with different remote Cloud providers simultaneously.

Having the API interoperability managed by the virtual infrastructure manager OpenNebula, the VMs still need a way to communicate with each other. The proposed solution is to use Virtual Private Network (VPN) technology to interconnect the different Cloud resources with the in-house data center infrastructure in a secure way. In particular, the authors propose OpenVPN software to implement Ethernet tunnels between each individual VM deployed in a remote Cloud and the local infrastructure LAN.

In this setup, which follows a client-server approach, the remote Cloud resources, configured as VPN clients, establish an encrypted VPN tunnel with the in-house VPN server, so that each client enables a new network interface which is directly connected to the data center LAN. In this way, resources located at different Clouds can communicate among them, and with local resources, as if they were located in the same logical network. This allows them to access common LAN services (NFS, NIS, etc.) in a transparent way, as local resources do.

It is obvious that the VPN software can introduce some extra latencies in the communication between the front-end and the remote back-end nodes, however, it also involves important benefits. First, although VMs deployed on Amazon

EC2 have a public network interface, they can be configured to only accept connections through the private interface implemented by the OpenVPN tunnel; this configuration provides the same protection degree to the remote back-end nodes than to the local ones, since the front-end can apply the same filtering and firewalling rules to prevent them from unauthorized or malicious access. Second, from the point of view of the virtualized service all nodes (either local or remote) are accessed in a similar way through the private local area network, what provides higher transparency to the service architecture.

One of the main challenges in a Hybrid setup is the image files management. The two use cases presented avoided to tackle that issue preparing the same images in the local infrastructure and the Cloud providers manually.

Use Cases

The previous architecture has been used to implement two use cases: the deployment of a Sun Grid Engine computing cluster (Moreno et al., 2011), and the implementation of a virtualized web cluster (Moreno et al., 2009).

Sun Grid Engine

The work "Multicloud deployment of computing clusters for loosely coupled MTC applications", by Moreno et al., 2011, applied the previously described Hybrid Cloud architecture to analyze the viability, from the point of view of scalability, performance and cost, of deploying large virtual cluster infrastructures distributed over different Cloud providers for solving loosely coupled Many-Task Computing (MTC) applications. In particular, to represent the execution profile of loosely-coupled applications, the chosen workload was the Embarrassingly Distributed (ED) benchmark from the Numerical Aerodynamic Simulation (NAS) Grid Benchmarks (NGB) suite (Frumkin & Van der Wijngaart, 2001). The

ED benchmark consists of multiple independent runs of a flow solver, each one with a different initialization constant for the flow field.

The first contribution of this work is the implementation of a real experimental testbed, consisting of resources from an in-house infrastructure and external resources from three different Cloud sites: Amazon EC2 (Europe and USA zones) and ElasticHosts. On top of this multi-cloud infrastructure spanning four different sites, a real computing cluster testbed was deployed.

The experimental testbed starts from a virtual cluster deployed in the local data center, with a queuing system managed by Sun Grid Engine (SGE) software, and consisting of a cluster front-end (SGE master) and a fixed number of virtual worker nodes. This cluster can be scaled-out by deploying new virtual worker nodes, which can be deployed on different sites (either locally or in different remote Clouds).

In this use-case the local resources are managed with OpenNebula. Images for the SGE worker nodes are registered both at the private cloud as well as uploaded to the Amazon EC2 and ElasticHosts Clouds. These images are pre-configured to establish a VPN connection to the private infrastructure when deployed remotely. The Amazon EC2 and ElasticHosts instances are managed through special virtualization and monitorization drivers that use the Cloud provider API, see Figure 2.

This scenario was used to analyze the performance of different cluster configurations, deploying the virtual worker nodes in different combinations of local and remote resources. For the cluster performance, the cluster throughput (i.e. completed jobs per second) was used as the metric. The resulting performance results, shown in Figure 3, prove that for the MTC workload under consideration (loosely coupled parameter sweep applications), multi-Cloud cluster implementations do not incur performance slowdowns compared to single-site implementations, and showing that the cluster performance (i.e. throughput) scales linearly when the local cluster infrastructure is complemented with external Cloud nodes. This fact proves that the multi-Cloud implementation of a computing cluster is viable from the point of view of scalability, and does not introduce important overheads, which could cause significant performance degradation

In addition, a study to quantify the cost of these cluster configurations was conducted, measuring the cost of the infrastructure per time unit. The performance/cost ratio was also analyzed, showing that some Cloud-based configurations exhibit better performance/cost ratio than local setup, so proving that the multi-Cloud solution is also appealing from a cost perspective.

Nginx

The paper "Elastic management of cluster-based services in the cloud", by Moreno et. al., 2009, evaluates the performance and scalability of the Hybrid Cloud architecture described above for deploying a distributed web server architecture. For this purpose, two different cluster-based web server architectures were implemented on top of

the OpenNebula-based Hybrid Cloud setup, using Amazon EC2 (US zone) as the remote provider.

The first web server cluster architecture considered in this work is a simple web server for serving static files, deployed on top of a Hybrid virtual infrastructure. It consists of a server front-end that runs the Nginx reverse proxy software ("Nginx", 2011) and distributes the user HTTP requests, using the round robin algorithm, among the different virtual back-end servers, which run the Nginx web server software.

The VMs hosting these back-end servers are registered in the OpenNebula local image repository, and uploaded to the Amazon EC2 Cloud; this way they can be deployed in the in-house physical resource pool or in Amazon EC2. This architecture is explained in Figure 2.

The VMs running on the local data center are deployed using the XEN hypervisor version 3.3.0, and have a 32-bit i386 architecture (equivalent to 1.0 GHz Xeon processor), 512 MB of memory, and Debian Etch OS. On the other hand, the remote VMs are based on an EC2 small standard instance (equivalent to 1.0-1.2 GHz Xeon processor), with 32-bit platform, 1.7 GB of memory, and Debian Etch OS. Although most modern

Figure 3. Throughput for simulated cluster configurations. Acronyms: L: Local infrastructure; AE: Amazon EC2 Europe; AU: Amazon EC2 USA; EH: ElasticHosts. The number preceding the site acronym represents the number of worker nodes.

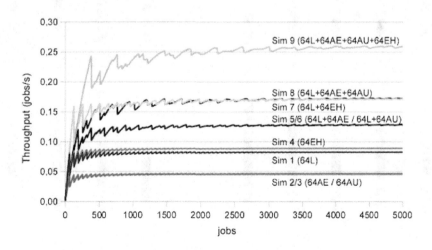

high-performance web servers are typically based on 64-bit platforms, for testing purposes in this simple architecture the authors chose the most basic instances provided by Amazon (small 32-bit instances) and similar hardware configuration for local nodes.

In the network infrastructure implemented for the virtual web server cluster, every virtual back-end node communicates with the front-end trough the private local area network. The local back-end nodes and the front-end are directly connected to this private network by means a virtual bridge configured in every physical host. On the other hand, the remote back-end nodes (deployed on Amazon EC2) are connected to the private network by means a virtual private network (VPN) tunnel, using the OpenVPN software. This tunnel is established between each remote node (OpenVPN client) and the cluster front-end (OpenVPN server). Although the OpenVPN tunnel can introduce some extra latencies in the communication between the front-end and the remote

back-end nodes; it offers the advantage that since communications are encrypted, it is possible to implement a SSL wrapper in the front-end, so that it can decrypt HTTPS requests from client browsers and pass them as plain HTTP to the back-end servers (either local or remote), without compromising privacy.

This scenario is used to analyze the cluster elasticity and throughput when it is scaled out with a growing number of remote back-end nodes deployed on Amazon EC2. To measure it, the experiment is conducted with a fixed number of 300 client HTTP requests of static files of different sizes; using different cluster configurations with increasing number of nodes (from 4 to 24 nodes), with different combinations of local and remote nodes. Two metrics are obtained: the time needed to complete all the client requests; and the cluster throughput (number of requests served per second).

Figure 4 shows clearly that, in spite of the obvious extra communication overheads to the remote

Figure 4. Web cluster throughput for 300 HTTP requests (different file sizes)

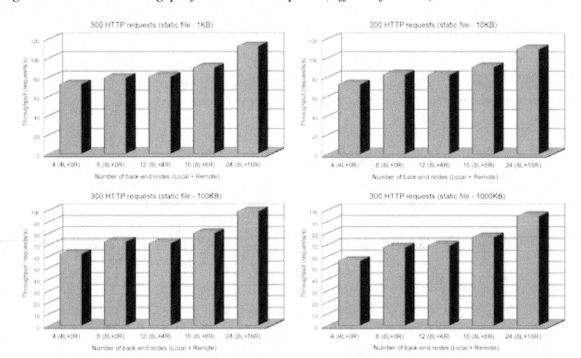

Amazon EC2 nodes, a sustained improvement in cluster throughput is obtained by adding an increasing number of remote nodes to the cluster, so proving the scalability of the proposed solution.

The second architecture considered in this work is a multi-tier server cluster adapted for the execution of the CloudStone benchmark ("Cloudstone", 2011). CloudStone, a project of the RAD Laboratory at UC Berkeley, is a toolkit consisting of an open-source Web 2.0 application, called Olio ("Olio", 2011), and a set of automation tools for generating load and measuring performance in different deployment environments (Sobel et al., 2008). The Olio project, launched by Sun and UC Berkeley, defines a typical Web 2.0 social application (in particular, a social-event calendar web application) and provides three initial implementations: PHP, Java EE and Ruby-on-Rails (RoR). The toolkit also includes an open-source workload generator ("Faban", 2011), and defines ways to drive load against the application in order to measure performance.

In this work the authors choose the RoR version of CloudStone, motivated by the fact that the preferred architecture for RoR deployment follows a proxy server based architecture. Following the architecture proposed by Sobel et al., 2008, they implement a multi-tier web server cluster deployed on top of a Hybrid virtual infrastructure which is composed by a front-end server (implemented by an Ngnix reverse proxy, with round robin load balancing), a variable number of virtual back-end nodes running the Rails application server processes (in particular, the Thin application server software), and a data base server (based on MySQL server). Again the back-end nodes are implemented as VMs, and can be deployed either on the in-house resource pool or remotely in Amazon EC2. In this case, the front-end and the database servers are also VMs deployed in the local data center.

This setup is tested using a single instance of the Faban-based workload driver. During a run, Faban records the response times of each request made by the load generator, from the time the request is issued by Faban until the time at which the last byte of the response is received. The request rate is measured between the initiations of successive operations. To test different benchmark loads, all the experiments are run for different number of concurrent users. Similarly to the previous use case, the scalability of the setup is tested by deploying a growing number of application server nodes in the local and remote Amazon EC2 infrastructure, each one running two Thin processes (one Thin process per CPU core). For each configuration, the throughput (total number of completed operations per second) is analyzed, showing that the proposed architecture exhibits a good scalability when it is deployed in a single data center, but worsens when the number of remote Amazon EC2 nodes increases.

Although the architecture worked, the outcome of the tests lead to the conclusion that the Hybrid setup does not result in a good scalability for this kind of highly interactive workloads with low time-out tolerance levels.

Importing Virtual Machines from Cloud Providers

This section introduces how OpenNebula can interact with external Cloud Storage providers in order to benefit from their services. It also describes how OpenNebula can download and register in the local infrastructure VMs from these remote Cloud providers.

OpenNebula orchestrates storage, network, virtualization, monitoring, and security technologies using specific drivers for each task. In Figure 2 the internal architecture of the OpenNebula core is shown.

When a new OpenNebula Image is registered in the Image Repository, the current OpenNebula Image Manager driver performs a regular file copy if the source is a local filesystem, or downloads the file to the Image Repository if its source is an HTTP URL.

In order to use images from external providers in OpenNebula there are two options. The first one is to adapt the Transfer Manager drivers to retrieve the image files from the external Cloud provider each time a VM is created. The other apporach is to import the external image files to the Open-Nebula Image repository once, and then use that imported image like any other OpenNebula image.

The first approach leverages the OpenNebula modular architecture, delegating the task of dealing with the Cloud provider to the transfer manager driver. The chapter has explained that a new Image can be registered in the image repository from a file hosted in a web server. Alternatively, the image can be registered with an URL as its source, without a local copy in the image repository, forcing the transfer manager driver to download a fresh copy from that URL each time the image is needed.

This mechanism can be extended to provide OpenNebula with the ability to interact with external Cloud storage providers. The drivers can be adapted to detect and process new URLs accordingly. For example, to interact with the Amazon Simple Storage Service (Amazon S3), the driver can detect URLs like this one s3://s3.amazonaws.com/mybucket/myimage.manifest.xml, and use the EC2 tools (ec2-download-bundle, ec2-unbundle, etc.) to download the image.

Delegating the interaction with the Cloud provider to the transfer manager forces OpenNebula to download the image each time a new VM is deployed. This is one of the biggest problems when dealing with external Cloud providers, if the provider is not in the same domain or network, the time that a client spends downloading the resource can lead to a very poor performance.

Although the chapter assumes that the images have to be downloaded from the Cloud provider, some storage solutions are prepared to export these storage resources. This is the case of the CDMI storage API which allows to mount an NFSv4 share or connect to an iSCSI or FibreChannel target the requested storage object. This option can also be supported by the OpenNebula core. Its development can be based on the existing LVM transfer manager driver in which the device is offered to the VM in the target path.

One of the advantages of delegating this task to the transfer manager is that each new VM will use the most up to date version of the image stored in the provider. This behaviour can benefit the user providing for example an image with an updated version of a database for a new VM, but it can also cause that the new VM fails to start due to an unstable or incomplete snapshot of the image.

The second option proposed above to deal with external Cloud providers, importing the image to the OpenNebula repository, can mitigate some of the problems shown in the previous section. Using this solution the image will only be downloaded once and included in the repository, saving a lot of time if one wants to use this resource in more than one VM.

As well as in the previous case OpenNebula allows us to easily implement this use case. In this solution the URL that identifies the resource must be defined as the path from where to copy the image, inside the image template.

The Image Manager drivers can be modified to understand the source and retrieve the file using the apropiate tools, in a similar way as it has been explained for the Transfer Manager drivers. The image files will be downloaded to the repository and included in the set of available local images. If a VM needs to use this image the transfer manager will copy it from the image repository instead of downloading it again.

As shown in the two previous examples Open-Nebula can be easily extended in order to interact with any external Cloud storage provider. One can even choose the best solution that fits the requirements between using the image repository or interacting with the external provider each time a VM is created.

Figure 5. Schematic view of the image files transfer mechanism from remote catalogs to the local repository

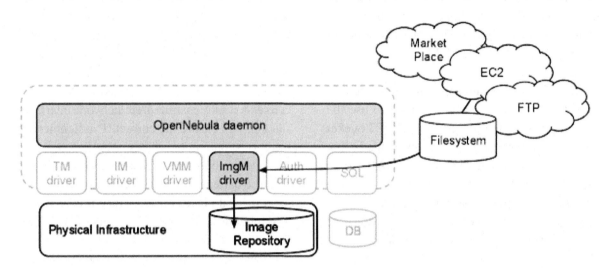

EC2 AMIs Use Case

The previous section has shown how to import images from external Cloud providers to Open-Nebula, assuming that these images were ready to run in OpenNebula without any modification. In this use case it will deal with images which are not prepared to run in OpenNebula such as the Amazon Machine Image (AMI), a special type of pre-configured operating system and virtual application software which is used to create a VM within the Amazon Elastic Compute Cloud (EC2).

This sub-section introduces the design of a new component for OpenNebula, based on the concept of catalogs. A catalog is a set of images offered by a Cloud provider or a partner. The high-level view of this new functionality is that OpenNebula will be able to manage a series of catalogs from where to list, import and adapt images to the local infrastructure. The administrators will be able to manage the available catalogs; and users will have the option to create a new VM in OpenNebula from one of the remote images.

In order to run an external image in Open-Nebula one must identify two main steps: first, the image is downloaded to the local repository,

and then adapted to benefit from the OpenNebula contextualization.

Although the architecture is extensible with different plug-ins, the given example is centered in Amazon EC2, as it is the Cloud provider with the most broadly used image catalog.

Amazon EC2 is used jointly with Amazon S3 for instances with root devices backed by local instance storage. This example considers images with a root device backed by Amazon S3

The first step to use an AMI in OpenNebula is to download the image from Amazon S3 so that it can be modified locally. In S3 all the objects are stored in buckets and the AMIs are bundled providing a manifest file that contains information about the bundling process and the AMI metadata.

As explained in the previous section, Open-Nebula can be modified in two different ways to retrieve images from external Cloud providers. On the one hand the transfer manager can be modified, and download the image each time a new VM is created. On the other hand the image repository can be extended and download the image to use it like any other local image. In this use case the authors have chosen the second option since it has to adapt the image before deploying it in any host, as will be seen later. Also this option mitigates the amount of time spent in downloading images from S3, since this process is performed once per image instead of once per VM.

Whereas the image driver normally copies or downloads files, to interact with the Amazon S3 API its workflow must be modified to use the AMI tools provided by Amazon. The S3 bucket that contains the target AMI is downloaded using the ec2-download-bundle command. After that, the AMI is unbundled in order to get a single file containing the whole image, using the ec2-unbundle command. These commands require the EC2 private key that was used to bundle the image.

At this point, the image file is ready to be registered in the OpenNebula repository, but its contents need to be contextualized. The Open-Nebula contextualization configures the network and allows to run custom user scripts at boot time.

When a new VM is started in Amazon EC2, specific user data information can be provided at start up in order to pass configuration information or even initialization scripts. This information is made available to the instance through a metadata server, only accessible for the instance. Therefore this information can be retrieved using any utility such as curl performing GET requests on the server. Inside this server one can also find metadata information of the instance itself.

As explained in the previous sections, Open-Nebula uses a CDROM device to provide specific instance information to the VMs; whereas the Amazon EC2 images expect a metadata server. Therefore the next step of the catalog component will be to adapt this image to the OpenNebula contextualization.

The first step of this process would be to set up the OpenNebula network init script that will configure the interfaces of the instance. This script depends on the OS distribution and should be executed at boot time before starting any network service. OpenNebula provides scripts for major GNU/Linux distributions such as Debian, Ubuntu, CentOS and openSUSE.

These contextualization scripts derive the IP address assigned to the VM from the MAC address, which is build as MAC_PREFIX:IP. Whenever the VM boots it will execute this script, which in turn would scan the available network interfaces, extract their MAC addresses, make the MAC to IP conversion and construct a /etc/network/interfaces file that will ensure the correct IP assignment to the corresponding interfaces.

Having done so, a VM based on this image could be started and it would be configured accordingly to the defined OpenNebula virtual network. The functionality of providing specific user data for each instance is still missing.

User specific information can be provided in OpenNebula instances using the CONTEXT section of the VM template. If OpenNebula detects this section in the template it will create a new ISO image containing the specified files and variables and it will be available from inside the instance in a CDROM device.

It would be easy to add a new init script that uses this information to configure the VM at start up. However, this task is not necessary because, as previously explained at the beginning of this section, the section deals with an EC2 AMI that is prepared to to be customized using a metadata server.

Instead of creating new scripts to interact with the OpenNebula context ISO it will serve this information in a local server to the instance, so that the instance will work as it was running in Amazon, combining both approaches without a substantial modification of the guest operative system. For this purpose the authors have chosen the SimpleHTTPServer provided by Python that allows us to serve the content of a directory in the desired URL. The CONTEXT section of the VM will contain the information required to fill this directory. All this process will be included in a init script inside the instance that will be executed before the EC2 script, that tries to use the metadata server located in the url http://169.254.169.254/ at boot time.

After that the image will be ready to be deployed in OpenNebula. The difference with other images is that an exact copy is still available in EC2, so the users can choose to deploy this VM locally or in Amazon, without further configuration. The user will only have to specify the specific user data to configure the instance and the public key to access from the outside.

With this use case the authors have seen that images can be moved from the public to the Private Cloud or even combine them, in a Hybrid Cloud, without substantial efforts. Therefore one can customize the cloud on-demand, using the Private or the Public Cloud when needed. It can run all the instances locally and if a host fails or it runs out of capacity it can deploy the same instances in a public cloud, enabling highly scalable hosting environments.

FUTURE RESEARCH DIRECTIONS

As seen in this chapter, interoperability is the main obstacle to the Hybrid Cloud model development. The authors believe that in the near future the efforts will be focused on the interoperability and standardization challenges. There are initiatives already working on this matter, such as the Open Grid Forum (OGF) group, who are developing a standard API for managing resources, called the Open Cloud Computing Interface (OCCI). Another promising efforts are SNIA's Cloud Data Management Interface (CDMI) storage API or DMTF's Open Virtualization Format (OVF) standard to import virtual environments.

CONCLUSION

This chapter has discussed the limitations and challenges that have to be faced before the Hybrid Cloud model can be developed to its fully potential. One of the main obstacles is the disparity of existing cloud interfaces, the options to interconnect VMs in different domains, the variety of image formats depending on the underlying hypervisor, and the heterogeneous resources of each provider.

The authors have proposed some solutions for these challenges, and have also presented a reference architecture based on OpenNebula. The viability of the proposed architecture has been proved with three Hybrid Cloud use cases: the deployment of a Sun Grid Engine computing cluster, the implementation of a virtualized web cluster, and the interaction with the Amazon S3 Cloud storage.

Although the Hybrid Cloud model is not yet fully developed, it has a great potential and the authors believe it will be one of the key research topics in the area of Cloud Federation.

REFERENCES

Amazon elastic compute cloud (amazon EC2)., (2011), Retrieved from http://aws.amazon.com/ec2/

Apache libcloud python library., (2011), Retrieved from http://libcloud.apache.org/

Bonfire (2011). Retrieved 11/20, from http://www.bonfire-project.eu/

Chef., (2011), Retreived from http://www.opscode.com/chef/

Cloudstone., (2011), Retrieved from http://radlab.cs.berkeley.edu/wiki/Projects/Cloudstone

Deltacloud., (2011), Retrieved from http://incubator.apache.org/deltacloud/

ElasticHosts., (2011), Retrieved from http://www.elastichosts.com/

Eucalyptus. (2011), Retrieved from www.eucalyptus.com

Faban., (2011), Retrieved from http://www.faban.org/

Flexiscale. (2011), Retrieved 11/20 from www.flexiscale.com

Frumkin, M., & Van der Wijngaart, R. F. (2001). NAS grid benchmarks: A tool for grid space exploration. *High Performance Distributed Computing, 2001. Proceedings. 10th IEEE International Symposium on,* 315-322.

FutureGrid. (2011), Retrieved from www.futuregrid.org

GoGrid. (2011), Retrieved from www.gogrid.com

Matos, M., Sousa, A., Pereira, J., & Oliveira, R. (2009). *CLON: Overlay network for clouds.* Nuremberg, Germany: ACM.

Moreno-Vozmedian, R., Montero, R. S., & Llorente, I. M. (2009). *Elastic management of cluster-based services in the cloud.* Barcelona, Spain: ACM.

Moreno-Vozmediano, R., Montero, R. S., & Llorente, I. M. (2011). Multicloud deployment of computing clusters for loosely coupled MTC applications. *Parallel and Distributed Systems. IEEE Transactions on, 22*(6), 924–930.

mOSAIC cloud. (2011), Retrieved from www.mosaic-cloud.eu

Nginx., (2011), from http://www.nginx.net/

Olio., (2011), from http://incubator.apache.org/olio/

Open cloud computing interface.,(2011), Retrieved from http://occi-wg.org/

Open cloud manifesto.org.,(2011),Retrieved from http://opencloudmanifesto.org/

Open virtualization format specification(2010). No. DSP0243)DMTF.

OpenStack. Retrieved 11/20, (2011), Retrieved from www.openstack.org

OpenVPN - open source VPN., (2011),Retrieved from http://openvpn.net/

Pearson, S. (2009). *Taking account of privacy when designing cloud computing services.* IEEE Computer Society.

Precision in IT infrastructure engineering - CFEngine., (2011) Retreived from http://cfengine.com/

Puppet labs., (2011) Retrieved from http://www.puppetlabs.com/

Rackspace., (2011),Retrieved from http://www.rackspace.com/

Rochwerger, B., Breitgand, D., Levy, E., Galis, A., Nagin, K., Llorente, I. M., et al. (2009). *The reservoir model and architecture for open federated cloud computing*

Sobel, W., Subramanyam, S., Sucharitakul, A., Nguyen, J., Wong, H., Klepchukov, A., et al. (2008). *Cloudstone: Multi-platform, multi-language benchmark and measurement tools for web 2.0*

Sotomayor, B., Montero, R. S., Llorente, I. M., & Foster, I. (2009). Virtual infrastructure management in private and hybrid clouds. *Internet Computing, IEEE, 13*(5), 14–22. doi:10.1109/MIC.2009.119

StratusLab. (2011)Retrieved from http://stratuslab.eu

Terremark.(2011)Retrieved from www.terremark.com

The QCOW2 image format. (2011) Retrieved from http://people.gnome.org/~markmc/qcow-image-format.html

Tsugawa, M., & Fortes, J. A. B. (2006). A virtual network (ViNe) architecture for grid computing. *Parallel and Distributed Processing Symposium, 2006. IPDPS 2006. 20th International,* 10 pp.

Virtual disk format specification. (2011)Retrieved from http://www.vmware.com/technical-resources/interfaces/vmdk.html

Virtual hard disk image format specification. (2011)Retrieved from http://technet.microsoft.com/en-us/library/bb676673.aspx

VMware vCloud director. (2011) Retrieved, from www.vmware.com/products/vcloud-director

VPN-cubed., (2011),Retrieved from http://www.cohesiveft.com/vpncubed/

ADDITIONAL READING

Bicer, T., Chiu, D., & Agrawal, G. (2011) "A Framework for Data-Intensive Computing with Cloud Bursting", in *Proceedings of the International Conference on Cluster Computing (Cluster'11)*

BioTeam. (2008). *Howto: Unicluster and Amazon EC2. Technical Report.* BioTeam Lab Summary.

Buyya, R., Ranjan, R., & Calheiros, R. N. (2010), InterCloud: Utility-Oriented Federation of Cloud Computing Environments for Scaling of Application Services, *Proceedings of the 10th International Conference on Algorithms and Architectures for Parallel Processing* (LNCS 6081, Springer), pp 13-31.

Ferrer, A. J., Hernández, F., Tordsson, J., & Elmroth, E. (2009). "OPTIMIS: a Holistic Approach to Cloud Service Provisioning". *Proceedings of the First International Conference on Utility and Cloud Computing, 2010*, pp. 1-8 K. Keahey, M. Tsugawa, A. Matsunaga, and J. Fortes. Sky computing. *IEEE Internet Computing, 13*(5), 43–51.

Llorente, I. M., Moreno-Vozmediano, R., & Montero, R. S. (2009)Cloud Computing for On-Demand Grid Resource Provisioning. *In Advances in Parallel Computing, Proceedings of HPC 2009)*, 18, 177-191

Mattess, M., Vecchiola, C., Garg, S. K., & Buyya, R. (2011). *Cloud Bursting: Managing Peak Loads by Leasing Public Cloud Services, Cloud Computing: Methodology, Systems, and Applications.* Boca Raton, FL, USA: CRC Press.

Montero, R.S., Moreno-Vozmediano, R., & Llorente, I.M.. An Elasticity Model for High Throughput Computing Clusters. (2011). *Journal of Parallel and Distributed Computing, 71*(6):750-757, R. Moreno-Vozmediano, R.S. Montero, I.M. Llorente (2011). Multi-Cloud Deployment of Computing Clusters for Loosely-Coupled MTC Applications. *IEEE Transactions on Parallel and Distributed Systems. Special Issue on Many Task Computing, 22*(6), 924–930.

Moreno-Vozmediano, R., Montero, R. S., & Llorente, I. M. (2011). Elastic management of web server clusters on distributed virtual infrastructures. *Concurrency and Computation, 23*(13), 1474–1490. doi:10.1002/cpe.1709

Nair, S. K., Porwal, S., Dimitrakos, T., Ferrer, A. J., Tordsson, J., Sharif, T., et al. (2010) Towards Secure Cloud Bursting, Brokerage and Aggregation, *The European Conference on Web Services (ECOWS)*

Sotomayor, B., Montero, R. S., Llorente, I. M., & Foster, I. (2010). Virtual Infrastructure Management in Private and Hybrid Clouds. *Internet Computing, 13*(5), 14–22. doi:10.1109/MIC.2009.119

Yan, S., Lee, B. S., Zhao, G., Ma, D., & Mohamed, P. (2011) "Infrastructure management of hybrid cloud for enterprise users". *Workshop on Systems and Virtualization Management (SVM)*

KEY TERMS AND DEFINITIONS

Cloud Computing: Computing paradigm consisting on the provisioning of computational resources as an on-demand service.

Hybrid Cloud: Combination of a Private Cloud, to satisfy the average demands, and Public Clouds, to outsource resources during peak demands.

IaaS Cloud: Cloud model that provides end-users with raw virtualized infrastructure.

Private Cloud: On-premise IaaS Cloud owned and managed by an organization.

Public Cloud: IaaS Cloud offered by a Cloud Provider to its customers.

Virtualization: Excution of Operating Systems on top of an abstraction of the hardware layer.

Chapter 12
CLEVER:
A Cloud Middleware Beyond the Federation

Francesco Tusa
Università degli Studi di Messina, Italy

Maurizio Paone
Università degli Studi di Messina, Italy

Massimo Villari
Università degli Studi di Messina, Italy

ABSTRACT

This chapter describes both the design and architecture of the CLEVER cloud middleware, pointing out the possibilities it offers towards enlarging the concept of federation in more directions. CLEVER is able to accomplish such an enlargement enabling the interaction among whatever type of electronic device connected to Internet, thus offering the opportunity of implementing the Internet of Things. Together with this type of perspective, CLEVER aims to "aggregate" heterogeneous computing infrastructure by putting together Cloud and Grid, as an example. The chapter starts with a description of the cloud projects related to CLEVER, followed by a discussion on the middleware components that mainly focuses on the innovative features they have, in particular the communication mechanisms adopted. The second part of the chapter presents a real use case that exploits the CLEVER features that allow easy creation of federated clouds' infrastructures that can be also based on integration with existing Grids; it is demonstrated thanks to the "oneshot" CLEVER deploying mechanism. It is possible to scale dynamically the cloud resources by taking advantage of the existing Grid infrastructures, and minimizing the changes needed at the involved management middleware.

INTRODUCTION

Cloud Computing is considered a successful technology that covers distributed computation infrastructures, able to strongly leverage the concept of Virtualization of physical resources for actuating a useful economy of scale. The Future Internet of services aims to enable the deployment and delivery of complex and large scale services to consumers with agreements upon quality of service (QoS) (Rochwerger et al., 2011).

Nowadays, in the Cloud scenarios, one can notice strong attention paid to the interoperability

DOI: 10.4018/978-1-4666-1631-8.ch012

Copyright © 2012, IGI Global. Copying or distributing in print or electronic forms without written permission of IGI Global is prohibited.

issues that need to be addressed for enabling cooperation among Clouds. This concept falls into a wide context of Cloud Federation and, in the near future, the dynamic setup of federated clouds will appear much more compelling.

Looking at these scenarios, this work describes a middleware able to build up an interoperable, heterogeneous cloud environment to accomplish resource federation: CLEVER (Tusa, Paone, Villari & Puliafito, 2010) has been designed and developed for managing virtual appliances (typically Virtual Machines). It is able to setup cross cooperating Cloud infrastructures, also using different VMMs technology. It allows for creating an abstraction layer during the management of virtual resources, even in clouds spread out on different administration domains. In particular, the middleware being introduced, presents several features enabling useful and easy management of private/hybrid clouds that, as will be pointed out in the last part of the chapter, can be also deployed on existing Grid infrastructures.

After a description of the current CLEVER architecture, in this Chapter, we will consider the opportunity of managing Virtualization Infrastructures exploiting Grid resources. Grid is

identified as the progenitor of Cloud Computing technology and it had a wide consensus in using it for non commercial applications. Due to the intrinsic nature of Grid and its incapability to attract enterprises needs, during the time, it has merely been confined in scenarios even less challenging.

The father of Grid Computing, Ian Foster, in (Foster, Zhao, Raicu & Lu, 2008) has tried to figure out what the main differences are between Cloud and Grid. Foster describes Cloud Computing as a large-scale distributed computing paradigm that is driven by economies of scale, in which a pool of abstracted, virtualized, and dynamically-scalable, managed computing power, storage, platforms, and services are delivered on demand to external customers over the Internet. Although the two paradigms are quite similar, Cloud Computing is acquiring a predominant position. Figure 1 (Google Trends: Cloud Computing vs Grid Computing. http://www.google.com/trends, 2011) highlights how Cloud Computing is widely gaining the interest against Grid computing.

Right now, the new perspective is coming out, consists of merging together the two computing paradigms, that is GRID and Cloud. Such a situation is happening because many worldwide

Figure 1. Google trend comparison between cloud and grid

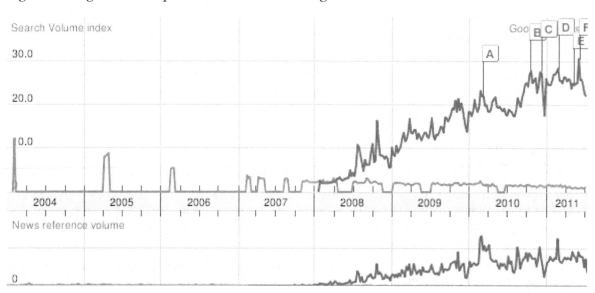

Governments in the last decade have spent a lot of money to provide Grid capabilities not only for scientific purposes but also for encouraging new businesses. In reality the recent Grid projects aimed to draw new IT business have faults in their goals. The authors believe the existing hardware infrastructures that support Grid have the overall characteristics for moving toward a more profitable IT technology that is the Cloud Computing paradigm. In order to reshape Grids the authors think it is necessary to partially maintain the current Grid middleware and enrich it with a Virtual Machine Manager (VMM: XEN ("Xen Hypervisor", 2011), VMware ("Virtualization", 2011), VirtualBox ("Virtualbox", 2011), etc.) at lower layer, with a new middleware able to manage VMs in Grid sites. The rest of the chapter will describe the middleware CLEVER, whose features well fit the "merged" scenario pointed out above.

Together with the aspect of federation exposed above, the Future Research also shows as the CLEVER architecture might be suitable for managing new, challenging scenarios like the Internet of Things (IoT). IoT, refers to "A world where physical objects are seamlessly integrated into the information network, and where the physical objects can become active participants in business processes. Services are available to interact with these 'smart objects' over the Internet, query and change their state and any information associated with them, taking into account security and privacy issues" ("SAP IoT Definition", 2011). In such a context, for instance, the smart and robust communication mechanism of CLEVER (see Section Communication details in CLEVER) may be employed for implementing the communication "logic" of a Sensor Network that gathers lot of data to be processed.

This chapter is organized as follows: Section Background provides a brief survey on the existing cloud middleware platforms, highlighting their strengths and weaknesses and also performing a comparison with the features made available from CLEVER. Section "CLEVER: motivations and ARCHITECTURE" introduces the motivation that lead us to design and implement a new cloud middleware and describes its main features, components and the mechanisms they employ for interacting and building an IaaS Cloud. After the description of the CLEVER architecture, in Section "Interdomain Federation" it points out the characteristics of CLEVER that allows the creation of federated clouds, exploiting the features made available from the XMPP. Section "a Concrete Use Case: Clever On Grid" provides a description of a real CLEVER use case that, thanks to its federation capabilities and zero-conf features, can be easily deployed on existing physical infrastructures managed according to the Grid computing paradigm. This Section provides some technical details on how the cloud infrastructure has been deployed on the INFN Grid infrastructure of Catania ("The COMETA Grid Infrastructure", 2011). Last Sections "Future Research: an enlarged federation" and "Conclusion" give some possible lights to the future and summarize the main concept learned from the CLEVER design.

BACKGROUND

In this Section, it provides a brief survey on the cloud middleware platforms that are similar to CLEVER. The authors developed CLEVER trying to overcome the issues that were identified on current cloud middleware. Since CLEVER is located at the IaaS level of the Cloud stack (IaaS, PaaS and SaaS), the comparison will be conducted at VIM layer of IaaS (See Figure 2), known as Virtual Infrastructure Manager. The Figure depicts the representation highlighted in Sotomayor, Montero, Llorente & Foster, 2009b.

The project OpenQRM ("OpenQRM", 2010) is an open-source platform for enabling flexible management of computing infrastructures. It is able to implement a cloud with several features that allows the automatic deployment of services. It supports different virtualization technologies

Figure 2. Representation of three-layered cloud stack

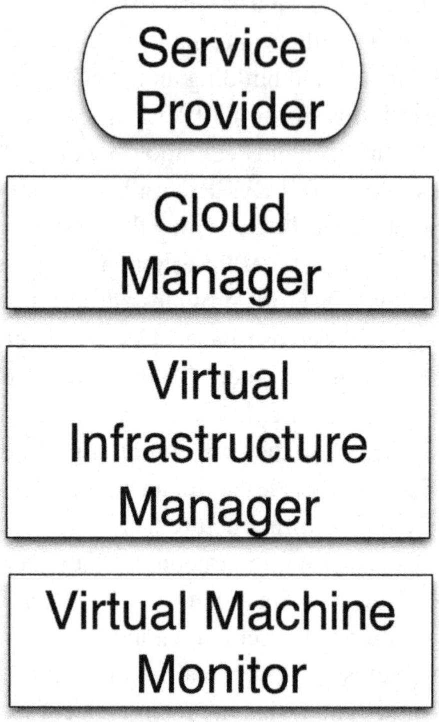

and format conversion during migration. This means VEs (appliances in the OpenQRM terminology) can not only easily move from physical to virtual (and back), but they can also be migrated from different virtualization technologies, even transforming the server image. OpenQRM is able to grant a complete monitor of systems and services by means of the Nagios tool ("Nagios, The Industry Standard" , 2010), which maps the entire OpenQRM network and creates (or updates) its corresponding configuration (i.e., all systems and available services). Finally, Open-QRM addresses the concepts related to High Availability (HA) systems: virtualization is exploited to allow users to achieve services failover without wasting all the computing resources (e.g. using stand-by systems).

OpenNebula (Sotomayor, Montero, Llorente & Foster, 2009a) is an open and flexible tool to build a Cloud computing environment. OpenNebula

can be primarily used as a virtualization tool to manage virtual infrastructures in a data-center or cluster, which is usually referred as Private Cloud. Only the more recent versions of OpenNebula are trying to supports Hybrid Cloud to combine local infrastructure with public cloud-based infrastructure, enabling highly scalable hosting environments. OpenNebula also supports Public Clouds by providing Cloud interfaces to expose its functionalities for virtual machine, storage and network management.

Still looking at the stack of Figure 2, other middleware work at an higher level than the VI Manager (High level Management) and provide high-level features (external interfaces, security and contextualization) but their VI management capabilities are limited and lack VI management features: this type of cloud middleware include Globus Nimbus (Hoffa et al., 2008) and Eucalyptus (Nurmi et al., 2009). Nimbus is an open source toolkit that allows to turn a set of computing resources into an Iaas cloud. Nimbus comes with a component called workspace-control, installed on each node, used to start, stop and pause VMs, implements VM image reconstruction and management, securely connects the VMs to the network, and delivers contextualization.

Nimbus's workspace-control tools work with Xen and KVM but only the Xen version is distributed. Nimbus provides interfaces to VM management functions based on the WSRF set of protocols. There is also an alternative implementation exploiting Amazon EC2 WSDL.

Eucalyptus (Nurmi et al., 2009) is an open-source cloud-computing framework that uses the computational and storage infrastructures commonly available at academic research groups to provide a platform that is modular and open to experimental instrumentation and study. Eucalyptus addresses several crucial cloud computing questions, including VM instance scheduling, cloud computing administrative interfaces, construction of virtual networks, definition and execution of service level agreements (cloud/user and cloud/

cloud), and cloud computing user interfaces. Not far past Eucalyptus was adopted as Virtualization Manager in the Ubuntu Core, but recently there is no longer support ("Canonical switches to OpenStack" , 2011) against OpenStack.

Sempolinski & Thain, (2010) provided an interesting comparison among the latest three architectures presented above. They remarked how the projects are aimed at different goals, but a clear convergence is recognizable. The authors posed three main questions, one about who has a complete cloud computing software stack. It is common in the three architectures that the actual cloud controller is only a small part of the overall system. The second one is who is really customizable. These are open-source projects, and the appeal of setting up a private cloud, as opposed to using a commercial one, is that the administrator can have more control over the system. They support standard API interfaces (i.e., front-end that uses a subset of the EC2 interface), and they are often one of these customizable components. The last one is about the degree of transparency in the user interface. One of the main shared opinions in the commercial cloud setting is the black-box nature of the system. The individual user, is not aware where, physically, his VMs are running. In a more customizable open-source setting, however, opportunities exist for a greater degree of explicit management with regard to the underlying configuration of physical machine and the location of VMs on them. Although the authors of this book agree with authors that the degree in which users can be permitted to examine and work on these underlying components varies among these systems. However, often they are so complicated needing to be fine tuned by administrators who customize the front-end. No any easy management is prefigured.

A separated analysis has to be faced with OpenStack middleware because it operates in the direction of an open ("Open Cloud Manifesto" , 2011) and advanced cloud framework. NASA leads the project aiming to: allow any organization to create and offer cloud computing capabilities using open source software running on standard hardware. In particular OpenStack Compute is software for automatically creating and managing large groups of virtual private servers. Open-Stack Storage is software for creating redundant, scalable object storage using clusters of commodity servers to store terabytes or even petabytes of data. It uses the shared nothing (SN) ("Shared Nothing (SN)" , 2011) philosophy in which the architecture is fully distributed where each node is independent and self-sufficient, and there is no single point of contention across the system. One can state a similar approach is used in our CLEVER architecture. Openstack is gaining certain notoriety in fact Canonical has recently announced ("Canonical switches to OpenStack", 2011): for Ubuntu, OpenStack, and not Eucalyptus will make up the core of the Ubuntu Cloud. Openstack has three sub-projects that is OpenStack Compute, OpenStack Object Store and OpenStack Imaging Service.

CLEVER: MOTIVATIONS AND ARCHITECTURE

CLEVER aims to provide Virtual Infrastructure Management services and suitable interfaces at the High-level Management layer to enable the integration of high-level features such as Public Cloud Interfaces, Contextualization, Security and Dynamic Resources provisioning.

Looking at the middleware implementations which act as High-level Cloud Manager (Hoffa et al., 2008; Nurmi et al., 2009), it can be said that their architecture lacks modularity: it could be a difficult task to change these cloud middleware for integrating new features or modifying the existing ones. CLEVER instead intends granting an higher scalability, modularity and flexibility exploiting the plug-ins concept. This means that other features can be easily added to the middleware just introducing new plug-ins or modules within its architecture without upsetting the organization. As will be better explained in the following Sections, this capability is particularly useful in Grid environments because all the times a specific Grid middleware needs one functionality, it can easily integrated in CLEVER without affecting the whole system organization.

The authors retain that some new features could be added within their implementation in order to achieve a system able to grant high modularity, scalability and fault tolerance. Our idea of cloud middleware, in fact, finds in the terms flexibility and scalability its key-concepts, leading to an architecture designed to satisfy the following requirements:

1. Persistent communication among middleware entities;
2. Transparency respect to "user" requests;
3. Fault tolerance against crashes of both physical hosts and single software modules;
4. Heavy modular design (e.g. monitoring operations, management of hypervisor and management of VEs images will be performed by specific plug-ins, according to different OS, different hypervisor technologies, etc);
5. Scalability and simplicity when new resources have to be added, organized in new hosts (within the same cluster) or in new clusters (within the same cloud);
6. Automatic and optimal system workload balancing by means of dynamic VEs allocation and live VEs migration.

In order to clarify the architecture on which CLEVER is based, let us consider a scenario formed by a set of physical hardware resources (i.e., a cluster) where VMs are dynamically created and executed on the hosts considering their workload, data location and several other parameters.

The basic operations our middleware should perform refer to:

1. Monitoring the VMs behavior and performance, in terms of CPU, memory and storage usage;
2. Managing the VMs, providing functions to destroy, shut-down, migrate and set network parameters;
3. Managing the VMs images, i.e., images discovery, file transfer and uploading.

Considering the concepts stated in (Sotomayor, Montero, Llorente & Foster, 2009b), such features can be analyzed on two different layers: Host Management (lower) and Cluster Management (higher). The middleware is based on the deployment scenario depicted in Figure 3, which shows a N-nodes cluster (also an interconnection of clusters could be analyzed) each containing a host level management module (Host Manager).

A single node may also include a cluster level management module (Cluster Manager). All the entities interact exchanging information by means of the Communication System based on the Extensible Messaging and Presence Protocol (XMPP) ("The Extensible Messaging" , 2011). The set of data necessary to enable the middleware functioning is stored within a specific Database deployed in a distributed fashion. The current CLEVER implementation is based on a specific plug-in able to interact with the Sedna native XML database ("Sedna" , 2011).

Figure 3 shows the main components of the CLEVER architecture, which can be split into two logical categories: the software agents (typical of the architecture itself) and the tools they exploit. To the former set belong both Cluster Manager and the Host Manager:

• Cluster Manager (CM) acts as an interface between the clients (software entities, which can exploit the cloud) and the HM agents. CM receives commands from the clients, performs operations on the HM agents (or on the database) and finally

Figure 3. CLEVER components deployment on the reference scenario

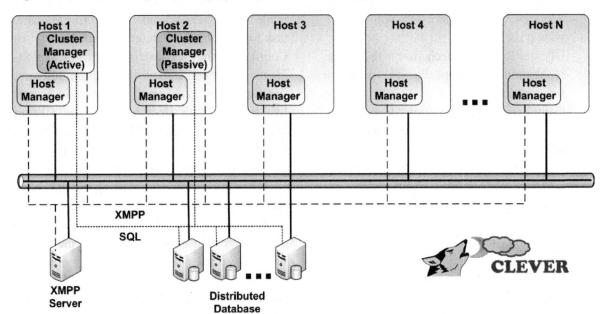

sends information to the clients. It also performs the management of VM images (uploading, discovering, etc.) and the monitoring of the overall state of the cluster (resource usage, VMs state, etc.). At least one CM has to be deployed on each cluster but, in order to ensure higher fault tolerance, many of them should exist. A master CM will exist in active state while the other ones will remain in a monitoring state.

- Host manager (HM) performs the operations needed to monitor the physical resources and the instantiated VMs; moreover, it runs the VMs on the physical hosts (downloading the VM image) and performs the migration of VMs (more precisely, it performs the low level aspects of this operation). To carry out these functions it must communicate with the hypervisor, hosts' OS and distributed file-system on which the VM images are stored. This interaction must be performed using a plug-ins paradigm.

The tools exploited by the middleware are the Database and the Communication System we have already pointed out above.

Strengths of a Cloud Middleware

In the "enlarged" federation view being considered, the communication system represents one of the most important parts of a cloud middleware and can became the way by means of new possibilities may be offered: any kind of data among the involved entities (i.e. hosts, sensors, real-life device connected to Internet), even belonging to different administration domains, might be exchanged while allowing the management of new challenging functionalities such as:

- New ways for Accounting and Billing even more tailored on end-users needs.
- The possibility to optimize the energy consumption in more datacenters, for Green computations.

- Mitigation of Distributed Denied of Services threats, addressed with world-wide policies.
- Disaster Recovery mechanisms: resilience, replication and fault-tolerance spread on many areas.
- Compliance and regulations faced in the same manner, against the datacenters locations.

For having such features, cloud middleware have to adopt technologies enabling:

- Scalability in data distribution avoiding bottlenecks.
- Security and Privacy as basis and not as add-on.
- Logging and Auditing with different granularity levels.
- Interactions with Sensors; i.e. sensor networks for catching the overall status data centers.

For all the points reported above, the communication system represents one of the strongest part of such a model. CLEVER was conceived having in mind these guidelines. It may appear more complex but the pluggable approach permits to configure an Agile framework. Plug-ins may enrich the collection of capabilities of this system when it is necessary. Hence, CLEVER can grow up, but at the same time it remains tiny to meet the needs of any infrastructure provider.

Communication Details in CLEVER

The main CLEVER entities, as already stated, are the Cluster Manager (CM) and the Host Manager (HM) modules, which include several sub-components, each designed to perform a specific task.

Host Manager and Cluster Manager include a specific module named respectively Host Coordinator and Cluster Coordinator. More specifically, the Host Coordinator manages the communica-

tion between the Host Manager internal modules while the Cluster Coordinator performs the same task for the Cluster Manager modules. The Host Coordinator and the Cluster Coordinator, exploiting the XMPP connection, allows the middleware functioning by exchanging messages in a chat-like fashion; both Host Manager and Cluster Manager(s) will attend a XMPP chat session for enabling operation of resource monitoring, VMs allocation.

When the middleware start-up phase begins, each software agent has to establish a connection to the XMPP server. The first agent booted will be the HM that, once connected to the server, will start a timer whose initial value is randomly chosen. When such timer expires, the HM will check the number of CMs available on the cluster. If this number is less than a given value, chosen evaluating the total number of hosts, the HM will start the initialization process of a new CM. In this manner, a set of CM agents will be created, in order to achieve the needed level of fault tolerance. This mechanism will persist while the middleware is up, allowing to maintain a proper number of instantiated CMs. In order to ensure as much as possible the middleware modularity, these sub-components are mapped on different processes within the Operating System of the same host, and communicate each other exchanging messages.

CLEVER has been designed for supporting two different types of communication: inter-module (external) communication and intra-module (internal) communication. Intra-module communication refers to the message exchanging protocol among components of the same module, whereas inter-module communication deals with the XMPP communication.

Inter-module communication (External): Intra-module communication refers to the message exchanging protocol among components of the same module, whereas *inter-module* communication deals with the XMPP communication.

To implement the *inter-module* communication mechanism, an XMPP server must exist within the CLEVER domain and all its entities must be connected to the same XMPP room. The authors believe that the best way to implement our proposed solution could take advantage of the XMPP. The XMPP protocol essentially was born to drive the communications in the heterogeneous instant messaging systems where it is possible to convey any type of data. In particular, the protocol has to guarantee the connectivity among different users even with restrictive network security policies (NAT transversal, firewalling policies, etc.). It is based on coupling of HTTP and XML, thus ensures the maximum level of flexibility. The XML versatility allows us to use the channel XMPP for the management, control data transfer in both intra-site and inter-site communications. In-fact the approach used does not show any difference in inter and intra site communication.

In order to better understand the difference between them, let us consider, for instance, the use case of an administrator that, using the CLI of the admin console client, requests to the Cluster Manager the instantiation of a Virtual Machine already registered in the CLEVER cloud (i.e. it is known the location on the associated disk-image). As the Figure 4 shows, in the top part of the picture, in order to start the requested VM, the CM has to send an XMPP message to the HM selected for its execution to notify the event. Moreover, within the HM, the component which receives the message (i.e. the Host Coordinator) will forward a request for VM execution to its component, using the intra-module communication mechanism.

Intra-module communication (Internal): intra-module communication involves sub-components of the same module. Since they essentially are

Figure 4. Inter-site and Intra-site communications

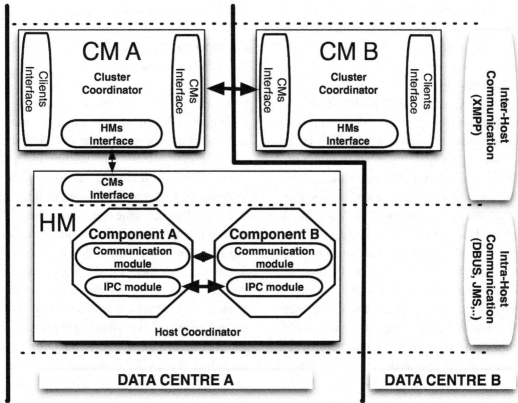

separated processes, a specific Inter Process Communication (IPC) has to be employed for allowing their interaction. In order to guarantee the maximum flexibility, the communication has been designed as depicted in Figure 4, in the bottom part of the picture. More specifically, two different modules exist: a low level one implementing the IPC, and an high-level one instead acting as interface with the CLEVER components, which allows access to the services they expose.

For implementing the communication mechanism, each module virtually exchanges messages (horizontally) with the corresponding peer exploiting a specific protocol (as the horizontal arrows indicate in Figure). However, the real message flow in the vertical ways: when the Component Communication Module (CCM) of the Component A aims to send a message to its peer on a different Component B, it will exploit the services offered by the underlying IPC module. Obviously, in order to correctly communicate, the CCM must be aware of the interface by means of these services are accessible. If all the IPC were designed according to the same interface, the CCM will be able to interact with them regardless both their technology and implementation.

Looking into the above mentioned mechanism, when the Component A needs to access a service made available from the Component B, it performs a request through its CCM. This latter creates a message which describes the request, then formats the message according to the selected communication protocol and sends it to its peer on the Component B by means of the underlying IPC module. This latter in fact, once received the message, forwards it to its peer using a specific container and a specific protocol. The IPC module on the Component B, after that such a container is received, extracts the encapsulated message and forwards it to the overlying CCM. This latter interprets the request and starts the execution of the associated operation instead of the Component A.

The services offered from a software component, according to the Object Oriented Programming, essentially consist of methods which can be accessed and invoked from external entities. This leads to the design and employment of XML serialization mechanisms of these requests: both the parameters and return values of the invoked methods, can be transmitted even though the associated data structure are complex, thanks to the employment of a specific set of libraries implementing the object serialization. In regards to the communication among the IPC modules, it is possible to employ different plug-ins, each based on a specific technology, but all implementing the same communication interfaces for interacting with the overlying CCM layer. Another condition each low-level plug-in must respect, refers to the employment of a synchronized, blocking communication mechanism: if a component wants to access a service made available by another one, whose invocation results is a return value, it is mandatory that the caller stays in a blocked state until the answer will be received.

Components of CLEVER with High Reliability

CLEVER presents a certain complexity in its architecture, but it allows an high modularity and independence among the components, thus enabling fault tolerance capability and a strong availability. As previously introduced, the first instantiated CM agent will remain in an active state (it will perform the operations about the VEs management) while the others will be in a monitoring state (they will receive the requests and will monitor the number of CM agents present in the cluster). If the active CM agent crashes, in order to maintain the service, another CM will change its own state to active. To select the active CM we adopt an algorithm similar to the one previously described for the CM instantiation. The main modules following such an approach, composing the Host Manager are described below:

- **Monitor:** provides information about the resource utilization of the physical host on which the Host Manager instance is running.
- **Hypervisor Interface:** is the CLEVER backend to the hypervisor running on the Operating System where the Host Manager is deployed. Since different Hypervisor technologies exist, different CLEVER Hypervisor backend have been implemented. CLEVER can be configured to load a given Hypervisor Interface plug-in during the start-up phase.
- **Image Manager:** manages the file transfer of the VM disk-images and provide them to the Hypervisor Interface when a VM allocation request is performed. It support different file transfer method and can access different storage service.
- **Network Manager:** gathers information about the host network state. Manages the network settings of the Host where the HM is deployed dynamically creating network bridges, routing and firewalling rules.

The Cluster Manager lies in the higher part of the same stack layer of the Host Manager and coordinates all the entities of the middleware (i.e. the HMs). Its internal composition is described in the following:

- **Database Manager:** is used for interacting with the Database where the cluster handling information is stored. It is implemented in the current CLEVER version for writing and retrieving information from the XML Sedna database using XQuery/ XPath.
- **Storage Manager:** manages the CLEVER logical file storage systems. It is respon-

sible of the registration and upload of VMs disk-images within the CLEVER storage.

- **Performance Estimator:** analysis the set of data collected from the hosts (e.g. CPU, memory) of the cluster and provide an estimation of the future trend for that measures.

Further details on the modules behavior and its internal composition can be found in Tusa F., Paone M., Villari M., and Puliafito A. (2010).

INTERDOMAIN FEDERATION

CLEVER has been designed with an eye toward federation. In fact, the choice of using XMPP for the intra-domain communication (i.e., external communication XMPP room) has been made thinking about the possibility to support in the future also inter-domain communication between different CLEVER administrative domains. The inter-domain communication is the base for the federation. Federation allows clouds to "lend" and "borrow" computing and storage resources to other clouds. In the case of CLEVER this means that a Cluster Manager of an administrative domain is able to control one or more Host Managers belonging other administrative domains. For example, if a CLEVER domain A runs out the resources of its own Host Managers, it can establish a federation with a CLEVER domain B, in order to allow the Cluster Manager of the domain A to use one or more Host Managers of the domain B. This enables the Cluster Manager of domain A to allocate Virtual Machines both in its own Host Managers and in the rented Host Manager of domain B. In this way, on one hand the CLEVER cloud of domain A can continue to allocate services for its clients (e.g., IT companies, organization, desktop end-users, etcetera), whereas on the other hand the CLEVER cloud of domain A earns money from the CLEVER cloud of domain B for the renting of its Host Managers.

As anyone may run its own XMPP server on its own domain, it is the interconnection among these servers which makes up the inter-domain communication. Usually, each user on the XMPP network has a unique Jabber ID (JID). To avoid requiring a central server to maintain a list of IDs, the JID is structured as an e-mail address with a user name and a domain name for the server where that user resides, separated by an at sign (@). For example, considering the CLEVER scenario a CM could be identified by a JID bach@domainB.net, whereas a HM could be identified by a JID liszt@domainA.net: *bach* and *liszt* respectively represent the host names of the CM and the HM, instead domainB.net and domainA.net represent respectively the domains of the cloud which "borrows" its Host Managers and of the cloud which "lends" Host Manager. Let us suppose that bach@domainB.net wants to communicate with liszt@domainA.net, *bach* and *liszt*, each respectively, have accounts on domainB.net and domain A XMPP servers.

A CLEVER cluster includes a set of HMs, orchestrated by a CM, all acting on a specific domain and connected to the same intra-domain communication XMPP room. Each Host Manager is deployed in a physical host and is responsible to manage its computing and storage resources according to the commands given by the CM. The idea of federation in CLEVER environments is founded on the concept that if a CLEVER cluster on a domain needs external resources of other CLEVER clusters, acting on different domains, a sharing of resources can be accomplished, so that the resources belonging to a domain can be logically included in another domain. Within CLEVER this is straightforward by means of the built-in XMPP features. Figure 5 depicts an example of inter-domain communication between two CLEVER administrative domain for the renting of two Host Managers from a domain to another.

Considering the aforementioned domains domainA.net and domainB.net, in scenarios without federation, they respectively include a different XMPP rooms for intra-domain communication (i.e., cleverRoom@domainA.net and cleverRoom@domainB.net) on which a single CM, responsible for the administration of the domain,

Figure 5. Example of inter-domain communication between two CLEVER administrative domains in a Host Manager renting scenario

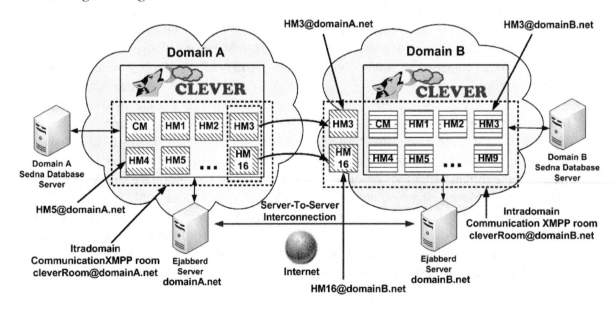

communicates with several HMs, typically placed within the physical cluster of the CLEVER domain.

Instead, considering a federated scenario among the two domains, if the Cluster Manager of the domainB.net domain needs of external resources, it could invite within its cleverRoom@ homeCloud.net room one or more HMs of the domainA.net domain. As previously stated, in order to accomplish such a task a trust relationship between the domainA.net and the domainB.net XMPP servers has to be established in order to enable a Server-to-Server communication allowing to HMs of domain A to join the external communication XMPP room of domain B.

As federation offers many business opportunities, an objective of the CLEVER project in future is the development of mechanisms enabling a Cluster Manager of a domain to find out other Cluster Manager federation-enabled belonging to other domains with which negotiate and establish a federation according to given SLAs for the renting of Host Managers.

A CONCRETE USE CASE: CLEVER ON GRID

As stated, nowadays the Cloud is increasing its popularity becoming one of the most widespread distributed computing paradigms. In order to provide cloud-based services to the users, a large number of computing resources are needed. This means that, a service provider that aims to increase its business opportunities through the cloud, basically may follows two different approaches: either it could buy some dedicated hardware resources that will be employed for this specific purpose or for achieving the costs optimization, the service provider may exploit computing resources that are employed for other purposes.

Even though the first approach is the easiest to implement, for granting the best cost/resource optimization and face the load peaks usually involved in cloud scenarios, a possibility could be to create an hybrid infrastructure where the physical cloud resources can dynamically scale according to the instantaneous workload requested by the cloud users, including external resources when needed. They may conveniently be part of the existing set of resources that are not assigned to the cloud: for example legacy hardware constituting the Grid infrastructure of the enterprise itself or other resources coming from external providers. In the first case the solution will be able to ensure a stronger security level also optimizing the resource usage of the enterprise because any further costs are not required for those resources.

In the second case, some security issues may arise due to the deployment of services on infrastructures that are not owned by the enterprise itself; furthermore new costs have to be faced from the enterprise for renting the required resources. According to the above-mentioned considerations, the most convenient approach seems to be the hybrid one. The following, in fact, considers the use case of an enterprise, which aims to offer cloud services to its users, by means of a set of dedicated resources that will be dynamically scaled considering the users' workload. The resources will be picked up from the existing Grid infrastructure that the enterprise already owns. Even though the approach of extending the cloud infrastructure over the Grid could appear easy to implement, considering the "stiffness" of the current Grid infrastructures and the requirements of the current middleware acting as Virtual Infrastructure Managers, such an approach will need some specific middleware modification and configuration to be accomplished.

Grid infrastructures, do not easily allow the users to manage the computing nodes for customizing its configurations. Furthermore, due to the firewalls, the network that interconnects the nodes is not flexible and do not allow the creation of connections accessible at the outside of the Grid infrastructure itself. In this scenario, the deployment of a cloud over the Grid could appear a very difficult task to accomplish: the different components of the cloud middleware have to be deployed on the Grid, to be properly configured and made accessible over the network. Looking at the existing cloud middleware, which have as strong requirement a preliminary installation and configuration phase, as stated, the integration operations will not be so trivial.

Besides the existing cloud middleware implementations, CLEVER tries to minimize the above mentioned issues thanks to its modularity (it is composed of two self-contained components: Host Manager and Cluster Manager). Moreover CLEVER does not need any particular configuration of the system on which it will be deployed (it only requires an Hypervisor and the corresponding plugin) and it is ready to run (only some parameters have to be specified such as the XMPP server).

The XMPP provides a solution for the firewalling and networking issues that are typical of the Grid infrastructures (thanks to SOCKS5 ("XEP-0065: SOCKS5" , 2011) it is possible to create direct TCP connections among entities belonging to different networks where direct routing does not exist). Indeed the XMPP enable the possibility of interconnecting hosts belonging to different networks. All the communications, in fact, are based on the transmission of messages through the server and will minimize the problems due to firewall and routing, because it is strongly un-linked to IP configurations. As introduced above, in this kind of environments also the file transfer might be affected by network problems. As well as the communication, also the file transfer might be based on the SOCKS5 solution offered by XMPP, that enable the communication among peer also in the case of routing and firewalling issues. Using these mechanisms, a cloud user can have the possibility of uploading files both in the cloud image repository or in the Grid file storage system. Figure 6 highlights the functionality of XMPP SOCKS5 Byte-stream.

In the top part of the picture, thanks to the modules of Network Manager (in HM) coordi-

Figure 6. Advanced networking control using CLEVER

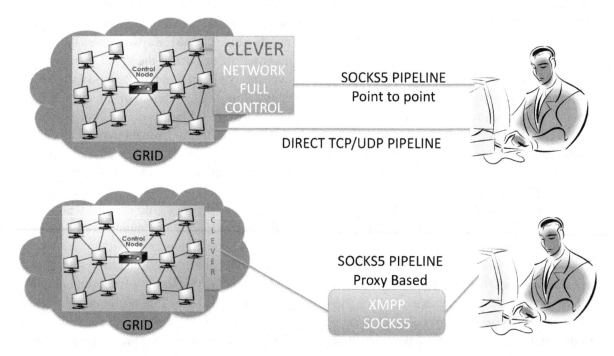

nated by the Cluster Manager, CLEVER is able to punctually setup the Grid network. However, if the network administration is complicated and the Grid security policy are too much problematic to configure, with CLEVER, it is possible to setup an alternative channel for end-users through the NAT-Transversal XMPP SOCKS5 and a Proxy Service (see the bottom part of Figure 6). The channel of communication allows users to interact with their VMs deployed in Grid. The interaction is aimed at the administration tasks (VNC, RDP, SSH shell, etc.) but also for exposing external services (HTTP/XMPP mapping).

Employed Mechanisms

The following will describe the mechanisms by means of it is possible to deploy a CLEVER-based cloud infrastructure on top of the Grid. The authors consider the enterprise is offering services to its users providing the resources reserved to the cloud. On the physical machines the CLEVER middleware is installed.

More specifically, on a given number of machines will be deployed the HM component whereas a subset of machines will run a CM instance. All the middleware components will interact using the same XMPP room. When the workload increases and there are not enough resources to satisfy the users' requests, in order to extend the cloud capabilities, it will be necessary to instantiate more Host Manager within the existing CLEVER room.

As introduced earlier, the Service provider may try to deploy the new HMs on the Grid infrastructure. This is accomplished submitting a given number of jobs, each containing the single .jar file representing CLEVER. This file contains all the packages of the middleware (both the HM and the CM) and the configuration files with the minimal required options.

Furthermore, in order to allow the CLEVER instances deployed on the Grid to take part of the already existing XMPP room, an authentication

mechanisms is needed: we employed the eJabber XMPP server ("eJabber", 2011) with the in-band registration support. Since these mechanisms will allow the creation of new users on the server without any control of the administrator, it allows the registration only of the users that have a X.509 certificate and can perform the mutual authentication. For this reason, a digital X.509 certificate will be also included within the job for authenticating the HM instances created. The XMPP user will be the name of the host on which the job is deployed while the Common Name of the certificate associated to the HM instance will be filled with a random generated identifier. As future work the authors plan to integrate this authentication mechanism with the current GSI implementation based on the proxy-certificates.

Since the XMPP server that is employed is located at the outside of the Grid infrastructure, a strong requirement for allowing the resource integration refers to the possibility of making a connection from the grid to the XMPP server.

This means that the firewalls have not dropped the network traffic coming from the Grid to the XMPP server. Another mandatory requirement for the Grid infrastructure consists in the installation of an Hypervisor that will be used for instantiating the requested VMs. During our experiments, the Virtualbox software package was installed ("Virtualbox", 2011) on the Grid Worker Nodes in order to allow the corresponding CLEVER plug-in to perform all the needed operation on the VMs. Figure 7 depicts what are the entity involved in the Grid infrastructure along with the elements necessary for setup the whole system. The deployment of CLEVER on Grid is partial, indeed the XMPP server, the Sedna Database and other elements (preexisting CLEVER environment) are external to Grid. This happens because we are considering Grid resources dynamically aggregated and temporary used. In the left side one can assume an enterprise having its private cloud CLEVER based. In the right side the Grid infrastructure is used by the enterprise with CLEVER for increasing its resources.

CLEVER environments need to be aware about the current and past configurations they assumed during the time. Snapshots of the system occur out of Grids. Finally the approach being used is invasive as less as possible, in order to reduce the deployment complexity at minimum level and encourage a wide deploy of VMs.

Our Testbed and Results

In the following the section is going to present how the mechanisms described above were implemented. More specifically, we interpreted the role of a cloud service provider with its own cloud dedicated resources that, in the case of heavy load generated from the users, has the possibility

of extending its computational capabilities exploiting its own resources assigned for the Grid. In our particular scenario, the cloud resources were organized in a cluster of physical machines managed by CLEVER. When more resources are needed, new HMs will be instantiated on the Grid as jobs and will be included within the already existing cloud infrastructure.

The new HMs will be configured (through the configuration file the .jar file contains) to join the external XMPP server, in particular the room where the other HMs are already connected.

During our tests, the authors assumed our cloud infrastructure, due to the users requests, has exhausted its own resources. For granting the SLA to the users we submitted a set of jobs to the COMETA Grid infrastructure managed by the Università degli Studi di Messina in cooperation

Figure 7. CLEVER deployment on the gLite GRID

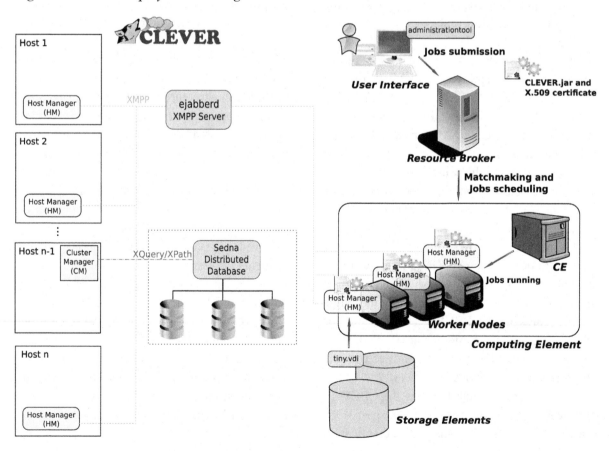

with the Catania INFN ("The COMETA Grid", 2011). Each of these jobs contain the .jar file of CLEVER and, once deployed will instantiate an HM instance on the worker node where it has been sent. Once the HM is up, through a Linux bash script we instantiate a VM on it and measure the amount of time elapsed between the job submission and the instant when the HM component has completed its start-up.

For better understanding all the mechanisms, in the following will quote the most interesting parts of the script that was used. After that the authentication phase is completed and the voms-proxy-certificate has been created, the first operation that has to be performed refers to the submission to the Grid of the job containing the CLEVER .jar file.

Together with this .jar file, another needed component is the cleverAdministration tool, that can be executed from whatever computer is available and is used both to interact with the active CM and send CLEVER commands to the new deployed HM.

```
#submit clever HM and CM
glite-wms-job-submit -d $USER -r
unime-ce-01.me.pi2s2.it:2119/jobman-
agerlcglsf-infinite -o job_id clever.
jdl
```

If the submission phase is correctly accomplished we wait for the HM initialization. Using the cleverAdministration tool we wait for the HM entrance within the CLEVER XMPP room. In particular we used the CLEVER command "getnotifypresence".

```
#waiting clever deploy
echo "Waiting clever connection ..."
java -jar dist/cleverAdministration.
jar getnotifypresence 2> /dev/null
#HM is now online
```

When the new HM is ready, within the script is retrieved its name (it depends on the worker node where it has been sent to) and the local path that will be used for performing the subsequent operations with the VM disk-image.

```
#retrieve HM name and local path
HM=$(java -jar dist/cleverAdminis-
tration.jar listhostmanager 2> /dev/
null|head  -n 1)
echo "HM found: $HM"
localpath=$(java -jar dist/clever-
Administration.jar getdefaultfolder
-h$HM 2> /dev/null)/
```

Now that all the needed information is collected, the VM can be created. The first step to be executed consists in the VM disk-image retrieval: through the Image Manager component of the Host Manager, it is downloaded from a repository where it has been previously registered. During this test we assumed the name of the image to download is stored within the variable "vmimage".

```
vmimage="tiny.vdi"
java -jar dist/cleverAdministration.
jar retrieveimg $vmimage 2> /dev/null
```

Once the disk-image has been downloaded, the VM can be created. We use the CLEVER command "startvm" of the cleverAdministration specifying: 1) the HM on which create the VM; 2) the name to assign to the created VM (clevergrid); 3) the full path of the disk-image retrieved (this is accomplished concatenating the local path obtained in the previous steps with the disk-image file name).

```
#create the VM
java -jar dist/cleverAdministration.
jar startvm -h $HM -onlycreate -nc-
levergrid -p${localpath}${vmimage}
echo "VM (clevergrid) created"
```

If the VM has been correctly created, it is ready to be started with the following CLEVER commands:

```
#start the VM
java -jar dist/cleverAdministration.
jar startvm -h$HM -onlyrun -nclever-
grid 2> /dev/null
echo "VM started:"
```

In order to have an estimation of the time needed for setting up new cloud computing nodes on the Grid, we performed a preliminary analysis deploying a set of five HMs (i.e. submitting five different jobs) on the Grid infrastructure. During the different tests we achieved some encouraging results since the amount of time needed for starting up the whole set of HMs is always lower than 5 minutes. The result obtained is quite impressive if one compares it with the time needed for achieving the same results using other cloud middleware. Thanks to the CLEVER features of modularity, auto-configuration and self-contained packaging, we were able to increase the number of computing resources of our cloud infrastructure in a few minutes.

If one supposes the employment of different cloud middleware that do not need provide "auto configuration" and need a preliminary installation phase, the whole time needed for performing the deployment of the new cloud computing nodes on the Grid will be certainly greater than the one we employed using CLEVER.

How to Allow Users to Managing Their VMs in GRID Environments Inside of Hidden Networks: The SOCKS5 and Remote Desktop in CLEVER

Thanks to CLEVER (in particular to its robust communication system) and its integration on GRID, it is possible to manage a considerable number of virtual machines. As mentioned above one of the main limitations in using GRID is the issue related to network administrations. CLEVER is able to overcome such problems leveraging the concept of firewall-pass-through of XMPP and SOCKS5 proxy. As Figure 6 has shown, the SOCKS5 protocol is able to reach VMs against all network restrictions. It is configured with XMPP and elected as external proxy all the times a network does not allow VMs' to be accessed from the Internet. One of the main advantages to deploying VMs on cloud is to provide users a full access to their machines without any limitation. GRID might be not particularly useful if these network constrains reduce the users' freedom. One of easiest way for controlling VMs is exporting Visual Desktops through different type of protocols; most widely protocols currently used are: VNC (with many versions), RDP (Remote Desktop Protocol, native protocol of Microsoft) and Linux XServer.

Figure 8 on the left side, edged by a dashed rectangle, shows the host with two parts: the Proxy (the circle shape) and a tiny version of CLEVER (the square shape). The latter looks like as a CLEVER Host Manager but with reduced functionalities. The proxy allows a dynamic configuration of the network along with the temporary setup for the web access enabling end-users. All users may access their machines without any further configuration; they have to simple use an HTML5 web browser, getting a transparent access to their machine. The proxy is able to translate the web communication to VNC (or RDP) protocol. The XMPP presents in the HM provide the needs to setup the SOCKS5 proxy service. The visual proxy being used is Guacamol and it shows a good visual interaction with a low data bit rate. The right side of Figure 8, inside the dashed rectangle, depicts the CLEVER modules interacting with Virtualbox and its VNC server installed into.

Figure 8. VM Desktop Remote control web based occurring through an inaccessible network

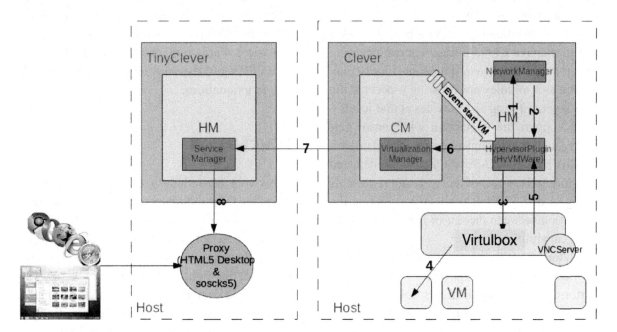

FUTURE RESEARCH: AN ENLARGED FEDERATION

This chapter has shown as a middleware aimed at clouds may allow the use of different computation resources, in this case the GRID physical resources. However, currently we are assisting to spasmodic autonomic control of Houses, Hospitals, Factories, enforcing the management of Smart Grids and Internet of Things initiatives (IoT), and so on. In this direction, sensor networks are becoming a pervasive technology that allows to monitor wide geographical areas to promptly detect critical operation conditions. The authors believe that sensor networks should be integrated as part of our Cloud Infrastructure, virtualized if needed, and accessed as any other resource in the cloud computing environment. Cloud computing exploits whatever virtual technologies for making an abstraction on data, processing, and storage. Virtual Machines (VMs) represent the typical example of how virtualization technology can be used in Cloud. Cloud costumers are able to pre-

configure VMs and to deploy them on the Cloud infrastructure, without any further configuration. VMs may collect data, execute their elaboration, migrate the data if necessary, expose APIs to be used from other VMs being executed in different Clouds and so on. In the near future, we will consider sensor networks as a virtual resource, which is accessible through a new cloud element that is the Virtual Pervasive Element (VPE). The collections of the VPEs are considered part of the Federated Clouds.

Thanks to the sensing technology one can practically collect whichever data as needed: a wide choice of sensors are already available in the market with many different typologies of acquisition. It can also be noted the evolution of sensors towards Smart Sensors and Actuator Sensors. In the former version, customers might change on-demand the sensors behaviour (i.e., data filtering, data aggregation, up to making local decision, etc.) thanks to customized programming code that can be instantiated on-demand in the sensor. In the latter version, that is Actuator Sensors, we consider such devices as elements able to perform remote actions on-demand.

As mentioned above, CLEVER provides a VIM able to manage Cloud infrastructures, covering aspects at the IaaS layer. At the same time, it may be seen as a middleware covering aspects at the PaaS layer, offering also services at that level.

To support the interaction with sensor networks, our idea is to implement a modified version of CLEVER, called C-SENSOR, which is depicted in Figure 9. It is part of the VPE and represents a plug-in of CLEVER necessary to endure the interaction between the sensor networks and the cloud capabilities.

On top of CLEVER and the VPE a new layer has been included that provides some specific platform oriented applications able to deliver advanced services for contributors of PaaS services. They include: smart monitoring, report services, data manipulation and aggregation. The

SaaS exposes the interfaces to access such services. The Federation among resources (Clouds, Grids and IoTs) is moving beyond the current scenario towards new challenging models, and CLEVER should be ready for accomplishing such new functionalities.

CONCLUSION

In this work, the authors described the design principles and the preliminary prototype implementation of our cloud middleware named CLEVER, giving a description of its main entities and of the mechanisms they employ to communicate. The work highlighted the most typical CLEVER features and compared them with the ones made available from other similar middleware, discussing the motivations that have lead us to design a new cloud VIM. In particular, it pointed out all

Figure 9. CLEVER for the near Future

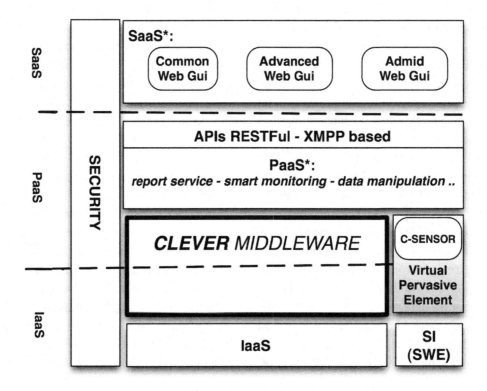

the strengths coming with the XMPP employment that easily allow the creation of dynamic (federated) cloud environments.

In the final part of the chapter it pointed out how CLEVER has been deployed in a GRID infrastructure: giving a look at the world wide picture of Grid infrastructure that currently are fully operating, one can see a huge number of datacenters exploiting GRID technology. The authors believe GRID might represent an opportunity for cloud operators, while at the same time GRID might have a remarkable sustain from cloud businesses.

Due to its design, CLEVER allows an easy setup in different administration domains. This is an important features if one considers GRID computation resource. Thanks to the wide usage of the XMPP protocol, our middleware overcomes the issues related to the GRID networks. The XMPP protocol essentially was born to drive the communications in the heterogeneous instant messaging systems where it is possible to convey any type of data. In particular, the protocol has to guarantee the connectivity among different users even with restrictive network security policies (NAT transversal, firewalling policies, etc.) existing in GRID. SOCKS5 Bytestreams of XMPP besides allows to transparently interconnect virtual networks among different domains.

REFERENCES

Canonical switches to OpenStack for Ubuntu Linux Cloud. (2011).Retrieved from: http://www.zdnet.com/blog/open-source/canonical-switches-to-openstack-for-ubuntu-linux-cloud/8875, eJabber: Jabber/XMPP instant messaging server. (2011)Retrieved from: http://www.ejabberd.im/.

Foster, I., Zhao, Y., Raicu, I., & Lu, S. (2008). Cloud Computing and Grid Computing 360-Degree Compared. *Grid Computing Environments Workshop, 2008. GCE '08,* (pp. 1–10).

Hoffa, C., Mehta, G., Freeman, T., Deelman, E., Keahey, K., Berriman, B., & Good, J. (2008). On the Use of Cloud Computing for Scientific Workflows. *Proceedings of SWBES 2008, Indianapolis.* New York, NY: Springer

Manifesto, O. C. dedicated to the belief that the cloud should be open, (2011) Retrieved from: http://www.opencloudmanifesto.org/.

Nagios, The Industry Standard in IT Infrastructure Monitoring: (2010) http://www.nagios.org.

Nurmi, D., Wolski, R., Grzegorczyk, C., Obertelli, G., Soman, S., Youseff, L., & Zagorodnov, D. (2009). The Eucalyptus Open-Source Cloud-Computing System. *Cluster Computing and the Grid, 2009. CCGRID '09. 9th IEEE/ACM International Symposium on.* (pp. 124–131). Washington, DC: IEEE Press.

OpenQRM official site: (2010) http://www.openqrm.com.

Rochwerger, B., Breitgand, D., Epstein, A., Hadas, D., Loy, I., & Nagin, K. (2011). RESERVOIR - when one cloud is not enough. *IEEE Computer, 44,* 44–51. doi:10.1109/MC.2011.64

SAP IoT Definition. (2011) Retrieved from: http://services.future-internet.eu/images/1/16/A4_Things_Haller.pdf.

Sedna, Native XML Database System: (2011) Retrieved from: http://modis.ispras.ru/sedna/.

Sempolinski, P., & Thain, D. (2010). A Comparison and Critique of Eucalyptus, OpenNebula and Nimbus. *The 2nd IEEE International Conference on Cloud Computing Technology and Science.* Washington, DC: IEEE Press.

Shared Nothing (SN) Architecture. (2011) http://en.wikipedia.org/wiki/Shared nothing architecture.

Sotomayor, B., Montero, R., Llorente, I. M., & Foster, I. (2009a). Resource Leasing and the Art of Suspending Virtual Machines. *High Performance Computing and Communications HPCC '09. 11th IEEE International Conference on.* (pp. 59–68). Washington, DC: IEEE Press

Sotomayor, B., Montero, R., Llorente, I. M., & Foster, I. (2009b). *Virtual Infrastructure Management in Private and Hybrid Clouds. Internet Computing, IEEE* (*Vol. 13*, pp. 14–22). Washington, DC: IEEE Press.

The COMETA Grid Infrastructure. (2011) Retrieved from: www.indicateproject.eu/getFile.php?id=173

The Extensible Messaging and Presence Protocol (XMPP) protocol: (2011) Retrieved from: http://tools.ietf.org/html/rfc3920

Trends, G. Cloud Computing vs Grid Computing. (2011) Retrieved from: http://www.google.com/trends.

Tusa, F., Paone, M., Villari, M., & Puliafito, A. (2010). CLEVER: A CLoud-Enabled Virtual EnviRonment. *15th IEEE Symposium on Computers and Communications ISCC '10. Riccione.* Washington, DC: IEEE Press.

Vàzquez, C., Huedo, E., Montero, R. S., & Llorente, I. M. (2009). Dynamic Provision of Computing Resources from Grid Infrastructures and Cloud Providers. *Proceedings of the International Conference on Hybrid Information Technology.* (pp. 113-119).

Virtualbox: x86 virtualization software package developed by Oracle. (2011) Retrieved from: http://www.virtualbox.org/

Virtualization: the essential catalyst for enabling the transition to secure cloud computing. (2011) Retrieved from: http://www.vmware.com/it/

Xen Hypervisor - Leading open source hypervisor for servers. (2011) Retrieved from: http://www.xen.org/

XEP-0065. SOCKS5 Bytestreams. (2011) Retrieved from: http://xmpp.org/extensions/xep-0065.html

ADDITIONAL READING

Ahlgren, B., Aranda, P. A., Chemouil, P., Oueslati, S., Correia, L. M., & Karl, H. (2011). Content, connectivity, and cloud: ingredients for the network of the future. *Communications Magazine, IEEE, 49*(7), 62–70. doi:10.1109/MCOM.2011.5936156

Bal, H. E., Maassen, J., van Nieuwpoort, R. V., Drost, N., Kemp, R., & van Kessel, T. (2010). Real-World Distributed Computer with Ibis. *Computer, 43*(8), 54–62. doi:10.1109/MC.2010.184

Celesti, A., Tusa, F., Villari, M., & Puliafito, A. (2010). "How to Enhance Cloud Architectures to Enable Cross-Federation, *Cloud Computing (CLOUD), 2010 IEEE 3rd International Conference on*, pp. 337-345.

Dikaiakos, M. D., Katsaros, D., Mehra, P., Pallis, G., & Vakali, A. (2009). Cloud Computing: Distributed Internet Computing for IT and Scientific Research. *Internet Computing, IEEE, 13*(5), 10–13. doi:10.1109/MIC.2009.103

Rehr, J. J., Vila, F. D., Gardner, J. P., Svec, L., & Prange, M. (2010). Scientific Computing in the Cloud. *Computing in Science & Engineering, 12*(3), 34–43. doi:10.1109/MCSE.2010.70

Tusa, F., Celesti, A., Paone, M., Villari, M., & Puliafito, A. (2011). "How CLEVER-based clouds conceive horizontal and vertical federations," *Computers and Communications (ISCC), 2011 IEEE Symposium on*, pp. 167-172.

KEY TERMS AND DEFINITIONS

cleverAdministration: Is the command line interface by means of a CLEVER cloud administrator can interact with the CLEVER infrastructure for sending specific commands to the active CM.

CLEVER Inter-Domain Communication: In a federated CLEVER scenario this is the mechanism that allows different clusters belonging to different administrative domains to interact exploiting the XMPP server-to-server communication.

CM: Cluster Manager is the CLEVER component that coordinates the HMs belonging to the cloud infrastructure.

Grid Worker Node: Is the computing node inside the Grid where the user's jobs submitted to the Computing Element are finally executed at a site.

HM: Host Manager is the CLEVER component running on each physical machine of the cluster where the cloud infrastructure takes place.

VIM: Virtual Infrastructure Manager is a type of cloud middleware whose main scope is the deployment and management of Virtual Machines.

XMPP Room: Is the "virtual room" where the XMPP entities "talk" each other exchanging messages.

Chapter 13
Monitoring Services in a Federated Cloud:
The RESERVOIR Experience

Stuart Clayman
University College London, UK

Giovanni Toffetti
University College London, UK

Alex Galis
University College London, UK

Clovis Chapman
University College London, UK

ABSTRACT

This chapter presents the need, the requirements, and the design for a monitoring system that is suitable for supporting the operations and management of a Federated Cloud environment. The chapter discusses these issues within the context of the RESERVOIR Service Cloud computing project. It first presents the RESERVOIR architecture itself, then introduces the issues of service monitoring in a federated environment, together with the specific solutions that have been devised for RESERVOIR. It ends with a review of the authors' experience in this area by showing a use-case application executing on RESERVOIR, which is responsible for the computational prediction of organic crystal structures.

INTRODUCTION

The emerging Cloud computing paradigm (Carr, 2008)(Wallis, 2008)(M. Armbrust et al., 2009) for hosting Internet-based services in virtualized environments, as exemplified by the Amazon Elastic Compute Cloud (EC2) or Google's AppEngine, aims to facilitate the creation of innovative Internet scale services without worrying about the computational infrastructure needed to support them. At present, no single hosting company can create a seemingly infinite infrastructure capable of serving the increasing number of on-line services, each having massive amounts of users and

DOI: 10.4018/978-1-4666-1631-8.ch013

Copyright © 2012, IGI Global. Copying or distributing in print or electronic forms without written permission of IGI Global is prohibited.

access at all times, from all locations. To cater to the needs of service creators, it is inevitable that the Service Cloud is going to be composed of a federation of sites from various infrastructure providers. Only by partnering and federating with each other, can infrastructure providers take advantage of the diversity factor and achieve the economies of scale needed to provide a seemingly infinite compute utility.

Service Clouds are just the latest incarnation of a concept that has been around since the 1960's, namely the manifestation of a general-purpose public computing utility. Throughout the history of computing we have seen such utilities appear in one form or another. Even though some success stories exist, such as in the area of high performance scientific computing, where Grid computing made significant progress over the past decade, none of these attempts materialized into a true general purpose compute utility that is accessible by anyone, at any time, from anywhere. Now however, the advent of new approaches utilizing an always-on Internet and virtualization, has brought about system designs which will enable the desired progress. An example of such a system design is the RESERVOIR *Service Cloud*, which is described in the next section.

RESERVOIR

The RESERVOIR FP7 project (Rochwerger et al, 2009)(Rochwerger et al, 2009b)(Rochwerger et al, 2011) aims to support the emergence of Service-Oriented Computing as a new computing paradigm and to investigate the fundamental aspects of Service Clouds as a fundamental element of the Future Internet.

RESERVOIR is a Service Cloud which has a new and unique approach to Service-Oriented Cloud computing. In the RESERVOIR model there is a clear separation between service providers and infrastructure providers. Service providers are the entities that understand the needs of particular

business and create and offer service applications to address those needs. Service providers do not need to own the computational resources needed by these service applications, instead, they lease resources from an infrastructure provider.

The infrastructure provider owns and leases out sections of a computing cluster, which supplies the service provider with a finite pool of computational resources. The cluster is presented as a Service Cloud site which is capable of allocating resources to many service providers at the same time. Through federation agreements, multiple infrastructure providers can factor together all of their compute resources thus offering a seemingly infinite resource pool for their customers - the service providers.

The high-level objective of RESERVOIR is to significantly increase the effectiveness of the compute and service utility model thus enabling the deployment of complex services on a Service Cloud that spans infrastructure providers and even geographies, while ensuring QoS and security guarantees. In doing so, RESERVOIR provides a foundation where resources and services are transparently and flexibly provisioned and managed like utilities.

RESERVOIR ARCHITECTURE

The essence of the RESERVOIR Service Cloud is to effectively manage a service specified as a collection of virtual execution environments (VEEs). A VEE is an abstraction representing both virtual machines running on a generic hypervisor infrastructure, as well as any application component that can be run (and/or migrated) on a leased infrastructure (e.g., Web applications on Google's App Engine, a Java based OSGi bundle). A Service Cloud, such as RESERVOIR, operates by acting as a platform for running virtualized applications in VEEs, which have been deployed on behalf of a service provider.

The service provider defines the details and requirements of the application in a Service Definition Manifest. This is done by specifying which virtual machine images are required to run, as well as specifications for (i) Elasticity Rules or performance objectives, which determine how the application will scale across a Cloud, and (ii) Service Level Agreement (SLA) Rules, which determine how and if the Cloud site is providing the right level of service to the application. Within each Service Cloud site there is a Service Manager (SM) and a VEE Manager (VEEM) which together provide all the necessary management functionality for both the services and the infrastructure. These management components of a Cloud system are shown in Figure 1 and are presented in more detail.

The Service Manager (SM) is the component responsible for accepting the Service Definition Manifest and the raw VEE images from the service provider. It is then responsible for the instantiation of the service application by requesting the creation and configuration of executable VEEs for each service component in the manifest. In addition, it is the Service Manager that is responsible for (i) evaluating and executing the elasticity rules and (ii) ensuring SLA compliance, by monitoring the execution of the service applications in real-time. Elasticity of a service is done by adjusting the application capacity, either by adding or removing service components and/or changing the resource requirements of a particular component according to the load and measurable application behaviour.

The Virtual Execution Environment Manager (VEEM) is the component responsible for the placement of VEEs into VEE hosts (VEEHs). The VEEM receives requests from the Service Manager to create VEEs, to adjust resources allocated to VEEs, and to also finds the best placement

Figure 1. RESERVOIR Service Cloud Architecture

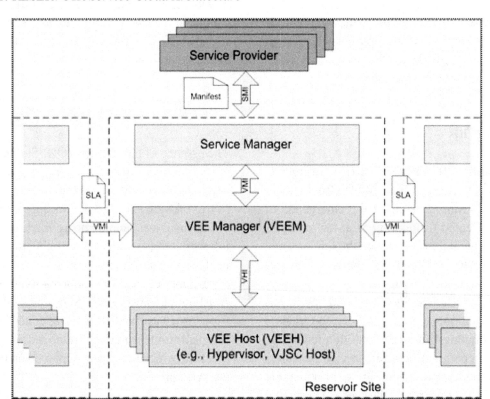

for these VEEs in order to satisfy a given set of constraints. The role of the VEEM is to optimize a site and its main task is to place and move the VEEs anywhere, even on remote sites, as long as the placement is done within the constraints set in the Manifest, including specifications of VEE affinity, VEE anti-affinity, security, and cost. In addition to serving local requests, the VEEM is the component in the system that is responsible for the migration of VEEs to and from remote sites. This is achieved by interacting with the VEEMs that manage other Clouds.

The Virtual Execution Environment Host (VEEH) is a resource that can host a certain type of VEEs. For example one type of a VEEH can be a physical machine with the Xen hypervisor (Barham et al., 2003) controlling it, whereas another type can be a machine with the KVM hypervisor (Kivity, 2007). In a Service Cloud hosting site there is likely to be a considerable number of VEEHs organised as a cluster.

These three main components of the Service Cloud architecture interact with each other using specific interfaces, namely SMI (service management interface), VMI (VEE management interface), and VHI (VEE host interface), within a site and also use the VMI interface for site-to-site federation via the VEEM. In Figure 1 the relationship between these components and interfaces is shown.

In the RESERVOIR platform, as can be seen in Figure 1, a Service Provider specifies the details and requirements of his application in the Service Definition Manifest. The Manifest also has the specifications of Elasticity Rules, which determine how the application will scale across the Cloud, and Service Level Agreement (SLA) objectives for the application as well as the infrastructure. The former specify which performance objectives should be attained by the service, the latter are used to determine if the platform is providing the right level of service to the application.

Federation and Networking

Apart from virtual execution environment requirements, the Service Definition Manifest also specifies the networking requirements of a service. In particular, the manifest can specify one or more private virtual networks called Virtual Area Networks (VANs), implemented as virtual Ethernet overlay services. Furthermore, the manifest specifies the public access points for the deployed service. Virtual execution environment interfaces can then be mapped to public IP addresses.

Public interfaces for a service are mapped to the available public IP addresses available at each compute Cloud, which allows users of the service to access it via the public IP address. However, virtual area networks (VANs) are implemented at the infrastructure level ensuring the VAN has separation, isolation, elasticity, and federation. The advantages of these attributes of the VAN are explained further:

- **Separation:** the service network and the infrastructure network are kept separate. RESERVOIR seeks to reduce mutual dependency between the infrastructure and the services. A VAN of a service, offered as part of RESERVOIR, needs to be separated from the infrastructure used by an infrastructure provider, similarly to the manner in which a virtual execution environment is separated from the physical host.
- **Isolation:** a VAN of one service is isolated from all VANs of other services. RESERVOIR seeks to isolate services such that possibly competing applications may securely share the infrastructure provider resources whilst being unaware of the other services. Isolated VAN services need to be offered side by side while sharing network resources of the infrastructure provider.

- **Elasticity:** a VAN can grow or shrink as necessary. RESERVOIR seeks to offer an elastic and extendable environment so that application providers will be able to adjust the size of their application on demand. A VAN service needs to enable application elasticity.
- **Federation:** a VAN can span over more than one Cloud provider. RESERVOIR seeks to form a federation of possibly competing infrastructure providers so that each provider offers an interchangeable pool of resources allowing service and resource migration without barriers. An interchangeable VAN service needs to be offered across administrative domains such that service providers would not be concerned by the identity of the infrastructure provider, the physical network used, or its configuration.

The VAN implementation of RESERVOIR provides the required virtual Ethernet overlay for each service. As a consequence of service elasticity and site management policies, some virtual machines belonging to a same service might be placed across different sites.

Figure 2 illustrates a simple federated scenario across two Service Clouds (Cloud A on the left and Cloud B on the right). Each site leases out compute resources to different service providers, in our example Cloud A is serving services 1 and 2 while Cloud B is managing service 3.

When virtual execution environments are placed on different sites, (as for Service 2 in Figure 2), the VEEMs at each participating site keep the VEEs connected by spawning the appropriate VAN proxies so that VANs stay connected and VEEs remain unaware of their actual placement. There are some network issues such as latency, jitter, and round trip time considerations that arise, but the important aspect is that connectivity is maintained across the federated domains. In a more complex scenario (such as, when more services and Service Clouds are participating in the federation) a single service can be scattered across several sites requiring multiple VAN proxies.

Once the VEEs are in place and the service is running, the Service Manager (SM) is responsible for managing all of the services on the Cloud. To undertake such management, a Cloud needs monitoring facilities.

MONITORING IN RESERVOIR

Monitoring is a fundamental aspect of a Service Cloud such as RESERVOIR because it is used both by the infrastructure itself and for service management. The monitoring system needs to be pervasive as:

- It is required by several components of the Service Cloud;
- It cuts across the layers of the Cloud system creating vertical paths; and
- It spans out across all the Service Clouds in a federation in order to link all the elements of a service.

For full operation of a RESERVOIR Service Cloud we observe that monitoring is a vital part of the full control loop that goes from the service management, through a control path, to the Probes which collect and send data, back to the service management which makes various decisions based on the data. The monitoring is a fundamental part of RESERVOIR as it allows the integration of components in all of the architectural layers.

The RESERVOIR monitoring system has a model of information consumers and information producers, connected by a monitoring data plane. The producers send measurements across the data plane, and these are read and processed by the consumers. In Figure 3 we show some of these producers and consumers, but this is not an exhaustive list.

Figure 2. VANs and services running on two RESERVOIR sites

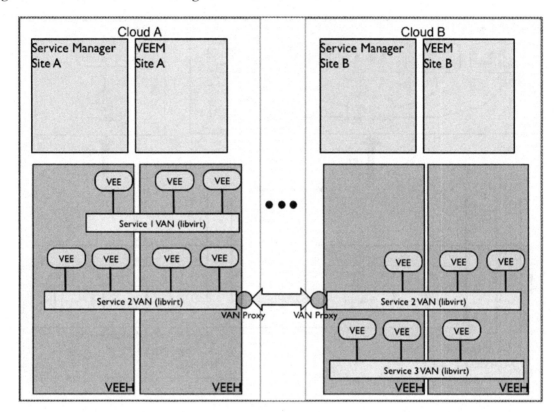

Information Consumers

Several RESERVOIR management functionalities have monitoring requirements. Some of these are presented here:

- **The VEE Placement:** within each RESERVOIR site, infrastructure resource utilization is monitored and the placement of VEEs is constantly updated to achieve optimal resource utilization according to policies set by the infrastructure provider. This is managed by Policy Engine of the VEEM;

- **Service Billing:** each infrastructure provider needs to collect resource (e.g., CPU, disk, memory, network) utilization over time, for each virtual execution environment of each service, in order to support its billing policy. This is managed by the

Billing and Accounts component of the Service Manager;

- **Service Elasticity:** the execution of the service applications is monitored and their capacity is constantly adjusted to meet the requirements specified in the service definition manifest. These on-going optimizations are done without human intervention by the management components in the Service Manager. There are several components, including the Elasticity Engine and the SLA Protection Engine, which dynamically evaluate elasticity and SLA rules and implement their actions in order to maintain the application running effectively. For these rules to be evaluated, a Service Cloud needs a monitoring subsystem which sends measurement data, collected from the whole architecture, to be fed into the rules.

Figure 3. Information producers and consumers in a single RESERVOIR Cloud

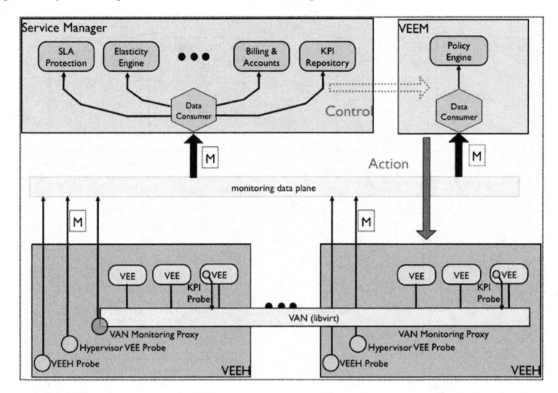

- **Infrastructural SLA Compliance:** service providers require reports on resource provisioning to assess compliance to SLAs by infrastructural providers;
- **Access Control:** infrastructure providers might use over-booking mechanisms to assign infrastructural resources to services based on a probabilistic model of resource usage derived from historical service traces. Hence, data about required VEEs and elasticity behaviour over time need to be stored and analysed.
- **Inter-Site Billing:** when virtual execution environments are migrated or spawned on a site belonging to a different service provider, billing across federated sites has to be supported according to federation agreements (e.g., billing on resource usage, or fixed amount)

For illustrative purposes, we gave just a high level overview of some of them.

Information Producers

Measurement data in RESERVOIR can come from the following sources (also depicted in Figure 3):

1. Raw data gathered from probes in the underlying infrastructure (VEEH). For example physical resource usage for each VEEH (VEEH Probe in Figure 3);

2. Raw data gathered from probes attached to the virtual machines (VEE). Used to monitor the amount of physical resources assigned to each VEE over time, mainly for billing (Hypervisor VEE Probe);

3. Data gathered from probes embedded in the application (application-specific probes), or data which is the combination of the raw data into composed Key Performance Indicators

(KPI Probe through a VAN Monitoring Proxy);

4. Data derived from the analysis of historical raw data and KPI data held in a data store (from the KPI Repository of the Service Manager in Figure 3)

RESERVOIR enforces a clear distinction between monitoring data coming from the infrastructure (VEEH Probes, Hypervisor Probes) and monitoring data coming from services (KPI probes). Apart from being information of different nature, the former being Cloud-specific and the latter being service/application-specific, another important reason for this choice is that monitoring data coming from inside the application should be as small in size and as refined as possible.

The rationale behind this choice is that each application will have a very specific behaviour that is in principle known only to the service provider. Therefore, instead on burdening the infrastructure provider with the responsibility of collecting and manipulating a vast amount of low-informative raw monitoring data, the design choice is to leave the service providers with complete freedom in the ways of collecting, aggregating, cleaning, and manipulating all the raw monitoring data they will see most fit for their application. To get the service specific monitoring data out of the service and into the environment of the Cloud management, there is monitoring infrastructure "on the outside" of a service, called the VAN Monitoring Proxy, which expects the internal KPI Probes of a service to publish highly aggregated, highly informative performance indicators to be used for triggering automated service elasticity decisions.

RESERVOIR provides a reference framework for service providers to implement their own application-specific probes. Once a probe is instantiated according to the framework, the data it produces is published on the VAN and sent to a specific multicast address. A monitoring proxy intercepts the published information in the VAN

and forwards it to the monitoring data plane for the local data consumers.

In a large distributed system, such as a RESERVOIR Service Cloud, there may be hundreds or thousands of measurement probes that can generate data. It would not be effective to have all of these probes sending data all of the time, so a mechanism is needed that controls and manages the relevant probes. Therefore, a Service Cloud requires a monitoring system that has a minimal runtime footprint and is not intrusive, so as not to adversely affect the performance of the Cloud itself or the running service applications. As a consequence, we need to ensure that components such as the VEEM, and Service Manager elements such as the Elasticity Rules Engine and the SLA Rules Engine only receive data that is of relevance and needed at a time.

Federated Monitoring

When Service Clouds are federated to accept each other's workload there needs to be a consideration of how monitoring will behave in the presence of the federated VEEs. Monitoring needs to continue to work correctly and reliably when a service executes across federated Clouds. When some VEEs are migrated to another Cloud, the monitoring data distribution mechanism will need to cross Cloud boundaries. It is essential that the interfaces and formats between Clouds be standardised in order that federation monitoring to work in heterogeneous environments. This will ensure that that the monitoring data for all the VEEs of a service will be connected, whether locally or remotely.

Monitoring in a Service Cloud presents us with some interesting issues. Although the Service Cloud infrastructure is a distributed system, it is structured in a very particular way, with one large Grid of machines acting as one Cloud. Most of the monitoring data stays within the site, as all of the consumers are within the site. The exception is for federated VEEs. With many monitoring systems the sources and consumers are often distributed arbitrarily across a network, and so the paths of data flow and the patterns of interaction are different. Within a Service Cloud the pattern is more predictable, and so we need to design and build for this. In Figure 3 we can see how the monitoring for the VEEs in one service are connected by the data distribution mechanism within a single Cloud, and how these are connected together to form a single service.

When a VEE is migrated from one site to a remote federated site, the monitoring data from that VEE still needs to be collected by the Service Manager at the originating Cloud. However, by migrating to a remote site the originating site loses direct control of the VEE. Therefore, in order to ensure a continuous monitoring capability, some fundamental issues need to considered. They are:

- How does monitoring behave when a VEE is sent to a remote Cloud
- What operations need to be done in each of the Clouds to activate this federation
- What components and objects need to be created and/or managed when federation occurs.

As we have seen in the 'Federation and Networking' section, once VEEs have crossed another Cloud's boundaries, the Ethernet overlay of the RESERVOIR VAN has the responsibility of instantiating the appropriate proxies so that VEEs belonging to the same service still have the perception of a single VAN spanning different Clouds. This connection between VAN parts on each Cloud is shown as the VAN Segment in Figure 4. If the service spans over 3 Clouds then there will be 3 Service VAN parts and 2 VAN Segments which comprise the whole service VAN.

Since there is a connection in place for each service, monitoring measurements from application-specific probes (KPI probes), on any VEE on any Cloud, will still reach the VAN Monitoring Proxy at the originating site. These measurements will be delivered to the originating site monitor-

ing consumers. There is no need to provide any other mechanism to route service/application monitoring information for application-specific probes. Furthermore, VAN isolation provides guarantees that service/application-specific monitoring information will only be available at the originating site Service Manager.

A different solution has to be taken for infrastructural monitoring information. One group of measurements (i.e., messages from VEEH Probes) are not intended to leave the Cloud managing each VEEH. In fact, monitoring information on the physical machines of a specific Cloud is needed for the Cloud management (e.g., placement, anomaly detection) and generally kept hidden from the outside. Data from Hypervisor VEE Probes, on the other hand, needs to be received both by the local Cloud Service Manager (e.g., for inter-Cloud billing) as well as by the Service Manager at VEE originating site (e.g., for Service Provider billing). As a consequence, the monitoring data plane has a per-service segment between federated sites, in order to transmit this monitoring data. This connection between monitoring data plane parts on each Cloud is shown as the Per-Service Segment in Figure 4.

These Per-Service Segments of the monitoring data plane are setup and shutdown, on-demand, as VEEs migrate from one Cloud to another. The setup is done when the first VEE of a service is migrated to a federated Cloud, and the shutdown is done when the last VEE of a service is migrated off a federated Cloud.

This allows the routing of Hypervisor Probe measurements to be delivered to the appropriate consumers.

When the first VEE of a service is about to be migrated across sites, a Federation Manager instantiates gateways for each service. A service gateway connects to the internal monitoring data plane of a RESERVOIR Cloud and forwards the relevant information to a matching gateway on the destination Cloud. In Figure 5 we see 3 such service gateways, for service A, service B, and

Figure 4. Monitoring across federated RESERVOIR Clouds

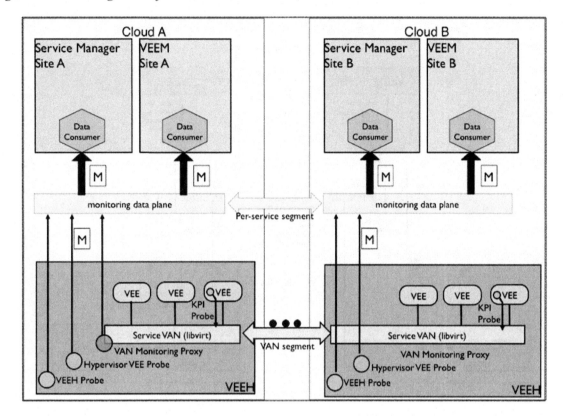

service C. Only monitoring data from service A VEEs crosses the service segment through the service A gateways. The same process applies for service B and service C.

The service gateways are under the control of the Federation Manager, which itself is controlled and managed by the VEEM. As service gateways are under administrative control of the Cloud that instantiates them, this enables:

1. Complete control over the information that is chosen to be forwarded over the gateway, as the VEEM and Federation Manager can adjust the settings of the gateway;
2. Gateways to be adaptable and implemented according to each Cloud monitoring data plane technology. This allows for a Cloud to use one technology internally for the monitoring data plane, and use a different

technology for the Cloud-to-Cloud transmission (e.g., multicast inside the Cloud and JMS over the gateway). Furthermore, two Clouds may have entirely different technologies for their monitoring data plane, but the gateways will provide the connection between them.

When VEEs are undeployed or migrated back to their originating site, and there are no more VEEs for a service still running on a Cloud, the federation managers on each Cloud have the responsibility of tearing down the appropriate service gateways.

The main requirements and issues regarding monitoring in a federated Cloud environment have been presented. In the next section we describe the design and implementation of a monitoring system that meets these requirements.

Figure 5. Federated monitoring management

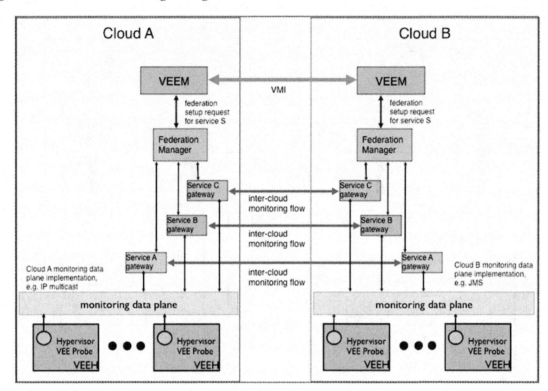

DESIGN OF A MONITORING SYSTEM

Existing monitoring systems such as Ganglia (Massie, Chun, & Culler, 2003), Nagios (Nagios, n.d.), MonaLisa (Newman, Legrand, Galvez, Voicu, & Cirstoiu, 2003), and GridICE (Andreozzi et al., 2005) have addressed monitoring of large distributed systems, but they have not addressed the rapidly changing and dynamic infrastructure seen in Service Clouds.

There is a cloud monitoring system called Amazon CloudWatch (CloudWatch, n.d.), that is available only through the Amazon AWS Cloud system. Amazon CloudWatch monitors AWS resources such as Amazon EC2 and Amazon RDS DB instances, and it can also monitor custom metrics generated by a customer's applications and services. It can be seen that its main goal is to provide data to the customer of the cloud about a running service, rather than providing data for infrastructure management.

Furthermore, there are two Cloud related projects that have also devised monitoring systems suitable for their needs. One is from the IRMOS project and the other is from the VISION project. The goal of the IRMOS project (Irmos, n.d.) is to design, develop, and validate Cloud solutions which will allow the adoption of interactive real-time applications, and especially multimedia applications, enabling a rich set of attributes with efficient integration into cloud infrastructures. The IRMOS monitoring system uses a two-layer approach which consists of six components. The goal of the VISION project (Vision, n.d.) is the setup and deployment of virtual data and storage services on demand, across disparate administrative domains, providing QoS and security guarantees. Its monitoring system design is very extensive and adaptable. At this time, both projects are still on-going and it is too early to determine any conclusions on their monitoring systems.

A monitoring system for Clouds needs to be designed and built to be fit for the purpose of both infrastructure and service monitoring. It needs to be for the whole of infrastructure and service management, and so it should cover SLA compliance, elasticity, QoS, etc. It is important to recognise that it is the monitoring mechanism that closes the loop from the initial deployment, through execution, and back to the Service Manager (as shown in Figure 3). The monitoring system is there to gather data from all the components within a Cloud architecture, and so monitoring is a fundamental aspect of a Service Cloud that is used by the infrastructure and for service management.

The monitoring system for a Service Cloud needs to feed data into the Service Manager so that it can manage the services deployed on the Cloud. Over time, it is expected that the management capabilities of the Service Manager will expand to include new functions. As a consequence we need the monitoring system to be adaptable, flexible, and extensible in order to support the expanding functionality.

To address all of the requirements and functionality of the Service Cloud environment, we have determined that the main features for monitoring that need to be considered are:

- **Scalability:** to ensure that the monitoring can cope with a large number of probes
- **Elasticity:** so that virtual resources created and destroyed by expanding and contracting networks are monitored correctly
- **Migration:** so that any virtual resource which moves from one physical host to another is monitored correctly
- **Adaptability:** so that the monitoring framework can adapt to varying computational and network loads in order not to be invasive
- **Autonomic:** so that the monitoring framework can keep running without intervention and reconfiguration

- **Federation:** so that any virtual resource which resides on another domain is monitored correctly
- **Isolation:** so that monitoring of VEEs from different services are not mixed and are not visible to other services

To establish such features in a monitoring framework requires careful architecture and design. The following section presents the Lattice Monitoring Framework which we have designed and built for the purpose of monitoring dynamic environments such as Service Clouds. Further details of the use of Lattice can be found in (Clayman et al., 2010) and (Clayman, Galis, & Mamatas, 2010).

In many systems, probes are used to collect data for system management (Cooke et al., 2003) (Massie et al., 2003). In this regard, Lattice also relies on probes. However, to increase the power and flexibility of the monitoring we introduce the concept of a data source. A data source represents an interaction and control point within the system that encapsulates one or more probes. A probe sends a well defined set of attributes and values to a data consumer at a predefined interval.

The goal for the monitoring system is to have fully dynamic data sources, in which each one can have multiple probes, with each probe returning its own data. The data sources will be able to turn on and turn off probes, or change their sending rate dynamically at run time. A further useful facility for a data source is the ability to add new probes to a data source at run-time. By using this approach we will be able to instrument components of the system without having to restart them in order to get new information.

It is also beneficial to interface with existing frameworks in order to collect data for Lattice. We would need these frameworks to fit in with the concept of data source and probe, and so they can be encapsulated with the relevant adapter in the implementation.

Such an approach for data sources and probes is important because in many systems that need monitoring, the Service Management needs to grow and adapt for new management requirements over time. If the monitoring system is a fixed point then Service Management will be limited.

To meet all the criteria outlined requires careful architecture and design. Many monitoring systems rely on simple data transmission. From a design point of view, this approach is successful, although, we have found it is better if the monitoring framework design encapsulates separate planes for data, for meta-data, and for control. This allows us to build a system that has the desired behaviour and meets the requirements.

In Lattice, the separate planes for connecting the monitoring framework are:

- **The data plane:** for distributing measurements from the Probes and Data Sources to the consumers. This is the same monitoring data plane shown in Figures 3, 4, and 5.
- **The control plane:** for distributing control messages to the Data Sources and the Probes.

- **The information plane:** which holds all the meta-data relating to measurements sent by Data Sources and Probes.

These three planes are shown in Figure 6, together with the Data Sources and Probes, Data Consumers, and a Regulator.

In a running system there will be multiple Data Sources, multiple Data Consumers, but only one Regulator.

The regulator's job is to ensure that the monitoring system does not flood the network or overload any applications.

Data Source

A Data Source can manage several Probes, and has plugins for the monitoring data plane, the control plane, and the information plane, so that it is possible to change the implementation of each plane easily and independently of the other planes. This will allow users to choose the best solution for different setup scenarios. We have a control interface so that Data Sources can be controlled from a Service Manager, via the control plane,

Figure 6. Multiple Planes

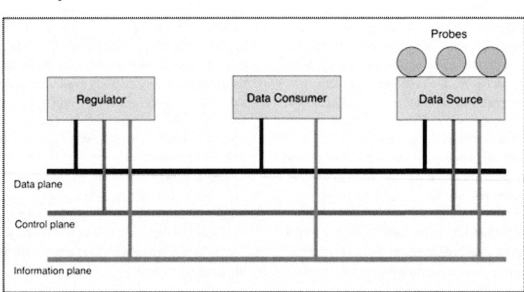

and Probes can also be controlled via the Data Source. We can then develop control strategies so that it is possible to manage the lifecycle of a Probe from a Service Manager rather than having everything programmed-in.

As there could be hundreds or thousands of probes in a Lattice system, it is important that each probe has a unique identity. Without an identity, it is not possible to identify individual probes. Using the identity it is possible for the Data Source to address the probe in order to turn it on, turn it off, change its rate of sending, or find its status. It is the probe's identity that also allows the combination of its data with other probe's data to create the complex information.

Probes

In many systems, the Probes collect data at a given data rate, and transmit measurements immediately, at exactly the same data rate. In Lattice we can decouple the collection rate and the transmission rate in order to implement strategies which aid in efficiency.

The collection of measurement data is a fundamental aspect of a Probe. The collection strategies will be:

- At data rate, which collects some measurement data at a regular data rate.
- On event, where a measurement is not collected at a specified rate, but is passed to the probe as an event from another entity. The transmission strategies are:
- At data rate, this is the main strategy, which transmits measurements at a regular data rate.
- On change, where a measurement is only transmitted when the data that is read is different from the previous data snapshot. This can be elaborated so that only a specific set of attributes are included when determining if there has been a change.

- Filtering, where a measurement is only transmitted if the filter passes the value. Examples of such filtering strategies are:
  - Above threshold, where a measurement is only transmitted when an attribute of the data that is read is above a specified threshold. Otherwise, nothing is transmitted.
  - Below threshold, where a measurement is only transmitted when an attribute of the data that is read is below a specified threshold. Otherwise, nothing is transmitted.
  - In band, where a measurement is only transmitted when an attribute of the data that is read is between an upper bound and a lower bound. Otherwise, nothing is transmitted.
  - Out of band, where a measurement is only transmitted when an attribute of the data that is read is above an upper bound or below a lower bound. Otherwise, nothing is transmitted.

although any kind of filter can be defined.

For a probe to be part of Lattice we can either write the probe from scratch or use existing sensors and instrumentation and adapt them for Lattice. The probes can be implemented in various ways to get the data they need to send. They can:

- Read the data directly from the relevant place
- Be an adaptor for an existing instrument by wrapping the existing one
- Act as a bridge for an existing instrument by allowing the existing one to send it data

in order to gather the required information.

Probe Data Dictionary

One of the important aspects of this monitoring design is the specification of a Data Dictionary for each probe. The Data Dictionary defines the attributes as the names, the types and the units of the measurements that the probe will be sending out. This is important because the consumers of the data can collect this information in order to determine what will be received. At present many monitoring systems have fixed data sets, with a the format of measurements being pre-defined. The advantage here is that as new probes are to be added to the system or embedded in an application, it will be possible to introspect what is being measured. This is important in a Service Cloud system such as RESERVOIR, because many of the Probes will not be known in advance.

The measurements that are sent will have value fields that relate directly to the data dictionary. To determine which field is which, the consumer can lookup in the data dictionary to elaborate the full attribute value set (see Figure 7).

Measurements

The actual measurements that get sent from a probe will contain the attribute-value fields together with a type, a timestamp, plus some identification fields. The attribute-values contain the information the probe wants to send, the type indicates what

kind of data it is, and the timestamp has the time at which the data was collected. The identification fields are used to determine for which component or which service, and from which probe this data has arrived from.

When using Lattice, if there are multiple components which need monitoring and there are multiple running services and any of these can have multiple probes, then the consumer of the data will be able to differentiate the arriving data into the relevant streams of measurements.

Data Plane

In order to distribute the measurements collected by the monitoring system, we use the Data Plane. For most Data Plane uses, we need a mechanism that allows for multiple submitters and multiple receivers of data without having vast numbers of network connections. For example, having many TCP connections from each producer to all of the consumers of the data for that producer would create a combinatorial explosion of connections. Solutions to this include IP multicast, Event Service Bus, or publish/subscribe mechanism. In each of these, a producer of data only needs to send one copy of a measurement (in a packet) onto the

Figure 7. Relationship of Probe to Measurement

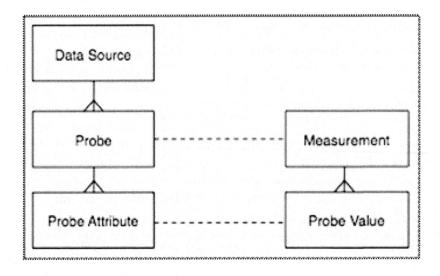

network, and each of the consumers will be able to collect the same packet of data concurrently from the network.

In order to avoid a reliance on any particular networking technology, there is a Data Plane plugin capability that allows the actual implementation for data distribution to be set at run time. Such an approach works well for Clouds and Grids because we have both multiple producers and multiple consumers.

One of the easiest solutions for the Data Plane is to use IP multicast because it has a very simple mechanism to distribution. However, IP multicast is a UDP based networking technology, and as such it has very similar attributes in terms of reliability and packet loss. It is possible to consider a more substantial framework which has higher reliability and more flexibility for the Data Plane as well.

Control Plane

In many monitoring systems, the probes are reporting their status at a fixed data rate and are always sending data onto the network. Such an approach is not scalable and does not fit with the design goals of Lattice. The monitoring system for Lattice requires both scalability and flexibility in order to operate effectively. Consequently, we need to have a level of control over all of the Data Sources and all of the Probes.

We have defined operations that allow individual Probes to be turned on and turned off independently of any other Probe. Furthermore, any Probe can have its data rate changed on-the-fly at run-time. It is by using these capabilities that we can achieve the scalability and flexibility we need from the monitoring system.

We have defined the Control Plane to support all of the above functionality. To enact this we have devised the following artefacts:

- A control protocol which sends the control messages,
- A controller-manager which decides which Probes to interact with,
- A policy engine which takes a global view of all the monitoring information and interacts with the controller-manager

Once these are built we have dynamic and autonomic control over the monitoring.

Information Plane

The Information Plane allows interaction with the Information Model for the monitoring framework. It holds all of the data about Data Sources, Probes, and Probe Data Dictionaries present in a running system. As Measurements are sent with only the values for the current reading, the meta-data needs to be kept for lookup purposes. By having this Information Plane, it allows consumers of measurements to lookup the meaning of each of the fields.

Within Lattice, there are key lifecycle points where data is added to the information model. They are when a Data Source is activated, and when a Probe is activated. This data can be looked up as required.

For example, if a measurement has a probe ID of 4272, as seen earlier, then a Service Manager can interact with the Information Plane to extract the actual name of the probe.

In many older monitoring systems this information model is stored in a central repository, such as an LDAP server. Newer monitoring systems use a distributed approach to holding this data, with MonAlisa using JINI as its information model store. For Lattice, the Information Plane also relies on a plugin component. Currently, we have an implementation which uses a Distributed Hash Table.

A MONITORING USE CASE

We have seen the RESERVOIR architecture, the monitoring requirements for RESERVOIR, and the design for an implementation of a monitoring system, we now present a service that executes on a Cloud in order to highlight how the monitoring is essential and how services need to be adapted to work on the Cloud. In this section, we give an overview of a service that can take full advantage of a RESERVOIR Cloud.

The selected service is a Grid-based application responsible for the computational prediction of organic crystal structures from the chemical diagram (Emmerich, Butchart, Chen, Wassermann, & Price 2005). The application operates according to a pre-defined workflow involving multiple web-based services and Fortran programs. Up to 7200 executions of these programs may be required to run, as batch jobs, in both sequential and parallel form, to compute various subsets of the prediction. Web services are used to collect inputs from a user, coordinate the execution of the jobs, process and display results, and generally orchestrate the overall workflow. The actual execution of batch jobs is handled by Condor (Thain, Tannenbaum, & Livny, 2002), a job scheduling and resource management system, which maintains a queue of jobs and manages their parallel execution on multiple nodes of a cluster.

This case study provides many interesting challenges when deployed on a Cloud computing infrastructure such as RESERVOIR. Firstly, the application consists of a number of different components with very different resource requirements, which are to be managed jointly. Secondly, the resource requirements of the services will vary during the lifetime of the application. Indeed, as jobs are created, the number of cluster nodes required to execute them will vary. Our goal in relying upon a Cloud computing infrastructure will be to create a virtualised cluster, enabling the size of the cluster to dynamically grow and contract according to load.

The service setup is illustrated in Figure 8, where the three main types of service components can be distinguished:

- The Orchestration Service is a web based server responsible for managing the overall execution of the application. It presents an HTTP front end enabling users to trigger predictions from a web page, with various input parameters of their choice. The Business Process Execution Language (BPEL), is used to coordinate the overall execution of the polymorph search, relying on external services to generate batch jobs, submit the jobs for execution, process the results and trigger new computations if required.
- The Grid Management Service is responsible for coordinating the execution of batch jobs. It presents a web services interface for the submission of jobs. Requests are authenticated, processed and delegated to a Condor scheduler, which will maintain a queue of jobs and manage their execution on a collection of available remote execution nodes. It will match jobs to execution nodes according to the workload. Once a target node has been selected it will transfer input files over and remotely monitor the execution of the job.
- The Condor Execution Service, which runs the necessary daemons to act as a Condor execution node. These daemons will advertise the node as an available resource on which jobs can be run, receive job details from the scheduler and run the jobs as local processes. Each node runs only a single job at a time and upon completion of the job transfers the output back to the scheduler, and advertises itself as available.

Packaged as individual virtual execution environments, the three components are deployed on the RESERVOIR infrastructure. The associated

Figure 8. Service on RESERVOIR

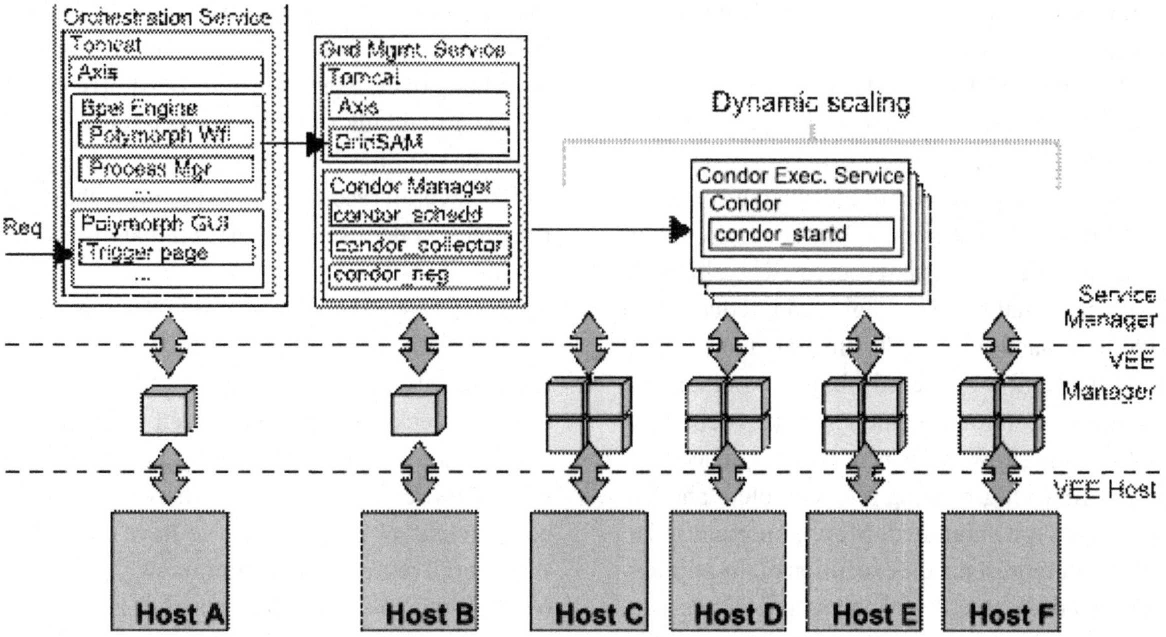

manifest describes the capacity requirements of each component, including CPU and memory requirements, references to the image files, starting order (based on service components dependencies), elasticity rules and customisation parameters. For the run shown here, the Orchestration and Grid Management Services will be allocated a fixed set of resources, with only a single instance of each being required. The Condor execution service however will be replicated as necessary, in order to provide an appropriate cluster size for the parallel execution of multiple jobs.

Elasticity rules will tie the number of required Condor execution service instances to the number of jobs in queue as presented by the Condor scheduler. This enables RESERVOIR to dynamically deploy new execution service instances as the number of jobs awaiting execution increases. Similarly, as the number of jobs in the queue decreases it is no longer necessary to use the resources to maintain a large collection of execution nodes, and VEEs can be released accordingly.

The elasticity rules will refer to key performance indicators that are declared within the manifest. All components and KPIs are declared in the manifest. This enables the infrastructure to monitor KPI measurements being published by specific components and associate them to the declared rules. In this particular instance, a monitoring Probe associated with the Grid Management Service will publish measurements under the uk.ucl.condor.schedd.queuesize qualified name every 30 seconds as integers.

When the Grid Management component is operational, the monitoring Probe, will begin the process of monitoring the queue length and transmit the number of jobs in the queue on a regular basis (every 30 seconds). These monitoring events will be recorded by the Service Manager to enforce elasticity rules. When conditions regarding the queue length are met, the Service Manager will request the deployment of an additional Condor Execution component instances. Similarly, when the number of jobs in queue falls below the selected threshold, it will request the deallocation of virtual instances.

An important metric to consider is that of resource usage. The goal of Cloud deployment is to reduce expenditure by allowing Service Providers to minimise over-provisioning. While the actual financial costs will be dependent on the business models employed by Cloud infrastructure providers, we can at the very least rely upon resource usage as an indicator of cost.

We compare resource usage obtained on RESERVOIR with that obtained in an environment with dedicated physical resources. The objective is to verify that there is a significant reduction in resource usage. The results illustrated in Figure 9 show the number of queued jobs plotted against the number of Condor execution instances deployed. Both charts show large increases in queued jobs as the first long running jobs complete and the larger sets are submitted. More importantly, the first chart represents the execution of the application in a dedicated environment and shows a set of 16 continuously allocated execution nodes. The second chart represents the execution of the application with RESERVOIR, shows the increase in the number of allocated nodes as jobs in queue increases, and a complete deallocation as these jobs complete.

There is little difference in execution times in the individual batches of jobs on either the dedicated or virtual RESERVOIR environment. A 10 minute increase of time, using RESERVOIR, can be constituted as reasonable considering the overall time frame of a search, which is well over 2 hours. This is particularly true as we consider the overall resource usage savings. Indeed as can be seen in Table 1, with respect to execution nodes, the overall resource usage decreases by 34.46% by relying on service elasticity. This is because the totality of the execution nodes are not required for the initial bulk of the run, where only 2 jobs are to be run.

The overall resource usage obtained showing run times, nodes used, and the summary is shown in Table 1.

The savings shown here are in the context of the run itself. If we consider the overall use of the application over the course of a randomly selected week on a fully dedicated environment where resources are continuously available, even more significant cost savings will exist. Based on cost savings obtained here, we have estimated that overall resource consumption would drop by 69.18%, due to the fact that searches are not run continuously; no searches were run on two days of the week, and searches, though of varying size, were run only over a portion of the day, leaving resources unused for considerable amounts of time. More details of this work can be found in (Chapman, Emmerich, Marquez, Clayman, & Galis, 2011).

FUTURE RESEARCH DIRECTIONS

There is much further work to do in the areas of service clouds and federated monitoring.

Table 1. Service on RESERVOIR

	Dedicated Environment	RESERVOIR Environment
Search run time (min) Complete shutdown time (min)	143.41 No shutdown	153.66 159.11
Average execution nodes: - for run - until shutdown	 16 No shutdown	 10.49 10.42
Percentage differences: - Resource usage saving - Extra run time (jobs)		 -34.46% 7.15%

Figure 9. Service on RESERVOIR

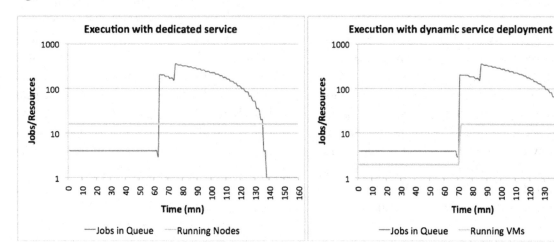

Within RESERVOIR, there is a full monitoring system lifecycle integration within the Service Manager, from the initial Service Definition Manifest presentation, through the first service deployment, and then the continual execution of the service. To support fully dynamic on-the-fly functionality these lifecycle and control functions will need to use a control plane of the monitoring framework. Using this control plane the Service Manager will be able to activate, deactivate, and set the data rate of probes, as necessary.

Furthermore, to ensure the continuous operation of the monitoring system, it needs to be self-aware of its operation and its effect on the whole RESERVOIR system. In order to make it this way, the monitoring system needs its own adaptable controller with policies which can control the whole of the monitoring system. All of these elements are considered as part of the further work. One main area of our future work will be to address the main features for monitoring in a virtualized network environment within the Lattice framework itself.

As we have shown, for full operation of a virtualized service cloud environment the monitoring is a vital part of the control loop. To ensure that this loop is effective we need to be confident that the measurements transmitted by probes are accurate. As such, we intend to investigate and evaluate the accuracy of the monitoring framework.

The mechanism of defining the measurements that probes will send using an information model is aligned with modelling approaches in many other areas. Consequently, we will examine how we can take information models for the service applications, and use this to create information models for the probes that will monitor these components. By doing this we could define and create the probes automatically from the service application's model.

A further goal for the Lattice monitoring system is to have fully dynamic data sources, in which the data source implementation will have the capability for reprogramming the probes on-the-fly. In this way, it will be possible to make probes send new data if it is required. For example, they can send extra attributes as part of the measurement. Yet another useful facility for a data source will be the ability to add new probes to a data source at run-time. By using this approach we will be able to instrument components of the virtual network without having to restart them in order to get this new information.

CONCLUSION

Monitoring in Service Clouds, such as RESER-VOIR, presents us with some interesting issues. Although the Service Cloud infrastructure is a distributed system, it is structured in a very particular way, with one large cluster of machines acting as one Cloud site. Most of the monitoring data stays within the site, as all of the consumers are within the site. The only exception to this is for federated VEEs. We see that the monitoring system is pervasive to a Service Cloud as:

1.   It is required by most of the components of the Service Cloud;
2.   It cuts across the layers of the Service Cloud creating vertical paths; and
3.   It spans out across all the Clouds in a federation in order to link all the VEEs of a service.

With many monitoring systems the sources and consumers are often distributed arbitrarily across a network, and so the paths of data flow and the patterns of interaction are different. Within a Service Cloud the pattern is more predictable, and so we have designed and built for this situation. In this chapter we have presented the issues that need to be addressed for a federated Cloud and we have shown how federated monitoring is designed and activated within RESERVOIR.

The use of the Lattice framework allowed us to build a monitoring infrastructure that collects, processes, and disseminates network and system information from/to the entities at real-time, acting as an enabler for service management functionality. We have seen that monitoring is a fundamental feature of any Service Cloud management system. We have also shown that Lattice can provide such monitoring for systems in which the virtualized resources are highly volatile as they can be started, stopped, or migrated atany time by the management in a federated environment.

We have shown that the implementation of these concepts is feasible and that a complete architecture can enable a Service Cloud infrastructure to realise significant savings in resource usage, with little impact on overall quality of service. Given that a Cloud can deliver a near similar quality of service as a dedicated computing resource, Clouds then have a substantial number of advantages. Firstly application providers do not need to embark on capital expenditure and instead can lease the infrastructure when they need it. Secondly, because the elasticity rules enable the application provider to flexibly expand and shrink their resource demands so they only pay the resources that they actually need. We have seen in the use-case example that the overall resource usage decreases by 34.46% by relying on service elasticity, as compared to a dedicated environment. Finally, the Cloud provider can plan their capacity more accurately because it knows the resource demands of the applications it provides.

ACKNOWLEDGMENT

This work is partially supported by the European Union through the RESERVOIR project of the 7th Framework Program. We would like to thank the members of the RESERVOIR consortium for their helpful comments. We also would like to thank Benny Rochwerger, Lars Larsson, Luis M. Vaquero, Luis Rodero Merino, Ruben S. Montero, Kenneth Nagin, Alessio Gambi, and Mario Bisignani for the technical discussions and support.

REFERENCES

Andreozzi, S., De Bortoli, N., Fantinel, S., Ghiselli, A., Rubini, G. L., Tortone, G., & Vistoli, M. C. (2005). GridICE: A monitoring service for Grid systems. *Future Generation Computer Systems*, *21*(4), 559–571. doi:10.1016/j.future.2004.10.005

Armbrust, M., Fox, A., Griffith, R., Joseph, A. D., Katz, R., Konwinski, A., et al. (2009). Above the Clouds: A Berkeley view of Cloud computing. *Technical Report UCB/EECS-2009-28*, Berkley, CA:University of California

Barham, P., Dragovic, B., Fraser, K., & Hand, S. (2003). Xen and the art of virtualization. *SIGOPS Oper. Syst. Rev.*, *37*(5), 164–177. doi:10.1145/1165389.945462

Carr, N. (2008). *The Big Switch - Rewiring the World from Edison to Google*. New York, NY: W. W. Norton.

Chapman, C., Emmerich, W., Marquez, F. G., Clayman, S., & Galis, A. (2011). *Software Architecture Definition for On-demand Cloud Provisioning*. Special Issue of Cluster Computing.

Clayman, S., Galis, A., Chapman, C., Toffetti, G., Rodero-Merino, L., Vaquero, L., et al. (2010). Monitoring Service Clouds in the Future Internet. In *Towards the Future Internet - Emerging Trends from European Research*, pp (115–126), Amsterdam, The Netherlands: IOS Press

Clayman, S., Galis, A., & Mamatas, L. (2010). Monitoring virtual networks with Lattice. In: *Management of Future Internet* - ManFI 2010, URL http://www.manfi.org/2010/

CloudWatch. Amazon CloudWatch, (n.d.) Retrieved from: http://aws.amazon.com/cloudwatch/

Cooke, A., Gray, A. J. G., Ma, L., Nutt, W., et al. (2003). R-GMA: An information integration system for Grid monitoring. In *Proceedings of the 11th International Conference on Cooperative Information Systems*, (pp. 462–481.) New York, NY: Springer

Emmerich, W., Butchart, B., Chen, L., Wassermann, B., & Price, S. L. (2005). Grid Service Orchestration using the Business Process Execution Language (BPEL). *Journal of Grid Computing, 3*(3- 4):283–304.

Irmos, IRMOS project, (n.d.) Retrieved from: http://www.irmosproject.eu/

Kivity, A. (2007). KVM: the linux virtual machine monitor," in *OLS '07: The 2007 Ottawa Linux Symposium*, (pp. 225–230)New York, NY: Springer

Massie, M. L., Chun, B. N., & Culler, D. E. (2003). The ganglia distributed monitoring system: Design, implementation and experience. *Parallel Computing*, 30.

Nagios, (n.d.) Retrieved from: http://www.nagios.org/

Newman, H. Legrand, I., Galvez, P., Voicu, R., & Cirstoiu, C. (2003). MonALISA: A distributed monitoring service architecture. In *Proceedings of CHEP03*, La Jolla, California.

Rochwerger, B., Breitgand, D., Levy, E., & Galis, A. (2009). The RESERVOIR model and architecture for open federated Cloud computing. *IBM Journal of Research and Development, 53*(4). doi:10.1147/JRD.2009.5429058

Rochwerger, B., Galis, A., Levy, E., Caceres, J. A., Breitgand, D., Wolfsthal, Y., et al. (2009b). Management technologies and requirements for next generation service oriented infrastructures. In 11th *IFIP/IEEE International Symposium on Integrated Management*. Washington, DC: IEEE Press.

Rochwerger, B., Tordsson, J., Ragusa, C., Breitgand, D., Clayman, S., & Epstein, A. (2011). RESERVOIR - When one Cloud is not enough. In *IEEE Computing*. Washington, DC: IEEE Press. doi:10.1109/MC.2011.64

Thain, D., Tannenbaum, T., & Livny, M. (2002). Condor and the Grid. In Berman, F., Fox, G., & Hey, T. (Eds.), *Grid Computing: Making the Global Infrastructure a Reality*. Hoboken, NJ: John Wiley & Sons Inc.

Vision, VISION project, (n.d.) Retrieved from: http://www.visioncloud.eu/

Wallis, P. (2008). Understanding Cloud computing, keystones and rivets., http://www.keystonesandrivets.com/kar/2008/02/Cloud-computing.html.

ADDITIONAL READING

Amazon, W. S. Amazon Web Services, http://aws.amazon.com/

Brewer, E. A. (2000) Towards robust distributed systems. In *Proceedings of the Annual ACM Symposium on Principles of Distributed Computing 19*, 7-10

4CaaSt. Building the PaaS Cloud of the Future, http://4caast.morfeo-project.org

Chapman, C., Emmerich, W., Marquez, F. G., Clayman, S., & Galis, A. (2010), *Elastic Service Management in Computational Clouds 19-23*, CloudMan 2010, IEEE/IFIP, Osaka, Japan

CIMI. Cloud Infrastructure Management Interface, DMTF, http://dmtf.org/sites/default/files/standards/documents/DSP0263_1.0.0b_0.pdf

Elmroth, E., Marquez, F. G., Henriksson, D., & Ferrera, D. P. (2009), Accounting and billing for federated cloud infrastructures, *8th Intl. Conf. Grid and Cooperative Computing*, (pp 268-275)

Jeery, K., and Burkhard, L., (2010), The Future of Cloud Computing: Opportunities For European Cloud Computing Beyond

Kang, C., and Wei-Min, Z.. (2009), Cloud Computing: System Instances and Current Research, *Journal of Software20*.(5)1337 1348

Legrand, I., Voicu, R., Cirstoiu, C., Grigoras, C., Betev, L., & Costan, A. (2009). Monitoring and Control of Large Systems With MonALISA. *Communications of the ACM, 52*(9), 49–55. doi:10.1145/1562164.1562182

McKinley, P. K., Samimi, F. A., Shapiro, J. K., & Tang, C. (2005). *Service Clouds: A distributed infrastructure for composing autonomic communication services. Technical Report, MSU-CSE-05-31*. East Lansing, Michigan: Department of Computer Science, Michigan State University.

Mejias, B., & Van Roy, P. (2010), *From Mini-clouds to Cloud Computing*. In Proceedings of the 2010 Fourth IEEE International Conference on Self-Adaptive and Self-Organizing Systems Workshop (SASOW '10). IEEE Computer Society, Washington, DC, USA, 234-238.

Milojicic, D. S., Llorente, I. M., & Montero, R. S. (2011). OpenNebula: A Cloud Management Tool. *IEEE Internet Computing, 15*(2), 11–14. doi:10.1109/MIC.2011.44

OCCI, Open Cloud Computing Interface, OGF

OpenNebula, The Open Source Toolkit for Data Center Virtualization. (OpenNebula), http://opennebula.org/

OVF. Open Virtualization Format, DMTF, http://dmtf.org/standards/cloud

RESERVOIR. Resources and Services Virtualization without Barriers, http://www.reservoir-fp7.eu

Rodero-Merino, L., Vaquero, L. M., Gil, V., Galan, F., Fontan, J., Montero, R. S., & Llorente, I. M. (2010). From infrastructure delivery to service management in clouds. *Future Generation Computer Systems, 26*(8), 1226–1240. doi:10.1016/j.future.2010.02.013

Tclouds, Tclouds Project, http://www.tclouds-project.eu/.

4WARD. The 4WARD Project - http://www.4ward-project.eu/

Youseff, L., Burtico, M., & Da Silva, D. (2008), *Toward a Unified Ontology of Cloud Computing*, Grid Computing Environments Workshop.

KEY TERMS AND DEFINITIONS

Elasticity: The growing and shrinking of resource usage at run-time.

Federated Cloud: A cloud that is made up more than one participant cloud. Each cloud is independent, but federates with other clouds to form a larger environment.

Infrastructure Provider: An organization that provides the infrastructure, (i.e servers and networks), that hosts and executes the virtual machines in a cloud. The infrastructure elements are leased out to service providers.

Service Cloud: A cloud that executes services on behalf of a service provider. This is different from a storage cloud or a network cloud.

Service Definition Manifest: The service provider defines the details and requirements of the application in a Manifest. This is done by specifying which virtual machine images are required to run.

Service Provider: An organization that creates an application and deploys it as a set of virtual machines on an infrastructure providers facilities. When the application executes, it will be a service for its end-users.

SM: The Service Manager is the component responsible for accepting the Service Definition Manifest and the raw VEE images from the service provider.

VAN: A Virtual Area Network, implemented as virtual Ethernet overlay services, connects services running in virtual machines with one or more private virtual networks in order to keep them independent of other services.

VEE: A virtual execution environment, which can be a virtual machine, executes the code of a service. A service cloud operates by acting as a platform for running virtualized applications in VEEs, which have been deployed on behalf of a service provider.

VEEH: A Virtual Execution Environment Host is a resource that can host a certain type of VEEs. For example one type of a VEEH can be a physical machine with the Xen hypervisor controlling it, whereas another type can be a machine with the KVM hypervisor.

VEEM: The Virtual Execution Environment Manager is the component responsible for the placement of VEEs into VEE hosts (VEEHs) and is responsible for optimization of a whole site.

Chapter 14
Achieving Flexible SLA and Resource Management in Clouds

Vincent C. Emeakaroha
Vienna University of Technology, Austria

Marco A. S. Netto
IBM Research, Brazil

Rodrigo N. Calheiros
The University of Melbourne, Australia

César A. F. De Rose
PUCRS, Brazil

ABSTRACT

One of the key factors driving Cloud computing is flexible and on-demand resource provisioning in a pay-as-you-go manner. This resource provisioning is based on Service Level Agreements (SLAs) negotiated and signed between customers and providers. Efficient management of SLAs and Cloud resources to reduce cost, achieve high utilization, and generate profit is challenging due to the large-scale nature of Cloud environments and complex resource provisioning processes. In order to advance the adoption of this technology, it is necessary to identify and address the issues preventing proper resource and SLA management. The authors purport that monitoring is the first step towards successful management strategies. Thus, this chapter identifies the SLA management and monitoring challenges in Clouds and federated Cloud environments, and proposes a novel resource monitoring architecture as a basis for resource management in Clouds. It presents the design and implementation of this architecture and presents the evaluation of the architecture using heterogeneous application workloads.

DOI: 10.4018/978-1-4666-1631-8.ch014

Copyright © 2012, IGI Global. Copying or distributing in print or electronic forms without written permission of IGI Global is prohibited.

INTRODUCTION

Cloud computing facilitates the implementation of scalable on-demand computing infrastructures combining concepts from virtualization, Grid, and distributed systems (Buyya et al., 2009; Elmroth & Tordsson, 2006). Cloud resources and services are provisioned based on Service Level Agreements (SLAs), which are contracts specified and signed between Cloud providers and their customers detailing the terms of the agreement including non-functional requirements, such as Quality of Service (QoS) and penalties in case of violations (Comuzzi et al., 2009). Self-manageable Cloud infrastructures are required in order to comply with users' requirements defined by SLAs and to minimize user interactions with the computing environment thereby enabling autonomic behavior (Kephart & Chess, 2003).

Flexible and reliable management of resource provisioning and SLA agreements in all IaaS, PaaS, and SaaS layers are of paramount importance to both Cloud providers and customers. It helps providers to avoid costly SLA penalties payable in case of violations, and to efficiently manage resources to reduce cost while optimizing the performance of customers' applications.

In order to guarantee SLA of customer applications, providers require sophisticated resource and SLA monitoring strategies to collect adequate information for the management process. The development of such monitoring strategies for Clouds is not trivial, and existing monitoring strategies are tailored toward either resource or SLA monitoring.

In this chapter, we identify the SLA management and monitoring challenges in Clouds and federated Cloud environments. We discuss existing monitoring strategies and the challenges they address. Finally, we present the Detecting SLA Violation infrastructure (DeSVi) architecture, which aims at detecting SLA violations through

resource monitoring in Cloud computing infrastructures. The DeSVi architecture is capable of managing the whole lifecycle of customer application provisioning in a Cloud environment, which includes resource allocation, application scheduling, and deployment. Cloud resources are monitored using a novel monitoring framework that is also capable of mapping low-level resource metrics to user-defined SLA parameters (Emeakaroha, Dustdar et al., 2010). The detection of possible SLA violations relies on the predefined service-level objectives and DeSVi relies on knowledge databases (Maurer, Dustdar et al., 2010) to manage such SLA violations.

The two key contributions of this chapter are i) the identification of resource monitoring, application monitoring, and SLA management challenges in Clouds and federated Cloud environments; and ii) the presentation of the novel DeSVi architecture for resource monitoring and SLA management in Cloud environments, which is also capable of suggesting optimal measurement intervals for efficient resource monitoring.

The rest of the chapter is organized as follows: In the background section, we identify some of the major challenges facing resource and SLA management in Clouds. In the management challenges and related work section, we discuss the existing solutions for monitoring in Clouds and federated Cloud environments. The section research motivation presents the FoSII project, which is the motivation for this research work. The DeSVi architecture description section presents our proposed and developed resource-monitoring infrastructure, which addresses some of the identified challenges in this chapter. In the evaluation section, we present the evaluation of our proposed monitoring architecture and some discussion about its applicability. We discuss some future research directions followed by the conclusions of the chapter in the last section.

BACKGROUND

In order for a Cloud provider to manage resources and enforce SLAs, there is a need for sophisticated monitoring techniques. Monitoring in Clouds can be carried out at different layers for different purposes.

Existing work on this topic focuses on various challenges hindering the capability of monitoring and SLA management in Cloud environments such as i) distributed application execution; ii) multi-tenancy application provisioning; iii) resource sharing between services; iv) the scalability of the monitoring mechanism; v) the establishment of SLA agreements; and vi) enforcement of the agreed SLA. The existing solutions we present in this chapter are focused on addressing some of these challenges. Resource and SLA monitoring in Clouds involves the use of monitoring agents embedded in the Cloud computing nodes to derive the appropriate information about the status of the computing node. The fact that an application can be executed in a distributed manner is a challenge to monitoring because the monitoring process of some component may fail, which can cause an inconclusive result that makes it impossible to determine the performance of the application and its resource consumption characteristics. Therefore, addressing this issue is an important research goal.

Most of the current Cloud providers are offering multi-tenant software as a service. That is, they provision one single application instance to multiple customers. This approach presents problems for monitoring regarding the issue of how to ensure SLAs for different customers. Another problem is resource sharing. Some Cloud providers use resource sharing when provisioning customer applications due to economic reasons. In such an environment, the execution of one application may affect the performance of the other. Thus, monitoring only Cloud resources is not enough to ensure the performance of distinct applications. Cloud environments can scale to thousands of nodes within a data center or can be distributed within geographical locations. Monitoring such an environment is not a trivial task because the Cloud provider has to ensure that the monitoring processes do not deteriorate the performance of the applications being provisioned. Furthermore, the scalability of the monitoring mechanism is another important issue to be considered. As already mentioned, Cloud environment can be of large-scale resources, which can be provisioned on-demand. Lack of scalable monitoring mechanism makes it impossible to monitor and manage such environments.

The establishment of SLAs between providers and customers electronically to reflect their wishes and terms of provisioning is not a trivial task. First of all, the provider and the customer must speak the same language in order to understand each other's terms before they could be able to negotiate and establish an agreement. After establishing the agreement, the provider must enforce the agreed terms while provisioning the customer application to avoid violating the agreement, which incurs penalty for the provider. The means of enforcing the agreed SLA is challenging because several problems may arise during application provisioning such as lack of resources or hardware failure.

MANAGEMENT CHALLENGES AND RELATED WORK

Regarding the fact that Cloud computing is a new trend, most of the existing monitoring strategies are based on the ideas used in related areas like distributed systems and Grid. In this section, we describe how each of the key challenges for monitoring and enabling SLAs in Cloud computing has been approached in such related areas.

Distributed Application Execution

In the area of distributed application execution, Gunter et al. (2000) present NetLogger, a distributed monitoring system that monitors and collects information of computer networks. Applications invoke NetLogger's API to survey the overload before and after some request or operation. This tool tackles the issue of distributed application execution monitoring and focuses mostly on network issues. Rellermeyer et al. (2007) propose the building, deploying, and monitoring of distributed applications with Eclipse. In their approach, they first analyse applications using Eclipse to determine the best way to deploy them in a distributed manner. After deploying the applications, they apply a tool to visualize the distributed execution of the applications and identify bottlenecks and failures. With this information they enforce the performance goals of the applications. Kilpatrick & Schwan (1991) present ChaosMon, an application for monitoring and displaying performance information for parallel and distributed systems. ChaosMon supports application developers in specifying performance metrics and to monitor these metrics visually to detect, analyse, and understand performance bottlenecks. This tool is a distributed monitor with a central control. It includes local monitors that reside on the target machines and communicate the monitored information to the central control. Wang et al. (2010) discuss a scalable run-time correlation engine for monitoring in a Cloud computing environment. Their approach is based on the use of log files to determine the behaviour of distributed applications. Thus, they developed a framework for run-time correlation of distributed log files in a scalable manner for enterprise applications in a Cloud environment. The correlation engine is capable of analysing and performing symptom matching with large volume of log data.

Multi-Tenancy Provisioning

Multi-tenancy application provisioning is becoming popular among Cloud providers that intend to cost-efficiently provision their single instance application to multiple customers. This market strategy is promising but there are still challenges in realizing it. Cheng et al. (2009) propose a multi-tenant oriented performance monitoring, detecting, and scheduling architecture based on SLAs. The authors aim at isolating and guaranteeing the performance goal of each tenant in the Cloud environment. This turns out to be complex because the provider is provisioning all the tenants with the same application instance but the SLAs for the applications are agreed on per tenant basis. In such a situation, the performance of some tenants' applications may be affected by abnormal resource consumptions by others since the Cloud hardware and software resources are shared by all tenants. To address these issues, the authors designed a dynamic SLA mechanism architecture, which monitors application grades, discovers abnormalities, and dynamically schedules shared resources to ensure tenants' SLAs and improve system performance.

Resource Sharing

Cloud computing technology is based on virtualization of physical machines to achieve mainly security and performance isolation. Therefore, VMs share resources of a physical machine in their operations. The VMs can be used to provision individual customer services and in some cases they are shared among customers. Efficient management of these shared resources to reduce cost and achieve high utilization is challenging. Huang & Wang (2010) present a combined push-pull model for resource monitoring in Cloud computing environments. Their approach is based on an extension of the prevailing push and pull model monitoring methods in Grids to Cloud computing. Their objective is to devise a monitoring framework capable to manage shared resources in Clouds. The motivation for this combination lies on the complementary characteristics of the two models. The push model has high consistency but low efficiency, whereas the pull model has low consistency but high efficiency. Thus, the authors combine these models by intelligently switching between them according to customer application requirements. Brandt et al. (2009) propose resource monitoring and management with OVIS to enable HPC in Cloud computing environments. The aim of the authors is to enable high performance computing in Cloud environments through sophisticated resource allocation mechanisms. The authors argue that intelligent resource utilization is a key factor for enabling HPC applications. In Clouds, these resources are heterogeneous and shared among users (particularly in virtualized environments) but there is a limited knowledge of the resource status. This can lead to overheads and resource contention among VMs, which brings down the overall performance. In their approach, the authors address this issue by using an advanced monitoring tool to dynamically characterize the resource and application state, and use the resulting information to optimally assign and manage resources. The degree to which the resources must be managed (i.e., monitored and analysed) depends on the resource usage model.

Scalability of Monitoring Mechanism

Scalable resource and application provisioning are among the key factors driving Cloud technology. Cloud computing promises scalable and on-demand resource provisioning in a pay-as-you-go manner. Cloud environments can scale to tens of thousands of computing devices. To manage such large-scale environments, scalable monitoring tools are paramount. Nevertheless, the development of such tools is not trivial. Soundararajan & Govil (2010) propose some techniques to tackle the challenges in building scalable virtualized datacenter management systems. The idea is to design a high-performance and robust management tool that scales from a few hosts to a large-scale Cloud datacenter. The design of the management

tool is driven by the need to create features that simplify daily operations, as datacenter grows in terms of hosts and the number of applications being provisioned, the management tool must scale to meet the increased demand. The authors showed how they realized a scalable management tool by addressing the following challenges: i) performance/fairness; ii) security; iii) robustness; iv) availability; and v) backward compatibility. Andreolini et al. (2011) present an assessment of overhead and scalability of system monitors for large data centers. The authors argue that there are several infrastructure monitoring tools designed to scale to very high number of physical machines, but such tools either collect performance measure at low frequency (missing to capture the dynamics of short-term task) or are not suitable for usage in Cloud environments. With such tools monitoring the correctness and efficiency of live migration is very difficult. The focus of the authors is to assess the scalability limits of a realistic monitoring infrastructure and to identify the bottlenecks in monitoring large-scale Cloud environments. To this effect, they designed and tested a monitoring infrastructure prototype. Voith et al. (2010) propose a path supervision framework for service monitoring in Infrastructure as a Service (IaaS) platforms. Their approach considers network applications and the monitoring of their metrics. The proposed framework takes measurements during the application execution to monitor the performance and detect SLA violations. To achieve high scalability, the measurement strategy is structured into stages for monitoring specific parts of the infrastructure. Fu & Huang (2006) propose GridEye, a service-oriented monitoring system with flexible architecture that is further equipped with an algorithm for prediction of the overall resource performance characteristics. The GridEye is designed to address scalability issues in monitoring distributed platforms considering the heterogeneity and distributed nature of Grid environments.

SLA Establishment

Cloud operations including resource and application provisioning are based on Service Level Agreements (SLAs). The specification and negotiation of such SLAs are still ongoing research. Koller & Schubert (2007) discuss autonomous SLA management using a proxy-like approach. They implemented an architecture that can be exploited to define SLA contracts. The architecture allows autonomous management of such contracts, once service providers and customers explicitly provide the requirements for the contracts. Based on the architecture, they outlined some guidelines on how such a system can be setup and reused. Their approach is based on WS-Agreement. Comuzzi et al. (2009) present an approach for establishment and monitoring of SLAs in complex service-based systems. They asserted that a service-provisioning infrastructure should allow the establishment of SLA contracts through coordinated negotiation among service providers and customers. In their approach, they define the process of SLA establishment adopted within the EU project SLA@SOI framework. They use WS-Agreement as the specification language and show the processes of negotiating electronic SLA between interested stakeholders. Debusmann & Keller (2003) propose SLA-driven management of distributed systems using the common information model. They describe their approach of mapping SLA definitions using the Web Service Agreement (WSLA) framework into common information model. In their approach, they present details of SLA establishment with WSLA language and discuss how the SLA objectives can be measured.

SLA Enforcement

To secure Cloud provider revenue and promote the attractiveness of Cloud computing, agreed SLAs must be guaranteed. The processes of enforcing the SLAs are complex and challenging. Ferretti et al. (2010) propose QoS-aware Clouds. In their approach they discuss the design and evaluation of a middleware architecture that enables SLA-driven dynamic configurations to respond effectively to the QoS requirements of the Cloud customer applications. The proposed architecture is proactive. It uses continuous monitoring and dynamic resource allocation to enforce the agreed SLA objectives for the customer applications. Skalkowski et al. (2010) present the application of the ESB architecture for distributed monitoring of the SLA requirements. The authors identified some issues affecting efficient SLA enforcement processes such as different technologies for the evaluation of the SLA documents, complex deployment processes, and scalability issues. Their SLA enforcement strategy is based on the continuous monitoring of the system to identify violation situations. Boniface et al. (2007) discuss dynamic service provisioning using GRIA (a Service Oriented Architecture framework) SLA. The authors explore how web service management using SLA and dynamic service provisioning can maximise resource utilization while fulfilling the QoS commitments to the existing customers. In their approach, they propose two possible policy enforcement strategies for handling SLA violation: i) prevention before violation and ii) reaction after violation. The prevention strategy is based on prediction of possible future violations, which can be obtained by monitoring predefined prevention thresholds. These prevention thresholds have to be defined on per SLA basis. With dynamic provisioning, when the prevention threshold is exceeded, a new service instance is started so that new requests are redirected to the new instance to ensure their SLA. The reaction strategy is only acceptable if the violation does not result in complete service failure. The service provider allows the violation of an SLA in order to enforce others. In such cases, it specifies priority for different SLAs based on business impact.

Federated Cloud Issues

The problems discussed so far are common for any type of Cloud infrastructure, which operates independently from other infrastructures. In this subsection, we discuss challenges that emerge when Cloud infrastructures are integrated in federated environments.

Currently, Cloud environments include dozens of independent, heterogeneous data centers, but many business operators have predicted that in the near future, the process of interoperable federated Clouds will start (Celesti et al., 2010). This is expected as a result of inefficiencies in the independent Cloud environments and the drive to exploit the full potentials of Cloud computing. For instance, if a provider does not have enough local resources to fulfil its customers' requirements, the provider will start denying the acceptance of new customers or cancelling some low-priority applications in order to guarantee the SLA of the high priority ones. This eventually leads to low profit for the provider and dissatisfaction for the customers.

The envisaged solution to this problem is Cloud federation (Rochwerger et al., 2009). Different Cloud providers running complementary service can mutually collaborate in sharing resources to fulfil their customers' demand. In this way, a provider could outsource resources from other providers when its local resources cannot sustain its workload. Through this means the provider obtains higher profit because it can serve more customers. Moreover, the expected revenue from these customers should be higher than the cost of borrowing extra resources in order to pay off (Goiri et al., 2010). Similarly, a provider that has underused resources can rent part of them to other providers to achieve higher utilization and increased profit. However, the expected benefit from renting out resources should be higher than the cost of maintaining them operative.

Based on the above discussion, determining the benefits of outsourcing or renting resources is a key factor to the success of federated Clouds. This is a new resource management challenge, which adds to the already existing resource management challenges in single Cloud environments.

To address the issue of resource management in federated Clouds, Goiri et al. (2010) propose a global scheduler to be used by all providers intending to collaborate. The scheduler is responsible for deciding where a customer application executes and manages the execution of the application. It decides the placement of the application on the provider's nodes and the amount of resource allocated to the nodes in order to guarantee the agreed SLA for the application while maximizing the profit of the provider. Clayman et al. (2010) tackle the issue of resource management in federated Clouds through service monitoring. They argue that the key factor hindering monitoring in federated environments is incompatible interfaces. For two Cloud providers to effectively exchange resources there is a need for standardized interfaces to support the exchange processes. Furthermore, they identified some issues to be considered in order to achieve federated monitoring such as: i) the setup of the federation in local and remote Cloud; ii) the setup of remote migration of computing nodes; iii) the connection for sending measurement information back to the local Cloud; and iv) the tear-down of remote connection in both the local and remote Cloud. Elmroth & Larsson (2009) propose technology-neutral interfaces for placement, migration, and monitoring of VMs in federated Clouds. The authors affirm that lack of interoperability impedes the advancement and adoption of Cloud computing technology. Overcoming this problem opens the door to varieties of business opportunities where customers are not burdened by vendor lock-in. They presented an algorithm for application placement and transfer of files, including VM images, between providers. Furthermore, they discussed their monitoring solution and how monitored data should be transferred among Cloud platforms. They also presented a novel approach for supporting application-level measurements in virtualized Cloud components.

Existing Monitoring Tools

In this section, we identify and differentiate some existing monitoring tools from our proposed DeSVi architecture. The aim is to show the contributions of our proposed monitoring framework.

GridEye (Fu & Huang, 2006) as described previously, is a service-oriented monitoring system. One of the limitations of this system is that it considers neither SLA management nor low-level metric mapping. Furthermore, we have described NetLogger (Gunther et al., 2000), which is a distributed monitoring system. However, it monitors only network resources.

Another interesting monitoring system is called Sandpiper (Wood et al., 2009). This system automates the process of monitoring and detecting hotspots and remapping/reconfiguring VMs whenever necessary. Sandpiper reminds DeSVi's goal, which is to avoid SLA violation. Similar to DeSVi, Sandpiper uses thresholds to check whether SLAs can be violated. However, it differs from our system by not allowing the mapping of low-level metrics, such as CPU and memory, to high-level SLA parameters, such as response time.

Balis et al. (2002) propose an infrastructure for Grid application monitoring. Their approach is based on OCM-G, which is a distributed monitoring system for obtaining information and manipulating applications running on the Grid. They aim to consider Grid-specific requirements and they design a suitable monitoring architecture to be integrated into the OCM-G system. Nevertheless, their approach does not support SLA enforcement in Clouds. RVision (Ferreto et al., 2002) is another monitoring system designed to be highly configurable. It supports monitoring sessions and dynamic linking of monitoring libraries and has low intrusion, which is necessary for environments

such as Cloud provider infrastructures. But they do not address mapping of low-level metrics to high-level SLAs.

Hershey & Runyon (2007) present SOA monitoring for enterprise computing systems. The authors strive to achieve comprehensive monitoring capabilities for federated environments in order to unite business requirements with emerging technologies and to facilitate service providers with the ability to respond proactively to events that occur during deployments. However, their approach is limited to monitoring only SOA metrics.

There are several other monitoring tools such as Bwatch, PARMON, SCMS and Ganglia. What distinguishes DesVi from these existing tools is that DesVi was designed with the focus on detecting SLA violations and it considers automatic mapping of low-level metrics, such as CPU, memory, and disk consumption to high-level QoS-related metrics such as throughput and response time.

Having discussed the challenges in resource and SLA management in Clouds and federated Clouds, and presented some existing solutions and approaches, we now present our novel resource monitoring architecture, which is a solution to scalable monitoring mechanism issues and shared resource-monitoring challenges. First of all, we describe our background and motivations in the next section before going into the proposed solution in Section 4.

RESEARCH MOTIVATION

One of the key advantages of using SLA in Cloud business is to guarantee customers a certain level of quality for accessing their services. In a situation where this level of quality is not met, the provider pays penalties for the breach of contract. In order to save Cloud providers from paying costly penalties and increase their profit, we devised the Low Level Metrics to High Level SLA (*LoM2HiS*) framework (Emeakaroha, Dustdar et al., 2010).

LoM2HiS is a building block of the FoSII (Foundations of Self-governing Infrastructures), which proposes models and concepts for autonomic SLA management and enforcement in Clouds. The FoSII infrastructure is capable of managing the whole lifecycle of self-adaptable Cloud services (Brandic, 2009). LoM2HiS is the FoSII component responsible for monitoring Cloud resources, mapping the low-level resource metrics to high-level SLA parameters, and detecting SLA violations as well as future SLA violation threats so as to react before actual SLA violations occur. FoSII is a research project funded by the Vienna Science and Technology Fund (WWTF) under the grant agreement ICT08-018. It is the motivation for the development of our proposed DeSVi architecture in this chapter. In the next section, we present an overview of the FoSII infrastructure.

FoSII Infrastructure Overview

The FoSII infrastructure relies on sophisticated monitoring techniques and advanced knowledge management strategies to achieve autonomic resource management and SLA enforcement. Figure 1 depicts the components of the FoSII infrastructure. It is divided into two parts: i) the monitoring part to determine the resource consumption behaviour and ii) the knowledge management part to analyse and provide reactive actions to manage the Cloud environment.

The self-management strategy in FoSII, as shown in Figure 1, consists of sensors for detecting changes in the desired state and for reacting to those changes. The host monitor sensors continuously monitor the infrastructure resource metrics (input sensor values arrow *a* in Figure 1) and provide the autonomic manager with the current resource status. The run-time monitor sensors

Figure 1. FoSII Overview

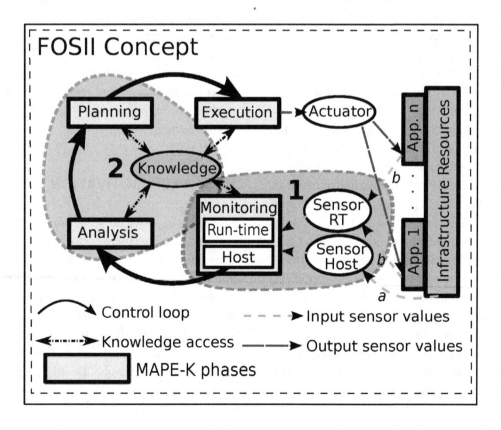

detect future SLA violation threats (input sensor values arrow *b* in Figure 1) based on resource usage experiences and predefined threat thresholds. We present below an overview of the FoSII components.

Monitoring

The LoM2HiS framework realizes the monitoring activities of FoSII. It comprises two core components, namely *host monitor* and *run-time monitor*. The former is responsible for monitoring low-level resource metrics, whereas the latter is responsible for metric mapping and SLA violation monitoring.

Cloud resource metrics are monitored by the *host monitor* using monitoring tools such as Gmond from Ganglia project (Massie et al., 2004). Resource metrics include downtime, uptime, and available storage. Based on the predefined mapping rules stored in a database, monitored metrics are periodically mapped to the SLA parameters. An example of an SLA parameter is service availability *Av*, which can be calculated using the resource metrics *downtime* and *uptime* as illustrated by the following mapping rule:

$$Availability = \left(1 - \frac{downtime}{uptime + downtime}\right) * 100.$$

The provider defines the mapping rules using appropriate Domain Specific Languages (DSLs). These rules are used to compose, aggregate, or convert the low-level metrics to form the high-level SLA parameter. The concept of detecting future SLA violation threats is designed by defining a more restrictive threshold than the SLA violation threshold known as threat threshold. Thus, calculated SLA values are compared with the predefined threat threshold in order to react before SLA violations happen.

The host monitor and the run-time monitor can be deployed on separate hosts. Thus, there is the need for a scalable communication mechanism facilitating the exchange of large numbers of messages.

Knowledge Management

The management aspect of FoSII is realized with a knowledge database component. This component is based on the Monitoring-Analysis-Plan-Execute cycle (Brandic, 2009). It receives the monitored information from the monitoring component and processes them in the different phases of the MAPE cycle to produce a reactive/management action to be executed by actuators (as shown in Figure 1) in the Cloud environment.

In our current approach, we have applied different strategies including Case-Based Reasoning (Maurer, Dustdar et al., 2010; Maurer, Sakellariou et al., 2010). CBR is the process of solving problems based on past experience. It tries to solve a *case* (a formatted instance of a problem) by looking for similar cases from the past and reusing the solutions of these cases to solve the current one. In general a typical CBR cycle consists of the following phases assuming that a new case has just been received: (i) retrieval of the most similar case or cases to the new one, (ii) reuse the information and knowledge in the similar case(s) to solve the problem, (iii) revision of the proposed solution, and (iv) retention of parts of this experience likely to be useful for future problem solving.

The proposed actions can be for example, to migrate a VM in a Cloud environment from one host to another or to increase the resource capacities of a certain VM in order to guarantee the SLA objectives of customer applications. The quality of the proposed action by the knowledge management is based on the accuracy of the monitored information. In this chapter, we concentrate on monitoring as the basic technique towards resource management and SLA enforcement in Cloud environments.

DESVI ARCHITECTURE DESCRIPTION

In this section we describe in details our proposed Detecting SLA Violation Infrastructure (DeSVi) architecture, its components, and the interactions among the components. The architecture is designed to manage the complete Cloud service provisioning lifecycle, which includes activities such as SLA monitoring, resource allocation, resource monitoring, and SLA violation detection.

The DeSVi architecture is depicted in Figure 2. The top-most layer represents the users (customers) who request service provisioning (step 1 in Figure 2) from the Cloud provider. The provider provisions the user services based on the agreed SLA parameters. The application deployer allocates necessary resources for the requested service and arranges its deployment on VMs (step 2). The VM Deployer and Configurator (Calheiros et al., 2010) takes care of the VM deployment processes and environmental configurations (step 3). The host monitor observes the metrics of the resource pool comprising VMs and physical hosts (step 4). The LoM2HiS framework performs the SLA violation detection.

In Figure 2 the arrow termed *Failover* indicates redundancy in the monitoring mechanism. The host monitor is designed to use monitoring agents like Gmond from Ganglia project (Massie et al., 2004), which are embedded in each node in the resource pool to monitor the metrics of the node. Such monitoring agents broadcast their monitored values to the other agents in the same resource pool, enabling access to the whole resource pool status from any node in the pool. The metric broadcasting mechanism is configurable and can be deactivated if necessary, even though it can obviate the problem of a bottleneck in the master node for accessing the monitored metrics of the resource pool.

The VM Deployer & Configurator and the Application Deployer are components for allocating resources and deploying applications in a Cloud environment. They are included in the architecture to show our complete solution. The Application Deployer is responsible for managing the execution of user applications, likewise *brokers* from Grid computing systems (Casanova, Wolski et al., 2000; Elmroth & Tordsson, 2006; Venugopal et al., 2006), focusing on parameter sweeping applications (Casanova, Berman et al., 2000). It simplifies the processes of transferring application input data to each VM, starting the execution, and collecting the results from the VMs to the front-end node. A scheduler located in the Application Deployer dynamically performs the mapping of the application tasks to VMs. The scheduler ensures that each slave process receives and processes tasks whenever the VM is idle. Extensive details on the Application Deployer and VM Deployer & Configurator are provided by (Emeakaroha, De Rose et al., 2010).

Monitoring Framework: Design

The LoM2HiS framework performs monitoring activities in our proposed architecture depicted in Figure 2. An overview of this monitoring framework is presented in Figure 3. The run-time monitor is designed to monitor services based on the negotiated and agreed SLAs. After agreeing on SLA terms, the service provider creates mapping rules for the LoM2HiS mappings (step 1 in Figure 3) using Domain Specific Languages (DSLs). An example rule is the availability equation presented earlier. Once the customer requests the provisioning of an agreed service (step 2), the run-time monitor loads the service SLA from the agreed SLA repository (step 3). Service provisioning is based on the infrastructure resources, which represent the hosts and network resources in a data center for hosting Cloud services. The monitoring agents measure the resource metrics, and the host monitor accesses the measured raw metrics for processing (step 4). The host monitor extracts the metric-value pairs from the raw metrics and transmits them periodically to the run-time

Figure 2. DeSVi Architecture

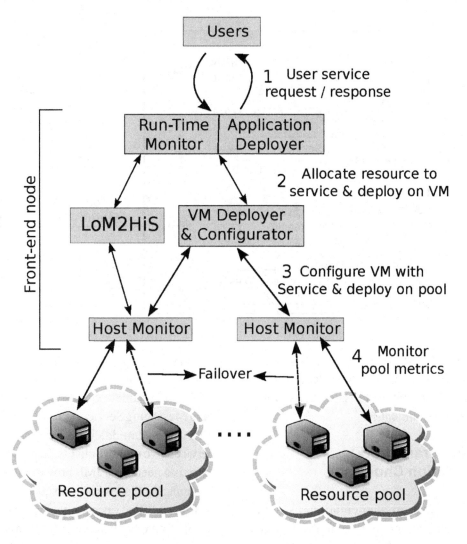

monitor (step 5) and to the knowledge component (step 6) using our designed communication model.

Upon reception of the measured metrics, the run-time monitor maps the low-level metrics based on predefined mapping rules to form an equivalent of the agreed SLA objectives. The resulting mapping is stored in the mapped metric repository (step 7), which also contains the predefined mapping rules. The run-time monitor uses the mapped values to monitor the status of the deployed services. In case future SLA violation threats are detected, it notifies (step 8) the knowledge com-

ponent to take preventive actions. The knowledge component also receives the predefined threat thresholds (step 8) for possible adjustments to environmental changes at run-time. This component works out an appropriate preventive action to avert future SLA violation threats based on the resource status (step 6) and defined rules. The knowledge component's decisions (e.g. assign more CPU to a virtual host) are executed on the infrastructure resources (step 9).

The separation of the host monitor and the run-time monitor makes it possible to deploy these

Figure 3. Monitoring Framework Overview

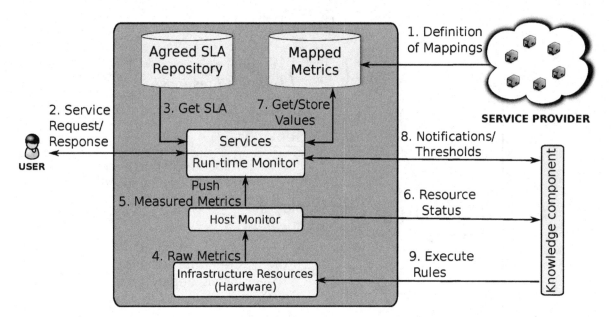

two components on different hosts. This decision is focused towards increasing the scalability of the framework and facilitating its usage in distributed and parallel environments.

Monitoring Framework: Implementation Choices

The *host monitor* implementation uses the standalone Gmond module from the Ganglia open source project (Massie et al., 2004) as its monitoring agent. Specifically, this component is used to monitor the low-level resource metrics. The monitored metric results are presented in an XML file and written to a predefined network socket. With our implemented Java routine, the host monitor listens to this network socket to access information about monitored metrics. Furthermore, we implemented an XML parser using the well-known open source SAX API (http://www.saxproject.org/) to parse the XML file in order to extract the metric-value pairs. These metric-value pairs are sent to the run-time monitor using a communication model.

We designed and implemented a scalable communication model for this purpose. Our communication model exploits the capabilities of the Java Messaging Service API, which is a Java message oriented middleware for sending messages between two or more clients. In order to use JMS, there is a need for a JMS provider that is capable of managing the sessions and queues. We used the well-established open source Apache ActiveMQ (http://activemq.apache.org/) for this purpose.

The *run-time monitor* implementation passes the received metric-value pairs into the ESPER engine (http://esper.codehaus.org/), which provides a filter to remove identical monitored values so that only changed values between measurements are delivered for further processing. This strategy drastically reduces the number of messages processed in the run-time monitor. The received metric-value pairs are stored in MySQL DB from where the mapping routine accesses them and applies the appropriate mappings. The agreed service SLA is also stored in the same DB accessible to the run-time monitor. Furthermore, we implemented a Java routine that checks for SLA violations by

Figure 4. Evaluation Testbed

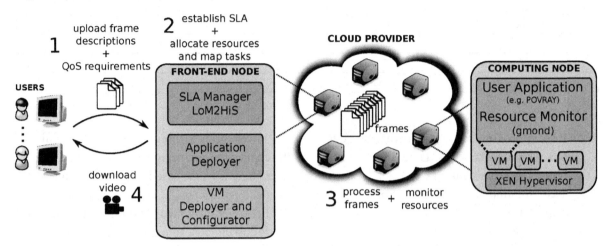

comparing the mapped SLA against the agreed service level objectives.

This framework was designed with the goal of being highly scalable. The JMS and ActiveMQ are used because they are platform-independent and because of the known scalability of the underlying ActiveMQ queues. Furthermore, the utilization of ESPER to filter out identical monitored information increases the efficiency of the framework. Especially in situations where the agents are monitoring in short time intervals.

EVALUATION AND DISCUSSION

This section presents evaluation results of the DesVi architecture. The goals of the evaluation are to test the capabilities of the proposed architecture in monitoring resources and detecting SLA violations and to show how DesVi can assist the monitoring process to determine the best cost-benefit measurement interval. It first presents the evaluation testbed and result analysis.

Achieved Results and Discussions

The evaluation testbed comprises a virtualized cluster composed of five Pentium 4 2.8GHz ma-

chines running Xen 3.4.0 on top of Oracle VM Server. One of the machines is used as the system front-end, which runs VM Deployer & Configurator, the application deployer, and LoM2His. Two VMs are deployed on each physical machine. The VMs are working nodes able to execute user applications. In this evaluation, we use POV-Ray workloads to represent user applications. The testbed and its components are presented in Figure 4.

As shown in Figure 4, users supply the QoS requirements in terms of SLOs (step 1 in Figure 4). At the same time the images with the POV-Ray applications and input data (frames) are uploaded to the front-end node. Based on the current system status, SLA negotiator establishes an SLA with the user. Thereafter, VM deployer starts configuration and allocation of the required VMs whereas application deployer maps the tasks to the appropriate VMs (step 3). In step 4 the application execution is triggered.

To evaluate DeSVi using heterogeneous load, three POV-Ray workloads were tested, each one with a different characteristic of time for rendering frames. The applications are:

1. **Fish:** rotation of fish on water. Time for rendering frames is variable.

279

Table 1. Application SLA Objective Definitions

SLA Parameter	Fish	Box	Vase
CPU	20%	15%	10%
Memory	297 MB	297 MB	297 MB
Storage	2.7 GB	2.6 GB	2.5 GB

2. **Box:** approximation of a camera to an open box with objects inside. Time for rendering frames increases during execution.
3. **Vase:** rotation of a vase with mirrors around. Time for processing frames is constant.

Three SLA documents are negotiated for the three POV-Ray workloads. These documents specify the level of Quality-of-Service that should be guaranteed for each workload during its execution. Table 1 presents the SLA objectives for each workload, which are used to monitor and detect SLA violations.

Table 2 presents the results of the experiments for 20-minute executions for each workload with different monitoring intervals. As it can be noticed,

the lower the measurement interval, the higher the chances of capturing an SLA violation. However, there is a cost associated with the measurements.

To evaluate this measurement cost, we defined the following cost function:

$$C = \mu * C_m + \sum_{\psi \in \{cpu, memory, storage\}} \alpha\left(\psi\right) * C_v$$

Where μ is the number of measurements, is the measurement cost, $\alpha(\psi)$ is the number of undetected SLA violations, and C_v is the cost of missing an SLA violation.

Table 2. Experimental Results

		Intervals	5s	10s	20s	30s	1min	2min
		Nr. of Measurements	240	120	60	40	20	10
Fish POV-Ray Application								
					Nr. of Violations			
SLA Parameter		**CPU**	105	90	42	28	16	8
		Memory	100	91	43	29	16	9
		Storage	97	91	43	29	17	9
Box POV-Ray Application								
SLA Parameter		**CPU**	85	37	22	17	12	7
		Memory	70	38	23	18	12	8
		Storage	65	38	23	18	11	8
Vase POV-Ray Application								
SLA Parameter		**CPU**	50	18	13	10	8	5
		Memory	45	19	14	11	9	6
		Storage	40	19	14	11	9	6

Figure 5. Measurement Costs for Each Workload

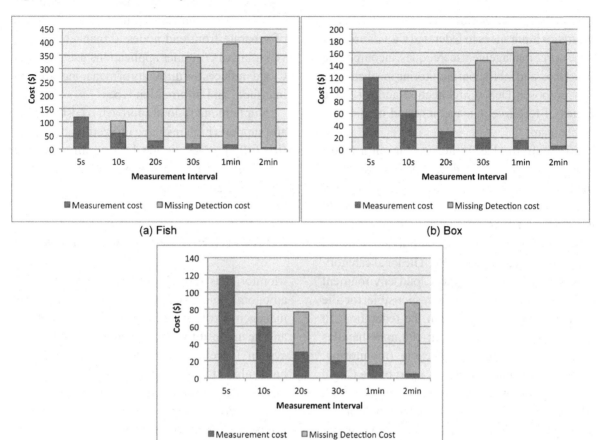

(a) Fish

(b) Box

(c) Vase

By applying the defined cost function onto the achieved outcome of Table 2, we obtained the results presented in Figure 5.

It can be noticed that the longer the measurement interval, the smaller the measurement cost, and that the higher the number of missed SLA violation detection, the higher the detection cost rises. This implies that to keep the detection cost low, the number of missed SLA violation must be low as well. In addition, there is no best-suited measurement interval for all workloads. Therefore, the architecture can sample the monitoring of a given workload in order to automatically define the best cost-benefit measurement interval.

From these evaluation results, we observe that different applications exhibit different resource consumption behaviours and consequently the optimal measurement interval varies. Our strategy of automatically determining the optimal measurement interval for different application types is key to achieving efficient application monitoring and resource management in Clouds.

Applying DeSVi in Federated Clouds

So far in the evaluation of our approach, we have concentrated in demonstrating the efficiency and usability of our approach in a single Cloud environment. In this section, we discuss the applicability of the DeSVi architecture in a federated Cloud environment. As described in Section 2.1, some of the major hindrances to federated Clouds are lack of resource management techniques, incompatible interfaces, and inefficient monitoring mechanisms. Our proposed DeSVi architecture addresses the issues of resource management and monitoring mechanism.

To apply the DeSVi architecture in a federated Cloud, we use a decentralized approach. In this approach, we create multiple front-end nodes (running the entire DeSVi architecture) to monitor and manage the application provisioning processes. The front-end nodes are divided into two categories – local and remote. The local category is responsible for the local Cloud environment and the remote category is responsible for the partner Clouds taking part in the federation. In the local category, each front-end node handles the whole provisioning lifecycle (monitoring, resource management, etc) in a part of the Cloud infrastructures while in the remote category, each front-end node is responsible for the whole provisioning lifecycle in a partner Cloud. The front-end nodes communicate with one another using our novel communication mechanism.

Customer application provisioning requests are first sent to the local front-end nodes for deployment. If none of the front-end nodes control enough resources to provision and manage the customer application execution, the request is forwarded to the remote front-end nodes for deployment in a partner Cloud environment. The remote front-end node deploys the customer application in a federated Cloud and arranges for the monitoring of the application execution using the monitoring framework and the return of the execution output to the customer.

With this approach, we achieve scalability and efficient management of resources and application provisioning in a federated Cloud environment. The division of the Cloud environment into parts whereby front-end nodes manage the parts overcomes the problem of a single bottleneck control unit and facilitates the scalability of the whole environment. Furthermore, the assignment of separate front-end nodes to manage the provisioning of customer applications using partner Clouds reduces the difficulty of managing different interfaces and information types.

Our federated Cloud approach is cost efficient and supports high resource utilization, because it first fully utilizes the local Cloud infrastructure resources before considering the utilization of remote Cloud resources.

FUTURE RESEARCH DIRECTIONS

Monitoring is the earliest step to be taken towards autonomic management of systems: no useful management of a system is possible without timely and accurate information about the underlying system. Therefore, the management system should be combined with other components in order to enable effective autonomous management of the system. For example, the DeSVi architecture can be combined with a knowledge management system to analyse the monitored data and predict future behaviour of the system.

Behaviour prediction and efficient autonomic management decision depend on robust intelligent systems able to analyse historical data in a timely manner and to extract useful information from them so the best decision for the given moment is taken. To achieve this, we foresee an evolution of advanced monitoring tools that include mapping rules to capture high-level requirements and translate them to precise low-level metrics based on previous observations of the system at work.

In the near future, we anticipate the introduction of architectures to support management at both PaaS and SaaS layers. These architectures shall be an extension of the existing ones (such as the DeSVi architecture), currently supporting only IaaS layer. The realization of management architectures at these layers will be based on the capabilities to collect information from software platforms supporting user applications (for the PaaS) and by directly monitoring the application offered at SaaS layer.

Another management challenge faced by Cloud providers is energy efficiency objectives. Large consumption of electricity is a major contributor to the rising of the atmospheric CO2 level, and Cloud data centres are at the forefront. There already exist some EU regulations and campaigns demanding cleaner businesses, therefore, Cloud providers must seek ways to improve their energy consumption. Monitoring strategies in our opinion will play a major role in energy management because it will help to detect unused physical and virtual resources that could be shut down to save energy.

Finally, we envision the development of advanced management systems in the future that will demand combination of resource, SLA, and energy consumption monitoring strategies for making better use of Clouds and federated Cloud environments.

CONCLUSION

Flexible and reliable management of SLA agreements and Cloud resources represent open research challenges in Cloud computing. Advantages of adequate management strategies are economically and ecologically indispensible. For instance, on the one hand it helps Cloud providers to prevent SLA violations thereby avoiding costly violation penalties and increasing their profits. On the other hand, it helps to reduce the cost of data center maintenance whereby unused resources are shutdown to save energy and reduce carbon oxide emission.

In this chapter, we identified the challenges facing SLA management and monitoring in Clouds and federated Cloud environments. The challenges recognized problems in Clouds such as the issue of distributed application execution, multi-tenancy application provisioning, resource sharing among applications or VMs, development of scalable monitoring tools, issues with SLA establishment and enforcement, and interoperability problems in federated Cloud environments. We discussed how these issues are affecting Cloud management and presented some existing approaches addressing them.

Furthermore, we proposed DeSVi - a novel resource monitoring architecture for monitoring Cloud resource metrics and detecting SLA violations. The DeSVi architecture is designed to manage the whole application provisioning lifecycle, which includes resource allocation, deployment, and monitoring processes. In this chapter, it represented a solution to scalable monitoring mechanism issues and shared resource-monitoring problems.

We evaluated the DeSVi architecture using three heterogeneous applications based on POV-Ray in a real Cloud testbed. From our experiments, we observed that the architecture was able to monitor resource status and detect SLA violations. Furthermore, we noticed that there are no single best measurement intervals for all types of applications. Therefore, the architecture can sample the monitoring of a given workload in order to automatically define the best cost-benefit measurement interval for efficient monitoring of the application execution.

REFERENCES

Andreolini, M., Colajanni, M., & Lancellotti, R. (2011). Assessing the overhead and scalability of system monitors for large data centers. In *Proceedings of the First International Workshop on Cloud Computing Platforms* (CloudCP '11). ACM, New York, NY, USA.

Balis, B., Bubak, M., Funika, W., Szepieniec, T., & Wismller, R. (2002). An infrastructure for grid application monitoring. In *Recent Advances in Parallel Virtual Machine and Message Passing Interface New York*. NY: Springer. doi:10.1007/3-540-45825-5_16

Boniface, M., Phillips, S. C., & Sanchez-macian, A. (2007). Dynamic Service Provisioning Using GRIA SLAs. In *Proceedings of the International Workshop on Service-Oriented Computing (IC-SOC'07)* Amsterdam, The Netherlands: IOS Press.

Brandic, I. (2009). Towards Self-Manageable Cloud Services, In *Proceedings of the 33rd Annual IEEE International Computer Software and Applications Conference, 2009. COMPSAC '09.,2*128-133, 20-24

Brandt, J., Gentile, A., Mayo, J., Pebay, P., Roe, D., Thompson, D., & Wong, M. (2009). Resource monitoring and management with OVIS to enable HPC in Cloud computing environments, In *Proceedings of the IEEE International Symposium on Parallel & Distributed Processing, 2009. IPDPS 2009.* 1-8, 23-29

Buyya, R., Yeo, C. S., Venugopal, S., Broberg, J., & Brandic, I. (2009). Cloud computing and emerging IT platforms: Vision, hype, and reality for delivering computing as the 5th utility. In *Future Generation Computing. System, 25*(6), 599–616.

Calheiros, R. N., Buyya, R., & De Rose, C. A. F. (2010). Building an automated and self-configurable emulation testbed for Grid applications. *Software, Practice & Experience, 40*(5), 405–429.

Casanova, H., Legrand, A., Zagorodnov, D., & Berman, F. (2000). Heuristics for scheduling parameter sweep applications in Grid environments. In *Proceedings of the Heterogeneous Computing Workshop (HCW'00)*, New York, NY: Springer.

Casanova, H., Obertelli, G., Berman, F., & Wolski, R. (2000). The AppLeS Parameter Sweep Template: User-level Middleware for the Grid. In *Proceedings of the Supercomputing (SC'00)*, New York, NY: ACM Press.

Celesti, A., Tusa, F., Villari, M., & Puliafito, A. (2010). How to Enhance Cloud Architectures to Enable Cross-Federation, In *Proceedings of the IEEE 3rd International Conference on Cloud Computing (CLOUD), 2010,*337-345, 5-10

Cheng, X., Shi, Y., & Li, Q. (2009). A multi-tenant oriented performance monitoring, detecting and scheduling architecture based on SLA, In *Proceedings of the 2009 Joint Conferences on Pervasive Computing (JCPC)* 599-604, 3-5

Clayman, S., Galis, A., Chapman, C., Toffetti, G., Rodero-Merino, L., & Vaquero, L. M. (2010). *Monitoring Service Cloud in the Future Internet. Towards the Future Internet - Emerging Trends from European Research, ISBN*. Amsterdam, The Netherlands: IOS Press.

Comuzzi, M., Kotsokalis, C., Spanoudakis, G., & Yahyapour, R. (2009). Establishing and Monitoring SLAs in Complex Service Based Systems. In *Proceedings of the 2009 IEEE International Conference on Web Services* (ICWS '09) 783-790 Washington, DC, USA IEEE Computer Society

Debusmann, M., & Keller, A. (2003). Sla-Driven Management Of Distributed Systems Using The Common Information Model, In *Proceedings of the IFIP/IEEE International Symposium on Integrated Management.*

Elmroth, E., & Larsson, L. (2009). Interfaces for Placement, Migration, and Monitoring of Virtual Machines in Federated Clouds, In *Proceedings of the Eighth International Conference on Grid and Cooperative Computing, 2009. GCC '09.*253-260, 27-29

Elmroth, E., & Tordsson, J. (2006). A Grid resource broker supporting advance reservations and benchmark-based resource selection. In *Applied Parallel Computing*. New York, NY: Springer. doi:10.1007/11558958_128

Emeakaroha, V. C., Brandic, I., Maurer, M., & Dustdar, S. (2010). Low level Metrics to High level SLAs - LoM2HiS framework: Bridging the gap between monitored metrics and SLA parameters in Cloud environments, In *Proceedings of the 2010 International Conference on High Performance Computing and Simulation (HPCS)*, 48-54

Emeakaroha, V. C., Calheiros, R. N., Netto, M. A. S., Brandic, I., & De Rose, C. A. F. (2010). DeSVi: An Architecture for Detecting SLA Violations in Cloud Computing Infrastructures. In *Proceedings of the International ICST Conference on Cloud Computing (CloudComp'10)*

Ferreto, T. C., De Rose, C. A. F., & De Rose, L. (2002). RVision: An open and high configurable tool for cluster monitoring. In *Proceedings of the 2nd IEEE/ACM International Symposium on Cluster Computing and the Grid (CCGRID)*, Washington, DC: IEEE Press

Ferretti, S., Ghini, V., & Panzieri, F. Pellegrini, & M., Turrini, E., (2010). QoS–Aware Clouds. In *Proceedings of the IEEE 3rd International Conference on Cloud Computing (CLOUD)*. 321-328

Fu, W., & Huang, Q. (2006). GridEye: A Service-oriented Grid Monitoring System with Improved Forecasting Algorithm, In *Proceedings of the Fifth International Conference on Grid and Cooperative Computing Workshops, 2006. GCCW '06*. 5-12

Goiri, I., Guitart, J., & Torres, J. (2010). Characterizing Cloud Federation for Enhancing Providers' Profit, In *Proceedings of the 2010 IEEE 3rd International Conference on Cloud Computing (CLOUD)* 123-130.

Gunter, D., Tierney, B., Crowley, B., Holding, M., & Lee, J. (2000). NetLogger: a toolkit for distributed system performance analysis, In *Proceedings of the 8th International Symposium on Modeling, Analysis and Simulation of Computer and Telecommunication Systems*. 267-273

Hershey, P., & Runyon, D. (2007). SOA Monitoring for Enterprise Computing Systems, In *Proceedings of the 11th IEEE International Enterprise Distributed Object Computing Conference (EDOC 2007)*, 443

Huang, H., & Wang, L. (2010). P&P: A Combined Push-Pull Model for Resource Monitoring in Cloud Computing Environment, In *Proceedings of the 2010 IEEE 3rd International Conference on Cloud Computing (CLOUD)*. 260-267.

Kephart, J. O., & Chess, D. M. (2003). The vision of autonomic computing, In *Computer*, *36*(1) 41- 50 Kilpatrick, C., & Schwan, K., (1991). ChaosMON —Application-specific Monitoring and Display of Performance Information for Parallel and Distributed systems. In *SIGPLAN Not. 26*(12) 57-67.

Koller, B., & Schubert, L. (2007). Towards autonomous SLA management using a proxy-like approach. In *Multiagent Grid System*, *3*(3), 313–325.

Massie, M. L., Chun, B. N., & Culler, D. E. (2004). The Ganglia distributed monitoring system: Design, implementation and experience. *Parallel Computing*, *30*(7), 817–840. doi:10.1016/j.parco.2004.04.001

Maurer, M., Brandic, I., Emeakaroha, V. C., & Dustdar, S. (2010) Towards Knowledge Management in Self-adaptable Clouds. In *Proceeding of the 4th International Workshop of Software Engineering for Adaptive Service-Oriented Systems (SEASS'10)*

Maurer, M., Brandic, I., & Sakellariou, R. (2010). Simulating Autonomic SLA Enactment in Clouds using Case Based Reasoning. In *Proceedings of the ServiceWave*, Ghent, Belgium

Prodan, R., & Ostermann, S. (2009). A survey and taxonomy of infrastructure as a service and web hosting Cloud providers, In *Proceedings of the 10th IEEE/ACM International Conference on Grid Computing* 17-25

Rellermeyer, J. S., Alonso, G., & Roscoe, T. (2007). Building, Deploying, and Monitoring Distributed Applications with Eclipse and R-OSGI. In *Proceedings of the 2007 OOPSLA workshop on eclipse technology eXchange* (eclipse '07). 50-54 New York, NY, USA: ACM

Rochwerger, B., Breitgand, D., Levy, E., Galis, A., Nagin, K., & Llorente, I. M. (2009). The Reservoir Model and Architecture for Open Federated Cloud Computing. *IBM Journal of Research and Development, 53*(4), 535–545. doi:10.1147/JRD.2009.5429058

Skalkowski, K., Sendor, J., Slota, R., & Kitowski, J. (2010). Application of the ESB Architecture for Distributed Monitoring of the SLA Requirements, In *Proceedings of the Ninth International Symposium on Parallel and Distributed Computing (ISPDC)*.203-210

Soundararajan, V., & Govil, K. (2010). Challenges in Building Scalable Virtualized Datacenter Management. In *SIGOPS Oper. Syst. Rev. 44*(4) 95-102.

Venugopal, S., Buyya, R., & Winton, L. (2006). A Grid Service Broker for Scheduling e-Science Applications on Global Data Grids. *Concurrency and Computation, 18*(6), 685–699. doi:10.1002/cpe.974

Voith, T., Oberle, K., Stein, M., Oliveros, E., Gallizo, G., & Kübert, R. (2010). A Path Supervision Framework A Key for Service Monitoring in Infrastructure as a Service (IaaS) Platforms, In *Proceedings of the 36th EUROMICRO Conference on Software Engineering and Advanced Applications (SEAA)* 127-130

Wang, M., Holub, V., Parsons, T., Murphy, J., & O'Sullivan, P. (2010). Scalable Run-Time Correlation Engine for Monitoring in a Cloud Computing Environment, In *Proceedings of the 17th IEEE International Conference and Workshops on Engineering of Computer Based Systems (ECBS)* Washington, DC: IEEE Press

Wood, T., Shenoy, P. J., Venkataramani, A., & Yousif, M. S. (2009). Sandpiper: Black-box and gray-box resource management for virtual machines. *Computer Networks, 53*(17), 2923–2938. doi:10.1016/j.comnet.2009.04.014

ADDITIONAL READING

Balakrishnan, P., & Somasundaram, T. S. (2011). SLA Enabled CARE Resource Broker. In *Proceedings of Future Generation Computer Systems, 27*(3), 265–279. doi:10.1016/j.future.2010.09.006

Balaton, Z., & Gombs, G. (2003). Resource and Job Monitoring in the Grid. In *Proceedings of Euro-Par '03*.

Balaton, Z., Kacsuk, P., & Podhorszki, N. (2001). Application Monitoring in the Grid with GRM and PROVE. In *Computational Science ICCS, 2073*

Balis, B., Bubak, M., Funika, W., Szepieniec, T., Wismüller, R., & Radecki, M. (2003). Monitoring Grid Applications with Grid-Enabled OMIS Monitor. In *Proceedings of European Across Grids Conference*. 230-239.

Chung, W. C., & Chang, R. S. (2009). A New Mechanism for Resource Monitoring in Grid Computing. In *Proceedings of Future Generation Computer Systems, 25*(1), 1–7. doi:10.1016/j.future.2008.04.008

De Chaves, S. A., Uriarte, R. B., & Westphall, C. B. (2011). Toward an Architecture for Monitoring Private Clouds. In Washington, DC:IEEE Communications Society. *Proceedings of IEEE Communications Magazine, 49*(12), 130–137. doi:10.1109/MCOM.2011.6094017

Dobson, G., & Sanchez-Macian, A. (2006). Towards Unified QoS/SLA Ontologies. In *Proceedings of the 2006 IEEE Services Computing Workshops (SCW '06)*

Emeakaroha, V. C., Netto, M. A. S., Calheiros, R. N., Brandic, I., Buyya, R., & De Rose, C. A. F. (2011). Towards Autonomic Detection of SLA Violations in Cloud Infrastructures. In *proceedings of Future Generation Computer Systems.*

Ferretti, S., Ghini, V., Panzieri, F., Pellegrini, M., & Turrini, E. (2010). Qos-Aware Clouds. In *Proceedings of 2010 IEEE 3rd International Conference on Cloud Computing (CLOUD)* 321 - 328

Krauter, K., Buyya, R., & Maheswaran, M. (2002). A Taxonomy and Survey of Grid Resource Management Systems for Distributed Computing. In *proceedings of Software Practice and Experience, 32*(2), 135–164. doi:10.1002/spe.432

Litke, A., Konstanteli, K., Andronikou, V., Chatzis, S., & Varvarigou, T. (2008). Managing Service Level Agreement Contracts in OGSA-based Grids. In *Proceedings of Future Generation Computer Systems, 24* (4 245 – 258

Sotomayor, B., Montero, R. S., Llorente, I. M., & Foster, I. (2009). Virtual Infrastructure Management in Private and Hybrid Clouds. In *Proceedings of IEEE Internet Computing, 13*(5), 14–22. doi:10.1109/MIC.2009.119

Theilman, W., Yahyapour, R., & Butler, J. (2008). Multi-level SLA Management for Service-Oriented Infrastructures. In *Proceedings of 1st European Conference on Towards a Service-Based Internet.*

Yeo, C. S., & Buyya, R. (2007). Pricing for Utility-driven Resource Management and Allocation in Clusters. In *Proceedings of International Journal of High Performance Computer Applications, 21*(4), 405–418. doi:10.1177/1094342007083776

KEY TERMS AND DEFINITIONS

Cloud Federation: The practice of connecting two or more independent Cloud computing environments for the purpose of load-balancing and cost-efficiently provisioning of services.

Cloud Resource Monitoring: The act of continually or periodically observing Cloud resources to determine changes and trends in their status. E.g., physical machines, virtual machines, storage.

Multi-Tenancy: The ability to provision one single application instance to multiple customers with the flexibility that each customer can have different configurations.

On-Demand Resource Provisioning: The flexibility of allocating extra resources automatically to a service at any point in time.

Self-Management: A process by which systems can manage their operations without human intervention.

SLA: Service Level Agreement is a contract signed between a Cloud provider and a Cloud customer, which states the terms of provisioning including non-functional requirements such as throughput, availability, etc; and penalties in case of violations.

SLA Management: The act of managing the agreed SLA terms to avoid violations thereby ensuring the performance of the customer service and the profit of the provider.

Chapter 15
Resource Management Mechanisms to Support SLAs in IaaS Clouds

David Breitgand
IBM Haifa Research Lab, Israel

Amir Epstein
IBM Haifa Research Lab, Israel

Benny Rochwerger
IBM Haifa Research Lab, Israel

ABSTRACT

In this chapter we focus on the Infrastructure as a Service (IaaS) model that epitomizes many of the generic resource management problems arising in cloud computing.

The authors consider elastic multi-VM workloads corresponding to multi-tier application and study the fundamental problems of VM placement optimization, subject to policy constraints, elasticity requirements, and performance SLAs. Numerous algorithmic and architecture proposals appeared recently in the area of resource provisioning in IaaS. The chapter provides a comprehensive review of related work in this field and presents the authors' recent scientific findings in this area obtained in the framework of an EU funded project, RESERVOIR. The chapter discusses horizontal elasticity support in IaaS, its relationship to SLA protection, VM placement optimization and efficient capacity management to improve cost-efficiency of cloud providers. Elastic services comprise multiple virtualized resources that can be added and deleted on demand to match variability in the workload. A Service owner profiles the service to determine its most appropriate sizing under different workload conditions. This variable sizing is formalized through a service level agreement (SLA) between the service owner and the cloud provider. The Cloud provider obtains maximum benefit when it succeeds to fully allocate the resource set demanded by the elastic service subject to its SLA. Failure to do so may result in SLA breach and financial losses to the provider. The chapter defines a novel combinatorial optimization problem called elastic services placement problem to maximize the provider's benefit from SLA compliant placement.

DOI: 10.4018/978-1-4666-1631-8.ch015

Copyright © 2012, IGI Global. Copying or distributing in print or electronic forms without written permission of IGI Global is prohibited.

It demonstrates the feasibility of our approach through a simulation study, showing that we are capable of consistently obtaining good solutions in a time efficient manner. In addition, we discuss how resource utilization level can be improved through an advanced capacity management leveraging elastic workload resource consumption variability.

INTRODUCTION

We consider a popular Infrastructure as a Service (IaaS) Cloud Computing paradigm where service providers rent VM instances on-demand from the IaaS provider on a "pay-as-you-go" basis to provide functionality (service) using these resources. In this model, the payment per VM instance comprises an initial fixed fee for ordering an instance and a variable usage based fee where usage is aggregated in each billing period.

To take advantage of the "pay-as-you-go" model, service providers strive to use just the needed capacity to satisfy the target end-user QoS at any given time. This is termed thin provisioning to differentiate it from the traditional over-provisioning methodology that plans capacity for peak workloads. Since workload applied to services varies with time, to match these variations with minimum capacity, VM instance sets comprising the services are *elastic*. The structure of an elastic service remains fixed, but the number of instances and/or size of the instances may vary.

The elastic behavior of the services is programmed using service-specific elasticity policies (also known as elasticity rules) that match workload variations with on demand capacity allotments ("Right Scale"; n.d., Rochwerger et al., 2009). In response to executing an elasticity rule, the IaaS provider needs to solve the service placement optimization problem to accommodate new VMs and already deployed ones to maximize profit from service provisioning. In any given billing period, each elastic service contributes to the total revenue of the IaaS provider via the per VM usage based payments aggregated over this period. Currently most IaaS providers offer VM instances from a diversified catalog suggesting a number

of discrete hardware configurations. For example, Amazon EC2 offers "small", "large", "extra large" and a few other VM configurations, where each configuration represents a different VM sizing and is charged using different instance hour rate[1]. Usually, VM types are provided under a single standard availability SLA. In ("RESERVOIR," 2008), availability SLA are further diversified and extended as follows. At any given time, the set of VMs mandated by the active elasticity rules has to be placed in its entirety to comply with the availability SLA of the service. We refer to this as *set requirements*.

The main focus of our study is SLA compliant placement of multi-VM elastic services under set requirements and placement constraints. In addition, we discuss leveraging statistical multiplexing, inherent to the elastic workloads to improve cost-effoiciency of the cloud provisioning.

Our proposed approach to placement is general and deals with a variety of placement restriction types. In this work, however, we focus on *anti-collocation* constraints that demand all VMs of the service to be placed on different physical hosts[2]. While deployment of VMs under placement constraints has received a significant attention in the literature, to the best of our knowledge, this problem was not considered in conjunction with the set requirements.

In this chapter we present Elastic Service Placement Problem (ESPP) that generalizes the model studied by Urgaonkar et al. (2007). The input to ESPP includes set of hosts and set of services, where each service is composed of a set of VMs. Each VM has size and profit that may depend on its type, SLA and the provider costs. In general, each VM may have different profit and capacity demands (size) when assigned to different hosts.

The goal of this optimization problem is to maximize the profit obtained from the placed VMs, while respecting the set requirements, placement constraints and resource capacity constraints.

Solving ESPP may entail VM migrations which incur various operational costs. In ESPP migration costs are directly incorporated into the placement problem by subtracting them from the profit of a migrated VM. Modeling of migration costs is highly non-trivial due to second order effects migrations might have on the migrated service and other running services. To the best of our knowledge, there is no single model thus far that accounts for all such effects caused by migrations. It should be noted that exact modeling of the migration costs in monetary terms is outside of the scope of this chapter. Rather than that we introduce synthetic migration costs used as a management lever to control the total number of migrations and potential profit loss caused by them. Although in the current practice of public cloud management, live migrations are not widely used, we believe that as technology underpinning migration improves, more providers will find the benefits of improved resource utilization offered by it attractive.

The IaaS model offers potential for higher resource utilization through resource pooling, which enables leveraging statistical multiplexing of the resource demands of the workloads and over-subscribe physical capacity. This approach is similar to over-subscribing of data communication links that has been used successfully for long time thanks to leveraging statistical multiplexing of the traffic.

Over-commit of the physical capacity is done transparently to the cloud customers, who expect to continue receiving a certain quality of service (possibly formalized through the Service Level Agreements) in spite of over-commit. Obviously, in an SLA based IaaS, over-committing physical resources exposes a cloud provider to a greater risk of decreasing quality of service and breaking Service Level Agreements (SLA) compliance.

Therefore, it is crucial to determine an overcommit level that allows to meet customers QoS expectations and comply with the SLA obligations using minimal physical capacity.

VM placement optimization and over-commit management are closely inter-related problems. These problems are generic to any cloud, be it public, private, hybrid, or generally federated. Although from the cloud customer's perspective, cloud provides infinite resources pool, the resources of any individual provider are always limited. As explained above, conditions of the perfect competition in the public cloud marketplace and the need to reduce the total cost of ownership in private and hybrid clouds, are the generic driving forces behind VM placement optimization and capacity management.

The rest of this chapter is organized as follows. In Section 2 we provide background and motivation for ESPP. In Section 3 we define our problem. We present a combinatorial auction view of ESPP and give a multi-unit combinatorial auctions formulation for ESPP in Section 4. The column generation method for solving ESPP is presented in Section 5. Numerical results for ESPP are presented in Section 6, showing that our method finds near-optimal solutions for large resource pools efficiently. We outline the future research directions in Section 7 and conclude our chapter in Section 8.

BACKGROUND

To put our discussion into a specific context, we abstract a generic management framework of an IaaS cloud as follows:

- **Service Manager:** receives service provisioning requests and presents Placement Optimizer with the VM sets that should be placed on the physical infrastructure at any point in time.

- **Placement Optimizer:** calculates an optimal placement to maximize the provider's profit from service placement (over all services).
- **Placement Planner:** calculates an optimal schedule of management actions required to move from the current placement to the new placement calculated by the Placement Optimizer.
- **Placement Actuator:** implements the placement schedule provided by the Placement Planner.

Current practices in cloud computing set customer expectations high, implying that service provisioning requests should be served very fast, usually on the scale of minutes. In this work we focus on the Placement Optimizer component developing efficient and scalable algorithms for a core optimization problem of maximizing profit while maximally satisfying availability SLAs and minimizing network overhead due to migrations.

Each service provisioning request contains the structure of the service including the number of VMs of each type, deployment constraints such as collocation and anti-collocation, elasticity rules that prescribe specific configurations under different environmental conditions, minimum and maximum number of instances of VMs of each type and availability Service Level Objectives (SLO) of the service. It is the responsibility of Service Manager to monitor performance of the service and change resource allotments in accordance with the elasticity rules. These rules may require scaling-up or scaling-down of the service by adding or removing VM instances subject to the maximal and minimal limits defined for the service.

Availability SLO specifies availability percentile that should be achieved for the VMs comprising the service *irrespectively of what elasticity rules are executed and when*, as long as resource demands are between the minimum and maximum limits contracted for the service. It

should be stressed that committing to availability SLO of an elastic service is especially challenging because the intervals over which availability of VMs are calculated may not even overlap for different VMs comprising an elastic service. To cope with this challenge, we propose a different approach to the management of availability guarantees. Namely, at any given moment we consider a VM set comprising the service (as mandated by the elasticity policy effective at this moment in time) as an indivisible whole that should be mapped on physical machines subject to capacity constraints and deployment constraints. In other words, elastic service concept implies a placement model where all VMs of the current service configuration should be placed for the service to be considered available[3].

Non-placing a service does not imply an immediate SLO violation as long as availability percentile of the service is not violated in this billing period.

The value generated by VM sets for the provider depends on the number of VMs in the set and VM types of the instances comprising the set. The direct consequence of the availability SLO protection model described above is that VM sets that are structurally the same (in terms of VM types and number of instances) may have different values at different points in time depending on their availability SLO compliance history. Namely, there are three options that should be considered by the Placement Optimizer w.r.t. every VM set:

- VM set is included in the next placement: the provider obtains revenue from the set calculated as a sum of per-VM revenues on the instance-hour basis;
- VM set is excluded from the next placement, but this does not violate availability SLA of the service yet: provider loses revenue from the service;
- VM set is excluded from the next placement, violating availability SLA of the service: the provider loses revenue from the

service and also compensates the customer with the service credit for the next billing period, which is a function of the service usage fee accumulated thus far in this billing period.

The tasks performed sequentially by Placement Optimizer, Placement Planner and Placement Actuator form a *management cycle*. At the beginning of each management cycle, Placement Optimizer receives input from the Service Manager in terms of VM of the newly arrived and already provisioned VM sets and their values at this point in time. The Placement Optimizer computes a placement to maximize profit from the service placement. As a part of this objective, Placement Optimizer minimizes the costs associated with availability SLO incompliance and VM migrations.

In case provisioning is performed on an initially empty host pool or on a partially loaded pool where VMs are not allowed to move from their current hosts due to workload sensitivity or other management concerns. There are no operational costs associated with migrations and the value of each VM is the same irrespective of the physical placement.

In many other practical scenarios, provisioning is being performed on the pre-loaded host pools where VMs can move within the pool or across different pools. Current virtualization technologies allow live migrating VMs across disparate physical hosts. The live migration of VMs may stress the data center network, which is a scarce shared resource, and incurs an overhead on both source and destination hosts in terms of CPU and memory. This overhead can be modeled as cost of migration between the source host of a VM and its feasible host destinations. While many factors affect the migration costs, the dominant factor is the cost of communication that depends on the available network bandwidth and network topology. While in this work we are not dealing with modeling the cost of VM migration, our problem

formulation explicitly accounts for these costs to maintain policy-based control over them.

It is important to stress that the quality of the placement produced by the Placement Optimizer directly influences duration and operational costs of the subsequent phases implemented by the Placement Planner and Placement Actuator. Obviously, the more migrations are implied by the new placement, the longer will be the scheduling and provisioning phases and higher will be the network overhead.

The model studied by Urgaonkar et al. (2007) is closest to our work. The authors consider non-elastic sets of application components corresponding to mandatory configurations that should be successfully placed in full on a cluster of physical hosts in order for the application to function. The objective is to maximize the number of successfully placed applications assuming all applications are equally important and generating the same revenue for the provider irrespective of the QoS and application sizing.

This problem is a special case of ESPP. We generalize the model of Urgaonkar et al. (2007) in the following important aspects.

- We consider variable values of VMs comprising the service sets due to diversified sizing and pricing and different SLA compliance histories.
- We consider variable profit from placing VMs on different hosts due to operational costs such as those incurred by migrations (we consider the use case where the placement optimization problem is solved repeatedly).
- We consider variable capacity requirements of the same VM when placed on different hosts possessing non-uniform processing capabilities.

We observe that ESPP problem can be viewed as a multi-unit combinatorial auction problem. In a combinatorial auction a number of non-identical goods are sold concurrently and bidders express preferences about combinations of goods and not just about single good. In a multi-unit combinatorial auction -- that extends this problem -- there are multiple copies of each good and the agents are allowed to bid on more than one unit of each good. The combinatorial auction problem is computationally hard and known approximation guarantees are not sufficiently good for most practical applications. Therefore, we explore scalable near optimal solutions by expressing ESPP as a multi-unit combinatorial auction using a standard set packing formulation. Since this formulation may have huge number of variables, we apply a column generation approach, which is a powerful tool for solving large scale integer problems. Instead of enumerating columns explicitly, the column generation method uses only a selected set. This method was first applied by Gilmore and Gomory (1963) for solving the cutting stock problem. Later column generation was successfully applied for several other application domains.

ELASTIC SERVICE PLACEMENT PROBLEM

We consider the following elastic service placement problem. We are given a set B of m bins and a set A of k services. Each bin i has capacity $c(i)$ and each service j contains n_j items, where each item l of service j has size p_{il}^j and value v_{il}^j to the provider when item l is assigned to bin i. The total value of each service equals the sum of the values of all its items if the whole service is packed and otherwise it equals zero.

The packing may be subject to deployment constraints. One especially challenging type of deployment constraints is given by the anti-collocation requirements where all items of a given service should be assigned to different bins[4]. The goal is to find a feasible assignment of the items' sets to bins to maximize the total value. In this

chapter we consider bin and VM capacity to be one dimensional. This represents a single resource, specifically, CPU power that can be expressed in compute units[5]. In practice, physical hosts (bins) and VMs (items) are multidimensional entities. Our proposed framework naturally extends to the multi-dimensional case. We defer the more involved study of the multidimensional model to the future work, however.

It is easy to see that ESPP generalizes the *Generalized Assignment Problem (GAP)*, which is defined as follows. Given a set of bins and a set of items, where the items may have different size and value for each bin. The goal is to find a feasible assignment of the items to bins to maximize the total value.

We now provide a direct integer programming formulation for ESPP. Let y_j be an indicator variable assuming 1 if service j is included into the placement and 0 otherwise. For each item l of service j and bin i, we have a decision variable x_{il}^j, which indicates whether item l is assigned to bin i.

$$\max \sum_{j=1}^{k} \sum_{l=1}^{n_j} \sum_{i=1}^{m} x_{il}^j \cdot v_{il}^j$$

$$s.t. \sum_{i=1}^{m} x_{il}^j = y_j \, \forall j \in A, \forall l \in \{1, \ldots, n_j\}$$

$$\sum_{j=1}^{k} \sum_{l=1}^{n_j} x_{il}^j \cdot p_{il}^j \leq c(i) \forall i \in \{1, \ldots, m\}$$

$$\sum_{l=1}^{n_j} x_{il}^j \leq 1 \forall j \in A, \forall i \in B$$

$$x_{il}^j \in \{0, 1\} \forall j \in A, \forall i \in B$$

$$y_j \in \{0, 1\} \forall j \in A.$$

In the integer program, the objective is maximizing the sum of values. The first set of constraints requires that for each service either the whole service is packed or none of its items is packed. The second set of constraints requires that the load of each bin does not exceed its capacity. The third set of constraints requires that the items of each service are assigned to distinct bins.

It is prohibitively expensive (in terms of running time and computation resources) to solve this IP formulation directly for large problem instances. Therefore, we turn to an alternative integer programming formulation that can be used to find near optimal solutions efficiently using column generation method. In the next section we show the relationship between ESPP and multi-unit combinatorial auctions and provide an alternative integer program formulation of ESPP using set packing formulation for multi-unit combinatorial auctions. This formulation is naturally amenable to column generation.

A COMBINATORIAL AUCTIONS APPROACH TO ESPP

Combinatorial Auctions Problem Description

In combinatorial auctions a number of non-identical goods are sold concurrently and bidders express preferences about combinations of goods and not just about the singletons. This problem can be viewed as a high level abstraction of complex resource allocation, and is the paradigmatic problem on the interface of economics and computer science (De Vries and Vohra, 2003; Nisan et al., 2007).

Formally, in combinatorial auctions there is a set of m non-identical goods that are concurrently auctioned to n bidders; in a multi-unit combinatorial auctions each good $i \in \{1, \ldots, m\}$

is available in $c(i) \in \mathbb{N}$ units. The combinatorial character of the auction comes from the fact that bidders have preferences regarding bundles of goods. A bundle of goods is a vector $(d_1, \ldots, d_m)$, where $0 \le d_i \le c(i)$ is the number of units of good i in the bundle. Each bidder j has a valuation function v_j that describes its preferences in monetary terms and assigns non-negative value for each bundle of goods, $v_j : \{0, \ldots, c(1)\} \times \ldots \times \{0, \ldots, c(m)\} \to R^+$. The goal of the auction is to find an allocation that maximizes the social welfare $\sum_j v_j(S_j)$ where S_j is the bundle of goods allocated to bidder j. Let us now turn to our problem. ESPP can be viewed as a multi-unit combinatorial auction as follows. The set of bins B is the set of non-identical goods and the capacity $c(i)$ of each bin i is the number of units of each good i. The set of services A is the set of bidders which bid on bundles of bin capacities. The goal is to maximize the sum of values of the bundles allocated to the bidders.

We define the load of a bin as the total size used by items (i.e., VMs) assigned to it. Each bundle S of service j is a load vector of the bins that corresponds to a feasible assignment of service j to the bins. We will abuse notation somewhat and also use S to refer to the corresponding assignment of service j to the bins. We denote by S_j the set of bundles of service j. Each service j has a profit function v_j, where $v_j(S)$ is the maximum profit of a feasible packing of service j with vector of loads that equals $S \in S_j$. We denote by $p(S,i)$ the total size of items that are packed in bin i according to bundle S.

The combinatorial auction problem is computationally hard and cannot be approximated to within a factor better than $m^{1/2-\varepsilon}$ for any constant $\varepsilon > 0$. This holds even for the special case of single-minded-bidders (Lehmann et al., 2002), which is also a special case of ESPP.

Integer Programming Formulation of Combinatorial Auctions for ESPP

We now model the ESPP problem using the integer programming formulation for multi unit combinatorial auctions. For a feasible assignment $S \in S_j$, let $x_{j,s}$ be an indicator variable that indicates whether assignment S is chosen for service j. We relax the $x_{j,s}$ variables to be in $[0,1]$ and obtain the following linear programming relaxation (LP2):

$$\max \sum_{j \in A} \sum_{S \in \mathcal{S}_j} x_{j,S} \cdot v_j(S) \qquad (1)$$

$$s.t. \sum_{S \in \mathcal{S}_j} x_{j,S} \leq 1 \forall j \in A \qquad (2)$$

$$\sum_{j \in A, S \in \mathcal{S}_j} x_{j,S} \cdot p(S,i) \leq c(i) \forall i \in B \qquad (3)$$

$$x_{j,S} \geq 0 \forall j \in A, S \in \mathcal{S}_j. \qquad (4)$$

In the linear program, the objective function is to maximize the sum of profits. Constraint (2) ensures that each service gets at most one assignment and constraint (3) ensures that the load of a bin does not exceed its capacity.

The corresponding dual linear program (DLP) is then:

$$\min \sum_{i \in B} c(i) \cdot y_i + \sum_{j \in A} z_j \qquad (5)$$

$$s.t. \sum_{i \in B} y_i p(S,i) + z_j \geq v_j(S) \forall j \in A, \forall S \in \mathcal{S}_j \qquad (6)$$

$$z_j \geq 0 \forall j \in A \qquad (7)$$

$$y_i \geq 0 \forall i \in B. \qquad (8)$$

The main reason for reformulating ESPP as a multi-unit combinatorial auction using set packing approach is that it naturally renders itself to column generation approach that can be used for solving the integer problem more efficiently.

COLUMN GENERATION

Column generation is a powerful technique for solving IP problems with huge number of variables. The idea of column generation is to solve the problem without considering explicitly all the variables. Column generation decomposes an LP relaxation of the problem into a master problem and subproblems. Initially a restricted LP formulation, called restricted master problem (RMP), that contains only a small subset of the variables of the full LP formulation is solved optimally. Then a subproblem called *pricing problem*, which is a separation problem for the dual linear program, is solved repeatedly to identify new variables that have positive reduced cost and can, therefore, potentially increase the objective value of the RMP. This process is referred to as the column generation phase. When no additional variables that can improve the objective value of the RMP can be identified, the column generation phase stops and the problem obtained in the column generation phase is solved as IP.

For (LP2) the pricing problem is to find a service j and assignment $S \in \mathcal{S}_j$ of positive reduced cost $v_j(S) - \sum_{i \in B} y_i p(S,i) - z_j$, where (y,z) is an optimal solution to the dual problem of the restricted master problem (RMP). For ESPP with anti-collocation constraints the pricing problem is the maximum weight bipartite matching problem that can be solved in polynomial time (see (Gabow, 1990)). For ESPP without the anti-collocation constraints, the pricing problem is GAP. In this chapter we focus on the variant of ESPP with the anti-collocation constraints.

For each $j \in A$, we define a bipartite graph $G_j = (B, I_j, E_j)$ in which we have an edge (i, l), if item l of service j can be assigned to bin i. The weight of edge (i, l) is $w_{il}^j = v_{il}^j - y_i p_{il}^j$. Thus, in order to find the highest reduced cost for every service j we have to solve the maximum weight bipartite matching that can be formulated as an integer program as follows.

$$\max \sum_{(i,l) \in E_j} w_{il}^j x_{il}$$

$$s.t. \sum_{i=1}^{m} x_{il}^j = 1 \forall l \in \{1, \ldots, n_j\}$$

$$\sum_{l=1}^{n_j} x_{il}^j \leq 1 \forall i \in \{1, \ldots, m\}$$

$$x_{il}^j \in \{0, 1\} \forall i \in B, \forall l \in \{1, \ldots, n_j\}.$$

If the value of the optimal solution to the above maximum weight bipartite matching problem for service j is greater than z_j then we have found a variable of service j that can be added to the LP. In our implementation, in every iteration of column generation, we solve the pricing problem for every service and if it has a positive reduced cost we add the corresponding column to the restricted master problem (RMP).

A generalization of branch-and-bound with LP relaxations, called branch-and-price (Barnhart et al., 1998), is often used for solving large IP problems. This scheme allows applying column generation throughout the branch-and-bound tree. However, our experiments show that simple column generation was capable of producing ESPP solutions very close to those of LP relaxation of ESPP where LP reflect the upper limit on the ESPP objective function for any given problem instance. Consequently we leave a more complex branch-and-price method out of the scope of this work.

IMPLEMENTATION AND SIMULATION RESULTS

The objective of our evaluation study is to compare the direct IP formulation to the proposed column generation method to get insights about the tradeoff between optimality and computational time under reasonable assumptions about the cloud settings.

One of the more challenging issues while evaluating algorithms on complex scenarios is generating representative input data sets. This data can come either from a real production environment or from a cloud simulator. In the cloud environment that we consider, the problem of the input data is exacerbated by having multiple independent dimensions characterizing our problem. Namely, one has to specify distribution of the physical hosts capacities, distribution of the resource demands by VMs, popularity distribution of VM sizes, distribution of the VM set sizes, birth-death stochastic process characterizing elasticity, distribution of value attributed to VM sets in accordance with specific SLA offerings and external workload. While recently some cloud simulation tools have appeared (Calheiros et al., 2010), these tools still need some input on the above mentioned aspects to drive the simulation. Given current production practices, we were not able to obtain sufficiently representative production data sets to extract all the needed data.

Therefore we resorted to implementing our own problem instance generator that abstracts the core features of the model important for the algorithmic evaluation. As one can easily verify, varying all aspects of the model described above quickly results in an unwieldy set of sub-instances that would be difficult to interpret and generalize. Thus, we decided to focus on a simple experimental setting that would be easy to follow and present, and which will be sufficiently informative to achieve the objective of this simulation study.

A single algorithm execution is performed on a random problem instance. We generate instances ranging from 10 to 700 bins representing physical hosts. We set the ratio by $\rho=n/m$ between the number of items (representing VMs) and bins in an instance and generate the number of items to satisfy this ratio. Item types are chosen uniformly from "Small", "Medium", "Large" which are the three typical sizes of virtual machine instances, where "Small", "Medium", and "Large" require 1, 3, and 7 compute units, respectively. Bin capacities are expressed in the same compute units as items. We uniformly draw bin capacities from [20, 40]. In most of our instances we used $\rho=10$. The number of items comprising each service is drawn uniformly from [1, 10]. We consider "Silver", "Gold" and "Platinum" SLA types with hourly compute unit price of 1, 2, 4, respectively. Each service SLA type is drawn uniformly from "Silver", "Gold" and "Platinum".

We partitioned our experiments into three sets. In the first set we considered small resource pools with the number of bins ranging from 10 to 220 and $\rho=10$. In this problem size range we explicitly compare our column generation algorithm to direct IP formulation and to the solution obtained by LP relaxation of ESPP. Beyond this range solving direct IP proved to be infeasible. Thus, we conducted the second set of experiments where we varied the number of bins from 250 to 700 with the same item-bin ratio as before. This set of experiments evaluates performance of our proposed method on the large resource pools. In these experiments we compare the results obtained by our solution to the LP relaxation only. In both sets of experiments we considered a use case where we start from an initially empty resource pool.

In the third set of experiments we study the use case where an initial assignment of items to bins already exists. We generate additional item sets simulating newly arrived service provisioning requests. Placement of the new services may cause migrations of items across bins. It is our objective in this set of simulations to validate that our migration costs modeling indeed controls the costs of migrations and get insights on the sensitivity of this mechanism.

In practical settings, timeliness of solving the placement problem is of paramount importance. Therefore in all our experiments we introduce two early stopping criteria. The first one is a time limit on the total computation time and the second one is target optimality gap that instructs the MIP solver to stop when the target is achieved. The optimality gap is defined as

$$100 \cdot \frac{LP\ optimum - Best\ known\ feasible\ solution}{Best\ known\ feasible\ solution}.$$

We implemented the column generation algorithm using CPLEX. We use CPLEX to solve the direct IP formulation of ESPP to compare performance and scalability of the direct approach to our column generation method. When evaluating the column generation method, we use CPLEX to solve the master problem, the subproblem and the IP resulting from the column generation algorithm.

It is known that the column generation method may suffer from the tailing-off effect where large number of iterations may be required to reach an optimal solution of the master problem LP. To reduce this effect, we impose a stopping condition as follows. The column generation halts when solution improves by less than certain percent between consecutive iterations. Our results show that the early stopping condition only marginally impacts solution optimality.

All our computational results are based on 5 randomly generated instances for each problem instance type. We compute average of these runs and also present the maximum value in the result set. We run all our simulations on a Linux machine with 2.5 GHz processor and 16 GByte of RAM.

Small Resource Pools

We present the full experimental results for small resource pools in (Breitgand and Epstein, 2010). Due to lack of space we highlight here the most important observations. Namely, we observe that the column generation algorithm becomes much faster than the direct IP formulation as the item-bin ratio increases. However, the optimality gap of the column generation algorithm is slightly worse than that of the direct IP formulation.

Our results for comparing column generation algorithm and direct IP formulation with time limit stopping condition of 15 minutes for resource pools of size 10 to 220 bins and $\rho=10$ show that if relatively long computation times are permissible, the direct IP formulation is slightly superior to the column generation method.

The big advantage of the column generation approach becomes evident in the next set of experiments where target optimality gap stopping condition is used. These simulations are summarized in Table 0.

As one can see the column generation algorithm is significantly faster than the direct IP formulation for the target optimality gap stopping condition. At the same time the optimality gap of the column generation algorithm is only slightly worse than that of the direct IP formulation.

Large Resource Pools

For large resource pools CPLEX was unable to find feasible solutions for the direct IP formulation within the time limit, hence in this section we show computational results only for the column generation algorithm. The results are summarized in Tables 1 and 2. The tables additionally display the average and maximum number of generated columns and the number of column generation iterations.

Our results show that for the time limit stopping condition the optimality gap increases with the problem size. We can see in Table 1 that for the problem instances of at most 500 bins, the average optimality gap obtained within the time limit is at most 10.29 and for larger instances of size at most 700 bins, the average optimality gap is at most 23.07.

As seen from Table 2, the obtained optimality gap of the column generation algorithm may occasionally exceed the target optimality gap of 10 percents. We can see in the table that the average optimality gap is at most 11.95. This happens because we use early stopping condition for column generation to mitigate the tailing-off effect as discussed earlier. Therefore we obtain near optimal LP solutions to the master problem rather than the optimal ones and this contributes to the overall optimality gap.

Placement with Migrations

In this section we consider the case of replacement, where the placement problem starts from an existing placement. In this case moving from the existing placement to the new placement may require live migrations of VMs. To take into account the operational costs incurred by live VM migrations, we subtract these costs from the value obtained from the migrated VMs. Thus, an already placed VM may produce different values when placed on different hosts.

We model migration cost of a VM with value v as αv, where $0 \leq \alpha \leq 1$. Thus, the real value that results from moving a VM from the original host to another host is $(1-\alpha)v$. In general α may vary for each VM and may depend on the communication cost between hosts in the host pool and between the host pools. In the presented experiments, we consider the homogenous case where communication costs between the hosts in the pool are uniform. We test the case of replacement by generating an instance for 250 to 700 bins. For each problem instance we compute an initial placement. Then, we generate new VMs that amount to $\beta=0.2$ fraction of the original number of VMs and run the placement algorithm for different values of α. We evaluate the quality of the new placement in terms of the total value to the provider and the number of VM migrations.

Figure 1 shows the effect of migration cost on the number of migrations performed when moving

Table 1. Target optimality gap of 10% for small resource pools

m	n	COLUMN GENERATION				DIRECT IP			
		Gap [%]		Time [s]		Gap [%]		Time [s]	
		Avg	Max	Avg	Max	Avg	Max	Avg	Max
10	100	6.75	8.63	0.18	0.26	3.15	5.61	0.03	0.05
40	400	8.85	9.34	1.56	1.66	5.59	7.62	1.31	2.07
70	700	7.58	9.21	4.72	5.25	3.86	6.9	7.16	7.73
100	1000	8.93	10.11	8.53	10.43	3.15	5.7	25.77	33.22
130	1300	9.13	10.01	17.90	22.03	3.11	4.79	60.04	73.97
160	1600	8.74	10.19	35.63	43.99	2.9	3.5	110.39	138.33
190	1900	8.8	9.29	42.58	45.21	3.0	4.82	256.74	409.91
220	2200	9.53	9.99	66.54	86.39	3.64	4.37	434.59	623.28

Table 2. Time limit of 15 minutes for large resource pools

m	n	Gap [%]		Time [s]		Columns		Iterations	
		Avg	Max	Avg	Max	Avg	Max	Avg	Max
250	2500	6.07	6.62	900	900	2387	2494	9	9
300	3000	6.81	7.11	900	900	2890.6	3102	9.4	10
350	3500	7.26	8.32	900	900	3369.4	3439	10	10
400	4000	8.676	9.63	900	900	4166.6	4434	11.4	12
450	4500	8.97	11.31	900	900	4928.8	5568	13	14
500	5000	10.29	11.92	900	900	5699.8	6084	13.2	14
550	5500	12.62	13.85	900	900	6677.6	7168	15.4	17
600	6000	13.65	14.95	900	900	7441.2	8022	16.6	17
650	6500	16.36	20.16	900	900	8597.6	9021	18.2	19
700	7000	23.07	23.9	900	900	9082.6	9346	17.2	18

Table 3. Target optimality gap of 10% for large resource pools

m	n	Gap [%]		Time [s]		Columns		Iterations	
		Avg	Max	Avg	Max	Avg	Max	Avg	Max
250	2500	11.10	12.2	62.506	65.19	2276.2	2457	9	9
300	3000	10.52	11.95	96.248	104.44	2947.4	3114	10	10
350	3500	11.04	11.87	141.578	158.07	3662	3805	10.8	11
400	4000	11.95	13.0	226.26	284.46	4307.4	4571	11.8	12
450	4500	10.34	12.32	406.194	459.99	5190.8	5532	13	14
500	5000	11.90	12.6	562.476	749.65	5603.4	5944	13.8	15
550	5500	11.41	13.37	910.94	1028.38	6710.8	7090	15.6	17
600	6000	11.83	13.21	1,167.27	1,250.96	7547.8	7925	16.4	17
650	6500	10.91	11.52	1,987.33	2,836.34	8065.6	8141	17.2	18
700	7000	11.61	12.35	2,072.33	2,364.51	9061.4	9791	17.2	18

from the initial placement to the new placement computed by the column generation algorithm with the time limit stopping condition of 15 minutes. As expected, the number of migrations decreases as the migration cost grows, which indicates that the cloud providers can control the operational cost of migrations using this method. Due to the lack of space we do not show the tabular data on the optimality gap. In general, the optimality gap obtained for the time limit of 15 minutes decreased from 10% to 4.5% as migration costs increased.

One may notice from Figure 1 that when the cost of migrations is zero, the number of migrations sharply decreases occasionally. At a first glance this appears to be counter-intuitive since zero migrations costs should have encouraged the solver to use more migrations when seeking for optimal solutions. The explanation for this effect is that when migration costs are non-zero, the solver starts with a smaller preferred candidate set for the already placed items giving placement preference to the bins where these items are placed at the moment. In the absence of migration costs

the solver needs to perform much more branching since there is no preferred placement for the items. Therefore 15 minutes might be too short a time limit and the optimality gap achieved in the case of zero migration costs is worse than in the case of non-zero migration costs.

To verify that in (Breitgand and Epstein, 2010), we repeated the same experiment with the time limit of 30 minutes. The results of these simulations show that when given more time, the optimality gap in case of zero migration costs improves and more migrations are performed as expected.

CAPACITY MANAGEMENT

The VM placement optimization mechanisms that we discussed so far, aim at protecting end user experience through leveraging elasticity in the Cloud with service tiers being scaled out on demand as prescribed by the elasticity rules. Guarantees on scaling out the service when required are stipulated by the elasticity SLAs in our approach.

Figure 1. Cost of migrations (time limit of 15 minutes)

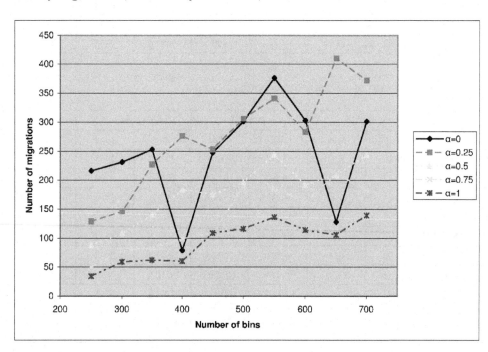

One way to guarantee elasticity SLAs and, therefore, also the end-user experience is making sure that the maximal total demand of all services deployed in the Cloud does not exceed physical capacity of the Cloud. In other words, by provisioning physical capacity according to the peak demand of the services.

As more elastic services are being deployed in the cloud, the probability that all of the services will simultaneously request their maximal capacity demands either through explicit elasticity rules or autonomic controller, diminishes. Moreover, as the system grows in size, the services can be viewed as independent. Therefore physical capacity of the data center can be multiplexed among the services allowing to accommodate more services with less physical capacity.

Multiplexing, however, increases the risk of resource allocation congestion. In our previous work (Lloriente et.al., 2011, Rochwerger et. al., 2011), drawing our inspiration from results in network bandwidth multiplexing, we define a notion of equivalent physical capacity required to host the given mix of services while keeping the probability of resource allocation congestion below the *acceptable risk level (ARL)*, which is set by the infrastructure provider in accordance with the business goals. A conservative approach would set ARL as the level of the strictest SLA availability percentile. As long as there is enough physical capacity to place equivalent capacity, the system would honor its SLA for all services.

Determining whether physical capacity is sufficient to place the equivalent capacity for VM allocation is a more difficult task than determining whether the network bandwidth is sufficient to accommodate equivalent bandwidth for multiplexing network transmissions. The reason for that is that VM placement is limited by a variety of capacity and assignment constraints. Therefore, a key aspect for equivalent capacity usage is the ability to compute feasible VM placements efficiently.

In RESERVOIR, we provide a management function, the *Admission Controller*, which calculates anonymous equivalent capacity based on the VM allocation statistics gathered for the services and then validates whether a feasible placement exists for this equivalent capacity, which is expressed in terms of the number of discrete VM sizes (also known as VM types) allocated to the workload mix as whole, capturing long-term statistical behavior of the workload.

The details on admission control functionality in RESERVOIR can be found in (Lloriente et.al., 2011). The basic and generic principles underpinning its operation can be summarized as follows. Each elastic service is allocated VMs from IaaS depending on the service manifest and the elasticity rules executed by the service management throughout its operation. IaaS usually provide VMs from a catalogue of discrete types. Thus, at any given moment, the number of VMs of each type can be regarded as a value of a random variable, whose distribution is unknown. As we consider multiple elastic services, the distribution of the random variable that represents the number of VMs of each type, which is the sum of the number of VMs of each type over all services, approaches Normal distribution because of the Central Limit theorem. Thus, if we set a target probability, ε for VM, allocation resource congestion, i.e., ARL, the number of VMs of each type i that would be allocated simultaneously in the Cloud for all the services, with probability 1-ε is obtained from Equatioin 9.

$$X_i = \sum_j \mu_j + \beta \sqrt{\sum_j \sigma_j^2}, \qquad (9)$$

where μ_j and σ_j are the mean and standard deviation, respectively, of the random variable representing the number of VMs of type i in service j. $\beta = \Phi^{-1}(1-\varepsilon)$ and the quantile function Φ^{-1} is the inverse function of the CDF Φ of $N(0,1)$.

Calculating equivalent capacity this way for each VM type, we obtain the total equivalent capacity for the Cloud. This equivalent capacity should have a feasible placement in order for SLAs be protected with the target probability 1-ε.

To develop some intuition, consider Figure 2. This figure presents a simplified simulation study of the multiplexing gain attainable for different ARL values ranging from 0.15 to 0.01. The simulation comprises three groups of experiments where the number of simulated services was 100, 200, and 300 respectively. Each service specifies 20 compute units as its maximal demand. To simulate either implicit or explicit automated elasticity, the actual number of resources for each service for any given time is drawn from the uniform distribution in the range [1. 20]. The stability periods between these resource allotment changes are exponentially distributed. The simulation comprises 5760 iterations that corresponds to two months worth of data points, where each data point is collected at 15 minutes interval. As one can observe, the equivalent capacity grows as ARL diminishes as smaller ARL means more strict requirements. The

actual multiplexing gain depends on the available physical capacity. Obviously, the physical capacity should at least equal equivalent capacity. If this is not the case, the system is over-committed beyond the desired ARL. However, a mere fact that there is more physical capacity than equivalent capacity cannot guarantee that a feasible placement of equivalent capacity (i.e., VMs hiding behind the compute units) on physical capacity (host platforms) exists.

Upon accepting a new service into the cloud, RESERVOIR's admission control policy calculates an impact on the equivalent capacity, assuming pessimistic estimation of resource usage for the new service, namely that it would use its maximal resources allocation as specified in the service manifest. The new service is accepted if and only if, the equivalent capacity resulting from service acceptance, can be feasibly placed on available physical resources.

Figure 2. Equivalent capacity in compute units as a function of the number of services and acceptable risk level probability

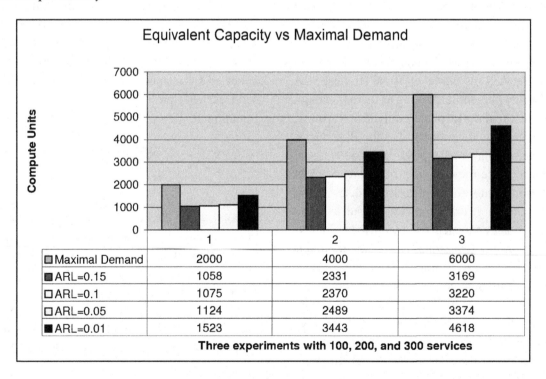

	Maximal Demand	ARL=0.15	ARL=0.1	ARL=0.05	ARL=0.01
1	2000	1058	1075	1124	1523
2	4000	2331	2370	2489	3443
3	6000	3169	3220	3374	4618

Three experiments with 100, 200, and 300 services

One of the problems with equivalent capacity approach just described, is that while equivalent capacity can be easily applied to some placement constraints such as migratability (we can just add additional VM types internally, representing the new types by the tuple <*size, migratability*>), it loses the notion of other deployment constraints such as, e.g., set constraints and anti-collocation constraints, for example. Therefore, equivalent capacity acts as a lower bound. Namely, if no feasible placement for equivalent capacity exists, there is also no feasible placement for equivalent capacity augmented by deployment constraints. Finding a feasible placement for equivalent capacity, however, does not guarantee that there is a feasible placement if additional deployment constraints exist. Another problem is that there are few placement algorithms that can effectively handle set and anti-collocation constraints. The placement algorithm presented earlier in this chapter is an example of an algorithm that can be used efficiently to validate feasibility of a placement for services with set and anti-collocation constraints.

One approach to deal with deployment constraints is based on the percentile analysis of VM tier (i.e., sets) allocation, finding out an 1-ε percentile for each VM type group per each service and then using this information as input for the placement algorithm of Section 3.

FUTURE RESEARCH DIRECTIONS

One future work direction that we explore is how to integrate the operational costs such as energy into the proposed framework. One promising approach is extending the multi-unit combinatorial auction modeling by adding the "opening cost" of bins. Another research direction that we will explore in the future is including storage resources assignment into the modeling. From the networking perspective, we will experiment with more sophisticated dynamic communication costs that reflect network topology and available

bandwidth. Another direction, we wish to better understand in the future is how different amount of anti-collocation constraints affect performance. On the one hand, anti-collocation requires more physical capacity to pack the same number of VMs, but simplifies the pricing problem (bipartite maximum weight matching). On the other hand, absense of anti-collocation constraints allows denser packings, but on the expense of a more complex pricing problem (GAP). Finally, we will explore partial VM set placement models, where different levels of SLA compliance are defined for different service configurations that contain the initially requested configuration as a proper subset.

Our future work in resources over-commit area focuses on over-subscribing capacity per individual host to allow vertical elasticity of the workloads with higher over-commit levels that would not be achievable otherwise. In addition we pursue a research direction that allows to use a simulation based approach instead of percentile analysis to account for deployment constraints in a more accurate manner.

CONCLUSION

We discussed management of elastic multi-tier workloads in IaaS.

Combining best SLA practices, we argue in favor of a non-obfuscated, diversified SLA model where multi-criteria SLA offerings are provided through SLA catalogues. Taking up clear and measureable commitments through SLA increases risks to the vendor, however. We propose a profit maximization approach to resource allocation that directly integrates costs due to SLA incompliance with other variable costs of production. We presented a novel approach to SLA-aware placement of elastic services in a cloud. We formulated a novel optimization problem, ESPP, and showed its relationship to GAP and multi-unit combinatorial auctions. We further developed an efficient computational methodology to solve

ESPP using column generation and demonstrated that the tradeoff between solution optimality and timeliness can be efficiently managed. We argue that the operational costs related to SLA provisioning and the network overhead incurred by live VM migrations can be modeled within the same framework. We evaluated our approach using simulations under the reasonable simplifying assumptions. As demonstrated by our results, the column generation method is capable of obtaining close to optimal solutions while controlling the tradeoff between the optimality gap of a solution and its timeliness.

Cost-efficiency of an IaaS provider depends on its ability to leverage statistical multiplexing inherent to the elastic workloads. We considered the problem of resources over-commit subject to our SLA model. We showed that our approach to ESPP can be used to improve the generic over-commit method previously reported by us, by better accounting for deployment constraints, such as anti-collocation. To the best of our knowledge, this problem have not received sufficient attention in the literature thus far, and our proposed methodology is the first step in this direction.

REFERENCES

Amazon Elastic Compute Cloud (EC2). (n.d.) http://aws.amazon.com/ec2.

Barnhart, C., Johnson, E. L., Nemhauser, G. L., & Savelsbergh, M. W. (1998). P. Branch-and-price: Column generation for solving huge integer programs. *Operations Research, 46*(3), 316–329. doi:10.1287/opre.46.3.316

Breitgand, D., & Epstein, A. (2010) SLA-aware Placement of Multi-Virtual Machine Elastic Services in Compute Clouds., IBM *Technical Report, H-0287*

Calheiros, R. N., Ranjan, R., Beloglazov, A., De Rose, C. A. F., & Buyya, R. (2010) CloudSim: A Toolkit for Modeling and Simulation of Cloud Computing Environments and Evaluation of Resource Provisioning Algorithms, Software: Practice and Experience.New York, NY. USAWiley Press.

De Vries, S., & Vohra, R. V. (2003). Combinatorial auctions: A survey. *INFORMS Journal on Computing, 15*(3), 284–309. doi:10.1287/ijoc.15.3.284.16077

Dobzinski, S., Nisan, N., & Schapira, M. (2010). Approximation algorithms for combinatorial auctions with complement-free bidders. *Mathematics of Operations Research, 35*(1), 1–13. doi:10.1287/moor.1090.0436

Gabow, H. N. (1990) Data structures for weighted matching and nearest common ancestors with linking. *In SODA*, (pp 434–443)

Gilmore, P. C., & Gomory, R. E. (1963). A linear programming approach to the cutting stock roblem-Part II. *Operations Research, 11*, 863–888. doi:10.1287/opre.11.6.863

IBM ILOG CPLEX 12.1.(n.d.) http://www-01.ibm.com/-software/integration/optimization/-cplex-optimizer.

Lehmann, D. J., O'Callaghan, L., & Shoham, Y. (2002). Truth revelation in approximately efficient combinatorial auctions. *Journal of the ACM, 49*(5), 577–602. doi:10.1145/585265.585266

Lloriente, I. M., Montero, R. S., Sotomayor, B., Breitgand, D., Maraschini, A., Levy, E., & Rochwerger, B. (2011). *Management of Virtual Machines for Cloud Infrastructures, Cloud Computing Principles and Paradigms, 157—191, Series on Parallel and Distributed Computing*. Wiley.

Nisan, N., Roughgarden, T., Tardos, E., & Vazirani, V. (2007). *Algorithmic Game Theory*. New York, NY, USA: Cambridge University Press. doi:10.1017/CBO9780511800481

RESERVOIR. The RESERVOIR project home page. (2008) http://www.reservoir-fp7.eu

Right Scale. Right scale. (n.d.) http://www.right-scale.com/m/.

Rochwerger, B., Breitgand, D., Epstein, A., Hadas, D., Loy, I., & Nagin, K. (2011). Reservoir - When One Cloud Is Not Enough. *IEEE Computer, 44*(3), 44–51. doi:10.1109/MC.2011.64

Rochwerger, B., Breitgand, D., Levy, E., Galis, A., Nagin, K., & Llorente, L. (2009). The RESERVOIR Model and Architecture for Open Federated Cloud Computing. *IBM Journal of Research and Development, 53*(4). doi:10.1147/JRD.2009.5429058

System Design and Implementation (NSDI'07), (2007) Cambridge, MA, USA,.

Urgaonkar, B., Rosenberg, A. L., & Shenoy, P. J. (2007). Application placement on a cluster of servers. *International Journal of Foundations of Computer Science, 18*(5), 1023–1041. doi:10.1142/S012905410700511X

ADDITIONAL READING

Bobroff, N., Kochut, A., & Beaty, K. (2007) Dynamic Placement of Virtual Machines for Managing SLA Violations. In *Integrated Network Management*, IM '07. 10th IFIP/IEEE International Symposium on Integrated Network Management, 119–128.

Briest, P., Krysta, P., & Vöcking, B. (2005) Approximation techniques for utilitarian mechanism design. *In STOC'05,* (pp. 39–48)

Chekuri, C., & Khanna, S. (2005). A polynomial time approximation scheme for the multiple knapsack problem. *SIAM Journal on Computing, 35*(3), 713–728. doi:10.1137/S0097539700382820

Desrochers, M., Desrosiers, J., & Solomon, M. (1992). A new optimization algorithm for the vehicle routing problem with time windows. *Operations Research, 40*(2), 342–354. doi:10.1287/opre.40.2.342

Desrochers, M., & Soumis, F. (1989). A column generation approach to urban transit crew scheduling. *Transportation Science, 23,* 1–13. doi:10.1287/trsc.23.1.1

Dobzinski, S., Nisan, N., & Schapira, M. (2010). Approximation algorithms for combinatorial auctions with complement-free bidders. *Mathematics of Operations Research, 35*(1), 1–13. doi:10.1287/moor.1090.0436

Feige, U., & Vondrák, J. J. (2006) Approximation algorithms for allocation problems: Improving the factor of 1 - 1/e. *In Proc. 47th IEEE Symp. on Found. of Comp. Science,* 667–676

Gmach, D., Rolia, J., Cherkasova, L., Belrose, G., Turicchi, T., & Kemper, A. (2008) An Integrated Approach to Resource Pool Management: Policies, Efficiency and Quality Metrics. In *38th Annual IEEE/IFIP International Conference on Dependable Systems and Networks (DSN'2008).*

Gupta, R., Bose, S. K., Sundarrajan, S., Chebiyam, M., & Chakrabarti, A. (2008) A Two Stage Heuristic Algorithm for Solving the Server Consolidation Problem with Item-Item and Bin-Item Incompatibility Constraints. In *IEEE International Conference on Services Computing (SCC'08), 2,* 39–46, Honolulu, HI, USA.

Kelly, T. (2003) Utility-Directed Allocation. In *First Workshop on Algorithms and Architectures for Self-Managing Systems,* http://ai.eecs.umich.edu/ tpkelly/papers/HPL-2003-115.pdf.

Khuller, S., Li, J., & Saha, B. (2010) Energy efficient scheduling via partial shutdown. In Proc. 21th *ACM-SIAM Symp. On Discrete Algorithms,* 1360–1372

Lehmann, B., Lehmann, D. J., & Nisan, N. (2001) Combinatorial auctions with decreasing marginal utilities. *In ACM Conference on Electronic Commerce*, 18–28

Mehta, S., & Neogi, A. (2008) Recon: A tool to recommend dynamic server consolidation in multi-cluster data centers. *In IEEE Network Operations and Management Symposium (NOMS 2008)*, 363–370, Salvador, Bahia, Brasil

Meng, X., Pappas, V., & Zhang, L. (2010). Improving the scalability of data center networks with traffic-aware virtual machine placement. *In INFOCOM*, Raghavan, P. (1998) Probabilistic construction of deterministic algorithms: Approximating packing integer programs. *Journal of Computer and System Sciences, 37*(2), 130–143.

Shmoys, D. B., & Tardos, E. (1993). An approximation algorithm for the generalized assignment problem. *Mathematical Programming, 62*, 461–474. doi:10.1007/BF01585178

Singh, A., Korupolu, M., & Mohapatra, M. (2008) Server-Storage Virtualization: Integration and Load Balancing in Data Centers. In *7th International Symposium on Software Composition* (SC 2008), Budapest, Hungary

Srinivasan, A. (1996) An extension of the Lovász local lemma, and its applications to integer programming. *In SODA '96: Proceedings of the seventh annual ACM-SIAM symposium on Discrete algorithms,* 6–15

Srinivasan, A. (1999). Improved approximation guarantees for packing and covering integer programs. *SIAM Journal on Computing, 29*(2), 648–670. doi:10.1137/S0097539796314240

Tang, C., Steinder, M., Spreitzer, M., & Pacifici, G. (2007) A Scalable Application Placement Controller for Enterprise Data Centers. In *16th International World Wide Web Conference* (WWW07), Bannf, Canada

Värbrand, P., Yuan, D., & Björklund, P. (2003) Resource Optimization of Spatial TDMA in Ad Hoc Radio Networks: A Column Generation Approach. *In INFOCOM,* 818–824

Verma, A., Ahuja, P., & Neogi, (2008) A. pmapper: power and migration cost aware application placement in virtualized systems. In *Middleware '08: Proceedings of the 9th ACM/IFIP/USENIX International Conference on Middleware*, 243–264, New York, NY, USA, Springer-Verlag New York, Inc. ISBN 3-540-89855-7.

Wang, X., Du, Z., Chen, Y., Li, S., Lan, D., Wang, G., & Chen, Y. (2008). An Autonomic Provisioning Framework for Outsourcing Data Center based on Virtual Appliances. *Cluster Computing, 11*(3), 229–245. doi:10.1007/s10586-008-0053-z

Wood, T., Shenoy, P., Venkataramani, A., & Yousif, M. (2007) Black-Box and Gray-Box Strategies for Virtual Machine Migration. *In USENIX Symposium on Networked System Design and Implementation (NSDI'07)*, Cambridge, MA, USA

KEY TERMS AND DEFINITIONS

Approximation Algorithm: An algorithm that is used to find an approximate solution to an optimization problem.

Capacity Over-Commit: A technique in resource management that allows increasing actual utilization of the physical resources by elevating resource sharing such that the total peak resource demand by all users may exceed actual physical capacity.

Cloud Computing: a style of utility computing, where computational, storage, and network resources are provided from a shared pool in a form of a metered service over the network.

Column Generation: A technique for solving large IP problems without considering explicitly all the variables.

Combinatorial Auction: An auction in which participants can place bids on combinations of discrete goods, rather than just individual goods.

IaaS: Infrastructure as a Service is a flavor of Cloud Computing, where the resources provided correspond to the basic infrastructure, such as Virtual Machines, Virtual Networks, and Block Storage.

Packing Problems: A class of optimization problems that require packing a finite set of items into a finite set of containers as densely as possible.

SLA: Service Level Agreement is a contract between service provider and service consumer that explicitly defines the provider's obligations and customer expectations in terms of the level of service.

Statistical Multiplexing: A phenomenon occurring in a system that shares resources among users with time-varying resource demand, causing the actual total demand at any given time to be smaller than the total possible peak resource demand by all users.

Virtual Machine Placement Optimization: A class of packing problems where Virtual Machines, items, should be placed on physical containers, hosts, racks, etc., as densely as possible to save physical resources.

ENDNOTES

[1]   It should be noted that usually the usage fee paid by the customer does not depend on the actual resource utilization. Under a typical IaaS chargeback scheme, such as that of EC2 or Rackspace, a VM instance that is utilized up to, say, 80% would be charged the same as an instance of the same type utilized, say, up to 1%, as long as both were powered up during the equal periods of time.

[2]   Collocation constraints are also handled by our framework. However, this type of restrictions is easily handled by creating pseudo-VMs, whose capacity requirements are the collective requirements of the VMs comprising a collocation group. Therefore, we do not discuss collocation constraints in this chapter.

[3]   An alternative approach to this "all-or-nothing" scale-up placement model is to define the levels of compliance as, e.g., as percentage of the VM superset that contains the initially requested configuration. The initially requested configuration still has to be placed in an all-or-nothing manner. We defer discussion of the partial placement model to future work.

[4]   The motivation for this type of constraints arises from the typical management scenarios such maintaining a specific level of fault tolerance mandated by regulations and SLAs.

[5]   The concrete definition of a compute unit differs from one provider to another. See, e.g., Amazon EC2. We use the term compute unit in a generic manner to refer to the CPU demand of a VM instance.

Chapter 16
Economic Analysis of the SLA Mapping Approach for Cloud Computing Goods

Michael Maurer
Vienna University of Technology, Austria

Vincent C. Emeakaroha
Vienna University of Technology, Austria

Ivona Brandic
Vienna University of Technology, Austria

ABSTRACT

Because of the large number of different types of service level agreements (SLAs), computing resource markets face the challenge of low market liquidity. The authors therefore suggest restricting the number of different resource types to a small set of standardized computing resources to counteract this problem. Standardized computing resources are defined through SLA templates. SLA templates specify the structure of an SLA, the service attributes, the names of the service attributes, and the service attribute values. However, since existing approaches working with SLA templates are static so far, these approaches cannot reflect changes in user needs. To address this shortcoming, the chapter presents a novel approach to adaptive SLA matching. This approach adapts SLA templates based on SLA mappings of users. It allows Cloud users to define mappings between a public SLA template, which is available in the Cloud market, and their private SLA templates, which are used for various in-house business processes. Besides showing how public SLA templates are adapted to the demand of Cloud users, the chapter also analyzes the costs and benefits of this approach. Costs are incurred every time a user has to define a new SLA mapping to a public SLA template that has been adapted. In particular, it investigates how the costs differ with respect to the public SLA template adaptation method. The simulation results show that the use of heuristics for adaptation methods allows balancing the costs and benefits of the SLA mapping approach.

DOI: 10.4018/978-1-4666-1631-8.ch016

Copyright © 2012, IGI Global. Copying or distributing in print or electronic forms without written permission of IGI Global is prohibited.

INTRODUCTION

Non-functional requirements, e.g., application execution time, reliability, and availability, are termed as quality of service (QoS) requirements and are expressed by means of service level agreements (SLAs). In order to facilitate SLA creation and SLA management, SLA templates have been introduced. SLA templates represent popular SLA formats. They comprise elements such as names of trading parties, names of SLA attributes, attribute metrics, and attribute values (Risch, Brandic, & Altmann, 2009). Sellers use SLA templates to describe their supply of resources. Buyers use them to describe their demand for resources.

However, as computing resources are described through different non-standardized attributes, e.g., CPU cores, execution time, inbound bandwidth, outbound bandwidth, and processor type, a large variety of different SLAs exists in the market (Risch & Altmann, 2009). The success of matching offers from sellers and bids from buyers becomes very unlikely, i.e., the market liquidity (the likelihood of matching offers and bids) becomes very low (Risch, Brandic, & Altmann, 2009). The same problem persists in Cloud federations, when different Cloud providers, who also offer and buy resources from each other, stick to their own SLA templates.

Approaches that tackle this plethora of SLA attributes include the use of standardized SLA templates for a specific consumer base (*Amazon Elastic Compute Cloud*, 2010, *Google App Engine*, 2010), downloadable predefined provider-specific SLA templates (*BRAIN*, 2010), and the use of ontologies (Oldham, Verma, Sheth, & Hakimpour, 2006, Dobson & Sanchez-Macian, 2006). These approaches clearly define SLA templates and require users to agree a priori on predefined requirements. In all these approaches, the SLA templates are assumed to be static, i.e., they do not change nor adapt over time due to market conditions.

Consequently, the existing approaches for the specification of SLA templates cannot easily deal with demand changes. Demand changes of users can be caused through different factors. For example, the emergence of multi-core architectures in computing resources required the inclusion of the new attribute "number of cores", which was not present in an SLA template a couple of years ago.

In this paper, we apply adaptive SLA mapping, a new, semi-automatic approach that can react to changing market conditions (Risch, Brandic, & Altmann, 2009). The adaptive SLA mapping approach adapts public SLA templates, which are currently used in the Cloud market, to the needs of users using the SLA mappings of users. These SLA mappings bridge the differences between existing public SLA templates and the private SLA template, i.e., the SLA template of the user. In our context, private templates do not necessarily imply that they are inaccessible to others, but the word "private" is used to differentiate it from the "public" SLA template of the (public) registry. Therefore, all consumers' and providers' templates are called "private", whereas the registry's template is called "public". Since a user cannot easily change the private SLA template due to internal or legal organizational requirements, an SLA mapping is a convenient workaround to integrate an external resource.

Our adaptive SLA mapping approach can use different adaptation methods. The benefit of using an adaptation method is decreased through some cost for the user for defining new SLA mappings. Within this paper, we investigate these costs. In particular, we investigate how public SLA templates can be adapted to the demand of Cloud users and how the costs and benefits differ with respect to the public SLA template adaptation method used.

After introducing a reference adaption method for our analysis, we compare two additional adaptation methods, which differ in the heuristics applied. The heuristics have been introduced in order to find a balance between the benefit of having a public SLA template that is identical to most of the private SLA templates and the cost of creating new SLA mappings and new public SLA templates. As the metrics for assessing the quality of the adaptation method, we use the overall system net utility of all users. The net utility considers the benefit of having the same attributes and attribute names in the public SLA template as in the private SLA template, as well as the cost of defining new SLA attribute mappings.

The benefits of the adaptive SLA mapping approach for market participants are threefold. Firstly, traders can keep their private templates, which might be required for other business processes. Secondly, based on their submitted mappings of private SLA templates to public SLA templates, they contribute to the evolution of the market's public SLA templates, reflecting all traders' needs. Thirdly, if a set of new products is introduced to the market, our approach can be applied to find a set of new public SLA templates. All these benefits result in satisfied users, who continue to use the market, therefore increasing liquidity in the Cloud market.

The four contributions of this paper are: (1) the definition of three adaptation methods for adapting public SLA templates to the needs of users; (2) the investigation of conditions under which SLA templates should be adapted; (3) the formalization of measures, i.e., utility and cost, to assess SLA adaptations and SLA adaptation methods; and (4) the introduction of an emulation approach for the defined use cases.

The work in this book chapter is based on Maurer, et al. (2012).

BACKGROUND

For placing our work in the context of the existing research, we briefly describe Cloud resource management, Cloud marketplaces, and the existing work on SLA matching.

Cloud Resource Management

There is a large body of work about managing resource provisions, negotiations, and federation of Cloud and Grid resources. An example is Cheng, Ooi, & Chan (2010). They designed agent technology to address the federation problems in Grids, i.e., the resource selection and policy reconciliation. Rodero-Merino et al. (2010) propose a new abstraction layer for managing the life cycle of services. It allows automatic service deployment and escalation depending on the service status. This abstraction layer can be positioned on top of different Cloud provider infrastructures. Hence, it mitigates the potential lock-in problem and allows the transparent federation of Clouds for the execution of services. Garg, Buyya, & Siegel (2010) investigate three novel heuristics for scheduling parallel applications on utility Grids, optimizing the trade-off between time and cost constraints. This related work on resource management considers resource provision from the provider's point of view. Little work has been performed on the management of Cloud resources in the context of a marketplace so far (Risch, Altmann, Guo, Fleming, & Courcoubetis, 2009, Quan & Altmann, 2009a).

Cloud Market

Currently, a large number of commercial Cloud providers have entered the utility computing market, offering a number of different types of services. These services can be grouped into three types: computing infrastructure services, which are pure computing resources on a pay-per-use basis (Altmann, Courcoubetis, & Risch, 2010, *Tsunamic Tech. Inc.*, 2010, *EMC Atmos Online*, 2010); software services, which are computing resources in combination with a software solution (*Google App Engine*, 2010, *Salesforce.com*, 2010); and platform services, which allow customers to create their own services in combination with the help of supporting services of the platform provider

(*Salesforce.com*, 2010, *Microsoft Azure*, 2010). The first type of services, which is also called Infrastructure-as-a-Service (IaaS), consists of a virtual machine, as in the case of Amazon's EC2 service, or in the form of a computing cluster, as offered by Tsunamic Technologies. The number of different types of virtual machines offered by a provider is low. For example, Amazon and EMC introduced only three derivations of their basic resource type (*Amazon Elastic Compute Cloud*, 2010). Examples for the second type of services, which are called Software-as-a-Service (SaaS) are services offered by Google (e.g., Google Apps (*Google App Engine*, 2010)) and Salesforce.com (*Salesforce.com*, 2010). These companies provide access to software on pay-per-use basis. These SaaS solutions can hardly be integrated with other solutions, because of their complexity. Examples for the third kind of Cloud services, which are called Platform-as-a-Service (PaaS), are Sun N1 Grid (*Sun Grid*, 2011), force.com (*Salesforce.com*, 2010), and Microsoft Azure (*Microsoft Azure*, 2010). In this category, the focus lies on provisioning essential basic services that are needed by a large number of applications. These basic services can be ordered on a pay-per-use basis. Although the goal of the PaaS service offerings is a seamless integration with the users' applications, standardization of interfaces is largely absent. Furthermore, big Cloud providers as the mentioned Azure or EC2 do not even provide their SLAs in a standardized format, e.g., XML. If they want to participate in markets with higher liquidity, as leveraged by our approach, they have to comply with the market rules and formalize their SLA templates in a machine-readable way.

The implementation of system resource markets have been discussed in several projects (Altmann, Courcoubetis, & Risch, 2010, Buyya, Abramson, & Giddy, 2001, Neumann, Stößer, & Weinhardt, 2008, Nimis, Anandasivam, Borissov, Smith, Neumann, & Wirström, 2008, Quan & Altmann, 2009b). Vouros et al. (2010) give an overview over information systems for traded resources in Grid markets and (Haque, Alhashmi, & Parthiban, 2011) deal with economic models of Grid computing markets. All in all, however, mentioned works either do not define the tradable goods, work with very simplified definitions, or do not take market liquidity into account.

A complementary approach to our work has proposed a common standardized, so called *Blueprint Template* (Nguyen et al., 2011). This is a tool to "provide a common structure, syntax and semantics for Cloud service providers to abstractly (…) and unambiguously describe their offerings on multiple abstraction layers". Our approach, however, goes further and also considers the SLA templates of the Cloud consumers and not only of the providers.

Service Level Agreement Matching

The main SLA matching mechanisms are based on OWL, DAML-S, or similar semantic technologies. Oldham et al. (2006) describe a framework for semantic matching of SLAs based on WSDL-S and OWL. Green (2006) describes another ontology-based approach based on OWL and SWRL. Dobson & Sanchez-Macian (2006) present a unified QoS ontology applicable to specific scenarios such as QoS-based Web services selection, QoS monitoring, and QoS adaptation. Ardagna, Giunta, Ingraa, Mirandola, & Pernici (2006) present an autonomic Grid architecture with mechanisms for dynamically reconfiguring service center infrastructures. It is exploited to fulfill varying QoS requirements.

Besides those ontology-based mechanisms, Koller & Schubert (2007) discuss autonomous QoS management, using a proxy-like approach for defining QoS parameters that a service has to maintain during its interaction with a specific customer. The implementation is based on WS-Agreement, using predefined SLA templates. However, they cannot consider changes in user needs, although this is essential for creating successful markets, as shown in our earlier work (Risch, Brandic, &

Altmann, 2009). Additionally, several works on SLA management have been presented by Buyya & Bubendorfer (2008). Besides, regardless of the type of approach used, these approaches do not evaluate and explain the benefits and costs through the introduction of SLA matching mechanisms.

Yarmolenko & Sakellariou (2007) make a case for increasing the expressiveness of SLAs. By achieving this, they can possibly increase market liquidity, when it comes to matching asks and bids in an environment where the semantics of parameters has already been agreed upon. Our approach could be seen as complimentary in the sense that it makes sure that their pre-condition of the agreement of the SLA parameter semantics holds.

ADAPTIVE SLA MAPPING

In this section, we present a use case for adaptive SLA mapping. In addition to this, we discuss the public SLA template life cycle, describe the three adaption methods, and introduce the utility and cost model for assessing SLA matching

approaches. Finally, we briefly discuss the application of the adaptive SLA mapping approach to federated Clouds.

SLA Mapping Use Case

At the beginning the registry administrator inserts the initial SLA templates into particular databases (step 0, DBs of public SLA templates, Figure 1).

As the next step, since resources can be exposed as services using typical Cloud deployment technologies (i.e., SaaS/PaaS/IaaS), we assume that the service provider of Figure 1 registers his resources, e.g., infrastructure, software, platforms, to the mentioned databases (step 1, DBs of public SLA templates, Figure 1).

If some differences between his resources, i.e., his private SLA templates, and the public templates exist, the provider defines SLA mappings. These SLA mappings can transform the private SLA template into the public SLA template and vice versa (step 2, Figure 1). Non-technical experts as, e.g., business experts, can easily create their mappings using Web interfaces or DSLs. They can define SLA mappings in the simple form "My

Figure 1. Use case of SLA mapping

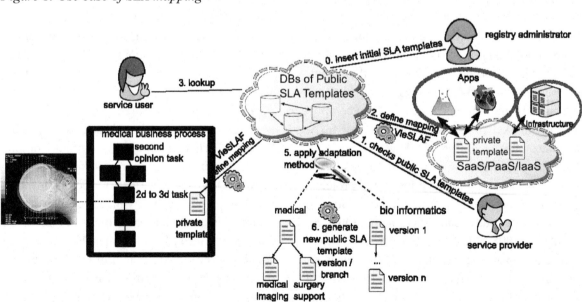

private template parameter *number of CPUs*" translates to "Public template parameter *CPU cores*". Afterwards, XSLTs can automatically be generated based on this information. The generation and management of SLA mappings, which is performed with VieSLAF, are explained in detail in (Brandic, Music, Leitner, & Dustdar, 2009).

In step 3 of Figure 1, Cloud users can look up Cloud services that they want to use in their workflow. Looking for public templates (steps 1 and 3) is not affected (slowed down) by the number of SLA mappings created, since users only look for the original public SLA template. For our use case, a business process (i.e., workflow) for medical treatments is assumed (Brandic, Benkner, Engelbrecht, & Schmidt, 2005). It includes various interactions with human beings, e.g., the task of getting a second opinion on a diagnosis, as well as an interaction with different infrastructure services. Some of these tasks, e.g., the reconstruction of 2-dimensional SPECT images to 3-dimensional SPECT images, can be outsourced to the Cloud (Brandic et al., 2005). Thereby, we assume that the private SLA template (representing the task) cannot be changed, since it is also part of some other local business processes and has to comply with different legal guidelines for electronic processing of medical data.

In case the user decides to outsource a task and discovers differences between the private SLA template and the public SLA template, the user defines an SLA mapping. In general, the SLA mapping describes the differences between the two SLA templates (step 4, Figure 1). A typical mapping is the mapping of an attribute name to another attribute name (e.g., *number of CPUs* to *cores*) or the inclusion of a new SLA attribute (e.g., *parallel programming models*) into the SLA template. Concerns like patient confidentiality can be enforced by an SLA compliance model (Brandic et al., 2010).

The public SLA templates are stored in searchable repositories using SQL and non-SQL-based databases (e.g., HadoopDB). The SLA mappings, which have been provided by users and providers to the registry administrator, are evaluated after certain time periods, in order to adapt the public SLA templates to the needs of the users. Then, the adapted public SLA templates replace the existing public SLA templates in the repository, constituting our novel approach of adaptive SLA mapping. The adaptation method, which adapts the public SLA templates, does this in a way such that the new public SLA templates represent user needs better than the old SLA templates (step 5, Figure 1).

The adaptation of attributes, attribute names, and attribute values cannot only replace SLA templates but also create new versions and branches of public SLA templates (step 6, Figure 1). A new branch of a public SLA template can be created, if specialization needs to be captured (e.g., a medical SLA template can be substituted by more specialized templates on medical imaging and surgery support). The creation of new branches using clustering algorithms has been examined by Breskovic, Maurer, Emeakaroha, Brandic, & Altmann (2011) in detail. The definition of different versions of a particular public SLA template occurs, if different attribute combinations in the templates are used frequently. Figure 1 shows n SLA template versions in the bioinformatics domain.

Public SLA Template Life Cycle

To illustrate the life cycle of public SLA templates, a brief example, as shown in Figure 2, is given first.

Initially, the SLA template registry only holds the initial public SLA template T_0. In iteration 1, all users define mappings from their private templates to T_0. Since the attribute names of the public SLA template *(A, B, C)* and the attribute names of the private template of each user differ, all users have to create 3 attribute mappings. Based on these mappings, the new version T_1 of the

Figure 2. SLA mapping process

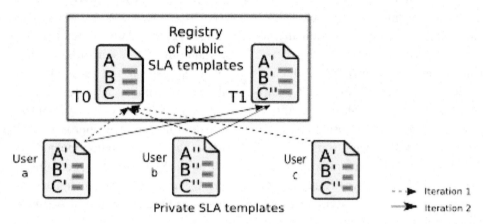

public template is generated (according to the adaptation method used), containing the attribute names *A', B', C"*.

Since the public SLA template has changed, users need to change their mappings as well (iteration 2). Consequently, user *a* only needs one attribute mapping, user *b* needs two attribute mappings, and user *c* does not need to issue any attribute mapping, since the public template is completely identical to her private template. This example shows how our adaptive SLA mapping approach adapts a public SLA template to the needs of users. In addition to this, since adapted public SLA templates represent the need of market participants, it is most likely that new requests of users need less attribute mappings, reducing the cost for these users.

The formalized public SLA template life cycle, which consists of five steps, is shown in Figure 3.

An initial template is created in the beginning of the life cycle (step 1, Figure 3). Afterwards,

consumers perform SLA mappings to their private SLA templates (step 2). Based on their needs, which are inferred from these mappings (step 3), and the predefined adaptation method, the public SLA template is adapted (step 4). Assuming that the demand of market participants does not change, a final template is generated (step 5). If the demand has changed during a fixed time period (i.e., new tasks have to be executed or new users joined the marketplace), the process continues with step 2. In practice, the time between two iterations could correspond to a time period of one week, e.g., but can be set to any value depending on the changes in the market. During that time new SLA mappings are solicited from consumers and providers.

Adaptation Methods

The adaptation methods determine for every attribute name of the public SLA template separately, whether the current attribute name should be

Figure 3. Formalized public SLA template life cycle

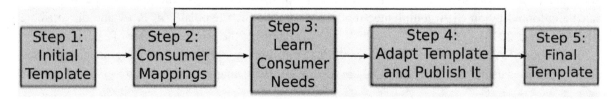

adapted or not. In this paper, we investigate three adaptation methods. The first adaptation method is the maximum method (which has been applied in the example shown in Figure 2). The remaining two adaptation methods apply heuristics, in order to find a balance between benefit and cost.

Maximum Adaptation Method

Applying this method, the SLA attribute name, which has the highest number of attribute name mappings, is selected (maximum candidate). The selected attribute name will become the next attribute name of the next public SLA template.

Example: If we assume that all attribute names have the same count, this method would select any of the four possible attribute names randomly. If a public SLA template already exists, the method will choose the attribute name that is currently used in the public SLA template.

Threshold Adaptation Method

In order to increase the requirements for selecting the maximum candidate, this method introduces a threshold value. If an attribute name is used more than this threshold (which can be adapted) and has the highest count, then this attribute name will be selected. If more than one attribute name is above the threshold and they have the same count, the method proceeds as described for the maximum method. If none is above the required threshold, then the method sticks to the currently used attribute name. Note, throughout the examples in this paper, we fix the threshold to 60%.

Example: Assuming an example, in which none of the attribute names has a mapping percentage above 60% and all counts are equal, the threshold method selects the attribute name that is listed in the public SLA template.

Maximum-Percentage-Change Adaptation Method

This method is divided into two steps. In the first step, the attribute name is chosen according to the maximum method.

In the second step, which comprises τ iterations, attribute names will be changed, only if the percentage difference between the highest count attribute name and the currently selected attribute name exceeds a threshold. The threshold σ_τ is set to *15%* within this paper. A low threshold leads to more mappings, whereas a high threshold leads on average to fewer mappings. After τ iterations (e.g., $\tau=10$), the method re-starts with executing the first step. This allows larger changes to the SLA template.

Example: Let us suppose the mapping count resulted in attribute name A' having the highest count. By applying the maximum method, A' is selected. In the next iteration, the number of mappings for each attribute name has changed. Attribute name A accounted for 10%, A' for 28%, A'' for 32%, and A''' for 30% of all mappings. Assuming a threshold of 15%, the chosen attribute does not change. The percentage difference between attribute name A' and the attribute name A'' with the highest count is only 32/28 - 1.0 = 14.3%.

Utility and Cost Model

Since the aim of this paper is to assess the benefit and the cost of using the adaptive SLA mapping approach for finding the optimal standardized goods in a Cloud market, we define a utility and cost model. At its core, the model defines the utility function and the cost function, which take attributes of the private SLA template of the customer and the attributes of the public SLA template as input variables.

The model assumes an increase in benefit, if an attribute (or attribute name or attribute value) of both templates is identical. This is motivated by the fact that the Cloud resource traded is identical to the need of the buyer (or, in the equivalent case, the provisioned resource of the provider). A trade could be executed faster. The model also captures the effort (i.e., cost) of changing an SLA mapping. The cost is only incurred, if the user needs to change its SLA mapping because of a change in the public SLA template.

To formally introduce the utility and cost functions, we introduce some definitions. The set of SLA attributes is defined as T_{var}. As an example, we set $T_{var} = \{\alpha, \beta\}$, where α represents *Number of Cores in one CPU* and β represents *Amount of CPU Time*. All possible attribute names that a user can map to $\pi \in T_{var}$ are denoted as $Var(\pi)$. Within our example, we set $Var(\alpha) = \{A, A', A'', A'''\}$, representing $Var("Number\ of\ Cores\ in\ one\ CPU") = \{CPU\ Cores,\ Cores\ of\ CPU,\ Number\ of\ CPUCores,\ Cores\}$, and $Var(b) = \{B, B', B'', B'''\}$. Note, in the same way as shown for attribute names, we could handle attribute values.

Assuming a set of private SLA templates $C = \{c_1, c_2, ..., c_n\}$ of customers, we can now define the relationship of a specific SLA attribute to a specific attribute name of this SLA attribute at a specific point in time (i.e., iteration) $i \in N$ for a SLA template p, $p \in C \cup \{T\}$ (i.e., private or public SLA template) as

$$SLA_{p,i} : T_{var} \rightarrow \bigcup_{\pi \in T_{var}} Var(\pi). \qquad (1)$$

With respect to our example, we assume $SLA_{T,0}(\alpha) = A$ and $SLA_{T,0}(\beta) = B$ as our initial public template T at time 0 (i.e., iteration 0).

Based on these definitions and the utility function exemplified in (Chen & Lu, 2008), we define the utility function $u_{c,i}^{+}(\pi)$ and the cost function

$u_{c,i}^{-}(\pi)$ for consumer c, attribute $\pi \in T_{var}$, and iteration $i \geq 1$ with $W^{+} \geq W^{-} \geq 0$ as

$$u_{c,i}^{+}(\pi) = \begin{cases} W^{+}, & SLA_{c,i}(\pi) = SLA_{T,i}(\pi) \\ 0, & SLA_{c,i}(\pi) \neq SLA_{T,i}(\pi) \end{cases} \qquad (2)$$

$$u_{c,i}^{-}(\pi) = \begin{cases} 0, & SLA_{c,i}(\pi) = SLA_{T,i}(\pi) \\ 0, & SLA_{c,i}(\pi) \neq SLA_{T,i}(\pi) \land \\ & SLA_{T,i-1}(\pi) = SLA_{T,i}(\pi) \\ W^{-}, & SLA_{c,i}(\pi) \neq SLA_{T,i}(\pi) \land \\ & SLA_{T,i-1}(\pi) \neq SLA_{T,i}(\pi) \end{cases} \qquad (3)$$

The utility function states that a consumer c receives a utility of W^{+}, if the name of the attribute of the private SLA template matches the name of the public SLA template attribute, and a utility of *0* otherwise.

With respect to the cost function, cost is defined as the effort of generating a new SLA mapping. The cost function states that a consumer has a cost of W^{-}, if the attribute names do not match and the public template attribute of the previous iteration has been adapted to a new one. In this case, the consumer has to define a new attribute mapping, as he cannot use the old one anymore. The cost of issuing a new mapping should be lower than the utility of standardizing SLA attributes through the same attribute names. This is why $W^{+} \geq W^{-}$. For our analysis, we set $W^{+}=1$ and $W^{-}=1/2$. In the other two cases of the cost function, the consumer has no cost, since either the attribute names match or the public template attribute name did not change since the previous iteration. That means he does not need any new mapping. Thus, for attribute π, the consumer c at iteration i gets the net utility

$$u_{c,i}^{o}(\pi) = u_{c,i}^{+}(\pi) - u_{c,i}^{-}(\pi) \qquad (4)$$

The net utility for all attributes at iteration i for consumer c is defined as the sum of the net utilities $u_{c,i}^{o}(\pi)$:

$$u_{c,i}^{o} = \sum_{\pi \in T_{var}} u_{c,i}^{o}(\pi) \qquad (5)$$

In addition to this, the overall utility and overall cost (i.e., the utility and cost of all consumers c and attributes π at iteration i) are defined as:

$$U_i^{+} = \sum_{c \in C} \sum_{\pi \in T_{var}} u_{c,i}^{+}(\pi) \qquad (6)$$

$$U_i^{-} = \sum_{c \in C} \sum_{\pi \in T_{var}} u_{c,i}^{-}(\pi) \qquad (7)$$

Consequently, the overall net utility at iteration i is defined as the difference between the overall utilities minus the overall cost or as the sum of the net utility of all consumers c for all attributes at iteration i:

$$U_i^{o} = U_i^{+} - U_i^{-} = \sum_{c \in C} u_{c,i}^{o} \qquad (8)$$

Application to Federated Clouds

This approach is highly suitable for federated Clouds. An important aspect of federations is that applications or virtual machines can be outsourced from one Cloud provider A to another Cloud provider B in the same federation. However, assuming that these providers use the same static SLA template to guarantee QoS goals to their consumers would limit and hinder the formation of meaningful Cloud federations. Our approach can be applied to this context by assuming that our Cloud consumers are actually other Cloud provider in need of additional resources. For example, with respect to Figure 1, we can identify the service provider of Figure 1 with a Cloud provider A that offers his resources and the service user of

Figure 1 with a Cloud provider B that is in need of resources to deploy its applications or virtual machines outside its own Cloud.

EXPERIMENT ENVIRONMENT

In order to analyze the performance of the three adaptation methods with respect to the balance between adapting the public SLA template to the current needs of all users and the cost of making new SLA mappings, we set up a simulation environment.

Simulation Testbed

For our simulation, we use a testbed that is composed of production-level software (*VieSLAF*) and software that simulates SLA mappings of users. Figure 4 illustrates our emulation testbed. The components that are drawn in white belong to *VieSLAF*. It comprises the knowledge base, the middleware for managing SLA mappings provided by consumers and providers, and the adaptation methods. The grey components indicate the components that simulate SLA mappings of users. A sample provider and a sample consumer are shown in the lower part of Figure 4.

The SLA mapping middleware, which follows a client-server design, facilitates the access for the provider and for the consumer to the registries. In detail, it provides to users a GUI for browsing public SLA templates. The SLA mapping middleware is based on different Windows Communication Foundation (WCF) services, of which only a few are mentioned in the following paragraph.

The *RegistryAdministrationService* provides methods for the manipulation of the database. This service requires administrator rights. An example for the use of these methods is the creation of template domains. Another service of the SLA mapping middleware is the *SLAMappingService*, which is used for the management of SLA mappings by service consumers and service providers

Figure 4. Adaptive SLA mapping architecture using VieSLAF

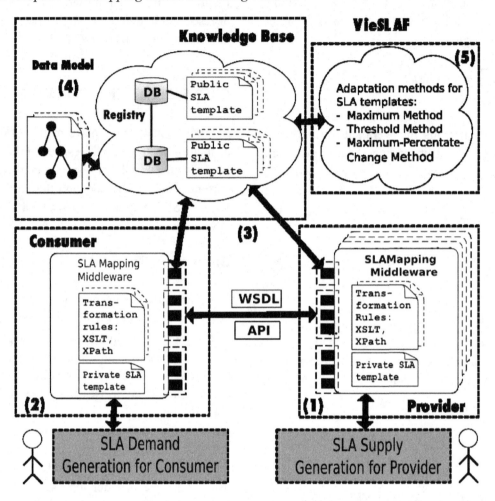

((3) of Figure 4). Providers and consumers may also search for appropriate public SLA templates through *SLAQueryingService* and define appropriate SLA mappings by using the method *createAttributeMapping*. With each service request, it is also checked whether the user has also specified any new SLA mappings. The SLA mappings (i.e., transformation rules) are stored in the private database of the user and can be reused by the user for her next SLA mapping.

The knowledge base for storing SLA templates in a predefined data model is implemented as registries representing searchable repositories ((4) of Figure 4). Currently, we have implemented an MS-SQL 2008 database with a Web service frontend. To handle scalability issues, we intend to utilize non-SQL DBs (e.g., HadoopDB) with SQL-like frontends (e.g., Hive (Thusoo, et al., 2009)). SLA templates are stored in a canonical form, enabling the comparison of XML-based SLA templates. The registry methods are also implemented as WCF services and can be accessed only with appropriate access rights. The access rights distinguish three access roles: *consumer*, *provider*, and *registry administrator*. The registry administrator may create new SLA templates. A service consumer and a service provider may search for SLA templates and can submit their SLA mappings.

Based on the submitted SLA mappings, public SLA templates are adapted by the registry administrator, using one of the adaptation methods ((5) of Figure 4), as introduced in section *Adaptation Methods*.

Simulation Parameters

For our simulation, we define five scenarios on how often attribute names occur in private SLA templates on average. In particular, each scenario defines an occurrence distribution of four different SLA attribute names. Our observations indicate that four different SLA attribute names seems to be a reasonable number, e.g., the SLA attribute names *CPU Cores, Cores of CPU, Number of CPUCores*, and *Cores*. However, this number can be increased without limitation.

With four different attribute names, we can partition all possible situations into exactly five different scenarios that are defined as follows:

- **Scenario a:** All attribute name counts for one attribute are equal.
- **Scenario b:** The counts of three attribute names are equal and larger than the remaining one.
- **Scenario c:** Two attribute name counts are equal and are larger than the other two, which are equal as well.
- **Scenario d:** One attribute name, which has been picked as the attribute name for the initial setting, has a larger count than the counts of the remaining three attribute names, which are equally large.
- **Scenario e:** One attribute name, which has not been picked as the attribute name for the initial setting, has a larger count than the counts of the remaining three attribute names, which are equally large.

The actual values of each of the five scenarios are shown in Table 1. The four attribute names chosen for this example are: *A, A', A''*, and *A'''*.

The initial setting of attribute α is the attribute name *A*.

As an example for the use of the scenarios, we take scenario *c*. If the attribute α (*Number of Cores in one CPU*) is distributed according to scenario *c*, then the four attribute names occur in average as follows: 10% of the attribute names is *A*, 10% of the attribute names is *A'*, 40% of the attribute names is *A''*, and 40% of the attribute names is *A'''*. However, as we intend to account for slight changes in the demand for attribute names by users, we draw randomly the attribute names according to the distribution given in Table 1 instead of generating the exact number of attribute names. Consequently, the actual counts of attribute names might vary compared to the average values shown in Table 1. As an example, the attribute names generated according to the distribution of scenario *c* might be 9%, 12%, 37%, and 42% instead of 10%, 10%, 40%, and 40%. This process of generation of attribute names is executed in each iteration.

Furthermore, three more simulation parameters need to be set. First, we limit the number of iterations to 20. This number is chosen, because from iteration to iteration the consumer base does not evolve (the consumers obey to the same distribution in each iteration, but the quite low number of users reveals different random samples of the distributions). 20 iterations are also sufficiently large to examine the market demand fluctuations. More iterations would not reveal any new information. In each iteration, 100 users perform SLA map-

Table 1. Average occurrence of attribute names in all scenarios

	Scenarios [%]				
	a	**b**	**c**	**d**	**e**
A	25	10	10	30.0	23.3
A'	25	30	10	23.3	30.0
A''	25	30	40	23.3	23.3
A'''	25	30	40	23.3	23.3

pings to all SLA attributes. The number is not set higher in order to mimic sufficiently large market demand fluctuations. At the end of an iteration, a new public SLA template is generated, which is based on the adaptation method and the SLA mappings of the user. As in our evaluation setting the market will not stabilize, a final template as described in Figure 3 will not be generated. For each of the three adaptation methods, we execute one separate simulation run. Moreover, the SLA template consists of 5 SLA attributes. The SLA attribute names of those 5 attributes are distributed according to scenarios a to e. Consequently, the utility and the cost will be averaged values over all five scenarios. Table 2 summarizes these settings.

SIMULATION RESULTS

Cost and Utilities of Three Adaptation Methods

Using our SLA mapping approach, the user benefits from having access to public SLA templates that reflect the overall market demand (i.e., the demand of all users). This benefit for a user is expressed with equation 2. However, this benefit comes with the cost for defining new SLA mappings whenever the public SLA template is adapted (equation 3).

Within this section, we investigate the cost for all users (equation 7), the utility of all users (equation 6), and the net utility of all users (equation 8) with respect to three adaptation methods. The net utility metric is used to decide which of the three adaptation methods investigated is superior.

The first adaption method that we investigate is the maximum method. It is our reference method, since it does not use any heuristics. The simulation uses the parameter settings that have been described in the previous Section.

Figure 5 shows the resulting public SLA templates for each of the 20 iterations. For every of the five attributes, a line indicates the SLA

Table 2. Simulation parameter settings

Simulation Parameter	Value
Number of scenarios	5
Number of users (consumers & providers)	100
Number of SLA attributes per SLA template	5
Number of SLA attributes names per attribute	4
Number of adaptation methods applied	3
Number of iterations	20

parameter names that have been chosen for a specific iteration.

Figure 6 shows, as expected, that the maximum method generates a high utility, since it achieves many matches of SLA attribute names of the public SLA template with those of the private SLA templates. Its utility stays around its initial utility value of about 170 in each iteration. However, as expected as well, it requires many new mappings and, thus, incurs high costs to the users. Consequently, the net utility is low. Consequently, we can state that the advantage of the maximum method is that the public SLA template generated with this method minimizes the differences to all private SLA templates of all users.

In order to address the issue of high cost of the maximum method, we use heuristics in adaptation methods. The heuristics help to find a balance between the utility of having a public SLA template, whose attribute names are identical to most of the attribute names of the private SLA templates, and the cost of creating new SLA attribute mappings. The first heuristics-based adaptation method, which we investigate, is the threshold method. The simulation results are shown in Figures 7 and Figure 8.

Figure 8 illustrates that the threshold method does not incur any cost to users at all. The reason is that this adaptation method does not cause any changes to the initially set parameter names at all (Figure 7). This is due to the high threshold (i.e., a threshold of 60%), resulting in no changes to the public SLA template attribute names.

Figure 5. Public templates for the maximum method

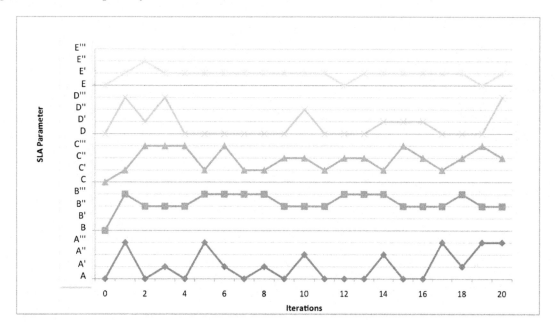

Nevertheless, the utility (and net utility) is not higher than the ones of the maximum method, just more stable across the 20 iterations. Therefore, the threshold method with a threshold of 60% could be considered the opposite strategy to the maximum method. That means, the initial public SLA template does not get adapted at all. By lowering the threshold parameter such that the threshold parameter for a few iterations is lower than the highest count of an attribute name, it is expected that the net utility improves. If the threshold parameter is lower than the minimum count of an attribute name in all iterations, then this method is identical to the maximum method.

Figure 6. Utility, cost, and net utility for the maximum method

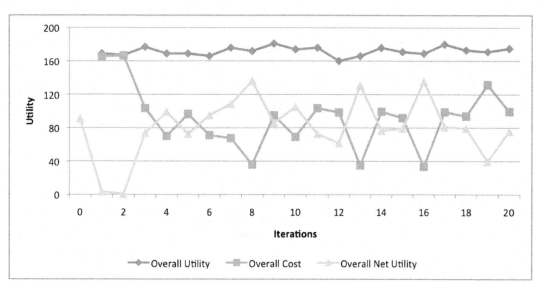

Figure 7. Public templates for the threshold method

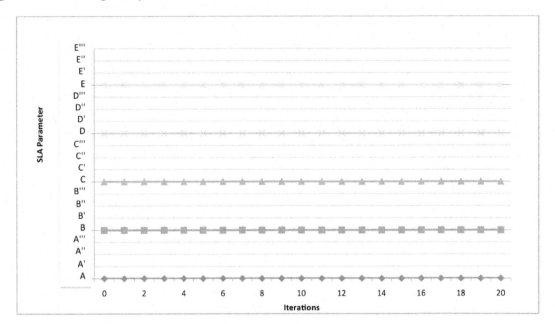

The maximum-percentage-change method is the second heuristics-based adaptation method that we investigate. The results are shown in Figures 9 and Figure 10. While Figure 9 shows the attribute names for each of the five attribute, Figure 10 shows the utility, the cost, and the net utility.

The simulation results show that in the first iteration and every tenth iteration $\tau=10$) the overall net utility decreases significantly due to the high amount of new SLA mappings needed (Figure 10). This is caused by the fact that the attribute names changed for many of the 5 attributes in these iterations (Figure 9). At these iterations, this

Figure 8. Utility, cost, and net utility, for the threshold method

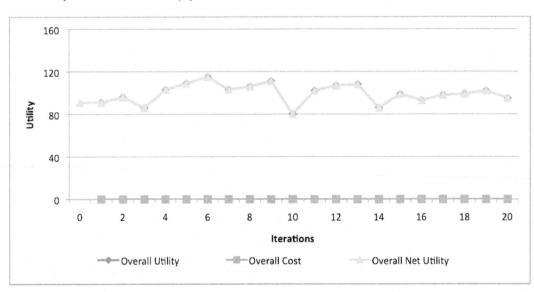

Figure 9. Public templates for the maximum-percentage-change method with τ=10

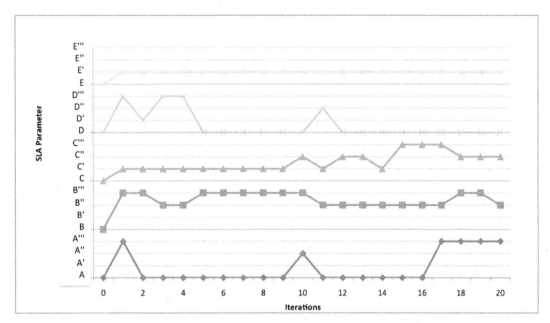

adaptation method chooses the attribute names with the maximum number of counts (not considering the threshold of *15%*). In the subsequent iterations, however, it considers the threshold of 15% again. Therefore, the cost is low and the overall net utility increases significantly. It achieves even higher values than the other two adaption methods.

Figure 10. Utility, cost, and net utility for the maximum-percentage-change method with τ=10

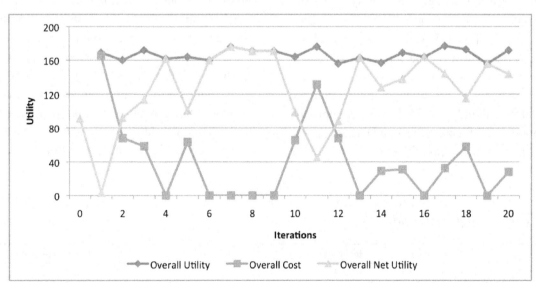

Average Net Utility

Table 3 shows the average overall utility, average overall cost, and the average overall net utility for all three adaptation methods. The averages are calculated over all iterations. The maximum method has achieved the highest average overall utility. It satisfies the largest number of users. However, since it also incurs the highest costs, it becomes the method with the lowest average overall net utility.

The threshold method does slightly better with respect to the average net utility than the maximum method. This is due to the zero cost. The threshold method (with a high threshold) stays with the initial SLA attribute name for the public SLA template.

The best adaptation method with respect to the average overall net utility is the maximum-percentage-change method. We observe that the average overall net utility is better than the ones of the other two adaptation methods, although the average overall utility is not the highest among the three adaptation methods. The reason is that the cost is low. The low cost is a result of the fact that the SLA attribute names of the public SLA template are not changed frequently. They are only changed in iterations $k\tau + 1, k \in N_0$ (i.e., when the method behaves like the maximum method) and whenever the threshold of *15%* is exceeded.

Based on the result shown in this section, we can state that the adaptive SLA mapping approach is a good way of generating standardized goods, which address the needs of the market. To reduce the cost of creating SLA mappings frequently, the introduction of heuristics into the adaptation methods is helpful. Our results show that a significant reduction of costs can be achieved while preserving the benefit of adapted public SLA templates.

FUTURE RESEARCH DIRECTIONS

Our future work will comprise an analysis of whether determining groups of users coming from different domains can increase the overall net utility even further than the maximum-percentage-change method. Furthermore, we will investigate other metrics (besides the quantity based mapping count) for the adaptation methods. This could be the number of SLAs newly established.

CONCLUSION

We have investigated cost, utility, and net utility of the adaptive SLA mapping approach. The adaptive SLA mapping approach requires market participants to define SLA mappings for translating their private SLA templates to public SLA templates. Contrary to all other available SLA matching approaches, the adaptive SLA mapping approach facilitates continuous adaptation of public SLA templates based on market trends.

However, the adaptation of SLA mappings comes with a cost for users in the form of effort for generating new SLA mappings to the adapted public SLA template. To calculate the cost and benefits of the SLA mapping approach, we uti-

Table 3. Overall utility, overall costs, and overall net utilities averaged across all iterations (The best values are highlighted in bold)

	Maximum	Threshold	Max.-Perc.-Change
avg. overall utility	**171.9**	99.5	166.6
avg. overall cost	91.3	**0.0**	39.95
avg. overall net utilities	80.6	99.5	**126.65**

lized the SLA management framework VieSLAF and simulated different market situations. Our findings show that the cost for SLA mappings can be reduced by introducing heuristics into the adaptation methods for generating adapted public SLA templates. The heuristic-based adaptation methods show cost reduction and an increase in average overall net utility. The best-performing adaptation method is the maximum-percentage-change method, which has been applied with a threshold of 15% and an iteration value $\tau = 10$.

ACKNOWLEDGMENT

The authors would like to thank Marcel Risch for his valuable discussions. The research was partially supported by the Korea Institute for Advancement of Technology (KIAT) within the ITEA 2 project 10014 EASI-CLOUDS and the Vienna Science and Technology Fund (grant agreement ICT08-018), Foundations of Self-governing ICT Infrastructures (FoSII).

REFERENCES

Altmann, J., Courcoubetis, C., & Risch, M. (2010). A marketplace and its market mechanism for trading commoditized computing resources *Annales des Télécommunications, 65*(11-12), 653–667. doi:10.1007/s12243-010-0183-1

Amazon Elastic Compute Cloud (Amazon EC2). (2010). Retrieved December 2011, from http://aws.amazon.com/ec2/.

Ardagna, D., Giunta, G., Ingraa, N., Mirandola, R., & Pernici, B. (2006). Qos-driven web services selection in autonomic grid environments. In *International conference on grid computing, high performance and distributed applications (gada)*. Montpellier, France.

BRAIN - business objective driven reliable and intelligent grids for real business. (2010). Retrieved December 2011 from http://www.eu-brein.com/.

Brandic, I., Anstett, T., Schumm, D., Leymann, F., Dustdar, S., & Konrad, R. (2010). Compliant cloud computing (c3): Architecture and language support for user-driven compliance management in clouds. In *The 3rd international conference on cloud computing (ieee cloud 2010)*. Miami, FL, USA.

Brandic, I., Benkner, S., Engelbrecht, G., & Schmidt, R. (2005). *Qos support for time-critical grid workflow applications. In 1st ieee international conference on e-science and grid computing*. Melbourne, Australia.

Brandic, I., Music, D., Leitner, P., & Dustdar, S. (2009). Vieslaf framework: Enabling adaptive and versatile sla-management. In *Gecon2009. in conjunction with euro-par 2009*. Delft, The Netherlands.

Breskovic, I., Maurer, M., Emeakaroha, V. C., Brandic, I., & Altmann, J. (2011). Towards autonomic market management in cloud computing infrastructures. In *International conference on cloud computing and services science - closer 2011*. Noordwijkerhout, the Netherlands.

Buyya, R., Abramson, D., & Giddy, J. (2001). A case for economy grid architecture for service oriented grid computing. In *Parallel and distributed processing symposium*.

Buyya, R., & Bubendorfer, K. (2008). *Market oriented grid and utility computing*. New Jersey, USA: John Wiley & Sons, Inc.

Chen, J., & Lu, B. (2008). An universal flexible utility function in grid economy. In *Ieee pacific-asia workshop on computational intelligence and industrial application*.

Cheng, W. K., Ooi, B. Y., & Chan, H. Y. (2010). Resource federation in grid using automated intelligent agent negotiation. *Future Generation Computer Systems, 26*(8), 1116–1126. doi:10.1016/j.future.2010.05.012

Dobson, G., & Sanchez-Macian, A. (2006). Towards unified qos/sla ontologies. In *Ieee services computing workshops (scw)* (pp. 18-22). Chicago, Illinois, USA.

EMC Atmos Online. (2010). https://mgmt.atmosonline.com/.

Garg, S. K., Buyya, R., & Siegel, H. J. (2010). Time and cost trade-off management for scheduling parallel applications on utility grids. *Future Generation Computer Systems, 26*(8), 1344–1355. doi:10.1016/j.future.2009.07.003

Google App Engine. (2010). Retrieved December 2011 from http://code.google.com/appengine/.

Green, L. (2006). *Service level agreements: an ontological approach. In 8th international conference on electronic commerce: The new e-commerce: innovations for conquering current barriers, obstacles and limitations to conducting successful business on the internet, icec '06.* New York, NY, USA.

Haque, A., Alhashmi, S. M., & Parthiban, R. (2011). A survey of economic models in grid computing. *Future Generation Computer Systems, 27*(8), 1056–1069. doi:10.1016/j.future.2011.04.009

Koller, B., & Schubert, L. (2007). Towards autonomous sla management using a proxy-like approach. *Multiagent Grid Systems, 3*(3).

Maurer, M., Emeakaroha, V. C., Brandic, I., & Altmann, J. (2012). Cost-Benefit Analysis of an SLA Mapping Approach for Defining Standardized Cloud Computing Goods. *Future Generation Computer Systems, 28*(1), 36–47. doi:10.1016/j.future.2011.05.023

Microsoft Azure. (2010). Retrieved December 2011 from http://www.microsoft.com/windowsazure/.

Neumann, D., Stößer, J., & Weinhardt, C. (2008). Bridging the adoption gap – developing a roadmap for trading in grids. *Electronic Markets, 18*(1), 65–74. doi:10.1080/10196780701797664

Nguyen, D., Lelli, F., Taher, Y., Parkin, M., Papazoglou, M., & van den Heuvel, W. J. (2011). Blueprint template support for engineering cloud-based services. In W. Abramowicz, I. Llorente, M. Surridge, A. Zisman, & J. Vayssière (Eds.), *Towards a service-based internet, 6994,* 26-37. Heidelberg, Germany: Springer Berlin.

Nimis, J., Anandasivam, A., Borissov, N., Smith, G., Neumann, D., & Wirström, N. (2008). SORMA - business cases for an open grid market: Concept and implementation. In Springer (Ed.), *5th international workshop on grid economics and business models (gecon '08)* (pp. 173-184).

Oldham, N., Verma, K., Sheth, A. P., & Hakimpour, F. (2006, May). *Semantic ws-agreement partner selection. In 15th international conference on world wide web, www 2006.* Edinburgh, Scotland, UK.

Quan, D. M., Altmann, J. (2009a). Resource allocation algorithm for the light communication Grid-based workflows within an SLA context. *International Journal of Parallel, Emergent and Distributed Systems, 24*(1).

Quan, D. M., & Altmann, J. (2009b). Grid business models for brokers executing SLA-based workflows. In *Rajkumar Buyya, Kris Bubendorfer. Market-Oriented Grid and Utility Computing.* New York, NY, USA: Wiley. doi:10.1002/9780470455432.ch7

Risch, M., & Altmann, J. (2009). Enabling open cloud markets through ws-agreement extensions. In *Service level agreements in grids workshop, in conjunction with grid 2009.*

Risch, M., Altmann, J., Guo, L., Fleming, A., & Courcoubetis, C. (2009). *The gridecon platform: A business scenario testbed for commercial cloud services. In 6th international workshop on grid economics and business models.* Delft, The Netherlands.

Risch, M., Brandic, I., & Altmann, J. (2009, November). Using sla mapping to increase market liquidity. In *Nfpslam-soc 2009 in conjunction with the 7th international joint conference on service oriented computing.* Stockholm, Sweden.

Rodero-Merino, L., Vaquero, L. M., Gil, V., Galan, F., Fontan, J., & Montero, R. S. (2010, October). From infrastructure delivery to service management in clouds. *Future Generation Computer Systems, 26*(8), 1226–1240. doi:10.1016/j.future.2010.02.013

Salesforce.com. (2010). Retrieved December 2011, http://www.salesforce.com.

Sun Grid. (2011) Retrieved December 2011 from http://wikis.sun.com/display/GridEngine/Home.

Thusoo, A., Sarma, J. S., & Jain, N. (2009). *Hive - a warehousing solution over a map-reduce framework.* Vldb.

Tsunamic Tech. Inc. (2010). Retrieved December 2011 from http://www.technology.ca.

Vouros, G. A., Papasalouros, A., Tzonas, K., Valarakos, A., Kotis, K., & Quiane-Ruiz, J. A. (2010). A semantic information system for services and traded resources in grid e-markets. *Future Generation Computer Systems, 26*(7), 916–933. doi:10.1016/j.future.2010.03.004

Yarmolenko, V., & Sakellariou, R. (2007). Towards increased expressiveness in service level agreements. *Concurrency and Computation, n.d.,* 19.

ADDITIONAL READING

Altmann, J., Hovestadt, M., & Kao, O. (2011). Business support service platform for providers in open cloud computing markets. *INC2011, IEEE 7th International Conference on Networked Computing,* Gumi, South-Korea.

Altmann, J., Rana, O. F., & Buyya, R. (2009) Grid economics and business models, 6th International Workshop, GECON 2009, LNCS 5745, Springer, Berlin, Heidelberg, Germany.

Mohammed, A., Altmann, J., & Hwang, J. (2009). Cloud computing value chains: understanding business and value creation in the cloud. In *Economic Models and Algorithms for Distributed Systems, Autonomic Systems book series, Birkhäuser.* Springer. doi:10.1007/978-3-7643-8899-7_11

Breskovic, I., Maurer, M., Emeakaroha, V. C., Brandic, I., & Altmann, J. (2011). *Achieving market liquidity through autonomic cloud market management. Special issue on Cloud Computing and Service Science.* Springer LNCS.

Neumann, D., Baker, M., Altmann, J., & Rana, O. F. (2009). Economic models and algorithms for distributed systems. Birkhäuser, Autonomic Systems series, ISBN 978-3-7643-8896-6.

KEY TERMS AND DEFINITIONS

Cost: The effort that is needed to perform a certain activity.

Heuristics: A rule which has been based on past experience when solving a problem.

IaaS: It is the abbreviation for Infrastructure-as-a-Service.

SLA: It is the abbreviation for service level agreement.

SLA Matching: The approach of checking whether two SLAs define the same good or service.

Utility: It is a measure for the benefit a user receives from the consumption of a service.

Chapter 17
Deploying and Running Enterprise Grade Applications in a Federated Cloud

Benoit Hudzia
SAP, UK

Jonathan Sinclair
SAP, UK

Maik Lindner
SAP, UK

ABSTRACT

The notion of cloud computing is a paradigm shift from local machines and networks to virtualization technologies with services as a technical and business concept. This shift introduces major challenges when using cloud for deploying and running enterprise applications in the current Enterprise ecosystems. For companies, picking and choosing the right cloud to meet requirements is hard, and no solution is likely to provide the end-to-end specific IT services delivery and an end-to-end IT solution. Conversely cloud federation assists in providing flexibility to the customer and enables them to lower their TCO by shifting from one cloud to another while mitigating risks associated with a single cloud approach. In order to create competitive differentiation, small businesses require multiple software systems to both meet minimal data management and creative expectations. At the other end of the enterprise ecosystem spectrum, large companies rely on thousands of services in order to meet the needs of everything from simple departmental database applications to core Enterprise Resource planning and Customer Relationship Management systems on which the enterprise itself is managed. As an optimal adoption decision cannot be established for all individual cases, the authors propose to analyze three different use cases for deployment of enterprise applications such as SAP, on the cloud in order to provide some valuable pointers to navigate the emerging cloud ecosystem: rapid provisioning, elasticity and live migration of enterprise applications.

DOI: 10.4018/978-1-4666-1631-8.ch017

Copyright © 2012, IGI Global. Copying or distributing in print or electronic forms without written permission of IGI Global is prohibited.

INTRODUCTION

Cloud computing is still in its early stages and constantly undergoing changes as new vendors, offers, services appear in the cloud market. This evolution of cloud computing model is driven by cloud providers bringing new services to the ecosystem or revamped and efficient exiting services primarily triggered by ever changing requirements by the consumers. However, as cloud computing is predominantly adopted by start-ups or SMEs so far and wide scale enterprise adoption of cloud computing model is still in its infancy. Enterprises are still carefully contemplating the various usage models where cloud computing can be employed to support their business operations. Often Enterprise Cloud Computing is understood as the outsourcing of business applications or data hosting to another organization's IT resources. While this is quite often the end result, it does not represent the overall objective and the complete set of possibilities for Enterprise Cloud Computing strategies.

Using cloud for deploying and running enterprise grade applications in the current Enterprise ecosystems faces major challenges. For example in order to create competitive differentiation, small businesses require multiple software systems to both meet minimal data management and creative expectations. At the other end of the scope scale, large enterprises rely on thousands of services in order to meet the needs of everything from simple departmental database applications to core Enterprise Resource planning (ERP) and Customer Relationship Management (CRM) systems on which the enterprise itself is managed. For companies, picking and choosing the right cloud to meet these needs it is hard, and no solution is likely to provide the end-to-end specific IT services deliver and end-to-end IT solution.

An optimal adoption decision cannot be established for all individual cases, as the types of resources (infrastructure, storage, software) obtained from a cloud depend on the size of the organization, understanding of IT impact on business, predictability of workloads, in optimal of existing IT landscape and available budget/resources for testing and piloting.

In this chapter, we first propose to analyze three different use cases. Second, we present the architecture deployed for the analysis. Third, we present the experimental results and finally propose a pragmatic approach to cloud for companies and their enterprise application in light of this analysis.

BACKGROUND: LARGE ENTERPRISE BUSINESS USE CASES

The business application's use case is about legacy applications in the datacenter. Its focus is rapid provisioning, flexible and effective operations in the datacenter and reduced Total Cost of ownership (TCO). Along these lines, the optimization of utilization of available hardware resources using virtualization technology is a goal of large independent software vendors (ISV) as well as of their customers. In addition, the enhanced flexibility given by virtualization technology for provisioning and maintenance of enterprise software instances is effecting today's datacenter operations for large-scale enterprise IT landscapes as shown by Ellahi, et al. (2011). The trend towards operational flexibility via virtualization of legacy applications is gaining momentum by customers.

Use Case Scenarios

This set of use cases are about classical or "pre-cloud era" applications in the datacenter. They focus on improving the rapid provisioning, flexible and effective operations in the datacenter. As the result, they demonstrate how to streamline and automate the life cycle management within cloud environment while reducing application TCO. Along these lines, the optimization of utilization of available hardware resources using virtualization technology is an important topic for ISV. Moreover, the enhanced flexibility given by virtualization technology for provisioning and maintenance of SAP instances is effecting today's datacenter operations for large-scale enterprise IT landscapes. This trend to increase the operational flexibility through the virtualization of legacy applications is gaining momentum by SAP customers. As a result, it became a subject of great interest inside SAP and among its customers.

Rapid Provisioning

In this scenario we demonstrated a completely unattended and fully automated deployment of an SAP ERP system starting from an Open Virtual Format (OVF) descriptor (Distributed Management Task Force, Inc., 2009) and Kernel Virtual Machine (KVM) images (Soh, et al. 2010). The challenge in this scenario is to demonstrate the flexibility provided by using OVF descriptor as a template and a VM image. Enabling us to be completely datacenter and cloud agnostic using the RESERVOIR-enabled framework, as presented in the following work by Reservoir Consortium (2011), Rochwerger et al. (2009), for deploying and running a large-scale enterprise application while reducing the provisioning lead-time drastically by several orders of magnitude. As output of such scenario, we created a datacenter-independent OVF appliance that can be deployed in a matter of minutes across a large variety of datacenters as opposed as the weeks it commonly takes as described by Dickersbach and Keller (2010).

Elasticity

An ERP Dialogue instance (DI) enables the ERP system to scale with the workload and by leveraging Reservoir stack; we were able to add another elastic dimension that was not available with standard operational environments. In this scenario, we dynamically added or removed VM hosting DI as the load increased or respectively decreased. This scenario makes use of the elasticity rules in the OVF descriptor developed by the Reservoir consortium as well as leveraging the Reservoir monitoring framework in order to enforce and validate of these rules.

Live Migration

Within a modern datacenter, operational flexibility requires the ability to live migrate an application between different physical hosts as presented in the work of Clark et al. (2005). However, due to limitations of the migration algorithms there is a high risk of service interruption when migrating large VMs or migrating VMs over low-bandwidth links.

So far live migration has focused on transferring the run-time memory state of the VMs with relative limited memory size in local area networks (LAN) and current techniques used for this transfer reach a certain limit and usability when Virtual Machine Monitors have to migrate more heavyweight VM containing large enterprise applications as explained by Hacking and Hudzia (2009).

In order to remediate this situation, SAP in cooperation with Umea University and IBM worked on optimization of the KVM live migration operation. As a result has obtained a tremendous impact on the performance of such operation with respect to large-scale VM migrations.

ARCHITECTURE

In this chapter, we present the typical Enterprise application and the cloud architecture:

Typical SAP Landscape Deployment

SAP systems are used for a variety of SAP applications that differ by version and functionality (e.g., CRM, ERP, and SCM). For a given application type, the SAP system components consist of generic parts that are customized by configuration, as well as parts that custom-coded for a specific instance. An SAP system used for a specific application is an example of a complex service application. Typically, an installation consists of several systems that differ by their target usage (e.g., production, test and development).

Certain SAP applications are composed of several loosely coupled systems. These systems are referred to as Deployment Units (DU). DUs have their independent databases and they communicate asynchronously by messages with each other.

A typical deployment of SAP systems contains (see Figure 1):

- IDES (Education System): purely for education purpose
- Development: where the consultants do the customization
- Quality: where the customization is tested
- Production systems: where the live data of the company is recorded

Some organizations may deploy additional systems in the landscape depending on its usage (Training, Data Migration, Pre Production, and Stress Test).

Note that, in the SAP common software deployment methodology the resources are sized and distributed in the following fashion:

- Development = some percentage of Production which is based on fair assumption
- QA = some percentage of Production which is based on fair assumption. However, QAS system ideally should be the same as Production; at the least disk capacity should be the same so that QAS can be refreshed with PRD system on regular interval/need basis.
- Production = Sized using one of the different sizing process

Hardware resource and optimal system configuration greatly depend on the requirements of the customer-specific project. This includes the implementation of distribution, security, and high availability solutions by different approaches using various third-party tools. In the case of high availability through redundant resources, for example, the final resource requirements must be adjusted accordingly. In sizing, you will determine how the individual systems should be designed so that the requirements for supporting business processes can be fulfilled in all situations. Realistic sizing must factor in hotspots and load peaks.

Figure 1. Typical staged deployment of SAP system, (© SAP used with permission)

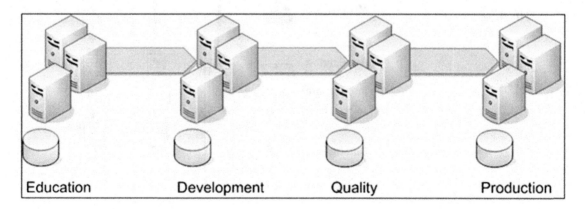

As a result, hardware sizing is influenced by various listed factors such as the number of systems involved in the landscape and its usage type i.e. OLTP or OLAP. During the sizing phase, you must estimate the hardware requirements such as:

- Architecture
  ◦ Centralized vs. Decentralized
  ◦ Consolidated vs. Discrete
  ◦ Heterogeneous vs. Homogenous
- Operating system \& Processor
  ◦ UNIX, Linux, Windows, Other; 32-bit, 64-bit
  ◦ CISC, RISC or EPIC
- Server Design [Workgroup, Enterprise]
- Storage Design, e.g. SAN
- Backup Design [Single Stage/two stage, online/offline]
  ◦ Network Design [LAN, WAN, Intranet]
- On-site Redundancy [Clustering \& pooling]

  ◦ DR site failover [Log Shipping, Storage Level Replication]
- Per year database growth

The number of users working with different applications, the volume of data created by that work, and the amount of data to be distributed externally from the system are factors determining the usage and hence the hardware and network resources required.

However, it is recommended to split production systems into multiple hosts in the form of instances (see Figure 2 each of them with a specific role assigned to them (Database, Central Instance (CI), Dialog Instance (DI), Batch, Application, Reporting, Etc.).

Note that additional infrastructure servers may include web, backup, load balancers, firewall, sap proxy, etc.

Figure 2. Typical Load and resource reparation of SAP system, (© SAP used with permission)

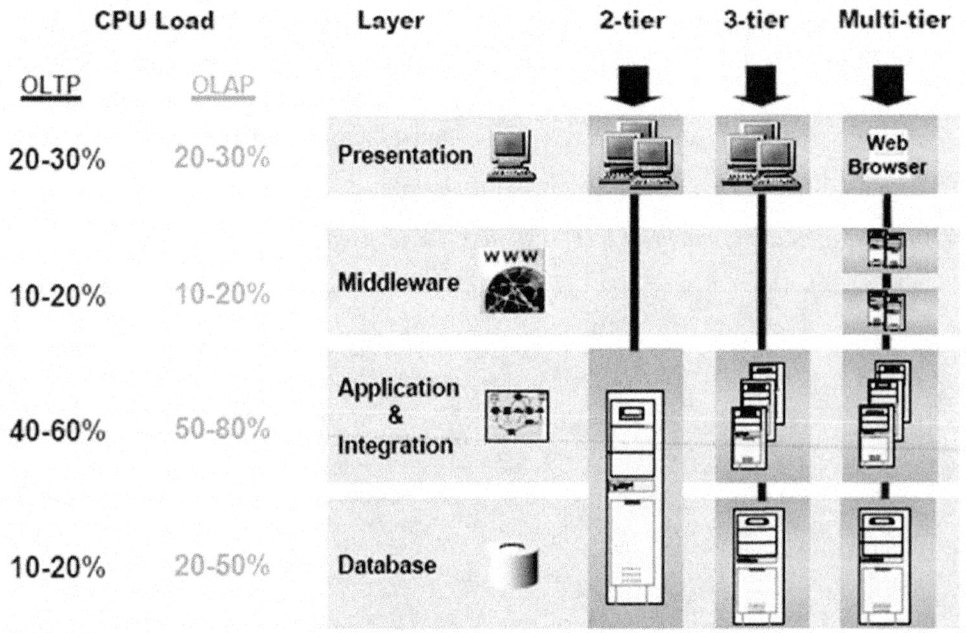

Abstraction of an "SAP System"

In order to limit the complexity of the setup for the use case we use an abstraction or subset of a typical system.

We consider an SAP system as a three-tier system consisting of a presentation layer, application layer and a database layer. Figure 3 shows the basic components of an SAP system.

The main components as depicted in Figure Figure 3 are:

*   **Central Instance:** The central instance is a concept that is unique to SAP. The central instance is a combination of hardware and software. It contains a physical server (the application server) and numerous software

components, including a message server, a database gateway (a pre-established connection between SAP and database), and various update, enqueue, dialog, and spool facility software. In most generic SAP architectures, there are numerous application servers but only a single central instance. However, in addition to managing the SAP interfaces, the central instance can also serve as an application server. Any computer is capable of running one or more application servers.

*   **Dialog Instance:** The Dialog Instance (DI) hosts the work processes that execute the ABAP programs as a response to user requests. The number of DIs can be configured for scalability. Moreover, the number

Figure 3. Typical SAP ERP subsystem architecture

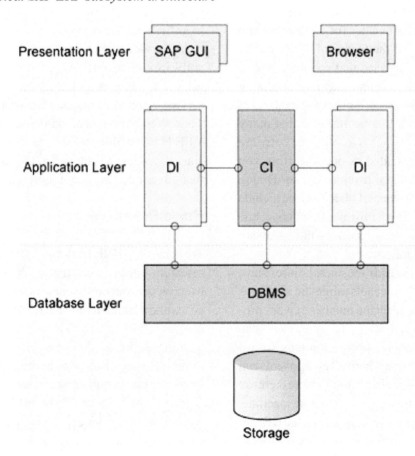

of work processes within each DI can be configured. It is important to emphasize that DIs maintain conversational and state full user sessions.

- **Database Management System:** A single Database Management System (DBMS) serves the SAP system. The DBMS accesses its storage either as a Network-Attached Storage or by a Storage Area Network It is important to emphasize that SAP applications require classic database transactions and strong data consistency.
- **Storage:** Network-Attached Storage (NAS) or by a Storage Area Network (SAN).

To put the concept into perspective, the Central Instance contains all different types of processes i.e. Dialog, Update, Enqueue, Batch, Message, Gateway, and spool. To an end user, Dialog process interacts with user during an on-line processing, and to cater for more users and enable scalability of the technical SAP system, additional Dialog instance that contain some of the processes such as updates, spool, and dialog to form a dialog instance. This being said, there can ONLY be ONE Central Instance, but many Dialog instance. Instance is a collection software component that is started as one; therefore you can start or stop Central Instance (CI) or Dialog (DI) as a software instance. Other instance include database instance. In a hardware perspective, one can see the application server as the hardware perspective of an instance.

From a scalability and robustness point of view, one can add and remove DIs while the system is running, as well as adapt the number of work processes of a specific DI or CI. The components can be arranged in a variety of configurations, from a minimal configuration where all components run on a single machine, to larger ones where there are several DIs, each running on a separate machine, and a separate machine with the CI and the DBMS.

Figure 4 depicts these configurations, where the components are realized as virtual machines in a virtual execution environment (VEE) host.

Cloud Setup for the Scenarios

We tested the different scenario using the RESERVOIR Infrastructure. This computing cloud is made up of cooperating RESERVOIR Sites that own and manage the physical infrastructure on which service applications execute. In order to optimise resource utilization we leverage the virtualization layer and use it and manipulate it under teh terminology of virtual execution environments (VEEs). This layer is a fully isolated run-time environment that abstract away the physical characteristics of the resource and enable sharing, partitions the computational resources within a site. The virtualized computational resources, alongside with the virtualization layer and all the management enablement components, are referred to as the VEE Host.

A Service or Service Application is a set of software components, which work collectively to achieve a common goal. Each component of such service application executes in a dedicated VEE. These VEEs are placed on the same or different VEE Hosts within the site, or even on different sites, according to automated placement policies that govern the site (see Figure 4).

Rapid Provisioning

We achieve to deliver, through the RESERVOIR research, a framework that enables the delivery of services on an on-demand basis, at competitive costs, and without requiring a large capital investment in infrastructure. Our research is inspired by a strong desire to liken the delivery of services to the delivery of utilities in the physical world. For example, a typical scenario in the physical world would be the ability of an electrical grid in one country to provide dynamically more electric

Figure 4. Federated Cloud architecture using Reservoir Framework

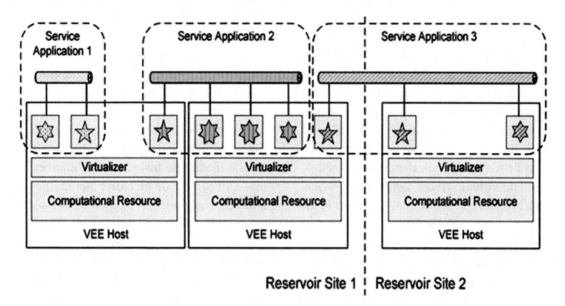

power to a grid in a neighbouring country to meet a spike in demand. We recognize that provisioning services from disparate service domains on-demand is arguably a more complex problem than the analogous problem of provisioning a utility in the physical world. For example, a service may be a composition of numerous distributed resources, including computing, storage and network elements. Provisioning a new service will consume physical resources, but cannot be allowed to cause an SLA violation of any other running application. Additionally, once initially provisioned, resources composing a service may be moved to other domains based on lower costs, performance or availability considerations. Our research will address those issues and minimize the barriers to delivering services as utilities.

Infrastructure orchestration enables organizations to rapidly provision infrastructure from pools of shared server and storage resources. In order to simplify the procurement task we use Reservoir automation capabilities and processes that are made available to users through the web-based, self-service portal as well as service manifests.

The service manifest, which is one of the key elements of the RESERVOIR model, is briefly reviewed in this subsection. First, the manifest specifies the structure of the service application in terms of component types that are to be deployed as virtual execution environments (VEEs).

For each of these component types, the manifest specifies a reference to a master image, i.e., a self-contained software stack (OS, middleware, applications, data and configuration) that fully captures the functionality of the component type. In addition, the manifest contains the information and rules necessary to create automatically, from a single parameterized master image, unique VEE instances that can run simultaneously without conflicts. The manifest also specifies the grouping of components into virtual networks and/or tiers that form the service applications. Given that the emerging Open Virtual Format (OVF) industry standard crafted by the Distributed Management Task Force, Inc. (2009) includes most of this information, the service manifest extends OVF.

Via the Reservoir portal, authorized users can select the resources they need from a list of virtual machine manifest (OVF based). From there they can request an infrastructure template for a specified lease period, which gives the assurance that the provisioned resources will be available for repurposing in a timely manner and that they will not sit idle after a user has completed a project.

Once approved, the requested infrastructure configuration is automatically created and provisioned. The Reservoir framework can automatically provision multiple tiers, multiple nodes, physical and virtual servers, network addresses, and attached storage. After that, users can manage their infrastructure via the self-service portal and its tools. Among other capabilities, users can suspend, resume, and delete resources and flex capacity or easily add or remove servers to an existing service to respond to changes in utilization.

Ultimately, we aimed to automate the provisioning of capabilities of available shared resources for IT administrators, application owners, test and development teams, and others who need timely access to IT infrastructure.

SCENARIO

We used a rather straightforward scenario but already one of the most complex for most enterprise applications:

1. OVF Processor parses OVF descriptor
2. Prepare an environment file for each VM of the appliance with all the customization and configuration parameter values that are specific to the actual deployment and VM (e.g., host names and IP addresses).
3. VEE Host places file as an ISO image on the CD drive of the to-be-booted VM
4. Service Provider prepared the Activation Engine and embeds it in the image. It is also the responsibility of the service Provider to prepare the OVF descriptor and images.

5. Pre-prepared software module (Activation Engine) is embedded in the image of the VM, reads this file and makes the appropriate settings for the starting image

The scenario is depicted in Figure 5.

The manifest specifies the capacity requirements for an explicitly sized service application. The minimum and maximum resource requirements of a single instance, e.g., number of virtual CPUs, size of memory, storage pool size, number of network interfaces and their bandwidth, are specified for each component. The dynamic and adaptive part of the capacity requirement is specified using a set of elasticity rules. These rules formally correlate monitored Key Performance Indicators (KPIs) and load parameters (e.g., response time, throughput, number of active sessions) with resource allocations (e.g., memory, CPU, bandwidth, etc...). These rules express how the resources allocated to the running VM can be dynamically adapted (increased or reduced) to satisfy the variable demand for the service application. It should be noted, that the term "usage" is not interchangeable with the term "utilization".

Finally, the manifest specifies KPIs that should be monitored by RESERVOIR in order to verify SLA compliance and in order to trigger the elasticity rules. This specification may include self-contained probes that periodically provide these KPIs.

A Sample Service Application and its Manifest

In order to illustrate the model and the manifest, we consider a complex business application, namely the SAP system under study. We first provide a brief description of an SAP system that is abstracted in order to emphasize only the relevant aspects.

A simplified service manifest for a SAP system is shown in Table 1. This manifest corresponds

Figure 5. Dynamic deployment Scenario workflow execution

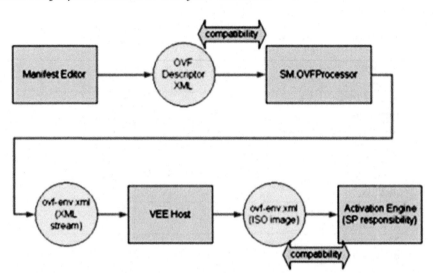

to the configuration where a DI and the DBMS each have a separate VEE, and the CI and Web Dispatcher are encapsulated on another VEE. Notice how the manifest fixes the CI and the DBMS as single instances, and declares the DI as the elastic entity by providing it with a range of instances. To optimize cost-effectiveness, the service manifest specifies resource requirements under normal load.

To enable dynamic matching of the application capacity to variable workloads, the manifest defines KPIs that are monitored as an indication for load that the SAP system serves.

The overall response time of a certain business transaction, or the number of concurrent active user session can be used for this purpose. An elasticity rule that triggers the addition of a new DI when this KPI exceeds a threshold value would adapt the resources allocated for the system as the workload increases. For example, if measured response time crossed a pre-specified threshold, then a new DI instance is added.

Moreover, we use the rapid deployment scenario to test the deployment of the SAP system across the WAN in multiple datacenters. The scenario was such that the CI was deployed in one location, and at least one DI was deployed in another datacenter located in another country. These experiments took place in the SAP network between Ra'anana, Israel and Belfast, Northern Ireland, and in the IBM network between Haifa, Israel, and Tel Aviv, Israel. In all cases, a Virtual Private Network was setup a-priori between the datacenters. If the VPN among the datacenters was fast enough, a reasonable sub-second response time from a user interface was achieved. Our conclusions from these preliminary experiments is that, assuming a reasonable network between the datacenters these scenarios become more and more reasonable, as the resultant operational flexibility across datacenters is quite beneficial.

Issues Encountered for Rapid Deployment

One of the biggest obstacles in our experiments for rapid provisioning related to the size of the images and the time it takes to create them, especially for the first time. SAP virtual machine image typically requires four hundred gigabyte to half a terabyte of storage space. As a result, loading,

Table 1. Service manifest for a SAP deployment

Component	Web Dispatcher, CI	DI	DBMS
Master Image	ci.img	di.img	db2.img
# of VCPUs (min/max)	2/4	4/8	8/8
Memory Size (min/max)	4G/8G	16G/32G	32G/64G
# of NICS	2	2	1
Additional disk size	None	100G	1000G
Minimum # of instances	1	4	1
Maximum # of instances	1	20	1

moving, storing image this size between different datacenters require moving them by postal mail.

In addition, in our experiments with the deployment of a real SAP system in RESERVOIR we realised that the licensing model of the current enterprise software can be a rather annoying aspect. It turns out that supporting the SAP licensing scheme requires some vertical architectural coordination that seems to be against the principle of separating the concerns among the horizontal layers in RESERVOIR. The SAP current licensing scheme works as follows: one has to acquire a license key before the system installation by providing a HW UUID for the hardware machine where the CI will be installed. In order to support this scheme, the VEE of the CI must be created with a predefined given UUID that matches the UUID for which the license was acquired. This means that support for a predefined virtual HW identifier is required. For the time being, we implemented a work-around where the VEEH gets the HW identifier and creates the VEE for the CI. The real problem is the fact that once we specify the HW identifier in the OVF descriptor we make, the descriptor cannot be reused as a template. We chose a scheme where the OVF descriptor points to a file, and the file holds the HW identifier. This way, the descriptor itself is reusable as a template. There are still issues regarding what is the nest way of passing the HW identified downstream to the VEEH. At present, we do have a working solution, and we are evaluating alternatives for improvements. We believe that this problem is representative of commercial applications that require a license.

Elasticity

In a cloud-computing context, automatic elasticity is the ability of a service designed by the Service Cloud Customer and deployed in some Service Cloud Provider to balance load by automatically replicating master images and create new virtual machines, gaining increased total throughput, increased availability and decreased failover and downtime. Alternatively, decommission idle virtual machines. Elasticity allows the Cloud Service Customers to benefit from reduced costs, and allows the Cloud Service Providers to increase resource sharing, reduce power consumption for idle resources, and as a whole benefit from reduced TCO. For example, the number of dialog

Figure 6. Sample SAP system deployments: (a) all components run in the same VEE; (b) the large components (CI and DBMS) run each on a dedicated VEE. VEEs are represented as rounded rectangles.

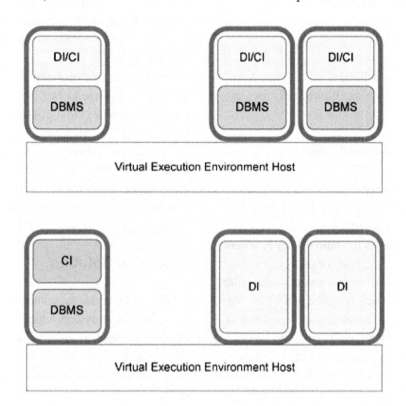

instance front-end virtual machines of a given service would be scale up and down depending on the client request load to those serves. Elasticity is an enabler for scalability.

Applications that are designed for scalability can benefit from this feature by making the corresponding Service elastic in the sense that required hardware resources can be allocated depending on the workload for the Service. Scalability is sustained by elasticity and can be achieved in two ways; firstly, by adapting the resources allocated to a particular virtual machine and secondly by adding or removing additional instances of virtual machines.

Elasticity may also be controlled by business needs, for example by allocation of resource in accordance to business cycles. For example, a Payroll Service that requires doubling its capacity on the last working day of every month. The

difference between automatic and not automatic scalability is that, in the former case (the one in which we focused in this section) the Customer does not deal with manually creating or destroying virtual machines as this process is done by the Service

Our work in Reservoir aimed at providing a way to specify rules to Business IT System, in order for them to automatically add and eliminate system components according to business load. We worked with colleagues from IBM and other for the Reservoir project to enhance the OVF standards for managing virtual instance. However, we faced multiple challenges:

- Define elasticity rules in OVF descriptor
- Add and eliminate Dialog Instances (DI) according to system load

- Elasticity rules rely on applicative KPIs that have to be monitored

Our Goals were to:

- Demonstrate elasticity
- Use the monitoring framework for rule enforcement

Limitations in Standard OVF

Standard OVF is limited to the fixed-size deployments and does not take dynamic scaling into account. This is a consequence of the <VirtualSystem> tag semantics in standard OVF, where each one of those tags represent exactly one virtual machine. So, if the Customer wants to scale up the service, e.g. to add a new instance of a webserver front-end to cope with increasing service demand. It has to issue a new OVF with an updated service description, i.e. with an added <VirtualSystem>, which would be almost equal to the previous one representing webserver front-end instances (even using the same virtual disk images). Therefore, the customers implement scalability as a sequence of OVF descriptors updated and submitted at the "right moments" to match changes in the service workload timely and efficiently.

The problem with this approach is that it increases the customer's effort by making it responsible, for maintaining a correct sequence of the OVF descriptors over time. In addition, depending on the cloud middleware ability to do seamless service upgrades, issuing a new OVF for an existing service could involve withdrawing of the previous version before deploying the new one. Therefore, the service would suffer an undue unavailability time.

One possible solution to dynamic scalability problem could be modifying the OVF semantics in such a way that a <VirtualSystem> would describe a component type rather than specific instance. The customer still has to monitor the status of the service in order to identify the "right

moments" mentioned above to issue the scalability operations. Note that this issue is orthogonal to whether a sequence of distinct OVF descriptors is used or some other means of service restructuring employed.

Summarizing the above, we observe that the standard OVF use to lack ability to specify the rules (i.e. policies) that govern the scalability of a service (if (conditions) then (actions)) along with the allowed bounds, e.g., the maximum and minimum number of VM instances of each type. Note that existing Cloud Providers have introduced this feature, but in proprietary and limited ways, i.e. through a reduced set of rules.

Proposed Solution

Firstly, we consider the semantic described above, so each <VirtualSystem> specifies an elastic array of almost identical virtual machines (except by the customization done through the OVF Environment) instead of individual VM instances. In order to govern the elasticity of such an array, a simple section has been defined, <ElasticArraySection>, consisting of a sequence of <Rule> tags. Within each <Rule> the following information is specified:

- **KPI name:** The KPI identifier whose value governs the scalability of the array. This KPI has to be defined within the <KPIsSection> described in Section 4.1.
- **Windows:** The time interval for sampling the KPI. The semantics of this window are that of a sliding window, e.g. 10 minutes.
- **Frequency:** The amount of samples to take in the window. For example, 60 samples per window, that is 6 samples per minute (1 sample each 10 seconds) for a 10 minutes window.
- **Quota:** The normalized "quantity of KPI" that a single VM instance can sustain in a steady state. The average KPI in the window will be compared with the defined

quota multiplied by the number of currently active VMs in order to decide if the array has to be expanded or shrunk.

So, the average value of the active Sessions KPI is continuously calculated for the last 10 minutes (60 samples) see Figure 7. Principle of sliding time widow for continuous evaluation of KPI. If the active Sessions divided by the number of current frontend instances is greater than 20, then assuming the load is balanced, each of the frontends is overloaded than what is considered acceptable to maintain the service quality. An additional frontend instance is therefore required. If, on the other hand, active Sessions divided by the number of current frontend instances is less than 20, then the service is over-provisioned and a single frontend instance should be removed to avoid unnecessary costs.

However while testing the automatic elastic features of the OVF extension we encountered an issue linked with the fact that SAP applications are state full which tend to be the minority of

application deployed within cloud environment. State full implies that once a session is opened with a specific user, a state is maintained for that user in a specific DI. Therefore, all requests of the same user have to be routed to the same DI. This behaviour poses a challenge when scaling down an SAP system. The problem rooted in the observation that even though the number of active sessions decreases, the sessions may be spread across DI in such a manner that is impossible to shutdown a DI.

There are several alternative solutions to this problem.

- Provide methods for designating some DI instances as candidates for shutdown. These candidates will not accept new sessions and will serve only on-going sessions. Once all on-going sessions are terminated it is possible to shutdown the DI.
- There is a way to move sessions between DIs.

Figure 7. Principle of sliding time widow for continuous evaluation of KPI

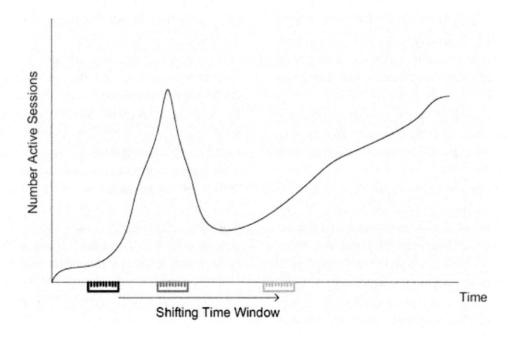

We are looking into both options in order to enable customers to leverage fully the benefit of elastic management of SAP systems within federated clouds.

Live Migration

Recent developments in virtualizations technology have resulted in its proliferation of usage across datacenters. Ultimately this technology goal is to more efficiently utilize server resources to improve TCO by virtualizing hardware and consolidating servers. These results in lower equipment costs and less electrical consumption for server power and cooling. But the TCO benefits of holistic virtualization extend beyond server assets. One of these aspects is related to the ability of being able to migrate a Virtual Machine (VM) across distinct physical hosts over a network. However, limitation of the current migration technology start to appear when they are applied on larger applications systems such as SAP ERP or SAP ByDesign. Such systems consume a large amount of memory and cannot be transferred as seamlessly as smaller one, creating service interruption. Limiting the impact and optimizing migration becomes even more important with the generalization of Service Level Agreement (SLA). In Reservoir we worked on a design and evaluation of a system that enables live migration of VMs running large enterprise applications without severely disrupting their live services, even across the Internet. By combining well-known techniques and innovative one we can reduce system downtime and resource impact for migrating live large virtual execution environments.

VM migration technologies such as the one developed by Barham et al. (2003), Bradford et al. (2007), Clark et al. (2005), Hacking and Hudzia (2009), Sapuntzaki et al. (2002), and Travostino (2006) focus on capturing and transferring the run time, in memory state of a VM over a LAN. Administrators can move live, running virtual machines from one host to another while maintaining near continuous service availability. Reconfiguring virtual machine hardware and migrating virtualized workloads to different hardware can be done by an administrator.

This increased efficiency makes it possible to manage the growing needs of the business with fewer physical servers and man-hours enabling small IT teams to contribute strategically rather than just tactically:

- **Live migration:** The VM continues to run while transferring its memory and local persistent state.
- **Minimal service disruption:** Migration should avoid to degrade significantly the performance of services running in the VM, as perceived by their users.
- **Transparency:** Services running in the migrated VM do not need to be migration-aware in any way, and can be out-of-the box. The VM's open network connections remain alive, even after an IP address change, and new connections are seamlessly redirected to the new IP address at the destination.

Our contribution is the design and evaluation of a system that enables live migration of VMs running large enterprise applications without severely disrupting their live services, even across the Internet. This work introduces modification to KVM originally developed by Soh, et al. (2010) live migration algorithm a novel memory transfer mechanism for live migration of virtual machines based on delta compression. We also added an adaptive warm up transfer phase in order to reduce the rigidity of migrating large VM. This work aim to increase transfer performance and reduce downtime, allowing system administrator to fully benefit from virtualization features with large business applications and appliances in minutes.

Our system is builds upon the KVM hypervisor live migration features. An extensive experimental evaluation highlights that our system offers an effective solution, featuring:

- Reduced interference with the running VM
- Reduced bandwidth usage
- Just In Time Live Migration behaviour
- Live Migration across WAN

In order to live migrate a VM, a hypervisors need to transfer the memory page of the VM across the network to the receptacle hypervisor. In the current live migration scenario the VM monitor will copy all the VM memory and then begin to re-send pages which have been dirtied (used since the last send). If it detects that the memory pages are being re-written faster than it can send it will freeze the VM and send the final changed memory and system state. The act of rewriting memory is known as page dirtying.

This is acceptable for normal use cases, but for large applications or applications which are memory intensive it is the case that the monitor cannot keep up with the rate of page dirtying as described by Harney et al. (2007). The VM is frozen too early and for an extended period of time. This period of inactivity often results in errors such as network timeouts and memory corruption. In serious cases it can crash the application or server.

One of the major drawbacks of live migration is that once you commit to it you must wait until the operation is complete. There is no guarantee of when it will be finished, and in addition, there is also the problems relating to the VM freeze. Due to these risks it is often safer to shut down the VM and restart it again on the second machine. This in itself will require a period of down-time.

Warm Up

In order to reduce the impact of these issues, we have implemented and extra phase in the migration process: A warm up phase which transfers memory in advance. This phase runs continuously in the background without disrupting the service

of the running application. Full live migration can be triggered after an unspecified amount of time. This functionality would be desirable to implement a hot-standby or instant-on Live Migration providing a cheap High Availability server.

The warm up is designed to run with as little overhead on performance as possible. If necessary it will need to give way to service related processes to avoid Disruption of Service. The amount of time that the VM is frozen for must be greatly reduced. Bringing it to within the thresholds for timeout will eliminate Disconnection of Services and mitigate the difficulty of maintaining consistency and transparency (For example, clocks running slow after migration). It should also be possibly to cancel the warm-up. The ability to decide not to migrate if the conditions look too risky will improve the predictability and Flexibility. Figure 8 shows the reasoning for this. If live migration is activated due to a spike in usage then we are committed to completing it, even if the usage drops. Warm-up allows the option to delay activating full live migration and cancel if it becomes unnecessary.

Warm-up also enable system administrator to tightly control the impact on the VM and provide a slower ramp-up than standard live migration operation. As a result it can reduce the overall downtime and prevent crash or errors after the completion of the operation (see Figure 9).

Delta Compression

A more subtle and cost-effective solution can be obtained by implementing the data compression mechanism also proposed in Meggiddo and Modha (2003); Potter (2005) and Pountain (1987), which, has the potential to alleviate the I/O bottleneck. By using delta compression on the original and updated memory pages, and to transmit the delta file we can drastically reduce the amount of downtime, making live migration a suitable feature for large business applications (see Figure 10).

Figure 8. Usage of warm-up in virtual machine operations

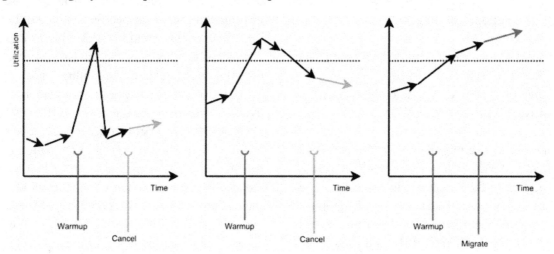

Figure 9. Performance comparison of live migration of ERP Systems with and without warm-up

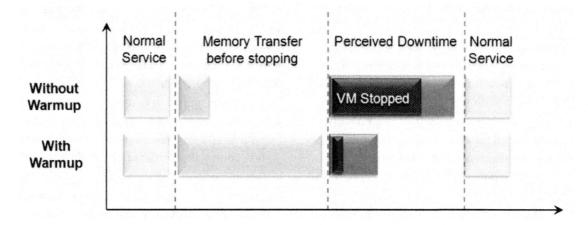

Transferring the Delta of memory pages allows us to optimise different resources aspect of the live migration:

- Reconstruction of the updated page file may be performed on resource-limited machines.
- Delta pages can be efficiently transmitted via slow or limited transport mediums.
- The use of Delta pages transfer allows limiting the live migration impact if the server migrating the VM is in high demand.

Gigabit Ethernet (ERP System) Scenario

We demonstrated the value of the delta compression scheme by VM running a SAP Central Instance ERP system was migrated over Gigabit Ethernet. We created a compression algorithm named XBRLE, as described by Hacking and Hudzia (2009), which reduce the total migration time from 235 s to 139 s, the suspension time was reduced from 3 s to 0.2 s, and the ping downtime from 5 s to 1 s, all illustrated in Figure

Figure 10. Principle of Delta compression for Live Migration of virtual machines

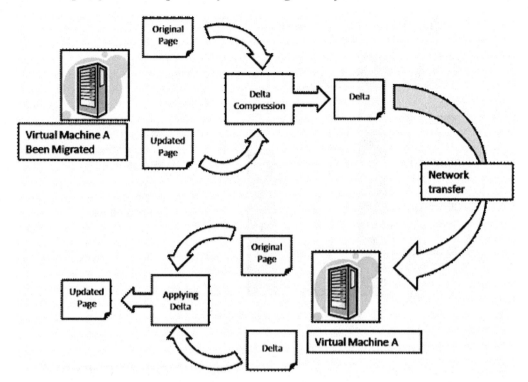

11. Performance comparison between standard and optimized live migration of ERP system. SAP is one of the most commonly used business intelligence applications. It puts a high load on the CPU and it is considered notoriously hard to migrate these kinds of systems live because of their dependency on transactions and time-out sensitive network connections. According to our experience with the SAP ERP system, fatal timing problems can occur already for migration downtimes as low as half a second. In our test, the total migration time was reduced with around 40% but as the system is very complex, the migration time can vary greatly depending on actual load during migration, etc. It is thus hard to draw any definitive conclusions regarding total migration time. More importantly, the migration downtime usually does not vary as much and even if the difference in downtime was not as dramatic as

in the two other scenarios, it was still reduced from 3s to 0.2s with the XBRLE algorithm. The smaller decrease in downtime compared to the earlier cases can partly be explained by the fact that the network is not as much of a bottleneck as in previous two cases.

Notably, in our test, the vanilla migration did not succeed. In this case, the system was resumed after migration but application CPU usage rose to 100% and the system was in an unstable state, probably due to timing errors. In the experiment, the KVM hypervisor constitutes the greater part of the system CPU usage.

This value was around 10% during the page transfer iterations, fluctuated substantially as the VM was shut down and resumed, and dropped almost to zero post migration. The I/O wait showed a similar pattern as the system CPU usage. In contrast, the XBRLE algorithm successfully migrate

Figure 11. Performance comparison between standard and optimized live migration of ERP system

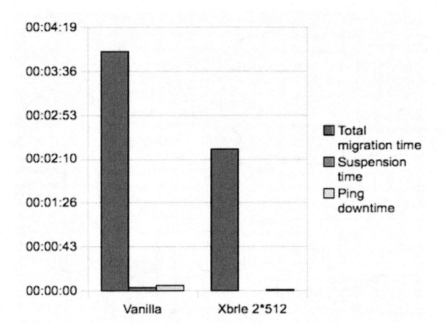

the ERP system, even at a higher load (70% application CPU) than where the vanilla algorithm failed (20% application CPU). This value fluctuate a bit as the VM was suspended and resumed, but returned to the 70% level after migration. As for system CPU usage, this value varied between 5% and 10% during the page transfer iterations. The spikes in this value can be attributed to the rather CPU-intensive compression of delta pages that are part of each iteration. These spikes got higher when more pages were compressed in later iterations, as the reduced amount of VM RAM remaining to transfer resulted in a higher cache hit ratio. I/O wait is low for the XBRLE algorithm, except for a short spike during the final shutdown and resume of the VM, which is linked to their buffering and release due to the switch over.

As the system CPU utilization on the VM was level at around 10% during migration in both cases, we conclude that the XBRLE migration algorithm had about the same impact on VM performance as the vanilla algorithm.

CONCLUSION: HYBRID ON-DEMAND ADD-ONS TO LEGACY APPLICATIONS

The use cases posed many challenges due to the inherent size and complexity of enterprise applications. The migration to the cloud architecture of existing or legacy applications is one of the main pain points for bringing large-scale business applications to the cloud. Applications that are at the centre of gravity of the enterprise are likely to remain on-premise for various reasons (e.g., security, criticality, and heavy integration with other applications). In addition, company ERP software has an expected average lifetime of 15 years, which means that companies will be reluctant to ditch their existing solution. However, application migration to the cloud is not a straightforward process. It is risky, and does not always guarantee a better service delivery.

As of today, the main adopter of cloud computing are small companies and start-ups that are not tied up to a legacy of IT investments. While for more mature enterprise, the cloud concept is new and hard to grasp. In addition, this IT model does not meet fully the criteria of enterprise IT yet, but it is getting there at an accelerated pace boosted by the rich and vibrant ecosystem being developed by start-up and now major IT vendors. Among the drawbacks of bringing large-scale business applications to the cloud, there is migration to the cloud architecture of existing or legacy applications. The expected average lifetime of ERP products is 15 years which means that companies will need to face this aspect sooner than later as they try to evolve toward the new IT paradigm as explained by Ellahi, et al.(2011). An application migration is not a straightforward process. It is risky, and does not always guarantee a better service delivery.

As we understood and overcame these obstacles and increased our expertise in the field, we were able to develop and refine a strategy for cloud adoption. We proposed a middle path solution enabling enterprises to adopt a hybrid model between on-premise and on-demand models in order to leverage fully the benefits of the cloud-computing paradigm whilst maintaining their current investment.

However, applications that are at the centre of gravity of the enterprise are likely to remain on-premise for various reasons (e.g., security, criticality, and heavy integration with other applications). Therefore, enterprises should adopt a model that is a hybrid of on-premise and on-demand models in order to leverage fully the benefits of the cloud-computing paradigm whilst maintaining their current investment. Such a hybrid model should support transitions between on-premise and on-demand modes of operation type of applications along with their data sets.

Future Research

In addition to the inherent problems of migrating large-scale business applications to the cloud, other non-functional requirements pose a hindrance to cloud adoption. Businesses today are required to comply with a litany of legislation, regulations and standards. The increasing utilization of the internet for delivering IT services gives rise to challenges in assessing and maintaining compliance. This becomes more apparent when companies interact in their federated cloud supply chain. IT is becoming a fundamental tool in enabling organizations to meet compliance. However, the development of internet-based IT infrastructures may result in current auditing standards becoming obsolete (for example, the transition from SAS70 to SSAE16 and ISAE3402). Auditors have traditionally relied on SAS 70 reports to audit and gain assurance that proper controls are in place. However, a number of factors have contributed to the need for new standards:

- The globalization of information technology and the practice of outsourcing business processes has generated the need for an international auditing standard.
- A dynamic regulatory landscape may create the need for additional information about internal control of financial reporting.
- U.S. convergence with international standards.

Most organisations manage their customer data through large-scale business applications such as a Customer Relationship Management (CRM) system. CRM systems are a widely adopted strategy for enhancing and maintaining customer relationships through the phases of marketing, sales and support. Storage of personal data in such systems poses the greatest problem in terms of auditing legislation from multiple jurisdictions. Therefore, further research into the multi-jurisdictional consequences needs to be carried out in context with research into the migration of large-scale business applications and federated cloud supply chains in order to address the problems discussed in this chapter.

REFERENCES

Barham, P., Dragovic, B., Fraser, K., Hand, S., Harris, T., Ho, A., et al. (2003). Xen and the art of virtualization. In *SOSP '03: Proceedings of the nineteenth ACM symposium on Operating systems principles*, (pp. 164–177) New York, NY: ACM.

Bradford, R., Kotsovinos, E., Feldmann, E., & Schioberg, H. (2007) Live wide-area migration of virtual machines including local persistent state. In *VEE '07: Proceedings of the 3rd international conference on Virtual execution environments*, (pp. 169–179) New York, NY: ACM

Clark, C., Fraser, K., Hand, S., Hansen, J. G., Jul, E., Limpach, C., et al. (2005). Live migration of virtual machines. In *Proceedings of the 2nd ACM/USENIX Symposium on Networked Systems Design and Implementation (NSDI)*, (pp. 273–286) New York, NY: ACM

Dickersbach, J. T., & Keller, G. (2010). *Production Planning and Control with SAP ERP* (2nd ed.). Singapore: SAP PRESS.

Distributed Management Task Force, Inc. (2009) Open Virtualization Format Specification, Version 1.0.0, document no. DAP0243; see http://www.dmtf.org/standards/published_documents/DSP0243_1.0.0.

Ellahi, T., Hudzia, B., Li, H., Lindner, M. A., & Robinson, P. (2011). The enterprise Cloud Computing Paragdim. In *Cloud Computing: Principles and Paradigms (Wiley Series on Parallel and Distributed Computing)*. Hoboken, NJ: Wiley. doi:10.1002/9780470940105.ch4

Hacking, S. & Hudzia. B. (2009) Improving the live migration process of large enterprise applications. In *VTDC '09: Proceedings of the 3rd international workshop on Virtualization technologies in distributed computing*, (pp. 51–58) New York, NY: ACM

Harney, E., Goasguen, S., Martin, J., Murphy, M., & Westall, M. (2007) The efficacy of live virtual machine migrations over the internet. In *VTDC '07: Proceedings of the 3rd international workshop on Virtualization technology in distributed computing*, (pp. 1–7) New York, NY: ACM, Kernel Based Virtual Machine. KVM - kernel-based virtualization machine white paper, (2006) Retrieved from: http://www.linux-kvm.org

Meggiddo, N., & Modha, D. S. (2003) ARC: A self-tuning, low overhead replacement cache. In *FAST '03: Proceedings of the 2nd USENIX Conference on File and Storage Technologies*, (pp. 115–130). Berkley, CA, USA: USENIX Association

Potter, S. (2005) Using binary delta compression (BDC) technology to update Windows XP and Windows Server 2003, Retrieved from http://www.microsoft.com/downloads/details.aspx

Pountain, D. (1987). Run-length encoding. *Byte*, *12*(6), 317–319.

Reservoir Consortium. (2011). RESERVOIR webpage, Retrieved from http://www.reservoir-fp7.eu/

Rochwerger, B., Breitgand, D., Levy, E., Galis, A., Nagin, K., & Llorente, I. M. (2009). The reservoir model and architecture for open federated cloud computing. *IBM Journal of Research and Development*, *53*(4), 535–545. doi:10.1147/JRD.2009.5429058

Sapuntzaki, C.P., Chandra, R., Pfaff, B.,Chow, J., Lam, M.S., and Rosenblum, M.. (2002) Optimizing the migration of virtual computers. *SIGOPS Oper. Syst. Rev.*, *36*(SI):377–390

Soh, C., Kien, S. S., & Tay-Yap, J. (2000). Enterprise resource planning: cultural fits and misfits: is ERP a universal solution? *Communications of the ACM*, *43*(4), 47–51. doi:10.1145/332051.332070

Travostino, F. (2006) Seamless live migration of virtual machines over the MAN/WAN. In *SC '06: Proceedings of the 2006 ACM/IEEE conference on Supercomputing*, (p. 290). New York, NY: ACM

KEY TERMS AND DEFINITIONS

ERP: Short for *enterprise resource planning*, ERP is business management software that allows an organization to use a system of applications to manage the business. ERP software integrates all facets of an operation, including development, manufacturing, sales and marketing.

Live Migration: Live migration is the movement of a virtual machine from one physical host to another while continuously powered-up. When properly carried out, this process takes place without any noticeable effect from the point of view of the end user. Live migration allows an administrator to take a virtual machine offline for maintenance or upgrading without subjecting the system's users to downtime.

OLAP: Stands for "Online Analytical Processing." OLAP allows users to analyze database information from multiple database systems at one time. While relational databases are considered to be two-dimensional, OLAP data is multidimensional, meaning the information can be compared in many different ways.

OLTP: Online transaction processing is a class of program that facilitates and manages oriented applications, typically for data entry and retrieval transactions in a number of industries, including banking, airlines, mail-order, supermarkets, and manufacturers.

SAP System Landscape: They system landscape basically is the set-up or arrangement of your SAP servers. Ideally, in an SAP environment, a three-system landscape exists. A three-system landscape consists of the Development Server, Quality Assurance Server and the Production Server. This kind of set-up is not primarily designed to serve as server clusters in case of system failure, the objective to enhance "configuration pipeline management".

SLA: A service-level agreement (SLA) is a contract between a service provider and a customer that specifies, usually in measurable terms, what services the service provider will furnish.

TCO: Total Cost of Ownership is a type of calculation designed to help consumers and managers assess both direct and indirect costs and benefits related to the purchase of any component. The intention is to arrive at a final figure that will reflect the effective cost of purchase, all things considered.

Virtual Machine: A virtual machine (VM) is a software implementation of a computing environment in which an operating system or program can be installed and run. The virtual machine typically emulates a physical computing environment, but requests for CPU, memory, storage, network and other hardware resources are managed by a virtualization layer which translates these requests to the underlying physical hardware.

Chapter 18
Towards Energy-Efficient, Scalable, and Resilient IaaS Clouds

Eugen Feller
INRIA Centre Rennes - Bretagne Atlantique, France

Louis Rilling
Kerlabs, France

Christine Morin
INRIA Centre Rennes - Bretagne Atlantique, France

ABSTRACT

With increasing numbers of energy hungry data centers, energy conservation has now become a major design constraint for current and future Infrastructure-as-a-Service (IaaS) cloud providers. In order to efficiently manage such large-scale environments, three important properties have to be fulfilled by the management frameworks: (1) scalability, (2) fault-tolerance, and (3) energy-awareness. However, the scalability and fault tolerance capabilities of existing open-source IaaS cloud management frameworks are limited. Moreover, they are far from being energy-aware. This chapter first surveys existing efforts on building IaaS platforms. This includes both, system architectures and energy-aware virtual machine (VM) placement algorithms. Afterwards, it describes the architecture and implementation of a novel scalable, fault-tolerant, and energy-aware VM manager called Snooze. Finally, a nature-inspired energy-aware VM placement approach based on the Ant Colony Optimization is introduced.

INTRODUCTION

Cloud computing has recently evolved as a new computing paradigm which promises virtually unlimited resources. Customers can rent resources based on the pay-as-you-go model. Resources are transparently provisioned by the cloud provider according to the customers' requirements. However, customers' growing demands for computing power are now facilitating the cloud service providers to deploy increasing amounts of energy hungry data centers (Greenpeace, 2010). Consequently, energy

DOI: 10.4018/978-1-4666-1631-8.ch018

Copyright © 2012, IGI Global. Copying or distributing in print or electronic forms without written permission of IGI Global is prohibited.

costs for operating and cooling the equipment of such data centers have increased significantly up to a point where they are able to surpass the hardware acquisition costs.

Besides the possibility to replace the hardware with more energy-efficient one, reducing the energy wasted because of hardware over-provisioning is crucial. Today's data centers infrastructure is typically over-provisioned in order to sustain the service availability during periods of peak resource demand. However, resource demand in current data centers is usually of a bursty nature and thus results in a low average utilization of approximately 15-20% (Vogels, 2008). Therefore, a big fraction of the resources can be used to take energy conservation decisions such as suspending or turning off unnecessary servers, while still preserving the customer's performance requirements.

Several open-source cloud projects have been recently started to provide alternative solutions to public Infrastructure as a Service (IaaS) cloud providers. Examples of such cloud management frameworks include Eucalyptus (Nurmi et al., 2009), OpenNebula (*OpenNebula*, 2011), and Nimbus (*Nimbus*, 2011).

Given that ubiquitous virtualization solutions are able to live migrate the VMs and servers can be turned on and off at any time, clusters can be turned into dynamic pools of resources by these frameworks. However, two main drawbacks exist which prevent existing cloud management frameworks to efficiently manage current and future large-scale infrastructures: (1) high degree of centralization, (2) lack of advanced energy and QoS-aware VM placement algorithms. While the first one leads to single point of failure (SPOF) and limited scalability, the latter results in high energy costs and heat dissipation. This in turn decreases the hardware reliability.

In order to solve the first drawback more decentralized IaaS management frameworks are required. Similarly, energy-conservation algorithms are needed which are able to operate efficiently in such dynamic large-scale environments.

One possible approach to conserve energy is to perform VM consolidation. VMs are packed on the least number of physical nodes and over provisioned servers are transitioned into a lower power state (e.g., suspend). This problem can be modeled as an instance of the well-known multi-dimensional bin-packing (MDBP) problem and has been mostly studied by means of simulations in several works (Stillwell et al., 2010; Li et al., 2009). Because of the NP-hard nature of the problem and the need to compute the solutions in a reasonable amount of time, approximation approaches (i.e., heuristics) have shown to provide good results. However, many of the existing approaches nowadays still: (1) ignore the multi-dimensional character of the problem (Buyya et al., 2010; Stillwell et al., 2010), (2) adapt simple greedy algorithms (e.g., FFD), which tend to waste a lot of resources (Setzer & Stage, 2010) and are highly centralized.

This chapter is organized as follows. In the first part recent achievements in designing and implementing IaaS cloud computing frameworks are reviewed. The VM placement problem is defined as an instance of the multi-dimensional bin-packing (MDBP) problem and some of the existing bin-packing algorithms including their application to the energy and QoS-aware VM placement problem are discussed.

The second part of the chapter presents the ongoing work towards enabling energy-efficiency, scalability, resilience and self-management in IaaS clouds. A novel VM manager called Snooze is introduced whose design was driven by these properties.

In addition, in order to overcome the drawbacks of current VM placement algorithms, a novel nature-inspired energy-aware VM placement algorithm based on the Ant Colony Optimization is introduced.

Finally, the chapter closes with conclusions and future research directions.

BACKGROUND

System Architectures

This section reviews the system architectures of three well-known open-source IaaS cloud management frameworks: Eucalyptus, OpenNebula and Nimbus. All these frameworks allow users to execute VMs on virtualized clusters. Thereby, a virtualized cluster is a set of physical machines which are managed by a virtualization solution such as Xen (*Xen*, 2011) or KVM (KVM, 2011).

Eucalyptus

Eucalyptus (Nurmi et al., 2009) has a hierarchical architecture and is composed of three components: node, cluster, and cloud controllers. The high-level overview of Eucalyptus' system architecture is depicted in Figure 1.

The node controller (NC) runs on each physical machine and manages the local VMs. All NCs interact with the hypervisor using the libvirt library (*LibVirt*, 2011) in order to discover the available server capacity (e.g. RAM, CPU), control VMs (e.g. start, stop), and learn about the state (e.g. terminated) of VMs on behalf of the cluster controller.

The cluster controller (CC) runs on the frontend node of a possibly geographically distributed cluster. It schedules VMs on the NCs. VM scheduling is based on the host information collected from the NCs.

The cloud controller (CLC) manages the CCs and implements the web services-based user interface. The CLC also interacts with the CCs in order to support monitoring information retrieval and resource allocation/deallocation enforcements.

The hierarchical architecture of Eucalyptus allows it to scale with the number of clusters. However, the management granularity is at cluster-level, and thus each CC is a SPOF and a potential performance bottleneck for its cluster. Moreover, fault tolerance is not addressed for the CLC. Finally, the preliminary power management features of Eucalyptus strictly rely on the *powernap* utility thus limiting the flexibility of the framework. It also remains unclear how to implement advanced energy-saving policies (e.g., consolidation) as the authors do not specify how VMs are continuously

Figure 1. Eucalyptus system architecture

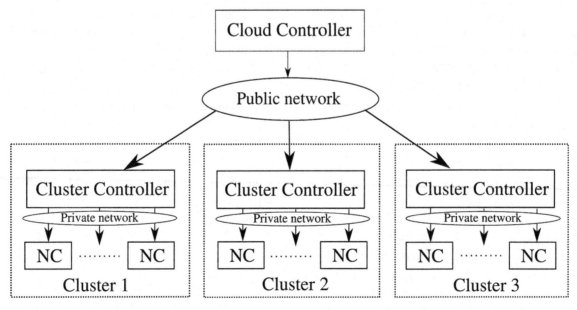

monitored and where monitoring data is stored for future analysis. Consequently, scalability, fault-tolerance and energy-awareness remain open issues for Eucalyptus.

OpenNebula

In contrast to Eucalyptus, OpenNebula (OpenNebula, 2011) is designed to manage a single cluster following the traditional frontend/backend model. The system architecture of OpenNebula is depicted in Figure 2.

OpenNebula's architecture is composed of three layers: tools, frontend and backend. Tools include a scheduler, the command line and RESTful interfaces, and are programmed using the frontend API. Custom schedulers can replace the default one and, for instance, use VM migration.

The frontend layer is composed of two components: core and drivers. The core implements the services necessary to control and monitor VMs, manage virtual networks, storage and hosts. The VM manager manages and monitors the VMs,

and uses pluggable drivers to support different hypervisors and monitoring frameworks. The host manager monitors and performs management actions on the physical machines, and also uses pluggable drivers. The internal data structure storage is provided by the database pool and is based on SQLite (*SQLite*, 2011).

The drivers component supports VM drivers to connect to the hypervisors (e.g., KVM), and information drivers to monitor the cluster nodes.

Finally, the backend layer provides the physical resources to execute VMs. VMs can be hosted locally (e.g., local cluster), remotely (e.g., public cloud), or both, which implements support for hybrid clouds.

Similarly to Eucalyptus' cluster controllers, OpenNebula's front-end node is a SPOF and a performance bottleneck for both management and monitoring. Moreover no power management component is available and no long term monitoring information about VMs is recorded, which makes it difficult to develop energy-aware scheduling policies like VM consolidation.

Figure 2. OpenNebula system architecture

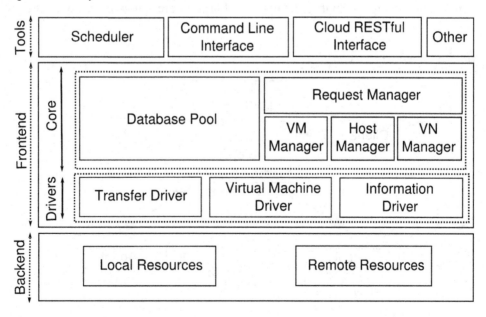

Nimbus

Similarly to OpenNebula, Nimbus' architecture follows the traditional frontend/backend model. Figure 3 gives a high-level overview of the Nimbus system architecture.

Clients contact the frontend node through web services, in order to perform VM operations (e.g., submission). The frontend node monitors and schedules VMs, and performs host/VM operations.

Each backend node runs an agent which executes VM management commands (e.g., start, stop) from the frontend node. Different hypervisors are supported using libvirt (*LibVirt*, 2011).

Analogously to Eucalyptus and OpenNebula, Nimbus suffers from the same scalability, fault-tolerance and energy efficiency problems.

Towards Decentralized Architectures

Recently several research works (Rouzaud-Cornabas, J., 2010; Quesnel & Lebre, 2011; Mastroianni et al., 2011), as well as the work described later in this chapter being among the first ones, have proposed more distributed frameworks. However, at most only preliminary simulation-based results are presented, with important implementation details

(e.g., fault-tolerance, scalability) being neglected. As this chapter focuses on working open-source systems and presents details of a working system, we let the reader investigate other approaches. Note that for space reasons the evaluation of our framework is out of the scope of this chapter and can be found in Feller et al., 2011.

Energy-Aware VM Placement

This section reviews some of the existing VM placement approaches targeting energy-conservation in IaaS clouds. First, assumptions of most of the VM placement algorithms are introduced and a formal definition of the VM consolidation problem as an instance of the multi-dimensional bin-packing (MDBP) is given. In particular, a binary integer programming (BIP) representation of the problem is introduced and the common algorithms to solve it are discussed.

Assumptions

Most of the existing VM placement algorithms assume a homogeneous environment in which all physical machines have the same capacity. Furthermore, knowledge about the VM and its

Figure 3. Nimbus system architecture

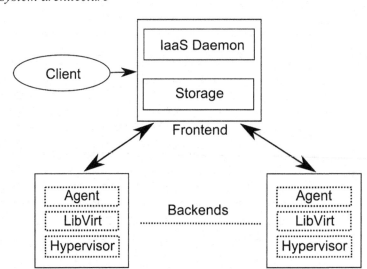

associated resource requirements is required in order to compute the placement. These resource requirements can be either seen as static or dynamic. In the static case it is assumed that a batch of VMs is submitted to the system and needs to be placed. Thereby, as no utilization information is available upon initial submission, given VMs resource requirements are considered static and VMs are scheduled according to this information. On the other hand, when time passes (i.e., sufficiently long) history resource utilization becomes available and can be used to estimate the resource demand. In that case, VM resource requirements can be seen as the dynamic estimates of the maximum resources required by the VMs over the predefined monitoring interval (e.g., week). The algorithms then take those values as input and dynamically overbook the resources when the VM resource demands permits it. Thereby, physical resource utilization is optimized. Consequently, it is assumed that VM resource utilization can be measured over predefined periods of time T (e.g., weeks) thus allowing the maximum VM resource demand to be estimated. Thereby, for the sake of simplicity the time t at which the maximum resource demand values are computed is not mentioned in the following formal definitions and is assumed to be the same as on which the VM consolidation algorithm is triggered. Moreover, in order to minimize the amount of migrations and limit the degree of performance degradation, the algorithms discussed in this chapter are assumed to be triggered after predefined, sufficiently long periods of time (e.g., weekly basis). More intelligent triggering decisions based on the analysis of VM characteristics (Setzer & Stage, 2010) are possible but go beyond the scope of this chapter. Finally, despite the relative long measurement periods, overbooking of resources can lead to performance degradation when VM resource demands suddenly start to increase. It is assumed that such changes can be detected and handled by the appropriate algorithm (Khanna et al., 2006).

Formal Problem Definition

The problem of mapping the VMs to physical machines can be modeled as an instance of the MDBP problem, in which the physical machines represent the bins and the VMs the items to be packed. Each bin has a predefined static resource (e.g., CPU cycles, CPU cores, RAM size, network bandwidth and disk size) capacity vector and each item is assigned with one time-varying resource demand vector.

Let $B := \{B_0, ..., B_v, ..., B_{n-1}\}$ denote the set of bins and $I := \{0, ..., m-1\}$ the set of items, with $n = |B|$ and $m = |I|$ representing the amounts of bins and items, respectively. Furthermore, available resources (i.e., CPU cycles, CPU cores, RAM size, network bandwidth and disk size) are defined by the set R with $d = |R|$.

Each bin B_v is assigned with a predefined static homogeneous d-dimensional bin capacity vector $\vec{C}_v := (C_{v,1}, ..., C_{v,k}, ... C_{v,d})$, in which each component defines the bin's capacity of resource $k \in R$. Moreover, all items $i \in I$ are represented by their time-varying d-dimensional resource demand vectors

$$\vec{r}_i := (\overline{r}_{i,1}, ..., \overline{r}_{i,k}, ..., \overline{r}_{i,d}) \in [0,1]^d$$

with each component of the vector being the items' maximum demand for resource $k \in R$ over the last measurement period T (e.g., week) relative to the corresponding dimension in the static bin resource capacity vector $\vec{C}_v$. Thereby, since we assume an homogenous set of bins/machines, without loss of generality it is assumed that the values of $\vec{C}_v$ have been normalized to 1 in the following definitions.

Finally, in order to complete the binary integer programming (BIP) model, two decision variables are defined:

- Bin allocation variable y_v equals 1 if the bin v is chosen and 0 otherwise.
- Item allocation variable $x_{i,v}$ equals 1 if the item i is assigned to the bin v, and 0 otherwise.

The ultimate goal is then to place all items such that, the number of bins used is minimized. This is reflected in the objective function:

$$\text{Minimize } f(y) = \sum_{v=0}^{n-1} y_v \qquad (1)$$

Subject to the following constraints:

$$\sum_{i=0}^{m-1} \overline{r}_{i,k} x_{i,v} \leq C_{v,k} y_v, \forall v \in \{0,\ldots,n-1\}, \forall k \in R \qquad (2)$$

$$\sum_{v=0}^{n-1} x_{i,v} = 1, \forall i \in \{0,\ldots,m-1\} \qquad (3)$$

Constraint (2) ensures that the capacity of each bin is not exceeded and constraint (3) guarantees that each item is assigned to exactly one bin.

VM Consolidation Algorithms

This section reviews commonly used approaches to solve the previously defined VM consolidation problem. Algorithms can be categorized as finding either approximate or exact solutions. Approximate solutions are typically obtained using greedy algorithms, and exact solutions can be obtained using linear programming or constraint programming. We present these three families of algorithms in the following paragraphs, and then discuss their advantages and drawbacks.

Greedy Algorithms

Typical greedy algorithms solving the VM consolidation problem are First-fit and First-fit decreasing. In First-fit, VMs are assumed to arrive sequentially and are scheduled on the first host which can accommodate them, starting from the first one sorted according to a predefined metric (e.g., resource capacity, power efficiency). For example, when a cluster spans three hosts having respectively 30, 50 and 40% of free capacity and a new VM is submitted which requires 20% of capacity, this VM is scheduled on the first host. Afterwards, the algorithm will try to schedule subsequent VMs starting again from the first host. Energy efficiency can be further optimized by presorting the hosts according to their power efficiency.

In First-fit decreasing, when a set of VMs is submitted the algorithm is improved by presorting the VMs in decreasing order prior allocation.

Note that since we represent VMs' resource demands and hosts' capacities as multi-dimensional vectors, sorting VMs and hosts requires to choose an ordering function like the L1 norm (L1, 2011).

Liner Programming and Constraint Programming

Linear programming (LP) (Murty, 1983), in particular Mixed-Integer-Linear-Programming (MILP) is one effective method to solve the VM consolidation problem. MILP is implemented by open-source (e.g., GLPK (GLPK, 2011)) and commercial solvers (e.g., IBM ILOG CPLEX (ILOG CPLEX, 2011)). Typically, in order to derive an optimal solution for the previously defined BIP model, currently branch-and-bound based algorithms (Murty, 1983) are implemented. Given the appropriate MILP model, such solvers can compute an optimal solution with exponential worst-case complexity. Consequently, most of the complexity goes into the problem formulation.

Note that variables of the model introduced in this chapter are integer valued. Assuming that the problem can be relaxed by allowing variables to be real valued, more efficient approaches such as the Simplex algorithm (Murty, 1983) can compute the results in polynomial time. However, the resulting solutions are likely infeasible (For example a VM could have to be split across multiple hosts.), and integer solutions that may be derived have no guarantee to be close to the optimal integer solutions.

Constraint programming (CP) (Rossi et al., 2006) is an alternative to LP. Similarly to LP, decision variables, objective functions to minimize or maximize, and constraints must be defined, which are then solved using a branch-and-bound algorithm. However, in contrast to LP, CP supports logical constraints and provides arithmetical expressions (e.g., integer division). Moreover, CP does not assume mathematical properties of the solution space (e.g., linearity) while LP requires the model to fall in a well-defined category (e.g., MILP). Nevertheless, both approaches are orthogonal and can be combined in order to achieve better results. For example, many Constraint Satisfaction Problems (CSPs) have been efficiently solved by such hybrid methods (Petrie et al., 2004).

Discussion

While approximate algorithms likely compute solutions faster than exact algorithms thanks to their quadratic complexity, the trade-off between these categories involves more than speed and amount of energy saved. Indeed, given that the appropriate mathematical model can be designed, placement constraints such as co- and anti-location of VMs can be easily added in CP, while heuristics are less flexible and would require significant modifications (e.g., to take into account graphs of dependencies). However, exact methods are highly centralized and memory-intensive as they need to keep a potentially large model (i.e., many

constraints) in memory, while a number of heuristic approaches (e.g., genetic algorithms, ant systems) can be easily distributed in order to provide better scalability and fault-tolerance. However, their application to VM consolidation is just starting to be investigated and will be discussed in the second part of this chapter.

Finally, the algorithms discussed in this chapter neither try to minimize the cost of VM migrations (Verma et al., 2010) when computing new mappings of VMs to hosts, nor compute reconfiguration plans (the order in which VMs should be migrated to transition to a new mapping). However, both tasks fall out of the scope of this chapter. Related literature includes (Hermenier et al., 2009; Murtazaev & Oh, 2011; Liu et al., 2011, and Ferreto et al., 2011).

TOWARDS ENERGY-EFFICIENT, SCALABLE, AND RESILIENT IAAS CLOUDS

Snooze: A Scalable and Autonomic Virtual Machine Management Framework for Private Clouds

One of the drawbacks of existing IaaS cloud management frameworks outlined in the previous section is their high degree of centralization. Consequently, they suffer from SPOFs and limited scalability. In order to overcome these limitations this section details the architecture of Snooze (Feller et al., 2011), a novel scalable, fault-tolerant and energy-aware VM management framework for private clouds. Thereby, several properties have to be fulfilled by Snooze in order to adapt such an environment. First, it has to scale across many thousands of nodes. Second, nodes and thus framework management components can fail at any time. Therefore, the system needs to self-heal and continue its operation despite of component failures. To scale across many thousands of nodes,

Snooze utilizes a self-organizing hierarchical and distributed architecture. Fault-tolerance is achieved with replication for the management framework components.

In the following paragraphs, first the system model and its assumptions are introduced. Afterwards, a global overview of the framework is given, and all system components including their implementation details are discussed. Finally, self-organization and self-healing mechanisms are described.

System Model and Assumptions

We assume a data center with possible multiple clusters whose nodes are interconnected with a high-speed LAN connection such as Gigabit Ethernet or Infiniband. Each cluster can be heterogeneous (i.e., different hardware and software). Each node is managed by a virtualization solution (e.g., Xen (*Xen*, 2011), KVM (*KVM*, 2011), OpenVZ (*OpenVZ*, 2011)) which supports VM live migration.

VMs are seen as black-boxes which are organized in so-called virtual clusters (VC) where each VC represents a collection of one or multiple VMs hosting one or multiple applications. We assume no restriction about applications: both compute and server applications are supported.

Multicast support is assumed to be available. Consequently, complex network topologies supporting multiple clusters are supported given that multi-cast forwarding can be enabled on the routers.

The current implementation of Snooze does not tolerate failures that partition the network. However appropriate leader election algorithms can replace the implemented one to tolerate such failures.

Finally hosts may fail, and failures are assumed to follow a fail-stop model.

Global System Overview

The global system overview of Snooze is shown in Figure 4.

Note, that for the ease of explanation this figure focuses on a single cluster while in a real scenario multiple clusters could be managed in the same manner. The architecture is partitioned

Figure 4. Layered system architecture

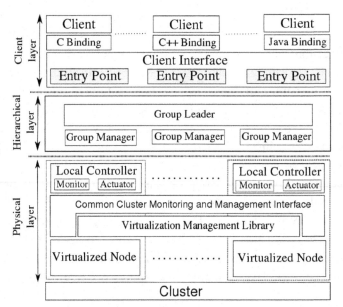

into three layers: physical, hierarchical and client. At physical layer, machines are organized in a cluster, in which each node is controlled by a so called Local Controller (LC).

A hierarchical layer allows to efficiently manage the cluster, and is composed of fault-tolerant components: Group Managers (GMs) and a Group Leader (GL). Each GM manages a subset of LCs, and the GL keeps the summary information of the GMs.

Finally, a client layer provides the user interface. This interface is currently implemented by a predefined number of replicated Entry Points (EPs) and is queried by the clients in order to discover the current GL. Clients can be implemented using the provided bindings in order to interact with the EPs. All the system components are implemented as Java RESTful web services. In the following sections the details of each component are discussed.

System Components

Local Controller (LC)

At the physical layer, the LC of a node is mainly in charge of the following tasks: (1) Joining the hierarchy during system boot and rejoining the hierarchy in case of GM failures, (2) Performing total host capacity retrieval (Total amount of CPUs/cores, memory and network capacity), (3) Performing VM monitoring (Current CPU, memory and network utilization), and (4) Enforcing host (e.g., suspend to ram) and VM management commands (start, suspend, resume, save, restore, shutdown, destroy, resize and migrate).

Therefore, an LC has two components: *Monitor* and *Actuator*. The *Monitor* implements all the logic required to monitor the host and its VMs (i.e., CPU, memory and network utilization) including reporting this information to the assigned GM. Similarly, the *Actuator* enforces the host and VM management commands coming from the GM. Both components rely on the Common Cluster

Monitoring and Management Interface (CCMMI), which allows to support different virtualization solutions, like the *libvirt* virtualization management library used in the current implementation, as well as external monitoring frameworks such as Ganglia (Ganglia, 2011).

Group Managers (GMs)

Each node (i.e., LC) of the physical layer is managed by one of the GMs within the hierarchical layer (see Figure 5).

This management mainly involves five tasks: (1) Receive, store and answer queries for host and VM monitoring information, (2) Estimate VM resource demands, (3) Schedule VMs, (4) Send host (e.g., suspend to ram) and VM management (e.g., start, stop) enforcement requests to the LCs and finally (5) Transmit GM summary information to the GL.

The host and VM monitoring information supporting the VM scheduling engine decisions is periodically sent to the GMs by the LCs and stored in an in-memory repository (other backends like Apache Cassandra (Cassandra, 2011) can implement this repository).

Based on this monitoring information, VMs' resource demand estimates, that are required by advanced optimization policies like consolidation, are performed by an integrated estimation engine using interfaces to plugin different CPU, memory, and network demand estimators. For instance an Exponentially Weighted Moving Average (EWMA) (resp. Double Exponential Moving Average (DEMA)) estimator can be used to estimate CPU (resp. memory) demand.

VM scheduling is performed on each GM by a generic engine that currently distinguishes between three types of policies implemented by the administrator: (1) scheduling, (2) optimization and (3) planning. While scheduling policies (e.g., round robin, load balance) are used for the incoming VMs, optimization and planning policies can be used as part of a system administrator configurable

Figure 5. Hierarchical layer

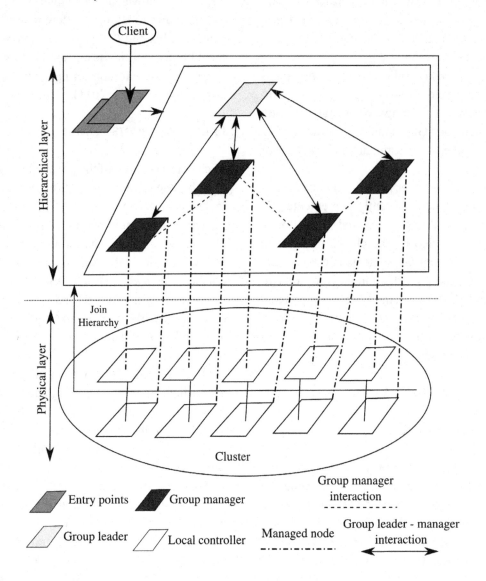

reconfiguration loop. The specified optimization policy computes the optimized VM placement and the planning policy computes a migration plan which gives the order of migrations required in order to move the system from the current state to the optimized one. For example, given that the administrator enables continuous optimization and specifies the proper reconfiguration interval (e.g., daily at 1 AM), Snooze attempts to optimize the current VM placement periodically using the specified optimization policy (e.g., consolidation).

To this end, the engine queries the estimation engine in order to get the current VM resource demand estimate vectors, triggers the optimization and planning policies and finally sends live migration requests to the actuators of the LCs.

When energy savings are enabled, each GM periodically observes the utilization of its LCs and triggers the specified power management actions (e.g., suspend to ram) when the LCs have become idle by sending the appropriate management commands. Therefore, a fixed idle time threshold exists above which the power management actions are triggered. Similarly, when LCs become overloaded, additional nodes are woken up. Finally, VMs on the overloaded LCs are rebalanced across the activated servers. In order to wake-up nodes each GM integrates a power management module which specifies the wake up logic (e.g., IPMI, Waken-On-LAN (WOL)). Finally, in order to rebalance the VMs, traditional scheduling policy is used (e.g., load balance). Note, that while we have briefly described how power management works, its details and evaluation are still ongoing work.

Finally, GM summary information is periodically sent by each GM to the current GL in order to support high-level scheduling decisions of the GL such as delegating VMs to be scheduled on the GMs, and to detect GM failures. This information is also used in case of GL failure to rebuild the GL system view. Currently, the GM summary includes the total amounts of used and free capacity available on all the managed LCs, as well as the VM networking related information (see the following Sections for more details).

Group Leader (GL)

The GL oversees the GMs and fulfills the following tasks: (1) Store incoming GM monitoring summary information, (2) Dispatch incoming VC submission requests, (3) Assign joining local controllers to GMs, (5) Manage VM network addresses, and (6) Periodically announce its presence. Note, that unlike on GMs, only lightweight (i.e., dispatching) VM placement decisions are performed.

GM summary information is received and stored in the GL repository in order to guide VC dispatching as well as LCs to GM assignment. Therefore, the GL integrates a scheduling engine using two types of policies. VC dispatching policies take as input a VM description as well as a repository reference and output the GM to which the VM start request should be delegated. The GL

then sends the VM start requests to the assigned GMs, waits for the replies and returns the output (i.e., status of VMs, assigned IP addresses, and GM descriptions) to the caller. GM assignment policies take as input an LC description as well as a repository reference and outputs the assigned GM. An LC needs to know which GM it is assigned to in order to join the hierarchy (see Section Self-Organization for the details of the join procedure).

VM network management is handled transparently to the user by Snooze. Each GL maintains a system administrator configurable subnet from which it is allowed to allocate IP addresses. When a VC is submitted to the GL, each of its VMs automatically gets an IP address from this subnet. A similar approach is applied in OpenNebula (*OpenNebula*, 2011).

In order to let the GL recycle IP addresses, the summary information of a GM includes a list of the IP addresses of its managed VM that have recently been terminated.

Entry Points

The EPs are used by the client software to discover the current GL. In order to keep track of the GL's address all EPs subscribe to the GL heartbeat multicast group and listen for current GL announcements.

Command Line Interface (CLI)

A Java-based CLI is implemented on top of the RESTful interfaces exported by the EPs, GL and GMs. It supports the definition and management of virtual clusters (VCs) as well as visualizing and exporting the current hierarchy organization in the GraphML format.

When a user defines a VC and attempts to start it, the CLI first tries to find an active EP by walking through the EPs list specified in its configuration file and testing the EP status. Given that an active EP exists, a GL lookup is sent in order to receive the current GL information. Finally, the request to submit the VC is delegated to the GL which dispatches the VMs on the available GMs. The result is returned to the CLI and presented to the user. Currently, the following information is provided: Assigned VM IP addresses, GM descriptions (i.e., hosts and ports), status (e.g., RUNNING) and an error code which is displayed if problems occurred during the submission. Finally, the GM information on which the VMs were dispatched is stored in the local CLI repository next to the VM definitions thus allowing the CLI to contact the GM directly whenever VC/VM management commands need to be performed. The following management commands are currently supported: starting, stopping, suspending, resuming, inter-GM migration, dynamic resizing (number of virtual cores and memory size) as well as retrieving the current live resource usage statistics of the VMs. Finally, it is important to mention that on GM failures the CLI repository information becomes obsolete. When the CLI detects that a GM is not reachable (e.g., during VM resource usage information retrieval) it first queries the EP in order to discover the current GL. Afterwards a GM discovery request including the VM identifier is sent to the GL. Upon reception of the request, the GL queries the currently active GMs in order to find the one assigned to the VM, and returns the result to the CLI. Thus the management command can be performed on the new GM. The following section details how self-organization and self-healing are performed.

Self-Organization and Healing of the Hierarchy

The core of the Snooze self-organization scheme includes a heartbeat-protocol and a leader election algorithm. Using the heartbeat protocol at all levels of the hierarchy allows components to detect failures of each other and rebuild the hierarchy.

The hierarchy join process of a GM works as follows. Each time a new GM attempts to join

the system, the leader election algorithm is triggered. Currently, our leader election algorithm is built on top of the Apache ZooKeeper (Hunt et al., 2010) highly available and reliable coordination system. Each time Snooze is deployed, the ZooKeeper service is installed on the EPs in replication mode. When a GM starts, it connects to the service, creates an ephemeral node in its hierarchical namespace and attaches to it the GM description (i.e., networking information and an internal Snooze identifier). This node is assigned a unique sequential identifier by the service in the namespace and is used by the GMs in order to discover the current GL and elect a new GL in case of failure. After the node creation each GM first tries to find another node in the namespace with a lower identifier (i.e., predecessor). If such node already exists the GM starts watching it and initiates the GL heartbeat multicast listener. Finally, upon the reception of a GL heartbeat message the GM sends a join request along with its description to the GL. Otherwise, if no node with a lower identifier could be detected, the current GM becomes the new GL and starts announcing its presence by sending multicast messages on the GL heartbeat multicast port.

GL and GM failures are handled as follows. Each time a failure of a GL or GM occurs an event is triggered on its successor GM as each node watches its predecessor. The successor GM becomes the new GL if its identifier is the lowest and stops all the GM related logic, otherwise it simply starts watching the next precessor GM. When a GM is promoted to be a GL it gracefully terminates all its tasks such as the heartbeat and monitoring data sender, its open LC connections, energy saver and the repository manager. Afterwards the GL logic is started along with the GL heartbeat sender. Finally, as all the existing GMs are still listening for GL heartbeat messages they receive the new GL information and automatically trigger the GL rejoin procedure. Note, that in case of a GL failure all its internal knowledge about the existing GMs as well as the distributed VM networking information (i.e., assigned IP addresses) is lost. In order to restore this knowledge, each time a GM rejoins the GL, the GM sends its description along with the VM networking information stored in its repository. Moreover, GM resource utilization summaries are periodically sent back to the GL thus making it completely recover the system view. Finally, as a GM has been promoted to become the new GL and thus has terminated all its GM related logic, LCs which were previously assigned to it fail to receive its heartbeat messages and trigger the system rejoin procedure.

The join process of a LC works as follows. Each time a LC attempts to join the hierarchy it starts listening for the GL multicast heartbeat messages. When it receives a heartbeat message, the join process is started by sending a GM assignment request with its current description (i.e., host address, port and total capacity) to the GL. The GL then triggers the GM assignment policy and dispatches the LC to an active GM. The contact information of the allocated GM is returned to the LC, which then initiates the actual GM join process by sending its description to the GM. Afterwards, it starts listening for GM heartbeat messages and periodically sends its own heartbeat, host and VM monitoring information to the GM. On an LC failure, the GM gracefully removes it from its database, and adds the IP addresses of the LC's VMs to the list of freed addresses. Finally, in case of a GM failure the LC rejoins the hierarchy by triggering again the join procedure. Because VM information (i.e., identifier, assigned IP address, etc.) stored by the previous GM might get lost, each time a LC joins the newly assigned GM, it also transfers its local state (i.e., information about currently running VMs), thus allowing the new GM to update its repository. This update is needed by the clients to discover the new VM location and by the GM to perform VM management operations as well as scheduling decisions.

Energy-Aware Nature-Inspired VM Consolidation

In order to overcome the limitations of the previously introduced heuristic-based VM consolidation algorithms, this section investigates bio-inspired VM placement approaches (e.g., genetic algorithms, ant systems). Such algorithms can bring significant improvements as they have the required properties (i.e., autonomy, scalability, and fault-tolerance) to efficiently manage large-scale infrastructures. Particularly, this section details a novel VM placement algorithm based on the Ant Colony Optimization (ACO) meta-heuristic and introduced by Feller et al. (2011). First a brief introduction to the ACO is given. Afterwards, algorithm details are discussed. The interested reader will find experimental results, showing near optimal solutions, in Feller et al. (2011).

Ant Colony Optimization

ACO is a meta-heuristic initially introduced by Dorigo et al. (1999) to solve the Traveling Salesman Problem (TSP). Since then it has been successfully adapted to solve many other complex combinatorial optimization problems like vehicle routing, quadratic assignment, dynamic job scheduling, graph coloring and bin packing.

The main inspiration for ACO was the natural food-discovery behavior of real ants. Because of the limited abilities of the ants to see and hear their environment they have developed a form of indirect communications (also called Stigmergy) using a chemical substance referred as pheromone. This substance is deposited by each ant on the path it traverses and evaporates over time. Other ants smell the concentration of this substance and tend to favor paths probabilistically according to the pheromone concentration on them. Surprisingly, after some time the entire ant colony converges towards the shortest path to the food source (Deneubourg et al., 1990). This behavior can be explained as follows. At the beginning, when starting from the nest ants choose a random path to follow. However, on the shortest path to the food source the ants return faster. Thereby, this path accumulates a stronger pheromone concentration thus being more attractive for subsequent ants to follow it. As time passes, pheromone concentration on the shortest paths continues to increase, while on the longer ones it keeps falling, making them less and less attractive.

When applied to combinatorial optimization problems such as TSP or Bin-Packing Problem (BPP), artificial ants act as a multi-agent system and construct a complex solution based on indirect low-level communication. The algorithm is composed of the following parts to imitate real ants. First ants decide which path or item to choose next. To this end a probabilistic decision rule has to be defined and should guide the ants choice towards the optimal solution. Second, artificial ants need a memory, used to record the local solution constructed so far. Finally, a pheromone update mechanism (1) simulates pheromone evaporation, and (2) deposits pheromone either, for TSP, on the visited paths or, for BPP, on the selected item-bin pairs. The design decisions of this work are discussed in the following paragraphs.

Algorithm Details

This section presents the design of the proposed ACO meta-heuristic based algorithm to solve the previously defined VM consolidation problem. After an overview of the algorithm, we detail the key parts. The pseudo code is depicted in Figure 6. A line-by-line description can be found in Feller et al. (2011).

Overview

In the following algorithm each ant receives all items (i.e., VMs), opens a bin (i.e., physical machine), assigns as many items as possible to the bin, and repeats with the next bin. The probabilistic decision rule thus describes the desirability for an ant to choose a particular item as the next one to pack in its current bin. This rule is based on the current pheromone concentration on the item-bin pairs and a heuristic which guides the ants towards choosing the most promising items. This stochastic nature of the algorithm allows the ants to explore a large number of potential solutions and thus compute better placements than a state-of-the-art greedy algorithm (Feller et al., 2011).

Probabilistic Decision Rule

The probability for an ant to choose an item i as the next one to pack in its current bin v is defined as follows:

$$p_v^i := \frac{[\tau_{i,v}]^\alpha \times [\eta_{i,v}]^\beta}{\sum\limits_{u \in N_v} [\tau_{u,v}]^\alpha \times [\eta_{u,v}]^\beta}, \quad \forall i \in N_v$$

(4)

where, $\tau_{i,v}$ denotes the pheromone based desirability of packing item i into bin v and $\eta_{i,v}$ the items heuristic information. Moreover, two parameters $\alpha, \beta > 0$ are used in order to either emphasize more the pheromone or the heuristic information. Finally, N_v defines the set of all items which qualify for inclusion into the current bin v. Hence, those are all items which have not been assigned to any bin yet and do not violate the bin capacity constraints in any dimension.

$$N_v := \{i \# \sum_{j=0}^{n-1} x_{i,j} = 0 \wedge \vec{b}_v + \vec{r}_i \leq \vec{C}_v\}$$

(5)

Thereby, $\vec{b}_v$ is defined as the load vector of bin v. It is computed as the sum of all item resource demand vectors currently assigned to the bin.

Figure 6. Algorithm pseudo code.

Algorithm 1 Energy-Aware ACO-based Workload Consolidation

1: Input: Set of items I and set of bins B with their associated resource demand vectors $\vec{r}_i$ and $\vec{C}_v$ respectively, Set of parameters
2: Output: Global best solution S_{best}
3:
4: Initialize parameters, Set pheromone value on all item-bin pairs to τ_{max}
5: **for all** $q \in \{0 \ldots nCycles - 1\}$ **do**
6:   **for all** $a \in \{0 \ldots nAnts - 1\}$ **do**
7:     $IS := I; v := 0$
8:     $S_a := [x_{i,j} := 0], \forall i \in \{0, \ldots, m - 1\}, \forall j \in \{0, \ldots, n - 1\}$
9:     **while** $IS \neq \emptyset$ **do**
10:       $N_v := \{i \mid \sum_{j=0}^{n-1} x_{i,j} = 0 \wedge \vec{b}_v + \vec{r}_i \leq \vec{C}_v\}$
11:       **if** $N_v \neq \emptyset$ **then**
12:         Choose item $i \in N_v$ stochastically according to probability $p_v^i := \frac{[\tau_{i,v}]^\alpha \times [\eta_{i,v}]^\beta}{\sum_{u \in N_v} [\tau_{u,v}]^\alpha \times [\eta_{u,v}]^\beta}$
13:         $x_{i,v} := 1$
14:         $IS := IS - \{i\}$
15:         $\vec{b}_v := \vec{b}_v + \vec{r}_i$
16:       **else**
17:         $v := v + 1$
18:       **end if**
19:     **end while**
20:   **end for**
21:   Compare ants solutions S_a according to the objective function $f \rightarrow$ Save cycle best solution as S_{cycle}
22:   **if** $q = 0 \vee IsGlobalBest(S_{cycle})$ **then**
23:     Save cycle best solution as new global best S_{best}
24:   **end if**
25:   Compute τ_{min} and τ_{max}
26:   **for all** $(i, B_v) \in I \times B$ **do**
27:     $\tau_{i,v} := (1 - \rho) \times \tau_{i,v} + \triangle\tau_{i,v}^{best}$
28:     **if** $\tau_{i,v} > \tau_{max}$ **then**
29:       $\tau_{i,v} := \tau_{max}$
30:     **end if**
31:     **if** $\tau_{i,v} < \tau_{min}$ **then**
32:       $\tau_{i,v} := \tau_{min}$
33:     **end if**
34:   **end for**
35: **end for**
36: **return** Global best solution S_{best}

$$\vec{b}_v := \sum_{i \in B_v} \vec{r}_i \qquad (6)$$

Heuristic Information

As the objective is to minimize the number of machines (i.e., maximize the resource utilization), the heuristic information is defined to favor items which utilize the bins better. This is achieved by using $\eta_{i,v}$ as the inverse of the scalar valued difference between the static capacity of bin v and the load of the bin after packing the item $i \in N_v$.

$$\eta_{i,v} := \frac{1}{\mid \vec{C}_v - (\vec{b}_v + \vec{r}_i) \mid_1} \qquad (7)$$

In order to compute the ratio the resulting d-dimensional resource demand vector needs to be mapped to a scalar value. Therefore, the L1-norm is used in this work. However, alternative methods such as taking the arithmetic mean are possible.

Pheromone Trail Update

After all ants have finished building a solution, pheromone trails on all item-bin pairs are updated in order to help guiding the ants towards the optimal solution. The pheromone trail update rule $\tau_{i,v}$ definition follows the MAX-MIN Ant System (MMAS) (Stutzle & Hoos, 1996) approach in which only the iteration's-best ant (i.e., ant whose solution's objective function value is minimal) is allowed to deposit pheromone. The pheromone update rule is defined as follows.

$$\tau_{i,v} := (1-\rho) \times \tau_{i,v} + \Delta\tau_{i,v}^{best}, \quad \forall\, (i, B_v) \in I \times B \tag{8}$$

where, the constant $\rho, 0 \leq \rho \leq 1$ is used to simulate pheromone evaporation (higher values simulate higher evaporation rates). $\Delta\tau_{i,v}^{best}$ is defined as the iteration's-best item-bin pheromone amount:

$$\Delta\tau_{i,v}^{best} := \begin{cases} \dfrac{1}{f(S_{best})} & if\ x_{i,v} = 1 \\ 0 & \text{otherwise} \end{cases} \tag{9}$$

Hence, pheromone concentration increases only for item-bin pairs belonging to the so far best solution S_{best}, and only those pairs become more attractive. A solution is defined as a binary matrix whose elements represent the mapping of items to bins.

The goal of the ACO-based algorithm is to minimize the amount of bins. Therefore, the amount of pheromone iteration's best ant deposits on the item-bin pair is defined to be inverse proportional to the value of the objective function f applied on the iteration's best-solution: the less bins are used, the higher amount of pheromone is deposited.

Finally, in ACO early stagnation can happen where the ants converge to a local minimum. In order to prevent this, MMAS constraints the pheromone values between lower and upper bounds $[\tau_{min}, \tau_{max}]$. τ_{max} is defined as $\tau_{max} := \dfrac{1}{f(S_{best}) \times (1-\rho)}$ and τ_{min} as $\tau_{min} := \dfrac{\tau_{max}}{g}$, respectively with factor $g > 1$ (Stutzle & Hoos, 1996).

FUTURE RESEARCH DIRECTIONS

Existing open source IaaS cloud management frameworks are highly centralized. Hence, their scalability is very limited. Moreover, they do not provide any means of fault-tolerance. First attempts to provide scalability and fault-tolerance (Feller et al., 2010; Rouzaud-Cornabas, 2010; Quesnel & Lebre, 2011, Thanakornworakij et al., 2011) have been recently made and need to be further investigated.

Similarly, a high degree of centralization can be observed in most of the existing VM placement algorithms as they require all the monitoring information to be available prior computation. In addition many of existing VM placement algorithms are limited to a single resource (e.g., CPU) and do not take into account possible migration costs (i.e., performance, energy). Hence, they ignore the multi-dimensional aspect of the problem. For example, networking is not considered by most of the existing works. Moreover, they are not able to estimate the impact of migrations on performance and energy. Thus decision-making aiming at minimizing the impact of migrations on both metrics is not possible. Many of the existing algorithms are not placement constraints aware. For example, cloud customers might require a set of VMs to be scheduled on the same host (e.g., performance reasons). On the other hand, security restrictions might enforce two VMs to be scheduled on different hosts. In addition, scheduling workloads with similar characteristics (e.g., memory bound) on the same host might result in performance degradation as caches are typically shared between workloads and thus should be avoided. Such co- and anti-location criteria's in conjunction with energy-saving objectives (e.g., minimize the number of hosts) remain to be investigated.

Last but not least, current algorithms are typically triggered at predefined time periods. However, these time periods do not relate to the time varying resource demands of the VMs. This can result in significant performance degradation due to migrations if the algorithm is started during period of high load. Consequently, approaches are needed, which can proactively trigger the algorithms during periods of low utilization.

CONCLUSION

This chapter has surveyed existing efforts on designing and implementing IaaS cloud management frameworks. In addition, the architecture and implementation details of a novel scalable, fault-tolerant, and energy-aware VM manager for heterogeneous virtualized clusters called Snooze were presented. Snooze is based on a self-organizing hierarchical architecture with replication thus it is scalable and fault-tolerant.

While the architecture of Snooze looks similar to the one of Eucalyptus, both frameworks are orthogonal and follow complementary goals. Eucalyptus utilizes a hierarchical architecture in order to efficiently manage federations of clusters while Snooze follows a simple design and focuses on enabling energy-awareness, scalability and fault-tolerance on a single cluster. Consequently, using the provided bindings Snooze can be coupled with Eucalyptus in order to act as a cluster controller

and thus provide energy-awareness, scalability and fault-tolerance at the cluster level. A first prototype of Snooze (Feller et al., 2011), was implemented and evaluated on the Grid5000 (Cappello, et al., 2005) experimental testbed.

Finally, a novel VM placement algorithm based on the Ant Colony Optimization (ACO) meta-heuristic to solve the first problem involved in the consolidation step (i.e., computing the optimized VM placement) was introduced. Even though the algorithm described in this chapter is implemented in a centralized manner, the autonomous nature of ants allows it to be implemented in a fully distributed environment thus avoiding SPOFs and providing properties such as scalability and fault-tolerance.

ACKNOWLEDGMENT

This research is funded by the French Agence Nationale de la Recherche (ANR) project EcoGrappe under the contract number ANR-08-SEGI-000.

REFERENCES

L1. (2011). Retrieved November 10, from http://mathworld.wolfram.com/L1-Norm.html

Buyya, R., Beloglazov, A., & Abawajy, H. J. (2010). *Energy-efficient management of data center resources for cloud computing: a vision, architectural elements, and open challenges.* Melbourne, Australia: Cloud Computing and Distributed Systems (CLOUDS) Laboratory.

Cappello, F., Caron, E., Dayde, M., Desprez, F., Jegou, Y., Primet, P., et al. (2005). Grid'5000: A large scale and highly reconfigurable grid experimental testbed. *6th IEEE/ACM International Workshop on Grid Computing.* 99–106.

Cassandra, A. (2011). Retrieved from http://cassandra.apache.org/

Deneubourg, L.-J., Aron, S., Goss, S., & Pasteels, M. J. (1990). The self-organizing exploratory pattern of the argentine ant. *Journal of Insect Behavior, 3*(2), 159–168. doi:10.1007/BF01417909

Dorigo, M., Caro, Di G., & Gambardella, M. L. (1999). Ant algorithms for discrete optimization. *Artificial Life, 5*(1), 137–172. doi:10.1162/106454699568728

Feller, E., Rilling, L., & Morin, C. (2011). Energy-Aware Ant-Colony Based Workload Placement in Clouds. *12th IEEE/ACM International Conference on Grid Computing (GRID-2011)*. Retrieved from: http://hal.inria.fr/inria-00626042/

Feller, E., Rilling, L., & Morin, C. (2011). Snooze: A Scalable and Autonomic Virtual Machine Management Framework for Private Clouds. *INRIA research report* (7833). Retrieved from http://hal.inria.fr/hal-00651542/en

Feller, E., Rilling, L., Morin, C., Lottiaux, R., & Leprince, D. (2010). Snooze: A Scalable, Fault-Tolerant and Distributed Consolidation Manager for Large-Scale Clusters. *2010 IEEE/ACM International Conference on Green Computing and Communications,* 125-132.

Ferreto, C. T., Netto, M., Calheiros, R., & De Rose, C. (2011). Server consolidation with migration control for virtualized data centers. *Future Generation Computer Systems, 27*(8), 1027–1034. doi:10.1016/j.future.2011.04.016

GLPK. (2011). *GNU linear programming kit.* Retrieved from http://www.gnu.org/s/glpk/

Greenpeace, I. (2010). *Make IT Green: Cloud computing and its contribution to climate change.* Retrieved from http://www.greenpeace.org/usa/Global/usa/report/2010/3/ make-it-green-cloud-computing.pdf

Hermenier, F., Lorca, X., Menaud, M.-J., Muller, G., & Lawall, J. (2009). Entropy: a consolidation manager for clusters. In *proceedings of the 2009 ACM SIGPLAN/SIGOPS international conference on Virtual execution environments.* (pp. 41–50) Washington DC, USA: Purdue

Hunt, O., Konar, M., Junqueira, P. F., & Reed, B. (2010). ZooKeeper: wait-free coordination for internet-scale systems. *2010 USENIX conference on USENIX annual technical conference (USENIXATC'10).*

IBM. (2011). Mathematical programming vs. Constraint programming. Retrieved from http://www-01.ibm.com/software/integration/optimization/cplex-cp-optimizer/mp-cp/

ILOG CPLEX. (2011). *High-performance software for mathematical programming and optimization.* Retrieved from http://www.ilog.com/products/cplex/

Khanna, G., Beaty, K., Kar, G., & Kochut, A. (2006). Application performance management in virtualized server environments. *10th IEEE/IFIP Network Operations and Management Symposium,* 373-381.

KVM. (2011). Kernel based virtual machine. Retrieved, from http://www.linux-kvm.org/

Li, B. Li, J., Huai, J., Wo, T., Li, Q. & Zhong, L. (2009). EnaCloud: An energy-saving application live placement approach for cloud computing environments. *2009 IEEE International Conference on Cloud Computing,* 17-24.

LibVirt. (2011). Libvirt: The virtualization API. Retrieved 6 July, 2011, from http://libvirt.org/

Liu, H., Xu, Z.-C., Jin, H., Gong, J., & Liao, X. (2011). Performance and energy modeling for live migration of virtual machines. 20th *international symposium on High performance distributed computing (HPDC '11).*

Mastroianni, C., Meo, M, Papuzzo, G. (2011). Self-economy in cloud data centers: statistical assignment and migration of virtual machines. *Euro-Par* (1) 407-418.

Murtazaev, A., & Oh, S. (2011). *Sercon: Server Consolidation Algorithm using Live Migration of Virtual Machines for Green Computing.* Available from: http://tr.ietejournals.org/text.asp?2011/28/3/212/81230

Murty, G. K. (1983). *Linear programming.* New York, NY: John Wiley & Sons.

Nurmi, D., Wolski, R., Grzegorczyk, C., Obertelli, G., Soman, S., Youseff, L., & Zagorodnov, D. (2009). The Eucalyptus open-source cloud-computing system. *9th IEEE/ACM International Symposium on Cluster Computing and the Grid.* Washington DC, USA: IEEE Press.

OpenVZ. (2011). Retrieved November 15, 2011, from http://wiki.openvz.org/Main_Page

OpenNebula. (2011). *OpenNebula 2.0 Architecture.* Retrieved July 12, 2011, from http://opennebula.org/documentation:archives:rel2.0:architecture

Petrie, E. K., Smith, B., & Yorke-smith, N. (2004). Dynamic symmetry breaking in constraint programming and linear programming hybrids. In *European Starting AI Researcher Symposium.*

Quesnel, F., & Lebre, A. (2011). Cooperative dynamic scheduling of virtual machines in *Distributed systems. 6th Workshop on Virtualization in High-Performance Cloud Computing (VHPC).*

Rossi, F., Beek, P., & Walsh, T. (2006). *Handbook of Constraint Programming (Foundations of Artificial Intelligence.* New York, NY: Elsevier.

Rouzaud-Cornabas, J. (2010). A distributed and collaborative dynamic load balancer for virtual machine. In *5th Workshop on Virtualization in High-Performance Cloud Computing (VHPC).*

Setzer, T., & Stage, A. (2010). Decision support for virtual machine reassignments in enterprise data centers. In *IEEE/IFIP Network Operations and Management Symposium Workshops,* (pp. 88-94.) Washington DC, USA: IEEE Press

SQLite. (2011). *SQLite.* Retrieved from http://www.sqlite.org/

Stillwell, M., Schanzenbach, D., Vivien, F., & Casanova, H. (2010). Resource allocation algorithms for virtualized service hosting platforms. *Journal of Parallel and Distributed Computing,* *70*(9), 962–974. doi:10.1016/j.jpdc.2010.05.006

Stutzle, T., & Hoos, H. (1996). Improvements on ant-system: Introducing max-min ant system. Research report. Retrieved from http://citeseerx.ist.psu.edu/viewdoc/summary?doi=10.1.1.41.6090

Thanakornworakij, T., Sharma, R., Scroggs, B., Leangsuksun, C. B., Greenwood, Z. D., Riteau, P., & Morin, C. (2011). High Availability on Cloud with HA-OSCAR. *4th Workshop on Resiliency in High Performance Computing (Resilience) in Clusters, Clouds, and Grids.*

Verma, A., Kumar, G., & Koller, R. (2010). The cost of reconfiguration in a cloud. *11th ACM International Middleware Conference (Industrial track),*(pp. 11-16) New York, NY: ACM Press

Vogels, W. (2008). Beyond Server Consolidation. *Queue,6*(1),20–26.doi:10.1145/1348583.1348590

Xen. (2011). *Xen hypervisor.* Retrieved July 20, 2011, from http://xen.org/

ADDITIONAL READING

Barbagallo, D., Di Nitto, E., & Dubois, J. Daniel., Mirandola, R. (2010). A bio-inspired algorithm for energy optimization in a self-organizing data center. *1st International conference on Self-organizing architectures,*(pp. 127-151) New York, NY: Springer Verlag

Barham, P., Dragovic, B., Fraser, K., Hand, S., & Harris, T. Ho., A., Neugebauer, R., Pratt, I., & Warfield, A. (2003). Xen and the art of virtualization. *19th ACM symposium on Operating systems principles.* (pp. 164–177) New York, NY: ACM Press

Beloglazov, A., & Buyya, R. (2010). Energy efficient allocation of virtual machines in cloud data centers. *IEEE International Symposium on Cluster Computing and the Grid*, (pp. 577–578) Washington DC, USA: IEEE Press

Beloglazov, A., & Buyya, R. (2010). Adaptive threshold-based approach for energy-efficient consolidation of virtual machines in cloud data centers. *8th International Workshop on Middleware for Grids, Clouds and e-Science (MGC)*, 4:1–4:6.

Bichler, M., Setzer, T., & Speitkamp, B. (2006). Capacity planning for virtualized servers. 16th Annual Workshop on Information Technologies and Systems, Milwaukee, Wisconsin, USA.

Bobroff, N., Kochut, A., & Beaty, K. (2007). Dynamic placement of virtual machines for managing sla violations. *10th IFIP/IEEE International Symposium on Integrated Network Management.* (pp. 119–128.) Washington DC, USA: IEEE Press

Breitgand, D., Maraschini, A., & Tordsson, J. (2011). Policy-Driven Service Placement Optimization in Federated Clouds. Research report. Retrieved July 6, 2011, from http://domino.watson.ibm.com/library/cyberdig.nsf/papers/8E35352121C147E9852578390058876E

Chekuri, C., & Khanna, S. (1999). On multidimensional packing problems. *10th ACM-SIAM symposium on Discrete algorithms*, (pp. 185–194) New York, NY: ACM Press

Coffman, G. E., Jr., Garey, R. M., & Johnson, S. D. (1997). Approximation algorithms for bin packing: a survey. (pp. 46–93) Boston, MA, USA: PWS Publishing Co.

Hermenier, F., Demassey, S., & Lorca, X. (2011). Bin Repacking Scheduling in Virtualized Datacenters. *17th International Conference on Principles and Practice of Constraint Programming; Application track*. Perugia, Italy.

Huebscher, C.M., & McCann, A. J. (2008). A survey of autonomic computing - degrees, models, and applications. *ACM Computing Surveys, 40*(3). doi:10.1145/1380584.1380585

Hwang, H.-C., & Wu, H.-C. A. (2000). A predictive system shutdown method for energy saving of event-driven computation. *ACM Transactions on Design Automation of Electronic Systems, 5*(2), 226–241. doi:10.1145/335043.335046

Lim, Y. M., Rawson, F., Bletsch, T., & Freeh, W. V. (2009). Padd: Power aware domain distribution. *International Conference on Distributed Computing Systems. 0*, (pp. 239–247) Washington DC, USA: IEEE Press

Nathuji, R., & Schwan, K. (2007). Virtualpower: coordinated power management in virtualized enterprise systems. *21st ACM SIGOPS symposium on Operating systems principles.* (pp. 265–278) New York, NY: ACM Press

Perera, S., & Gannon, D. (2009). Enforcing User-Defined management logic in large scale systems. *2009 Congress on Services - I*, (pp. 243–250) Washington DC, USA: IEEE Press

Pottier, R., Léger, M., & Menaud, M-J. A Reconfiguration Language for Virtualized Grid Infrastructures. *10th IFIP international conference on Distributed Applications and Interoperable Systems (DAIS), 6115.*

Srikantaiah, S., Kansal, A., & Zhao, F. (2008). Energy aware consolidation for cloud computing. *Workshop on Power Aware Computing and Systems (HotPower).*

Verma, A., Ahuja, P., & Neogi, A. (2008). pmapper: power and migration cost aware application placement in virtualized systems. *9th ACM/IFIP/ USENIX International Conference on Middleware.* (pp. 243–264) New York, NY: ACM Press

Xu, J., Zhao, M., & Fortes, B. A. José. (2009). Cooperative Autonomic Management in Dynamic Distributed Systems. *11th International Symposium on Stabilization, Safety, and Security of Distributed Systems,* (pp. 756–770) New York, NY: Springer

KEY TERMS AND DEFINITIONS

Ant Colony Optimization (ACO): A probabilistic meta-heuristic for solving combinatorial optimization problems.

Consolidation: Packing of multiple virtual machines on the least number of physical ones.

Fault-Tolerance: A system which is designed to resume its operation despite system component failures.

Infrastructure-as-a-Service (IaaS): A provisioning model which provides virtual resources on demand.

Scalability: Ability of a system, or algorithm to efficiently manage increasing number of resources.

Self-Organization: Ability of a system to autonomically configure without external intervention.

Self-Healing: Ability of a system to automatically reconfigure and continue its operation in case of system component failures.

Virtualization: Division of a physical machine into multiple virtual ones.

Chapter 19
Self–Management of Applications and Systems to Optimize Energy in Data Centers

Frederico Alvares de Oliveira Jr.
ASCOLA Research Team (INRIA-Mines Nantes, LINA), France

Adrien Lèbre
ASCOLA Research Team (INRIA-Mines Nantes, LINA), France

Thomas Ledoux
ASCOLA Research Team (INRIA-Mines Nantes, LINA), France

Jean-Marc Menaud
ASCOLA Research Team (INRIA-Mines Nantes, LINA), France

ABSTRACT

As a direct consequence of the increasing popularity of cloud computing solutions, data centers are grow-ing amazingly and hence have to urgently face with the energy consumption issue. Available solutions are focused basically on the system layer, by leveraging virtualization technologies to improve energy efficiency. Another body of works relies on cloud computing models and virtualization techniques to scale up/down applications based on their performance metrics. Although those proposals can reduce the energy footprint of applications and by transitivity of cloud infrastructures, they do not consider the internal characteristics of applications to finely define a trade-off between applications Quality of Service and energy footprint. In this paper, the authors propose a self-adaptation approach that consid-ers both application internals and system to reduce the energy footprint in cloud infrastructure. Each application and the infrastructure are equipped with control loops, which allow them to autonomously optimize their executions. The authors implemented the control loops and simulated them in order to show their feasibility. In addition, the chapter shows how the solution fits in federated clouds through a motivating scenario. Finally, it provides some discussion about open issues on models and implementa-tion of the proposal.

DOI: 10.4018/978-1-4666-1631-8.ch019

Copyright © 2012, IGI Global. Copying or distributing in print or electronic forms without written permission of IGI Global is prohibited.

INTRODUCTION

Over the last few years, cloud computing has received a lot of attention in both industry and academia. First, from the application provider point of view, cloud computing permits to precisely request/release resources on the fly. It means that the infrastructure provider can deliver computational and storage resources in a flexible and elastic manner, while charging the application only for what it actually consumes (Mirashe & Kalyankar, 2010). This is particularly interesting for applications that need to cope with a highly variable workload (e.g. web application). Second, from the infrastructure provider point of view, cloud computing has shown to be a very powerful model to mutualize resources and thus face the problem of energy consumption in IT infrastructures. Recent techniques like virtualization enable the provisioning of resources through virtual machines that can be placed in the same physical machine. As a consequence, the workload of several applications can be consolidated in a few physical machines, which allows one to turn off some and hence reduce the energy consumption (Hermenier, Lorca, Menaud, Muller & Lawall, 2009).

However, since the beginning of the popularization of cloud computing platforms, the total energy consumption has grown dramatically (*Energy Star*, 2007; Koomey, 2007) and it is important to provide resources that applications require and not much to autonomously reduce the energy footprint of applications hosted on cloud infrastructures as much as possible. Concretely, it consists in determining the right trade-off between the Quality of Service (QoS) of applications' end-users and the resources they consume (Brandic, 2009). The provisioning of additional resources can be non relevant for the profit of the application provider if the renting fees (and by transitivity the energy footprint) are not satisfactory.

Several works have been proposed to manage both applications QoS and the overall energy consumption of the infrastructure through a unique system (Kephart et al., 2007; Nguyen Van, Dang Tran & Menaud, 2010; Wang & Wang, 2010; Petrucci, Loques, & Mossé, 2011). The objective is to maximize applications' QoS while minimizing the costs due to the infrastructure (e.g. energy consumption). Although it enables to scale up/down applications by querying/releasing resources according to their incoming charge, applications are considered as black boxes. This restrains the adaptation capability of applications in the sense that they are only able to add or remove resources based on performance attributes. From our point of view, it is not sufficient since applications may have specific requirements in terms of reactivity, fault-tolerance and others concerns. The QoS of one application is not only related to performance criteria such as response time but also to internal aspects that may differ from one application to another (Comuzzi & Pernici, 2009). For example, the definition of the QoS of a HomeBanking application may be different than that of a Video-on-Demand application. The QoS of the former may be defined based on details about encryption, whereas the latter may consider aspects like image resolution and encoding characteristics. Since the application internals directly drive the resources requested to the infrastructure provider, it is important to consider the application as a white box.

This work focuses on extending the usual elasticity capability (scaling up/down) by considering also applications internals (i.e. components). The way applications are composed (i.e. which components are used and how they are connected) may lead to different application configurations and by consequence to different energy footprints. Providing a unique framework generic enough to take into account every application configuration in addition to the infrastructure constraints seems to be too difficult. Instead, we advocate a per application autonomic system coupled to an infrastructure one: each application is equipped with one autonomic loop in charge of determining the minimum amount of resources necessary to provide the best QoS possible while an additional loop autonomously manages the physical resources at the infrastructure level. Thus, the objective of the per-application autonomic loop is to switch from one internal configuration to another according to the incoming charge, the QoS expectations and the infrastructure constraints. As a result, adaptation processes will be triggered in order to query/release VMs to the infrastructure manager, which can finely manage the resources.

As a proof of concept, we implemented a prototype and validated it through simulation. Our system relies on Service-Oriented Architectures to model and implement applications. Regarding the optimization problems, we rely on Constraint Programming to model and solve them.

The rest of this article is organized as follows: First, we discuss the current state of the art. Second, we present our approach for energy-aware self-management of applications in cloud infrastructures. Then, we provide some discussion about how the proposed approach fits on federated cloud scenarios. Finally, we present some perspectives on the topic by outlining our on-going research and then we conclude the work.

BACKGROUND

In this section, we discuss a selection of recent and relevant work about self-management on applications and cloud computing to address the problem of energy consumption in data centers.

Nguyen Van, Dang Tran & Menaud (2010) proposed a Service Level Agreement (SLA)-based approach for cloud resources management running several applications at the same time. In their system, each application is profiled with its performance functions (based on the income workload and the amount of resources allocated to it) and a utility-based SLA. The objective is to determine the number of VMs necessary so that the utility is maximized and thereafter to pack those VMs into the minimum number of Physical Machines (PMs). This objective was split into two

separate optimization problems that were modeled and solved by using Constraint Programming techniques. Our work extends this approach by allowing internal application adaptations.

In (Arnaud & Bouchenak, 2009), an approach to improve the performance in multi-tier-based applications was proposed. It takes into account two levels of configuration (architectural and local) in order to improve the system performance. The architectural configuration means the cost in terms of physical machines and the local configuration corresponds to the maximum number of concurrent clients the servers can admit. The approach makes use of *Mean Value Analysis* queuing approach to model the performance (i.e. the latency and abandon rate) in each tier. Based on those parameters and on the configuration cost, an objective function is provided. Two algorithms are provided: one to implement the model which is used to predict the latency, cost and abandon rate based on a given configuration and workload; and another one to find the optimal solution based on the objective function. The adaptation may occur in two levels: (i) degrade the application QoS by increasing the abandon rate (admission control); (ii) or by adding/suppressing PMs. Apart from the fact that we define our infrastructure in terms of VMs, we take into consideration that applications can internally be adapted. So, instead of controlling the QoS by admission control, we internally change the application to improve or decrease its QoS. In fact, that approach can be seen as a particular case of the proposed approach in this chapter, where the QoS criterion considered is the availability.

In (Petrucci, Loques, & Mossé, 2011), the authors proposed an approach to optimize the energy consumption in a multi-application heterogeneous cluster environment. They rely on Dynamic Voltage Frequency Scaling (DVFS) and server consolidation techniques to reduce the power consumption. Performance and power models are defined in terms of frequency and utilization rate of physical machines. The proposed approach consists in determining the number of VMs needed for each application under a given workload in a way the overall energy consumption is minimized. The problem was modeled and solved by using *Mixed-Integer Programming*. Contrary to our work, the optimization problems (to determine the number of VMs and placing them) are performed in a single decision module. We believe that applications, having different kinds of workload may have different needs in terms of reconfigurations (different periods). Moreover, dealing with it as a single and more complex problem may lead to serious problems of scalability, and by transitivity reactivity.

In the same way, Kephart et al. (2007) proposed a framework for managing power and performance using a joint utility function in the context of web servers. This framework composed of two separate agents that manage performance and power. The former sends performance information to the latter, which in turn manage the tradeoff between performance and power consumption. After receiving state information from the performance manager, which has its own power-unaware policies, the power manager tries to optimize the joint utility by applying its power policy to manage the trade-off between performance and power. The work makes use of DVFS to implement its power management policies, which are related to a specific machine.

In (Kansal, Liu, Singh, Nathuji & Abdelzaher, 2010), the authors propose an interface-based coordinated method for multiple applications and system layer. The idea is that only semantic-less numbers (i.e. numbers that can be increased or decreased) representing QoS levels and energy (i.e. processors frequency levels) are shared among applications and system. The application has no information about the system power management modules, and similarly, the system has no details about the application QoS levels. Hence, a coordination algorithm is provided to combine all applications' needs in terms of QoS and system's energy requirements. However, in order to trigger a reconfiguration process at the infrastructure level, it is necessary that all applications sharing a PM degrade their QoS so it is possible to decrease the PM's frequency levels. That process may take too long to converge so the adaptation is no longer needed. Furthermore, that approach does not rely on virtualization techniques. In our approach, on the other hand, we benefit from virtualization in the sense that QoS degradation of application hosted by different machines may trigger to a consolidation, which, in turn, may result in energy savings.

Ardagna, Panicucci, Trubian & Zhang (2010) proposed an autonomic approach to tackle several energy-related sub-problems in two different control loops: short-term, for problems whose solutions have a low overhead; and long-term, for problems whose solutions have a high overhead. The two control loops share some decision variables, which ensure a better exploitation of the tradeoff energy costs and applications QoS. The work classifies the adaptations with regards to their complexities and overheads. For instance, the same control loop is in charge of performing application-level adaptations (by reconfiguring business processes) and infrastructure adaptation (by using DVFS mechanisms), because both kinds of adaptations imply a low overhead in comparison to other kinds of adaptation such as VM migration. Differently, in our proposal, we focus on cloud-based environments, in which applications are not aware of the infrastructure, which in turn, considers applications as black boxes. For this reason, several per-application and one infrastructure control loops are defined. Furthermore, our proposal takes into account application internal reconfiguration in order to either reduce the energy footprint and/or meet the resources restrictions.

SAFDIS (Gauvrit, Daubert, & André, 2010) is a multi-level framework for self-adaptable distributed applications. The problem of adaptation is managed in a traversal way, from the application to the infrastructure, in the sense that applications and infrastructure are monitored and thereafter the adaptation takes place at the upper level (application) considering the current state of lower levels (infrastructure). For instance, a sensor may detect that an application is overloaded. The framework will then try to migrate the application from one resource to a more powerful one. Although the work proposes a cross-layered approach to adapt applications and infrastructure in function of their QoS, it is not the focus to deal with the energy issue.

BrownMap (Verma et al., 2010) is a methodology to enforce power budget in data centers. The objective is to cope with temporary reduction of power available in data centers (brown-out). The authors proposed an approach based on VM live migration and VM resizing to adapt shared data centers when brownouts happen. Based on a power model and utility-based SLA specification, the methodology analyzes every server (one-by-one) by performing VM resizing and/ or VM replacement until a global power budget is met. In summary, the methodology aims at adapting the infrastructure to meet the power budget while minimizing utility drops of the infrastructure. While the work focuses on the infrastructure adaptation to cope with power supply interruptions, our work goes further by allowing the infrastructure provider to raise information to applications about a possible resource shrink situation. The per-application control loop captures this information in order to make the application adaptable the infrastructure restrictions. In the other way around, the application control loop is also able to make request/release of resource to infrastructure provider in an autonomic manner.

In summary, to the best of our knowledge, there is no work that leverages the fact that applications may have several internal configurations to cope at the same time with applications' QoS, the infrastructure constraints and by transitivity with the energy footprint of the cloud infrastructure.

SELF-MANAGEMENT OF APPLICATIONS AND SYSTEMS TO REDUCE ENERGY FOOTPRINT

Motivating Scenario

In this section, we present a motivating scenario that aims at making the understanding of the proposed approach easier. The objective is to show that applications deployed on cloud infrastructures can be adapted not only in terms of performance, as it is usually applied, but also in terms of application internals.

The applications that we consider are composed of a set of *components*. According to the workload, the expected QoS and the cost implied by the usage of the infrastructure, each component can be stopped/started or replaced by other *components* during runtime. Hence, applications can operate in different *configurations* depending on which components are running and how they are connected. One component can be defined either as a single software unit, or as a composition of other components (i.e. *composites*). For each component that takes part in a given configuration there may be one or several *instances* of it executing at the same time. Applications are hosted on cloud infrastructures whose physical resources are offered in terms of Virtual Machines (VM). Each VM can host only one component instance. As VMs can be allocated/released in an on-demand manner, the application can be dynamically scaled up/down by adjusting the number of *instances* (and consequently the number of VMs) for each component of a given *configuration*.

The motivating scenario consists of a 3-tier web application (frontend, application server and database). As any web-application, the responsiveness is of major importance: the Service-Level Agreement (SLA) between the application provider and his clients establishes the price that should be paid for each level of response time delivered. In addition to responsiveness, our application requires High Availability (HA) of services, since there are no revenues while services are down. For that, our application uses fault-tolerance mechanisms, which make the application able to reconfigure its architecture to avoid periods of unavailability. As a consequence, the application's QoS is composed of two criteria: the response time and the HA degree.

Figure 1 shows six possible configurations for the application and their respective QoS (in terms of responsiveness and HA). We indicate the impact on the resource from the energy footprint (the more resources we use, the more energy is used). In this example, we use stars to quantify the QoS. Be it positive such as performance and HA, or negative such as the energy footprint. Classically, the HA degree varies according to the number of replicas associated to each application component. For the sake of simplicity, we consider a constant workload and that each *component* has only one *instance*, which means that there is one VM per component.

Configuration 1 (k_1) is the configuration with best HA and performance, because it is composed of two components (replicas) for each tier. However, due to number of VMs (six in our case) necessary to execute, its energy footprint is the highest one.

Configuration 2 (k_2) has the same HA degree than k_1, since there is a replica for each component. The performance is slightly worse than in k_1, because in this configuration, components FE and AS are expressed as a composite component and for this reason share the same VM. Because of this, the k_2 has a lower energy footprint than k_1.

In Configuration 3 (k_3), the HA degree is lower than in k_2 because there is no fault-tolerance in tiers FE and AS, whereas the performance and energy footprint remains the same.

Configuration 4 (k_4) has the same HA degree than k_3, whereas its performance is slightly worse than in comparison to k_3 thanks to the fact that components FE and AS share the same VM. As a result, k_4 has a lower energy footprint than k_3.

Configuration 5 (k_5) has no mechanism of fault-tolerance and hence has a lower HA degree than k_4. Its performance is also slightly worse than in k_4, since it has fewer DB components. With respect to the energy footprint, k_5 consumes less VM, and hence has a smaller energy footprint.

Finally, Configuration 6 (k_6) does not have any mechanism of fault-tolerance. k_5 has a better performance than k_6, since the latter encapsulates all components in a composite, which means that they will share the same VM.

The objective of the application provider is to maximize its revenues and minimize its costs. The revenues are determined by the QoS (response time and HA degree), whereas its costs are due to hosting fees. Therefore, the problem is to find the best trade-off between QoS and the number of VMs needed to host the application. We claim that only the application provider knows particularities (e. g. HA degrees) and under which situations it is pertinent to degrade/upgrade (i.e. switch from one configuration to another) taking into its impact in terms renting fees and by transitivity energy consumption.

System Architecture

This section presents the system architecture overview of the proposed framework. We describe the two kinds of parts involved and how interact.

The application provider aims at increasing its applications' QoS while reducing the hosting costs. The infrastructure provider, in turn, aims to sell as much resources (e.g. CPU and RAM) as possible, while reducing its the power consumption costs. For this purpose, we rely on autonomic computing in order to conceive a system consisting of two kinds of control loop: the Application Manager (AM) and the Infrastructure Manager (IM). As aforementioned, the choice for several control loops (one per application) instead of only one is justified by the fact that applications may have different characteristics and because of that the autonomic phases (i.e. monitoring, analysis,

Figure 1. Six possible application configurations and their Quality of Service

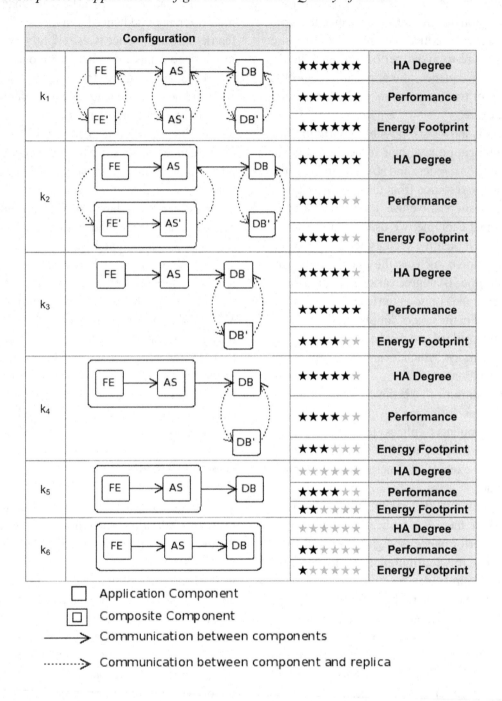

planning and execution) may differ significantly from one application to another. For instance, the loop frequency of an application that performs scientific calculus might be different than for a web application.

Figure 2 shows the global architecture. For each application there is one AM in charge of maintaining the correct amount of resource according to the different configurations and the workload. At the low level, the IM manages the overall energy footprint by consolidating VMs on a minimum number of servers and arbitrates the allocation of resources according to the application demands (Nguyen Van, Dang Tran, & Menaud, 2010).

In practice, the AM gathers information about the application activity such as the application workload. It then analyzes information by deciding whether it is necessary to adapt the application. The AM relies on an *objective function* to find the right application configuration for the current workload so the cost (due to VMs allocated to it) is minimized and the application QoS is maximized. The difference between the number of VMs currently used and the number of VMs required for the new solution is requested/released from the IM. Nevertheless, when the IM does not manage to provision more VMs, or when it is more profitable to avoid the demand of more

resources, the AM receives a notification and should switch from one configuration to another more compliant, (e.g. by switching components off or replacing them). For instance, in our motivating scenario, the AM may decide to switch from configuration k_1 to k_3 without impacting on the performance, but only on the HA degree criterion.

Having the new application configuration, the AM identifies the components that should be deployed, started/stopped, connected/disconnected, and determines in which order those actions should happen. Based on that it performs the reconfiguration.

The IM, in turn, gathers some information about the infrastructure such as the resource utilization rates for each VM and the data center power availability. With this information the IM performs two tasks: (i) it arbitrates about the distribution

Figure 2. Interaction between Application Manager and Infrastructure Manager

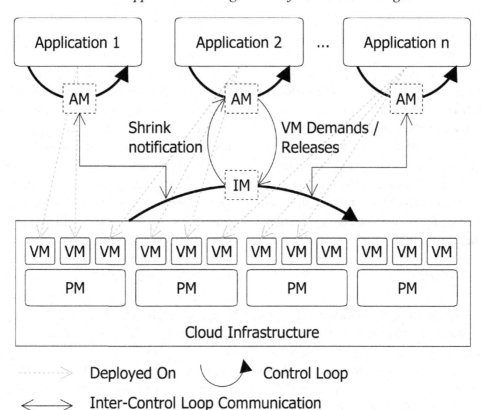

of resources among all applications in periods of low availability of resources; and (ii) handle the applications demands for allocation/release of resources. In the first task, the IM arbitrates on which applications should be more penalized based on a pre-defined arbitration policy. For instance, by defining different classes of clients (e. g. diamond, gold, silver, etc.). Then, the IM notifies those applications by informing them about the constraints in terms of infrastructure they must meet. In the second task, based on the new resources requirements and the current state (mapping VM/PM), the IM consolidates these new VMs along with other applications' VMs so that the number of PMs that need to be on is minimized (Hermenier, Lorca, Menaud, Muller & Lawall, 2009). The result of this procedure is a new and optimized mapping VMs/PMs.

It is noteworthy that due to the strong dependencies among the component instances and the hosting VMs, the executions at both levels must be synchronized. For instance, the VM that hosts one component (instance) cannot be stopped before the component has been disconnected from the rest of the application. These issues have not yet been addressed, as they are part of an ongoing work (see section FUTURE RESEARCH DIRECTIONS).

With respect to the optimization problems, we model the consolidation problem at the IM and the resource provisioning and application reconfiguration problems at the AM as Constraint Satisfaction Problems and solve them with Constraint Programming techniques. The next section describes this approach.

Constraint Model

The choice for Constraint Programming (Rossi, Van Beek & Walsh, 2009) to model and solve the optimization problems is due to several reasons. It allows one to completely abstract the problem model from the solver implementation. Furthermore, it allows composition of constraints:

constraints can be dynamically added/removed without posing any side effect on the global model. A Constraint Programming Model is roughly composed of three elements: a set of variables of the problem, a domain function, which associates to each variable its domain, and a set of constraints. Given that, the solver engine is in charge of finding the possible solutions. For optimization problems, an objective function is defined and an optimal solution is then a solution that minimizes (or maximizes) that function. In this section, we present the definition of the constraint models we use to solve the optimization problems previously described. As explained, these two optimization problems are independently solved, although the results produced by one (e.g. the number of VMs needed to host the application) may sometimes be used as input for the other (e.g. to find the optimal placement of those VMs).

Application Constraint Model

One application is composed of a set of components (primitive or composite) expressed by the vector $C = (c_1, c_2, ..., c_n)$. The application might have o (one or several) configurations $K = (k_1, k_2, ..., k_o)$, where each configuration k_i is defined by the sub-set of components $S_i \subseteq C$ that should be used and the way those components are connected. In order to consume the application, end users pay an amount according to the quality delivered by the application's services. Thus, the QoS in general have an impact on the application provider's revenues. One configuration k_i has its QoS described in terms of performance $Q_i^{perf} \in [0,1]$ and its internal configuration specific attribute $Q_i^{spec} \in [0,1]$. The former corresponds to the number of client requests the application is able to serve, whereas the latter is the quality implied by the application configuration.

As an example, let us consider the application described in Section MOTIVATING SCENARIO. The components are $C = (FE, AS, DB, FE', AS', DB', (FE, AS), (FE, AS)')$ and configurations $K =$

$(k_1, k_2, ..., k_6)$. Q^{spec}, in this example, corresponds to the HA degree of each configuration. Thus, $Q_1^{spec} = Q_2^{spec} > Q_3^{spec} = Q_4^{spec} > Q_5^{spec} = Q_6^{spec}$, where Q_i^{spec} is the Q^{spec} of configuration k_i.

In order to apply techniques like load balancing to improve the performance, to each component can be assigned one or several instances and each instance should be hosted by one VM. There may be one or several classes of VM $M = (m_1, m_2, ..., m_q)$, which are expressed in terms of CPU (m_i^{cpu}), RAM (m_i^{ram}) and cost (m_i^{cost}, expressed in terms of currency, e.g. \$0.10) for $1 \leq i \leq q$. Considering the vectors C and M, the chosen configuration k_w, $1 \leq W \leq o$ corresponds to an allocation of VMs (number of instances) for each component $c_j \in S_W$ taking part of the configuration. This allocation is espressed by matrix N (Equation 1), where each element e_{ij} corresponds to the number of VMs of class, m_i allocated to component c_j.

$$\mathbf{N} = \begin{pmatrix} e_{11} & e_{12} & \cdots & e_{1q} \\ e_{21} & e_{22} & \cdots & e_{2q} \\ & & \cdots & \\ e_{n1} & e_{n2} & \cdots & e_{nq} \end{pmatrix} \quad (1)$$

In addition, we define a constraint (Equation 2) stating that if a configuration k_l is chosen, there should not be any VM ($e_{ij} = 0$) for all classes of VM m_j and for any component c_j, which is not part of configuration k_l ($c_i \notin S_l$).

$$W = l \Leftrightarrow (\forall c_i \in C: c_i \notin S_l (\forall j: 1 \leq j \leq q (e_{ij} = 0))) \quad (2)$$

It is straightforward that the performance of one component service varies according to the resource capacity allocated to it and its demands. Thus, for each component $c \in C$, we define a function $perf_j: (\lambda, \rho_j) \to \aleph$ in terms of response time, where λ corresponds to the workload and ρ_j to the total amount of CPU allocated to component c_j. Finally, the QoS performance value Q^{perf} is determined

by a utility function $u: \aleph \to [0,1]$ of the global response time. In other words, both Q^{spec} and Q^{perf} are normalized values that estimates the utility in terms of revenues of a given application configuration k running under a certain infrastructure configuration N. Indeed, the higher the response time the lower is the revenue. Similarly, the lower the specific QoS (Q^{spec}), the lower is the revenue.

For each application, a maximum cost ($cost^{max}$) is defined to express the maximum amount of money each application intends to spend. The constraint expressed by Equation 3 states that the application total cost cannot exceed $cost^{max}$. The cost function $cost(N)$ is defined as percentage of $cost^{max}$ (Equation 4).

$$cost^{max} \geq \sum_{i=1}^{n} \sum_{j=1}^{q} e_{ij} * m_i^{cost} \quad (3)$$

$$cost(N) = \frac{\sum_{i=1}^{n} \sum_{j=1}^{q} e_{ij} * m_i^{cost}}{\cos t^{max}} \quad (4)$$

In the example described in Section MOTIVATING SCENARIO, the cost corresponds to the energy footprint due to the number of instances assigned to each component. For example, let us consider that there is only one VM class that costs \$1 per VM and the application has a budget ($cost^{max}$) of \$6. As there is one instance per component, there would be necessary 6, 4, 4, 3, 2 and 1 VMs for configurations k_1, k_2, k_3, k_4, k_5 and k_6, which lead to a normalized cost of 1, 0.6, 0.6, 0.5, 0.3 and 0.16, respectively.

The objective function is therefore defined as in Equation 5.

$$O_{N,W} = \max(w_{perf} * Q_W^{perf}(\sum_{\forall c_j \in S_w} perf_j(\lambda, \rho_j)) + w_{spec} * Q_W^{spec} + w_{cost} * (1 - cost(N))) \quad (5)$$

where $0 \leq w_{spec} + w_{perf} + w_{cost} \leq 1$, where w_{spec}, w_{perf} and w_{cost} correspond to weights for the Q^{spec}, Q^{perf} and *cost*, respectively.

Infrastructure Constraint Model

The infrastructure constraint model relies on the previous work Entropy (Hermenier, Lorca, Menaud, Muller & Lawall, 2009), an autonomic data center manager. The infrastructure consists of a set of PMs expressed by vector $P = (pm_1, pm_2, ..., pm_p)$, where pm^{cpu} and pm^{ram} define respectively the CPU and RAM capacities of machine $pm \in P$. There might be several VM instances $V = (vm_1, vm_2, ..., vm_r)$, which host components of different applications. vm_j^{cpu} and vm_j^{ram} express the CPU and RAM capacities of VM vm_j. The matrix H (Equation 6) defines which VM are hosted by each PM, where $h_{ij} = 1$ if and only if vm_j is hosted on pm_i, $h_{ij} = 1$, otherwise.

$$\mathbf{H} = \begin{pmatrix} h_{11} & h_{12} & ... & h_{1r} \\ h_{21} & h_{22} & ... & h_{2r} \\ & & ... & \\ h_{p1} & h_{p2} & ... & h_{pr} \end{pmatrix} \tag{6}$$

where $1 \leq i \leq p$, $1 \leq j \leq r$.

The constraints 7 and 8 state that the CPU and RAM demands of VMs hosted in one PM should not exceed its CPU and RAM capacities.

$$pm_i^{cpu} \geq \sum_{j=1}^{r} h_{ij} * vm_j^{cpu} : \forall 1 \leq i \leq p \tag{7}$$

$$pm_i^{ram} \geq \sum_{j=1}^{r} h_{ij} * vm_j^{ram} : \forall 1 \leq i \leq p \tag{8}$$

Finally, the objective is to minimize the number of nodes necessary to host the VMs instances in *V*, as is can be seen in Equation 9.

$$O_H = \min(\sum_{i=1}^{p} u_i),$$

where

$$u_i = \begin{cases} 1, \exists vm_j \in V \mid h_{ij} = 1 \\ 0, otherwise \end{cases} \tag{9}$$

The result of this optimization problem is a reconfiguration plan with a set of VM migration operations. As migration operations are very costly (especially in comparison with application adaptation), it is important to take into consideration the cost of each operation in the reconfiguration plan. In Entropy, the cost model of a virtual machine migration is basically calculated based on the amount of memory allocated to it. Due to space constraints, we do not explain here how the reconfiguration plan is calculated. For further details, please see (Hermenier, Lorca, Menaud, Muller & Lawall, 2009).

Experimental Results

In this section, we present preliminary results based on a Java-based simulator, which implements the Infrastructure and the Application Managers. We relied on Choco (2008), a Constraint Programming Java library, to model and solve the optimization problems (at the application and infrastructure layers) presented in last section.

In order to evaluate whether it is possible to reduce the energy footprint without interfering on the Application Provider revenues, we executed our simulator over the motivating application. As we claim, there is a direct relation between the QoS delivered by applications and their revenues, the simulation aims at observing the ratio QoS/Cost for a given application with and without the possibility of adaptation.

Simulation Setup

The experiments were performed on an Intel Core 2 Duo (2.53 GHz) computer with 4GB of RAM. We set the waiting times of AMs and IM to 3 and 1 seconds, respectively. As previously stated, the application is defined as vector of available components $C = (FE, AS, DB, FE', AS', DB')$. For sake of simplicity, we consider only two configurations $K = (k_1, k_4)$ so $S_1 = (FE, AS, DB, FE', AS', DB')$ and $S_4 = ((FE, AS), (FE, AS)', DB, DB')$. $Q_1^{spec} = 1$ and $Q_4^{spec} = 0.85$ quantify the HA degree of both configurations. Last, we weighted arbitrarily the QoS criteria and the cost as follows: $w_{perf} = 0.5$, $w_{spec} = 0.25$ and $w_{cost} = 0.25$. Figure 3 describes the utility function for the performance criterion (Figure 3a) and the performance functions for all components involved (Figure 3b, 3c and 3d). As mentioned before, these functions give the response time in function of the workload and there exist several functions, one for a different portion of CPU allocated to the component in question.

The simulated infrastructure is composed of 30 physical machines $P = (pm_1, ..., pm_{30})$, for each $pm_i \in P$, $pm_i^{cpu} = 4GHz$ and $pm_i^{ram} = 4GHz$. There are two classes of VMs $M = (m_1, m_2)$, with $m_1^{cpu} = 1GHz$, $m_1^{ram} = 1GHz$, $m_1^{cost} = 0.18$, $m_2^{cpu} = 2GHz$, $m_2^{ram} = 2GB$ and $m_2^{cost} = 0.27$.

Results

In order to analyze more in details how application's characteristics and consequently its reconfigurations impact on the energy footprint, we firstly performed the experiments over a single application scenario. Hence, there exists only one AM and one IM. Figure 4 shows the number of PMs necessary to execute the application under a given workload (defined by the dotted curve). The other two curves represent: (i) the number of PMs when only one configuration (k_1) is considered; and (ii) when two configurations (k_1 and k_4) are considered. The initial placement of VMs on PMs is based on an initial workload pre-defined for the application (in this case 600 requests/s). As it can be seen, there is an important energy saving when the application switches between k_1 and k_4 in comparison to when the application stays only on configuration k_1.

The energy savings are important, but it is straightforward that when degrading the QoS less resource is needed and hence less energy is consumed. Figure 5, on the other hand shows the ratio QoS per cost when considering only one configuration (k_1) and when considering the two configurations (k_1 and k_4). The ratio is used as a metric to compare the two approaches (considering k_1 and k_1/k_4) in terms of incomes (QoS) and expenses (cost). Figure 5d shows when the application switches from one configuration to another during the execution. Figure 5a shows the ratio Q^{perf} per cost. We can observe that there is a significant difference between the two curves in favor of the approach that considers configuration switch. In effect, when one application operates in a degraded mode (configuration with $Q_4^{spec} = 0.85$), it might require less resource for the same workload (i.e. to attend to the same amount of clients) in comparison to when it operates on a non-degraded mode (configuration with $Q_1^{spec} = 1$). Alternatively, the application operating on a degraded mode might be able to serve more clients with the same amount of resources than the application operating on a non-degraded mode. Concerning the Q^{spec} (Figure 5b), we can also observe better results for the approach that allows switching between configurations. This is also true when we compare the two approaches by considering the ratio of the average of both QoS criteria per cost (Figure 5c). The conclusion that can be drawn from the simulation is that the Application Provider can save a significant amount of energy by internally adapting its application according to clients' demands and application-specific QoS. Moreover, this saving does not impact negatively on the overall ratio revenues/cost.

Figure 3. (a) The SLA function for the application; (b) The set of performance functions of components FE, FE', AS and AS'; (c) The set of performance functions of components DB and DB'; (d) and the set of performance functions of composites (FE, AS) and (FE, AS)'

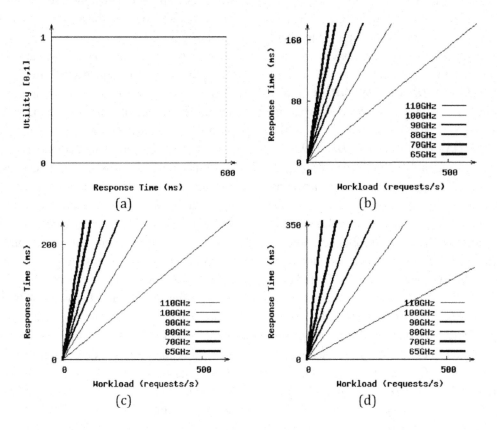

Figure 4. Resources consumed (in terms of PM) by the application under a certain workload

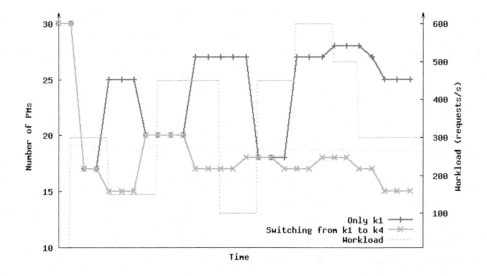

We have also simulated our framework in a multi-application scenario by launching four AMs. Although any different kinds of application with specific QoS and characteristics could be used in this kind of scenario, we decided, for the sake of clarity and simplicity, to reuse the same application definition for the four applications. We redefined the performance functions for all components in order to accommodate all four applications in the same infrastructure capacity (Figure 6). Figure 7 shows the number of PMs consumed when four application are launched simultaneously under a certain workload. It is important to notice that each application was given a different workload (the dotted line shows the sum of all workloads). As it can be seen, there is a significant improvement in terms of energy savings when considering a multi-application scenario. However, since our approach does not consider any special policy to improve the trade-off between QoS and energy consumption at the infrastructure layer, the ratio QoS per cost remains the same regardless the approach (considering only k_1 or switching from k_1 to k_4). This limitation is currently being addressed as an on-going work.

Scalability Evaluation

Finally, we evaluated the scalability of both constraint programming-based optimization solutions. Figure 8 shows the execution time of the AM optimization algorithm based on the number of components and VMs allocated to each component. The algorithm takes approximately 2 seconds to find a solution for 10-component application, each component having up to 30 VMs. We believe that better results can be achieved by applying heuristics to select tree nodes in the search space during the execution. We plan to exploit this aspect as future works.

As previously mentioned, we rely on Entropy for the IM optimization problem. Although, it is perfectly is suitable for small and medium-sized data centers (Hermenier, Lorca, Menaud, Muller & Lawall, 2009), we are aware that it does not scale for large-sized ones. To this end, we are currently working on a completely distributed approach for VM management whose objective is to be able to manage a large number of VMs and PMs in distributed manner. For further details, please see (Quesnel & Lèbre, 2011).

TOWARDS SELF-MANAGEMENT OF APPLICATIONS ON FEDERATED CLOUDS

Federated clouds are used to get additional resources or services in order to meet particular needs of applications that cannot be satisfied by only one cloud. These additional resources can be used to improve the QoS (performance or application specifics). For example, in a scenario of security, constraints can state that a given application component should not be deployed on some cloud infrastructures for security reasons. In scenarios of SLA management, when a violation occurs, applications providers may decide switch its applications or part of them to another cloud infrastructure provider. Furthermore, the application provider might also search for best offers amongst all cloud infrastructure providers in order to choose the one that offers the best trade-off computing power and cost. Finally, one can imagine that in a renewable energy-aware scenario, there might be a constraint ensuring that at least a certain percentage of the application components must be deployed on renewable-energy supplied cloud infrastructures.

To address the federation of cloud computing systems, we extended the architecture illustrated in Figure 2 in order to accommodate one infrastructure manager per cloud infrastructure (Figure 9). Each IM is in charge of managing the resources delivered by each cloud. According to the availability and cost of the resources offered by different cloud infrastructure providers, the AMs interact with one or several IMs. Concretely, the AMs

Figure 5. (b) Ratio Q^{perf} per cost; (b) Ratio Q^{spec} per cost; (c) Ratio Average QoS per cost; (d) Periods of time when the application operates on configurations k_1 or k_4.

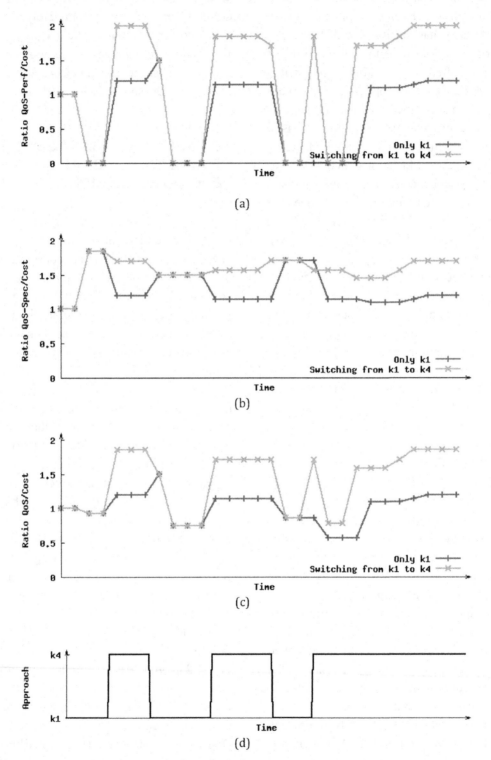

(a)

(b)

(c)

(d)

Figure 6. (a) The set of performance functions of components FE, FE', AS and AS'; (b) The set of performance functions of components DB and DB'; and (c) the set of performance functions of composites (FE, AS) and (FE, AS)'

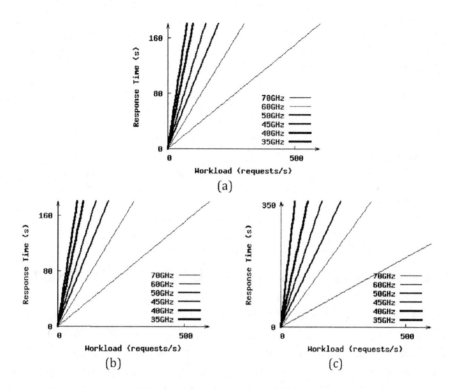

Figure 7. Resources consumed (in terms of PM) by the all applications under a certain workload

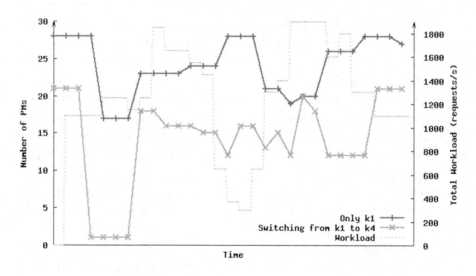

Figure 8. Execution time of the Application Manager Optimization Algorithm according to the number of components and virtual machines

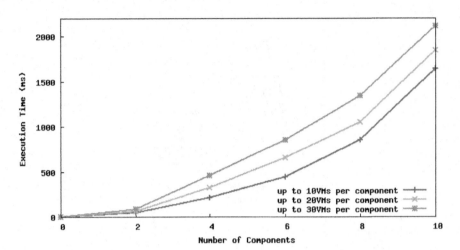

estimate the amount of resources necessary for their applications based on VM classes that may belong to different cloud infrastructures. From the point of view of our model, the only change is the size of vector M, which now considers more VM classes that can be delivered by several cloud infrastructures (see Section CONSTRAINT MODEL).

Going back to our motivating scenario, components and replicas are deployed on different cloud infrastructure in order to increase the HA criterion (keeping in mind potential network overhead issues). Thus, a constraint should be defined to guarantee that two components c_i, c_j should never be deployed in the same cloud infrastructure (Equation 10). To this end, constraint programming is very suitable, since it offers compositionality: constraints can be easily added/removed depending on the application requirements without posing any side effect on the existing model. Therefore, the proposed approach can fit to one or several cloud platforms.

$$\forall m_k, m_l \in M \mid m_k^{prov} = m_l^{prov} ((e_{ik} > 0 \vee e_{il} > 0)$$
$$\Leftrightarrow (e_{jk} = 0 \wedge e_{jl} = 0)) \quad (10)$$

where m_l^{prov} corresponds to the provider of VM class m_l.

FUTURE RESEARCH DIRECTIONS

The objective of this work is to propose a framework for self-optimization of cloud applications to cope with the problem of resource provisioning and by transitivity the energy consumption. Although we have presented some interesting preliminary results, there is still a lot of work to be done. In this section, we discuss future perspectives for this work in particular as well as some emerging trends related to energy efficiency in cloud infrastructures.

• **Synchronization/transaction:** as previously discussed, synchronization of operations becomes a critical point when we deal with concurrent but interdependent control loops. In our particular case, there are several control loops intending to optimize applications by internally reconfiguring them or by scaling up/down their resources. It turns out that when a reconfiguration takes place at application level, all the underlying operations should be synchronized in order to avoid component disruption. For instance, if one application decides to replace one component by another, there

Figure 9. Infrastructure and Application Managers in a Federated Cloud Environment

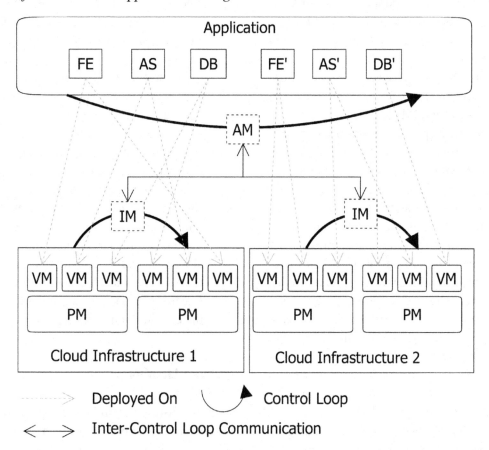

must be mechanisms to guarantee that there will be an infrastructure to support the component to be replaced until the new component has been properly bound to the rest of the application (Ledoux & Lèger, 2010). In other words, VM create/destroy operations should be synchronized with component start/stop operations. This is particularly important in the case of federated clouds.

- **Overhead and Reconfiguration costs**: The costs due to the reconfigurations at the application level (start, stop, deploy, bind, unbind) were not modeled and thus not taken into account in our optimization model. We believe that the impact, compared to the costs at the infrastructure layer (migration costs) is negligible. However,

we did not take into account the impacts of a reconfiguration performed at application level on the infrastructure level. In fact, it is hard to consider such aspects while having the infrastructure as a black box. In this context, the only thing AMs see are VMs being offered by IMs, but not how those VMs are placed and how an action performed at application level will impact on the underlying infrastructure. One possibility would be to raise information from IM that will somehow guide the decision taken at AM. For instance, a pricing policy where prices are dynamic according to the state of placement of VMs on PMs may encourage AMs to request/release or reconfigure at a certain moment. A first proposal of such an idea can be found in (Alvares de Oliveira Jr. & Ledoux, 2011). In summary, we believe this is an issue of major importance and we plan to deal with in more detail.

- **Extend the API between AMs and IMs**: Currently in this work, the interface between AMs and IM consists only in create/destroy VM operations. We envision several situations where only those operations are not enough and some requirements specific to each application should be translated into constraint at the infrastructure level. For instance, in our motivating scenario, it is reasonable to think that one component should never be co-hosted (in the same PM) along with its replica. To this end, we believe that Plasma (Hermenier, F., Lawall, J., Menaud, J. M. & Muller, G., 2011), an approach for managing high available web applications based on dynamic consolidation of virtual machines and placement constraint descriptions, is a good start point.

- **Power Model:** In this work, we consider as power consumption unit the number of PM switched on. We are aware that the energy consumption within one machine can vary significantly and hence more fine-grained power models would help to achieve better results. Several works (Bohra & Chaudhary, 2010) (Koller, Verma, & Neogi, 2010) (Kansal et al., 2010) propose more detailed power models that deal with power consumption in a per process/application/VM basis. As result, the power variation within a single PM can be more easily detected.

- **Pricing Policy:** In this work, we consider a static pricing policy, since the price paid by Application Providers for physical resources remains the same and depends only on the amount of resource. However, the cost implied by the execution of one VM may vary for several reasons. As dis-

cussed in the previous topic, the energy consumption can vary significantly in function of the workload. In addition, the energy footprint of a VM i.e. the impact on the overall energy consumption may also vary according to its placement. Therefore, it is important to consider these dynamic aspects (load, placement, etc) in order to determine the price of infrastructures and hence make applications more aware of the infrastructure current state.

- **Storage and Data Management:** We currently consider only the CPU and RAM dimensions for virtual machines resources. However, this is not suitable for applications whose main focuses are data storage. For this reason, we plan to add storage to the existing dimensions.

CONCLUSION

Energy consumption in IT and especially in data center has been given a lot of attention in the last years. The popularization of new provisioning has driven the recent increase of the energy consumption in IT infrastructures. On the other hand, these kinds of models permit to provision physical resources in a "pay-as-you-go" manner. Along with virtualization techniques it allows to mutualize resources and consequently to improve their utilization.

Current approaches leverage autonomic computing to automatically provision resources to application. The idea is that applications can be auto-scalable in the sense that they are capable to demand the minimum amount of resources to maintain their Quality of Service (QoS). The QoS in this case is basically defined in terms of performance and hence does not take into consideration the internal characteristics of application to define application-specific QoS. In this chapter, we presented an approach that goes deeper in the adaptation process by taking into account application internals and their impact on the energy footprint. We argue for software platform based on autonomic computing in which each application has its own control loop whose objective is to find the best trade-off between QoS and the amount of resources needed. Another control loop at the infrastructure layer takes care of applications demands in order to manage the energy consumption. To this end, we provided Constraint Programming-based model for this Constraint Satisfaction Problem. We showed through simulation scenarios that our approach enables to find solutions with better trade-off between QoS and energy footprint. Moreover, we showed that our approach is well suited for both single and federated clouds. Finally, we provided some discussion on the work limitations and open issues regarding synchronization, power model, and reconfiguration cost among others, which will guide our future research.

REFERENCES

Alvares de Oliveira Jr. & F., Ledoux, T. (2011). Self-management of applications QoS for energy optimization in datacenters. *Proceedings of the 2st Workshop on Green Computing Middleware (GCM'2011)*. New York, NY: ACM.

Ardagna, D., Panicucci, B., Trubian, M., & Zhang, L. (2010). Energy-Aware Autonomic Resource Allocation in Multi-tier Virtualized Environments. *IEEE Transactions on Services Computing*, 1-36. Published by the IEEE Computer Society. Retrieved from http://www.computer.org/portal/web/csdl/doi/10.1109/TSC.2010.42

Arnaud, J. (2009). MoKa: Modelisation et planification de capacite pour les systemes multi-etages. [MoKa: Modeling and capacity planning systems for multi-storey] *Les NOuvelles TEchnologies de la REpartition - Notere 2009 [New Technologies of Distributed Systems]*, Montreal, Canada.

Bohra, A. E. H., & Chaudhary, V. (2010). VMeter: Power modelling for virtualized clouds. *2010 IEEE International Symposium on Parallel Distributed Processing Workshops and Phd Forum IPDPSW*, 1-8. Retrieved from http://ieeexplore.ieee.org/lpdocs/epic03/wrapper.htm?arnumber=5470907

Brandic, I. (2009). Towards Self-Manageable Cloud Services. *33rd Annual IEEE International Computer Software and Applications Conference*, 2(iv), 128-133. Retrieved from http://ieeexplore.ieee.org/lpdocs/epic03/wrapper.htm?arnumber=5254138

Choco. (2008). Choco: an Open Source Java Constraint Programming Library. *White Paper 14th International Conference on Principles and Practice of Constraint Programming CPAI08 Competition*, (10-02-INFO). Retrieved from http://www.emn.fr/z-info/choco-solver/pdf/choco-presentation.pdf

Comuzzi, M., & Pernici, B. (2009). A framework for QoS-based Web service contracting. *ACM Transactions on the Web, 3*(3), 1-52. Retrieved from http://portal.acm.org/citation.cfm?doid=1541822.1541825

Energy Star. (2007). *Report to Congress on Server and Data Center Energy Efficiency Public Law 109-431*. Environmental Protection, 109, 431. US Environmental Protection Agency: ENERGY STAR Program. Retrieved from http://www.osti.gov/energycitations/product.biblio.jsp?osti_id=929723

Gauvrit, G., Daubert, E., & André, F. (2010). SAFDIS: A Framework to Bring Self-Adaptability to Service-Based Distributed Applications. *36th EUROMICRO Conference on Software Engineering and Advanced Applications*, 211-218. Retrieved from http://ieeexplore.ieee.org/lpdocs/epic03/wrapper.htm?arnumber=5598099

Haq, I. U., Brandic, I., & Schikuta, E. (2010). SLA Validation in Layered Cloud Infrastructures. LNCS, 6296, 153-164 Retrieved from http://www.springerlink.com/content/4j22m37153275444/

Hermenier, F., Lawall, J., Menaud, J. M., & Muller, G. (2011). Dynamic Consolidation of Highly Available Web Applications. *Research Report*. INRIA. Retrieved from http://hal.inria.fr/inria-00567102/PDF/RR-7545.pdf

Hermenier, F., Lorca, X., Menaud, J. M., Muller, G., & Lawall, J. (2009). Entropy: a consolidation manager for clusters. *The 2009 International Conference on Virtual Execution Environments VEE09*, (41), 41-50. Retrieved from http://portal.acm.org/citation.cfm?id=1508300

Kansal, A., Liu, J., Singh, A., Nathuji, R., & Abdelzaher, T. (2010). Semantic-less coordination of power management and application performance. *ACM SIGOPS Operating Systems Review*, 44(1), 66. Retrieved from http://portal.acm.org/citation.cfm?doid=1740390.1740406

Kansal, A., Zhao, F., Liu, J., Kothari, N., & Bhattacharya, A. A. (2010). Virtual machine power metering and provisioning. Proceedings of the *1st ACM symposium on Cloud computing*, Retrieved from http://portal.acm.org/citation.cfm?doid=1807128.1807136

Kephart, J. O., Chan, H., Das, R., Levine, D. W., Tesauro, G., Rawson, F., & Lefurgy, C. (2007). Coordinating multiple autonomic managers to achieve specified power-performance tradeoffs. *Fourth International Conference on Autonomic Computing ICAC07*, 24-24. Retrieved from http://ieeexplore.ieee.org/lpdocs/epic03/wrapper.htm?arnumber=4273118

Koller, R., Verma, A., & Neogi, A. (2010). WattApp: an application aware power meter for shared data centers. *Proceeding of the 7th international conference on Autonomic computing* (p. 31–40). ACM. Retrieved from http://portal.acm.org/citation.cfm?id=1809049.1809055

Koomey, J. G., & D, P. (2007). *Estimating Total Power Consumption by the U. S. and the World*. Analytics Press. Retrieved from https://files.me.com/jgkoomey/98ygy0

Léger, M., Ledoux, T., & Coupaye, T. (2010). Reliable Dynamic Reconfigurations in a Reflective Component Model. *ComponentBased Software Engineering*, 74-92. Retrieved from http://www.springerlink.com/index/58HQ758200009817.pdf

Mirashe, S. P., & Kalyankar, N. V. (2010). Cloud Computing. *Communications of the ACM*, 51(7), 9. Retrieved from http://arxiv.org/abs/1003.4074

Nguyen Van, H., Dang Tran, F., & Menaud, J.-M. (2010). Performance and Power Management for Cloud Infrastructures. *IEEE 3rd International Conference on Cloud Computing*, 329-336. Retrieved from http://ieeexplore.ieee.org/lpdocs/epic03/wrapper.htm?arnumber=5557975

Petrucci, V., Loques, O., & Mossé, D. (2010). Dynamic optimization of power and performance for virtualized server clusters. *Proceedings of the 2010 ACM Symposium on Applied Computing SAC*, 10, 263. Retrieved from http://portal.acm.org/citation.cfm?doid=1774088.1774144

Pottier, R., Léger, M., & Menaud, J. (2010). A Reconfiguration Language for Virtualized Grid Infrastructures. *Distributed Applications and Interoperable Systems* (p. 42–55). Retrieved from http://www.springerlink.com/index/L65456V26417MH71.pdf

Quesnel, F., & Lebre, A. (2011): Cooperative Dynamic Scheduling of Virtual Machines in Distributed Systems. In *VHPC'11: 6th Workshop on Virtualization in High-Performance Cloud Computing.* New York, NY: Springer.

Rossi, F., Van Beek, P., & Walsh, T. (2006). *Handbook of Constraint Programming.* Amsterdam, The Netherlands: Elsevier.

Verma, A., De, P., Mann, V., Nayak, T., Purohit, A., Gargi, D., & Ravi, K. (2010). BrownMap: Enforcing Power Budget in Shared Data Centers. *Proceedings of the ACM/IFIP/USENIX 11th International Middleware Conference - Middleware 2010* (pp. 42-63). New York, NY: Springer.

Verma, A., & Koller, R. (2010). The cost of reconfiguration in a cloud. *Proceedings of the 11th International Middleware Conference Industrial track on Middleware Industrial Track 10,* 11-16. Retrieved from http://portal.acm.org/citation. cfm?doid=1891719.1891721

Wang, X., & Wang, Y. (2010). Coordinating Power Control and Performance Management for Virtualized Server Clusters. *IEEE Transactions on Parallel and Distributed Systems, 22*(2), 245–259. Retrieved from http://ieeexplore.ieee.org/lpdocs/epic03/wrapper.htm?arnumber=5467056 doi:10.1109/TPDS.2010.91

ADDITIONAL READING

Ardagna, D., Cappiello, C., Lovera, M., Pernici, B., & Tanelli, M. (2008). Active Energy-Aware Management of Business-Process Based Applications. *Proceedings of the 1st European Conference on Towards a Service-Based Internet.* Vol. 5377, pp. 183-195. Springer-Verlag. Retrieved from http://dx.doi.org/10.1007/978-3-540-89897-9_16

Barroso, L. A., & Hölzle, U. (2007). *The Case for Energy-Proportional Computing. Computer* (*Vol. 40,* pp. 33–37). IEEE Computer Society.

Beloglazov, A., & Buyya, R. (2010). Energy Efficient Resource Management in Virtualized Cloud Data Centers. *10th IEEE/ACM International Conference on Cluster Cloud and Grid Computing,* 826-831. IEEE. Retrieved from http://ieeexplore.ieee.org/lpdocs/epic03/wrapper. htm?arnumber=5493373

Breskovic, I., Maurer, M., Emeakaroha, V. C., Brandic, I., & Altmann, J. (2010). Towards Autonomic Market Management in Cloud Computing Infrastructures. *International Conference on Cloud Computing and Services Science - CLOSER 2011,* 7-9 Noordwijkerhout, the Netherlands.

Buyya, R., Yeo, C., Venugopal, S., & Broberg, J. (2009). Cloud computing and emerging IT platforms: Vision, hype, and reality for delivering. *Generation Computer.* Retrieved from http://linkinghub.elsevier.com/retrieve/pii/ S0167739X08001957

Li, Z., Grosu, R., Sehgal, P., Smolka, S. A., Stoller, S. D., & Zadok, E. (2010). On the Energy Consumption and Performance of Systems Software. *Proceedings of the 2010 international conference on Service-oriented computing - ICSOC'10.* Haifa, Israel. 8:1--8:12. Retrieved from http://portal.acm. org/citation.cfm?id=1987827

Maurer, M., Brandic, I., & Sakellariou, R. (2010). Simulating Autonomic SLA Enactment in Clouds Using Case Based Reasoning. *Proceedings of the 2010 ServiceWave Conference,* 25-36. Retrieved from http://www.springerlink.com/ index/315G60451341M26K.pdf

Nathuji, R., & Schwan, K. (2007). VirtualPower: coordinated power management in virtualized enterprise systems. *Proceedings of the 21st ACM Symposium on Operating Systems Principles (SOSP)*, 41(6), 265-278. Retrieved from http://portal.acm.org/citation.cfm?id=1323293.1294287

Raghavendra, R., Ranganathan, P., Talwar, V., Wang, Z., & Zhu, X. (2008). No " Power " Struggles: Coordinated Multi-level Power Management for the Data Center. *Proceedings of the 13th international conference on Architectural support for programming languages and operating systems*, 43(3), 48-59. Retrieved from http://portal.acm.org/citation.cfm?id=1346281.1346289

Soundararajan, V., & Anderson, J. M. (2010). The impact of management operations on the virtualized datacenter. *Proceedings of the 37th annual international symposium on Computer architecture ISCA*, 326. Retrieved from http://portal.acm.org/citation.cfm?doid=1815961.1816003

KEY TERMS AND DEFINITIONS

Autonomic Computing: A concept that refers to computer systems equipped with self-management mechanisms.

Constraint Programming: Programming paradigm in which the variables and the relationships among them are defined in terms of constraints.

Energy Efficiency: A metric defined in terms of amount work compared to the energy consumed.

Performance: A metric defined in terms of amount of work performed compared to the time and resource consumed.

Quality of Service: A set of quantitative and qualitative properties of a system necessary to achieve both the required functionality of the application and user satisfaction.

Utility Computing: A model based on service provisioning in which computing resources are made available to customers as needed.

Virtualization: The creation of a software-based representation of hardware resources (e.g. CPU, DRAM, storage, etc.) that hides the specific characteristics of the underlying hardware.

Chapter 20
Access Control in Federated Clouds:
The Cloudgrid Case Study

Valentina Casola
University of Naples "Federico II", Italy

Antonio Cuomo
University of Sannio, Italy

Umberto Villano
University of Sannio, Italy

Massimiliano Rak
Second University of Naples, Italy

ABSTRACT

Resource sharing problem is one of the most important aspects of Cloud architectures whose primary goal is to fully enable the concept of accessing computing resources on-demand. Access control and resource federation are hot research topics and a lot of open issues should be addressed on functionalities, technological interoperability, quality of services and security of the federated infrastructures. This chapter aims at offering a view on the problems of access control on federated Clouds; since they strongly depend on chosen architectures and platforms, the chapter will discuss some solutions applied on a real case study: the PerfCloud framework, which is based on the integration of Grid and Cloud platforms. The proposed architecture is based on the adoption of an interoperability system to cope with identity federation and access control, it is strictly related to the adopted framework nevertheless it helps the reader to have an idea of the involved open issues and available solutions in commercial or experimental clouds.

DOI: 10.4018/978-1-4666-1631-8.ch020

Copyright © 2012, IGI Global. Copying or distributing in print or electronic forms without written permission of IGI Global is prohibited.

INTRODUCTION

Cloud Computing is undoubtedly an innovation that is going to change every business area. As a matter of fact, the possibility to access computing resources on-demand creates many opportunities and economic efficiencies. On the minus side, Cloud services may be vulnerable to malicious attacks; attackers can potentially locate where data are physically stored within the Cloud, and use clever strategies to obtain access to them.

The Cloud Security Alliance points out a set of 15 different security domains related to the Cloud paradigm that are primary related to the "security management and governance" (to be able to manage the risk associated with a particular provider) and to the security "operational aspects" (as access control privacy, confidentiality and data integrity, business continuity, disaster recovery,...). Each of these domains involves a great number of open issues, which strongly depend on the Cloud architecture and the delivery and deployment model (IaaS, ...) adopted. According to these considerations and despite of many Cloud providers policies, to cope with security issues, we need to characterize any Cloud architecture as a complex layered system; in fact, any architectural choices and service provision activities imply the adoption of proper security policies and mechanisms to guarantee data integrity, privacy and user confidentiality.

In this chapter we will illustrate and discuss two primary security problems, actively investigated by the scientific community today: (i) *identity federation* to enable authentication and security cooperation among the untrusted domains that build up the Cloud environment and (ii) *access control* to properly protect physical and virtual resources.

As for identity federation, it is crucial for Cloud providers to support the overall lifecycle management of users in a completely automated way; this includes user identity management, provisioning/ de-provisioning and, in general, access control policies. It is not uncommon for a Cloud provider to delegate authentication to external trusted identity providers using federation standard such as SAML. This model offers the flexibility to enforce the appropriate authentication strength according to the customer's information protection and data classification policies and standards. Unfortunately, many providers are not ready to be compliant with these new standards and *ad hoc* solutions are enforced, not enabling security monitoring and auditing capabilities.

As for access control, Cloud customers should be aware that fine-grain authorization models are also immature. Where they do exist, they are usually implemented in a proprietary fashion, specific to the Cloud provider. Nevertheless, in many distributed environments role-based access control models and their standard implementation (as XACML) are now commonly adopted and they can be used even in the Cloud environment.

The above described security problems can be found in a very large number of situations and when solutions are implemented, they strongly depend on the technological choices done on specific requirements. In this chapter we will classify cloud architectures from a security point of view, showing that for some of them, it is possible to generalize security solutions to access control and federation.

The first assumption we will do is that cloud users can access services that are offered "on the top" of many different independent providers, each provider having its own security domain (i.e. each of them has its own set of users, being able to authenticate, profile and authorize them to access specific resource).

To enable access to all providers, a federation approach is needed; providers face this problem by federating the security domains. The federation implies the possibility to authenticate users even if they where identified in different domains, to associate them a specific role and finally to grant fine-grain access to their resources. This activity can be performed with the adoption of Trusted

Third parties whose primary goal is to extent the validity of user credentials and their permissions, it is accomplished with the adoption of common standard for interoperability purposes but also with explicit agreements among the involved parties. Such agreements should be accomplished in a completely transparent way respect to cloud users. As a practical example, we will consider a digital certificate based authentication mechanism where different users are authenticated by different Certification Authorities and the interoperability among their security domains is accomplished with automatic cross certification processes.

In the reminder of the chapter, we will illustrate how the adoption of an Interoperability System can be useful to federate untrusted domains in the cloud and we will illustrate its adoption in a special Platform as a Service Cloud (PaaS) model, named PerfCloud, whose implementation is based on the integration of a physical and virtual Grids to offer cloud services.

The reminder of the chapter is organized as follows: the *Background* section is logically divided into two parts, in the first we will introduce two kinds of cloud architectures "classified" from a security point of view and we will introduce a special cloud platform, named *cloudgrid,* that provides an innovative PaaS solution; in the second part we will focus on the related security problems and in particular on identity federation and access control. In the section 3 we will focus on cloudgrid architectures and illustrate a general solution for authentication and access control for accessing federated resources, we will also present an implementation of such architectures named PerfCloud. The chapter ends with a brief description of the future research directions and a conclusion section.

BACKGROUND

Looking at available commercial solutions and in progress research projects, one of the main open issues that could potentially limit the wide adoption of Cloud architectures is the protection of data and applications. Protection involves many aspect and requirements related to security so, a Cloud provider should care not only access control, data confidentiality, privacy, back up and other operational stuffs, but also all organizational aspects that are related to the management of such complex infrastructures that, usually, are the main causes of security breaks. There is a great number of open issues, and they strongly depend on the Cloud architectures and the delivery and deployment models (IaaS, PaaS, …) adopted. Indeed, any architectural choices and service provision activities imply the adoption of proper security policies and mechanisms to guarantee security requirements.

As already said, the main security issues on Cloud architectures are primary related to the "security management and governance" (to be able to manage the risk associated with a particular provider) and to the security "operational aspects" (as access control privacy, confidentiality and data integrity, business continuity, disaster recovery,...). The scientific community has begun to investigate the latter aspect and commercial solutions try to enforce proper access control mechanisms.

For example, available Cloud solutions offer a large set of different mechanisms for access control. Among the others, Google, which is essentially a PaaS provider, adopts a number of industry-standard mechanisms to authenticate users (including LDAP, Active Directory-based authentication and single sign-on systems (SSO)). It requires the use of a unique User ID, based on standards like OpenID (Recordon, 2006) or OAUTH (Hammer, 2010). Besides being used to identify the activity of each person on the Google network, this ID is used to control access to every system at Google. Access rights are based on user's role and enable the authorization of users on many different platforms by a fine grain access control that is enforced by a central authorization service compliant to SAML standards, solving, in this way, the interoperability among authorization mechanisms implemented by different resources.

Another interesting example is given by Amazon, it enforces access control through a fully centralized Identity and Access Management (IAM) system that lets administrators to manage users, groups of users, and access permissions for services and resources. The authentication protocols are mainly based on the adoption of Public Key Certificates.

On the other hand, Cloud platforms that integrate Grid infrastructures mainly enforce security mechanisms that are provided by the underlying security system (i.e., Grid GSI). As a matter of fact, in these architectures, public key infrastructures are configured and used in different ways to provide security features (e.g., user certificates, Grid proxy certificates, encryption/decryption functions, secure protocols…).

It is quite difficult to generalize the security issues that arise in the different solutions, nevertheless the available architectures have many points in common even if security mechanisms and their implementation may strongly be different.

Even if there is not a clear taxonomy in the literature, according to our experience, two main approaches exist for building PaaS solutions, we call them *integrated solutions* and *deploy-based solutions*.

Integrated solutions, like Google App Engine (GAE), are web accessible development environments, which enable the developer to build an application in a given language (Java or Python for the GAE applications) using a set of libraries and loading the code on the remote system. The management of the execution is completely up to the Cloud provider. Developers do not control the machines on which the application runs, they cannot directly manage threads or use system-related functionalities, they only have a set of APIs (Task API in GAE) which offer a limited control on the coordination of code execution.

Deploy-based solutions, like the ones that IBM, Oracle and Microsoft as commercial providers

and OPTIMIS (Optimis, 2010; Tordsson, 2011), CONTRAIL (Jégou, 2011; *CONTRAIL*, 2010) and MOSAIC as European project are proposing, follow a different approach: they build a system which enable the deployment of middlewares on the top of resources acquired from an IaaS Cloud provider, offering a service interface for it. The deployed middleware is the same that is usually adopted on physical and standard machines, but the deployment services automatize the process of installation and configuration of the software on cloud resources (both computational and storage resources). Such PaaS solutions are then able to offer a set of functionalities as, for example, the ability of automatically change the number of machines to be adopted and self-scaling according to their usage. Deploy-based solutions programming interfaces are based on the deployed software stack and many possibilities are available.

In general, integrated solutions define a single trusted domain and the mechanisms to extend it to cooperate with other cloud providers are not visible to cloud users (and even it is not possible to control or monitor them). On the other hand, deploy-based solutions offer explicit mechanisms to federate different security domains; it is possible to gather infrastructure resources from a collection of different cloud providers and, at the same time, they offer a single unified view of them trough the deployed software. The potentialities of the deploy-based model are paid with a higher architectural complexity and management.

According to these considerations, to cope with such complexity, we need to look at any Cloud architecture as a complex layered system made of virtual and physical resources, any layer and their interactions should be protected with proper mechanisms.

In such layered view, we mainly locate a Cloud layer, managed by administrator users, whose role and activity is defined by the Cloud providers according to the available physical resources, their distribution and deployment, and a resource layer that should be accessible to generic Cloud users, that can use or modify resources according to predefined agreements with the provider. The Cloud layer may be, in turn, made of federated resources that can be accessible only to trusted users to provide a unique view of the physical resources; on the other hand, the resource layer can be a platform or an infrastructure itself and there is the need to enable and control the cooperation among virtual and physical resources.

With this perspective, the primary security problems of a Cloud architecture are related to: *(i)* the opportunity to share virtual and physical resources by creating federated infrastructures and *(ii)* the need of enabling the access to them only to authorized users, both with a PaaS and an IaaS model, provided with an integrated solution or a deploy-based solution,

As for access control, this is implemented in two different steps: the first step consists of authentication of different users that joined the Cloud; authentication mechanisms variegate from set of credentials (login and password over secure channels) to strong authentication mechanisms (based on digital signatures combined with secret password) that widely adopt digital certificates and encryption protocols. Authenticated users can play different roles within the Cloud and they must be authorized before performing any action (second step).

Authorization mechanisms are usually "locally" enforced by the resources; this means that before enabling a Cloud approach, some interoperability issues should be faced: security policies should be updated to regulate the access to the resource in the Cloud, interoperability mechanisms should be put in place to guarantee the consistency of policies and mechanisms, one of these mechanisms is provided, for example, by the SAML standard, that enable interoperability among different authorization services.

The adoption of digital certificates, implicitly define trusted domains; in the fact, users that have been authenticated by a Certification Authority can access resources under the security domain defined by the corresponding Public Key Infrastructure.

Indeed, to fully enable the Cloud approach, it is desirable to grant cooperation among users and virtual resources even when they are offered by potentially untrusted domains. In this case, authentication and authorization are not enough to enforce access control, in fact there is the need to implement a secure way to access shared resources; in other terms, different resources can be seen as different security domains as they locally enforce different security policies for authentication and authorization and there is the need to establish federated mechanisms to let them be available.

This problem is strictly related to Identity Federation among distributed domains and cannot be solved by traditional access control mechanisms. At the state of the art, when a Cloud infrastructure has to accept a new virtual site as part of the infrastructure (or platform), a complex evaluation procedure usually takes place. This involves human interaction and manual evaluation of the security policies adopted by the site to enable cooperation and to trust each other. But, as one of the objectives of any Cloud system is to automatize all procedures (on-demand self-service (Mell, 2009)), the safe "manual" admission procedure is not a reasonable solution, and a federated approach to security and, more specifically, to identity management is required (*Cloud Security Alliance*, 2009).

Federating the Cloud providers means federating their security domains, while the above cited projects have the focus on federating the technological solutions (i.e. let them interoperate) the problem of what are the effects of building a federated security domains are less investigated.

Some solutions, as CONTRAIL (*CONTRAIL*, 2010) which build a complex distributed Cloud Provider on the basis of federation, build up their own security domain with their own authentication system: users are CONTRAIL users, and all technological and security aspects of the underlying providers are completely hidden.

Some projects rely on the underlying physical infrastructure technologies; for example, in the Cloud on Grid approach, to federate Grid resources an interoperability system has been proposed as an extension of the Globus toolkit (Casola, 2007b); it is based on an automatic technique to validate digital certificates even when issued by untrusted Certification Authorities so enabling identity federation to access federated resources.

In both architectures, administration roles are played by specific users "against" the philosophy of the cloud but what are the effects of such an indirect delegation of responsibilities?

Trying to give an answer is not easy; as already said, the complexity depends on the chosen architecture and, as a consequence, the security features and requirements can be analysed and discussed only when a reference model and architecture are chosen. For this reason, in the next sections, we will introduce and discuss the security issues of a Cloud infrastructure that provides a PaaS and a IaaS; it is build on the integration of a Grid infrastructure that provides the Cloud physical infrastructural environment (Cloud on Grid) and a Grid infrastructure that provides the platform virtual environment (Grid on Cloud); we named this *cloudgrid* and we will discuss some interesting solutions to the security issues in the solution and recommendation section.

Access Control and Identity Federation in the Cloudgrid

In this chapter we aims at offering a practical approach to facing security problems, so will focus on a special case of deploy-based solution: the *cloudgrid* solution. The key idea is that the software deployed on the infrastructure resources is a grid middleware, which represent the Platform as a Service middleware: *cloudgrid* users can develop their application using the globus toolkit and consumer resources modelled in terms of GRID resources. PerfCloud is the prototype implementation of such a system.

Figure 1 details the proposed cloudgrid approach. The bottom layer is a common physical Grid, on the top of which services have been deployed to instantiate virtual machines. This is a simple implementation of IaaS offering on Grid resources (a *cloud-on-grid*), serving virtual machines which are intrinsically general purpose and can be used for different applications. Perf-Cloud offers such virtual machines both as single machines and in terms of Virtual Clusters, i.e. a set of virtual machines interconnected through a (virtualized) dedicated network.

On these resources, it is perfectly reasonable to install a Grid middleware on them to create a virtual Grid infrastructure (a *grid-on-cloud* approach). In the following we call Virtual Grid, a GRID environment built on the top of virtual resources.

What distinguishes a cloudgrid from simple cloud-on-grid or grid-on-cloud architectures is the support to automatically federate the Virtual Grids among them and with the underlying physical Grid. In other words both physical and virtualized resources can be used by the user transparently trough the Grid middleware, which represent the PaaS interface of our solution.

A Grid User, i.e. an user which has obtained a set of valid credential from a Virtual or a Physical Grid, has the right of accessing, through his applications, to resources offered by any of the Grids composing the *cloudgrid* infrastructure. As it will be detailed later, this has a lot of security implications.

The motivation for the integration of Grid and Cloud models is twofold. The cloud-on-grid model offers Cloud IaaS services, but the leased computing resources (e.g., the virtual clusters) are basic infrastructures not ready to interoperate.

On the other hand, the grid-on-cloud model makes it possible to build interoperable systems, but these systems are built from resources leased from clouds and cannot exploit the great potential of existing scientific grids. A cloudgrid grants its users the advantages of both cloud-on-grid and

Figure 1. The cloudgrid layers

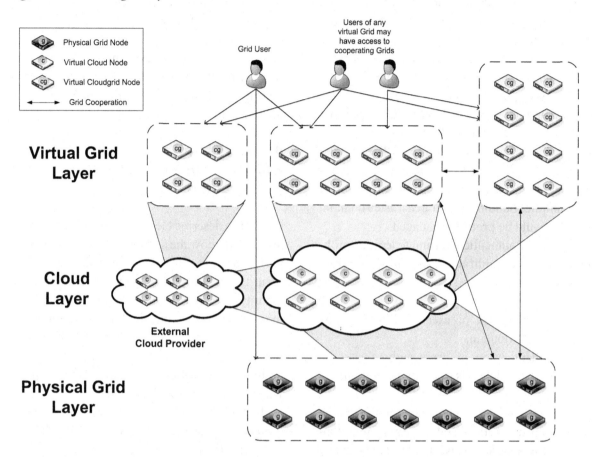

grid-on-cloud models (management flexibility and interoperability, respectively).

These evident benefits do not come at no cost, anyway: as it will be shown, this architecture exhibits a lot of security issues which will be object of next sections, related to the protection of virtual and physical resources, and to the desire to share resources among untrusted domains.

As a matter of fact, any virtual cluster administrator, who is for the Grid a standard user with no physical resource management grants, can act as a Grid administrator once the virtual cluster is integrated in the Grid, and this potentially is very dangerous. On the other hand, any virtual resource can be shared with other trusted users if proper federation rules are enforced.

Security Requirements in CloudGrid

As already mentioned, security requirements are strongly related to both the delivery and deployment model of the Cloud, because architectural choices and service provision activities imply the adoption of proper security policies to guarantee data integrity, privacy and user confidentiality. In the remainder of this chapter, we will consider *authentication, federation* and *authorization* issues in Cloud services build on top of Grid infrastructures, that provide a PaaS and an IaaS. In particular we will refer to services implemented on the integration of a Grid infrastructure that provides the Cloud physical infrastructural environment (Cloud on Grid) and a Grid infrastructure that provides the platform virtual environment (Grid on Cloud) through the adoption of Virtual Clusters, i.e. virtual resources that can be directly managed by Cloud users; we named this *cloudgrid* and we will discuss some interesting architectures in the solution and recommendation section.

We explicitly note that such considerations can be applied to every kind of Deploy-based PaaS solution based on IaaS federation: each time resources are acquired from different cloud provider they belong to different trust domains and deploying cooperating software on the top of them implies building a federated trusted domain, which should be properly managed.

As for the authentication and federation problem, we have to split this issue in two different aspects:

1. Authentication of users within the same security domain,
2. Authentication of users authenticated in untrusted domains (identity federation).

From a technical point of view, there are many technological solutions and some available standards for authentication within the same security domain. When the authentication is based on the adoption of digital certificates, these authentication mechanisms are respectively named: *basic path authentication* and *extended path validation*.

The second point is also known as the identity federation problem; it is still an open problem to face when untrusted resources need to cooperate as it is traditionally based on not-automatic procedures; this issue is of fundamental importance to be addressed in the Cloud when virtual and physical resources need to cooperate to provide wide infrastructures.

We will illustrate a possible solution based on the adoption of digital certificates.

As for the authorization problem, the security policies at the Cloud layer involve many different users who can play different roles within the Cloud platform. For example, in a Grid environment resources are often provided for free so, it is necessary to differentiate users, introducing figures with higher privileges to perform administration tasks. We will discuss an access control policy for Cloud services and in next section we will illustrate how to enforce it with proper security mechanisms within the underlying Grid infrastructure.

Authentication and Identity Federation in a CloudGRID Infrastructure

In order to describe clearly the problem, we summarize here how the authentication process takes place in a Grid environment with users of the same security domain (authentication) or of different security domains (identity federation). The following considerations are valid for all authentication mechanisms that are based on digital certificates but, for completeness, we will focus our attention on the authentication procedures that take place when requesting GRID services.

In a Grid environment, users have a set of Grid credentials consisting of a X.509 v3 digital certificate (Housley, 2002) and a private key. The certificate is digitally signed by a Certification Authority that guarantees for the binding of a subject distinguished name (DN) to its private key. The authentication mechanism involves the presentation of the certificate and the possession of the corresponding private key. A known problem in such a protocol is the protection of the private key. At this aim, two strategies are commonly adopted: i) the key is protected with encryption or by storing it on a hardware token (e.g., a smart card); ii) the private key has limited lifetime, after which it is no longer valid.

The Globus Toolkit security implementation, known as the Grid Security Infrastructure (GSI) (*Globus Security Team*, 2005), follows the second strategy, using Proxy Certificates (Welch, 2004). Short-term credentials created by a user can successively be used in the place of traditional long-term credentials to authenticate him. The proxy certificate has its own private key and certificate, and is signed using the user long-term credential.

A typical session with the GSI would involve the Grid user (End-Entity) using its passphrase and the GSI command grid-proxy-init creating a proxy certificate from its long-term credential. The user could then use a GSI-enabled application to invoke a service operation from a Globus Toolkit Grid Services Container (Globus Security Team, 2005).

From the Grid resource point of view, to fully perform the authentication process, a certificate validation service interface should be defined and used within the Open GRID Services Architecture (OGSA) (Foster, 2002) implementation to:

1. Parse a certificate and to verify desired attribute values, as the validity period, the Distinguished Name and so on,
2. Perform path validation (basic and extended) (Housley, 2002) on a certificate chain and verify the revocation status according to updated certificate revocation lists (CRLs) or through an on-line Certificate Status Protocol,
3. Return attribute information for different usage.

Available Grid implementations, as the Globus Toolkit (GT4) (Foster, 2006), provide static mechanisms to perform a "basic certificate path validation" process, i.e.:

1. Cryptographic verifications over the certificate path (verifying the digital signature of each certificate).
2. Verification of each certificate validity period.
3. Verification that the root certificate in the chain is trusted.
4. Verification of the certificates status to ensure that they have not been revoked or suspended.

In particular, in GT4 the first certificate in the chain is considered a Trust Anchor if it has been stored into the Grid node /etc/grid-security/certificates/directory, while the certificate status is retrieved from a locally-stored Certificate Revocation List (CRL).

When a Grid user has been authenticated by an untrusted Certification Authority and he tries to access untrusted Grid resources, an "extended path validation" (Casola, 2007b) must be enforced to validate a digital certificate issued by any other CA.

The main idea behind the extended path validation mechanism is to define an approach that enables any Grid relying-party to validate in real-time a digital certificate issued by any other CA, even if they do not belong to the same trusted domain, enabling in this way an identity federation mechanism. So, the identity federation problem in authentication mechanisms based on digital certificates mainly consists of the need to evaluate and to extend trust to the authority that issued such certificates. If we are able to automatically perform the extended path validation, we are able to perform Identity Federation since we can accept and validate credentials from any domain. Our approach is to build a dynamic federation of CAs by automatically evaluating their certificate policies (automatic cross-certification) (Casola, 2007a). In (Casola, 2007b) we introduced an Interoperability System (IS) that acts as an intermediary between the certificate verifiers (relying parties) and the issuing CAs by managing (retrieving, elaborating and updating) the information needed to perform the extended path validation: the list of accredited CAs, the list of revocation sources and the Certificate Policies. In Figure 2 the logical blocks of the Interoperability System (IS) are shown.

The IS may be allocated within the Trusted Third Party domain. In our case, it will be offered as a service by the Physical Grid site, and must perform two main tasks:

1. On-line validation of the certificate status,
2. Evaluation of the issuing CA security level.

Figure 2. Interoperability System (IS) main components

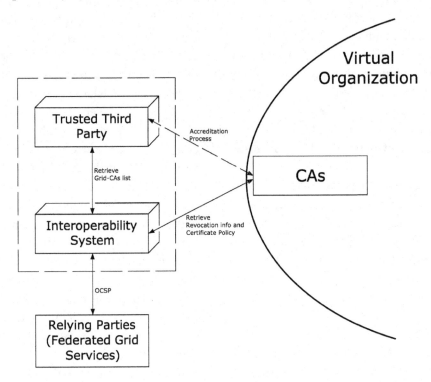

For the first task we can use a Grid Validation System able to retrieve the status of a digital certificate through the OCSP protocol in a CA federation. This feature has been implemented as an extension of Globus Toolkit, and it is named OGRO (Luna, 2006a, 2006b). As regards the second task, for evaluating a CA security level we have adopted the Reference Evaluation Methodology (REM), a policy-based evaluation technique that was primary proposed for evaluating Certification Authorities in the cross-certification process (Casola, 2007a).

The REM approach is based on the formalization of a Grid-CA Certificate Policy i) to determine if this Authority is compliant with another CA Certificate Policy and ii) to quantitatively evaluate the Global Security Level (GSL) of this CA. The GSL is a quantitative measure of the CA trust degree, and it will be compared with the other CA level to decide to extend or not the trust to an incoming user request. The GSL will be retrieved and evaluated by a Grid Service before extending trust (to federate an identity).

In (Casola, 2007b) we proposed the use of a Policy and OCSP based Interoperability System (POIS) to enable Identity Federation among Cloud users. Figure 3 shows the main actors and the system components during the invocation of a service offered by a Grid container that supports federation (Federated Grid Container).

At a coarse view, POIS offers the following features:

1. Manages (retrieves, updates) the list of Virtual Organizations CAs (accredited by the root-VO).
2. Manages (retrieves, updates) the accredited CAs Certificate Policies.
3. Manages (retrieves, updates) the accredited CAs CRLs.
4. Communicates validation information to relying parties over OCSP.

Figure 3. Service request to a Federated Grid Service through POIS

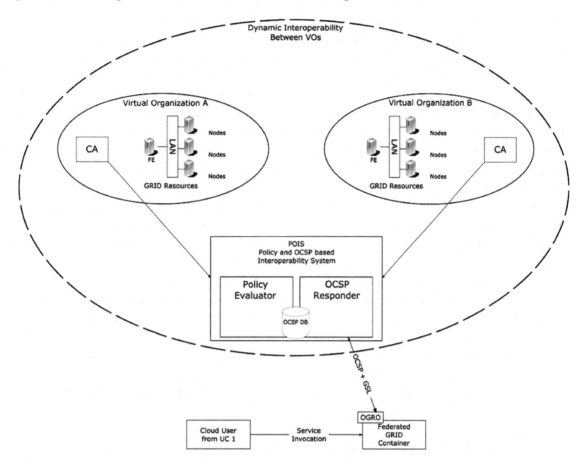

As for the features 1 and 2, we assume that the database with the list of accredited CA and their Certificate Policies is manually and off-line managed by system administrators (in particular by the Grid Administrator). The CRLs (feature 3) from each accredited CA are retrieved by using CertiVeR CRL Updater module, as in (CertiVer, 2006), so they can be used in the Extended Path Validation process. The Policy Evaluator subsystem implements the REM evaluation technique to evaluate the GSL on any VO CA Policy. The GSL is then communicated to relying parties by the OCSP protocol (feature 4).

To summarize, POIS is able to perform the Identity Federation thanks to a specific client (like OGRO (OGRO,2006)) which provides the following two enhancements to the GT4 basic path validation algorithm: i) certificate status is extracted from the OCSP response and ii) the GSL evaluated by POIS is compared against the GSL value required by the Grid Service for trusting the request from a different Virtual Organization. In next section we will illustrate its adoption with an example for accessing federated resources.

Authorization in the CloudGRID Infrastructure

The security policies at the Cloud layer involve many different users who can play different roles within the Cloud platform. For example, in a Grid environment resources are often provided for free so, to perform administration tasks and differentiate services, it is necessary to differentiate users by introducing figures with higher privileges. It is important to point out that the administration role cannot be played by physical machine administrators, since resources to be administered are location-transparent Grid resources.

Users need different privileges on system resources (physical and virtual). At this level, fine-grain access control mechanisms are needed to guarantee access to service administrators, system administrators and end-users. We have analyzed the different roles and corresponding security policies for the access to Cloud services (both administration and user services), and pointed out four different roles:

- **System Administrator:** manages the physical architecture and software components (turns on/off servers, installs services and applications, secures operating systems and virtual machines, manages and updates systems,...).
- **Grid User:** can access Grid services and resources that are hosted on different servers.
- **Cloud Administrator**: can perform administration tasks on Cloud services (e.g., create/delete virtual machines and clusters, assign clusters to Cloud Users, manage Cloud Users, maintain the integrity and consistency of the Cloud environment...) but he is not the owner of the created resources, as they are assigned to Cloud Users.
- **Cloud User:** can access and manage Cloud resources (virtual services and resources) and administrate his own virtual cluster(s). He is authorized by passing a fine-grain access control.

Some example of security rules and policy will be discussed in next sections.

In the Grid there are system administrators who manage physical machines from the hardware up to the Globus layer, and Grid users who just access and use the grid-exposed resources. In the Cloud, instead, there are different classes of resources to protect (physical and virtual ones). They are "assigned" to external users and must be independently managed and protected at different architectural levels (container, service, resource).

Furthermore, according to the Cloud NIST definition of "on-demand self-service" the Cloud administration tasks should be performed by automated procedures or may be supervised by humans in "free" environments as, for example, in the academic context; since the Grid platforms are widely adopted in academic context, we decided to include the Cloud administrator role in our analysis.

To enforce role based access control mechanisms, many standard architectures and proprietary solutions are available. In next section we will discuss the standard solutions implemented in the underlying Grid infrastructure.

The PerfCloud Security Solution

We applied the just described mechanisms to PerfCloud, our cloudgrid prototype.

The approach can be summarized as follows: every Virtual Grid comes with an access control module that guards access to the resources: its XACML based implementation for role-based access control will be discussed in next paragraphs. To support authentication (federated or not), the Virtual Grids are instrumented with a POIS Client in addition to their own Certificate Authority.

Thanks to the authorization and access control mechanisms integrated on each Physical and Virtual Grids every user will be able to access to all the resources offered by the cloudgrid infrastructure, but his authorization level (i.e. the services to which he has right to access) depends on the credentials he owns and on the Grid Infrastructure which effectively released them.

To better describe the architecture, a final paragraph has been included with a working scenario that stimulates all the security building blocks.

Access Control

Even if offering to users full rights on their virtual resources is one of the aims of Cloud systems, this can have a side effect in a cloudgrid: in fact, a Virtual Cluster administrator has full right access to the Virtual Cluster but he can also manage the new Grid site that is hosted by the physical Grid site. This represents a big security issue: a user of a hosted Cloud site could access physical resources if the Cloud administrator does not enforce proper security policies in issuing credential or delegating rights, or if he wants to abuse of his role on the physical resources. As a consequence, a cloudgrid requires a powerful role-based authorization mechanism.

PerfCloud relies on Globus Toolkit 4 (GT4) as Grid middleware. So we customized and enriched the default Globus configurations in order to meet the security requirements described in the previous sections. As regards access control, GT4 offers a flexible but poor mechanism for both authentication, as previously illustrated, and for authorization and data confidentiality (Globus Security Team, 2005). In particular, GT4 uses the concept of Security Descriptors as standard method for configuring the security requirements and policies of clients and services. The Security Descriptors are XML files which are deployed together with the services. They can be enforced to protect different resources, as a Globus container, a service or a specific resource.

GT4 authentication founds on PKI and the adoption of X.509 digital certificates with basic path authentication. The standard GT4 implementation is not configurable and does not allow to supply additional parameters for the authentication procedure. However, the Security Descriptor (SD) makes it possible to specify the communication protocols that an authenticated user must adopt in order to access a resource. It is possible to specify four (non-exclusive) options:

- **None**, in which no secure communication is enforced;
- **Secure Message**, which provides per-message secure communication in accordance with the WS-Security specification (Atkinson, 2002);
- **Secure Conversation**, which provides a secure session in accordance with the WS-SecureConversation specification.
- **Secure Transport**, in which a secure communication channel is adopted (i.e., SSL/TSL transport protocols are used)

For example, if the SD of a service specifies the adoption of SecureTransport and SecureMessage, the only service invocations accepted will be those with a SOAP message encrypted according to the SecureMessage WS-security standard over a TLS channel. Everything else will be rejected.

As for Authorization, by default GSI offers only simple mechanisms:

- **Mapfile**, in which no authorization is performed except for the container-wide Grid mapfile;
- **Embedded PDP**, in which it is possible to define a per-container, a per-service or per-resource mechanism handled by a Local Policy Decision Point (PDP).

However, GSI also offers a set of APIs to integrate an external PDP, as XACML (OASIS, 2005) or shibboleth (Barton, 2006), to support more expressive authorization policies.

The default security solutions offered by Globus do not meet all the security requirements we outlined in the previous section; we extended the authorization mechanism in order to support XACML and, consequently, role-based policies (Ferraiolo,1992), then we forced the security descriptor to adopt secure communication channels for all the cloud-related service and resources (Casola, 2010, 2011).

Exhibit 1.

1. Example XACML Condition

```
<Condition FunctionId="urn:oasis:names:tc:xacml:1.0:function:
string-is-in">
<Apply FunctionId="urn:oasis:names:tc:xacml:1.0:function:
string-one-and-only">
<SubjectAttributeDesignatorDataType="http://www.w3.org/2001/
XMLSchema#string"
AttributeId="urn:oasis:names:tc:xacml:1.0:subject:subject-id"/>
</Apply>
<ResourceAttributeDesignatorDataType="http://www.w3.org/
2001/XMLSchema#string" AttributeId="urn:oasis:names:tc:xacml:
1.0:resource:owner-id"/>
</Condition>
```

2. Example XACML Subject

```
<Subject>
<SubjectMatchMatchId="urn:oasis:names:tc:xacml:1.0:function:
string-equal">
<AttributeValueDataType="http://www.w3.org/2001/
XMLSchema#string">administrator</AttributeValue>
<SubjectAttributeDesignatorDataType="http://www.w3.org/2001/
XMLSchema#string" AttributeId="urn:oasis:names:tc:xacml:2.0:
subject:role"/>
```

In Exhibit 1, there are two simple examples of XACML rules. The first allows only the owner to access his own resources (enforced thanks to the Condition tag in the XACML syntax). The latter allows any user with an Administrator role to access a resource (enforced thanks to the role attribute of the Subject tag in the XACML syntax).

In (Casola, 2010) we showed through a comprehensive set of experiments that the introduction of role based access control logic has negligible impact on the response time of Grid services.

Federation

Federating the virtual grids with the physical one proves to be a valuable solution to the interoperability problems. With a federative approach, the leased Virtual Clusters have their own Certificate Authority, through which they are able to release certificates that are verified through an extended path validation procedure. Another possibility would have been to integrate the new grids in the Virtual Organization of the underlying physical Grid, but this requires the sharing of the root Grid Certification Authority with the unsecure virtual grids, which is not recommended.

The invocation of a service is shown in Figure 4: interoperability is dynamically granted as we can perform in an automatic way the cross certification via the REM methodology. As already said, the REM methodology is able to quantitatively evaluate a Certificate Policy and it is useful to understand if a CA is trusted or not. Furthermore, the OCSP responder is able to evaluate the certificate status of any certificate issued by any Certification Authority.

Figure 4. Request for a Federated Grid Service through POIS

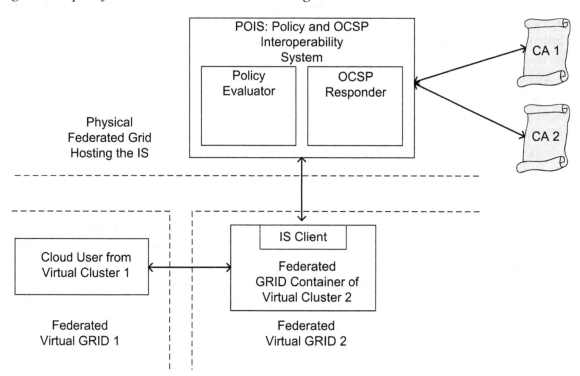

We wish to point out that it is up to the Grid Container to interact with the Interoperability System. It can perform such an operation if it has been federated and has a suitable client, like OGRO (Luna, 2006), that provides the following two enhancements to the GT4 basic path validation algorithm: i) the certificate status is extracted from the OCSP response and ii) the GSL evaluated by POIS is compared against the GSL value required by the Grid Service for trusting the request from a different Virtual Organization. We will denote such container as a Federated Grid Container (and, consequently, we will refer to Federated Grid Services and Federated Resources). When a customer asks for a Virtual Cluster, the Cloud Administrator will create a new Virtual Cluster and configure images and services with or without federated facilities according to the customer request.

Once federated services are available, different scenarios may occur. They are strictly related to the relations between the different grids (both Virtual and Physical). In particular:

1. The new Virtual Grid has a pre-configured Certification Authority that has a hierarchical relation with the Root Certification Authority of the Physical Grid;
2. The new Virtual Grid CA has not any relations with the other Virtual Grids or with the Physical Grid.

In the first case, basic path validation is enough to extend trust to Cloud users whose certificates have been issued within the hierarchy (the Certification Path validation process does not fail as the Root CA acts as the Trust Anchor). Nevertheless, the adoption of a hierarchical approach should be discouraged (i) to enable Cloud Administrators to configure their own Certification Authorities and (ii) to avoid that a Cloud Administrator issues to its users digital credentials that can be directly validated and accepted by all physical Grid resources.

In the second case, an explicit federation mechanism is needed to cooperate. Identity Federation does not automatically mean to grant access to a federated resource. In fact, once a user has been authenticated by an external Virtual Grid, its identity will be mapped to a specific (federated) role and the defined role-based access control policy will be enforced at resource level (Casola, 2011). For example, a user from the Virtual Grid 1 that has a role of Cloud Administrator can access to specific resources of Virtual Grid 2 but, possibly, with a non-administrator role.

In the following, we will describe in detail the second scenario, including the role mapping and authorization aspects.

Accessing Federated Resources: An Example Scenario

This final paragraph will introduce a practical case of resource access in the federated cloudgrid. As the sequence diagram in Figure 5 shows, the interaction starts when User@VC1, an user of Virtual Cluster 1 belonging to Virtual Grid 1, requests a Grid service offered by the physical cluster, part of the Root Physical Grid and denoted with FGC@Root. The interoperability is made possible because the Grid Services Container has been federated. This means that the Certificate Policies from all the interoperable Virtual Grids have been previously submitted to the POIS, they have been evaluated by the Policy Evaluator subsystem and the corresponding GSL has been stored into OCSP Responder DB along with the CA data (this step is not shown in the diagram).

The steps of this scenario are:

1. When a Cloud user from the Virtual Grid 1 (user@VC1) requests a Grid service offered by the Physical Grid, its Federated Grid Container (FGC@Root) performs extended path validation:

   ◦ Basic path validation on the proxy certificate is performed;
   ◦ The digital certificate status is evaluated on-line through the OCSP Responder;
   ◦ The GSL value is directly retrieved from the POIS (that maintains a database with all pre-evaluated Certification Authorities of the accredited Virtual Clusters).
   ◦ The GSL of the Cloud user's CA is compared against the minimum required-GSL defined by the Federated Grid Container to extend trust, and if GSLV C1 > GSLGC, the validation is successful.

2. If the extended path validation is successful, the Cloud user is mapped to a "federated user".

3. The role granted to the federated user is retrieved from a role repository.

4. Role-based access control mechanism is performed by using the XACML Policy Decision Point (PDP) configured at Resource Level (Welch, 2004).

5. Resource is accessed if the user has suitable authorization for its use.

In Table 1, we report different cases of federation and the corresponding "federated role" that is assigned considering who requests a resource and where the resource is hosted.

We can note that if an user from the Virtual Grid 1 (denoted User@VC1) requests a service of the Physical Grid (denoted Root in the table), it is recognized as a federated limited user and a limited set of rights will be granted in the rbac policy (for example, we could grant computing resources, but not administration ones). If the same user from the Virtual Grid 1 (User@VC1) requests a service of the Virtual Grid 2 (denoted VC2), it will be recognized as a federated user and the rbac policy will grant services according to the agreements between parties. If a user from

Figure 5. Extended Path Validation with POIS

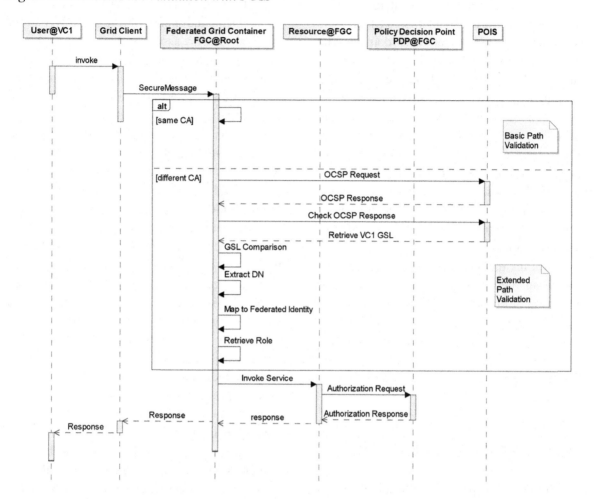

the Root (or a user from Virtual Grid 1) requests a service of the Root (or of the VC1) - this is a trivial case - basic path validation is performed and the user role does not change as the requester is not federated but "internal" and so does not require the extended validation mechanism. The

last case is when a user from the Physical Grid requests services offered by a Virtual Grid. Once again, extended path validation is performed and the assigned role and the policy will depend on the agreement between the parties.

Table 1. Roles Mapping

Requester	Resource Location	Identity Mechanism	Role mapped
User@VC1	Root	Extended Validation	Federated limited user
User@VC1	VC2	Extended Validation	Federated user
User@Root	Root	Basic Validation	Same role
User@VC1	VC1	Basic Validation	Same role
User@Root	VC1	Extended Validation	Federated user

In conclusion, thanks to the Interoperability System we are able to extend trust to Cloud users even when they come from untrusted domains. The whole mechanism works because we are able to automatically validate any digital certificate and to assign it a degree of trust (the Global Security Level). On the basis of this trust degree, we are also able to assign a dynamic profile to users coming from the outside world, to let them access computing or even administration resources. We think that this is a very important issue in a Cloud environment, as identity federation is an open issue that still limits the wide adoption of these infrastructures.

One of the main drawbacks of this approach may be an inevitable performance penalty, as complex authorization mechanisms or the use of secure channels may heavily increase the overhead on service invocation and some interesting works have been presented to evaluate the trade-off among different architectural and security solutions.

FUTURE RESEARCH DIRECTIONS

In addition to the problems illustrated in this chapter, many open issues should be taken in consideration to completely face the security problems that may arise in Cloud infrastructures.

We have identified some research problems we consider of great interest for the scientific community on the next years.

The first research direction of great interest is a User-Centric approach to Security. At the state of the art the main focus on security issues are related to integration of security mechanisms into the Cloud engines, this is a traditional approach to security: the goal is to integrate well-known security solutions in order to build up a "Secure Cloud Provider". Note that traditional does not mean simple, as outlined in the chapter, all security issues became more complex due to the nature of Cloud computing.

But Cloud Computing introduces additional requirements and opportunities to security; indeed, the final users are assuming a more relevant role, solutions start to be configured around the needing of each final users, and security as well as quality are becoming primary points to contract and there is the need to proper define, evaluate and monitor Service Level Agreements (SLAs) and Service Level Management. From a security point of view this is a really interesting new challenge: how to build user-centric solutions? How to enable a user to identify its own security requirements in a clear and negotiable way, in order to choose (among a federation of Cloud providers) the one that fits its own needs? What about the privacy issues and guarantees about data protection even when the final user does not know where in the world the provider has its physical servers?

Security oriented SLA involve new set of problems, like the needing of formally and clearly describe the security features (the security policies) and, even more important, a clear way to measure and evaluate the quality of the security solution being offered.

Security is often evaluated on the basis of human experience and on the basis of qualitative parameters, in a context which automates every procedure (the self-service approach of NIST Cloud definition) how to approach the security evaluation?

The above proposals are just few of the number of new challenges that are arising in the Cloud environment, but in our opinion the security aspects that strongly impact on organizational and management aspects will be among the hot research topics for the next few years, as they will represent the difference in the quality of the infrastructures and services provided.

CONCLUSION

In this chapter we have illustrated some examples of commercial Cloud infrastructures and Cloud research projects that address the security problems in different ways.

In particular, we focused our attention on access control and identity federation as we think that there is the need of new models and architectures to fully enable the secure sharing and cooperation of resources to effectively provide Cloud infrastructures.

Many Cloud solutions leverage services without integrating identity management and access control mechanisms; others are beginning to address these points with proprietary solutions. Trying to generalize has not been easy, nevertheless, we have located some common critical points and discussed them by adopting a real case study that provides the Cloud services with the integration of Grid and Cloud resources, we named this approach CloudGrid.

We have discussed the access control problems and identity federation starting from users requirements to access both virtual and physical Grid sites without abusing the privileges linked to their role in their own domain.

The proposed Identity Federation approach relies on an underlying Grid infrastructure and it is based on the definition of an Interoperability System that validates certificates by dynamically building a federation among untrusted Certification Authorities (we adopted the REM methodology to evaluate and compare the trust level of a Certification Authority) and by evaluating on-line the status of a digital certificate (we proposed the adoption of the OCSP protocol and a Grid OCSP client named OGRO). To illustrate in details the proposed architecture we also presented a typical scenario where users from a virtual cluster request resources hosted by other clusters (virtual or physical), illustrating the federation process and the enforcement of access control policies that are specific for "federated users".

In our opinion these topics will be of great interest in the next future for the whole scientific community; in fact they have a strong impact on the overall quality of data protection that a Cloud provider can guarantee to its users and customers and we believe this will be the difference in many business area.

REFERENCES

Atkinson, B. (2002). *WS-Security Specification, Web Services Security 1.0*. Mendeley.

Barton, T., Basney, J., Freeman, T., Scavo, T., Siebenlist, F., Welch, V., et al. (2006). Identity federation and attribute-based authorization through the globus toolkit, shibboleth, gridshib, and myproxy. *In Proc. of 5th Annual PKI R&D Workshop*. Gaithersburg, MD: NIH

Casola, V., Cuomo, A., Rak, M., & Villano, U. (2010). *Security and performance trade-off in perfcloud. In the Proc. of VHPC2010*. New York, NY: Springer.

Casola, V., Lettiero, R., Rak, M., & Villano, U. (2010). *Access control in Cloud on grid: the PerfCloud case study. In the Proc. of SPCC2010*. New York, NY: Springer.

Casola, V., Luna, J., Manso, O., Mazzocca, N., Manel, M., & Rak, M. (2007). Interoperable grid pkis among untrusted domains: an architectural proposal. *In Proc. of the 2nd Grid and Pervasive Conference* (GPC2007) New York, NY: Springer

Casola, V., Mazzeo, A., Mazzocca, N., & Vittorini, V. (2007).A security metric for public key infrastructures. *Journal of Computer Security, vol. 15, no. 2*.

CertiVeR. (2006). *Certificate revocation and validation service*. Retrieved from www.certiver.com/.

Cloud Security Alliance (2009). *Security guidance for critical areas of focus in cloud computing*.

CONTRAIL Consortium. (2010). *CONTRAIL-Project Homepage*. Retrieved from http://contrail-project.eu/

Craciun, C. D., Petcu, D., & Rak, M. (2011). TOWARDS A CROSS PLATFORM CLOUD API Components for Cloud Federation. *In Proc. of CLOSER 2011*, Noordwijkerhout, The Netherland

Ferraiolo, D., & Kuhn, D. R. (1992). Role-based access control. *In Proc. of the 15th National Computer Security Conference*, pp. 554-563. Baltimore, MD: The Institute

Foster, I. (2006). Globus toolkit version 4: Software for service oriented systems. *Journal of Computer Science Technology, 21*(4), 513–520. doi:10.1007/s11390-006-0513-y

Foster, I., Kesselman, C., Nick, J. M., & Tuecke, S. (2002). The physiology of the Grid: An open grid services architecture for distributed systems integration. Retrieved from http://www.globus.org/research/papers/ogsa.pdf.

Foster, I., Welch, V., Kesselman, C., Mulmo, O., Pearlman, L., Tuecke, S., et al. (2004). X.509 proxy certificates for dynamic delegation. *In Proc. of the 3rd Annual PKI R&D Workshop*. Gaithersburg, MD: NIH

Foster, I., Zhao, Y., Raicu, I., & Lu, S. (2008). Cloud Computing and Grid Computing 360-Degree Compared. *In Grid Computing Environments Workshop*, (pp 1-10) New York, NY: Springer

Hammer-Lahav, E. (2010). Rfc5849. *The oauth 1.0 protocol*. Retrieved from http://tools.ietf.org/rfc/rfc5849.txt.

Housley, R., et al. (2002). *Internet Engineering Task Force, Rfc3280 internet x.509 public key infrastructure certificate and certificate revocation list (crl) profile*. Retrieved from www.ietf.org/rfc/rfc3280.txt.

Jégou, Y. (2011). *Contrail Approach. In 2nd Workshops on Software Services*. Timisoara, Romania: Open Computing Infrastructures for Elastic Services.

Luna, J., Manso, O., & Manel, M. (2006). Ocsp for grids: Comparing prevalidation versus caching. *In Proc. of 7th IEEE/ACM International Conference on Grid Computing*, Barcelona.

Luna, J., Manso, O., & Manel, M. (2006). Using ogro and certiver to improve ocsp validation for grids. *In Proc. of the 1st Grid and Pervasive Conference* (GPC2006). New York, NY: Springer

Mancini, E. P., Rak, M., & Villano, U. (2009). Perfcloud: Grid services for performance-oriented development of cloud computing applications. *In S. Reddy (Ed.).* (pp. 201-206.) New York, NY: WETICE, IEEE Computer Society

Mell, P., & Grance, T. (2009). *The NIST Definition of Cloud Computing*. New York, NY: Springer.

mOSAIC Consortium (2010). *mOSAIC Project Homepage*. Retrieved from http://www.mosaic-cloud.eu

OGRO. (2006). *The open grid ocsp client api*. Retrieved from http://globusgrid.certiver.com/info/ogro.

Optimis Consortium. (2010). OPTIMIS Project Homepage. Retrieved from http://www.optimis-project.eu/

Recordon, D., & Reed, D. (2006). Openid 2.0: a platform for user-centric identity management. *In Proc. of the second ACM workshop on Digital identity management*, (pp. 11-16) New York, NY: ACM.

The Globus Security Team. (2005). *Globus toolkit version 4 grid security infrastructure: A standards perspective*. Retrieved from www.globus.org/toolkit/docs/4.0/security/GT4-GSI-Overview.pdf

The Globus Security Team. (2005). *Globus toolkit version 4 grid security infrastructure: Authorization framework*. Retrieved from http://www.globus.org/toolkit/docs/4.0/security/authzframe/.

The OASIS technical committee. (2005). *Xacml: extensible access control markup language.* Retrieved from http://www.oasisopen.org/committees/xacml/repository/

Tordsson, J. (2011). *OPTIMIS - towards holistic cloud. In 2nd.* Timisoara, Romania: Workshops on Software Services.

ADDITIONAL READING

Adabala, S., Matsunaga, A., Tsugawa, M., Figueiredo, R., & Fortes, J. A. (2004). Single sign-on in in-vigo: Role-based access via delegation mechanisms using short-lived user identities. *Parallel and Distributed Processing Symposium, 2004. Proceedings. 18th International* (p 22). Washington, DC: IEEE.

Armbrust, M., Fox, A., Griffith, R., Joseph, A. D., Katz, R. H., Konwinski, A., et al. (2009). *Above the clouds: A berkeley view of cloud computing.* Technical Report UCB/EECS-2009-28, Berkeley, CA: EECS.

Berger, S., Cáceres, R., Goldman, K., Pendarakis, D., Perez, R., Rao, J. R., Rom, E., et al. (2009). Security for the cloud infrastructure: Trusted virtual data center implementation. *IBM Journal of Research and Development, 53*(4), 6: 1-6: 12.

Bidgoli, H. (2006). *Handbook of information security (Vol. 3).* Wiley.

Buyya, R., Ranjan, R., & Calheiros, R. (2010). *Intercloud: Utility-oriented federation of cloud computing environments for scaling of application services. Algorithms and Architectures for Parallel Processing* (pp. 13–31). New York, NY: Springer.

Demchenko, Y., Cristea, M., & de Laat, C. (2009). XACML policy profile for multidomain network resource provisioning and supporting authorisation infrastructure. *Policies for Distributed Systems and Networks, 2009. POLICY 2009. IEEE International Symposium on* (pp. 98-101). Washington, DC: IEEE.

Elmroth, E., Marquez, F. G., Henriksson, D., & Ferrera, D. P. (2009). Accounting and billing for federated cloud infrastructures. *Grid and Cooperative Computing, 2009. GCC'09. Eighth International Conference on* (pp. 268-275). Washington, DC: IEEE.

Foster, I., Freeman, T., Keahy, K., Scheftner, D., Sotomayer, B., & Zhang, X. (2006). Virtual clusters for grid communities. *Cluster Computing and the Grid, 2006. CCGRID 06. Sixth IEEE International Symposium on 1*, 513-520

Gouglidis, A., & Mavridis, I. (2010). On the definition of access control requirements for grid and cloud computing systems. *Networks for Grid Applications*, 19-26.

Hughes, J., & Maler, E. (2005). Security Assertion Markup Language (SAML) V2. 0 Technical Overview. *OASIS SSTC Working Draft sstc-saml-tech-overview-2.0-draft-08.*

Jensen, M., Schwenk, J., Gruschka, N., & Iacono, L. L. (2009). On technical security issues in cloud computing. *Cloud Computing, 2009. CLOUD'09. IEEE International Conference on* 109-116

Krutz, R. L., & Vines, R. D. (2010). *Cloud security: A comprehensive guide to secure cloud computing.* Wiley.

Lang, B., Foster, I., Siebenlist, F., Ananthakrishnan, R., & Freeman, T. (2006). A multipolicy authorization framework for grid security. *Network Computing and Applications, 2006. NCA 2006. Fifth IEEE International Symposium on* (pp 269-272). Washington, DC: IEEE.

Li, W., & Ping, L. (2009). Trust model to enhance security and interoperability of cloud environment. *Cloud Computing*, 69-79.

Mather, T., Kumaraswamy, S., & Latif, S. (2009). *Cloud security and privacy: an enterprise perspective on risks and compliance.* Sebastopol, CA: O'Reilly Media, Inc.

Mell, P., & Grance, T. (2009). *Effectively and securely using the cloud computing paradigm.* NIST, Information Technology Lab.

Nagaratnam, N., Janson, P., Dayka, J., Nadalin, A., Siebenlist, F., & Welch, V. (2002). The security architecture for open grid services. *Open Grid Service Architecture Security Working Group, Global Grid Forum* Naqvi, S., Villari, M., Latanicki, J., & Massonet, P. (S.d.). From Grids to Clouds-Shift in Security Services Architecture. *Cracow, 9,* 12–14.

Rochwerger, B., Breitgand, D., Levy, E., Galis, A., Nagin, K., Llorente, I. M., Montero, R., et al. (2009). The reservoir model and architecture for open federated cloud computing. *IBM Journal of Research and Development, 53*(4), 4: 1-4: 11.

Rochwerger, B., Vázquez, C., Breitgand, D., Hadas, D., Villari, M., Massonet, P., Levy, E., et al. (2010). An architecture for federated cloud computing. *Cloud Computing*, 391-411.

Sandhu, R. S., Coyne, E. J., Feinstein, H. L., & Youman, C. E. (1996). Role-based access control models. *Computer, 29*(2), 38–47. doi:10.1109/2.485845

Stanoevska-Slabeva, K. (2009). *Grid and cloud computing: a business perspective on technology and applications.* Berlin, Germany: Springer Verlag.

Suess, J., & Morooney, K. (2009). Identity management and trust services: Foundations for cloud computing. *EDUCAUSE Review*, 11.

Takabi, H., Joshi, J. B., & Ahn, G. (2010). Security and privacy challenges in cloud computing environments. *Security & Privacy, IEEE, 8*(6), 24–31. doi:10.1109/MSP.2010.186

Tuecke, S., Welch, V., Engert, D., Pearlman, L., & Thompson, M. (2004). Internet X. 509 public key infrastructure (PKI) proxy certificate profile. *RFC3820, June.*

Welch, V., Siebenlist, F., Foster, I., Bresnahan, J., Czajkowski, K., Gawor, J., et al. (2003). Security for grid services. *High Performance Distributed Computing, 2003. Proceedings. 12th IEEE International Symposium on* (pp 48-57). Washington, DC: IEEE.

Yan, L., Rong, C., & Zhao, G. (2009). Strengthen cloud computing security with federal identity management using hierarchical identity-based cryptography. *Cloud Computing*, 167-177.

KEY TERMS AND DEFINITIONS

Cloudgrid: Cloud and GRID computing paradigms have many points in common; both adopt large datacenters, both offer resources to users, both aim at providing a common environment for distributed resources. The integration of the two environments is a state of fact and a big opportunity to reuse available GRID infrastructure. The cloudgrid approach was proposed to offer a complete PaaS cloud infrastructure and to face the related security issues.

PerfCloud: PerfCloud is a framework that provides performance prediction services in an e-science cloud. The design relies on the adoption of a set of grid services able to create a Virtual Cluster (VC) and to predict the performance of a given target application on that particular VC.

Interoperability Systems: The Interoperability System (IS) acts as an intermediary between a certificate verifiers (relying parties) and the issuing CAs by managing (retrieving, elaborating and updating) the information needed to perform the extended path validation: the list of accredited CAs, the list of revocation sources and the Certificate Policies. The IS must perform two main tasks: (1) Online validation of the certificates' status, (2) Evaluation of the issuing CA's security level.

Reference Evaluation Methodology (REM): The REM is a security evaluation methodology to automatically evaluate the security level associated to a security infrastructure; it is made of three different components: (1) The policy formalization: defines how to express a security policy in a rigorous way, (2) The evaluation technique: the process to evaluate a previously formalized policy, (3) The reference levels: denotes how to get a security level relative to a minimum policy used as reference.

Policy and OCSP Based Interoperability System (POIS): POIS is an identity validation system, it is comprised of three basic elements: an OCSP Responder's database, a Policy Evaluator and an OCSP Responder itself. POIS offers the following features: Manage (retrieve, update) the list of CAs accredited in the federation; Manage (retrieve, update) the accredited CAs' Certificate Policies; Manage (retrieve, update) the accredited CAs' CRLs; Communicate validation information to relying parties over OCSP; Perform Extended Path Validation; Perform Basic Path Validation; Evaluate and/or Compare Certificate Policies through precomputed Security Levels.

418

Compilation of References

10 gen (2011) *10gen PAAS* Retreived from: www.10gen. com

About OpenNMS. (n.d.). Retrieved from http://www. opennms.org/about/

Achemlal, M., Gharout, S., & Gaber, C. (2011). Trusted platform module as an enabler for security in cloud computing. *Network and Information Systems Security Conference*, 1-6.

Alhamad, M., Dillon, T., & Chang, E. (2010). Conceptual SLA framework for cloud computing. *4th IEEE International Conference on Digital Ecosystems and Technologies (DEST)*, 606-610, doi:10.1109/DEST.2010.5610586

Altmann, J., Courcoubetis, C., & Risch, M. (2010). A marketplace and its market mechanism for trading commoditized computing resources *Annales des Télécommunications*, *65*(11-12), 653–667. doi:10.1007/ s12243-010-0183-1

Alvares de Oliveira Jr. & F., Ledoux, T. (2011). Self-management of applications QoS for energy optimization in datacenters. *Proceedings of the 2st Workshop on Green Computing Middleware (GCM'2011)*. New York, NY: ACM.

Amazon CloudWatch. (2011). Website, retrieved July 20, 2011 from http://aws.amazon.com/cloudwatch/

Amazon EC2. (2011). Retrieved from: http://aws.amazon. com/ec2.

Amazon Elastic Compute Cloud (Amazon EC2). (2010). Retrieved December 2011, from http://aws.amazon.com/ ec2/.

Amazon Inc. (2011), *Amazon Web Services, Amazon Corporation Inc*, Retrieved from: http://aws.amazon.com

Amazon Web Services LLC. (2011). Amazon elastic compute cloud. Website, retrieved July 20, 2011 from http://aws.amazon.com/ec2/

Anderson, C. (2011). *The Long Tail: How Endless Choice Is Creating Unlimited Demand*. New York, NY: Random House Business Books.

Anderson, D. P., & Fedak, G. (2006). The computational and storage potential of volunteer computing. In *CCGRID '06* (pp. 73–80). Washington, DC: IEEE Computer Society.

Andreolini, M., Colajanni, M., & Lancellotti, R. (2011). Assessing the overhead and scalability of system monitors for large data centers. In *Proceedings of the First International Workshop on Cloud Computing Platforms (CloudCP '11)*. ACM, New York, NY, USA.

Andreozzi, S., De Bortoli, N., Fantinel, S., Ghiselli, A., Tortone, G., & Vistoli, C. (2003). GridICE: A Monitoring Service for the Grid. In *Third Cracow Grid Workshop* (pp. 220–226).

Andreozzi, S., De Bortoli, N., Fantinel, S., Ghiselli, A., Rubini, G. L., Tortone, G., & Vistoli, M. C. (2005). GridICE: A monitoring service for Grid systems. *Future Generation Computer Systems*, *21*(4), 559–571. doi:10.1016/j.future.2004.10.005

Andrieux, A., Czajkowski, K., Dan, A., Keahey, K., Ludwig, H., Nakata, T., et al. (2011). GFD-R.192: Web Services Agreement Specification (WS-Agreement). *The Open Grid Forum Full Recommendation*. Retrieved November 15, 2011, from http://www.ogf.org/documents/ GFD.192.pdf.

Andrzejak, A., & Xu, Z. (2002). Scalable, Efficient Range Queries for Grid Information Services. In *Second IEEE International Conference on Peer-to-Peer Computing*. Washington, DC: IEEE Press.

Andrzejak, A., Kondo, D., & Anderson, D. (2010), Exploiting non-dedicated resources for cloud computing, in: *Network Operations and Management Symposium (NOMS* (pp. 341–348). doi:10.1109/NOMS.2010.5488488.

Apache libcloud python library., (2011), Retrieved from http://libcloud.apache.org/

Apache Software Foundation. (2011). *The Apache Hadoop Project* Retrieved from: http://www.hadoop.apache.org

Ardagna, D., Giunta, G., Ingraa, N., Mirandola, R., & Pernici, B. (2006). Qos-driven web services selection in autonomic grid environments. In *International conference on grid computing, high performance and distributed applications (gada).* Montpellier, France.

Ardagna, D., Panicucci, B., Trubian, M., & Zhang, L. (2010). Energy-Aware Autonomic Resource Allocation in Multi-tier Virtualized Environments. *IEEE Transactions on Services Computing*, 1-36. Published by the IEEE Computer Society. Retrieved from http://www.computer.org/portal/web/csdl/doi/10.1109/TSC.2010.42

Armbrust, M., Fox, A., Griffith, R., Joseph, A. D., Katz, R., Konwinski, A., et al. (2009). Above the Clouds: A Berkeley view of Cloud computing. *Technical Report UCB/EECS-2009-28*, Berkley, CA: University of California

Arnaud, J. (2009). MoKa: Modelisation et planification de capacite pour les systemes multi-etages. [MoKa: Modeling and capacity planning systems for multi-storey] *Les NOuvelles TEchnologies de la REpartition - Notere 2009 [New Technologies of Distributed Systems]*, Montreal, Canada.

Atkinson, B. (2002). *WS-Security Specification, Web Services Security 1.0.* Mendeley.

Automated Monitoring. (n.d.). Retrieved from http://www.logicmonitor.com/features/automated-configuration/

Babcock, C. (2009, 01 21). *Intel, Citrix To Collaborate On Virtualized Desktops.* Retrieved 04 25, 2011, from InformationWeek: http://www.informationweek.com

Baker, S. (2008), Google and the Wisdom of Clouds. *BusinessWeek* Retrieved from: http://www.businessweek.com/magazine/content/07 52/b4064048925836.htm

Baldoni, R., Querzoni, L., & Virgillito, A. (2005). *Distributed Event Routing in Publish/Subscribe Communication Systems: a Survey. Technical Report TR-1/06.* Rome, Italy: Universita´ di Roma

Balis, B., Bubak, M., Funika, W., Szepieniec, T., & Wismller, R. (2002). An infrastructure for grid application monitoring. In *Recent Advances in Parallel Virtual Machine and Message Passing Interface New York.* NY: Springer. doi:10.1007/3-540-45825-5_16

Bangeman, E. (2006, 09 07). *Microsoft and Cisco hook up on network security.* Retrieved 11 09, 2011, from Security: http://arstechnica.com

Baresi, L., Miraz, M., & Plebani, P. (2008). A Flexible and Semantic-Aware Publication Infrastructure for Web Services. In *Proceedings of the 20th international conference on Advanced Information Systems Engineering (CAiSE '08).* New York, NY: Springer

Barham, P., Dragovic, B., Fraser, K., Hand, S., Harris, T., Ho, A., et al. (2003). Xen and the art of virtualization. In *SOSP '03: Proceedings of the nineteenth ACM symposium on Operating systems principles*, (pp. 164–177) New York, NY: ACM.

Barnhart, C., Johnson, E. L., Nemhauser, G. L., & Savelsbergh, M. W. (1998). P. Branch-and-price: Column generation for solving huge integer programs. *Operations Research, 46*(3), 316–329. doi:10.1287/opre.46.3.316

Barton, T., Basney, J., Freeman, T., Scavo, T., Siebenlist, F., Welch, V., et al. (2006). Identity federation and attribute-based authorization through the globus toolkit, shibboleth, gridship, and myproxy. *In Proc. of 5th Annual PKI R&D Workshop.* Gaithersburg, MD: NIH

Baumann, A., & Peter, S. Schüpbach, A., Singhania, A., Roscoe, T., Barham, P., and Isaacs. R., (2009). Your computer is already a distributed system. Why isn't your OS? *In 12th Workshop on Hot Topics in Operating Systems*, May.

Baumann, A., Barham, P., Dagand, P., Harris, T., Isaacs, R., Peter, S., et al. (2010) *The Multikernel:* A new OS architecture for scalable multicore systems, *In the 22nd ACM Symposium on OS Principles*, Big Sky, MT, USA, October.

Bellur, U., Rao C. S. & S.D, M. K. (2010). Optimal Placement Algorithms for Virtual Machines. *Arxiv preprint arXiv10115064, (Vm)*, pp 1-16. Retrieved from http://arxiv.org/abs/1011.5064

Berger, S., Caceres, R., Goldman, K. A., Perez, R., Sailer, R., & Doorn, L. v. (2006). vTPM: Virtualizing the Trusted Platform Module. *USENIX SS'06 - USENIX Security Symposium - Vol. 15.* Boston: Association for Computing Machinery.

Bermbach, D., Klems, M., Tai, S., & Menzel, M. (2011). MetaStorage: A Federated Cloud Storage System to Manage Consistency-Latency Tradeoffs. In *IEEE 4th Conference on Cloud Computing (CLOUD). 2011.* Washington, DC: IEEE Press.

Bernstein, D., & Vij, D. (2010), Intercloud Security Considerations, In 2010 *IEEE Second International Conference on Cloud Computing Technology and Science*, (pp. 537-544), Nov. 2010

Bernstein, D., Ludvigson, E., Sankar, K., Diamond, S., & Morrow, M. (2009). Blueprint for the Intercloud – Protocols and Formats for Cloud Computing Interoperability. In *Proceedings of The Fourth International Conference on Internet and Web Applications and Services.* 328-336.

Bertino E, Paci F, Ferrini R, and Shang N (2009), Privacy-preserving digital identity management for cloud computing, *Data Engineering 32*,(1)

Bessani, A., Correia, M., Quaresma, B., Andre, F., & Sousa, P. (2011). DEPSKY: Dependable and Secure Storage in a Cloud-of-Clouds, *Proceedings of the sixth conference on Computer systems, EuroSys'11*, (, pp. 31—46) Salzburg, Austria: ACM

Bharambe, A. R., Agrawal, M., & Seshan, S. (2004). Mercury: Supporting scalable multi-attribute range queries. In *Proceedings of the ACM SIGCOMM*, New York, NY: ACM Press.

Bohra, A. E. H., & Chaudhary, V. (2010). VMeter: Power modelling for virtualized clouds. *2010 IEEE International Symposium on Parallel Distributed Processing Workshops and Phd Forum IPDPSW*, 1-8. Retrieved from http://ieeexplore.ieee.org/lpdocs/epic03/wrapper.htm?arnumber=5470907

Bonfire (2011). Retrieved 11/20, from http://www.bonfire-project.eu/

Boniface, M., Nasser, B., Papay, J., Phillips, S. C., Servin, A., Xiaoyu, Y., et al. (2010, 9-15 May 2010). *Platform-as-a-Service Architecture for Real-Time Quality of Service Management in Clouds.* Paper presented at the Internet and Web Applications and Services (ICIW), 2010 Fifth International Conference on.

Boniface, M., Phillips, S. C., & Sanchez-macian, A. (2007). Dynamic Service Provisioning Using GRIA SLAs. In *Proceedings of the International Workshop on Service-Oriented Computing (ICSOC'07)* Amsterdam, The Netherlands: IOS Press.

Bonvin, N., Papaioannou, T. G., & Aberer, K. (2009). Dynamic cost efficient replications in data Clouds. In *1th ACM Workshop on Automated Control for Datacenters and Clouds* (ACDC) (pp. 49-56), Barcelona, Spain: ACM Press.

Bradford, R., Kotsovinos, E., Feldmann, E., & Schioberg, H. (2007) Live wide-area migration of virtual machines including local persistent state. In *VEE '07: Proceedings of the 3rd international conference on Virtual execution environments*, (pp. 169–179) New York, NY: ACM

BRAIN - business objective driven reliable and intelligent grids for real business. (2010). Retrieved December 2011 from http://www.eu-brein.com/.

Brandic, I. (2009). Towards Self-Manageable Cloud Services. *33rd Annual IEEE International Computer Software and Applications Conference*, 128-133.

Brandic, I., Anstett, T., Schumm, D., Leymann, F., Dustdar, S., & Konrad, R. (2010). Compliant cloud computing (c3): Architecture and language support for user-driven compliance management in clouds. In *The 3rd international conference on cloud computing (ieee cloud 2010).* Miami, FL, USA.

Brandic, I., Music, D., Leitner, P., & Dustdar, S. (2009). Vieslaf framework: Enabling adaptive and versatile sla-management. In *Gecon2009. in conjunction with euro-par 2009.* Delft, The Netherlands.

Brandic, I., Benkner, S., Engelbrecht, G., & Schmidt, R. (2005). *Qos support for time-critical grid workflow applications. In 1st ieee international conference on e-science and grid computing*. Melbourne, Australia.

Brandt, J., Gentile, A., Mayo, J., Pebay, P., Roe, D., Thompson, D., & Wong, M. (2009). Resource monitoring and management with OVIS to enable HPC in Cloud computing environments, In *Proceedings of the IEEE International Symposium on Parallel & Distributed Processing, 2009. IPDPS 2009*. 1-8, 23-29

Breitgand, D., & Epstein, A. (2010) SLA-aware Placement of Multi-Virtual Machine Elastic Services in Compute Clouds., IBM *Technical Report, H-0287*

Breskovic, I., Maurer, M., Emeakaroha, V. C., Brandic, I., & Altmann, J. (2011). Towards autonomic market management in cloud computing infrastructures. In *International conference on cloud computing and services science - closer 2011*. Noordwijkerhout, the Netherlands.

Bruneo, D., Longo, F., & Puliafito, A. (2011). Evaluating energy consumption in a Cloud infrastructure. In *Proceedings of the 2011 IEEE International Symposium on World of Wireless, Mobile and Multimedia Networks* (WoWMoM) (pp. 1-6), Lucca, Italy: IEEE Computer Society.

Bugiel, S., Nürnberger, S., Sadeghi, A. R., & Schneider, T. (2011). TwinClouds - Secure Cloud Computing with Low Latency, In *Communications and Multimedia Security (CMS'11) conference*, LNCS.

Buyya, R., Abramson, D., & Giddy, J. (2001). A case for economy grid architecture for service oriented grid computing. In *Parallel and distributed processing symposium*.

Buyya, R., Beloglazov, A., & Abawajy, H. J. (2010). *Energy-efficient management of data center resources for cloud computing: a vision, architectural elements, and open challenges*. Melbourne, Australia: Cloud Computing and Distributed Systems (CLOUDS) Laboratory.

Buyya, R., Ranjan, R., & Calheiros, R. N. (2010). Inter-Cloud: Utility-Oriented Federation of Cloud Computing Environments for Scaling of Application Services. In *Proceedings of the 10th International Conference on Algorithms and Architectures for Parallel Processing (ICA3PP 2010)*, New York, NY: Springer.

Buyya, R., & Bubendorfer, K. (2008). *Market oriented grid and utility computing*. New Jersey, USA: John Wiley & Sons, Inc.

Buyya, R., Ranjan, R., & Calheiros, R. N. (2010). Lecture Notes in Computer Science: *Vol. 6081. InterCloud: Utility-Oriented Federation of Cloud Computing Environments for Scaling of Application Services*. Algorithms and Architectures for Parallel Processing.

Buyya, R., Yeo, C. S., Venugopal, S., Broberg, J., & Brandic, I. (2009). Cloud computing and emerging IT platforms: Vision, hype, and reality for delivering computing as the 5th utility. In *Future Generation Computing. System*, *25*(6), 599–616.

Calheiros, R. N., Ranjan, R., Beloglazov, A., De Rose, C. A. F., & Buyya, R. (2010) CloudSim: A Toolkit for Modeling and Simulation of Cloud Computing Environments and Evaluation of Resource Provisioning Algorithms, Software: Practice and Experience. New York, NY. USA Wiley Press.

Calheiros, R. N., Buyya, R., & De Rose, C. A. F. (2010). Building an automated and self-configurable emulation testbed for Grid applications. *Software, Practice & Experience, 40*(5), 405–429.

Camenisch, J., Hohenberger, S., Kohlweiss, M., Lysyanskaya, A., & Meyerovich, M. (2006), How to win the clonewars: efficient periodic n-times anonymous authentication, in *Proceedings of the 13th ACM conference on Computer and communications security, 2006*, (pp. 201–210.) New York, NY: ACM Press

Cameron, K. (2005). *The Laws of Identity*, Retrieved July 26, 2011, from http://www.identityblog.com/?p=352/#lawsofiden_topic3

Canonical switches to OpenStack for Ubuntu Linux Cloud. (2011). Retrieved from: http://www.zdnet.com/blog/opensource/canonical-switchesto-openstack-for-ubuntu-linux-cloud/8875, eJabber: Jabber/XMPP instant messaging server. (2011) Retrieved from: http://www.ejabberd.im/.

Cantor, S., et al. (2005) Assertions and Protocols for the OASIS Security Assertion Markup Language (SAML) V2.0. *OASIS Standard*, March 2005. Document ID saml-core-2.0-os http://docs.oasis-open.org/security/saml/v2.0/saml-core-2.0-os.pdf

Cappello, F., Caron, E., Dayde, M., Desprez, F., Jegou, Y., Primet, P., et al. (2005). Grid'5000: A large scale and highly reconfigurable grid experimental testbed. *6th IEEE/ACM International Workshop on Grid Computing.* 99–106.

Carr, N. (2008). *The Big Switch - Rewiring the World from Edison to Google.* New York, NY: W. W. Norton.

Carroll, S. B. (2005). *The New Science of Evo Devo - Endless Forms Most Beautiful.* New York: W. W. Norton & Co.

Casanova, H., Legrand, A., Zagorodnov, D., & Berman, F. (2000). Heuristics for scheduling parameter sweep applications in Grid environments. In *Proceedings of the Heterogeneous Computing Workshop (HCW'00),* New York, NY: Springer.

Casanova, H., Obertelli, G., Berman, F., & Wolski, R. (2000). The AppLeS Parameter Sweep Template: User-level Middleware for the Grid. In *Proceedings of the Supercomputing (SC'00),* New York, NY: ACM Press.

Casola, V., Luna, J., Manso, O., Mazzocca, N., Manel, M., & Rak, M. (2007). Interoperable grid pkis among untrusted domains: an architectural proposal. *In Proc. of the 2nd Grid and Pervasive Conference* (GPC2007) New York, NY: Springer

Casola, V., Mazzeo, A., Mazzocca, N., & Vittorini, V. (2007). A security metric for public key infrastructures. *Journal of Computer Security, vol. 15, no. 2.*

Casola, V., Cuomo, A., Rak, M., & Villano, U. (2010). *Security and performance trade-off in perfcloud. In the Proc. of VHPC2010.* New York, NY: Springer.

Casola, V., Lettiero, R., Rak, M., & Villano, U. (2010). *Access control in Cloud on grid: the PerfCloud case study. In the Proc. of SPCC2010.* New York, NY: Springer.

Cassandra, A. (2011). Retrieved from http://cassandra.apache.org/

Catteddu, D., & Hogben, G. (2009). Cloud Computing-Benefits, risks and recommendations for information security. In *ENISA.* Heraklion, Greece: ENISA. doi:10.1007/978-3-642-16120-9_9

Celesti, A., Tusa, F., Villari, M., & Puliafito, A. (2010). How to Enhance Cloud Architectures to Enable Cross-Federation. In *IEEE 3rd Conference on Cloud Computing (CLOUD). 2010.* Washington, DC: IEEE Press.

Celesti, A., Tusa, F., Villari, M., & Puliafito, A. (2010). Security And Cloud Computing: Intercloud Identity Management Infrastructure. In *Proceedings of The 19th IEEE International Workshops on Enabling Tech- nologies: Infrastructures for Collaborative Enterprises (WETICE 2010) - ETNGRID,* Washington, DC: IEEE Press

CertiVeR. (2006). *Certificate revocation and validation service.* Retrieved from www.certiver.com/.

Chadwick, D. (2009). Federated identity management. *Foundations of Security Analysis and Design, V,* 96–120. doi:10.1007/978-3-642-03829-7_3

Chaitanya, S., Butler, K., Sivasubramaniam, A., McDaniel, P., & Vilayannur, M. (2006). Design, implementation and evaluation of security in iSCSI-based network storage systems. *Storage Security and Survivability (StorageSS 2006).* Alexandria, USA. doi: 10.1145/1179559.1179564

Chan, G. (2011, 11 05). *Storage Virtualization & Scale-out Technology.* Retrieved 11 08, 2011, from Enterprise Features: http://enterprisefeatures.com

Chandra, A., & Weissman, J. (2009), Nebulas: using distributed voluntary resources to build Clouds, in: *Proceedings of the 2009 conference on Hot topics in cloud computing,* (p 2) Berkley, CA: USENIX Association

Chapman, C., Emmerich, W., Marquez, F. G., Clayman, S., & Galis, A. (2011). *Software Architecture Definition for On-demand Cloud Provisioning.* Special Issue of Cluster Computing.

Chappell, D. (2006). Introducing Windows CardSpace". MSDN. April 2006. Retrieved July 26, 2011, from http://msdn.microsoft.com/en-us/library/aa480189.aspx

Chef.,(2011), Retrieved from http://www.opscode.com/chef/

Chen, D., Dharmaraja, S., Chen, D., Li, L., Trivedi, K. S., Some, R. R., & Nikora, A. P. (2002). Reliability and availability analysis for the JPL remote explora-tion and experimentation system. In *Proceedings of the International Conference on Dependable Systems and Networks* (DSN) (pp. 337-342), Bethesda, MD, USA: IEEE Computer Society.

Chen, H., Zhou, C., & Xiong, N. (2010). Petri net modeling of the reconfigurable protocol stack for Cloud computing based control systems. In *Proceedings of the 1st International Conference on Cloud Computing* (CLOUDCOM) (pp. 393-400), Indianapolis, IN, USA: IEEE Computer Society.

Chen, J., & Lu, B. (2008). An universal flexible utility function in grid economy. In *Ieee pacific-asia workshop on computational intelligence and industrial application.*

Cheng, X., Shi, Y., & Li, Q. (2009). A multi-tenant oriented performance monitoring, detecting and scheduling architecture based on SLA, In *Proceedings of the 2009 Joint Conferences on Pervasive Computing (JCPC)* 599-604, 3-5

Cheng, W. K., Ooi, B. Y., & Chan, H. Y. (2010). Resource federation in grid using automated intelligent agent negotiation. *Future Generation Computer Systems, 26*(8), 1116–1126. doi:10.1016/j.future.2010.05.012

Choco. (2008). Choco: an Open Source Java Constraint Programming Library. *White Paper 14th International Conference on Principles and Practice of Constraint Programming CPAI08 Competition,* (10-02-INFO). Retrieved from http://www.emn.fr/z-info/choco-solver/pdf/choco-presentation.pdf

Ciardo, G., Blakemore, A., Chimento, P. F., Muppala, J. K., & Trivedi, K. S. (1993). Automated generation and analysis of Markov reward models using stochastic reward nets. In *Linear Algebra, Markov Chains and Queuing Models* (pp. 145–191). New York, NY, USA: Springer. doi:10.1007/978-1-4613-8351-2_11

Cisco Inc. (2011). *Cisco Cloud Computing* Retrieved from: http://www.cisco.com/en/US/netsol/ns976/index.html

Clark, C., Fraser, K., Hand, S., Hansen, J. G., Jul, E., Limpach, C., et al. (2005). Live migration of virtual machines. In *Proceedings of the 2nd ACM/USENIX Symposium on Networked Systems Design and Implementation (NSDI),* (pp. 273–286) New York, NY: ACM

Clayman, S., Galis, A., & Mamatas, L. (2010). Monitoring virtual networks with Lattice. In: *Management of Future Internet* - ManFI 2010, URL http://www.manfi.org/2010/

Clayman, S., Galis, A., Chapman, C., Toffetti, G., Rodero-Merino, L., Vaquero, L., et al. (2010). Monitoring Service Clouds in the Future Internet. In *Towards the Future Internet - Emerging Trends from European Research,* pp (115–126), Amsterdam, The Netherlands: IOS Press

Clayman, S., Galis, A., Chapman, C., Toffetti, G., Rodero-Merino, L., & Vaquero, L. M. (2010). *Monitoring Service Cloud in the Future Internet. Towards the Future Internet - Emerging Trends from European Research, ISBN.* Amsterdam, The Netherlands: IOS Press.

Cloud Computing Use Case Discussion Group. (2010). Cloud Computing Use Cases http://cloudusecases.org

Cloud Data Management Interface. (CDMI, 2011) Specification Version 1.0.1. Retrieved September 15, 2011, from: http://cdmi.sniacloud.com/

Cloud Security Alliance. (2009). *Security guidance for critical areas of focus in cloud computing.* New York, NY: Springer.

Cloud Security Alliance. (2011): Retrieved 06 21, 2011 from: https://cloudsecurityalliance.org/

Cloudstone., (2011), Retrieved from http://radlab.cs.berkeley.edu/wiki/Projects/Cloudstone

CloudWatch. Amazon CloudWatch, (n.d.) Retrieved from: http://aws.amazon.com/cloudwatch/

Collectd - The system statistics collection daemon. (n.d.). Retrieved from http://collectd.org/

Colling, D. J., Martyniak, J., McGough, A. S., Krenek, A., Sitera, J., & Mulac, M., & Dvorák, F. (2010). Real time monitor of grid job executions. *Journal of Physics: Conference Series, 219*(6). doi:10.1088/1742-6596/219/6/062020

Colmenares, J. A., Bird, S., Cook, H., Pearce, P., Zhu, D., Shalf, J., et al. (2010). Tesselation: Space-Time Partitioning in a Manycore Client OS *In 2nd* USENIX Workshop on Hot Topics in Parallelism (HotPar'10). Berkeley, CA, USA. June.

Computing (CLOUD), vol., no., pp.123-130, 5-10 July 2010.

Comuzzi, M., & Pernici, B. (2009). A framework for QoS-based Web service contracting. *ACM Transactions on the Web, 3*(3), 1-52. Retrieved from http://portal.acm.org/citation.cfm?doid=1541822.1541825

Comuzzi, M., Kotsokalis, C., Spanoudakis, G., & Yahyapour, R. (2009). Establishing and Monitoring SLAs in Complex Service Based Systems. In *Proceedings of the 2009 IEEE International Conference on Web Services* (ICWS '09) 783-790 Washington, DC, USA IEEE Computer Society

CONTRAIL Consortium. (2010). *CONTRAIL Project Homepage*. Retrieved from http://contrail-project.eu/

Cooke, A., Gray, A. J. G., Ma, L., Nutt, W., et al. (2003). R-GMA: An information integration system for Grid monitoring. In *Proceedings of the 11th International Conference on Cooperative Information Systems*, (pp. 462–481.) New York, NY: Springer

Craciun, C. D., Petcu, D., & Rak, M. (2011). TOWARDS A CROSS PLATFORM CLOUD API Components for Cloud Federation. *In Proc. of CLOSER 2011*, Noordwijkerhout, The Netherland

Crump, G. (2010, 10 21). *Articles*. Retrieved 6 14, 2011, from Storage switzerland: http://www.storage-switzerland.com

Dawkins, R. (1989). *The Selfish Gene*. New York: Oxford University Press.

De Vries, S., & Vohra, R. V. (2003). Combinatorial auctions: A survey. *INFORMS Journal on Computing, 15*(3), 284–309. doi:10.1287/ijoc.15.3.284.16077

Debusmann, M., & Keller, A. (2003). Sla-Driven Management Of Distributed Systems Using The Common Information Model, In *Proceedings of the IFIP/IEEE International Symposium on Integrated Management.*

Dell Inc. (2011), *Dell cloud computing solutions* http://www.dell.com/cloudcomputing

Deltacloud., (2011), Retrieved from http://incubator.apache.org/deltacloud/

Demir, O., Head, M. R., Ghose, K., & Govindaraju, M. (2007). Securing Grid Data Transfer Services with Active Network Portals. In *Proc. of the IEEE International Parallel and Distributed Processing Symposium*, (pp. 1-8.) Washington, DC: IEEE CS.

Deneubourg, L.-J., Aron, S., Goss, S., & Pasteels, M. J. (1990). The self-organizing exploratory pattern of the argentine ant. *Journal of Insect Behavior, 3*(2), 159–168. doi:10.1007/BF01417909

Di Nitto, E., Ghezzi, C., Metzger, A., Papazoglou, M., & Pohl, K. (2008). A journey to highly dynamic, self-adaptive service-based applications. Automated Software Engineering Journal, 2008.

Di Nitto, E., Ghezzi, C., Metzger, A., Papazoglou, M., & Pohl, K. (2008). A journey to highly dynamic, self-adaptive service-based applications. *Automated Software Engineering, 25*, 313–341. doi:10.1007/s10515-008-0032-x

Di Stefano, A., Morana, G., & Zito, D. (2009). A P2P strategy for QoS discovery and SLA negotiation in Grid environment. In *Future Generation Computer Systems Journal 25*, (8)862-875

Dickersbach, J. T., & Keller, G. (2010). *Production Planning and Control with SAP ERP* (2nd ed.). Singapore: SAP PRESS.

Dimitrakos, T. (2010), Common Capabilities for Service Oriented Infrastructures and Platforms: An Overview, In *Eighth IEEE European Conference on Web Services*, (pp.181-188), Washington, DC: IEEE Press.

Distefano, S., Cunsolo, V., Puliafito, A., & Scarpa, M. (2010). Cloud@Home: A New Enhanced Computing Paradigm. In Furht, B., & Escalante, A. (Eds.), *Handbook of Cloud Computing*, (pp. 575–594). New York, NY: Springer. doi:10.1007/978-1-4419-6524-0_25

Distributed Management Task Force, Inc. (2009) Open Virtualization Format Specification, Version 1.0.0, document no. DAP0243; see http://www.dmtf.org/standards/published_ documents/DSP0243_1.0.0.

DMTF. (2003). CIM Concepts White Paper CIM Versions 2.4+. *Technical Report DSP0110*, Distributed Management Task Force

DMTF's Open Virtualization Format. (OVF, 2011), Retrieved November 30, 2011 from: http://www.dmtf.org/standards/ovf

Dobson, G., & Sanchez-Macian, A. (2006). Towards unified qos/sla ontologies. In *Ieee services computing workshops (scw)* (pp. 18-22). Chicago, Illinois, USA.

Dobzinski, S., Nisan, N., & Schapira, M. (2010). Approximation algorithms for combinatorial auctions with complement-free bidders. *Mathematics of Operations Research, 35*(1), 1–13. doi:10.1287/moor.1090.0436

Dorigo, M., Caro, Di G., & Gambardella, M. L. (1999). Ant algorithms for discrete optimization. *Artificial Life, 5*(1), 137–172. doi:10.1162/106454699568728

Dyson, G. B. (1997). *Darwin among the Machines, the evolution of global intelligence*, Reading, MA, Helix Books, Addition Wesley Publishing Company

EDGeS 3G Bridge (2011). Website: http://sourceforge.net/projects/edges-3g-bridge/

Edmonds A., Sam Johnston, Thijs Metsch, Gary Mazzaferro (2010) Open Cloud Computing Interface - Core & Models. Retrieved from ttp://occi-wg.org/about/specification/

EGEE Consortium. (2004). *Enabling Grid for E-sciencE (EGEE) Portal*. Retreived from http://www.eu-egee.org

ElasticHosts., (2011), Retrieved from http://www.elastichosts.com/

Ellahi, T., Hudzia, B., Li, H., Lindner, M. A., & Robinson, P. (2011). The enterprise Cloud Computing Paragdim. In *Cloud Computing: Principles and Paradigms (Wiley Series on Parallel and Distributed Computing)*. Hoboken, NJ: Wiley. doi:10.1002/9780470940105.ch4

Elmroth, E., & Larsson, L. (2009). Interfaces for Placement, Migration, and Monitoring of Virtual Machines in Federated Clouds, In *Proceedings of the Eighth International Conference on Grid and Cooperative Computing, 2009. GCC '09.*253-260, 27-29

Elmroth, E., & Tordsson, J. (2006). A Grid resource broker supporting advance reservations and benchmark-based resource selection. In *Applied Parallel Computing*. New York, NY: Springer. doi:10.1007/11558958_128

EMC Atmos Online. (2010). https://mgmt.atmosonline.com/.

Emeakaroha, V. C., Brandic, I., Maurer, M., & Dustdar, S. (2010). Low level Metrics to High level SLAs - LoM2HiS framework: Bridging the gap between monitored metrics and SLA parameters in Cloud environments, In *Proceedings of the 2010 International Conference on High Performance Computing and Simulation (HPCS),* 48-54

Emeakaroha, V. C., Calheiros, R. N., Netto, M. A. S., Brandic, I., & De Rose, C. A. F. (2010). DeSVi: An Architecture for Detecting SLA Violations in Cloud Computing Infrastructures. In *Proceedings of the International ICST Conference on Cloud Computing (CloudComp'10)*

Emig, M., Brandt, F., Kreuzer, S., & Abeck, S. (2007). *Identity as a Service–Towards a Service-Oriented Identity Management Architecture, Dependable and Adaptable Networks and Services* (pp. 1–8). Belin, Germany: Springer.

Emmerich, W., Butchart, B., Chen, L., Wassermann, B., & Price, S. L. (2005). Grid Service Orchestration using the Business Process Execution Language (BPEL). *Journal of Grid Computing, 3*(3- 4):283–304.

Energy Star. (2007). *Report to Congress on Server and Data Center Energy Efficiency Public Law 109-431.* Environmental Protection, 109, 431. US Environmental Protection Agency: ENERGY STAR Program. Retrieved from http://www.osti.gov/energycitations/product.biblio.jsp?osti_id=929723

Engates, J. (2009, 07 27). *Hybrid clouds the way to go.* Retrieved 04 20, 2011, from NETWORK WORLD: http://www.networkworld.com

ENISA. (2009). *Cloud Computing Risk Assessment.* ENISA.

ENISA. (2011). *Security and Resilience in Governmental Clouds. Making an informed decision.* ENISA.

Enomaly Inc. (2011), *Enomaly Elastic Computing Platform (ECP)* Retrieved from: http://www.enomaly.com/

EnStratus. (2011). Website, retrieved July 20, 2011 from http://www.enstratus.com/

Eucalyptus. (2011), Retrieved from www.eucalyptus.com

Eu-Emi Consortium. (2011). *Europen Middleare Initiative (Eu-Emi) Portal*. Retreived from http://www.eu-emi.eu

EUGRIDPMA. (2008). *EU Grid PMA Charter*. Retrieved from http://www.eugridpma.org/charter

European Network and Information Security Agency. ENISA (2011). Security & Resilience in Governmental Clouds. Making an informed decision. Annex III Reservoir Architecture Description. Retrieved May 15, 2011, from http://www.reservoir-fp7.eu/uploads/Documents/Security%20%20Resilience%20in%20Governmental%20Clouds_ENISA.pdf

Faban., (2011), Retrieved from http://www.faban.org/

Fedak, G., Germain, C., Neri, V., & Cappello, F. (2001): Xtremweb: a generic global computing system. Cluster Computing and the Grid, 2001. In *Proceedings. First IEEE/ACM International Symposium* (pp. 582–587) Washington, DC: IEEE Press

Feller, E., Rilling, L., & Morin, C. (2011). Energy-Aware Ant-Colony Based Workload Placement in Clouds. *12th IEEE/ACM International Conference on Grid Computing (GRID-2011)*. Retrieved from: http://hal.inria.fr/inria-00626042/

Feller, E., Rilling, L., & Morin, C. (2011). Snooze: A Scalable and Autonomic Virtual Machine Management Framework for Private Clouds. *INRIA research report* (7833). Retrieved from http://hal.inria.fr/hal-00651542/en

Feller, E., Rilling, L., Morin, C., Lottiaux, R., & Leprince, D. (2010). Snooze: A Scalable, Fault-Tolerant and Distributed Consolidation Manager for Large-Scale Clusters. *2010 IEEE/ACM International Conference on Green Computing and Communications*, 125-132.

Ferg, B., & Associates. (2007). OpenID Authentication 2.0 - Final. Retrieved July 26, 2011, from http://openid.net/specs/openid-authentication-2_0.html

Ferraiolo, D., & Kuhn, D. R. (1992). Role-based access control. *In Proc. of the 15th National Computer Security Conference*, pp. 554-563. Baltimore, MD: The Institute

Ferrer, A. J. (2012). OPTIMIS: a Holistic Approach to Cloud Service Provisioning. *Future Generation Computer Systems, 28*(1), 66–77. doi:10.1016/j.future.2011.05.022

Ferreto, T. C., De Rose, C. A. F., & De Rose, L. (2002). RVision: An open and high configurable tool for cluster monitoring. In *Proceedings of the 2nd IEEE/ACM International Symposium on Cluster Computing and the Grid (CCGRID)*, Washington, DC: IEEE Press

Ferreto, C. T., Netto, M., Calheiros, R., & De Rose, C. (2011). Server consolidation with migration control for virtualized data centers. *Future Generation Computer Systems, 27*(8), 1027–1034. doi:10.1016/j.future.2011.04.016

Ferretti, S., Ghini, V., & Panzieri, F. Pellegrini, & M., Turrini, E., (2010). QoS–Aware Clouds. In *Proceedings of the IEEE 3rd International Conference on Cloud Computing (CLOUD)*.321-328

Ficco M. (2010). Achieving Security by Intrusion-Tolerance Based on Event Correlation,in Special Issue on Data Dissemination for Large scale Complex Critical Infrastructures, *International Journal of Network Protocols and Algorithms (NPA), 2*,(3,). 70-84.

Ficco, M., & Rak, M. (2011). Intrusion Tolerant Approach for Denial of Service Attacks to Web Services. In *Proc. of the 1st Inter. Conference on Data Compression, Communications and Processing, 2011*. Washington, DC: IEEE CS.

Flexiscale. (2011), Retrieved 11/20 from www.flexiscale.com

Floyer, D. (2010, 08 12). *Integrating Storage and Network Virtualization: A prerequisite for an effective Cloud Computing Model*. Retrieved 11 07, 2011, from Wikibon: http://wikibon.org

Fontan, J., Vazquez, T., Gonzalez, L., Montero, R., & Llorente, I. (2008). OpenNebula: The open source virtual machine manager for cluster computing. In: *Open Source Grid and Cluster Software Conference* New York, NY: Springer

Ford, M., Lew, K., Spanier, S., & Stevenson, T. (1997). *Internetworking Technologies Handbook*. Indianapolis, IN: Cisco Press.

Forgy, C. L. (1979). *On the efficient implementation of production systems*. Pittsburg, PA: Carnegie Mellon University.

Foster, I., Kesselman, C., Nick, J. M., & Tuecke, S. (2002). The physiology of the Grid: An open grid services architecture for distributed systems integration. Retrieved from http://www.globus.org/research/papers/ogsa.pdf.

Foster, I., Welch, V., Kesselman, C., Mulmo, O., Pearlman, L., Tuecke, S., et al. (2004). X.509 proxy certificates for dynamic delegation. *In Proc. of the 3rd Annual PKI R&D Workshop.* Gaithersburg, MD: NIH

Foster, I., Zhao, Y., Raicu, I., & Lu, S. (2008). Cloud Computing and Grid Computing 360-Degree Compared. *In Grid Computing Environments Workshop,* (pp 1-10) New York, NY: Springer

Foster, I. (2005). Globus Toolkit Version 4: Software for Service-Oriented Systems. In Jin, H., Reed, D., & Jiang, W. (Eds.), *Journal of Computer Science and Technology* (Vol. 3779, pp. 2–13). New York, NY: Springer. doi:10.1007/11577188_2

Frumkin, M., & Van der Wijngaart, R. F. (2001). NAS grid benchmarks: A tool for grid space exploration. *High Performance Distributed Computing, 2001. Proceedings. 10th IEEE International Symposium on,* 315-322.

Fu, W., & Huang, Q. (2006). GridEye: A Service-oriented Grid Monitoring System with Improved Forecasting Algorithm, In *Proceedings of the Fifth International Conference on Grid and Cooperative Computing Workshops, 2006. GCCW '06.* 5-12

FutureGrid. (2011), Retrieved from www.futuregrid.org

Gabow, H. N. (1990) Data structures for weighted matching and nearest common ancestors with linking. *In SODA,* (pp 434–443)

Garg, S. K., Buyya, R., & Siegel, H. J. (2010). Time and cost trade-off management for scheduling parallel applications on utility grids. *Future Generation Computer Systems, 26*(8), 1344–1355. doi:10.1016/j.future.2009.07.003

GATNER. (2008), Seven cloud-computing security risks. Retrieved November 30, 2011, from: http://www.gartner.com/

Gauvrit, G., Daubert, E., & André, F. (2010). SAFDIS: A Framework to Bring Self-Adaptability to Service-Based Distributed Applications. *36th EUROMICRO Conference on Software Engineering and Advanced Applications,* 211-218. Retrieved from http://ieeexplore.ieee.org/lpdocs/epic03/wrapper.htm?arnumber=5598099

Geer, D. (2009). The OS faces a brave new world. *Computer, 42*(10), 15–17. doi:10.1109/MC.2009.333

Ghemawat, S., Gobioff, H., Leung, S.T. The Google File System. *SIGOPS Oper. Syst. Rev. 37*(5) 29–43

Ghosh, R., Longo, F., Naik, V. K., & Trivedi, K. S. (2010). Quantifying resiliency of IaaS Cloud. In *Proceedings of the IEEE Symposium on Reliable Distributed Systems (SRDS)* (pp. 343-347), Los Alamitos, CA, USA: IEEE Computer Society.

Ghosh, R., Trivedi, K. S., Naik, V. K., & Kim, D. S. (2010). End-to-End Performability analysis for Infrastructure-as-a-Service Cloud: An interacting stochastic models approach. In *Proceedings of the Pacific Rim International Symposium on Dependable Computing* (PRDC) (pp. 125-132), Tokyo, Japan: IEEE Computer Society.

Gillespie, M. (2009, June 1). *Intel Trusted Execution Technology.* Retrieved 4 15, 2011, from Intel Software Network: http://software.intel.com

Gilmore, P. C., & Gomory, R. E. (1963). A linear programming approach to the cutting stock roblem-Part II. *Operations Research, 11,* 863–888. doi:10.1287/opre.11.6.863

Gkantsidis, C., & Mihail, M. (2005). Hybrid search schemes for unstructured peer-to-peer networks. In *INFOCOM 2005, 24th Annual Joint Conference of the IEEE Computer and Communications Societies.* Washington,DC: IEEE Press

GLPK. (2011). *GNU linear programming kit.* Retrieved from http://www.gnu.org/s/glpk/

Gogouvitis, S., Konstanteli, K., Waldschmidt, S., Kousiouris, G., Katsaros, G., & Menychtas, A. (2012). Workflow management for soft real-time interactive applications in virtualized environments. *Future Generation Computer Systems, 28*(1), 193–209. doi:10.1016/j.future.2011.05.017

GoGrid. (2011), Retrieved from www.gogrid.com

Goiri, I., Guitart, J., & Torres, J. (2010). Characterizing Cloud Federation for Enhancing Providers' Profit, In Proceedings of the 2010 IEEE 3rd International Conference on Cloud

Google App Engine. (2010). Retrieved December 2011 from http://code.google.com/appengine/.

Google Inc. (2011), *Google app engine* Retrieved from: http://code.google.com/appengine/

Gopalakrishnan, A. (2009). Cloud Computing Identity Management. *SETLabs Briefings.*, *7*, 45–54.

Graffi, K., Stingl, D., Gross, C., Nguyen, H., & Kovacevic, A. Steinmetz, R. (2010), Towards a p2p cloud: Reliable resource reservations in un-reliable p2p systems, In: *Parallel and Distributed Systems (ICPADS), IEEE 16th International Conference* (pp. 27–34)doi:10.1109/ICPADS.2010.34.

Green, L. (2006). *Service level agreements: an ontological approach. In 8th international conference on electronic commerce: The new e-commerce: innovations for conquering current barriers, obstacles and limitations to conducting successful business on the internet, icec '06*. New York, NY, USA.

Greenpeace, I. (2010). *Make IT Green: Cloud computing and its contribution to climate change*. Retrieved from http://www.greenpeace.org/usa/Global/usa/report/2010/3/ make-it-green-cloud-computing.pdf

Gruschka, N., & Jensen, M. (2010). Attack Surfaces: Taxonomy for Attacks on Cloud Services. In *proc. of the 3rd Int. IEEE Conf. on Cloud Computing, 2010*, (pp. 279-279). Washington, DC: IEEE CS Press.

Gruschka, N., & Lo Iacono, L. (2009). Vulnerable Cloud: SOAP Message Security Validation Revisited. In Proc. of the IEEE Int. Conf. on Web Services. Los Angeles, 2009. IEEE CS Press.

Gunter, D., Tierney, B., Crowley, B., Holding, M., & Lee, J. (2000). NetLogger: a toolkit for distributed system performance analysis, In *Proceedings of the 8th International Symposium on Modeling, Analysis and Simulation of Computer and Telecommunication Systems*.267-273

Hacking, S. & Hudzia. B. (2009) Improving the live migration process of large enterprise applications. In *VTDC '09: Proceedings of the 3rd international workshop on Virtualization technologies in distributed computing*, (pp. 51–58) New York, NY: ACM

Hammer-Lahav, E. (2010). RFC 5849: The OAuth 1.0 protocol *Internet Engineering Task Force, 54*, 1–39.

Hanna, S., & Molina, J. (2010, 03 24). *Cloud Security Questions?* Retrieved 11 07, 2011, from Cloud Computing Jornal: http://cloudcomputing.sys-con.com

Han-Zhang, W., & Liu-Sheng, H. (2010). An improved trusted cloud computing platform model based on daa and privacy ca scheme. In International Conference on Computer Application and System Modeling (ICCASM),pp. V13–33 – V13–39, 2010.

Haq, I. U., Brandic, I., & Schikuta, E. (2010). SLA Validation in Layered Cloud Infrastructures. LNCS, 6296, 153-164 Retrieved from http://www.springerlink.com/content/4j22m37153275444/

Haque, A., Alhashmi, S. M., & Parthiban, R. (2011). A survey of economic models in grid computing. *Future Generation Computer Systems*, *27*(8), 1056–1069. doi:10.1016/j.future.2011.04.009

Haring, G., Marie, R., Puigjaner, R., & Trivedi, K. S. (2001). Loss Formulae and Their Application to Optimization for Cellular Networks. In *IEEE Transaction on Vehicular Technology* (pp. 664–673). Washington, DC, USA: IEEE Computer Society.

Harney, E., Goasguen, S., Martin, J., Murphy, M., & Westall, M. (2007) The efficacy of live virtual machine migrations over the internet. In *VTDC '07: Proceedings of the 3rd international workshop on Virtualization technology in distributed computing*, (pp. 1–7) New York, NY: ACM, Kernel Based Virtual Machine. KVM-kernel-based virtualization machine white paper, (2006) Retrieved from: http://www.linux-kvm.org

Harris, D. (2011, 06 16). *Cloud legislation takes center stage on Capitol Hill*. Retrieved 06 29, 2011, from Gigaom: http://gogaom.com

Hasselmeyer, P. (2007). Removing the Need for State Dissemination in Grid Resource Brokering. In *5th International Workshop on Middleware for Grid Computing (MGC 2007)*.New York, NY ACM Press.

Hasselmeyer, P., & d'Heureuse, N. (2010). Towards Holistic Multi-Tenant Monitoring for Virtual Data Centers. In *2010 IEEE/IFIP Network Operations and Management Symposium Workshops* (pp. 350-356). Piscataway, NJ: IEEE.

Hermenier, F., Lawall, J., Menaud, J. M., & Muller, G. (2011). Dynamic Consolidation of Highly Available Web Applications. *Research Report*. INRIA. Retrieved from http://hal.inria.fr/inria-00567102/PDF/RR-7545.pdf

Hermenier, F., Lorca, X., Menaud, J. M., Muller, G., & Lawall, J. (2009). Entropy: a consolidation manager for clusters. *The 2009 International Conference on Virtual Execution Environments VEE09*, (41), 41-50. Retrieved from http://portal.acm.org/citation.cfm?id=1508300

Hershey, P., & Runyon, D. (2007). SOA Monitoring for Enterprise Computing Systems, In *Proceedings of the 11th IEEE International Enterprise Distributed Object Computing Conference (EDOC 2007)*,443

Hirel, C., Tuffin, B., & Trivedi, K. S. (2000). SPNP: Stochastic Petri Nets. Version 6. In *Proceedings of the 11th International Conference on Technology of Object-Oriented Languages and Systems* (TOOLS) (p.354), Malaga, Spain: Springer.

Hoffa, C., Mehta, G., Freeman, T., Deelman, E., Keahey, K., Berriman, B., & Good, J. (2008). On the Use of Cloud Computing for Scientific Workflows. *Proceedings of SWBES 2008, Indianapolis*. New York, NY: Springer

Housley, R., et al. (2002). *Internet Engineering Task Force, Rfc3280 internet x.509 public key infrastructure certificate and certificate revocation list (crl) profile*. Retrieved from www.ietf.org/rfc/rfc3280.txt.

HP. Intel, Yahoo! (2011), *Open Cirrus Open Cloud Computing Research Testbed* Retrieved from: https://opencirrus.org/

Hu, F., Qiu, M., Li, J., Grant, T., Tylor, D., McCaleb, S., et al. (2011). A Review on Cloud Computing: Design Challenges in Architecture and Security. *Journal of Computing and Information Technology - CIT*, 25-55.

Huang, H., & Wang, L. (2010). P&P: A Combined Push-Pull Model for Resource Monitoring in Cloud Computing Environment, In *Proceedings of the 2010 IEEE 3rd International Conference on Cloud Computing (CLOUD)*.260-267.

Hunt, O., Konar, M., Junqueira, P. F., & Reed, B. (2010). ZooKeeper: wait-free coordination for internet-scale systems. *2010 USENIX conference on USENIX annual technical conference* (USENIXATC'10).

IBM ILOG CPLEX 12.1.(n.d.) http://www-01.ibm.com/-software/integration/optimization/-cplex-optimizer.

IBM SmatCloud Enterprise™ (2001). Retrieved from: www.ibm.com/services/us/en/cloud-enterprise/

IBM. (2011). Mathematical programming vs. Constraint programming. Retrieved from http://www-01.ibm.com/software/integration/optimization/cplex-cp-optimizer/mp-cp/

ILOG CPLEX. (2011). *High-performance software for mathematical programming and optimization*. Retrieved from http://www.ilog.com/products/cplex/

Inc, I. B. M. (2011), *IBM Cloud* Retrived from: http://www.ibm.com/ibm/cloud/

INCITS. (2006, 02 17). *Fiber Channel Security Protocols*. Retrieved 11 05, 2011, from T11 Project: http://www.t10.org

IPXE. (2010). *Open Source Boot Firmare*. Retrieved 11 12, 2011, from Ipxe: http://ipxe.org/

Irmos, IRMOS project, (n.d.) Retrieved from: http://www.irmosproject.eu/

Jacobson, V., Smetters, D. K., Thornton, J. D., Plass, M. F., Briggs, N. H., & Braynard, R. L. (2009), Networking named content. In: *Proceedings of the 5th international conference on Emerging networking experiments and technologies*. (pp. 1–12)., New York, NY: ACM, http://doi.acm.org/10.1145/1658939.1658941

Javadi, B., Kondo, D., Vincent, J., & Anderson, D. (2010). Discovering statistical models of availability in large distributed systems: An empirical study of seti@home. In *IEEE Transaction on Parallel and Distributed Systems* (pp. 1896–1903). Washington, DC, USA: IEEE Computer Society. doi:10.1109/TPDS.2011.50

Jclouds (2010). Jclouds Homepage. Retrieved from http://code.google.com/p/jclouds/

Jégou, Y. (2011). Open Computing Infrastructures for Elastic Services: Contrail Approach. Invited Speak presented at the meeting 2nd Workshops on Software Services, West University of Timisoara, Timisoara, Romania

Jégou, Y. (2011). *Contrail Approach. In 2nd Workshops on Software Services*. Timisoara, Romania: Open Computing Infrastructures for Elastic Services.

Jensen, M., & Gruschka, N. (2008). Flooding Attack Issues of Web Services and Service-Oriented Architectures. *In Proc. of the Workshop on Security for Web Services and Service-Oriented Architectures (SWSOA'08)*, (pp. 117–122.)

Jensen, M., & Schwenk, J. (2009). The accountability problem of flooding attacks in service-oriented architectures. In Proc. of the 4th Int. Conf. on Availability, Reliability *and Security (ARES'09)*, (pp. 25-32). Washington DC, USA: IEEE CS.

Jensen, M., Gruschka, N., & Luttenberger, N. (2008). The Impact of Flooding Attacks on Network-based Services. In *Proceedings of the IEEE Int. Conf. on Availability, Reliability and Security (ARES), 2008.* Washington, DC: IEEE Press

Jensen, M., Schwenk, J., Gruschka, N., & Lo Iacono, L. (2006). On Technical Security Issues in Cloud Computing. In *Proc. of the IEEE Inter. Conference on Cloud Computing,* (pp.109-116.) Washington, DC: IEEE CS.

Joshi, K. R., Bunker, G., Jahanian, F., Moorsel, A. P. A. V., & Weinman, J. (2009). Dependability in the Cloud: Challenges and opportunities. In *Proceedings of the 39th annual IEEE/IFIP International Conference on Dependable Systems and Networks* (DSN) (pp. 103-104), Lisbon, Portugal: IEEE Computer Society.

Kansal, A., Liu, J., Singh, A., Nathuji, R., & Abdelzaher, T. (2010). Semantic-less coordination of power management and application performance. *ACM SIGOPS Operating Systems Review*, 44(1), 66. Retrieved from http://portal. acm.org/citation.cfm?doid=1740390.1740406

Kansal, A., Zhao, F., Liu, J., Kothari, N., & Bhattacharya, A. A. (2010). Virtual machine power metering and provisioning. Proceedings of the *1st ACM symposium on Cloud computing,* Retrieved from http://portal.acm.org/citation.cfm?doid=1807128.1807136

Kantara Initiative. (2009). The Kantara Initiative. Retrieved July 26, 2011, from http://kantarainitiative.org/

Katsaros, G., & Gallizo, G. Kübert, R., Wang, T., Fitó, J.O., & Henriksson, D. (2011). A Multi-level Architecture for Collecting and Managing Monitoring Information in Cloud Environments. In *1st International Conference on Cloud Computing and Services Science (CLOSER 2011).*

Katsaros, G., Kousiouris, G., Gogouvitis, S., Kyriazis, D., & Varvarigou, T. (2010). *A service oriented monitoring framework for soft real-time applications.* Paper presented at the Service-Oriented Computing and Applications (SOCA), 2010 IEEE International Conference on. Washington, DC: IEEE Press

Katsaros, G., Kübert, R., & Gallizo, G. (2010). Building a Service-Oriented Monitoring Framework with REST and Nagios. In *IEEE International Conference on Services Computing (SCC)* Washington, DC: IEEE Press.

Kecskemeti, G., Terstyanszky, G., Kacsuk, P., & Nemeth, Zs. (2011). An approach for virtual appliance distribution for service deployment. *Future Generation Computer Systems*, 27(3), 280–289. doi:10.1016/j.future.2010.09.009

Kephart, J. O., & Chess, D. M. (2003). The vision of autonomic computing, In *Computer, 36*(1)41- 50Kilpatrick, C., & Schwan, K., (1991). ChaosMON —Application-specific Monitoring and Display of Performance Information for Parallel and Distributed systems. In *SIGPLAN Not. 26*(12)57-67.

Kephart, J. O., Chan, H., Das, R., Levine, D. W., Tesauro, G., Rawson, F., & Lefurgy, C. (2007). Coordinating multiple autonomic managers to achieve specified power-performance tradeoffs. *Fourth International Conference on Autonomic Computing ICAC07*, 24-24. Retrieved from http://ieeexplore.ieee.org/lpdocs/epic03/wrapper.htm?arnumber=4273118

Keren, D., Sharfman, I., Schuster, A., & Livne, A. (2011). Shape Sensitive Geometric Monitoring. *Knowledge and Data Engineering, IEEE Transactions on, PP*(99), 1-1.

Kertesz, A., Kacsuk, P., Iosup, A. & Epema, D. H.J. (2008). Investigating peer-to-peer meta-brokering in Grids, *Technical report*, TR-0170, Institute on Resource Management and Scheduling, *CoreGRID – Network of Excellence.*

Kertesz, A., Kecskemeti, G., & Brandic, I. (2011). Autonomic SLA-aware Service Virtualization for Distributed Systems, In proceedings of the 19th Euromicro International Conference on Parallel, Distributed and Network-Based Computing, *IEEE Computer Society*, 503-510.

Kertesz, A., & Kacsuk, P. (2010). GMBS: A new middleware service for making grids interoperable. *Future Generation Computer Systems, 26*(4), 542–553. doi:10.1016/j.future.2009.10.007

Khanna, G., Beaty, K., Kar, G., & Kochut, A. (2006). Application performance management in virtualized server environments. *10th IEEE/IFIP Network Operations and Management Symposium*, 373-381.

Kim, D. S., Machida, F., & Trivedi, K. S. (2009). Availability Modeling and Analysis of a Virtualized System. In *Proceedings of the Pacific Rim International Symposium on Dependable Computing* (PRDC) (pp. 365-371), Seoul, Korea: IEEE Computer Society.

Kirby, G., Dearle, A., Macdonald, A., & Fernandes, A. (2010). *An Approach to Ad hoc Cloud Computing.* St. Andrews, Scotland: University of St Andrews.

Kiril (2011). *Top 25 European Cloud PRoviding Rising Stars to Watch - Complete List.* Retrieved 11/08/2011 from http://www.cloudtweaks.com/2011/04/top-25-european-cloud-providing-rising-stars-to-watch-complete-list/

Kivity, A. (2007). KVM: the linux virtual machine monitor," in *OLS '07: The 2007 Ottawa Linux Symposium,* (pp. 225–230) New York, NY: Springer

Kivity, A., Lublin, U., & Liguori, A. (2007). kvm: the Linux Virtual Machine Monitor. *Reading and Writing, 1*, 225–230.

Ko M, and G, Shehab M. (2009) Privacy-Enhanced User-Centric Identity Management, *Proc. IEEE Int'l Conf. Communications,* (pp. 998–1002) Washington DC, USA: IEEE Press.

Koller, B., & Schubert, L. (2007). Towards autonomous sla management using a proxy-like approach. *Multiagent Grid Systems, 3*(3).

Koller, R., Verma, A., & Neogi, A. (2010). WattApp: an application aware power meter for shared data centers. *Proceeding of the 7th international conference on Autonomic computing* (p. 31–40). ACM. Retrieved from http://portal.acm.org/citation.cfm?id=1809049.1809055

Koller, B., & Schubert, L. (2007). Towards autonomous SLA management using a proxy-like approach. In *Multiagent Grid System, 3*(3), 313–325.

Kolodner, E. K., Shulman-Peleg, A., Naor, D., Brand, P., Dao, M., & Eckert, A. (2012). Data-intensive Storage Services on Clouds: Limitations, Challenges and Enablers. In Petcu, D., & Poletti, J. V. (Eds.), *European Research Activities in Cloud Computing New Castle upon Tyne.* UK: Cambridge Scholars Publishing.

Koomey, J. G., & D, P. (2007). *Estimating Total Power Consumption by the U. S. and the World.* Analytics Press. Retrieved from https://files.me.com/jgkoomey/98ygy0

Kulkarni, V. G. (2010). *Modeling and Analysis of Stochastic Systems.* Boca Raton, FL, USA: CRC Press - Taylor & Francis Group.

Kumaraswamy, S., Lakshminarayanan, S., Stein, M. R. J., & Wilson, Y. (2010), "Domain 12: Guidance for Identity & Access Management V2. 1," Retrieved July 26, 2011, from http://www.cloudsecurityalliance.org/.

KVM. (2011). Kernel based virtual machine. Retrieved, from http://www.linux-kvm.org/

Kyriazis, D., Menychtas, A., Kousiouris, G., Oberle, K., Voith, T., & Boniface, M. (2011). *A Real-time Service Oriented Infrastructure. Control, 1(2).* Global Science and Technology Forum.

L1. (2011). Retrieved November 10, from http://mathworld.wolfram.com/L1-Norm.html

Lancki, B., Dixit, A., & Gupta, V. (1996, 08 01). *Mobile-IP: Transparent Host Migration on the Internet.* Retrieved 04 21, 2011, from LinuxJournal: http://www.linuxjournal.com

Langton, C. G. (1989). Artificial Life. In *Santa Fe Institute Studies in the Sciences of Complexity (Vol. 6).* Addison Wesley.

Latanicki, J., & Villari, M. Massonet P., and Naqvi S. (2009). From Grids To Clouds Shift In Security Services Architecture, In *CGW'09 - Cracow Grid Workshop*, Krakow, Poland.

Léger, M., Ledoux, T., & Coupaye, T. (2010). Reliable Dynamic Reconfigurations in a Reflective Component Model. *ComponentBased Software Engineering*, 74-92. Retrieved from http://www.springerlink.com/index/58HQ758200009817.pdf

Legrand, I. C., Newman, H. B., Voicu, R., Cirstoiu, C., Grigoras, C., Toarta, M., & Dobre, C. (2009). MonALISA: An agent based, dynamic service system to monitor, control and optimize distributed systems. *Computer Physics Communications*, *180*(12), 2472–2498. doi:10.1016/j.cpc.2009.08.003

Lehmann, D. J., O'Callaghan, L., & Shoham, Y. (2002). Truth revelation in approximately efficient combinatorial auctions. *Journal of the ACM*, *49*(5), 577–602. doi:10.1145/585265.585266

Lemos, R. (2006, 01 26). *Researchers: Rootkits headed for BIOS*. Retrieved 11 12, 2011, from Security Focus: http://www.securityfocus.com

Lewis, K. D., & Lewis, J. E. (2009). Web Single Sign-On Authentication using SAML. *Internationl Journal ofComputer Science Issues*, *2*, 41-48.

Li, B. Li, J., Huai, J., Wo, T., Li, Q. & Zhong, L. (2009). EnaCloud: An energy-saving application live placement approach for cloud computing environments. *2009 IEEE International Conference on Cloud Computing*, 17-24.

Li, L. E., & Woo, T. (2010). VSITE: A scalable and secure architecture for seamless L2 enterprise extension in the cloud. *Secure Network Protocols (NPSec)*, *5*, pp. 31-36. Kyoto. doi: 10.1109/NPSEC.2010.5634451

LibVirt. (2011). Libvirt: The virtualization API. Retrieved 6 July, 2011, from http://libvirt.org/

Lindner, M., Marquez, F. G., Chapman, C., Clayman, S., Henriksson, D., & Elmroth, E. (2010). The Cloud Supply Chain: A Framework for Information, Monitoring, Accounting and Billing. In *2nd International ICST Conference on Cloud Computing (CloudComp 2010)*.

Liu, H., Xu, Z.-C., Jin, H., Gong, J., & Liao, X. (2011). Performance and energy modeling for live migration of virtual machines. 20th *international symposium on High performance distributed computing (HPDC '11)*.

Lloriente, I. M., Montero, R. S., Sotomayor, B., Breitgand, D., Maraschini, A., Levy, E., & Rochwerger, B. (2011). *Management of Virtual Machines for Cloud Infrastructures, Cloud Computing Principles and Paradigms, 157—191, Series on Parallel and Distributed Computing*. Wiley.

Longo, F., Ghosh, R., Naik, V. K., & Trivedi, K. S. (2011). A Scalable Availability Model for Infrastructure-as-a-Service Cloud. In *Proceedings of the 41st annual IEEE/IFIP International Conference on Dependable Systems and Networks* (DSN) (pp. 335-346), Hong Kong, China: IEEE Computer Society.

Loutas, N., Peristeras, V., Bouras, T., Kamateri, E., Zeginis, D., & Tarabanis, K. (2010). Towards a Reference Architecture for Semantically Interoperable Clouds. In Cloud Computing Technology and Science (CloudCom), 2010 IEEE Second International Conference on.

Lucas-Simarro, J. L., Moreno-Vozmediano, R., Montero, R. S., & Llorente, I. M. (2011). Dynamic Placement of Virtual Machines for Cost Optimization in Multi-Cloud Environments. *In Proceedings of the 2011 International Conference on High Performance Computing & Simulation (HPCS 2011)*. 1-7.

Luna, J., Ghani, H., Germanus, D., & Suri, N. (2011), A Security Metrics Framework for the Cloud, Proceedings of the SECRYPT 2011 Conference.

Luna, J., Manso, O., & Manel, M. (2006). Ocsp for grids: Comparing prevalidation versus caching. *In Proc. of 7th IEEE/ACM International Conference on Grid Computing*, Barcelona.

Luna, J., Manso, O., & Manel, M. (2006). Using ogro and certiver to improve ocsp validation for grids. *In Proc. of the 1st Grid and Pervasive Conference* (GPC2006). New York, NY: Springer

Lv, Q., Cao, P., Cohen, E., Li, K., & Shenker, S. (2002). Search and replication in unstructured peer-to-peer networks. In Proceedings of the 16th international conference on Supercomputing (ICS '02).

Mainkar, V., & Trivedi, K. S. (1996). Sufficient conditions for existence of a fixed point in stochastic reward net-based iterative models. In *IEEE Transactions on Software Engineering* (pp. 640–653). Washington, DC, USA: IEEE Computer Society. doi:10.1109/32.541435

Malone, T. W. (1990). Organizing information systems: Parallels between human organizations and computer systems. Scott P. Robertson (Ed.), *Cognition, Computing and Cooperation*. Greenwood Publishing Company.

Mancini, E. P., Rak, M., & Villano, U. (2009). Perfcloud: Grid services for performance-oriented development of cloud computing applications. *In S. Reddy (Ed.).* (pp. 201-206.) New York, NY: WETICE, IEEE Computer Society

Manifesto, O. C. dedicated to the belief that the cloud should be open, (2011) Retrieved from: http://www.opencloudmanifesto.org/.

Mao, O., Kaashoek, F., Morris, R., Pesterev, A., Stein, L., Wu, M., et al. (2008) Corey: an operating system for many cores, *In the 8th USENIX Symposium on Operating Systems Design and Implementation* OSDI '08, San Diego, California, December.

Markoff, J. (1999, 2 29). Intel Goes to Battle as Its Embedded Serial Number Is Unmasked. *The New York Times*, p. Retrieved from www.nyt.com on 6/7/2001.

Marosi, A. Cs. & Kacsuk, P. (2011). Workers in the clouds. In *Proceedings of the 2011 19th Euromicro Conference on Parallel, Distributed and Network-based Processing*, 519–526.

Marsan, M. A., Balbo, G., & Conte, G. (1984). A class of generalized stochastic petri nets for the performance evaluation of the multiprocessor systems. In *ACM Transactions on Computer Systems* (pp. 93–122). New York, NY, USA: ACM Press.

Marshall, P., Keahey, K., & Freeman, T. (2010). Elastic site: Using clouds to elastically extend site resources. In *Proceedings of the 2010 10th IEEE/ACM International Conference on Cluster, Cloud and Grid Computing.* 43–52.

Martin, R. (2007), The Red Shift Theory. *InformationWeek* Retrieved from: http://www.informationweek.com/news/hardware/showArticle.jhtml?articleID=201800873

Massie, M. L., Chun, B. N., & Culler, D. E. (2004). The Ganglia distributed monitoring system: Design, implementation and experience. *Parallel Computing, 30*(7), 817–840. doi:10.1016/j.parco.2004.04.001

Mastroianni, C., Meo, M, Papuzzo, G. (2011). Self-economy in cloud data centers: statistical assignment and migration of virtual machines. *Euro-Par* (1) 407-418.

Matos, M., Sousa, A., Pereira, J., & Oliveira, R. (2009). *CLON: Overlay network for clouds.* Nuremberg, Germany: ACM.

Maurer, M., Brandic, I., & Sakellariou, R. (2010). Simulating Autonomic SLA Enactment in Clouds using Case Based Reasoning. In *Proceedings of the ServiceWave*, Ghent, Belgium

Maurer, M., Brandic, I., Emeakaroha, V. C., & Dustdar, S. (2010) Towards Knowledge Management in Self-adaptable Clouds. In *Proceeding of the 4th International Workshop of Software Engineering for Adaptive Service-Oriented Systems (SEASS'10)*

Maurer, M., Emeakaroha, V. C., Brandic, I., & Altmann, J. (2012). Cost-Benefit Analysis of an SLA Mapping Approach for Defining Standardized Cloud Computing Goods. *Future Generation Computer Systems, 28*(1), 36–47. doi:10.1016/j.future.2011.05.023

Meggiddo, N., & Modha, D. S. (2003) ARC: A self-tuning, low overhead replacement cache. In *FAST '03: Proceedings of the 2nd USENIX Conference on File and Storage Technologies*, (pp. 115–130). Berkley, CA, USA: USENIX Association

Mell, P., & Grance, T. (2009). The NIST Definition of Cloud Computing. *National Institute of Standards and Technology, 53(6)*, 50. NIST. Retrieved from http://csrc.nist.gov/groups/SNS/cloud-computing/cloud-def-v15.doc

Mell, P., & Grance, T. (2009). *The NIST Definition of Cloud Computing.* New York, NY: Springer.

MeSsAGE Lab-Monash eScience and Grid Engineering Laboratory (2011), *Nimrod/G* Retrieved from: http://www.messagelab.monash.edu.au/NimrodG

Messner, E. (2009, 03 31). *Cloud Security Alliance Formed to Promote Best Practices*. Retrieved 06 21, 2011, from Cloud Computing: http://www.networkworld.com

Microsoft Azure. (2010). Retrieved December 2011 from http://www.microsoft.com/windowsazure/.

Microsoft Corp. (2011). Windows Live ID. Retrieved July 26, 2011, from https://accountservices.passport.net/ppnetworkhome.srf?lc=1033&mkt=EN-US

Microsoft Inc. (2011), *Azure services platform* Retrieved from: http://www.microsoft.com/cloud/

Microsoft. (2011, 10 10). *Hardware.* Retrieved 11 05, 2011, from Microsoft MSDN: http://msdn.microsoft.com/en-us/windows/hardware/gg463149

Mikkilineni, R., Seyler, I., (2011), *"Parallax - A New Operating System Prototype Demonstrating Service Scaling and Service Self-Repair in Multi-core Servers,"* Enabling Technologies: Infrastructure for Collaborative Enterprises (WETICE), 2011 20th IEEE International Workshops on, vol., no., pp.104-109, 27-29.

Milojicic, D., Lorente, I. M., & Montero, R. S. (2011). OpenNebula: A Cloud Management Tool. *IEEE Internet Computing, 15*(2), 11–14. doi:10.1109/MIC.2011.44

Mirashe, S. P., & Kalyankar, N. V. (2010). Cloud Computing. *Communications of the ACM, 51*(7), 9. Retrieved from http://arxiv.org/abs/1003.4074

Mironov, I. (2005, November). *Hash functions: Theory, attacks, and applications.* Retrieved 06 22, 2011, from Microsoft Research: http://research.microsoft.com

Mitchell, W. M. (1992). *Complexity: The Emerging Science at the Edge of Order and Chaos* (p. 218). London: Penguin Books.

Mohamed, A. (2009, 06 10). *A history of cloud computing.* Retrieved 05 09, 2011, from computerweekly.com: http://www.computerweekly.com

Morana, G., Mikkilineni, R., (2011), *"Scaling and Self-repair of Linux Based Services Using a Novel Distributed Computing Model Exploiting Parallelism,"* Enabling Technologies: Infrastructure for Collaborative Enterprises (WETICE), 2011 20th IEEE International Workshops on, vol., no., pp.98-103, 27-29

Moreno-Vozmediano, R., Montero, R. S., & Llorente, I. M. (2011). Multicloud deployment of computing clusters for loosely coupled MTC applications. *Parallel and Distributed Systems. IEEE Transactions on, 22*(6), 924–930.

Moreno-Vozmedian, R., Montero, R. S., & Llorente, I. M. (2009). *Elastic management of cluster-based services in the cloud.* Barcelona, Spain: ACM.

Morgan, R. L., Cantor, S., Carmody, S., Hoehn, W., & Klingenstein, K. (2004). Federated Security: The Shibboleth Approach. *EDUCAUSE Quarterly, 27*(4).

Morris, C. (2011). *Sony PlayStation Facing Yet Another Security Breach,* New York, from http://www.cnbc.com/id/43079509

mOSAIC cloud. (2011), Retrieved from www.mosaic-cloud.eu

mOSAIC Consortium (2010). *mOSAIC Project Homepage.* Retrieved from http://www.mosaic-cloud.eu

Murtazaev, A., & Oh, S. (2011). *Sercon: Server Consolidation Algorithm using Live Migration of Virtual Machines for Green Computing.* Available from: http://tr.ietejournals.org/text.asp?2011/28/3/212/81230

Murty, G. K. (1983). *Linear programming.* New York, NY: John Wiley & Sons.

Nagios, The Industry Standard in IT Infrastructure Monitoring: (2010) http://www.nagios.org.

National Institute of Standards and Technology (NIST), Guidelines on Security and Privacy in Public Cloud Computing. Retrieved September 15, 2011, from http://csrc.nist.gov/publications/drafts/800-144/Draft-SP-800-144_cloud-computing.pdf

Neumann, D., Stößer, J., & Weinhardt, C. (2008). Bridging the adoption gap – developing a roadmap for trading in grids. *Electronic Markets, 18*(1), 65–74. doi:10.1080/10196780701797664

Newman, H. B., Legrand, I. C., & Bunn, J. J. (2001). A distributed agent-based architecture for dynamic services. *CHEP2001 Beijing Sept.*

Newman, H. B., Legrand, I. C., Galvez, P., Voicu, R., & Cirstoiu, C. (2003). MonALISA: A Distributed Monitoring Service Architecture. *Arxiv preprint cs0306096,* cs.DC/0306, 8.

Newman, H. Legrand, I., Galvez, P., Voicu, R., & Cirstoiu, C. (2003). MonALISA: A distributed monitoring service architecture. In *Proceedings of CHEP03*, La Jolla, California.

Nginx., (2011), from http://www.nginx.net/

Nguyen Van, H., Dang Tran, F., & Menaud, J.-M. (2010). Performance and Power Management for Cloud Infrastructures. *IEEE 3rd International Conference on Cloud Computing*, 329-336. Retrieved from http://ieeexplore.ieee.org/lpdocs/epic03/wrapper.htm?arnumber=5557975

Nguyen, D., Lelli, F., Taher, Y., Parkin, M., Papazoglou, M., & van den Heuvel, W. J. (2011). Blueprint template support for engineering cloud-based services. In W. Abramowicz, I. Llorente, M. Surridge, A. Zisman, & J. Vayssière (Eds.), *Towards a service-based internet, 6994*, 26-37. Heidelberg, Germany: Springer Berlin.

Nicol, D. M., Sanders, W. H., & Trivedi, K. S. (2004). Model-based evaluation: From dependability to security. In *IEEE Transactions on Dependable and Secure Computing* (pp. 48–65). Washington, DC, USA: IEEE Computer Society.

Nimbus (2011). *The Nimbus Cloud.* Retrieved July 26, 2011, from http://www.nimbusproject.org/

Nimis, J., Anandasivam, A., Borissov, N., Smith, G., Neumann, D., & Wirström, N. (2008). SORMA - business cases for an open grid market: Concept and implementation. In Springer (Ed.), *5th international workshop on grid economics and business models (gecon '08)* (pp. 173-184).

Nisan, N., Roughgarden, T., Tardos, E., & Vazirani, V. (2007). *Algorithmic Game Theory.* New York, NY, USA: Cambridge University Press. doi:10.1017/CBO9780511800481

NIST. (2011). *NIST Cloud Computing Standards Roadmap (NIST SP 500-291)* Retrieved 12/8/2011 from http://www.nist.gov/itl/cloud/

Núñez D., Agudo I., Drogkaris P., and Gritzalis S. (2011), Identity Management Challenges for Intercloud Applications, in C. Lee, J.-M. Seigneur, J. J. Park, and R. R. Wagner, Eds *Secure and Trust Computing, Data Management, and Applications, vol. 187,.* (pp. 198-204.) Berlin Heidelberg, Germany: Springer.

Nurmi, D., Wolski, R., Grzegorczyk, C., Obertelli, G., Soman, S., Youseff, L., & Zagorodnov, D. (2009). The Eucalyptus Open-Source Cloud-Computing System. *Cluster Computing and the Grid, 2009. CCGRID '09. 9th IEEE/ACM International Symposium on.* (pp. 124–131). Washington, DC: IEEE Press.

Nyren, A., Edmonds, A., Papaspyrou, A., & Metsch, T. (2011). GFD-P-R.183: Open Cloud Computing Interface - Core. *The Open Grid Forum Proposed Recommendation.* Retrieved August 8, 2011, from http://www.ogf.org/documents/GFD.183.pdf.

OASIS. (2007, 03 19). *WS-Trust 1.3.* Retrieved 06 06, 2011, from OASIS: http://docs.oasis-open.org

OASIS. (2011). *The Organization for the Advancement of Structured Information Standards.* Retrieved July 26, 2011, from http://www.oasis-open.org/

OCCI Work Group. (2011), *The Open Cloud Computing Interface* Retrieved from: http://occi-wg.org/

OGRO. (2006). *The open grid ocsp client api.* Retrieved from http://globusgrid.certiver.com/info/ogro.

Oldham, N., Verma, K., Sheth, A. P., & Hakimpour, F. (2006, May). *Semantic ws-agreement partner selection. In 15th international conference on world wide web, www 2006.* Edinburgh, Scotland, UK.

Olio., (2011), from http://incubator.apache.org/olio/

Open Cloud Computing Interface. (OCCI, 2011) An open community-lead specifications delivered through the Open Grid Forum (OGF). Retrieved November 30, 2011, from: http://occi-wg.org/

Open Cloud Manifesto. (2009). *Open Cloud Manifesto.* Retrieved from http://www.opencloudmanifesto.org

Open virtualization format specification(2010). No. DSP0243)DMTF.

Open, I. D. (2007, 12 05). *OpenID Authentication 2.0 - Final.* Retrieved 11 12, 2011, from Openid: http://openid.net

OpenFlow. (2011). *OpenFlow.* Retrieved 07 19, 2011, from http://www.openflow.org

OpenNebula. (2011). *OpenNebula 2.0 Architecture.* Retrieved July 12, 2011, from http://opennebula.org/documentation:archives:rel2.0:architecture

OpenQRM Developer Community. (2011), *openQRM open-source Data-center management platform* Retrieved from: http://www.openQRM.com

OpenQRM official site: (2010) http://www.openqrm.com.

OpenStack. Retrieved 11/20, (2011), Retrieved from www.openstack.org

OpenVPN - open source VPN., (2011),Retrieved from http://openvpn.net/

OpenVZ. (2011). Retrieved November 15, 2011, from http://wiki.openvz.org/Main_Page

Optimis Consortium. (2010). OPTIMIS Project Homepage. Retrieved from http://www.optimis-project.eu/

ORACLE Inc. (2011), *ORACLE Cloud Computing* Retrieved from: http://www.oracle.com/us/technologies/cloud/index.htm

Ortega, J. M., & Rheinboldt, W. C. (1970). *Iterative Solution of Nonlinear Equations in Several Variables*. New York, NY, USA: Academic Press.

Paletta, M., & Herrero, P. (2009). A MAS-Based Negotiation Mechanism to Deal with Service Collaboration in Cloud Computing. *International Conference on Intelligent Networking and Collaborative Systems*,147-153, doi: 10.1109/INCOS.2009.21.

Parizo, E. (2011, 06 27). *Gartner: Prepare today or face cloud computing security problems tomorrow*. Retrieved 07 02, 2011, from SearchCloudSecurity: http://searchcloudsecurity.techtarget.com

Paton, N., De Aragão, M., Lee, K., Fern, A., & Sakellariou, R. (2009). *Optimizing utility in cloud computing through autonomic workload execution*. IEEE Data Eng. Bull.

Pauley, W. A. (2010, November-December 8(6)). *Cloud Provider Transparency*. Retrieved 6 14, 2011, from Security & Privacy, IEEE: http://ieeexplore.ieee.org. doi: 10.1109/MSP.2010.140

Pearson, S. (2009). *Taking account of privacy when designing cloud computing services*. IEEE Computer Society.

Pegasus Communications. (2010). The *Systems Thinker*, from www.thesystemsthinker.com

Petcu, D., Craciun, C. D., & Rak, M. (2011). TOWARDS A CROSS PLATFORM CLOUD API Components for Cloud Federation. *Paper presented at the meeting CLOSER 2011*, Noordwijkerhout, The Netherland

Petrie, E. K., Smith, B., & Yorke-smith, N. (2004). Dynamic symmetry breaking in constraint programming and linear programming hybrids. In *European Starting AI Researcher Symposium*.

Petrucci, V., Loques, O., & Mossé, D. (2010). Dynamic optimization of power and performance for virtualized server clusters. *Proceedings of the 2010 ACM Symposium on Applied Computing SAC*, 10, 263. Retrieved from http://portal.acm.org/citation.cfm?doid=1774088.1774144

Potter, S. (2005) Using binary delta compression (BDC) technology to update Windows XP and Windows Server 2003, Retrieved from http://www.microsoft.com/downloads/details.aspx

Pottier, R., Léger, M., & Menaud, J. (2010). A Reconfiguration Language for Virtualized Grid Infrastructures. *Distributed Applications and Interoperable Systems* (p. 42–55). Retrieved from http://www.springerlink.com/index/L65456V26417MH71.pdf

Pountain, D. (1987). Run-length encoding. *Byte*, *12*(6), 317–319.

Precision in IT infrastructure engineering - CFEngine., (2011) Retreived from http://cfengine.com/

Prodan, R., & Ostermann, S. (2009). A survey and taxonomy of infrastructure as a service and web hosting Cloud providers, In *Proceedings of the 10th IEEE/ACM International Conference on Grid Computing* 17-25

Puppet labs., (2011) Retrieved from http://www.puppetlabs.com/

Quan, D. M., Altmann, J. (2009a). Resource allocation algorithm for the light communication Grid-based workflows within an SLA context. *International Journal of Parallel, Emergent and Distributed Systems, 24*(1).

Quan, D. M., & Altmann, J. (2009b). Grid business models for brokers executing SLA-based workflows. In *Rajkumar Buyya, Kris Bubendorfer. Market-Oriented Grid and Utility Computing*. New York, NY, USA: Wiley. doi:10.1002/9780470455432.ch7

Querna, P. (2010). *Apache LibCloud*. Presented at the meeting Velocity Ignite 2010. Retrieved from: http://paul.querna.org/slides/libcloud-ignite.pdf

Quesnel, F., & Lebre, A. (2011): Cooperative Dynamic Scheduling of Virtual Machines in Distributed Systems. In *VHPC'11: 6th Workshop on Virtualization in High-Performance Cloud Computing*. New York, NY: Springer.

Rackspace Cloud. (2011). Website, retrieved July 20, 2011 from http://www.rackspace.com/cloud/

Rackspace., (2011),Retrieved from http://www.rackspace.com/

Ranjan, R., & Buyya, R. (2009). *Decentralized Overlay for Federation of Enterprise Clouds. Handbook of Research on Scalable Computing Technologies* (Li, K., Eds.). USA: IGI Global.

Recordon, D., & Reed, D. (2006). Openid 2.0: a platform for user-centric identity management. *In Proc. of the second ACM workshop on Digital identity management,* (pp. 11-16)New York, NY: ACM.

Rellermeyer, J. S., Alonso, G., & Roscoe, T. (2007). Building, Deploying, and Monitoring Distributed Applications with Eclipse and R-OSGI. In *Proceedings of the 2007 OOPSLA workshop on eclipse technology eXchange* (eclipse '07). 50-54 New York, NY, USA: ACM

Reservoir Consortium. (2011). RESERVOIR webpage, Retrieved from http://www.reservoir-fp7.eu/

RESERVOIR. The RESERVOIR project home page. (2008) http://www.reservoir-fp7.eu

Right Scale. Right scale. (n.d.) http://www.rightscale.com/m/.

RightScale. (2011). Website, retrieved July 20, 2011 from http://www.rightscale.com/

Risch, M., & Altmann, J. (2009). Enabling open cloud markets through ws-agreement extensions. In *Service level agreements in grids workshop, in conjunction with grid 2009.*

Risch, M., Brandic, I., & Altmann, J. (2009, November). Using sla mapping to increase market liquidity. In *Nfpslam-soc 2009 in conjunction with the 7th international joint conference on service oriented computing.* Stockholm, Sweden.

Risch, M., Altmann, J., Guo, L., Fleming, A., & Courcoubetis, C. (2009). *The gridecon platform: A business scenario testbed for commercial cloud services. In 6th international workshop on grid economics and business models.* Delft, The Netherlands.

Rochwerger, B., Breitgand, D., Levy, E., Galis, A., Nagin, K., Llorente, I. M., et al. (2009). *The reservoir model and architecture for open federated cloud computing*

Rochwerger, B., Galis, A., Levy, E., Caceres, J. A., Breitgand, D., Wolfsthal, Y., et al. (2009b). Management technologies and requirements for next generation service oriented infrastructures. In 11th *IFIP/IEEE International Symposium on Integrated Management*. Washington, DC: IEEE Press.

Rochwerger, B., Berltgand, D., Epstein, A., Hadas, D., Loy, I., & Nagin, K. (2011). Reservoir – When One Cloud is not enough. *Computer, 44*(3), 44–51. doi:10.1109/MC.2011.64

Rochwerger, B., Breitgand, D., Levy, E., Galis, A., Nagin, K., & Llorente, L. (2009). The RESERVOIR Model and Architecture for Open Federated Cloud Computing. *IBM Journal of Research and Development, 53*(4). doi:10.1147/JRD.2009.5429058

Rodero-Merino, L., Vaquero, L. M., Gil, V., Galan, F., Fontan, J., & Montero, R. S. (2010, October). From infrastructure delivery to service management in clouds. *Future Generation Computer Systems, 26*(8), 1226–1240. doi:10.1016/j.future.2010.02.013

Rodriguez, J., & Klug, J. (2011). Federated Identity Patterns in a Service-Oriented world. *The Architecture Journal*. Retrieved July 26, 2011, from http://msdn.microsoft.com/en-us/library/cc836393.aspx

Romano, L., & Ficco, M. (2011). A Generic Intrusion Detection and Diagnoser System Based on Complex Event Processing. In *Proc. of the 1th International Conference on Data Compression, Communications and Processing, 2011*, (pp. 275-284.) Washington, DC:IEEE CS Press.

Rossi, F., Van Beek, P., & Walsh, T. (2006). *Handbook of Constraint Programming*. Amsterdam, The Netherlands: Elsevier.

Rouzaud-Cornabas, J. (2010). A distributed and collaborative dynamic load balancer for virtual machine. In *5th Workshop on Virtualization in High-Performance Cloud Computing (VHPC)*.

Rubens, P. (2011, 06 16). *Does Virtualization Deliver on Its Promise?* Retrieved 11 08, 2011, from Trends: http://www.serverwatch.com

Sahai, A., Graupner, S., Machiraju, V., & Van Moorsel, A. (2003). Specifying and monitoring guarantees in commercial grids through SLA. *CCGrid 2003 3rd IEEE ACM International Symposium on Cluster Computing and the Grid 2003 Proceedings*, 292-299. Washington, DC: IEEE.

Sahin, O. D., Gupta, A., Agrawal, D., & El Abbadi, A. (2004). A Peer-to-peer Framework for Caching Range Queries. In *20th International Conference on Data Engineering (ICDE'04)*, Washington, DC: IEEE Press.

Salehi, M. A., & Buyya, R. (2010). Lecture Notes in Computer Science: *Vol. 6081. Adapting market-oriented scheduling policies for cloud computing* (pp. 351–362). Algorithms and Architectures for Parallel Processing.

Salesforce.com. (2010). Retrieved December 2011, http://www.salesforce.com.

Samimi, F. A., McKinley, P. K., & Sadjadi, S. M. (2006). Mobile service clouds: A self-managing infrastructure for autonomic mobile computing services. In *LCNS 3996* (pp. 130–141). Berlin, Germany: Springer-Verlang.

SAMLLibertyDiffs. (2010). *Differences Between SAML V2.0 and Liberty ID-FF 1.2*. Retrieved July 26, 2011, from https://wiki.shibboleth.net/confluence/display/SHIB/SAMLLibertyDiffs

SAP IoT Definition. (2011) Retrieved from: http://services.future-internet.eu/images/1/16/A4_Things_Haller.pdf.

Sapuntzaki, C.P., Chandra, R., Pfaff, B.,Chow, J., Lam, M.S., and Rosenblum, M.. (2002) Optimizing the migration of virtual computers. *SIGOPS Oper. Syst. Rev.*, 36(SI):377–390

Scavo, T., Cantor, S., & Dors, N. (2005, 06 02). *Shibboleth Architecture*. Retrieved 11 08, 2011, from Internet2: http://shibboleth.internet2.edu

Schmidt, M., Fallenbeck, N., Smith, M., & Freisleben, B. (2010). Efficient distribution of Virtual Machines for cloud computing. In *Proceedings of the 2010 18th Euromicro Conference on Parallel, Distributed and Network-based Processing.* 564-574.

Schopf, J. M., Raicu, I., Pearlman, L., Miller, N., Kesselman, C., Foster, I., & D'Arcy, M. (2006). *Monitoring and Discovery in a Web Services Framework: Functionality and Performance of Globus Toolkit MDS4.* MCS Preprint #ANL/MCS-P1315-0106. Retrieved August 8, 2011, from http://www.mcs.anl.gov/uploads/cels/papers/P1315.pdf.

Schubert, L., Jeffery, K., & Neidecker-Lutz, B. (2010). *The Future of Cloud Computing*. Brussels, BE: European Commission.

Sedna, Native XML Database System: (2011) Retrieved from: http://modis.ispras.ru/sedna/.

Segal, B., Buncic, P., Quintas, D., Gonzalez, D., Harutyunyan, A., Rantala, J., & Weir, D. (2009). Building a volunteer Cloud. In *Conferencia Latinoamericana de Computacion de Alto Rendimiento*. CLCAR.

Sempolinski, P., & Thain, D. (2010). A Comparison and Critique of Eucalyptus, OpenNebula and Nimbus. *The 2nd IEEE International Conference on Cloud Computing Technology and Science*. Washington, DC: IEEE Press.

Setzer, T., & Stage, A. (2010). Decision support for virtual machine reassignments in enterprise data centers. In *IEEE/IFIP Network Operations and Management Symposium Workshops*, (pp. 88-94.) Washington DC, USA: IEEE Press

Shared Nothing (SN) Architecture. (2011) http://en.wikipedia.org/wiki/Shared nothing architecture.

Sharfman, I., Schuster, A., & Keren, D. (2007). A geometric approach to monitoring threshold functions over distributed data streams. *ACM Transactions on Database Systems*, 32(4), 23. doi:10.1145/1292609.1292613

Shen, Z., Li, L., Yan, F., & Wu, X. (2010). Cloud computing system based on trusted computing platform. *International Conference on Intelligent Computation Technology and Automation (ICICTA)*, 942 –945.

Sheth, A., & Ranabahu, A. (2010). Semantic Modeling for Cloud Computing, Part I & II. In *IEEE Internet Computing Magazine, 14*, 81-83.

Silvera, E., Sharaby, G., Lorenz, D., & Shapira, I. (2009). *IP mobility to support live migration of virtual machines across subnets. SYSTOR 2009.* Haifa.

Skalkowski, K., Sendor, J., Slota, R., & Kitowski, J. (2010). Application of the ESB Architecture for Distributed Monitoring of the SLA Requirements, In *Proceedings of the Ninth International Symposium on Parallel and Distributed Computing (ISPDC)*.203-210

Skene, J., Lamanna, D., & Emmerich, W. (2004). *Precise Service Level Agreements*. In Proc. of the *26th nt. Conference on Software Engineering*, (pp. 179–188), Washington, DC: IEEE Computer Society Press.

Smith, W. E., Trivedi, K. S., Tomek, L. A., & Ackaret, J. (2008). Availability analysis of blade server systems. In *IBM Systems Journal* (pp. 621–640). Indianapolis, IN, USA: IBM Press.

SNIA. (2010). Cloud Data Management Interface. Retrieved from www.snia.org

SNIA. Cloud Storage Reference Model (2009). Retrieved from http://www.snia.org/tech_activities/publicreview/CloudStorageReferenceModelV03.pdf

Sobel, W., Subramanyam, S., Sucharitakul, A., Nguyen, J., Wong, H., Klepchukov, A., et al. (2008). *Cloudstone: Multi-platform, multi-language benchmark and measurement tools for web 2.0*

Soh, C., Kien, S. S., & Tay-Yap, J. (2000). Enterprise resource planning: cultural fits and misfits: is ERP a universal solution? *Communications of the ACM, 43*(4), 47–51. doi:10.1145/332051.332070

Solomon, B., Ionescu, D., Litoiu, M., & Iszlai, G. (2010). Designing autonomic management systems for cloud computing. *International Conference on Computational Cybernetics and Technical Informatics*, 631-636, doi: 10.1109/ICCCYB.2010.5491335

Sotomayor, B., Montero, R., Llorente, I. M., & Foster, I. (2009a). Resource Leasing and the Art of Suspending Virtual Machines. *High Performance Computing and Communications HPCC '09. 11th IEEE International Conference on.* (pp. 59–68). Washington, DC: IEEE Press

Sotomayor, B., Montero, R., Llorente, I. M., & Foster, I. (2009b). *Virtual Infrastructure Management in Private and Hybrid Clouds. Internet Computing, IEEE* (*Vol. 13*, pp. 14–22). Washington, DC: IEEE Press.

Soundararajan, V., & Govil, K. (2010). Challenges in Building Scalable Virtualized Datacenter Management. *ACM SIGOPS Operating Systems Review, 44*(4), 95–102. doi:10.1145/1899928.1899941

Sperb Machado, G., Hausheer, D., & Stiller, B. (2009). *Considerations on the Interoperability of and between Cloud Computing Standards. In 27th Open Grid Forum (OGF27), G2CNet Workshop: From Grid to Cloud Networks.* New York, NY: Springer.

SpringSource Hyperic. (n.d.). Retrieved from http://www.springsource.com/files/uploads/all/datasheets/S2_DataSheet_Hyperic_USLET_EN.pdf

SQLite. (2011). *SQLite.* Retrieved from http://www.sqlite.org/

Sriram, I., & Khajeh-Hosseini, A. (2010, 01 19). *Research Agenda in Cloud Technologies.* Retrieved 05 20, 2011, from Cornell University Library: http://www.arxiv.com/abs/1001.3259

Srirama, S. N., Jarke, M., & Prinz, W. (2006), Mobile web service provisioning. In: *AICT-ICIW '06: Proceedings of the Advanced Int'l Conference on Telecommunications and Int'l Conference on Internet and Web Applications and Services.* (p. 120) Washington, DC: IEEE Computer Society

Staggs, D., Saldhana, A., & DeCouteau, D. (2011). *Cross-Enterprise Security and Privacy Authorization (XSPA) TC, OASIS.* Retrieved July 26, 2011, from http://www.oasis-open.org/

Stavridou, V., Dutertre, B., Riemenschneider, R. A., & Saidi, H. (2001). Intrusion tolerant software architectures. In *Proc. of DARPA Information Survivability Conference \& Exposition II (DISCEX '01)* 2230-241.

Stillwell, M., Schanzenbach, D., Vivien, F., & Casanova, H. (2010). Resource allocation algorithms for virtualized service hosting platforms. *Journal of Parallel and Distributed Computing, 70*(9), 962–974. doi:10.1016/j.jpdc.2010.05.006

StratusLab Consortium. (2010). StratusLab Project Homepage. Retrieved from http://stratuslab.eu/

StratusLab. (2011)Retrieved from http://stratuslab.eu

Sturdevant, C. (2010, 02 10). Cisco OTV Extends Layer 2 Between Data Centers. Retrieved 11 07, 2010, from Data Storage - eWeek: http://www.eweek.com

Stutzle, T., & Hoos, H. (1996). Improvements on ant-system: Introducing max-min ant system. Research report. Retrieved from http://citeseerx.ist.psu.edu/viewdoc/summary?doi=10.1.1.41.6090

Sun Grid. (2011) Retrieved December 2011 from http://wikis.sun.com/display/GridEngine/Home.

Symantec Co. (1999, 03 19). Symantec Detects and Eliminates Recent Pentium III Serial Number Exploit. Retrieved 06 22, 2011, from Symantec News Release: http://www.symantec.com

System Design and Implementation (NSDI'07), (2007) Cambridge, MA, USA,.

Takabi H, Joshi J B D, and Ahn G, Security and Privacy Challenges in Cloud Computing Environments, Security & Privacy, IEEE8, (6) 24-31.

Tan, Y., Gu, X., & Wang, H. (2010). Adaptive system anomaly prediction for large-scale hosting infrastructures. In Proceedings of the 29th ACM Symposium on Principles of distributed computing (PODC) (pp. 173-182), Zurich, Switzerland: ACM Press.

Tanenbaum, A. S., & van Steen, M. (2002). Distributed Systems Principles and Paradigms. Saddle River, New Jersey: Prentice Hall.

TCG. (2010, 09 13). Open Standards from TNC. Retrieved 10 21, 2011, from Trusted Computing Group: http://www.trustedcomputinggroup.org

Tenschert, A., et al. (2011). VERSION II der Architektur der SLA-Schicht; Official Report from the SLA4D-Grid project. Retrieved August 8, 2011, from http://www.sla4d-grid.de/sites/default/files/SLA4D-Grid_Version-II_Architektur.pdf.

Terremark.(2011) Retrieved from www.terremark.com

Thain, D., Tannenbaum, T., & Livny, M. (2002). Condor and the Grid. In Berman, F., Fox, G., & Hey, T. (Eds.), Grid Computing: Making the Global Infrastructure a Reality. Hoboken, NJ: John Wiley & Sons Inc.

Thanakornworakij, T., Sharma, R., Scroggs, B., Leang-suksun, C. B., Greenwood, Z. D., Riteau, P., & Morin, C. (2011). High Availability on Cloud with HA-OSCAR. 4th Workshop on Resiliency in High Performance Computing (Resilience) in Clusters, Clouds, and Grids.

The COMETA Grid Infrastructure. (2011) Retrieved from: www.indicateproject.eu/getFile.php?id=173

The Extensible Messaging and Presence Protocol (XMPP) protocol: (2011) Retrieved from: http://tools.ietf.org/html/rfc3920

The Globus Security Team. (2005). Globus toolkit version 4 grid security infrastructure: A standards perspective. Retrieved from www.globus.org/toolkit/docs/4.0/security/GT4-GSI-Overview.pdf

The Globus Security Team. (2005). Globus toolkit version 4 grid security infrastructure: Authorization framework. Retrieved from http://www.globus.org/toolkit/docs/4.0/security/authzframe/.

The Gomez Platform: Overview. (n.d.). Retrieved from http://www.compuware.com/application-performance-management/the-gomez-platform.html

The OASIS technical committee. (2005). Xacml: extensible access control markup language. Retrieved from http://www.oasisopen.org/committees/xacml/repository/

The Open Group. (2010). Single Sign-On. Retrieved July 26, 2011, from http://www.opengroup.org/security/sso/

The Openstack Community. (2011), OpenStack Cloud Software: open source software for building private and public clouds. Retrieved from: http://www.openstack.org/

The Programmable Web. (2011) Retrieved from: http://www.programmableweb.com

The QCOW2 image format. (2011) Retrieved from http://people.gnome.org/~markmc/qcow-image-format.html

The RESERVOIR Consortium. (2011), RESERVOIR Project Retrieved from: www.reservoir-fp7.eu/

Thibodeau, P., & Vijayan, J. (2011). Amazon EC2 service outage reinforces Cloud doubts. *Computerworld* from http://www.computerworld.com/s/article/356212/

Thusoo, A., Sarma, J. S., & Jain, N. (2009). *Hive - a warehousing solution over a map-reduce framework*. Vldb.

Tierney, B., Aydt, R., Gunter, D., Smith, W., Swany, M., Taylor, V., & Wolski, R. (2002). *GFD-I.7: A Grid Monitoring Architecture*. The Open Grid Forum Informational Document. Retrieved August 8, 2011, from http://www.ogf.org/documents/GFD.7.pdf.

Tiffany, E., & Madsen, P. (2009). *Level of Assurance Authentication Context Profile for SAML 2.0*. OASIS.

Tim O'Reilly. (2006), *What is WEB 2.0* Retrieved from: http://www.oreillynet.com/pub/a/oreilly/tim/news/2005/09/30/what- is-web-20.html

Tomek, L., Muppala, J., & Trivedi, K. S. (1993). Modeling Correlation in Software Recovery Blocks. In *IEEE Transactions on Software Engineering* (pp. 1071–1086). Washington, DC, USA: IEEE Computer Society.

Tomek, L., & Trivedi, K. S. (1991). Fixed-Point Iteration in Availability Modeling. In *Informatik-Fachberichte (Vol. 283*, pp. 229–240). Berlin, Germany: Springer-Verlag.

Tordsson, J. (2011). *OPTIMIS - towards holistic cloud*. Invited Speak presented at the meeting 2nd Workshops on Software Services, Timisoara, Romania

Travostino, F. (2006) Seamless live migration of virtual machines over the MAN/WAN. In *SC '06: Proceedings of the 2006 ACM/IEEE conference on Supercomputing*, (p. 290). New York, NY: ACM

Trends, G. Cloud Computing vs Grid Computing. (2011) Retrieved from: http://www.google.com/trends.

Trivedi, K. S., Kim, D. S., Roy, A., & Medhi, D. (2009). Dependability and security models. In *Proceedings of the 7th International Workshop on the Design of Reliable Communication Networks* (DRCN) (pp. 11-20), Washington, DC, USA: IEEE Computer Society.

Trivedi, K. S., Vasireddy, R., Trindade, D., Nathan, S., & Castro, R. (2006). Modeling High Availability Systems. In *Proceedings of the Pacific Rim International Symposium on Dependable Computing* (PRDC) (pp. 154-164), Riverside, CA, USA: IEEE Computer Society.

Trivedi, K. S., Wang, D., Hunt, D. J., Rindos, A., Smith, W. E., & Vashaw, B. (2008). Availability Modeling of SIP Protocol on IBM WebSphere. In *Proceedings of the Pacific Rim International Symposium on Dependable Computing* (PRDC) (pp. 323-330), Taipei, Taiwan: IEEE Computer Society.

Trivedi, K. S. (2001). *Probability and Statistics with Reliability, Queuing, and Computer Science Applications*. New York, NY, USA: John Wiley and Sons.

Trivedi, K. S., & Sahner, R. (2009). SHARPE at the age of twenty two. In *Sigmetrics Performance Evaluation Review* (pp. 52–57). New York, NY, USA: ACM Press. doi:10.1145/1530873.1530884

Tsugawa, M., & Fortes, J. A. B. (2006). A virtual network (ViNe) architecture for grid computing. *Parallel and Distributed Processing Symposium, 2006. IPDPS 2006. 20th International,* 10 pp.

Tsunamic Tech. Inc. (2010). Retrieved December 2011 from http://www.technology.ca.

Tusa, F., Celesti, A., & Mikkilineni, R. (2011), "*AAA in a Cloud-Based Virtual DIME Network Architecture (DNA),*" Enabling Technologies: Infrastructure for Collaborative Enterprises (WETICE), 20th IEEE International Workshops on, vol., no., pp.110-115, 27-29 June 2011

Tusa, F., Paone, M., Villari, M., & Puliafito, A. (2010), Clever: A cloud-enabled virtual environment. In: Computers and Communications (ISCC), 2010 IEEE Symposium on. pp. 477 –482

UEFI. (2011). Retrieved 04 21, 2011, from http://www.uefi.org

Uemura, T., Dohi, T., & Kaio, N. (2009). Availability analysis of a scalable intrusion tolerant architecture with two detection modes. In *Proceedings of the 1st International Conference on Cloud Computing* (CLOUDCOM) (pp. 178-189), Beijing, China: Springer.

Universidad Complutense de Madrid. (2011), *Distributed Systems Architecture Research Group: OpenNEbula Project* Retrieved from: http://www.opennebula.org/

University Masaryk of Chicago - University of Florida - Purdue University. (2011), *Nimbus – Stratus – Wispy - Kupa Projects* Retreived from: http://workspace.globus.org/clouds/nimbus.html/, http://www.rcac.purdue.edu/teragrid/resources/#wispy, http://www.acis.ufl.edu/vws/, http://meta.cesnet.cz/cms/opencms/en/docs/clouds

Urgaonkar, B., Rosenberg, A. L., & Shenoy, P. J. (2007). Application placement on a cluster of servers. *International Journal of Foundations of Computer Science*, *18*(5), 1023–1041. doi:10.1142/S012905410700511X

Vàzquez, C., Huedo, E., Montero, R. S., & Llorente, I. M. (2009). Dynamic Provision of Computing Resources from Grid Infrastructures and Cloud Providers. *Proceedings of the International Conference on Hybrid Information Technology.* (pp. 113-119).

Vázquez, C., Huedo, E., Montero, R. S., & Llorente, I. M. (2011). On the use of clouds for grid resource provisioning. *Future Generation Computer Systems*, *27*(5), 600–605. doi:10.1016/j.future.2010.10.003

Venezia, P. (2010, 02 16). *First glimpse: Cisco OTV.* Retrieved 05 20, 11, from Reuters: http://www.reuters.com

Venugopal, S., Buyya, R., & Winton, L. (2006). A Grid Service Broker for Scheduling e-Science Applications on Global Data Grids. *Concurrency and Computation*, *18*(6), 685–699. doi:10.1002/cpe.974

Verma, A., & Koller, R. (2010). The cost of reconfiguration in a cloud. *Proceedings of the 11th International Middleware Conference Industrial track on Middleware Industrial Track* 10, 11-16. Retrieved from http://portal.acm.org/citation.cfm?doid=1891719.1891721

Verma, A., De, P., Mann, V., Nayak, T., Purohit, A., Gargi, D., & Ravi, K. (2010). BrownMap: Enforcing Power Budget in Shared Data Centers. *Proceedings of the ACM/IFIP/USENIX 11th International Middleware Conference - Middleware 2010* (pp. 42-63). New York, NY: Springer.

Verma, A., Kumar, G., & Koller, R. (2010). The cost of reconfiguration in a cloud. *11th ACM International Middleware Conference (Industrial track)*,(pp. 11-16) New York, NY: ACM Press

Villari, M., Latanicki, J., Massonet, P., & Naqvi, S. Rochwerger, B. (2010), Scalable Cloud Defenses For Detection, Analysis and Mitigation Of DDOS Attacks, chap. 13, pp. 127–137. FIA book, IOS Press, towards the future internet - emerging trends from european research 2010 edn.

Villari, M., Tusa, F., Massonet, P., Naqvi, S., & Latanicki, J. (2009). Mitigating Security Threats To Large-scale Cross Border Virtualization Infrastructures, *International Conference on Cloud Computing*, 19-21 Munich, Germany

Villari, M., Rochwerger, B., Massonet, P., & Latanicki, J. (2010). Scalable Cloud Computing Defenses for Detection and Analysis of DDOS attacks. In Tselentis, G. (Eds.), *Towards The Future Internet* (pp. 127–137). Amsterdam, The Netherlands: IOS Press.

Villinger, S. (2011, 08 22). The 30-year-long Reign of BIOS is Over: Why UEFI Will Rock Your IT. *HP Feature Articles* Retrieved 11 07, 2011, from: http://h30565.www3.hp.com

Virtual disk format specification. (2011)Retrieved from http://www.vmware.com/technical-resources/interfaces/vmdk.html

Virtual hard disk image format specification. (2011)Retrieved from http://technet.microsoft.com/en-us/library/bb676673.aspx

Virtualbox: x86 virtualization software package developed by Oracle. (2011) Retrieved from: http://www.virtualbox.org/

Virtualization: the essential catalyst for enabling the transition to secure cloud computing. (2011) Retrieved from: http://www.vmware.com/it/

Vishwanath, K. V., & Nagappan, N. (2010). Characterizing Cloud computing hardware reliability. In *Proceedings of the ACM Symposium on Cloud Computing* (SOCC) (pp. 193-204), Indianapolis, IN, USA: ACM Press.

Vision, VISION project, (n.d.) Retrieved from: http://www.visioncloud.eu/

VMWare Inc. (2011), *Vmware vcloud* Retrieved from: http://www.vmware.com/products/vcloud/

VMware vCloud director. (2011) Retrieved, from www.vmware.com/products/vcloud-director

Vogels, W. (2008). Beyond Server Consolidation. *Queue*, *6*(1), 20–26. doi:10.1145/1348583.1348590

Voith, T., Oberle, K., Stein, M., Oliveros, E., Gallizo, G., & Kübert, R. (2010). A Path Supervision Framework A Key for Service Monitoring in Infrastructure as a Service (IaaS) Platforms, In *Proceedings of the 36th EUROMICRO Conference on Software Engineering and Advanced Applications (SEAA)* 127-130

von Neumann, J. (1987). *General and Logical Theory of Automata*. William Aspray and Arthur Burks (Ed.), MIT Press

von Neumann, J. (1987). *Papers of John von Neumann on Computing and Computing Theory, Hixon Symposium*, September 20, 1948, Pasadena, CA, The MIT Press, p454, p457

von Neumann, J. (1966). *Theory of Self-Reproducing Automata* (Burke, A. W., Ed.). Chicago, Illinois: University of Illinois Press.

Vouros, G. A., Papasalouros, A., Tzonas, K., Valarakos, A., Kotis, K., & Quiane-Ruiz, J. A. (2010). A semantic information system for services and traded resources in grid e-markets. *Future Generation Computer Systems*, *26*(7), 916–933. doi:10.1016/j.future.2010.03.004

VPN-cubed., (2011),Retrieved from http://www.cohesiveft.com/vpncubed/

Waldburger, M., & Stiller, B. (2006) Toward the mobile grid: service provisioning in a mobile dynamic virtual organization. In: *IEEE International Conference on Computer Systems and Applications.* (pp. 579–583) Washington, DC: IEEE Press

Wallis, P. (2008). Understanding Cloud computing, keystones and rivets., http://www.keystonesandrivets.com/kar/2008/02/Cloud-computing.html.

Wang, C., Wang, Q., Ren, K., & Lou, W. (2010). Privacy-Preserving Public Auditing for Data Storage Security in Cloud Computing. *INFOCOM 2010. 14*, 1-9. San Diego, CA: IEEE Press. doi: 10.1109/INFCOM.2010.5462173

Wang, M., Holub, V., Parsons, T., Murphy, J., & O'Sullivan, P. (2010). Scalable Run-Time Correlation Engine for Monitoring in a Cloud Computing Environment, In *Proceedings of the 17th IEEE International Conference and Workshops on Engineering of Computer Based Systems (ECBS)* Washington, DC: IEEE Press

Wang, D., Fricks, R. M., & Trivedi, K. S. (2003). Dealing with non-exponential distributions in dependability models. In *Performance Evaluation - Stories and Perspectives* (pp. 273–302). Vienna, Austria: Oesterreichchische Computer Gessellschaft.

Wang, L., Tao, J., Kunze, M., Castellanos, A. C., Kramer, D., & Karl, W. (2008). Scientific Cloud Computing: Early Definition and Experience. In *HPCC '08* (pp. 825–830). Washington, DC: IEEE Computer Society. doi:10.1109/HPCC.2008.38

Wang, X., & Wang, Y. (2010). Coordinating Power Control and Performance Management for Virtualized Server Clusters. *IEEE Transactions on Parallel and Distributed Systems*, *22*(2), 245–259. Retrieved from http://ieeexplore.ieee.org/lpdocs/epic03/wrapper.htm?arnumber=5467056doi:10.1109/TPDS.2010.91

Web Service Description Language – WSDL. (2011), Website, retrieved July 20, 2011 from http://www.w3.org/TR/wsdl

Wegner, P., & Eberbach, E. (2004). New Models of Computation. *The Computer Journal*, *47*(1). doi:10.1093/comjnl/47.1.4

Welch, V., Foster, I., Kesselman, C., Mulmo, O., Pearlman, L., Tuecke, S., et al. (2004), X.509 proxy certificates for dynamic delegation, in *Proc. of the 3rd Annual PKI R&D Workshop*. New York, NY: Springer

Wentzlaff, D., & Agarwal, A. 2009). Factored operating systems (fos): the case for a scalable operating system for multicores. *In SIGOPS Operating System Review*, vol 43(2):pp. 76–85.

What is ntop ? (n.d.). Retrieved from http://www.ntop.org/overview.html

Winter, R., & McConnell, D. (n.d.). *Security Through Maturity: A Brief on Securing iSCSI Networks.* Retrieved 11 04, 2011, from http://www.dell.com/downloads/global/power/ps2q09-20090225-McConnell.pdf

Wood, T., Shenoy, P. J., Venkataramani, A., & Yousif, M. S. (2009). Sandpiper: Black-box and gray-box resource management for virtual machines. *Computer Networks, 53*(17), 2923–2938. doi:10.1016/j.comnet.2009.04.014

WS-Federation. (2007). *Web Services Federation Language.* Retrieved July 26, 2011, from http://www.ibm.com/developerworks/library/specification/ws-fed/

XACML. (2011). eXtensible Access Control Markup Language (XACML), OASIS. Retrieved July 26, 2011, from http://www.oasis-open.org/committees/tc_home.php?wg_abbrev=xacml

Xen Hypervisor - Leading open source hypervisor for servers. (2011) Retrieved from: http://www.xen.org/

Xen. (2011). *Xen hypervisor.* Retrieved July 20, 2011, from http://xen.org/

XEP-0065. SOCKS5 Bytestreams. (2011) Retrieved from: http://xmpp.org/extensions/xep-0065.html

Yang, B., Tan, F., Dai, Y. S., & Guo, S. (2009). Performance evaluation of Cloud service considering fault recovery. In *Proceedings of the 1st International Conference on Cloud Computing* (CLOUDCOM) (pp. 571-576), Beijing, China: Springer.

Yarmolenko, V., & Sakellariou, R. (2007). Towards increased expressiveness in service level agreements. *Concurrency and Computation, n.d.,* 19.

Yin, L., Fricks, R. M., & Trivedi, K. S. (2002). Application of semi-Markov process and CTMC to evaluation of UPS system availability. In *Proceedings of the Annual Reliability and Maintainability Symposium* (pp. 584-591), Seattle, WA, USA: IEEE Computer Society.

Zadok, E., Iyer, R., Joukov, N., Sivathanu, G., & Wright, C. P. (2006). On incremental file system development. *ACM Transactions on Storage, 2*(2), 161–196. doi:10.1145/1149976.1149979

Zanikolas, S., & Sakellariou, R. (2005). A Taxonomy of Grid Monitoring Systems. *Future Generation Computer Systems, 21,* 163–188. doi:10.1016/j.future.2004.07.002

Zhou, F., Goel, M., Desnoyers, P., & Sundaram, R. (2010). Scheduler Vulnerabilities and Coordinated Attacks in Cloud Computing. In *Proc. of the Int. IEEE Symposium on Network Computing and Applications,* (pp. 123-130) Washington DC, USA: IEEE CS Press

Zimmer, V. J., Dasari, S. R., & Brogan, S. P. (2009, 09). *Trusted Platforms.* Retrieved 11 5, 2011, from EFI: http://download.intel.com/technology/efi/SF09_EFIS001_UEFI_PI_TCG_White_Paper.pdf

Zisman, A., Spanoudakis, G., & Dooley, J. (2008). A Framework for Dynamic Service Discovery. In *Proceedings of the 2008 23rd IEEE/ACM International Conference on Automated Software Engineering (ASE '08)* Washington, DC: IEEE Press.

About the Contributors

Massimo Villari is an Aggregate Professor in Computer Engineering at the Università degli Studi di Messina, Italy. In 2003 he received his PhD in Computer Science School of Engineering. Since 2006 he is an Aggregate Professor at Università degli Studi di Messina. He is actively working as IT Security and Distributed Systems Analyst in cloud computing, virtualization and Storage for the European Union Projects "RESERVOIR" and "VISION-CLOUD". Previously, he was an academic advisor of STMicroelectronics, help an internship in Cisco Systems, in Sophia Antipolis, and worked on the MPE-G4IP and IPv6-NEMO projects. He investigated issues related with user mobility and security, in wireless and ad hoc and sensor networks. He is IEEE member. Currently he is strongly involved on EU Future Internet initiatives, specifically Cloud Computing and Security in Distributed Systems. His main research interests include virtualization, migration, security, federation, and autonomic systems. In UniME is also the Cloud Architect of CLEVER; a cloud middleware aimed at federated clouds.

Ivona Brandic is Assistant Professor at the Distributed Systems Group, Information Systems Institute, Vienna University of Technology (TU Wien). Prior to that, she was Assistant Professor at the Department of Scientific Computing, Vienna University. She received her PhD degree from Vienna University of Technology in 2007. From 2003 to 2007 she participated in the special research project AURORA (Advanced Models, Applications and Software Systems for High Performance Computing) and the European Union's GEMSS (Grid-Enabled Medical Simulation Services) project. She is involved in the European Union's SCube project and she is leading the Austrian national FoSII (Foundations of Self-governing ICT Infrastructures) project funded by the Vienna Science and Technology Fund (WWTF). She is Management Committee member of the European Commission's COST Action on Energy Efficient Large Scale Distributed Systems. From June-August 2008 she was visiting researcher at the University of Melbourne. Her interests comprise SLA and QoS management, Service-oriented architectures, autonomic computing, workflow management, and large scale distributed systems (Cloud, Grid, Cluster, etc.).

Francesco Tusa was born in Messina on Feb 5th 1983. In 2008, he received a Master Postdegree in "Open Source and Computer Security", and started his PhD studies in "Advanced Technologies for Information Engineering" at the Università degli Studi di Messina. On April 2011 he defended his PhD thesis "Security in distributed computing systems: from Grid to Cloud". He have been actively working as IT Security and Distributed Systems Analyst in cloud computing, virtualization and Storage for the European Union Projects "RESERVOIR" and "VISION-CLOUD". He is involved in the design and implementation of the CLEVER cloud middleware. His scientific activity has been focused on studying distributed systems, grid and cloud computing. His research interest are in the area of security, virtualization, migration, federation of distributed computing systems. He is one of the members of the MDSLab Computer Engineering group at the Università degli Studi di Messina.

* * *

Frederico Alvares de Oliveira Jr. is a PhD student in the ASCOLA research group (INRIA-Mines Nantes, LINA), in Nantes, France. He received his master degree in 2009 at the Aeronautics Institute of Technology - ITA, in São José dos Campos, São Paulo, Brazil, where he performed research on Dynamic Composition of Semantic Web Services. Currently, he is working on dynamic adaptation of component-based software in the context of cloud computing and energy efficiency. More precisely, he is studying the impacts of applications on cloud-based infrastructures and how such kinds of (component-based) applications should interact with underlying infrastructures to optimize their QoS and dynamically reconfigure to cope with energy constraints.

David Breitgand is a research staff member at the IBM Haifa Research Lab. Dr. Breitgand has a Ph.D. in Computer Science from the Hebrew University, Jerusalem. His research interests include cloud computing, end-to-end performance analysis, and management of networked systems. Since joining IBM in 2003, he worked on business driven IT optimization, SLA management, networked storage, and cloud computing.

Nicolò Maria Calcavecchia received the MSc degree in computer science from the University of Illinois at Chicago, and the MSc degree in computer science engineering from the Politecnico di Milano in a joint degree program. He is working toward the PhD degree at the Politecnico di Milano. His main research interests focus on large decentralized systems, and in particular the study of self-organizing systems.

Rodrigo N. Calheiros is a Post-Doctoral Research Fellow in the Cloud Computing and Distributed Systems Laboratory (CLOUDS Lab) in the University of Melbourne, Australia. He completed his PhD degree in Computer Science in 2010 at PUCRS, Brazil, and his MSc degree in 2006 at the same University. In 2008, Dr. Calheiros started research and development in the area of Cloud computing with the CloudSim simulation toolkit. Since them, he contributed in other Cloud projects and products such as InterCloud, LoM2HiS, and Manjrasoft Aneka. His research interests include scheduling, provisioning and integration of Cloud Computing systems and simulation and emulation of distributed systems, with emphasis in Grids and Clouds.

Valentina Casola is an Assistant Professor at the University of Naples Federico II. She received the Laurea degree in Electronic Engineering cum laude from the University of Naples in 2001 and she received her Ph.D. in Electronic and Computer Engineering from the Second University of Naples in 2004. Her research activities are both theoretical and experimental and are focused on security methodologies to design and evaluate distributed and secure infrastructures.

Antonio Celesti received the Master's degree in Computer Science from the Faculty of Mathematical, Physical and Natural Sciences, Università degli Studi di Messina, Italy, in 2008. From 2009, he is attending his Ph.D. studies in "Advanced Technologies for Information Engineering" at the Faculty of Engineering - Università degli Studi di Messina. From April 2009 e is one of the members of the Multimedia and Distributed Systems Laboratory (MDSLab). His scientific activity has been focused on studying distributed systems and cloud computing.

Clovis Chapman received an M.Sc. in Data Communication and Distributed Systems and a Ph.D. in 2009 from the Department of Computer Science at University College London. He has been involved in several UK and European wide research projects focusing on Grid and Cloud computing technologies and has authored over 25 papers in international conferences and journals on the subject. His primary research interests include the management of large scale distributed computing infrastructures, with specific focus on virtualisation technologies and service oriented computing.

Vincent Chimaobi Emeakaroha (M.Sc. B.Sc) is a research assistant at the Distributed Systems Group, Information Systems Institute, Vienna University of Technology (TU Wien). He received a Bachelor degree in Computer Engineering in 2006 and gained double Masters in Software Engineering & Internet Computing in 2008 and in Computer Science Management in 2009 all at Vienna University of Technology. He is currently involved in the Austrian national FoSII (Foundations of Self-governing ICT Infrastructures) project funded by the Vienna Science and Technology Fund (WWTF) while pursuing his PhD studies. His research areas of interest include Cloud computing, autonomic computing, energy efficiency in Cloud, SLA, and QoS management.

Massimo Civilini is manager of Engineering at Cisco Systems Inc. in San Jose, CA since 1998 keeping R&D and applied research positions in Internet Services, Network Management and Server Access and Virtualization divisions. His focus has been on firmware development for high end switches and routers, green computing and data center software provisioning and virtualization. He has a degree in Physics from the University of Pisa (Italy) and kept management and technical positions with Olivetti R&D and American Megatrends, Inc. authoring papers on computer architecture. He holds two patents on sensor management and network security. His current interests include storage virtualization, sensor control and Cloud management.

Stuart Clayman received his PhD in Computer Science from University College London in 1994. He has worked as a Research Lecturer at Kingston University and is now a Senior Research Fellow at UCL. He co-authored 30 conference and journal papers. His research interests and expertise lie in the areas of software engineering and programming paradigms; distributed systems; cloud systems, systems management; networked media; and knowledge-based systems. He also has previous extensive experience in the commercial arena undertaking architecture and development for software engineering and networking systems.

Antonio Cuomo is a Ph.D. student at the University of Sannio, Benevento, Italy. His research activities focus on performance evaluation and prediction of parallel and distributed computer systems, including Cloud Computing, Grid Computing and their integration. He received the Laurea Specialistica degree cum laude in Computer Science Engineering from the University of Sannio in 2009.

César De Rose has a B. Sc. degree in Computer Science from the Catholic University of Rio Grande do Sul – (PUCRS, Porto Alegre, RS, Brazil, 1990) a M.Sc. in Computer Science from the Federal University of Rio Grande do Sul – (CPGCC-UFRGS, Porto Alegre, RS, Brazil, 1993) and a Doctoral degree from Karlrsruhe University (Karlsruhe, Germany, 1998). Since 1998 he is an Associate Professor at PUCRS and member of the Parallel and Distributed Processing Group. His research interests include resource management in parallel and distributed architectures. Since 2009 he is lead researcher at the PUCRS High Performance Laboratory (LAD-PUCRS).

Elisabetta Di Nitto is an Associate Professor at Dipartimento di Elettronica e Informazione at Politecnico di Milano. Her expertise lies in the area of large-scale, open, service-oriented systems with a special attention to self-adaptable techniques. She has published and presented various papers on the most important international journals and conferences and has served in the program committee of various international conferences. She has been also program co-chair of ASE 2010 (Automated Software Engineering Conference) and of ServiceWave 2010. She is member of the Editorial Board of IEEE Transactions on Software Engineering, of the SOCA journal and of the Journal of Software: Evolution and Process.

Salvatore Distefano is an assistant professor at the Politecnico di Milano. His research interests include performance evaluation, parallel and distributed computing, software engineering, and reliability techniques. Distefano received his PhD in "Advanced Technologies for the Information Engineering" from the Università degli Studi di Messina.

Amir Epstein is a research staff member at the IBM Haifa Research Lab. Dr. Epstein has a Ph.D. in Computer Science from the Tel Aviv University, Israel. His research interests include approximation methods, algorithmic game theory and cloud computing. Since joining IBM in 2008, Amir has worked on image management, networking, and cloud computing.

Eugen Feller is a Ph.D. student at the INRIA Myriads research team in Rennes (France). He holds a Bachelor's and Master's degree with honors in computer science from the Heinrich-Heine University of Duesseldorf (Germany). During his studies he focused on operating and distributed systems. In particular, fault tolerance techniques for distributed applications. From late 2007 till early 2009 he has worked as a research assistant at the operating system / distributed systems group in Duesseldorf. Here, he has contributed to the grid checkpointing service of XtreemOS and the Kerrighed checkpointer. Currently, he focuses his research on scalable, fault-tolerant and energy-aware resource management in cloud computing infrastructures.

Massimo Ficco is Assistant Professor at Department of Information Engineering of the Second University of Naples (SUN). He received the degree in Informatics Engineering in 1999 from the University of Naples "Federico II", and his PhD in "Electronic Engineering" from the "Università Parthenope". From 2000 to 2010, he was senior researcher at Italian University Consortium for Computer Science (CINI). Form 2004, he taught courses in "Software Engineering" in regular and master courses. His current research interests include software engineering architecture, dependability aspects of critical infrastructure, and mobile computing. He has been involved in several EU funded research projects in the area of security and reliability of critical infrastructures, including: CADENUS (FP5-IST-1999-11017), INTERSECTION (FP7-SEC-2007-216585), CRITICAL-STEP (FP7-PEOPLE-2008-IAPP), INSPIRE (FP7-SEC-2008-225553), OSMOSIS(FP7-SEC-2009-10.7.0.2), and mOSAIC ().

Alex Galis is a Visiting Professor at University College London. He has co-authored 7 research books and more that 190 publications in journals and conferences in the Future Internet areas: networks, services and management. He acted as PTC chair of 14 IEEE conferences and reviewer in more than 100 IEEE conferences (www.ee.ucl.ac.uk/~agalis). He worked as a Vice-Chairman ITU-T Focus Group on Future Networks, which is defining design goals and requirements the Future Network (www.itu.int/ITU-T/focusgroups/fn/index.html).

Hamza Ghani received his Licence des sciences économiques from the University of Fez in 2002 and his MS in Computer Science with Business Administration from TUD in 2009 and thereon he joined the DEEDS group of Prof. Suri as PhD assistant. His research interests include economic-driven security metrics and security in financial critical infrastructures. He is involved in the FP7 EC projects CoMiFin and ABC4Trust.

Rahul Ghosh is a Ph.D. candidate in Electrical and Computer Engineering at Duke University, USA. He received M.S. in Computer Engineering from Duke University in 2009. Prior to this, he received B.E. in Electronics and Telecommunication from Jadavpur University, India, in 2007. His research interests include stochastic processes, queuing systems, Markov chains, performance and dependability analysis of large scale computer systems. Rahul's Ph.D. thesis research is focused on developing scalable analytic models for Infrastructure-as-a-Service Cloud. During his Ph.D., he worked as a research intern at IBM T. J. Watson Research Center. At IBM Research, his work was focused on cost optimization, capacity planning and risk analysis of Cloud systems.

Spyridon V. Gogouvitis was born in Athens, Greece in 1982. He received the Dipl.-Ing. from the School of Electrical and Computer Engineering of the National Technical University of Athens (NTUA) in 2006. He is currently pursuing his Ph.D. while working as a Researcher in the Telecommunication Laboratory of the Institute of Communication and Computer Systems (ICCS) and is involved in the VISION Cloud EU project. In the past he has been actively involved in several EU and National funded projects such as the Interactive Realtime Multimedia Applications on Service Oriented Infrastructures (IRMOS) project. He has also worked as a developer for the Hellenic Army Information Systems Support Centre and as a consultant for the General Secretariat for Information Systems of the Hellenic Ministry of Economy and Finance. His research interests include Grid and Cloud Computing, Workflow Management, as well as Mobile and Ubiquitous Computing.

Peer Hasselmeyer has many years of experience in the field of service-oriented architectures and distributed computing. He received a MS degree in Computer Science from the University of Colorado at Boulder, USA, and a Ph.D. from the Darmstadt University of Technology, Germany. He is currently working as a senior researcher at NEC Laboratories Europe in Heidelberg, Germany. His main research interests are service-oriented architectures, cloud computing, software-defined networking, and data center and service management. Peer has contributed to many EU-co-funded projects and is a frequent program committee member of various conferences. He published numerous research papers at international conferences and in magazines.

Benoit Hudzia is Senior Researcher at SAP Research, CEC Belfast (United Kingdom),his research is focused on Technology infrastructure, Cloud and Distributed Systems. In the past, he was leading the UK funded project Virtex on virtualization technologies, participates in the EU-funded Cloud Computing project Reservoir, and is involved in the SAP internet of services framework research programme. He received a PhD from the University College Dublin in the field of parallel and distributed computing with focus on P2P and grids systems. During his studies in Electronics and Computer Science Engineering at the University of Paris 6 (Msc) and the engineering School EFREI(Paris) (Meng), his main emphasis was on Distributed systems and parallelism for enterprise applications.

Peter Kacsuk is the Head of the Laboratory of Parallel and Distributed Systems in MTA SZTAKI, Hungary. He received his MSc and university doctorate degrees from the Technical University of Budapest in 1976 and 1984, respectively. He received the Kandidat degree (equivalent to Ph.D.) from the Hungarian Academy in 1989. He habilitated at the University of Vienna in 1997. He received his professor title from the Hungarian President in 1999 and the Doctor of Academy degree (DSc) from the Hungarian Academy of Sciences in 2001. He has been a part-time full professor at the Cavendish School of Computer Science of the University of Westminster and the Eotvos Lorand University of Science Budapest since 2001. He has published two books, two lecture notes and more than 200 scientific papers on parallel computer architectures, parallel software engineering and Grid computing. He is co-editor-in-chief of the *Journal of Grid Computing* published by Springer.

Gregory Katsaros received his diploma from the Department of Electrical and Computer Engineering of the National Technical University of Athens, Athens, Greece in 2006 and the M.S. degree in Techno-Economic Systems (MBA) co-organized by the Electrical and Computer Engineering Department–NTUA, Economic Sciences Department–National Kapodistrian University of Athens, Industrial Management Department–University of Piraeus, in 2008. Currently, he is a Ph.D. candidate focusing in Service Oriented infrastructures and monitoring frameworks, while he is also working as a Researcher in the Telecommunications Laboratory of the Institute of Communications and Computer Systems (ICCS) of NTUA. He has been involved in several European funded research projects such as NextGRID, BEinGRID, EchoGRID, IRMOS, OPTIMIS VISION and more.

Gabor Kecskemeti (Ph.D. University of Westminster, 2011) is the leader of the Cloud Computing research group of the Laboratory of Parallel and Distributed Systems in MTA SZTAKI Computer and Automation Research Institute, Hungary. He was involved in several successful European research projects (e.g., S-Cube, EDGeS, ePerSpace). He has published over 30 scientific papers (including 3 journal articles) in the area of cloud and grid computing particularly from the field of virtual appliance delivery in IaaS cloud systems.

Attila Kertesz, PhD, is a Research Fellow at the Laboratory of Parallel and Distributed Systems of MTA SZTAKI, Hungary. He graduated as a program-designer mathematician, and received his PhD in the field of Grid Computing at the University of Szeged, Hungary. His research interests include resource management and interoperability issues of Cloud and Grid systems. He has participated in several European projects (SHIWA, EDGI, EGI-InSPIRE, EGEE FP6 and 7 projects, and S-Cube and CoreGRID Network of Excellence projects), and published over 40 scientific papers.

Bastian Koller (Dr.-Ing.) received 2011 a PhD in mechanical engineering from the University of Stuttgart and a diploma in computer science from the University of Würzburg in 2004. He worked in many national and international research activities realizing Grid and Cloud Computing frameworks as well as improving the usage of HPC Resources. Main projects he is or was involved are on a European Level: OPTIMIS, BonFIRE, IRMOS and CRESTA. From 2006 to 2010 he was Technical Manager of the IST BREIN project. Since 2007 he leads the Service Management and Business Processes Group of the High Performance Computing Centre Stuttgart.

Stefanos Koutsoutos was born in Athens, Greece in 1981. He received his Degree in Mathematics from the Department of Mathematics at the University of Athens (UOA) in 2005. He then received his MSc in Software Engineering from Athens Information Technology Institute. Currently, he is a Working Researcher at the Telecommunications Laboratory of the Institute of Communication and Computer Systems (ICCS) in the National Technical University of Athens (NTUA), where he is a Ph.D. student. He has been involved in several EU and National funded projects, such as ASNWER and iTacitus. Currently he is part of the NTUA team undertaking the VISION project. He has worked with several companies, providing services as a senior developer and software designer.

Dimosthenis Kyriazis received his diploma from the school of Electrical and Computer Engineering of the National Technical University of Athens (NTUA) in 2001 and his MSc degree in "Techno-economics" in 2004 (co-organized by the Electrical and Computer Engineering Dept – NTUA, Economic Sciences Dept – National Kapodistrian University of Athens, Industrial Management Dept – University of Piraeus). Since 2007, he holds a PhD in the area of Service Oriented Architectures with a focus on quality aspects and workflow management from the school of Electrical and Computer Engineering Department of NTUA. His expertise lies with service-based, distributed and heterogeneous systems, software and service engineering. As a Senior Research Engineer of the Institute of Communication and Computer Systems (ICCS) of NTUA, he has participated in several EU and National funded projects (e.g. VISION Cloud, 4CaaSt, BEinGRID, NextGRID, AkoGRIMO, HPC-Europa, EchoGRID, CHALLENGERS, HellasGRID, USNES) leading research for addressing issues related to quality of service provisioning, fault tolerance, workflow management, performance modeling in service oriented environments and application domains such as multimedia, post-production, virtual reality, finance, e-health and others. He also serves as the QoS & SLAs EU Collaboration Working Group leader.

Adrien Lèbre is an Associate Professor in the ASCOLA Research Group of Ecole des Mines of Nantes (France). He received his Ph.D. from Grenoble Institute of Technologies and his master degree from University of Grenoble. His research activities aim at designing and implementing new distributed systems leveraging recent programming models (such as event or component programming). Currently, he's working on two specific domains: the study of new distributed file system models and the use of virtualization technologies for Cluster, Grid and Cloud architectures. Since 2008, Adrien is the chair of the virtualization working group of the Grid'5000 infrastructure. He is also involved in the consortium of the European Marie Curie Initial Training Network (MCITN) "SCALing by means of Ubiquitous Storage (SCALUS)."

Thomas Ledoux is an Assistant Professor at Ecole des Mines de Nantes. Previously, he worked as a full-time researcher at INRIA from 2008-10. He is a member of the Ascola research team (EMN-INRIA) and member of the Laboratoire Informatique de Nantes Atlantique (LINA, UMR CNRS). Thomas's main research interests include Component-Based Software Engineering (CBSE), Domain Specific Languages (DSL) for autonomic computing, green computing and cloud computing. Currently, he investigates self-adaptive component-based applications for large-scale distributed systems. He held a PhD from University of Nantes in 1998. He has served on a number of conference program committees and is a member of the board of the Regional Doctoral School STIM. Finally, he headed several national projects for the Ascola team.

Maik A. Lindner is a Senior Manager at SAP Labs, LLC. and is focused on infrastructure and related strategy topics. In the past, Maik worked as a business development manager and senior researcher for SAP Research Belfast. In his function as a researcher, Maik led the SAP team of the European Union FP7 funded project RESERVOIR. For this he dealt with aspects of large-scale enterprise software on on-demand IT resources including the importance of standardization. During his time in Belfast he led and contributed to several successful project proposals in the area of smart electricity grids and cloud computing. His research resulted in many international publications and patent efforts. In his role as a business development manager, he built an interface between SAP's internal development and business groups and researchers for future ICT systems and architectures. Maik holds a PhD from the University of Muenster (Germany) in Information and Controlling Systems with a focus on Business Intelligence. Prior to his PhD he finished his MSc in Information Systems. The cores of Maik's research interests are business aspects and business/market models for emerging technologies such as cloud computing.

Ignacio M. Llorente is a full Professor and the head of the Distributed Systems Architecture Research group at the Complutense University of Madrid. His research interests include advanced distributed computing and virtualization technologies, architecture of large-scale distributed infrastructures, and resource-provisioning platforms. Llorente has a PhD in computer science from the Complutense University of Madrid and an Executive Master in business administration from the Instituto de Empresa Business School.

Jesus Luna received his Bachelor's degree from the "Instituto Politécnico Nacional" (IPN, Mexico 1995), a Master's degree in Computer Science from the "Tecnológico de Monterrey" (ITESM CEM, Mexico 2002) and a PhD in Computer Architecture from the "Universidad Politécnica de Cataluña" (UPC, Spain 2008). He was a postdoctoral researcher with the CoreGRID Network of Excellence (Greece/Cyprus, 2008-2009) and has more than 15 years of experience in the field of computer security working with both public and private companies and, universities in Mexico and southern Europe. Since 2009 is an active member of the "Cloud Security Alliance" (CSA) and in 2010 became part of the Board of

Directors from its Spanish Chapter (CSA-ES). Currently he is the head of the security research group at TU Darmstadt's DEEDS, and his topics of interest include security metrics, Cloud and Grid security, botnets mitigation, VANETs and WSN security+privacy, and PKI-related security.

Francesco Longo was born in Messina on November 16th 1982. He received his Degree in Computer Engineering from the Università degli Studi di Messina (Italy) in November 2007, final score 110/110 summa cum laude. The title of his thesis was "Symbolic representation of the reachability graph of non-Markovian stochastic Petri net". From September 2007 to June 2008 he worked at the Università degli Studi di Messina within the PON Project "Progetto per l'Implementazione e lo Sviluppo di una e-Infrastruttura in Sicilia basata sul paradigma della grid (PI2S2)" with the aim of designing and implementing a QoS management system in Grid environment. In June 2008 he received a Master's degree in Open Source and Computer Security. He received his Ph.D in "Advanced Technologies for Information Engineering" at the Università degli Studi di Messina in April 2011. Between May 2010 and October 2010 he spent a period as a visiting scholar in the United States at the Duke University (Durham, NC) where he had the opportunity to collaborate with Prof. Kishor S. Trivedi in the modeling of Cloud systems and in the quantitative evaluation of their performance and availability. Since 2010 he is teaching assistant for the subject "Valutazione delle prestazioni" (Performance evaluation) at the Faculty of Engineering, Università degli Studi di Messina. He is now a post doc Researcher within the Vision Cloud European project at the Università degli Studi di Messina. The project has the aim of building a new storage cloud infrastructure and framework. His main research interests include performance and reliability evaluation of distributed systems (mainly Grid and Cloud) with main attention to the use of non-Markovian stochastic Petri nets.

Attila Csaba Marosi is a Research Associate at the Laboratory of Parallel and Distributed Systems of MTA SZTAKI, Hungary. He graduated as an electrical engineer and currently doing his PhD studies at Budapest University of Technology and Economics, Hungary. His research interests include dynamic resource provision, cloud federations, and volunteer computing. He was involved in several successful European projects (CoreGrid, EGEE, EDGeS, EDGI) and published more than 20 scientific papers.

Michael Maurer is currently working as a Project Assistant at the Distributed System Group, Information Systems Institute, Vienna University of Technology (TU Wien). He studied the diploma program Applied Mathematics with a focus on Computer Science (first M.Sc) and the Masters program Computational Intelligence (second M.Sc), which he finished both with distinction in November 2007 and April 2009 respectively. Furthermore, he studied at the City College of New York in New York USA during the winter term 2008. He has been working on the FoSII (Foundations of Self-governing ICT Infrastructures) project funded by the Vienna Science and Technology Fund (WWTF) since 2009. His research areas of interest include Cloud Computing, Autonomic Computing, Service Level Agreements, and Knowledge Databases. He is especially interested in the autonomic governing of Cloud Computing infrastructures.

Jean-Marc Menaud is an Associate Professor at the Ecole des Mines de Nantes. He has defended his habilitation in 2011. Prior, he obtained his PhD on distributed system at university of Rennes and got an assistant Professor position at the Ecole des Mines de Nantes in 2000. He is a member of the ASCOLA

EMN-INRIA, LINA project-team and his recent research focuses on the dynamic and complex strategies for cluster and cloud management. In the context of virtualized data center, he proposed btrScript, a domain specific language to virtual machines placement and an open-source system named Entropy, which reconfigures the placement of virtual machine according to high-level constraints. The flexibility of the reconfiguration algorithm is provided by the usage of a constraint solver.

Rao Mikkilineni received his PhD from University of California, San Diego in 1972 working under the guidance of prof. Walter Kohn (Nobel Laureate 1998). He later worked as a research associate at the University of Paris, Orsay, Courant Institute of Mathematical Sciences, New York and Columbia University, New York. He is currently the Founder and CTO of Kawa Objects Inc., California, a Silicon Valley startup developing next generation computing infrastructure. His past experience includes working at AT&T Bell Labs, Bellcore, U S West, several startups and more recently at Hitachi Data Systems. He currently chairs IEEE conference track on "Convergence of Distributed Clouds, Grids, and their Management" in WETICE2012. He has published several papers on POTS (Plain Old Telephone Service), PANS (Pretty Amazing New Services) using the Internet, and SANs (Storage Area Networks).

Daniel Molina received his M.E. in Computer Science (2010) and his MSc in Computer Science Research (2011) from Universidad Complutense de Madrid (UCM), where he is currently a PhD student. His interests are in cloud and virtualization technologies. In 2009 he joined the Distributed Systems Architecture Group at UCM as part of the development team of the virtual infrastructure manager, OpenNebula, that was used in the RESERVOIR project, flagship of the European Union cloud computing projects. He is now part of the NUBA project.

Giovanni Morana is a temporary researcher at University of Catania, where he obtained his PhD in Information and Telecommunication Engineering in 2009 (with the thesis "QoS management in Wide-Area Distributed Systems"). His research activity is mainly focused in designing algorithms for an optimal management of resources on distributed environments, including Clouds, Grid and P2P systems. He was co-chair of IEEE Workshop on "Enabling technologies for Next Generation Grids" (ETNGRID09/10) and, currently, he is co-chair of the track on "Convergence of Distributed Clouds, Grids, and their Management" in the IEEE WETICE conference. From 2010, he has a scientific collaboration with Kawa Objects Inc., CA, USA, working on distributed computing discipline.

Rafael Moreno-Vozmediano received the M.S. degree in Physics and the Ph.D. degree from the Universidad Complutense de Madrid (UCM), Spain, in 1991 and 1995 respectively. In 1991, he joined the Department of Computer Science of the UCM, where he worked as a Research Assistant and Assistant Professor until 1997. Since 1997 he is an Associate Professor of Computer Science and Electrical Engineering at the Department of Computer Architecture of the UCM, Spain. He has about 19 years of research experience in the fields of High-Performance Parallel and Distributed Computing, Grid Computing and Virtualization.

Christine Morin received the engineering degree in computer science from the Institut National des Sciences Appliques (INSA), of Rennes (France), in 1987 and Master and PhD degrees in computer science from the University of Rennes I in 1987 and 1990, respectively. In 1998, she got the Habilitation ˆ Diriger des Recherches in computer science from the UniversitŽ de Rennes 1. She holds a senior research position at INRIA and leads the Myriads research team on the design and implementation of autonomous distributed systems. She is the coordinator of the Contrail project on cloud computing funded the European Commission. Her main research interests are in operating systems, distributed systems, fault tolerance, cluster, grid and cloud computing.

Rubén S. Montero, PhD is an associate professor in the Department of Computer Architecture at Complutense University of Madrid, and Chief Technology Advisor and co-founder of C12G Labs, a cloud technology start-up. Over the last years, he has published more than 80 scientific papers in the field of High-Performance Parallel and Distributed Computing, and contributed to more than 20 research and development programmes. He has also held appointments as independent expert for several international and regional research agencies. Currently, he is the chief architect and co-leader of the OpenNebula project. He is the Technical Coordinator for StratusLab, the European initiative to integrate Grid and Cloud; and he is also heavily involved in organizing the Spanish e-science infrastructure as a member of the infrastructure expert panel of the national e-science initiative.

Vijay K. Naik is Research Staff Member at IBM T. J. Watson Research Center. He has been an active researcher in the area of distributed & fault tolerant computing and service computing. Over the past few years, he has been providing leadership in developing innovative technologies for cloud computing that are now incorporated in IBM provided solutions. Currently, he is leading research teams to advance the frontiers of hybrid cloud computing, workload migration to cloud systems, transformation of enterprise IT to cloud computing, performance modeling and analysis of cloud based services & systems, and quantifying the economics of cloud computing. He received his Ph.D. degree in computer science from Duke University in 1988. Previously he has worked at Google and ICASE, NASA Langley Research Center.

Marco Netto has over 12 years of experience on resource management for distributed systems. He is currently with IBM Research Brazil. Marco has published over 30 scientific publications, including journals, conference papers, and book chapters, and has filed over 10 patents. He is a regular reviewer of several conferences and journals such as *IEEE Transactions on Parallel and Distributed Systems, Journal of Parallel and Distributed Computing, Future Generation Computer Systems*, and *Concurrency and Computation: Practice and Experience*. He is also a member of IEEE Computer Society. Marco obtained his Ph.D. in Computer Science at the University of Melbourne (2010), Australia and his M.Sc. (2004) and B.Sc (2002) degrees at PUCRS, Brazil. His research interests are Cluster/Grid/Cloud Computing with focus on SLA management, virtualization, performance evaluation, job scheduling, rescheduling, Quality-of-Service, optimization issues, simulation, workload migration, and resource monitoring.

Silviu Panica has more than eight years of experience in distributed computing being involved in several European funded projects related to Grid and Cloud computing. He was Research Assistant in the Computer Science Department of West University of Timisoara from 2005 until 2007. During this period his research interest was in remote sensing field using Grid computational power combined with the high performance infrastructure to optimize the overall processing time of the satellite images. Starting with 2007 he is a PhD student at West University of Timisoara. His current research interest is in Cloud computing area focusing on the resource identification protocols applied in heterogeneous unstable distributed systems.

Maurizio Paone was born in Messina on March 20th 1973. He received his Degree in Electronic Engineering from the Engineering Faculty of the Università degli Studi di Messina (Italy) in 2003. Since then he has been engaged in research on Quality of Service (QoS) in wireless networks and ad-hoc networks. In December 2006, he received the Ph.D. degree in Advanced Technologies for Information Engineering from the Università degli Studi di Messina. Scientific activity of Dr. Paone has been focused on studying mobile networks systems. His research interests include QoS management in mobile wireless networks (infrastructure and ad-hoc topologies) and routing in Wireless Sensor Networks by adopting the Swarm Intelligence paradigm. Recently Dr. Paone has started researching in the field of Cloud Computing, contributing to the design of the CLEVER cloud middleware and working on virtualization and storage issues for the European Union Projects "RESERVOIR" and "VISION-CLOUD".

Dana Petcu is Professor at Computer Science Department of West University of Timisoara and Director of the private research Institute e-Austria Timisoara. Her research experience is related to the topics of parallel and distributed computing, and computational mathematics. She has authored more than two hundreds reviewed articles and ten textbooks. She is chief editor of the international journal Scalable Computing: Practice and Experiences and co-editor of over fifteen conference proceedings. She leads three European Commission's projects in Software Services, HPC and Cloud Computing and was involved as team leader in more than ten others related to distributed and parallel computing. She received the international Maria-Sybilla-Merian award for women in science and an IBM award, and is nominated Romanian representative in several forums at European level.

Antonio Puliafito is a full Professor of Computer Engineering at the Università degli Studi di Messina. He is also Vice President of Consorzio Cometa, which is currently managing the Sicilian Grid infrastructure. His interests include parallel and distributed systems, networking, wireless, and grid and cloud computing. Puliafito received his PhD in electrical engineering from the University of Palermo. He's a member of IEEE and the IEEE Computer Society.

Massimiliano Rak is an Assistant Professor at Second University of Naples. He received his degree in Computer Science Engineering at the University of Naples Federico II in 1999. In November 2002 he received Ph.D. in Electronic Engineering at Second University of Naples. He is Assistant Professor at Second University of Naples from 2002. He is author of more than seventy scientific publication and he is member of many scientific committee of international conferences. He acts as general chair for the Fourth Edition of the IAS International Conferences and participate to regional, national and European funded research project with responsibility roles. His scientific activity is mainly focused on the analysis and design of High Performance System Architectures, methodologies and techniques for Distributed Software development, Performance and Security evaluation in Distributed System, Cloud Computing.

Louis Rilling received a PhD in computer science from the University of Rennes in 2005. During his PhD, he has studied operating system foundations for distributed data sharing, high availability, and scalability in dynamic grids. He was a postdoctoral research guest at Vrije Universiteit Amsterdam in 2005, where he has studied high-availability for a scalable web server. From 2006 to Fall 2011 he has led research and development at Kerlabs. His research activities and interests mainly focus on operating systems, especially on distributed scheduling, fault-tolerance, high availability, and scalability. He has studied scalable fault-tolerance techniques for petaflop-scale applications of high energy physics simulation within the PetaQCD project, funded by the French ANR (National funding Agency for Research). Since 2009 he is also involved in the EcoGrappe project, funded by the French ANR, in which he has led the study of operating system mechanisms for energy savings in clusters of workstations.

Benny Rochwerger has an M.S. degree in computer science from the University of Massachusetts Amherst, and a B.Sc. degree in computer engineering from the Technion– Israel Institute of Technology. Since joining IBM in 1995, he has worked in virtualization management, autonomic computing, event processing, grid computing, distributed graphics, and networking. Benny was the lead architect for the Reservoir project. Presently Benny manages a research group focusing on advanced network virtualization technologies.

Carlos Martín Sánchez received his M.E. in Computer Science (2009) and his MSc in Computer Science Research (2010) from Universidad Complutense de Madrid (UCM), where he is currently a PhD student. His interests are in cloud and virtualization technologies. In 2009 he joined the Distributed Systems Architecture Group at UCM as part of the development team of the virtual infrastructure manager, OpenNebula, that was used in the RESERVOIR project, flagship of the European Union cloud computing projects. He is now part of the NUBA project.

Ian Seyler is the founder and CEO of Return Infinity Inc., a Canadian software R&D company devoted to creating a new generation of operating systems that overcome the scaling challenges posed by many-core servers. Return Infinity is partnering with Kawa Objects Inc. in the development of Parallax, a new operating system which implements scalable, distributed, and parallel computing to take advantage of the new generation of 64-bit multi-core processors using Distributed Intelligent Managed Element (DIME) network architecture. He has co-authored several papers on Parallax and its potential use in next generation data centers.

Jonathan Sinclair is a Research Associate with SAP Research Belfast. He is currently working as a PhD student in collaboration with Queen's University Belfast, in the research area of legal compliance auditing for distributed computer systems. As a research associate, Jonathan has worked on European Union FP7 funded project RESERVOIR and is currently engaged in the OPTIMIS project. He has contributed to efforts in different legal aspects of Cloud Computing research. Jonathan obtained his MEng from Queen's University Belfast in Computer Science in 2009. Jonathan's research interests include topics such as GRC (Governance, Risk & Compliance), Security & Privacy, Service Level Agreements and Argumentation.

Neeraj Suri received his PhD. from the University of Massachusetts at Amherst. He currently holds the TU Darmstadt Chair Professorship in "Dependable Systems and Software" at TU Darmstadt, Germany. His earlier appointments include the Saab Endowed Professorship, faculty at Boston University, and sabbaticals at Microsoft Research. His interests span the design, analysis and assessment of trustworthy software and systems focusing on composite issues of dependability and security. His group's research has garnered sustained support from the EC, Microsoft, IBM etc. Suri is a recipient of the NSF CAREER award, Microsoft Research Awards and the 2008 IBM Faculty Award. Suri currently serves as the associate Editor-in-Chief for IEEE Trans. on Dependable and Secure Computing (TDSC), on the editorial boards for *IEEE Security & Privacy, IEEE Transactions on Software Engineering, ACM Computing Surveys*, and *Journal of Security and Networks*. He is currently the Chair-Elect for IEEE TC on Dependability and Fault Tolerant Computing.

Giovanni Toffetti is currently a Research Associate at University College London. He received a European Ph.D. in Ingegneria dell'Informazione from Politecnico di Milano in 2007. He is author of several articles published in international conferences and workshops in the Web and software engineering field. His research interests include modeling and automatic code generation for data-intensive Web applications, event-driven systems, content-based routing, model-based testing, distributed systems, cloud computing and mobile applications.

Kishor S. Trivedi holds the Hudson Chair in the Department of Electrical and Computer Engineering at Duke University. He has been on the Duke faculty since 1975. He is the author of a well known text entitled, Probability and Statistics with Reliability, Queuing and Computer Science Applications, published by John Wiley. He has also published two other books entitled, Performance and Reliability Analysis of Computer Systems, published by Kluwer Academic Publishers and Queueing Networks and Markov Chains, John Wiley. He is a Fellow of the Institute of Electrical and Electronics Engineers. He has published over 470 articles and has supervised 43 Ph.D. dissertations. He is the recipient of IEEE Computer Society Technical Achievement Award for his research on Software Aging and Rejuvenation. He works closely with industry in carrying our reliability/availability analysis, providing short courses and in the development and dissemination of software packages such as SHARPE and SPNP.

Theodora A. Varvarigou received the B. Tech degree from the National Technical University of Athens, Athens, Greece in 1988, the MS degrees in Electrical Engineering (1989) and in Computer Science (1991) from Stanford University, Stanford, California in 1989 and the Ph.D. degree from Stanford University as well in 1991. She worked at AT&T Bell Labs, Holmdel, New Jersey between 1991 and 1995. Between 1995 and 1997 she worked as an Assistant Professor at the Technical University of Crete, Chania, Greece. Since 1997 she was elected as an Assistant Professor while since 2007 she is a Professor at the National Technical University of Athens, and Director of the Postgraduate Course "Engineering Economics Systems". Prof. Varvarigou has great experience in the area of semantic web technologies, scheduling over distributed platforms, embedded systems and grid computing. In this area, she has published more than 150 papers in leading journals and conferences. She has participated and coordinated several EU funded projects, related to subject of the IRMOS project such as POLYMNIA, Akogrimo, NextGRID, BEinGRID, Memphis, MKBEEM, MARIDES, CHALLENGERS, FIDIS, and other.

Umberto Villano is full Professor at the University of Sannio at Benevento, Italy, where he is Director of the Department of Engineering. His major research interests concern performance prediction and analysis of parallel and distributed computer architectures, tools and environments for parallel programming and distributed algorithms. He received the Laurea degree in Electronic Engineering cum laude from the University of Naples in1983.

Philipp Wieder is working as a scientist at the Gesellschaft fuer Wissenschaftliche Datenverarbeitung mbH Goettingen (GWDG). He graduated in 2000 from RWTH Aachen University with a diploma in electrical engineering. After his studies, he entered the area of high performance computing and distributed systems, contributing intensively to research topics like MPP systems, grids, SOA, virtualization, and currently cloud computing. From 2000 until 2007 Philipp Wieder was affiliated with the Central Institute for Applied Mathematics (ZAM), now called Juelich Supercomputing Centre (JSC), of the Research Centre Juelich. From 2007 to 2011 he was with the Service Computing Group at the TU Dortmund University. After a long history of European projects, he currently manages the German project SLA4D-Grid.

Index

A

Active Management Technology (AMT) 163
Amazon S3 16, 43, 212-215
Ant Colony Optimization (ACO) 363
appliance instantiation 24, 31-32, 35
approximation algorithm 306
autonomic computing 10, 16, 47, 75, 285, 370, 377, 390-392, 394

B

Binary Integer Programming (BIP) 354
BitTorrent 22
brokerage 39
Broker Property Description Language (BPDL) 27
business process modeling 18

C

capacity over-commit 306
Central Instance 333
certificate revocation lists (CRLs) 403
ChaosMon 269, 285
CLEVER cloud middleware 219
Cloud architecture 122, 127, 159-160, 168, 196-198, 201, 208-209, 244-245, 253, 330, 335, 346-347, 396, 398-399
Cloud-Brokers 18-20, 25-27, 31, 33, 35
cloud computing 1-3, 5, 7-19, 33-38, 41, 46, 52-57, 59, 72-75, 78-83, 88, 90-96, 98, 101, 103-104, 113-116, 132, 135, 153-155, 158-161, 172-174, 177-181, 185, 188-194, 196-199, 205, 215-217, 219-223, 236-237, 239-240, 242-243, 258, 263-264, 266-272, 283-289, 291, 304-308, 325-329, 346, 348, 350-351, 367-370, 372-374, 385, 392-393, 396, 412-416
cloud computing ecosystem 3, 36-37, 185

cloud federation 1-5, 10-11, 13, 16-17, 20, 36-38, 41-47, 51-52, 54-55, 82, 99, 104, 130, 151, 158, 176, 178-180, 182-183, 187-190, 193, 197, 215, 220, 272, 285, 287, 328, 414
cloud federation brokerage 46-47
cloudgrid 395, 397, 400-402, 405-407, 410, 413, 416
Cloud@Home 43, 55, 79-93
Cloud Incubator Initiative 14
cloud infrastructure 2-3, 10-11, 15, 26, 52, 75, 79, 88-89, 98, 106, 123, 133, 136, 151-152, 156, 158-160, 165-166, 168-169, 171, 221, 231, 233-234, 236-237, 241, 249, 260, 262, 264, 272, 282, 372, 376, 385, 388, 399-400, 415-416
Cloud Infrastructure Management Interface (CIMI) 15
Cloud interoperability 43, 88, 198
Cloud Market 310
cloud match-making 50
Cloud monitoring 8, 97, 99-100, 103-108, 110, 112-114, 118, 120-123, 127, 129-130, 133, 251-252
cloud paradigm 8, 54, 79, 92, 99, 176, 183, 197, 396
cloud providers 1-5, 8-11, 15-16, 18-22, 24, 26, 33, 36-54, 70, 81, 89, 91, 99-100, 102, 112-114, 120, 133-135, 152, 160, 173, 177, 180, 182, 189, 196-208, 211-213, 218, 240, 246, 262, 267-269, 271-273, 276, 283, 286-288, 290, 300, 309-311, 317, 329, 338, 340, 350-351, 396-399, 402, 412-413
Cloud Resource Management 310
Cloud Security Alliance (CSA) 12, 17, 160, 165, 172-173, 177, 190-191, 396, 399, 413
CloudWatch 22, 33, 100, 122, 131, 252, 263
cloud world 14
Cluster Manager (CM) 224, 226
combinatorial auction 290, 292-295, 303, 307
combined replication 30-31, 35
Condor Execution Service 258-259
Consolidation 356

constraint programming 356-357, 368-370, 374, 380, 382, 388, 391, 393-394
Content Delivery Network (CDN) 5
Continuous Time Markov Chains (CTMC) 136
Control Plane 254, 257, 261
Cost 320
Cross-Cloud 14, 21-23, 42, 178
Cross-Cloud Federation Manager (CCFM) 42
cyber attacks 5, 176, 178, 189-190

D

Data Plane 161, 246, 249-251, 254, 256-257
data segregation 12, 170
decentralized brokerage 38, 40-41, 44-46, 52
Delta Compression 343
DeSVi architecture 267, 273-274, 276-277, 279, 282-283
Dialogue Instance (DI) 333
DIME Network Architecture (DNA) 63, 66, 77
directed acyclic graph (DAG) 64, 66, 78
Discrete Time Markov Chains (DTMC) 136
distributed cloud service 4-5
Distributed Intelligent Managed Element (DIME) 57, 59
distributed service composition 4
Domain Specific Languages (DSLs) 275-276

E

Elastic Computing Cloud (EC2) 196
ElasticHosts infrastructure 200
Elasticity 330
Elastic Service Placement Problem (ESPP) 289
Energy Conservation 354
Enterprise Resource Planning (ERP) 328-329
Eucalyptus 352

F

Factored Operating System (FOS) 68
Fault-tolerance 357
FCAPS (Fault, Configuration, Accounting, Performance and Security) management 58
Federated Cloud Management (FCM) 24
Federated clouds 3, 18, 21, 42, 53-54, 102-103, 112, 127-128, 177, 219-221, 237, 249, 272-273, 281-282, 284, 312, 317, 342, 370, 372, 385, 389, 391, 395
fixed point iteration 135, 145, 147, 151
FoSII infrastructure 274

Future Internet 1, 79-81, 83, 89-90, 93, 96, 114-115, 117, 131, 133, 194, 219, 243, 263, 284

G

Generic Meta Brokering Service (GMBS) 25
Globus Monitoring and Discovery Service (Globus MDS) 101
Google App Engine (GAE) 398
Greedy Algorithm 356
GridEye 270, 273, 285
Grid infrastructures 22, 219-220, 231-232, 240, 370, 392, 398, 401
Grid Management Service 258-259
Grid Monitoring 100-102, 115, 122, 133, 263, 285
Grid Monitoring Architecture (GMA) 102
Grid Security Infrastructure (GSI) 402

H

Heuristics 309
Host manager (HM) 225-226
hybrid clouds 43, 70, 83, 104, 158-160, 169-172, 177, 180, 196-198, 201, 205, 208-209, 215-218, 220, 222, 240, 287, 290, 353
Hypervisor Management 100-101

I

IaaS Cloud systems 19, 22-23, 152
Identity and Access Management (IAM) 178, 398
identity federation 176, 395-397, 399-400, 402-405, 410, 412-413
identity provider (IdP) 184-185
Identity Provider/Service Provider (IdP 7, 54
Infrastructure-as-a-Service (IaaS) 3-4, 8-10, 13-14, 18-33, 36-39, 42-44, 82, 88, 98-99, 101, 103-105, 113, 117-118, 123-124, 134-135, 137-140, 151-153, 156, 177, 179-180, 182, 189-190, 196-197, 199, 206, 218, 221-222, 238, 267, 270, 282, 286, 288-290, 301, 303-304, 307, 311-312, 327, 350-352, 354, 357, 366-367, 371, 396-402
InterClouds 20-21
Internet Engineering Task Force (IETF) 167
Interoperability System (IS) 403-404, 416

L

large cloud providers 3, 36-37
Linear Programming (LP) 356
Live Migration 330, 342

M

Management Interface Layer (MIL) 127
Management Operating Layer (MOL) 127
Markov Regenerative Process (MRGP) 136
Master Boot Record (MBR) 162, 203
Mean Value Analysis 374
meta-brokering 18-19, 26, 28, 33-35
MetaStorage 43, 55
middleware development 84
middlewares 6-7, 82, 183, 398
Mixed-Integer-Linear-Programming (MILP) 356
Mixed-Integer Programming 375
monitoring 7
Monitoring Framework Service (MFS) 123
Monitoring Service Instance (MSI) 124
Multi-Cloud use 18, 24
Multi-Dimensional Bin-Packing (MDBP) 354
multi-tenancy 12, 69-70, 73, 75, 105, 113, 187, 190, 268-269, 283, 287

N

Nimbus 354

O

Open Cloud Computing Interface (OCCI) 15, 17, 88, 96, 103, 113, 115, 177, 191, 199, 215-216, 264
Open Grid Forum (OGF) 15, 17, 102, 215
OpenNebula 353
OpenStack 23, 30, 80, 82, 96, 199, 216, 223, 239
Open Virtual Format (OVF) 14, 330, 335
Orchestration Service 258
Overlay Transport Virtualization (OTV) 167

P

p2p interactions 6
Parallax Operating System 68, 72
PerfCloud framework 395
Platform-as-a-Service (PaaS) 3-4, 8-9, 13-14, 36-39, 42-44, 81-82, 95, 113, 117-118, 123, 177, 179-180, 183, 188-189, 221, 238, 264, 267, 282-283, 311-312, 397-402, 416
Policy and OCSP Based Interoperability System (POIS) 404, 417
Private Clouds 3, 24, 29, 70, 82, 104, 115, 149, 162, 170, 184, 196-198, 287, 357, 368
privileged user access 12

Public Clouds 29, 70, 96, 151, 187, 196-197, 200, 218, 222

Q

QEMU Copy On Write (QCOW) 203
Quality of Service (QoS) 2, 9, 80, 118, 219, 267, 309, 311, 373, 390

R

Reference Evaluation Methodology (REM) 404, 417
regulatory compliance 12-13
reliability block diagram (RBD) 135
Representational State Transfer (REST) architecture 182
RESERVOIR 21, 42, 80, 82, 92, 96, 103, 123, 125-127, 180, 198, 239, 242-251, 256, 258-264, 288-289, 301-302, 305, 334-336, 338, 348
resource capability brokers 3
restricted master problem (RMP) 295-296
Rule Engine 129, 133

S

SAP System 333
SAP System Landscape 330
Scalability 357
Security Assertion Markup Language (SAML) 170, 191, 415
Security Domains Federation 180, 185-187
self-CHOP 1, 10-11, 45
self-management 1-2, 10-11, 45, 64-65, 68, 71, 78, 159, 274, 287, 351, 372, 374, 376, 385, 391, 394
Self-Organization 362
Semi-Markov Process (SMP) 136
service brokerage 2, 10
Service Clouds 91, 96, 103, 114-115, 117, 131, 243, 246, 249, 252-253, 260, 262-264
service composition 2, 4, 38, 58-59
Service Level Agreements (SLA) 4, 290, 311
service level specification (SLS) 12
service migration 2, 4-5
service negotiation 2, 10
SLA Mapping 312
SLA Matching 311
SLA Template Life Cycle 313
smaller/medium cloud providers 3, 37
Snooze 357

Software-as-a-Service (SaaS) 3-4, 8-9, 13-14, 23, 36-39, 43-44, 113, 117-118, 123, 188-189, 221, 238, 267, 282-283, 311-312
software isolation 13
statefulness 165
statistical multiplexing 289-290, 304, 307
Stochastic Reward Nets 153, 156-157
Storage 334
storage modules 161, 168
storage virtualization 168-169, 172
structured networks 48, 51
System Architecture 352

T

Technological Federation 179, 182-183, 186, 188, 190
techno-utility complex 80
Telecom Grade Trust 59, 71-72, 75, 78
Total Cost of Ownership (TCO) 131, 329
transport layer security (TLS) 169
trusted computing 2, 17, 54, 164-165, 174-175
Trusted Execution Environment (TXT) 163
Turing machines 60, 76

U

Unified Extensible Firmware Interface (UEFI) 163, 171
unstructured networks 48, 51
Utility 324
utility computing 306, 310, 325-326, 394

V

VEE Manager (VEEM) 126, 244
virtual appliance 18-20, 24-27, 30-35, 202
Virtual Area Networks (VANs) 245
Virtual Desktop Image (VDI) 203
Virtual Execution Environment Hosts (VEEHs) 126, 245
Virtual Execution Environment Manager (VEEM) 126, 244
virtual execution environments (VEEs) 42, 126, 243, 334-335
Virtual Hard Disk (VHD) 202
Virtual Infrastructure Management (VIM) 216-217, 223, 240, 287
Virtualization 351
Virtual Machine Manager (VMM) 206
Virtual Machines (VM) 19, 342, 351, 354, 376
Virtual Machine Units (VMUs) 123
VISION CLOUD 127-130
VM Management Framework 357
volunteer-Cloud 79, 81
Volunteer computing 38, 43, 79-83, 90-94

W

Web Services Security (WSS) 170

X

XMPP Room 227, 229-231, 233, 235, 241